D1556766

The Symphony

Robert Greenberg, Ph.D.

THE GREAT COURSES

PUBLISHED BY:

THE GREAT COURSES
Corporate Headquarters
4840 Westfields Boulevard, Suite 500
Chantilly, Virginia 20151-2299
Phone: 1-800-832-2412
Fax: 703-378-3819
www.thegreatcourses.com

Robert Greenberg, Ph.D.

San Francisco Performances

Robert Greenberg was born in Brooklyn, New York, in 1954 and has lived in the San Francisco Bay Area since 1978. He received a B.A. in music, magna cum laude, from Princeton University in 1976. His principal teachers at Princeton were Edward Cone, Daniel Werts, and Carlton Gamer in composition; Claudio Spies and Paul Lansky in analysis; and Jerry Kuderna in piano. In 1984, Greenberg received a Ph.D. in music composition, *With Distinction*, from the University of California, Berkeley, where his principal teachers were Andrew Imbrie and Olly Wilson in composition and Richard Felciano in analysis.

Greenberg has composed more than 45 works for a wide variety of instrumental and vocal ensembles. Recent performances of his works have taken place in New York, San Francisco, Chicago, Los Angeles, England, Ireland, Greece, Italy, and the Netherlands, where his *Child's Play* for String Quartet was performed at the Concertgebouw of Amsterdam.

Greenberg has received numerous honors, including three Nicola de Lorenzo Composition Prizes and three Meet-the-Composer Grants. Recent commissions have been received from the Koussevitzky Foundation at the Library of Congress, the Alexander String Quartet, the San Francisco Contemporary Music Players, guitarist David Tanenbaum, the Strata Ensemble, and the XTET ensemble. Greenberg is a board member and an artistic director of COMPOSERS, INC., a composers' collective/production organization based in San Francisco. His music is published by Fallen Leaf Press and CPP/Belwin and is recorded on the *Innova* label.

Greenberg has performed, taught, and lectured extensively across North America and Europe. He is currently music historian-in-residence with San Francisco Performances, where he has lectured and performed since 1994, and resident composer and music historian to National Public Radio's "Weekend All Things Considered." He has served on the faculties of the University of California at Berkeley, California State University at Hayward, and the San Francisco Conservatory of Music, where he chaired the Department of Music, History and Literature from 1989–2001 and served as the Director of the Adult Extension Division from 1991–1996. He has lectured for some of the most prestigious musical and arts organizations in the United States, including the San Francisco Symphony (where for 10

i

years, he was host and lecturer for the symphony's nationally acclaimed "Discovery Series"), the Lincoln Center for the Performing Arts, the Van Cliburn Foundation, and the Chautauqua Institute. He is a sought-after lecturer for businesses and business schools, speaking at such diverse organizations as the Commonwealth Club of San Francisco and the University of Chicago Graduate School of Business, and has been profiled in various major publications, including the *Wall Street Journal*, *Inc.* magazine, and the *Times of London*.

Table of Contents
The Symphony

Table of Contents
The Symphony

The Symphony

Scope:

The symphony is the most important genre of orchestral music. It evolved from certain instrumental practices of early opera—its two essential Baroque precursors were the Italian opera overture and the *ripieno* concerto. By the 1730s, Italian-style opera overtures had evolved as multi-section *sinfonias*, substantial enough to be performed independently of the operas they were originally created to precede. The influence of the Italian opera sinfonia was felt in Vienna, Austria, where, during the 1740s, composers began creating self-standing, three-part orchestral works. By the 1760s and 1770s, the Baroque Italian overture had evolved into the Classical-era symphony, the single most important orchestral genre of its time.

In the hands of its greatest practitioners—Joseph Haydn and Wolfgang Mozart—the Classical-era symphony became a transcendent art form. It was a work for a large instrumental ensemble (an *orchestra*) and consisted of four distinct sections, or *movements*, each with its own beginning, middle, and end. Generally speaking, the Classical-era symphonic template was the standard for 40 years or more, in thousands of symphonies written across Europe during the mid- to late 18th century—until Beethoven. For the iconoclastic Beethoven, neither the expressive restraint nor the symphonic template of the Classical era stood a chance. As far as the French composer, Claude Debussy, was concerned, the symphony reached its apogee with Beethoven's Ninth Symphony (1824), and the ensuing 19th-century symphonic repertoire was a mere shadow of Beethoven—an opinion Debussy shared with many of his contemporaries.

Although many 19th-century symphonists were content to compose relatively conservative works based on the Classical-era template, others pushed the genre to the far limits of musical expression, from the autobiographical *Symphonie fantastique* of Berlioz to the multimedia symphonic extravaganzas of Gustav Mahler. As the symphony progressed across the span of the 20th century, it displayed originality, ambiguity, individuality, and variety, with a healthy number of masterpieces emerging from Moscow to Manhattan, by composers such as Ralph Vaughan Williams, Charles Ives, Dmitri Shostakovich, and Roy Harris.

This course claims three criteria for its selection of composers and symphonies. First, our selection of symphonies will include only major works for orchestra. Second, we will study only works that are entitled "symphony" by their composers. Finally, with a couple of exceptions, we will study symphonies by composers who awarded the symphonic genre a major, if not pre-eminent position in their musical output, and made significant contributions to its development. Along with their compositions, we will also study the lives of these artists.

Lecture One
Let's Take It From the Top!

Scope: After a brief look at the etymology of the word *symphony*, this lecture outlines the basic template of the Classical-era symphony. This template was the standard for 40 years in 18th-century Europe, until Beethoven revolutionized the genre. After Beethoven, the symphony could not return to the rituals and expressive restraint of the Classical era, and it came to encompass a far wider range of musical expression. This course traces the development of the symphony, beginning with its roots in the opera of the Baroque period.

Outline

I. To begin, let's look at the etymology of the word *symphony*.

A. In ancient Greek, the word *sumphonos* meant "sounding together," "harmonious," "in agreement," or "sounds in concordance." The Romans appropriated the word, converting it to *symphonia*. The Latin word then became, in Old French, *symphonie*; in Old English, *symphonye*; and in modern Italian, *sinfonia*.

B. The word first took on a specifically musical meaning in Italian. During the late 1500s and early 1600s—the end of the Renaissance and the beginning of the Baroque era—the word *sinfonia* was used to identify instrumental introductions, episodes, and interludes in otherwise vocal compositions.

1. After 1630, the word *sinfonia* (along with the word *sonata*) was used more often to designate separate, specifically instrumental compositions, the usage implying that multiple instrumental melodies were sounding together, or in agreement with each other. On the basis of this meaning, Johann Sebastian Bach called his "Three Part [or "Three Voice"] Inventions" of circa 1723 for harpsichord "*Sinfonias*" (or, more properly, "*Sinfonie*"). (**Musical selection**: Bach, Sinfonia [Three Part Invention] in F Major, BWV 794 [c. 1723].)

2. In the late 1600s, thanks largely to an Italian opera composer named Alessandro Scarlatti (1660–1725), the word *sinfonia* had come to represent—in Baroque Italy—a particular type of instrumental opera introduction that we now refer to as an *Italian overture*. We hear the opening section of Scarlatti's overture to the opera *La Griselda* of 1721. (**Musical selection**: Scarlatti, Overture to *La Griselda* [1721].)

C. By the 1760s and 1770s, the Baroque Italian overture had evolved into the Classical-era symphony, the single most important genre of orchestral music of its time. In the hands of its greatest practitioners—Joseph Haydn and Wolfgang Mozart—the Classical-era symphony became a transcendent art form.

D. A Classical-era symphony was a work for a large instrumental ensemble (an *orchestra*) that consisted of four distinct sections, or *movements*, each movement with its own beginning, middle, and end. In general, the four movements of a Classical symphony exhibit a ritual progression of contrasting *tempi* ("speeds"), expressive moods, and formal structures. Using Wolfgang Mozart's Symphony no. 29 in A Major of 1774 as an example, we will look at the basic large-scale template of a Classical-era symphony.

1. The first movement has a fast tempo and its structure is in sonata form, meaning that, over the course of the movement, we hear two contrasting themes expressed, developed, and recapitulated. Such a *sonata-form* movement is intellectually challenging and expressively varied. (**Musical selection**: Mozart, Symphony no. 29 in A Major, movement 1, theme 1/transition/theme 2, beginning.)

2. Movement 2 has a slow tempo and a lyric and gentle mood, providing a bit of a break after the intellectual and expressive rigors of the first movement. (**Musical selection**: Mozart, Symphony no. 29 in A Major, movement 2, opening.)

3. Movement 3 has a moderate tempo; its structure is that of a minuet and trio; and its mood is dancing and gracious. The third movement of a Classical symphony is meant to reactivate the body after the songlike lyricism of the second movement. (**Musical selection**: Mozart, Symphony no. 29 in A Major, movement 3, minuet.)

4. In movement 4, the tempo is fast to very fast, and the mood is brilliant and upbeat, meant to leave us with a smile. (**Musical**

selection: Mozart, Symphony no. 29 in A Major, movement 4, opening.)

E. Like any template, this Classical-era symphonic model was meant to be tweaked. After all, much great art is based on the manipulation of an audience's expectations and the creation of something unexpected. But the unexpected is meaningful only if it is understood as unexpected, if it is perceived as being contrary to something with which we are familiar.

F. Generally speaking, the Classical-era symphonic template was the standard for 40 years or more, in thousands of symphonies written across Europe during the mid- to late 18th century—until Beethoven.

II. Neither the expressive restraint nor the symphonic template of the Classical era stood a chance with Beethoven. Beethoven's symphonies provoked an unheard-of degree of excitement and criticism.

A. In terms of broadening the definition of what constituted a symphony, no symphony Beethoven ever composed had a more far-reaching influence than the Ninth of 1824.

1. For comparison, we listen to selections from the revolutionary Third, the expressionistic Fifth, and the brilliant Seventh. (**Musical selections**: Beethoven, Symphony no. 3 in Eb Major, op. 55, movement 1, opening; Symphony no. 5 in C Minor, op. 67, movement 1; Symphony no. 7 in A Major, op. 92, movement 4.)

2. Why did the Ninth have a greater influence than these other works? The answer is that Beethoven included voices in its fourth movement. (**Musical selection**: Beethoven, Symphony no. 9 in D Minor, op. 125, movement 4, vocal entry [from orchestral introduction].)

Chorus:
Oh friends, not this tone!
Rather let us sing more pleasantly
and more joyfully.
Joy! Joy!

Oh joy, thou lovely spark of God,
Daughter of Elysium,
we enter, drunk with fire,

immortal goddess, thy holy shrine.

Thy magic does again unite
what custom has torn apart;
all men shall be brothers,
where thy gentle wing is spread.

3. Beethoven's obliteration of the line between the orchestral genre of symphony and the vocal, storytelling genres of opera and cantata was earth-shattering.

B. In 1903, the great French composer Claude Debussy expressed his belief that the relevance of the symphony as a genre ended with Beethoven's Ninth. For Debussy, the symphony reached its apogee with the Ninth in 1824, and the ensuing 19th-century symphonic repertoire was a mere shadow of Beethoven—an opinion he shared with many of his contemporaries. Admittedly, after Beethoven, music could not return to the urbanity and restraint of the Classical style.

C. Certainly, Debussy's ancestor, the French composer Hector Berlioz, believed completely in Beethoven's vision of the symphony as an ever more inclusive genre, a genre that must be unhindered by convention and formula.

1. Berlioz's *Symphonie fantastique* of 1830 is a strange and wonderful work that tells (in purely instrumental terms) an explicit and autobiographical story over the course of its *five* movements—the story of a young, unhappy, and ultimately suicidal lover.

2. The most famous movement is the fourth, the "Scaffold March." It depicts the unhappy lover being carted to the scaffold and his subsequent execution by the blade of the guillotine. The theme that depicts this "march to the scaffold" is one of the most familiar in the repertoire. (**Musical selection**: Berlioz, *Symphonie fantastique*, movement 4, "march" theme.)

3. Is this huge, programmatic, five-movement work of Berlioz still a symphony? Of course, but it is a symphony by a composer with a vivid imagination living in that post-Beethoven, expression-crazed artistic environment that we today call the Romantic era.

D. Although many 19th-century symphonists were content to compose relatively conservative works based on the Classical-era template, still others pushed the genre to the far limits of musical expression, from the autobiographical *Symphonie fantastique* of Berlioz to the multimedia symphonic extravaganzas of Gustav Mahler.

III. Despite Debussy's pessimism regarding its future, the symphony, as a genre, lived on, and across the span of the 20th century, it displayed originality, ambiguity, individuality, and variety.

    A. We return to the original definition of the word *symphony*: "sounding together," "harmonious," or "sounds in concordance."

        1. With that definition in mind, we listen to the central section of the fourth and final movement of Charles Ives's Symphony no. 4 of 1916. (**Musical selection**: Ives, Symphony no. 4, movement 4 [1916].)

        2. Certainly, Ives had a rather unconventional sense of what constituted "harmonious concord." For Ives, "concordance" and "harmony" were products of the democratic spirit, a reflection of his abject belief that true freedom was a product of "the will to argue together and the will to work together."

    B. During the 20th century, one of the most time-honored aspects of the symphony—its organization as a multi-movement construct—was called into question by some composers. Any number of 20th-century composers wrote single-movement orchestral works that they called "symphonies." Lacking the inherent contrast between multiple movements, such symphonies display tremendous contrast within their single movements.

    C. Of course, during the 20th century, to a degree greater than ever before, we also find that the expressive content of many symphonies mirrors the feelings, beliefs, and worldviews of their composers with startling explicitness and originality.

        1. We see, for example, the Hindu vision of ecstatic, all-encompassing love that is the inspiration behind Olivier Messiaen's *Turangalîla Symphony*. (**Musical selection**: Messiaen, *Turangalîla Symphony*, movement 5, "Joy of the Blood of Stars.")

        2. We find another example in the brutal and terrifying portrait of Joseph Stalin painted by Dmitri Shostakovich in the second movement of his Symphony no. 10 of 1953. (**Musical**

selection: Shostakovich, Symphony no. 10 in E Minor, op. 93.)

D. We will be flexible in our approach to what constitutes a "symphony," because clearly, the symphony is an evolving genre that has changed tremendously since its invention.

IV. We have three criteria for selecting which composers and symphonies to include in this course.

A. First, a *symphony*, as we will define it, is a major work for orchestra. In Lecture Two, we will define what constitutes an *orchestra*, and we will observe that like *symphony*, the *orchestra* is an evolving entity, one that has changed dramatically since its first incarnation in the mid- to late 1600s.

B. The second criterion is that we will study only works that are entitled "symphony" by their composers. This excludes orchestral poems or tone poems; suites and concert overtures; and serenades, *sinfoniettas*, and ballets.

C. Finally, with a couple of exceptions, we will study symphonies by *symphonists*, that is, composers who seriously cultivated the genre. Along with their compositions, we will also study the lives of these artists.

V. We begin our examination in the Baroque era.

A. During the 17th century, culture and science had conspired to greatly expand the musical and expressive resources available to the composers of the time, with two stunning achievements among the results: the invention of opera (around the year 1600) and the growth and development of instrumental music as a major musical tradition.

B. Opera—the setting to music of an entire stage drama—demanded extraordinary instrumental resources to accompany the voices and provide scenic tone painting. As we will see in Lecture Two, the orchestra owes its existence to opera, as do any number of seemingly "non-operatic" instrumental genres, such as the concerto and suite.

C. Like the concerto and the orchestral suite, the early history of the symphony is a story of how certain instrumental practices of opera became detached from their vocal surroundings. The two essential Baroque precursors to the symphony were the Italian-style overtures that preceded the performance of Italian operas and a type of concerto called the *ripieno concerto*.

D. By the late 17th century, there were two essential types of opera overtures, the *French overture* and the *Italian overture*. For all intents and purposes, the French overture was invented by an Italian-born violinist and dancer named Jean-Baptiste Lully.

1. Lully was humbly born in Florence in 1632 and, through a series of complicated events and machinations, was appointed Superintendent of Music and Composer of Music for the Royal Chamber in 1661, at the age of 29. At the height of his career and fame, Lully was one of the most hated men in France.

2. Lully standardized the style and structure of the instrumental introductions, or *overtures*, that preceded the operas, ballets, and masques he composed for the king and court. These overtures typically consist of two main sections: a moderately slow, pomp-filled opening section, featuring sweeping strings and long-short rhythms, followed by a faster section. We listen to the majestic opening of Lully's overture to his opera *Armide*. (**Musical selection**: Lully, Overture to *Armide* [1686].)

3. Despite its international popularity during the Baroque era, the French overture was doomed to extinction. The type of Baroque overture that was to live on was the Italian-style opera overture.

E. The Italian overture, the *sinfonia*, was originally a four-part construct, the four parts following a slow-fast-slow-fast scheme. The Sicilian-born composer Alessandro Scarlatti is usually credited with having set the pattern for the 18th-century Italian overture and, by association, its descendent: the self-standing concert symphony.

1. Scarlatti tightened and intensified the dramatic scheme of the four-part Italian overture by reducing it to three parts—fast-slow-fast—with each of these three parts having its own beginning, middle, and end.

2. Scarlatti's overtures generally consisted of a fast, fanfarish first movement; a second, slower movement; and a fast, dance-like third movement in triple meter. As an example, we turn to the overture to Scarlatti's opera *La Griselda* of 1721.

(**Musical selection**: Scarlatti, Overture to *La Griselda* [1721].)

a. The first *section* (or *movement*; we will use these terms interchangeably) runs about 50 seconds. It is typical of the "curtain-raising music" of the period: *through composed* (meaning that the music develops as it goes), filled with rhythmic hustle and bustle, and lacking almost entirely any memorable melodies.

b. The second movement slows the action, featuring two oboes and running about 45 seconds in length. Like section one, it is through composed, although there is a greater sense of melodic substance here than in the first section.

c. The third movement brings back the fast tempo and celebratory mood of the first. Unlike the first two movements of the overture, this third one has a specific musical form. It is in *binary dance form*, meaning that it consists of two distinct and contrasting parts, with each part being immediately repeated, creating a large-scale ‖a a b b‖ structure. Binary dance form was the single most ubiquitous instrumental form of the Baroque. In the performance we hear, the opening part, "a", is repeated, but part "b" is not.

Welcome to *The Symphony*. This is Lecture One and it's entitled "Let's Take It from the Top!"

The History of a Word and a Musical Genre

Symphony—a brief etymological excursion is called for. In ancient Greek, the word *sumphonos* meant "sounding together," "harmonious," "in agreement," or "sounds in concordance." The Romans appropriated the word (as they did indeed appropriate so much of Greek culture), converting it slightly in the process to the word *symphonia*. The Latin word, *symphonia*, became in Old French the word *symphonie*, in Old English *symphonye* and in modern Italian, *sinfonia*. It was in its Italian permutation, *sinfonia*, that the word first took on a specifically musical meaning. During the late 1500s and very early 1600s, a period that we now refer to as the end of the Renaissance and the beginning of the Baroque era, the word *sinfonia* was meant to identify instrumental introductions, episodes, and interludes in otherwise vocal compositions. After 1630 or so, the word *sinfonia* (along with the word *sonata*) was used with increasing frequency to designate separate, specifically instrumental compositions, the usage implying that multiple instrumental melodies were sounding together, in concordance, in agreement, in symphony with each other. It was based on the meaning of this word, *sinfonia*, that led Johann Sebastian Bach to call his so-called "Three Part [or "Three Voice"] Inventions" of circa 1723 for harpsichord "*Sinfonias*" (or properly, "*Sinfonie*").

[Musical example from Symphonia, J.S. Bach]

Now, back to the late 1600s. By that time, thanks in greatest part to a Palermo-born and Naples-based Italian opera composer named Alessandro Scarlatti, who lived from 1660 to 1725, the word *sinfonia* had come to represent—in Baroque Italy—a particular type of instrumental opera introduction, or overture, a type of opera overture we now refer to as an *Italian overture*. We hear the opening section of Scarlatti's overture to the opera *La Griselda* of 1721.

[Musical example from Overture, La Griselda, Scarlatti]

By the 1750s and 1770s, Baroque Italian overture had evolved into something quite more extensive. The Classical sinfonia—or symphony—had become the single most important genre of orchestral music of its time. And in the hands of its practitioners, Joseph Haydn and Wolfgang Mozart, the Classical-era symphony became a transcendent art form. A Classical-era symphony was a work for a large instrumental ensemble called an *orchestra* that consisted of four distinct sections, or *movements*, each movement with its own beginning, middle, and end. In general, the four movements of a Classical symphony exhibit a ritual (meaning predictable) progression of contrasting *tempi* (meaning speeds), expressive moods, and formal structures. Using Wolfgang Mozart's Symphony no. 29 in A Major in 1774 as an example, I present to you the ritual: the basic large-scale template of a Classical-era symphony.

Movement 1: Tempo? Fast. Structure? *Sonata form*, meaning that, over the course of the movement, we will hear typically two contrasting forms expressed, developed, and recapitulated. Such a sonata form will be intellectually challenging and expressively varied as befits a formal structure based on contrasting themes and their ongoing development. Please, the beginning of the first movement of Mozart's Symphony no. 29 in A Major.

[Musical example from Symphony no. 29 in A, K201, Mozart: I]

Movement 2 of the Classical-era symphonic template: tempo is slow; mood and spirit is lyric and gentle, providing a bit of a break after the intellectual and expressive rigors of the first movement. Mozart's Symphony no. 29 in A Major, second movement.

[Musical example from Symphony no. 29 in A, K201, Mozart: II]

Movement 3 of the Classical-era symphonic template: tempo is moderate; structure is minuet and trio; mood and spirit is dancing and gracious. The third movement of a Classical symphony is meant to reactivate the body after the song like lyricism of the second movement. Mozart's Symphony no. 29 in A Major, third movement opening.

[Musical example from Symphony no. 29 in A, K201, Mozart: III]

And finally, movement 4 of the Classical-era symphonic template. Tempo is fast to very fast; mood and spirit is brilliant and upbeat, meant to leave us with a smile on our faces and a bounce in our steps. This is Mozart's Symphony no. 29 in A Major, fourth movement opening.

[Musical example from Symphony no. 29 in A, K201, Mozart: IV]

Now, like any template, this Classical-era symphonic model was meant to be tweaked. So much great art is after all about tweaking the givens. It's about manipulating the audience's expectations and creating something otherwise unexpected. But the unexpected is only meaningful if it is understood as such, if it is perceived as being contrary to something with which we are already familiar and comfortable. An extraordinary Rice Krispies Treat can only be appreciated as such if we already know what your basic Rice Krispies Treat is supposed to taste like. We can't know we've gone outside of the box if we never perceived a box to begin with. So, generally and accurately speaking, tweaks aside, the classical era symphonic template was the overwhelmingly standard rule for 40 years or more, in thousands of symphonies written across Europe during the mid to late 18th century—until Beethoven.

Oh my goodness, he was an irksome, brilliant, unhappy and extraordinarily original man. Neither the expressive restraint nor the symphonic template of the Classical era stood a chance with Beethoven. Beethoven's symphonies, like just about everything else he composed, provoked an unheard of degree of excitement and criticism. In terms of broadening forever the definition of what constituted a symphony, no symphony Beethoven ever composed, not the revolutionary Third [an excerpt of Beethoven's Third Symphony is played] nor the expressionistic Fifth [an excerpt of Beethoven's Fifth Symphony is played], not the brilliant Seventh [an excerpt of Beethoven's Seventh Symphony is played], my friends, no symphony of Beethoven's had a greater and more far-reaching influence—as a symphony—than the Ninth of 1824. And why? Well, such a simple thing really—voices. Beethoven put singers singing words into the fourth and last movement of his Ninth Symphony. Please, the words in English translation that we first hear in that fourth movement:

Chorus:

Oh friends, not this tone!
Rather let us sing more pleasantly
and more joyfully.
Joy! Joy!

Oh joy, thou lovely spark of God,
Daughter of Elysium,
we enter, drunk with fire,
immortal goddess, thy holy shrine.

Thy magic does again unite
what custom has torn apart;
all men shall be brothers,
where thy gentle wing is spread.

[Musical example from Symphony no. 9, Beethoven; IV]

Land o' Goshen, where do we start? Voices in a symphony. The presence of these voices in the final movement of Beethoven's Ninth is like Barry Bonds taking his cuts with a wiffle ball bat, like Slobodan Milosevic replacing the late and great Fred Rogers in a new children's show, "Mr. Milosevic's Neighborhood", like W. C. Fields doing a "Got Milk?" ad, like Margaret Thatcher taking up residence at the Playboy mansion, like a Teaching Company course not being informative and entertaining. "Incredible!" we cry. "Out of the question!" we insist.

In a culture where the nature and substance of the symphony was as intrinsic to its self-image as baseball and the movies and The Teaching Company are to ours, Beethoven's obliteration of the line between the orchestral genre of symphony and the vocal story-telling genres of opera and cantata was, very simply, earth shattering—a 9.8 on the cultural Richter Scale.

In 1903, the great French composer Claude Debussy—and a great, if reluctant, admirer of Beethoven (Beethoven was, after all, a German)—in 1903, Debussy expressed his belief that the relevance of symphony as a genre ended with Beethoven's Ninth. We quote Debussy:

A fog of criticism and verbiage surrounds [Beethoven's] Ninth. It is amazing that it has not been buried [entirely] under the mass of prose that it has provoked. Nothing is superfluous in this stupendous work, not even the Andante, declared by modern aestheticians to be overly long. [In his Ninth, Beethoven] determined to surpass himself. I can scarcely see how the success can be questioned. [Unfortunately], it seems to me that the proof of the futility of this symphony has been well established since Beethoven. We must conclude [in 1903] that the symphony, in spite of so many attempted transformations [since Beethoven], belongs to the past by virtue of its studied elegance, its formal elaboration, and the philosophical attitude of its audience.

For Monsieur Debussy, the symphony as a genre was a Classical-era construct, one that reached its apogee with Beethoven's Ninth back in 1824. Debussy's opinion that the 19th-century symphonic repertoire was a mere shadow, an impotent echo of Beethoven, was one he shared with many of his contemporaries. Now admittedly, after Beethoven, there could be no going back to the urbanity and restraint of the Classic style. Not that such a thing would have happened anyway, in the increasingly middle-class dominated "me"-oriented, "I-must-express-myself" mentality of 19th-century Romanticism.

Certainly, Debussy's ancestor, the French composer Hector Berlioz, believed completely in Beethoven's vision of the symphony as an evermore inclusive genre, a genre that must contain whatever expressive content a composer put into it, unhindered by convention and formula. Berlioz's *Symphonie fantastique* of 1830 is a strange and wonderful work that tells (in purely instrumental terms) an explicit and autobiographical story over the course of its five movements—the story of a young, unhappy, and ultimately suicidal lover. The most famous movement is the fourth, the so-called "Scaffold March." It depicts the unhappy lover being carted to the scaffold and his subsequent execution at the blade of the guillotine. The theme that depicts this "march to the scaffold" is one of the most familiar in the repertoire.

[Musical example from Symphony Fantastique, Berlioz: IV]

A question: Is this huge, programmatic, five-movement work of Berlioz's still a symphony? Well, of course it is, but it's still not your great-grandfather's symphony. It's a symphony by a composer with a very vivid imagination living in that post-Beethoven, expression-crazed environment that we today call the Romantic era. And while many, many 19th-century symphonists were content to compose relatively conservative works based on the Classical-era symphonic template, still others, like Berlioz, pushed the genre to the far limits of musical expression as they understood it, from the autobiographical *Symphonie fantastique* of Berlioz to the multi-media symphonic extravaganzas of Gustav Mahler. (Oh yes, yes, extravaganzas my friends. Mahler's Eighth Symphony for example, the so-called "Symphony of a Thousand" required so many performers when it was first produced in Munich, in 1910, over a thousand performers in reality, that the running joke said that there would be no one available to attend the premiere, as everybody within fifty miles of Munich would already be on stage, playing or singing. Yes, a "Symphony of a Thousand" indeed!)

The nicknames—yes the nicknames! We cannot ignore the multitudinous number and varieties assigned to symphonies, often for no other reason than to break the generic monotony of simply calling a work "symphony." There's Haydn's "Surprise" Symphony; Mozart's "Linz," "Prague" and "Jupiter" Symphonies; Beethoven's "Eroica" and "Pastoral" Symphonies; Schumann's Symphony no. 1, the so-called "Spring" Symphony and Schumann's Third, the "Rhenish" Symphony (that's as in "Rhineland Symphony"); Mahler's "Titan" (the First), the "Resurrection" (his Second), and of course his Eighth, the "Symphony of a Thousand."

Frankly, some symphonic nicknames might have been best done without. For example, Carl Nielsen's Symphony no. 4, "The Inextinguishable" of 1916. Well, more than one très cruel wag has referred to the piece as "The Undistinguished," a sentiment that, I trust, we will not share after having examined the piece in Lecture Seventeen. And how about Aaron Copeland's Symphony no. 2 of 1933, the so-called "Short Symphony"? So what happens if it's performed really slowly? Does it become the "Not-so-Short Symphony", perhaps even the "Longish Symphony"? And then there's Camille Saint-Saens Symphony no. 3 of 1866, the so-called "Organ" Symphony. My friends, color me sophomoric, but I for one have made it a policy never to use such words as "quaff," "boot," "chug," "groin," or "organ" (to name but a few) in any title I want the world to take seriously.

If Claude Debussy was disappointed by the post-Beethoven symphony in the 19th century, well, we can only rue the fact that he didn't have an opportunity to turn his ear, and his pen, onto the symphonies of the 20th century. The symphony, as a genre, has lived on, and across the span of the 20th century it displayed all the originality, ambiguity, individuality, and variety as every other sort of music during that magnificent and troubled time.

Symphony: We return to the original definition, the meaning of the word: "sounding together," "harmonious," or "sounds in concordance." With that basic definition ringing in our ears, we hear the central section of the fourth and final movement of Charles Ives's Symphony no. 4 of 1960.

[Musical example from Excerpt from Symphony no. 4, Ives]

Certainly, the gentleman from Connecticut (we refer here to Mr. Ives) had a rather unconventional sense of what constituted "harmonious concord." For Ives, concordance and harmony were a product of the democratic spirit, a reflection of his abject belief that true freedom—personal, artistic, political true freedom—was a product of "the will to argue together and the will to work together." For example, on January 10, 1931, Ives heard a performance of his orchestral work, *Three Places in New England*, performed in New York City. Conducted by Nicolas Slonimsky, the performance was, technically, terrible, a complete mess. But Ives was thrilled with the spirit behind the performance, and after the concert he told the conductor Slonimsky, "This was just like a town meeting—everyone for himself! Wonderful how it came out!" One can only wonder what Claude Debussy would have said about that.

During the 20th century, one of the most time-honored aspects of the symphony was called into question by some of the composers. A multi-movement construct since its invention, any number of 20th-century symphony composers wrote single-movement orchestral works that they called "symphonies." Roy Harris's Symphony no. 3 of 1937 and Samuel Barber's Symphony no. 1 of 1943 are two such single-movement symphonies that we will examine. Lacking the inherent contrast between multiple movements, such symphonies will display tremendous contrasts within their single movement. And of course, during the 20th century, to a degree greater than ever before, the expressive contents of many symphonies mirrored, as demonstrative just moments ago in Ives's Fourth, the feelings and the worldviews of their composers with startling explicitness and originality.

From the Hindu vision of ecstatic all-encompassing love that is the inspiration behind Olivier Messiaen's Turangalila Symphony:

[Musical example from Turangalila Symphony, Messiaen]

To the brutal and terrifying portrait of Joseph Stalin painted by Dmitri Shostakovich in the second movement of his Symphony no. 10 of 1953:

[Musical example from Symphony no. 10, Shostakovich]

From Messiaen's Hindu-inspired joy to Shostakovich's Stalin-inspired brutality, the 20th-century symphony will take us to expressive places that would have curled the hair on Debussy's head and straightened it everywhere else.

What's In and What's Out

We're going to have to be very flexible in our approach to what constitutes a symphony because clearly the symphony is an evolving genre that has changed tremendously since its invention. Our criteria for selecting which composers and symphonies are to be included in this course are three in number. Number one: a *symphony* as we will define it is a major work—yes, a subjective definition that—a major work for orchestra. Soon enough, in Lecture Two, we will define what constitutes an *orchestra* and we will observe that like *symphony*, the *orchestra* is an evolving entity, one that's changed dramatically since its first incarnation in the mid- to late 1600s.

During the course of this survey, then, we will only study works that were composed for more-or-less full orchestras, whatever that meant at the given time. We will not study any *chamber* or *Kammer* symphonies; no "symphonies for wind ensembles," sackbut consorts, or piccolo ensembles—heaven save us from phone solicitors and piccolo ensembles! Criteria number two: we will only study works entitled "symphony" by their composers. No orchestral poems or tone poems, no suites or concert overtures, no serenades, *sinfoniettas*, or ballets. If it's not called a "symphony" somewhere in its title by its very own composer, it's not on our menu.

The third criteria for the works in this survey is, for the most part, we will study symphonies by symphonists, that is, composers who seriously cultivated the genre. Now, there will be a couple of exceptions to this as we will examine symphonies by such one-shot wonders as Cesar Franck and Olivier Messiaen. But, with those composers excepted, we will study symphonies that came from the pens and pencils of practiced symphonists—from Giovanni Battista Sammartini's 68 surviving symphonies and Luigi Boccherini's 26, to Joseph Haydn's surviving 104 and Wolfgang Mozart's 41. And since we need to know something about the people who actually created these symphonies, from Beethoven's Nine to Schubert's Nine to Dvorak's Nine to Bruckner's Nine to Mahler's Nine—yes, I know, it's all a little scary, this nine stuff—this will also be a course about the symphonists themselves.

Beginnings

In the beginning there was the Baroque era, and musically, it was very good. During the 17th century, the 1600s, culture and science had conspired together to expand greatly the musical and expressive resources available to composers of the time with two stunning achievements being among the results: the invention of opera around the year 1600 and the growth and development of instrumental music as a major musical tradition unto itself.

Please, a sidebar regarding the development of instrumental music during the Baroque era. This is not to say that some instrumental music did not exist before the Baroque; it did. But pre-Baroque instrumental music was a nascent tradition, generally limited to dance music and instrumental compositions that were based on vocal (meaning choral) practice. Accurately speaking, the overwhelming majority of pre-Baroque (meaning Renaissance) music was vocal music, vocal music that served both spiritual and secular verse. Truly, it wasn't until the 17th century and the standardization of string instruments, of tuning practice and the whole emergence of major-minor systems of tonality, and a musical community increasingly conditioned by the emotional immediacy of opera that a general instrumental tradition could and did evolve.

Back, then, please to the concurrent development of opera and instrumental music during the 17th century. Opera—the setting to music of an entire stage drama from beginning to end—demanded extraordinary instrumental resources to accompany the voices and provide scenic tonal painting. Look—if there's a thunderstorm on stage, it's not the singers who are going to provide the sounds of thunder, lightning and rain. As we will find out in Lecture Two, the orchestra owes its very existence to opera, as do any number of "non-seeming operatic" instrumental genres. For example, opera was the inspiration for those Italian composers who transferred the lyric solo-voice dominated character of opera to the world of instrumental music and in doing so created the genre of *concerto*.

The influence of opera on the development of instrumental practice is amazing. Another example: In order to flexibly accompany the half-sung, half-spoken recitatives of early opera, a new sort of practice emerged. It was performed by a group of instruments called, collectively, the *basso continuum*, a musical element that went on to become the essential underpinning of almost every instrumental composition for the next 150 years, well into the mid-18th century. The dance episodes that were so overwhelmingly popular in 17th-century French operas and masques were arranged for keyboard and instrumental ensembles, were published and performed as self-standing entities, and thus gave rise to an entirely new genre of instrumental compositions entitled *suites* and *partitas* and *orchestral suites*.

Like the concerto and orchestral suite, the early history of the symphony is a story of how certain instrumental practices of opera became detached from their vocal surroundings and cut free to develop on their own. The two essential Baroque precursors to the symphony were the so-called *Italian-style overtures* that preceded the performance of Italian operas and the type of concerto called the *ripieno concerto*.

Overtures

By the late 17th century there were two essential types of opera overtures: the so-called *French overture* and the *Italian overture*. For all intents and purposes, the French overture was invented by an Italian-born violinist and dancer-turned-French-court composer named Jean-Baptiste Lully. Lully was humbly born in Florence in 1632. When, through a series of events and machinations way too complicated to even attempt to explain here and now, he was appointed Superintendent of Music and Composer of Music for the Royal Chamber in 1661, at the age of 29, the appointment being made by the 23 year-old King Louis XIV himself. At the height of his career and fame, Lully was one of the most hated men in all of France. Of Lully, the contemporary poet Jean de La Fontaine wrote, "He is lewd and evil minded, and he devours all." According to the English historian, Alistair Horne, Lully was "the ugly Italian, dirty, untidy, coarse, a heavy drinker who later became wholly debauched. But he was the father of French opera, and it was thanks to his genius that it had its first golden age."

Lully standardized the style and structure of the instrumental introductions, or *overtures*, that preceded the operas, ballets and masques he composed for the king and the court. These overtures typically consisted of two sections, a moderately slow pomp-filled opening section featuring sweeping strains and long-short rhythms, followed by a faster section. We listen to the majestic opening of Lully's opening to his opera *Armide* of 1686.

[Musical example from Armide; Lully]

Despite its phenomenal international popularity during the Baroque, the French overture was ultimately the Dodo bird of Baroque orchestral genres, a species headed for extinction. The type of Baroque overture that was to live on into the future, its musical seed potent and its symphonic progeny legion, was the Italian-style overture.

Unlike the two different parts of the French overture, the Italian overture (what the Italians called *sinfonia*) was originally a four-part construct, the four parts following a slow-fast-slow-fast scheme. While it's impossible to give anyone credit for having invented the Italian overture, it was the Sicilian-born composer, Alessandro Scarlatti, who set the pattern for the 18th-century Italian overture and, by association, its descendant, the self-standing concert symphony. Scarlatti tightened and intensified the dramatic scheme of the four-part Italian overture by reducing it to three parts—fast-slow-fast—with each of these three parts having its own beginning, middle and end. Scarlatti's overtures then generally consisted of a fast fanfarish first movement, a second slower movement and a fast, dance-like third movement in triple meter. As an example, we turn to the overture of Scarlatti's opera *La Griselda* of 1721.

Please note the following: One, the first *section* (or *movement*—we're using these terms interchangeably here) runs about 50 seconds. It is typical of the "curtain-raising music" of the period: through composed and filled with rhythmic hustle and bustle, and lacking almost entirely any memorable melodies.

Two, the second movement slows the action and features two oboes and runs about 45 seconds in length. Like section one, it is through composed, meaning that the music develops as it goes, although there is a greater sense of melodic substance here than in the first movement.

Three, the third movement brings back the fast tempo and celebratory mood of the first. Unlike the first two movements of the overture, this third one has a specific musical form. It is in *binary form*, meaning it consists of two distinct and contrasting parts, with each part being immediately repeated creating a large scale a a b b structure. Binary form was the single most ubiquitous instrumental form of the Baroque. In our performance, the opening part "a" is indeed repeated, but part "b" is not. Alessandro Scarlatti, Overture to *La Griselda* of 1721.

[Musical example from Overture to La Griselda, Scarlatti]

Unless you're an early opera freakazoid—the numbers of who are fewer than Raiders fans who eat with untensils—you will not be familiar with the music of Alessandro Scarlatti. He was eclipsed by his own son, Domenico, the sixth of his ten children, and Alessandro's music has been relegated to almost complete obscurity. This is most unfortunate because Alessandro Scarlatti was a first-rate composer who created a tremendous body of work—including over 100 operas and nearly 700 cantatas, not counting his other religious and instrumental compositions. According to Donald Grout:

From the present viewpoint, it seems most accurate to regard [Alessandro] Scarlatti [rather than Antonio Vivaldi] as the outstanding composer of the late Italian Baroque period. [He was a composer] whose work marks the historical consummation of the era. He was no more a conscious innovator than Bach; [like Bach,] he surpassed his contemporaries by virtue of his superior genius and skill in the handling of a common musical language.

For anyone wanting to hear more of Alessandro Scarlatti, I would suggest that the perfect place to start is with his opera *La Griselda*, the Italian-style overture of which we just heard. Typical of Scarlatti's best work, *La Griselda* of 1721 offers an extraordinary variety of arias, with each creating its own little musical world, each demonstrating Scarlatti's inexhaustible melodic invention and his great sensitivity in setting text.

When we return, we'll turn to the ripieno concerto, itself an outgrowth of Baroque opera, the genre that along with the Italian overture was the immediate predecessor of the concert symphony.

Thank you.

Lecture Two

The Concerto and the Orchestra

Scope: In this lecture, we examine another Baroque-era precursor to the symphony, the *ripieno concerto*, which is generally defined as a self-standing, three-movement composition for a string orchestra. What, then, differentiates the ripieno concerto from a symphony? As we'll see, these concerti feature certain Baroque stylistic traits that set them apart from the later treatment of melody, harmony, contrast, and development of the 18th-century symphony. We also take a look at the development of the orchestra in the 17th century and the early art of orchestration. By the 1730s and 1740s, these parallel developments began to come together in the popular *style galant* of the Italian opera sinfonia, which would, in turn, give rise to the first true symphonies.

Outline

I. Before we begin to discuss the first genuine concert symphonies—three-movement orchestral works created to be performed as self-standing entities—we must first take a look at a Baroque-era instrumental genre called the *ripieno concerto*, a three-movement work for string orchestra composed as a self-standing entity.

A. Along with the French and Italian-style overtures and the orchestral dance suites (all of which evolved from Baroque operatic practice), the other most important type of orchestral music in the mid- and late-Baroque era was the *concerto*. Three types of concerto appeared during the Baroque era, all of which were invented in Italy.

1. The most common type of Baroque concerto is the *solo concerto*, which features a single solo instrument accompanied by the orchestra. The second type is the *concerto grosso*, or "large concerto," in which a group of solo instruments—typically three—is accompanied by the orchestra. The third type is the so-called "full," or *ripieno*, concerto, a work for a string orchestra that uses the formal constructs of a concerto but does not feature any particular solo instrument or instruments.

2. We think of a concerto as a work for a solo instrument or group of soloists accompanied by an orchestra, but during the Baroque era, the genre was defined more generally than it is today. The word comes from the Latin *concertare*, which means "to be in concert or agreement with." During the Baroque era, when terminology dealing with instrumental music was evolving, any combination of instruments playing together could be called a "concerto."

3. Such Italian composers as Giuseppe Torelli and Tomaso Albinoni wrote many ripieno concerti, and Antonio Vivaldi—the quintessential Venetian composer of the High Baroque—wrote more than 50 of them.

B. Indeed, it was from his study of the concerti of Vivaldi that Johann Sebastian Bach composed what is now known as his Brandenburg Concerto no. 3, one of the few ripieno concerti produced outside of Italy. (**Musical selection**: Johann Sebastian Bach, Brandenburg Concerto no. 3 in G Major, BWV 1048, movement 3 [c. 1721].)

1. Like its Italian models, Bach's Brandenburg no. 3 is written for strings alone, including, of course, the ubiquitous basso continuo part, played by a harpsichord. Although some Italian ripieno concerti had as many as five movements, the progressive trend was toward works in three movements, such as Bach's: fast-slow-fast.

2. The first movement is, like its Italian models, a *ritornello*- (meaning "return" or "refrain") form movement. It follows a formal procedure in which the opening theme returns, in whole or in part, after various developmental and contrasting episodes. (**Musical selection**: Johann Sebastian Bach, Brandenburg Concerto no. 3 in G Major, BWV 1048, movement 1.)

3. The second, slow movement of Bach's Brandenburg no. 3 is quite brief. In the score, it consists of the word *adagio*, meaning "slow," and just two chords. Bach no doubt intended one or more instruments to improvise a solo here and provide some textural contrast with the non-soloistic outer movements. In our recording, the second movement is performed as a brief cadenza for violin. (**Musical selection**: Johann Sebastian Bach, Brandenburg Concerto no. 3 in G Major, BWV 1048, movement 2.)

4. The third and final movement is, like the first, a brisk *allegro* in ritornello form. As we listen to this movement, be aware of its monothematic and non-transformational nature.

   a. It is monothematic, because the only melodic structure that stands out as a memorable tune is the opening theme. The contrasting episodes do not offer any new thematic material but are, rather, episodes built from fragments of the opening theme, episodes that separate the ongoing reiterations of that opening theme.

   b. The movement is non-transformational, because there is no metamorphic alternation and re-integration of the thematic material during the course of the movement; when the theme is reiterated, whether in whole or in part, we hear it in much the same way every time.

   c. This is in no way a denigration of Bach; thematic contrast and transformation are innovations of the future. Bach's musical language demanded continuity, not contrast; thematic fragmentation, not transformation. As we listen, be aware of the kaleidoscopic, rather than transportive, nature of the music.

C. Taken together, then, Bach's Third Brandenburg is a self-standing, three-movement composition for string orchestra. Why aren't this and similar ripieno concerti called *symphonies*?

   1. First, we don't call them symphonies because their composers didn't call them symphonies. Second, and more important, these ripieno concerti exhibit musical stylistic traits that anchor them firmly in the Baroque tradition, including their melodic style, harmonic usage, formal structures, and lack of contrast and thematic development in individual movements.

   2. The genre of music that we will call a *symphony* is one that will demonstrate a different approach to melody, harmony, contrast, and development, a genre that will eventually do away with the basso continuo and mirror a new musical style, one wrought by the Enlightenment during the mid- to late 18th century.

II. Parallel with the development of opera was the birth and development of the instrumental ensemble that we call the *orchestra*.

A. The word *orchestra* comes from the Greek term for the semicircular space around the stage of a Greek theater, the space in which the chorus chanted during the course of a theatrical production. The Romans appropriated the word to refer to the front-row seats immediately around the stage.

   1. The use of the word *orchestra* to designate a group of instruments first became common in France before spreading across Europe. In 1768, with the publication of Jean-Jacques Rousseau's *Dictionary of Music*, the word was authoritatively attached to the instrumental ensemble itself, rather than the location from where it played.

   2. We will define *orchestra* as generally as possible, that is, as any instrumental ensemble in which there is more than one player on one or more instrumental parts. Thus, if an ensemble has two or three violinists playing the same part—*doubling* or *tripling* the part—it will be considered an orchestra. Conversely, an ensemble featuring only one player per part, such as a string quartet, will be considered a *chamber group*.

B. Opera and orchestra evolved side by side. Although large instrumental ensembles existed before the invention of opera, they typically did not perform as a single coherent entity, nor was music composed for such a group as a single coherent entity. Rather, the musicians were combined into various ensembles, what were then called *consorts* and what we would call *chamber ensembles*.

C. Early operas tended to use this same sort of instrumental mixing. As an example, we turn to the first operatic masterwork, Claudio Monteverdi's *Orfeo*, composed in 1607, only seven years after the staging of Jacopo Peri's *Euridice*, a work that is acknowledged today as the first opera.

   1. Monteverdi's *Orfeo* calls for more than 40 instruments, a huge number for its time. Typically, however, Monteverdi did not use these 40 players as a single coherent ensemble but, instead, drew from his resources various smaller combinations of instruments.

   2. For example, the introduction—a blaring, brilliant fanfare announcing the start of the opera—features heraldic trumpets (*cornetts*), early trombones (*sagbutts*), winds, and drums, organized into separate consorts. The introduction consists of the same phrase played three times in succession; the cornett

and sagbutt consort play the first iteration of the phrase, a woodwind consort plays the second, and the cornetts and sagbutts return to play the third iteration. (**Musical selection**: Monteverdi, Overture to *Orfeo*.)

3. Monteverdi did not use his 40 instruments as an integrated orchestral ensemble. That ensemble would evolve with opera and at its heart would be the strings.

III. The eventual dominance of the strings in the evolving orchestra was a result of two factors, one practical and the other historical.

A. On the practical side, stringed instruments—especially the relatively new violin family, consisting of the violin, viola, and 'cello—were capable of sustaining their sound indefinitely. As a group, they create a rich, homogeneous, and seamless sound from very high to very low. Historically, long before the invention of opera, groups of stringed instruments had been used in Italy to accompany singers in church and secular settings and in France, where string consorts provided the music for courtly dancing.

B. In 17th-century France, concurrent with the development of early opera, courtly and theatrical dancing—*ballet*—became something of a mania. In 1626, King Louis XIII created the *Grande Bande* of the French court, an ensemble to accompany royal dance parties. This ensemble consisted of 8 violins, 12 violas, and 4 'cellos, and its creation was a landmark event in the history of the orchestra.

C. Parallel events were taking place at this time in the opera houses of Italy, particularly in Venice, where the first public opera house opened in 1637. As the number and seating capacity of these theaters grew, an ever-greater number of instruments was required simply to fill the physical space. Thus, based partly on the French model and partly on physical necessity, the string section of a typical Venetian opera house grew. By the mid-17th century, the typical opera orchestra used 12 to 14 string instruments of various sizes, along with a harpsichord, a large lute called a *chitarrone*, and 1 or 2 trumpets.

D. As opera became increasingly popular in the 17th century, more instruments were added by composers as novelties, that is, to create special effects and indulge in tone painting. For example, if a pastoral effect was needed for a particular scene, a composer might include a passage for recorders or a flute; a royal stage scene might require the musical presence of a cornett and trombone choir. However, such "novelty" instruments rarely played simultaneously with the strings, mainly because wind instruments of the late 16th and early 17th centuries were made in one piece and could not be tuned. Such instruments could be played alone, but it was difficult to combine unlike instruments and be in tune.

E. The tuning problems inherent in combining wind instruments with strings were solved in France where, by the mid-17th century, woodwind instruments joined the strings as "permanent" members of the orchestra. Flute and bassoon designs were altered to make them tunable and, therefore, practical for use in the orchestra. As quickly as these wind instruments were modernized and brought into the orchestral fold in France, Italian composers added them to their opera orchestras, as well.

F. By the first decades of the 18th century, not only had wind and brass instruments become part of the "standard" opera orchestra but a new and equally important concept had developed, that of *orchestration.*

1. This term refers to the manner in which a composer assigns instruments to the melodic and accompanimental parts of a composition. When wind instruments first began entering the orchestra in the 1650s, what passed for orchestration was rather crude, because the winds, when they weren't being used to create some special effect, simply doubled the string parts; that is, they added body to the string sound by playing the same notes as the strings, surrendering their own unique tone-color.

2. By the 1720s, the art of orchestration had truly been born: Winds and brass, in various combinations, might be asked to supply harmonic accompaniment to string melodies; winds and brass might play the principal melody while being accompanied by the strings; or some combination of winds and brass might be asked to play countermelodies of equal importance to the string parts.

3. Thus, the art of orchestration came to rest in having the instruments of the orchestra play discontinuously. That is, no single instrumental group should be allowed to play all the time, but individual instruments and groups of instruments in various combinations should enter and depart, constantly

altering the weight and color of the music as it unfolds. The art of orchestration treats the instruments of the orchestra like colors on a palette; tasteful and judicious use of coloristic shading, of instrumental complement and contrast determine whether an orchestral canvas shines and breathes or lies flat and lifeless.

G. As an example of the early art of orchestration, we return to the overture of Alessandro Scarlatti's opera *La Griselda* of 1721.

   1. Scarlatti scored his overture for strings, two oboes, and two trumpets. In the first 13 measures of the overture—the opening 40 seconds—Scarlatti deploys the oboes and trumpets in three different ways. For the first 7 measures, the oboes and trumpets function as harmonic support—as background—sustaining chords, while the violins play the thematic music in the foreground. (**Musical selection**: Scarlatti, Overture to *La Griselda*, measures 1–7.)

   2. Immediately following this, in measures 8–9 (and, again, in measures 12–13), the oboes and trumpets move into the foreground and play the thematic music, while the violins supply the harmonic support. (**Musical selection**: Scarlatti, Overture to *La Griselda*, measures 8–9.)

   3. In measures 11–12, the oboes play countermelodies to the strings that are equal to what the strings are playing. (**Musical selection**: Scarlatti, Overture to *La Griselda*, measures 11–12.)

   4. Let's put this all together and hear the entire first *allegro* of Alessandro Scarlatti's Italian-style overture to *La Griselda*. Pay special attention to the ebb and flow of the orchestration and Scarlatti's ability to create a sense of constantly shifting musical weight, emphasis, and color. (**Musical selection**: Scarlatti, Overture to *La Griselda*, section/movement 1.)

IV. By the 1730s, the concurrent evolution of the orchestra as a performing ensemble and the Italian-style opera overture as a genre of music to be performed by that ensemble had reached a point where the multi-section sinfonias had become substantial enough to be performed as compositions separate from the operas they were originally created to precede.

A. Such a sinfonia is Giovanni Battista Pergolesi's overture to his opera *L'Olimpiade* of 1735. Typically, Pergolesi's overture is a three-movement composition, which follows the tempo plan fast-slow-fast. Pergolesi scores his sinfonia for strings, oboes, horns, harpsichord continuo, and in the third-movement finale, trumpets. As we listen, please note the following points:

1. As we would expect, the first movement—in D major—is an energized curtain raiser. But it is also exhibits the brilliant, straightforward melodic material that will be much more characteristic of the coming Classical era than the more complex melodic surfaces of the Baroque era. Having said that, typical of Baroque practice, the movement is monothematic and the theme goes undeveloped.

2. The slow second movement—in D minor—is substantial in itself and goes far beyond the simple, relatively inconsequential middle movements of so many earlier Italian-style overtures. About a minute into the movement, a genuine contrasting theme is introduced in the key of F major. The movement ends back in D minor, with both themes stated in that key.

3. The third and final movement is the most advanced in the overture, featuring not just a contrasting theme in a new key but also a brief development section. The addition of trumpets, for the first time in the sinfonia, also imbues this final movement with a festive spirit and instills the orchestration with a sense of growth and development unto itself.

B. As we listen to this opera "overture," consider whether the piece is a satisfying musical experience by itself. Does it exhibit those musical aspects that render a composition complete—a sense of beginning, middle, and end; an adequate degree of contrast between the movements and, perhaps, even within the movements? Are there recognizable themes that ground and give gravity to this as a piece of music in itself, and do any of those themes undergo the process of development? (**Musical selection:** Pergolesi, Overture to *L'Olimpiade* [1735].)

C. This new and evolving Italian style of lyric music of the early and mid-18th century was called the *style galant* and was wildly popular. By the 1730s and 1740s, the Italian overture became the single most popular orchestral genre in Europe. In particular, the influence of the Italian opera sinfonia was felt in Vienna, the capital of the Habsburg Empire, where during the 1740s, composers began creating self-standing, three-part orchestral works—the first true symphonies.

Lecture Two—Transcript
The Concerto and the Orchestra

Welcome back. This is Lecture Two entitled "The Concerto and the Orchestra." Well, it's accurate to say that the symphony as a genre came into existence during the mid-18th century. It's virtually impossible to fix on a specific date, to point a finger at one or even two works and say (as we can in the case of opera), "Ah ha! That's it; that's the first symphony." And why not? Well, for starters, as we observed in Lecture One, the word *sinfonia*, the Italian word for "symphony," had already been in use for a century or more to designate a variety of musical genres including the overtures that preceded Italian operas.

In the 1720s and 1730s, composers of these multi-sectioned Italian-style overtures designed them so that they could be separated from the opera that they were created to precede, and performed as self-standing works unto themselves. Should we call such an operatic overture a concert symphony as well? You see the problem. At what point do these dual-use opera *sinfonia* become purely concert symphonies? Of that we can't be sure. And before we can begin to discuss the first genuine concert symphonies, three-movement orchestral works created as self-standing entities, we must first take a look at a Baroque-era instrumental genre called the *ripieno concerto*, a three-movement work for string orchestra composed as a self-standing entity.

Now we'll backtrack. Along with the French and Italian-style overtures and the orchestral dance suites (all of which evolved from Baroque operatic practice), the other most important type of orchestral music in the mid- and late Baroque was the *concerto*. Three types of concerti appeared during the Baroque era. All three types were invented in Italy, where such operatic techniques as recitative, aria and ensemble were adapted to the world of instrumental composition. The first and most common type of Baroque concerto is the *solo concerto*, a type of concerto that features a single solo instrument, a single solo voice accompanied by the orchestra. The second type of Baroque concerto is the *concerto grosso*, or "large concerto" in which a group of solo instruments, typically three in number, is accompanied by the orchestra. The third type of Baroque concerto is the *ripieno concerto*. A ripieno concerto was, and still is, a work for a string orchestra that utilizes the formal constructs of a concerto but does not feature any particular solo instrument or solo instruments.

Yes, it's true that today we understand a concerto as being a work for a solo instrument or group of soloists accompanied by an orchestra. However, this wasn't the understanding during the Baroque era, which defined the genre concerto much more generally than we do today. Please, the word *concerto* comes from the Latin (and Italian) *concertare*, a word that is virtually synonymous with the Greek-rooted word "symphony." *Concertare*, like "symphony," means "to be in concert with," "to be in agreement with," "to be in accordance with," "in harmony with." During the Baroque era when terminology dealing with instrumental music was just beginning to evolve, any combination of instruments playing together could be called a "concerto," just as in English, any group of instruments playing together might be called a "consort," and the venue in which they play called a "concert."

Back then to the ripieno concerto. Such Italian composers as Giuseppe Torelli and Tomaso Albinoni wrote many such ripieno concerti and Antonio Vivaldi, the quintessential Venetian composer of the High Baroque, wrote over 50 of them himself. This brings us to the man. It was from his study of the concerti of Vivaldi that Johann Sebastian Bach, living and working in what amounted to the Baja of central Germany—the tiny principality of Anhalt-Köthen, in Saxony—composed what is now known as his Brandenburg Concerto no. 3. It is a ripieno concerto, one of the very few such concerti produced outside Italy. As it is a wise thing to use any excuse to listen to the music of Sebastian Bach, we will examine his third Brandenburg Concerto in G Major as an example of a ripieno concerto.

Like his Italian models, Bach's Brandenburg no. 3 is written for strings alone, including of course, the ubiquitous basso continuo part, here played by a harpsichord. While some Italian ripieno concerti had as many as five movements, the progressive trend was towards works in three movements like Bach's: fast-slow-fast. The first movement of Bach's Brandenburg no. 3 is, like its Italian models, a *ritornello*, meaning a "return" or "refrain" form movement. It's a formal procedure that sees the opening return in whole or in part after various developmental and contrasting episodes. Let's listen to the opening minute of this six-minute first movement of Bach, Brandenburg Concerto no. 3.

[Musical example from Brandenburg Concerto no. 3, Bach: I]

The second, slow movement of Brandenburg no. 3 is a bit of an oddity, brief frankly to the point of atomic. In the score, it consists of the word *adagio* (meaning "slow") and two chords. That's it—two chords. Without a doubt, Bach intended one or more instruments to improvise a little solo here and in doing so provide some contrast with the decidedly non-soloistic outer movements. In our recording, the second movement is performed as a brief cadenza for violin.

[Musical example from Brandenburg Concerto no. 3, Bach: II]

The third and final movement is, like the first, a brisk *allegro* in ritornello form. We are going to listen to this wonderful movement in its entirety and here's why: I want us to be aware of the monothematic and non-transformational nature of this music. It is monothematic because the only melodic structure that stands out as a memorable tune is the opening theme. The contrasting episodes do not offer any new thematic material, but are rather episodes built from fragments of the opening theme, episodes that separate the reiterations of that opening theme. The movement is non-transformational, because there is no metamorphic alteration and re-integration of the thematic material during the course of the movement. When the theme is reiterated, whether in whole or in part, we hear it pretty much the same way every time. Now please, this is in no way meant to denigrate Bach. The sort of thematic contrast and transformation we're talking about is still a thing of the far future. Bach's musical language demanded continuity, not contrast; thematic fragmentation, not transformation. We should no more expect Bach to write a sonata-form type movement than we would expect him to warm up a day-old cabbage knish in a microwave.

Let's hear the movement and let's be aware, then, of the kaleidoscopic, rather than the transportive nature of this music.

[Musical example from Brandenburg Concerto no. 3, Bach: III]

So, taken all together, what do we have here? A self-standing, three-movement composition for string orchestra. Why not, then, are ripieno concerti like Bach's Third Brandenburg simply called *symphonies*? Reason one: we don't call them symphonies because their composers didn't call them symphonies. They called them concerti and so will we; an unsatisfying explanation, I know. So here's the real reason, reason number two: These ripieno concerti exhibit musical stylistic traits that anchor them firmly within the Baroque. Their melodic style, their harmonic usage, formal structures and most importantly their lack of contrast and thematic development within individual movements all together identify them as being firmly within Baroque tradition. The genre of music that we will call a *symphony* is one that will demonstrate a very different approach to melody, harmony, contrast, and development, a genre that will eventually do away with the basso continuo, a genre that will mirror a new musical style, one wrought by the Enlightenment of the mid- to late 18th century.

The Orchestra

Parallel with the development of opera was the birth and development of that instrumental ensemble we call the *orchestra*. Again, let's first deal with the word. The word orchestra comes from the Greek term for the semi-circular space around the stage of a Greek theater. It's the space in which the famed Greek chorus stood and chanted their commentary during the course of a theatrical production. The Romans appropriated the word, although in a Roman theater, the word orchestra referred to the front row seats immediately around the stage like ringside seats at a major boxing match. The orchestra seats at a Roman theater were reserved for the wealthy, for senators and other political bigwigs, important visitors and so forth.

The first recorded use of the word orchestra to designate a group of instruments rather than a location in a theater, is found in an article written in 1702 by a Parisian cleric named François Raguenet in which he refers to the "*Orchestre de notre Opera,*" "our opera orchestra." This use of the word *orchestra* as a reference to the band of instruments that performed from the foot of the stage from an opera theater first became common in France, and from there it spread across Europe. In 1768, Jacques Rousseau's authoritative *Dictionary of Music* was published in Paris, and it was as a result of the definition of the word *orchestra* contained therein that the word was attached finally and authoritatively to the instrumental ensemble itself, rather than the location from where it played.

Up until then, instrumental ensembles were called all sorts of names. In Italy, the word *concerto* was used to indicate virtually any grouping of instruments from small to large. In both England and France, the word *band* was used for the same purpose. For example, the king's musicians in London were called the Royal Band. In France, Louis XIV's royal ensemble was called *Le Grande Bande*. Whatever we choose to call it, a band or an orchestra, the instrumental ensemble represented by these terms is an approximation, with no specific number of instruments implied. The only implication is that a band or an orchestra will constitute a large ensemble, but then what was considered a large ensemble in 1720 would have been considered miniscule in 1890.

For our purposes then, we will define an *orchestra*—as generally as possible—as any instrumental ensemble in which there is more than one player on one or more instrumental parts. So if there are two or three violinists playing the same part—*doubling* or *tripling* the part as we say—the ensemble will be considered an orchestra. Conversely, an ensemble featuring only one player per part, like a string quartet for example, such an ensemble would be considered a *chamber group*.

Like dogs and early humans, opera and the instrumental ensemble that accompanied the singers, the orchestra evolved side by side. Yes, large instrumental ensembles existed before the invention of opera. For example, in 1550, the English royal musicians, the king's musicians consisted of a band of 80 players who played violins, violas, flutes, trumpets, trombones, shawms (the ancestor of the oboe) and drums. But typically, "Ye Olde Royal Bande" did not perform as a single coherent entity, nor was music composed for it as a single coherent entity. Rather, the musicians of the Royal Band were combined, depending on the occasion, into various smaller ensembles into what were then called *consorts* and into what we would call today *chamber ensembles*.

Early operas tended to use the same sort of instrumental mix and matching. As an example, we turn to the first operatic masterwork, Claudio Monteverdi's *Orfeo* composed in 1607, only 7 years after the staging of Jacopo Peri's *Euridice*, a work that we today acknowledge as the first opera. Monteverdi's *Orfeo* calls for over 40 instruments, a gigantic number of instruments for its time. They must have had to hire every competent musician in Lombardy to fill out such a band. But typical of the time, 1607, Monteverdi did not employ these 40 players as a single coherent ensemble. Instead, he drew from his resources various smaller combinations of instruments. So, for example, the introduction—a blaring, brilliant fanfare announcing the start of the opera—the introduction features heraldic trumpets (or *coronetts*), *sagbutts* (yes, you read that correctly, they were early trombones), winds, and drums organized into separate consorts. The introduction of Monteverdi's *Orfeo* consists of the same phrase played three times in succession. In our performance we will hear the coronett and sagbutt consort play the first iteration of the phrase, a woodwind consort play the second, after which the coronett and sagbutts return to play the third and final iteration.

[Musical example from Orfeo, Monteverdi]

The point—Monteverdi's forty instruments did not an integrated ensemble make. That ensemble would evolve with opera and its heart would be the strings.

The Strings

The eventual dominance of the strings in the evolving orchestra was a result of two factors, one entirely practical and the other historical. On the practical side, stringed instruments—especially the relatively new violin family, consisting of the violin, viola, and cello—were and indeed still are capable of sustaining their sound indefinitely. As a group, they create a rich homogeneous and seamless sound from very high to very low. As for the historical reason for the dominance of the strings in the developing orchestra, long before the invention of opera, groups of string instruments had been used already in Italy to accompany singers both in church and in secular settings, as well as in France, where string consorts provided the music for courtly dancing.

In 17th-century France, concurrent with the development of early opera, courtly and theatrical dancing—*ballet* as the French called it—became something of a genuine mania. In 1626, King Louis XIII of France created the *Grande Bande* of the French Court, the so-called "Twenty-four Strings of the King," an ensemble created to accompany royal dance parties and such. The "Twenty-four Strings of the King" consisted of eight violins, twelve violas and four cellos. Its creation was a landmark event in the history of the orchestra. In 1656, John-Baptiste Lully reorganized the *Grande Bande* for his king, Louis XIV. Lully added oboes and bassoons and began using the ensemble as the opera orchestra at the *Academie Royale de Musique*. The opening of Lully's overture to *Armide*, which we listened to in Lecture One, was scored for just this ensemble.

While Lully was thus expanding his string-dominated orchestra in France, parallel events were taking place in the opera houses of Italy, in particular in Venice, where the first public opera house—the Teatro San Cassiano—opened its doors in 1637. The subsequent explosion of public opera theaters in Venice—and the ever increasing seating capacity of these public opera theaters—required an ever-greater number of instruments to fill the physical space of the theaters. And so, based partly on the French model and partly on physical necessity, the string section of the typical Venetian opera house grew as well. By the mid-17th century, a typical Venetian opera orchestra consisted of twelve to fourteen string instruments of various shapes and sizes. The standard Venetian opera orchestra also included a harpsichord, a large lute called a *chitarrone*, and one or two trumpets.

As the 17th century went on, and as opera became an increasingly popular entertainment all throughout Europe, so ever more instruments were added by composers to the opera orchestras as novelties, in order to create special effects and indulge in tone painting. For example, if a pastoral effect was needed for a particular scene, a composer might include a passage for recorders and/or a flute; a royal and magnificent stage scene might require the musical presence of a cornett and trombone choir. However—and this is a really important point—such "novelty" instruments rarely played simultaneously with the strings. One major reason for this had to do, in the case of wind instruments, with tuning. You see, late 16th and early 17th century wind instruments were made in one piece and were literally "untunable." When such instruments were used by themselves, there was no problem. But it was very difficult, if not impossible, to combine unlike instruments and stay in tune.

The tuning problems inherent in combining wind instruments with strings was solved in France, where by the mid-17th century woodwind instruments joined the strings as permanent members of the orchestra. We can rack this event up to good old Gallic technological ingenuity and the fact that necessity, the need for more and more varied instrumental resources in the opera houses was here *la mère* of invention. Flute and bassoon designs were altered to make them tunable, and therefore practical for usage in the orchestra. The shawm was converted into the modern oboe sometime around 1650 by a member of the famed Hotteterre family, an entire clan of musicians employed by the French court. And as quickly as these instruments were modernized and brought into the orchestral fold in France, well, so Italian composers seized upon them and added them to their orchestras as well.

By the first decades of the 18th century, the 1700s, wind and brass instruments were not only part of the standard opera orchestra, but a new and equally important concept had developed: the concept of *orchestration*. Orchestration, my friends, refers to the manner in which a composer assigns instruments to the melodic and accompanimental parts of a composition. When wind instruments first began entering the orchestra in the 1650s, what passed for orchestration was a pretty rude affair, as the winds, when they weren't being used to create some special effect, simply doubled the string parts, that is they added body to the string sound by playing the same notes as the strings, surrendering as they did their own unique tone color for the greater good of a buffed out string section.

By the 1720s, the art of orchestration had truly been born. Winds and brass in various combinations might be asked to supply harmonic accompaniment to string melodies. Winds and brass in various combinations might play the principle melody while being accompanied by the strings. Or, some combination of winds and brass might be asked to play countermelodies of equal importance to the string parts. Lastly, and perhaps most importantly from an artistic point of view, the art of orchestration as practiced by the early 1700s and indeed to this very day, lay in having the instruments of the orchestra play discontinuously. That is, no single instrumental group should be allowed to play all the time, but rather individual instruments and groups of instruments in various combinations should enter and depart, constantly altering the weight and color of the music as it unfolds. Like the art of painting, the art of orchestration treats the instruments of the orchestra like colors on a palette. Certainly the strings are the most common colors; but they do not, they must not, predominate all the time. Tasteful and judicious use of colors and shading, of instrumental complement and contrast will determine whether an orchestral contrast shines and breathes or lies there like a monochromatic lump. That's what the art of orchestration is all about, and it is a product of the early 18th century.

As an example of the early art of orchestration, we return to the overture of Alessandro Scarlatti's opera *La Griselda* of 1721. Scarlatti scored his overture for strings, two oboes and two trumpets. In just the first 13 measures of the overture, the opening 40 seconds or so, Scarlatti deploys the oboes and trumpets three different ways. For the first seven measures, the oboes and trumpets function as harmonic support, as background, sustaining chords while the violins play the thematic music, the foreground music.

[Musical example from Overture, La Griselda, Scarlatti]

Immediately following this in measures 8 through 9, and then a few measures later in measures 12 and 13, the oboes and trumpets move into the foreground and play the thematic music while the violins take a back seat and supply the harmonic support.

[Musical example from Overture, La Griselda, Scarlatti]

And immediately following that, in measures 11 and 12, the oboes play countermelodies to the strings that are the equal to what the strings are playing.

[Musical example from Overture, La Griselda, Scarlatti]

Now, let's put this together and hear the entire first *allegro*—the entire first movement—of Scarlatti's Italian-style overture to *La Griselda*. Let us pay special attention to the ebb and flow of the orchestration, and how Scarlatti's deft use of his little orchestra creates a sense of constantly shifting musical weight, emphasis, and color—this my friends is what orchestration is all about.

[Musical example from Overture, La Griselda, Scarlatti: I]

Putting it all together!

By the fourth decade of 18th century, the 1730s, the concurrent evolution of the orchestra as a performing ensemble and the Italian-style opera overture or sinfonia as a genre of music to be performed by that ensemble, had reached a point where the multi-sectioned symphonias had become substantial enough as pieces of music unto themselves to be performed as compositions separate from the opera they were originally created to precede.

Such a sinfonia is Giovanni Battista Pergolesi's overture to his opera *L'Olimpiade* of 1735. Typically, Pergolesi's overture is a three-part, that is a three-movement composition, which follows the typical tempo plan of fast-slow-fast. Pergolesi scores his sinfonia for strings, oboes, horns, harpsichord continuo, and in the third movement finale, trumpets. We're going to listen to the sinfonia in its entirety, start to finish.

Please, please, note the following: The first movement—in D major—is an energized curtain raiser. But it's also something more. It exhibits the sort of brilliant, straightforward melodic material that would be much more characteristic of the coming Classical era than the more complex melodic surfaces of the Baroque era. Having said that, typical of Baroque practice, the movement is monothematic, and the theme goes undeveloped.

The slow second movement—in D minor—constitutes a substantial chunk of music in itself and goes far beyond the simple, relatively inconsequential middle movements of so many earlier Italian-style overtures. About a minute into the movement, a genuine contrasting theme is introduced in the key of F major. The movement ends back in D minor, with both themes stated in that key.

The third and final movement is the most advanced in the overture, featuring as it does not just a contrasting theme in a new key but a brief development section as well. The addition of trumpets for the first time in the sinfonia also imbues this final movement with a festive spirit, and it's just that sort of device that gives an orchestration a sense of growth and development unto itself.

While we listen to this opera "overture," I'd like us to ask ourselves as to whether or not the piece makes a satisfying musical experience unto itself. Does it exhibit those musical aspects that render a composition complete unto itself—a sense of beginning, middle and end? Does it have an adequate degree of contrast between the movements and perhaps even within the movements? Are there recognizable themes that ground and give gravity to this as a piece of music unto itself? And do any of those themes undergo the process of development? Well, let's listen. Giovanni Battista Pergolesi, *L'Olimpiade*, 1735.

[Musical example from Giovanni Battista Pergolesi, *L'Olimpiade*, 1735.]

So, is Pergolesi's sinfonia *L'Olimpiade* a satisfying listen all by itself? Well, you bet it is. Musicologist Preston Stedman writes:

> [Pergolesi's sinfonia *L'Olimpiade*] is a veritable treasure trove of style mannerisms that foreshadow the 18th century concert symphony. Whereas the first movement fits more into the concept of a rousing curtain-raiser, the two remaining [movements] contain several progressive traits. Clarity of structure, some well-defined themes, abbreviated development sections, an absence of [the sort of] counterpoint and imitation [so typical of Baroque era music] and a complete surrender to the *style galant* [that is the new, elegant, light, and more frankly tune-full, pre-Classical melodic style evolving there in Italy] show the extent to which the Italian sinfonia provided the basic raw materials for the concert symphony.

The *Style Galant*

My friends it is virtually impossible to overstate the popularity of the new and evolving Italian style of indiscernible music of the early and mid 18th century. As never before, the popularity of Italian music, particularly I would tell you of Italian opera, swept across Western Europe and the British

Isles. In process, the Italian overture, the sinfonia, became by the 1730s and 1740s, the single most popular orchestral genre in Europe. In particular, the influence of the Italian opera sinfonia was felt in Vienna, the great capital of the Habsburg Empire where during the 1740s composers began composing self-standing three-part orchestral works that they called "sinfonias."

In Lecture Three, we will attack with all the intensity of a sumo wrestler at an all-you-can-eat buffet the so-called pre-Classic symphony. But before we do, we will first have to deal with some terminological garble that makes a conversation between Sylvester Stallone and Yoda sound like Shakespearean dialogue. Ha ha. I know a tease line when I hear one.

Until then, thank you!

Lecture Three
The Pre-Classical Symphony

Scope: In this lecture, we discuss such pre-Classical symphonists as
Giovanni Battista Sammartini, Carl Philip Emanuel Bach, and
Georg Christoph Wagenseil, composers whose music embodies
the *galant* style in Italy (Sammartini) and the *empfindsam* style in
Germany (C. P. E. Bach) and Austria (Wagenseil). As we learn
about these composers, we'll also define a number of associated
musical terms, including *binary form*, *sonata form*, *exposition*,
development, *recapitulation*, and others. We close with the
Viennese Classical style, which combined features of the Italian
and German styles and made use of the instrumental techniques of
the Mannheim orchestra.

Outline

I. At the end of Lecture Two, we noted that the so-called *galant* style
swept across Europe in the 1730s and 1740s. Because the earliest true
symphonies are a product of this time, we will quickly address some of
the names and terms that are applied to the period that lay between the
High Baroque and Viennese Classicism, an era roughly spanning the
years 1730–1770.

A. According to the textbooks, the Baroque era ended in 1750 with
the death of J. S. Bach; presumably, then, the Classical era began
immediately afterward. Of course, in reality, the transition from
Baroque to Classical was evolutionary, and a variety of terms and
names has been applied to the incremental stylistic changes that
marked this evolution.

B. For a number of young Italian composers working during the
1720s and 1730s, the complicated melodies, stiff and inflexible
phrase structures, and often polyphonic textures of the High
Baroque style seemed outdated and out of touch with the mood of
the time and the increasingly middle-class audiences.

1. Such Naples-based composers as Alessandro Scarlatti,
Leonardo Leo Nicola Antonio Porpora, and Giovanni Battista
Pergolesi increasingly sought to cultivate a music that was
melodically tuneful, homophonic in texture, light in mood,

and direct in expression; a music as free and graceful in effect as they believed High Baroque music to be academic and ponderous.

2. The term *galant style* came to be associated with this refined and pleasing Neapolitan music. This style, with its emphasis on clarity, directness of expression, and beauty of line, was a proto-Classical musical style. The galant style must also be distinguished from *Rococo*, a French design style.

C. The *empfindsam Stil*, meaning, literally, the "sensitive" or "sentimental style," was the mid-18th–century German equivalent to the galant style, characterized by melodic tunefulness, simplicity of utterance, and directness of expression.

II. Time and history have been unkind to Giambattista Sammartini (c. 1700–1775), whom we might call the "inventor" of the concert symphony. He was the first composer to write a piece in *sonata form*, a leading figure in the development of the Classical style, and a first-rate composer who wrote at least 68 symphonies, among many other works, yet we rarely hear his name or his music.

A. Sammartini's father, Alexis Saint-Martin, was a French oboist who emigrated from France to Italy; his mother was a native Italian named Girolama de Federici. Their son, Giovanni Battista, was born in or near Milan in late 1700 or early 1701, and he lived and worked in that city for the rest of his life.

B. In 1726, by the age of 26, Sammartini was being referred to locally as "our very famous" composer. By the 1730s, he was acknowledged as Milan's leading composer, and by the 1740s, with his music being published and performed in Paris, London, Vienna, and Amsterdam, his international reputation was firmly established.

C. In 1732, Sammartini composed his first opera, entitled *Memet*, and by the late 1730s, he had begun to compose self-standing *sinfonie*, "overtures-without-operas," as they were called, for private performance in the homes of Milan's elite. As an example, we turn to Sammartini's Symphony no. 32 in F Major for strings, composed around 1744.

D. Sammartini's F Major is a three-movement work, organized along the lines of an Italian opera overture: fast-slow-fast. Having said that, the sophisticated treatment of the musical materials within each of the three movements marks this work as a true self-standing symphony. The first movement *presto* is no mere curtain raiser but a proto-sonata–form movement in the guise of binary form.

1. *Sonata form*, sometimes called *sonata-allegro*, is a *musical form*, that is, the internal structure of a movement of music. Sonata form is one of the great inventions of the 18th century, and many composers continued to use it well into the 20th century.

2. In spirit, sonata form grew out of operatic practice. An opera, as we all know, is the setting to music of a stage play. Drama and comedy—flip sides of the same human coin—are about characters and their interactions, as is sonata form.

3. A sonata-form movement features at least two contrasting themes or key areas. The introduction of, and interaction between, these contrasting musical "characters" is the essential substance of the sonata-form movement. The themes are first introduced, separately, in a section called the *exposition*; they are then fragmented, metamorphosed, and manipulated in a section called the *development*; finally, they are reintegrated and restated in their original order in a section called the *recapitulation*.

4. Technically, sonata form grew out of Baroque binary form, the single most common of all Baroque instrumental procedures. *Binary form* consists of two sections of music, each of which is immediately repeated, yielding a large-scale structure of ‖aa|bb‖.

5. As the High Baroque progressed, composers began to elongate, extend, and make more substantial and interesting this time-honored and well-used formal procedure. Most notably, the second section, "b", came to begin in a contrasting key. This harmonic innovation necessitated three corresponding developments.

   a. First, to begin section "b" in a new key, the second half of section "a" had to *modulate*, that is, "change key," so that when section "b" began, the new key would already be comfortably established.

   b. Second, after having begun section "b" in the new key, the music had to eventually modulate and return to where it began so that the piece could end in the same key in which it started.

  c. Finally, having changed back to the original key about halfway through part "b", the music that began part "a" would be reprised (or recapitulated) to confirm for the listener that it had indeed returned to where it had begun. Part "b" of the binary form, then, came to be longer than part "a."

6. This High Baroque extension of binary form was the last evolutionary step before the development of sonata form. All that was necessary was the composition of a contrasting theme to go along with the contrasting key established near the end of part "a." The beginning of part "b" would then take on the character of a development section, as the music modulates back toward the home key, using melodic fragments of both themes as it goes. Finally, both themes would be recapitulated at the conclusion of part "b" in the home key.

E. Returning, then, to Sammartini's Symphony no. 32 in F Major for strings, remember that it is a proto-sonata–form movement in the guise of binary form.

1. The movement starts with a bold, hammer-blow theme in F major. In terms of sonata form, this is theme 1. In terms of binary form, it's the opening of part "a." (**Musical selection**: Sammartini, Symphony no. 32 in F Major, movement 1 [1744].)

2. Keep in mind that we are currently in the key of F major. *Major* and *minor* are the two essential *modes*, or "pitch palettes," of European tonal music. Major is perceived as being the brighter sounding of the two, and minor, the darker sounding.

3. Immediately following this bright and bold opening theme in F major, there ensues a transitional passage, during which the music modulates from the home key (F major) to a new key (C major). (**Musical selection**: Sammartini, Symphony no. 32 in F Major, movement 1.)

4. Having established the new key, a brief, rising melodic idea leads to a vigorous conclusion, a musical "punctuation mark" called a *cadence*, bringing part "a" of the binary form to its

conclusion. (**Musical selection**: Sammartini, Symphony no. 32 in F Major, movement 1.)

5. Using the terminology of sonata form, we have heard the *exposition*, consisting of theme 1; followed by the modulating transition, or bridge, to theme 2; followed by closing material in the new key. Using the terminology of binary form, we have just heard part "a," which according to convention, is now repeated in its entirety. (**Musical selection**: Sammartini, Symphony no. 32 in F Major, movement 1.)

6. We now begin part "b" of the binary form or the development section of a sonata form. Beginning in the new key (C major) and using fragments of the themes just heard in part "a" (the exposition), the music modulates back toward the home key of F major. (**Musical selection**: Sammartini, Symphony no. 32 in F Major, movement 1.)

7. In the second half of part "b" or the recapitulation of the sonata form, the themes are now heard in their original order and in the home key of F major. (**Musical selection**: Sammartini, Symphony no. 32 in F Major, movement 1.)

8. Finally, the entire "b" section or the development and recapitulation is repeated. We listen to the entire movement from beginning to end. (**Musical selection**: Sammartini, Symphony no. 32 in F Major, movement 1.)

9. The second movement of Sammartini's Symphony no. 32 is a ravishing *andante*. (**Musical selection**: Sammartini, Symphony no. 32 in F Major, movement 2.)

10. The third movement is a quirky and wonderful dance in binary form. Because this movement does not introduce a second theme, it is not called sonata form. Note the odd, irregular, and wonderful tag that Sammartini adds to the theme after each of its first two iterations (part "a" and its repetition). (**Musical selection**: Sammartini, Symphony no. 32 in F Major, movement 3.)

F. Sammartini's music played an essential role in the creation of what we now think of as the *Classical style*. He was among the most advanced and experimental composers of his time and the first master of the symphony. Along with his influence on subsequent composers, the consistently high quality of his music places him among the most important composers of the 18th century.

III. From Italy, the popularity of the "overture-without-an-opera," the new *sinfonia*, spread rapidly.

    A. Exhibiting the melodic and expressive characteristics of the new galant style, the genre of symphony embodied all that was considered musically modern in the 1740s–1760s. Because it was a new musical genre, the symphony was free to be experimental, and as such, it came to epitomize the new musical spirit of the Enlightenment.

    B. For the rest of this lecture, let us a take a brief tour of some Europe's pre-Classic symphonic "hot spots" and sample a range of movements by a range of composers.

IV. Johann Sebastian Bach's two most famous sons, Carl Philip Emanuel Bach (1714–1788) and Johann Christian Bach (1735–1782), represent perfectly what is called "the north-south divide" of the pre-Classic symphonic tradition.

    A. Carl Philip Emanuel, or C. P. E., Bach was the second surviving son of Johann Sebastian and his first wife, Barbara. He remains the most famous of Bach's sons and, as a composer, the one who stayed closest to his north German roots.

        1. North German music, rooted in the Lutheran tradition, experienced a golden age from 1650–1725. But that golden age blinded many north Germans to the merits of the new music coming out of Italy in the 1730s–1740s, music they dismissed as frivolous and self-indulgent, light and unserious.

        2. In 1740, C. P. E. was hired as court harpsichordist for Frederick the Great. For 28 years, he played the harpsichord in Berlin and Potsdam, performing music that reflected the emperor's arch-conservative (and most certainly anti-Italian) taste. C. P. E.'s own compositions were rarely performed at court.

        3. Georg Philipp Telemann, C. P. E.'s godfather and music director for the city of Hamburg, died in 1767. In early 1768, C. P. E., who was 54 at the time, managed to obtain his release from the emperor and took the post of *Kapellmeister* for the city of Hamburg.

        4. Hamburg, despite being a "north German" city, was musically much less conservative than the Charlottenburg Palace in Berlin. C. P. E.'s compositional style underwent a metamorphosis, one beautifully reflected in his six Hamburg Symphonies of 1773, which exhibit a lightness and melodic grace far beyond anything he had composed in Prussia.

5. We listen to the first movement of C. P. E.'s Hamburg Symphony no. 6 in E Major. It is a compact sonata-form movement with an ending so abrupt and harmonically shocking as to leave us unsure as to whether it has really ended! (**Musical selection**: C. P. E. Bach, Symphony no. 6 in E Major, movement 1 [1773].)

B. C. P. E.'s half-brother, Johann Christian, or J. C. Bach, was Johann Sebastian's youngest son, the 11th child of Bach's second wife, Anna Magdalena. The difference between C. P. E. and J. C. Bach's symphonies embodies the contrast between the German north and the Italian south; where C. P. E.'s music is abrupt, dramatic, and filled with contrasts of mood, J. C. Bach's music is smooth, polished, elegant, and sensuous.

1. J. C. was swept away by the new Italian *galant* style. In 1754, at the age of 19, he moved to Italy, where he studied composition with Padre Giambattista Martini, one of the most famous Italian musicians of the time.

2. In 1757, Christian converted to Catholicism and, three years later, was appointed as one of the two organists at the Milan Cathedral. He also composed Italian-language operas, which were extremely popular. Word of his work spread quickly, and offers from opera houses in Venice and London began to pour into the cathedral.

3. In May of 1762, Christian asked for and received a year's leave of absence to compose two operas for the King's Theater in London, a leave of absence from which he never returned.

4. The first of his commissioned operas, a work entitled *Orione*, premiered on February 19, 1763, and was a great success. The English queen, Charlotte, a German by birth, became Bach's essential patron. Within a year, he was appointed "music master to the Queen," a position that guaranteed his fame and fortune.

5. Christian Bach's first set of symphonies—the six symphonies published as op. 3—are a perfect example of the smooth,

urbane, Italian opera–inspired lyric charm that made J. C. Bach one of the finest exponents of the galant style.

6. As an example, we turn to Bach's Symphony in D Major, op. 3, no. 1, scored for strings, two oboes, and two horns. We listen to the third and final movement, a rousing and concise *presto* in sonata form. (**Musical selection**: Johann Christian Bach, Symphony in D Major, op. 3, no. 1, movement 3 [1765].)

V. In closing, we turn to Vienna, where the northern and southern European musical styles, represented by the *empfindsam* style of C. P. E. Bach and the galant style of J. C. Bach, were blended into a single musical language of virtually perfect balance—a balance of heart and head, feeling and intellect, lyric melody and subtle harmony. The city gave its name to this musical style, which became the *Viennese Classical style*.

A. The most important Viennese composer of pre-Classic symphonies was Georg Christoph Wagenseil (1715–1777), who was born in Vienna.

1. Wagenseil was a prolific composer whose symphonies combine the lyric grace of the Italian galant style, the discipline and expressive depth of the German *empfindsam* style, and the orchestral techniques of the Mannheim composers, of whom we will speak in Lecture Four.

2. Wagenseil composed a total of 63 symphonies between about 1745 and 1762, and they were performed widely in his lifetime, from Sweden to Italy, Bohemia to North America.

3. Like those of the brothers Bach, Wagenseil's symphonies followed the three-movement plan of the Italian overture. We will listen to the first movement of his Symphony in Bb Major, composed around 1764. The movement is a sonata-form/binary-form hybrid, meaning that Wagenseil has indicated that the exposition ("a" in the binary form) be repeated, as well as the development and recapitulation ("b" in the binary form).

4. The sonata-form structure of the movement reveals itself with crystal clarity. The exposition repeat begins 1 minute, 12 seconds, into the movement; the development, at 2 minutes, 25 seconds; and the recapitulation, at 3 minutes, 7 seconds.

(**Musical selection**: Wagenseil, Symphony in Bb Major, WV 441, movement 1 [1764].)

B. Along with Georg Matthias Monn (1717–1750) and Florian Gassman (1729–1774), who were the other leading composers of symphonies in Vienna during the 1740s–60s, Wagenseil's symphonic music synthesized the lyricism of the south; the compositional discipline, harmonic technique, and expressive power of the north; and the instrumental techniques of the orchestra of the court of Mannheim to the west, to which we turn in the next lecture.

Lecture Three—Transcript
The Pre-Classical Symphony

Welcome back to *The Symphony*. This is Lecture Three—it is entitled "The Pre-Classical Symphony."

Terms

As we concluded Lecture Two, we noted that the so-called *galant* style, a new, lyric pre-Classical Italian style, epitomized by the music of Giovanni Pergolesi, swept across Europe in the 1730s and the 1740s. The earliest true symphonies are a product of this time. So let us quickly but vigorously deal with some of the names and terms that are routinely applied to the period that lay between the High Baroque and Viennese Classicism, an era roughly spanning the years between 1730 and 1770.

According to our textbooks, the Baroque era ended in 1750 with the death of Johann Sebastian Bach in Liepzig early in the evening on July 28, 1750. Presumably then, the Classical era began immediately after, sometime later that same evening. Of course, in reality, the transition from Baroque to Classical was evolutionary—not sudden and revolutionary as that date of 1750 might lead us to think. Aspects of the Classical style began to appear in some Italian music as early as the 1720s. And what we now refer to as the *Viennese Classical* style wasn't completely in place until the 1770s. And to the enduring confusion of music history students everywhere and music fans alike, a whole slew of terms and names has been applied to the incremental stylistic changes that mark the evolution of the Baroque to the Classical.

For any number of young Italian composers working during the 1720s and 1730s, the complicated melodies, stiff and inflexible phrase structures, and often polyphonic textures of the High Baroque style seemed hopelessly out of touch and out of date with the mood of their time and their increasingly middle-class audiences. Such Naples-based composers as Alessandro Scarlatti, Leonardo Leo Nicola Antonio Porpora, and Giovanni Battista Pergolesi increasingly sought to cultivate a music that was melodically tuneful, homophonic in texture, light in mood, and direct in expression; a music as free and graceful in effect as they believed High Baroque music to be academic and ponderous.

The term *galant style* came to be associated with this Neapolitan music. In colloquial 18th century usage, the term *galant* denoted something that was pleasing, especially to the ladies—refined, elegant, witty, natural, enjoyable, sophisticated, polite and in good taste. The galant musical style with its emphasis on clarity, directness of expression, and beauty of line was a genuinely proto-Classical musical style. As opposed to *Rococo*, a stylistic term which is often used synonymously with galant, but is—we have to be sticklers for accuracy—something rather different.

Rococo was a French design style that maintained the detailed, ornamental characteristic of Baroque design but on a frankly less monumental scale. The term has been applied to the music of the early and mid-18th century as well, but not, in the measured and elegant words of Donald Michael Randel in the *New Harvard Dictionary of Music*:

> [But] not always judiciously. Attempts by musicologists to extend the term 'Rococo' to all European music [of the early to mid-18th century] has met with a number of difficulties. In the first place, the new galant or early Classical style had its origins in Italy, specifically in Italian opera, and not in France. Second, the patronage enjoyed by [gallant] Italian opera of the period was mixed and partly public, whereas the patronage of the French Rococo was aristocratic and mostly private. Finally, the new Italian style represented a [genuine] break with the past, whereas true Rococo maintains strong links with the Baroque.

Terms: Finally, we turn to the term *empfindsam* style, or in German, the *empfindsamer Stil*, meaning, literally, the "sensitive" or "sentimental" style. The *empfindsam* style was the German equivalent to the galant style, a mid-18th-century German musical style characterized by melodic tunefulness, simplicity of utterance, and directness of expression. As we discuss such pre-Classical symphonists as Giovanni Battista Sammartini, Carl Philip Emanuel Bach, and Georg Christoph Wagenseil, we will be discussing composers whose music embodies the galant style in Italy and the *emfindsam* style in Germany and Austria.

Giovanni Battista Sammartini (ca. 1700-1775)

History, my friends, has been unkind to Sammartini. If we had to choose one person as the de facto "inventor" of the concert symphony, it would have to be Sammartini. He was the first composer to write something that we today recognize as *sonata form*. He was a leading figure in the development of the Classical style. He was a really first-rate composer who wrote at least 68 symphonies, among many, many other works. And when-oh-when do we ever hear his name or his music? Let us do our bit to correct this unfortunate inequity.

Sammartini's father, Alexis Saint-Martin (Saint-Martin equals, in Italian, Sammartini) was a French oboist who immigrated to Italy. His mother was a native Italian named Girolama de Federici. Their son, Giovanni Battista, was born in or near Milan in late 1700 or early 1701, and he lived and worked in that city for the rest of his life. By the age of 26, in 1726, Sammartini was being referred to locally as "our very famous" composer Giambattista Sammartini. Now, I would tell you that not everyone was as enthusiastic about Sammartini's early music. When the German composer and flute player Johann Joachim, or J.J. Quantz visited Milan in 1726, the most he could bring himself to admit was that Sammartini's music "is not bad."

Well, truth be told, Sammartini's music was a whole lot better than "not bad." By the 1730s, he was Milan's leading composer, and by the 1740s with his music being published and performed in Paris, London, Vienna and Amsterdam (where Antonio Vivaldi conducted one of Sammartini's symphonies in 1738), his international reputation was firmly established. Copies of Sammartini's symphonies could be found in the music library of Prince Nicholas Esterhazy, where without any doubt they would have been studied by the young Joseph Haydn.

In 1732, Sammartini composed his first opera, a work entitled *Memet*. By the late 1730s, he began to compose self-standing *sinfonie*—"overtures without operas" as they were called—for private performance in the homes of Milan's elite. As an example, we turn to Sammartini's Symphony no. 32 in F Major for strings, composed around 1744.

Typical of all early symphonies, Sammartini's F Major is a three-movement work, organized along the lines of an Italian overture: fast-slow-fast. Having said that, it's the sophisticated treatment of the musical materials within each of the three movements that marks this work as a true self-standing symphony and not just an overture. The first movement *presto* is no mere curtain-raiser, but a proto-sonata-form movement in the guise of binary form.

Okay, listen up because all this "form" stuff is really important. *Sonata form,* sometimes called *sonata-allegro,* is a *musical form,* that is, the internal structure of a movement of music. Sonata form is one of the great inventions of the 18th century, and many composers continue to use it with significant success well into the 20th century. In spirit, sonata form grew out of operatic practice. An opera, as we all know, is the setting to music of a stage play, a drama, or a comedy. Drama and comedy—flip sides of the same human coin really—are all about people (characters) and their interaction. And so is sonata form.

A sonata-form movement features at least two contrasting themes and/or key areas, and it is the introduction and interaction between these contrasting musical "characters" that is the essential substance of a sonata-form movement. The themes are introduced, separately, in an *exposition*; they are then fragmented, metamorphosed, and manipulated in a section called the *development*; and finally, they are reintegrated and restated in their original order in a section called the *recapitulation*.

Technically, sonata form grew out of Baroque binary form, that single most common of all musical forms. *Binary form* consists of two sections of music, each of which is immediately repeated, yielding a large-scale structure of ‖aa|bb‖. Now, as the High Baroque progressed, composers began to elongate, extend, and make more substantial and interesting this time-honored (meaning boring) and well-trod (meaning used up) formal procedure. Most notably, the second section, "b", came to begin in a new key, a contrasting key, a key other than the one that began section "a". This harmonic innovation necessitated three corresponding developments. Number one, in order to begin section "b" in a new key, the second half of section "a" had to *modulate*, that is "change key." Then when section "b" began, the new key would already be comfortably established. Musical development number two: After having begun section "b" in the new key, the music had to eventually modulate again (change key) and return to where it began so that the piece could end the same key in which it began. Three, having transited back to the original key, about halfway through part "b", the music that began part "a" would be reprised (or recapitulated) in order to confirm for the listener that the music had indeed returned to where it had begun. What with the modulation back to the home key and the reprise of the original thematic material in that home key, these second sections (part "b" of the binary form) came to be longer, sometimes substantially longer, than part "a".

This High Baroque extension of binary form was the last evolutionary step before the development of sonata form. All that was necessary was for a composer to compose a new theme, a second theme—a contrasting theme— to go along with a new key, the second key, the contrasting key established near the end of part "a". The beginning of part "b" would then take on the character of the development section, as the music modulates back towards the home key, using melodic fragments of both themes as it goes. Finally, both themes would be recapitulated at the conclusion of part "b" in the home key. That's how sonata form works, my friends.

Back then to Sammartini's Symphony no. 32 in F Major, for strings, composed around 1744. Immediately preceding our little sidebar into sonata form and its evolution, I had stated that the first movement *presto* is no mere curtain raiser but a proto-sonata-form in the guise of binary form. Yes it is. The movement starts with a bold, hammer-blow type theme in F major.

[Musical example from Symphony No. 32 in F Major for Strings, Sammartini: I]

In terms of sonata form, this is theme one. In terms of the binary form, it's the opening of part "a". Let's hear it again.

[Musical example from Symphony No. 32 in F Major for Strings, Sammartini: I]

Terms, terms, terms. We are presently in the key of F major. *Major* and *minor* are the two essential *modes* or "pitch palattes" of European tonal music. Major is perceived as being the brighter sounding of the two, and minor, the darker sounding of the two. Now, immediately following this bright and bold opening theme in F major, there ensues a transitional passage during which the music modulates from the home key (F major) to a new key, which happens here to be C major. Let's hear it.

[Musical example from Symphony No. 32 in F Major for Strings, Sammartini: I]

Having established this new key, a brief, rising melodic idea leads to a conclusion, a musical punctuation mark, something we call a *cadence*.

[Musical example from Symphony No. 32 in F Major for Strings, Sammartini: I]

Now using the terminology of sonata form, we have just heard the *exposition,* consisting as it does of theme 1, the modulating translation or bridge, to a new key which is what we would now call theme 2, followed by closing material in that new key. Using the terminology of binary form, we have just heard part "a", which according to convention, is now repeated in its entirety.

[Musical example from Symphony No. 32 in F Major for Strings, Sammartini: I]

We now begin part "b" of the binary form, or the development section of a sonata form. Beginning in the new key of C major and using fragments of the themes as just heard in part "a" (or the exposition), the music modulates back towards the home key of F major. Let's hear that portion of the movement.

[Musical example from Symphony No. 32 in F Major for Strings, Sammartini: I]

And now the second half of part "b", or in the parlance of the sonata form, the recapitulation. The themes are now heard in their original order and in the home key of F major.

[Musical example from Symphony No. 32 in F Major for Strings, Sammartini: I]

Finally, the entire "b" section, or the development and the recapitulation of the sonata form, is repeated. To repeat myself, this movement is a proto-sonata-form movement in the guise of binary form. Let's hear the entire movement from beginning to end. Sammartini's Symphony no. 32 in F Major, movement one.

[Musical example from Symphony No. 32 in F Major for Strings, Sammartini: I]

The second movement of Sammartini's Symphony no. 32 is a ravishing *andante*. We hear its opening moments.

[Musical example from Symphony No. 32 in F Major for Strings, Sammartini: II]

The third and final movement is a quirky and wonderful dance in binary form. This movement introduces no second theme, so we would not and should not call it sonata form. However, we can and will call it "swingin' great stuff." Note the odd and utterly wonderful little tags, how Sammartini adds to the theme after each of its first two iterations (that would be part "a" and its repetition). Sammartini's Symphony no. 32 in F Major, movement three.

[Musical example from Symphony No. 32 in F Major for Strings, Sammartini: III]

No doubt about it my friends, Giambattista Sammartini had mad skills. Sammartini's music played an essential role in what we now think of as the Classical style. He was one of the most advanced and experimental composers of his time, and the first great master of the symphony. Along with his influence on subsequent composers, the consistently high quality of his music places him among the most important composers of the 18th century.

Off and Running

From Italy the popularity of the "overture-without-an-opera," the new concert-sinfonia, or just sinfonia, or symphony spread like wildfire. Exhibiting those melodic and expressive characteristics of the new and incredibly popular galant style, the genre of symphony embodied all that was considered musically hip, current, and modern in the 1740s, '50s and '60s. Because it was a brand new musical genre, the symphony was not limited by any particular tradition. And so, like early opera, like jazz in the 1920s and rock and roll in '50s and '60s, it was free to be an experimental art form. As such, the symphony was the genre of music that, along with opera buffa, came to epitomize the new music and the new musical spirit, the great mid-18th century social revolution called the Enlightenment.

The number of symphonies written in the 18th century—by geniuses, slobs, and everyone in between—is mind-boggling. According to the Union Thematic Catalog of Eighteenth Century Symphonies, as of 1975, more than 12,350 had been counted, a number that has undoubtedly grown since then. For the remainder of this lecture, we will take a brief but enthusiastic tour of some of Europe's pre-Classic symphonic "hot spots" and sample a range of movements by a range of composers, saving the hottest of these spots, the Electoral court at Mannheim, for our next lecture.

Sebastian Bach's Boys and the North-South Divide

Johann Sebastian Bach's two most famous sons, Carl Philip Emanuel Bach (1714–1788) and Johann Christian Bach (1735–1782), represent perfectly what is called "the north-south divide" of the pre-Classic symphonic tradition. Carl Philip Emanuel, or C. P. E. Bach was the second surviving son of Johann Sebastian and his first wife, Barbara. He was, and remains, the most famous of Bach's sons, and as a composer, the one who stayed closest to his north German roots. Yes, his north German roots.

North German music, rooted in the Lutheran tradition, experienced a golden age between about 1650 and 1725. But that golden age went a long way towards blinding many north Germans to the merits of the new music—the style galant—coming out of 1730s and 1740s, music they dismissed as prettified, dandified, Italian music—music to be treated with contempt.

In 1740, C. P. E. was hired as court harpsichordist for Frederick the Great. For 28, years he played the harpsichord in Berlin and Potsdam, performing music that reflected the emperor's arch-conservative (and most certainly anti-Italian taste). As for C. P. E.'s own compositions, well, they were rarely performed in court. He was, in his way of thinking, never properly appreciated by his boss. So he quit. In 1767, the great Georg Philipp Telemann, C. P. E.'s godfather and music director for the city of Hamburg, died at the age of 86. In early 1786, C. P. E., no spring chicken himself at 54 years of age, managed to obtain his release from "Freddy the G," and took the plump post of *Kapellmeister* for the city of Hamburg.

Well, talk about a breath of fresh air. Hamburg, despite being a "north German" city was musically an infinitely less conservative place than the Charlottenburg Palace in Berlin. C. P. E.'s compositional style underwent a metamorphosis, one beautifully reflected in his six so-called Hamburg Symphonies of 1773, which exhibit a lightness and melodic grace far from anything he had composed in Prussia. According to musicologist Allan Badley, "C. P. E. Bach's most characteristic touches could be found in these symphonies: energetic tuttis, sudden contrast in mood, extreme modulations, and abrupt endings, hallmarks of the so-called *empfindsamer Stil* [the "sensitive" or "sentimental" style] of which [C. P. E. Bach] is the supreme representative."

As an example, let's listen to the first movement of C. P. E.'s Hamburg Symphony no. 6 in E Major. It's a compact little sonata-form movement with an ending so abrupt and harmonically shocking as to leave us unsure as to whether the movement has really ended. Let's hear it. Carl Philip Emanuel Bach, Symphony no. 6 in E Major, movement 1 of 1773.

[Musical example from Symphony No. 6 in E Major, C. P. E. Bach; 1]

A great sidebar: Emanuel Bach's Hamburg Symphonies were commissioned by Baron Gottfried von Swieten, who would go on to become one of Mozart's most important patrons and to write the libretti for Haydn's oratorios *The Creation* and *The Seasons*. Von Swieten was a huge fan of Johann Sebastian Bach at a time when it had fallen into near total obscurity. Sometime around 1772, the baron traveled to Holland to meet C. P. E. Bach in the hopes of acquiring some of his father's musical manuscripts. C. P. E. and the baron became good friends, and the commission for the six symphonies was one of the immediate fruits of that friendship.

C. P. E. Bach's half-brother, Johann Christian, or J. C. Bach, was Johann Sebastian's youngest son, the eleventh child of Bach's second wife, Anna Magdalena. (A lot of kids!) The difference between C. P. E. and J. C. Bach's symphonies embodies the contrast between the German north and the Italian south; where C. P. E.'s music is abrupt and dramatic and filled with contrasts of mood, J.C. Bach's music is smooth, polished, elegant, and sensuous.

J. C. or Christian Bach was swept away by the new Italian galant style in a manner typical of his time, but not typical for a member of the Bach family. In 1754, at the age of 19, four years after his father's death, Christian moved to Italy where he studied composition with Padre Giambattista Martini, one of the most famous Italian musicians of the time. In 1757, Christian converted to Catholicism, and three years later, in 1760, he was appointed as one of the two organists at Milan's Cathedral. When he wasn't tickling the ivories, J. C. was composing, Italian language operas mostly, and they proved to be extremely popular and widely performed. Word of this marvelous young Bach spread quickly, and offers from opera houses in Venice and London began to pour into the organ loft at the Cathedral. Would you have stayed in Milan? No. Neither did J. C. In May of 1762, he asked for and received a year's leave of absence to compose two operas for the King's Theater in London, a leave of absence from which he never returned.

The streets of London might have been covered with slime and offal, but for Christian Bach they were paved in gold. The first of his commissioned operas, a work entitled *Orione*, premiered on February 19, 1763—and it was a huge hit! Charles Burney, the single most important music writer in London declared that in this opera, "Every judge of music perceived the emanations of genius." And even more important than Burney's approbation was that of the English queen, Charlotte, a German by birth, who soon became Christian Bach's essential patron. Within a year, Bach was appointed "music master to the Queen," and with that his fame and fortune were guaranteed.

Please, another side bar: It was exactly at this time—in April of 1764—that a teeny-tiny 8-year-old *wunderkind extraordinaire* from Salzburg named Wolfgang Mozart arrived in London with his family. Mozart spent the next

15 months in London, and despite their age differences, Wolfgang Mozart and Christian Bach became fast friends. And while a formal teacher-student relationship never existed between them, their musical relationship was such that the eminent Bach scholar, Ernest Warburton has no qualms writing that, "[J. C. Bach's compositional] style, which was largely derived from Italian opera, was the most important single influence on Mozart's [own compositional development]."

Christian Bach's first set of symphonies—the six symphonies published as op. 3—were composed and published while Mozart was there living in London. They are a perfect example of the smooth, urbane, Italian opera-inspired lyric charm that made J. C. Bach one of the finest exponents of the galant style. As an example, we turn to Bach's Symphony in D Major, op. 3, no. 1, scored for strings, two oboes, and two horns. Let's hear the third and final movement, a rousing and concise *presto* in sonata form.

[Musical example from Symphony in D Major, Opus 3, No. 1; J.C. Bach]

Vienna

In closing, we turn to Vienna, an imperial city whose geographic location at the crossroads of Europe assured a cultural confluence unmatched anywhere else in Europe. It was in Vienna that the northern and southern musical styles, as represented by the *empfindsam* style of C. P. E. Bach and the galant style of J. C. Bach were blended into a single musical language of virtually perfect balance—a balance of head and heart, of intellect and feeling, lyric melody and subtle harmony, a musical style to which the city gave its name—the *Viennese Classical style*. But, we get ahead of ourselves. By far, the most important Viennese composer of pre-Classic symphonies was Georg Christoph Wagenseil, who was born in Vienna in 1715 and died there in 1777. Wagenseil was a prolific composer whose symphonies combined the lyrical grace of the Italian galant style, the discipline and expressive depth of the German *empfindsam* style, and the orchestral techniques of the Mannheim composers, of whom we will speak in Lecture Four.

Wagenseil, my friends, was also a favorite of the Empress Maria Theresa, her personal accompanist on those occasions when she waddled forth to sing at her private recitals, the Florence Foster Jenkins of her time. One can only marvel at the discipline of the choir to keep a straight face at such times. Anyway, Wagenseil composed a total of 63 symphonies between about 1745 and 1762, and they were performed widely, I mean really widely, in his own lifetime from Sweden to Italy, from Bohemia to North

America. Like those of the brothers Bach, Wagenseil's symphonies followed the three-movement plan of the Italian overture. We will listen to the first movement of his Symphony in Bb Major, composed around 1764. The movement is in sonata form/binary form, meaning that Wagenseil has indicated that the exposition (or "a" in the binary form) be repeated as well as the development and recapitulation ("b" in the binary form). For the sake of time, we will not listen to the repetition of the development and the recapitulation.

The sonata-form structure of the movement reveals itself with crystal clarity. The exposition repeat begins one minute and twelve seconds (1:12) into the movement; the development at two minutes, twenty-five seconds (2:25), and the recapitulation at three minutes and seven seconds (3:07). Please, Georg Christoph Wagenseil's Symphony in Bb Major, movement 1 of 1754.

[Musical example from Symphony in Bb Major, Baggencile; I]

This is by any standard thoroughly engaging music. And the second and third movements of this music, well they're just as good. Along with Georg Matthias Monn and Florian Gassman, who were the other leading composers of symphonies during the 1740s, '50s, and '60s, Wagenseil's symphonic music synthesized the lyricism of the south; the compositional discipline, harmonic technique and expressive oomph of the north; and the instrumental techniques of the orchestra of the court of Mannheim to the west.

We have already discussed the galant style of the south and the *empfindsam* style of the north. Now it's time to meet the so-called "army of generals," the orchestra at the court of Mannheim and the composers who wrote for it.

Thank you.

Lecture Four
Mannheim

Scope: Under the directorship of Jan Vaclav Stamitz, the court orchestra at Mannheim gained a reputation for unprecedented virtuosity across Europe in the mid-18th century. This lecture explores Stamitz's contribution to the development of the symphony and surveys his compositions for the orchestra, which featured the renowned Mannheim crescendi. We also look at the work of Stamitz's successors in composing for the orchestra, including Franz Xaver Richter, Ignaz Holzbauer, and Johann Christian Cannabich.

Outline

I. Mannheim, in west-central Germany, was founded in 1606 as a fortress, and it remained a military installation until 1720, when it was designated an electoral seat of the Holy Roman Empire.

   A. The elector, Carl Philipp, brought to Mannheim musicians from Breslau, a German-speaking city just north of Bohemia.

   B. Carl Philipp initiated a major building program at Mannheim that included a gigantic palace. Life at the court quickly gained a reputation as being among the most brilliant in Germany. By 1723, the musical establishment at the Mannheim court included 56 full-time musicians, most of whom were Bohemian, with a few native Germans.

   C. In 1742, Elector Carl Philipp died and was succeeded by Prince Carl Theodor (1724–1799). Carl Theodor was only 18 at the time of his accession, but he was an enlightened patron of science, business, the arts, and especially, music.

   D. Prince Carl Theodor, an excellent musician himself, immediately began adding musicians to the large number he had inherited; eventually, the Mannheim court had 90 musicians.

   E. The leader in this deep pool of talent was the violinist, conductor, and composer Jan Vaclav Antonin Stamitz (1717–1757).
   1. Stamitz was born in Bohemia, where he was educated at the Jesuit Gymnasium. He was a genuine violinistic phenomenon,

and after attending Prague University for a year, he began to travel in search of fame and fortune.

2. In 1741, at the age of 24, Stamitz was hired to play in the orchestra in Mannheim. A year later, Prince Carl Theodor succeeded his uncle Carl Philipp as elector, and Stamitz's meteoric rise through the musical ranks at Mannheim began.

3. In 1743, he was appointed first violinist of the court. By 1744, at the age of 27, he was the highest paid musician in Mannheim. In 1745, he was awarded the title of concertmaster, the position that we today would regard as the conductor of the orchestra.

4. As concertmaster, it was Stamitz's job to prepare and conduct the orchestral concerts held in the Rittersaal (the "knight's hall") of the electoral palace. Stamitz led the orchestra from his seat at the front of the violin section, using his bow, shoulders, hands, head, and elbows to signal and direct his band.

5. Stamitz turned the Mannheim musicians into an orchestral unit of unmatched skill. He drilled the strings endlessly, and it was the unique ability of the string section to play as a unit that lay at the heart of the Mannheim orchestra's sound and reputation. Their precision, their uniform bowing, and the fact that Stamitz had personally trained each one of his performers created an unprecedented level of orchestral virtuosity.

6. In addition to his directorship duties, Stamitz was expected to create orchestral compositions. Inspired by a string section that could play with all the nuance of a soloist and surrounded by some of the best musicians in Europe, Stamitz wrote orchestral music that treated the orchestra like a virtuoso ensemble. In doing so, he virtually created the standards by which orchestras and orchestral music were measured for the next 50 years.

7. In 1750, Elector Prince Carl Theodor created a new title and post for his prized concertmaster/composer, that of instrumental music director. Without a doubt, much of what we still consider "modern orchestral practice" can be traced to Stamitz and the composers that followed him in Mannheim, including Franz Xaver Richter, Ignaz Holzbauer, and Christian Cannabich.

II. Fifty-eight of Stamitz's symphonies have survived; we will sample an early one and a late one.

    A. We begin with the first movement of his Symphony in A Major, one of his three "Mannheim" Symphonies, which were written sometime between 1741 and 1746 and are among the first works Stamitz composed for the electoral court. The symphony is scored for strings and continuo. Overall, it follows the three-movement, Italian overture–style design, although the structure and substance of each of the movements mark the piece as a true symphony. We turn to the first-movement allegro.

        1. The first movement is a hybrid sonata form/binary form, with the exposition of the sonata form ("a" of the binary structure) immediately repeated, and the development and recapitulation ("b" of the binary structure) then also immediately repeated.

        2. Theme 1 is a "Joy to the World"–type melody, a two-octave scalar descent in A major. We listen to this modest but memorable theme, followed by the transitional material (called the *modulating bridge*) that will effect the change of key in preparation for theme 2. (**Musical selection**: Stamitz, Symphony in A Major, movement 1, theme 1, and modulating bridge [c. 1741–1746].)

        3. Theme 2 and—of equal importance—key area 2 now ensues. (**Musical selection**: Stamitz, Symphony in A Major, movement 1, theme 2.)

        4. The following *cadential* music now brings this exposition to its close. As we listen, please note two important elements. (**Musical selection**: Stamitz, Symphony in A Major, movement 1, cadence music.)

            a. This closing material begins with an orchestral *crescendo*—that is, the music gradually goes from soft to loud—which is the sort of device that would have made Stamitz's audiences rise from their seats. Stamitz didn't invent the crescendo, but through him, orchestral crescendi came to be called "Mannheim crescendi" across Europe.

            b. The other element to note is what happens after the crescendo—a series of phrases during which the orchestra alternates between playing very loud and very soft.

Again, this device would have driven contemporary audiences wild with excitement.

5. Now the entire exposition (or part "a" in binary form) is repeated. (**Musical selection**: Stamitz, Symphony in A Major, movement 1, exposition.)

6. The development section (or the first half of "b" of the binary structure) begins with a brief reiteration of theme 1. This music is *harmonically unstable*, because it is almost continually *modulating*, or "changing key." The effect is one of almost constant forward momentum. Stamitz's development section is substantial, and it uses melodic materials drawn from both themes 1 and 2 and the modulating bridge. (**Musical selection**: Stamitz, Symphony in A Major, movement 1, development.)

7. The recapitulation follows, during which both themes are heard in the home key of A major. Be aware that the recapitulation is no mere repetition of the exposition; Stamitz expands the modulating bridge between themes 1 and 2 and very slightly shortens the cadential material following theme 2. (**Musical selection**: Stamitz, Symphony in A Major, movement 1, recapitulation.)

8. Not long after Stamitz's time, most sonata-form movements will end at this point. Soon enough, the practice of following the structural prescription of the old binary form by repeating what would have been "b" (what is now, in sonata form, the development and recapitulation) will come to be regarded as tedious and unnecessary.

9. But in 1746, this development had not yet occurred. In this first movement of his Symphony in A Major, Stamitz goes back and repeats the development and recapitulation in their entirety. (**Musical selection**: Stamitz, Symphony in A Major, movement 1, development and recapitulation.)

B. None of Stamitz's symphonic innovations was more important than his treatment of the large-scale scheme of the symphony; he essentially created the four-movement structure. Around 1748 or 1749, he began inserting a minuet between the slow second movement and the fast final movement of his symphonies and was the first to use this four-movement scheme consistently. As his fame grew and his symphonies were played and published across

Europe, the influence of his four-movement symphonies became pervasive.

C. As an example of one of Stamitz's later, four-movement symphonies, we turn to his Symphony in D Major, op. 3, no. 2, composed around 1753 and published in Paris in 1757. The symphony is scored for strings, horns, and oboes.

1. We don't have to wait long for one of Stamitz's trademark crescendi; following the six opening orchestral hammer blows—the "*premiere coup d'archets*" ("first attack of the bows")—the first crescendo is off and running and, with it, the movement! We hear the exposition in its entirety; theme 2, a chipper and engaging tune, appears 54 seconds into the exposition. (**Musical selection**: Stamitz, Symphony in D Major, op. 3, no. 2, movement 1, exposition [c. 1753].)

2. The second movement, labeled *andantino*, offers a lyric, moderately paced respite from the rigors of the first. We will listen to the first half of the movement. Note the orchestral writing here: The strings first play the thematic material, followed by the oboes and horns. (**Musical selection**: Stamitz, Symphony in D Major, op. 3, no. 2, movement 2, opening.)

3. The third movement is a gracious and engaging minuet, a fashionable and recognizable dance type of the time. This sort of movement would have been perceived as having a genuinely "popular" appeal. (**Musical selection**: Stamitz, Symphony in D Major, op. 3, no. 2, movement 3, minuet.)

4. The fourth and final movement is a *prestissimo* (meaning "very fast"). We hear it in its entirety of 1 minute, 48 seconds. (**Musical selection**: Stamitz, Symphony in D Major, op. 3, no. 2, movement 4, *prestissimo*.)

D. Stamitz died in March of 1757 at age 39. His innovations laid the groundwork for much of the great symphonic music that was to come, including the work of Haydn and Mozart, who studied Stamitz's music and profited from its example.

III. Jan Stamitz's premature death in 1757 did not bring down the curtain on the Mannheim orchestra or the Mannheim school of orchestral composers.

A. Among the most of important of these composers was Franz Xaver Richter (1709–1789), who was born to German parents in Bohemia.

    1. Richter was trained as a singer and a violinist and was hired as a singer by the court at Mannheim sometime around the year 1747. He was also a composer of considerable talent and was granted the title of chamber composer to the elector by Carl Theodor in 1768.

    2. In general, Richter's symphonic music is not nearly as adventurous as Stamitz's, and he avoided the sort of extreme virtuosity and musical effects (such as the crescendo) that were so closely associated with the Mannheim style. Nevertheless, he was considered one of the leading Mannheim composers.

    3. Let's sample the first movement of his three-movement Symphony in G Major, a relatively early work, composed at the time he was hired to sing at Mannheim. We hear the exposition of this sonata-form movement. (**Musical selection**: Richter, Symphony in G Major, movement 1, exposition.)

B. The Elector Prince Carl Theodor also built a magnificent opera theater and imported productions from Milan, Rome, and Vienna. On June 15, 1753, when an opera entitled *Il figlio delle selve* ("*The Son of the Forests*") was produced for the elector, he decided that he must have its composer, Ignaz Holzbauer (1711–1783), in his employ. Prince Carl Theodor created the post of music director of the opera at Mannheim and installed Holzbauer within the month.

    1. Holzbauer was born in Vienna in 1711. His father was in the leather business, and his mother died when he was 17. As a young man, he learned to play a number of musical instruments and taught himself to compose. In the 1730s, he traveled to Italy to study and became an exponent of the new galant style.

    2. Holzbauer's duties in Mannheim were to compose and produce operas and sacred music, but he also wrote for the orchestra. Sixty-five of his symphonies have survived, most of them based on the three-movement scheme of the Italian opera overture. We will sample the first movement of his Symphony in D Major, op. 3, no. 4, published in Paris 1772 and most likely written in 1771.

3. Holzbauer begins the movement in a genuinely original way, *pianissimo*, with a rising D-major scale, rather than with a loud opening chord, the *premier coup d'archet* so typical of most Mannheim symphonies. This rising opening sounds, virtually, like a rising curtain, and it becomes louder as it progresses. (**Musical selection**: Holzbauer, Symphony in D Major, op. 3, no. 4, movement 1 [c. 1771].)

C. No examination of the Mannheim group would be complete without mention of Johann Christian Cannabich (1731–1798).

1. Cannabich was born and raised in Mannheim, and he profited from the musical education establishment created by the elector. Cannabich was a violinist and became the prize student of Jan Stamitz. In 1743, at the age of 12, he was allowed to enter the Mannheim orchestra as a "scholar," with special permission from the elector. In 1850, at the age of 19, Cannabich traveled to Italy to study composition and violin at the elector's expense.

2. When Stamitz died unexpectedly in 1757, Cannabich was recalled to Mannheim and appointed concertmaster of the Mannheim orchestra. In 1774, he was appointed to Stamitz's old position of instrumental music director and became the sole conductor and what was called the "trainer" of the orchestra.

3. Cannabich was also a prolific composer; as an example of his work, we turn to his Symphony no. 50 in D Minor, op. 10, no. 5, published in Mannheim in 1778. We hear the first movement of this most uncharacteristic work—a Mannheim symphony that begins in minor! It is a stirring movement in sonata form, and in our performance, without an exposition repeat. (**Musical selection**: Symphony no. 50 in D Minor, op. 10, no. 5, movement 1 [c. 1778].)

IV. In 1778–1779, Prince Carl Theodor inherited the title of elector of Bavaria and moved his court from Mannheim to Munich. The Mannheim court orchestra was merged with the existing Munich orchestra, and the merger brought an end to the golden age of music at Mannheim.

Lecture Four—Transcript
Mannheim

We return to *The Symphony*. This is Lecture Four, entitled "Mannheim." Okay, Paris, London, Vienna, Berlin, we could all understand a lecture dedicated to the establishment of any one of those cities. But Mannheim? Mannheim Germany? It's about as unexpected as putting the Rock & Roll "Hall of Fame" in Cleveland. But yes, Mannheim, in west-central Germany. The city was founded in 1606 as a fortress, and it remained a military installation until 1720, when it was designated an electoral seat of the Holy Roman Empire.

Turning the backwater fortress of Mannheim into a seat of one of the seven electors of the Holy Roman Empire was like converting a malarial swamp on the east bank of the Potomac River into Washington, D.C.—expensive and time consuming, but a gold mine for the local economy. The elector himself was a gent by the name of Carl Philipp who brought with him to Mannheim musicians to whom he had become inordinately attached, musicians hired during a previous assignment to the city of Breslau. Breslau was a German-speaking city just north of Bohemia, in what is today southwest Poland. This is very important because the great bulk of musicians that Elector Carl Philipp imported to Mannheim were Bohemians—they were Czechs.

Carl Philipp initiated a huge building program at Mannheim that included a truly gigantic palace, the largest Baroque structure in all of Germany. Life at the court of Mannheim quickly gained a reputation as being among the most brilliant in all of Germany. By 1723, the musical establishment at the Mannheim court included no less than 56 full-time musicians, a huge number for the time. The great bulk of these musicians were Bohemian, with a few native Germans added for good measure. In 1742, Elector Carl Philipp died, and he was succeeded by Prince Carl Theodor, who lived from 1724 to 1799. Carl Theodor, who was only 18 years old at the time of his accession, was a genuinely enlightened man living in an age of enlightenment, a patron of science, business, the arts, and especially, most especially, a patron of music.

Christian Schubart, a contemporary of the new elector, Prince Carl Theodor, wrote in reference to the prince: "It would be hard to find another great man who had woven music so tightly into his life as this one. He awoke to music; music accompanied him to his table, music resounded when he went hunting; music heightened his worship in church, music lulled him in balmy slumber."

When the great Francois Voltaire visited Mannheim in 1753, his secretary Collini observed afterwards: "The [Mannheim] court was probably the most brilliant in Germany. Festivity followed upon festivity, and the good taste that was thereby developed lent them ever-new charms. There were hunts, operas, French plays and musical performances by the first virtuosos of Europe." Yes, they were indeed the first virtuosos of Europe.

Once having become elector, the young Prince Carl Theodor, an excellent musician himself, immediately began adding musicians to the large number he had inherited. Eventually there were 90 musicians on the Mannheim palace payroll, an astonishing number. And we're not talking, my friends, about hacks hired to fill in the ranks. Oh, no, no. Prince Carl Theodor spared no expense in hiring some of the best musicians in all of Europe, all of them major 18th-century orchestral dogs. And the big dog, the alpha dog in this deep pool of talent was the violinist, conductor, and composer Jan Vaclav Antonin Stamitz (or, in German, Johann Wenzel Anton Stamitz), who lived from 1717 to 1757. Stamitz was born in Bohemia where he was educated at the Jesuit Gymnasium in Jihlava, a big deal, as the Jesuit schools of Bohemia were famous for their rigorous musical training and turned out many of Europe's finest musicians during the 18th century.

Stamitz was a genuine violinistic phenom, and after attending Prague University for a year, he hit the road in search of fame and fortune. It did not elude him for very long. In 1741, at the age of 24, he was hired to play in the orchestra in Mannheim. A year later, Prince Carl Theodor succeeded his uncle Carl Philipp as the elector and Stamitz's meteoric rise through the musical ranks in Mannheim began. In 1743, he was appointed first violinist of the court. By 1744, at the age of 27, he was the highest paid musician in Mannheim. In 1745, at the ripe age of 28, he was awarded the title of concertmaster, the position that we today would regard as the conductor of the orchestra. As concertmaster, it was Stamitz's job to prepare and conduct the orchestral concerts held in the Rittersaal (the knight's hall) of the electoral palace. Stamitz led his orchestra from his seat at the front of the violin section, using his bow, his shoulders, his hands, his head, and elbows to signal and direct his orchestra.

Stamitz made the Mannheim orchestra into an orchestral unit the likes of which had never existed before. The Mannheim court orchestra became not only the best orchestra in Europe, but the best orchestra that had ever existed up to its time. Stamitz drilled the strings endlessly. It was the unique ability of the string section to play as a unit that lay at the very heart of the Mannheim orchestral sound and reputation. Their precision, their utterly uniform bowing and the fact that Stamitz had personally trained each and every one of his performers created an unprecedented level of orchestral virtuosity. They simply blew their audiences away.

The previously quoted Christian Schubart had the opportunity to hear the Mannheim orchestra itself, and he has left us with this rather breathless description: "One believed oneself to be transported to a magic island of sound. No orchestra in the world ever equaled the Mannheimer's execution. Its forte is like thunder; its crescendo like a mighty waterfall; its diminuendo a gentle river disappearing into the distance; its piano is a breath of Spring." "The wind instruments are everything that they should be: the raise and carry or fill and inspire the storm of the strings."

The estimable Charles Burney was equally swept away by the orchestra at Mannheim. Burney wrote that: "there are more solo players and good composers in this than perhaps in any other orchestra in Europe; it is an army of generals, equally fit to plan a battle as to fight it."

"Good composers" notes Master Burney. It would seem that everyone at the court of Mannheim composed. And chief among those "good composers," the one who gave the Mannheim Orchestra its distinct sound and popularized such famous and widely imitated techniques as the "Mannheim crescendo" and the "Mannheim Rocket" was the violinist-turned-conductor-turned-composer Jan Vaclav Stamitz."

In addition to his directorship duties, Stamitz was expected to provide orchestral compositions of his own creation. Inspired by a string section that—thanks to his own good offices—could play with all the nuance of a soloist, and surrounded as he was by some of the best musicians in Europe, Stamitz wrote orchestral music that for the first time treated the orchestra like a virtuoso ensemble. In doing so, he virtually created the standard by which orchestras and orchestral music were measured for the next 50 years.

In 1750, Elector Prince Carl Theodor created an entirely new post for his prized concertmaster/composer, a post called instrumental music director. Stamitz was only 33 years old, though by this time he was known across the continent. Without a doubt, much of what we still consider to this day "modern orchestral practice" can be traced to Stamitz and the composers that followed him there in Mannheim, including Franz Xaver Richter, Ignaz Holzbauer, and Christian Cannabich.

Stamitz: Symphonies

Fifty-eight of Stamitz's symphonies have survived, and we're going to sample two of them, an early one and a late one. We begin with the first movement of his Symphony in A Major, one of his so-called "Mannheim Symphonies," which were written sometime between 1741 and 1746 and are therefore among the first works he composed for the electoral court. The symphony is scored for strings and continuo. Over all, it follows the three-movement Italian-overture style design, although the structure and substance of each of the movements mark the piece as a true symphony. We turn to the first-movement allegro.

Typical of its time, this movement is a hybrid sonata-form/binary-form movement, with the exposition of the sonata form ("a" of the binary structure) being immediately repeated, and then the development and recapitulation ("b" of the binary structure) then also being immediately repeated. Theme 1 is a "Joy to the World"-type melody, a two-octave scalar descent in A major.

[Musical example from Symphony in A Major, Stamitz]

A modest theme indeed, but memorable enough. We hear it again from the beginning, but this time we will continue through the traditional material that follows it, transitional material called a *modulating bridge* that will effect a change of key in preparation for theme 2.

[Musical example from Symphony in A Major, Stamitz: I; Theme I and Modulating Bridge]

Theme 2, and my friends, of equal importance, key area 2 now ensues.

[Musical example from Symphony in A Major, Stamitz: I; Theme II and Key Area II]

The following closing (or *cadential*) music now brings this exposition to a close. Please note the following two most important elements. This closing material begins with an orchestral *crescendo*—the music gradually goes from soft to loud—and this is just the sort of device that literally would have made Stamitz's audiences rise from their seats. Obviously, Stamitz didn't invent the crescendo, but he did make such orchestral crescendi famous such that they were referred to across Europe as "Mannheim crescendi." The second thing that I want you to be aware of is what happens after the crescendo—a series of phrases follows during which the orchestra alternates between playing very soft and very loud, back and forth, just the sort of device that would have driven contemporary audience wild with excitement. Oh, these were the good old days when you didn't have to bite the head off to get an audience reaction. Let's hear this exposition, the exposition closing cadential music beginning with the crescendo.

[Musical example from Symphony in A Major, Stamitz: I; Exposition closing]

And now the entire exposition (or part "a" in the binary form) is repeated. Let's hear it straight through from the beginning.

[Musical example from Symphony in A Major, Stamitz: I]

The development section (or the first half of "b" of the binary structure) begins with a brief reiteration of theme 1. This music is *harmonically unstable* as it is almost continually *modulating* or "changing key." The effect is one of almost constant forward momentum. Stamitz's development section is quite substantial, running 41 seconds in our recording and it employs melodic materials drawn from both themes 1 and 2 and the modulating bridge in addition. Let's hear the development section. Stamitz, Symphony in A Major, movement 1, development.

[Musical example from Symphony in A Major, Stamitz: I; Development]

The recapitulation follows, during which time both themes, 1 and 2, are heard in the home key of A major. Be aware please that Stamitz's recapitulation is no mere repetition of the exposition. He expands the modulating bridge between themes 1 and 2 and ever so slightly shortens the cadential material following theme 2. We hear the recapitulation.

[Musical example from Symphony in A Major, Stamitz: I; Recapitulation]

Now this is where, in the not-too-far-distant future, most sonata-form movements will end. Soon enough, the practice of following the structural prescription of the old binary form by repeating what would have been "b" (but what is now, in sonata form, the development and recapitulation) will come to be regarded as tedious and necessary. But not yet, not in 1746. In this first movement of the Symphony in A Major, Stamitz does indeed go back and repeat development and recapitulation in their entirety. Let's hear them.

[Musical example from Symphony in A Major, Stamitz: I; Development and Recapitulation]

Of all of Stamitz's symphonic innovations, none was more important than his treatment of the large-scale scheme of the symphony. You see, it was Stamitz, that for all intents and purposes, created the four-movement symphony. Around 1748 or 1749, he began inserting a dance, a minuet, between the slow second movement and the fast final movement of his symphonies. Well, here and there other composers had experimented with four-movement schemes. Stamitz was the first to use it consistently in over half of his symphonies—as it turned out, a large number. And as his fame grew, and as his symphonies were played and published across Europe, the influence of his four-movement symphonies became pervasive.

As an example of one of Stamitz's later, four-movement symphonies, we turn to his Symphony in D Major, op. 3, no. 2, composed around 1753 and published in Paris in 1757. The symphony is scored for strings, horns, and oboes. Once the first movement begins, we don't have to wait very long for one of Stamitz's trademark crescendi; following the six opening orchestral hammer blows—the *"premiere coup d'archets"* (the "first attack of the bows" as the gesture would have been called)—the first crescendo is off and running, and with it, the movement. We hear the exposition in its entirety. For our information theme 2—a chipper and engaging little tune—occurs 54 seconds into the exposition.

[Musical example from Symphony in D Major, Opus 3, No. 2, Stamitz: I]

The second movement, labeled *andantino*, offers a lyric, moderately paced respite from the rigors of the first. Note please the orchestral writing here. The strings first play the thematic material followed by the oboes and horns. Very tasteful, very tasty.

[Musical example from Symphony in D Major, Opus 3, No. 2, Stamitz: II]

The third movement, the new movement, the extra movement is a gracious and engaging minuet, without a doubt the single most popular and recognizable dance type of the time. As such, this sort of movement would have been perceived as having a genuinely "popular" appeal.

[Musical example from Symphony in D Major, Opus 3, No. 2, Stamitz: III (Minuet opening)]

The fourth and final movement is a zesty *prestissimo* (*prestissimo* meaning "very fast" and presumably, "very zesty"). We hear this final movement in its entirety.

[Musical example from Symphony in D Major, Opus 3, No. 2, Stamitz: IV]

Stamitz died, all too young, in March of 1757, at the age of 39. His innovations laid the groundwork for much of the great symphonic music that was to come. And here we refer directly to Haydn and Mozart, who studied Stamitz's music and profited mightily from his example. Writing in 1772, fifteen years after Stamitz's death, Charles Burney offered this appraisal of his music:

> [Stamitz], like another Shakespeare, broke through all difficulties and discouragements; and pushed [symphonic] art further than anyone had done before him. His genius was truly original [and] bold; invention, fire and contrast in the quick movements; a tender, graceful, and insinuating melody in the slow; ingenuity and richness of the accompaniments characterized his productions; all replete with great effects, produced by an enthusiasm of genius, refined, but not repressed by cultivation.

Franz Xaver Richter (1709-1789)

Johann Stamitz's premature death in 1757 did not bring down the curtain on the Mannheim orchestra, or the Mannheim school of orchestral composers. The elector, Prince Carl Theodor, did more than just collect great instrumentalists. He also collected great composers, composers who were colleagues and students of Stamitz's, composers whose responsibilities increased after Stamitz's death.

Among the most important of these composers was Franz Xaver Richter. Richter was born in Bohemia to German parents in 1709. He was trained as a singer and as a violinist, and it was in his capacity as a singer—a *basso*— that he came to be hired by the court of Mannheim sometime around 1747. He was also a composer of considerable talent and eventually he was granted the title of chamber composer to the elector by Carl Theodor in 1768. While he was best remembered for his chamber music, particularly his string quartets, which had a powerful influence on Haydn, Richter composed extensively for the Mannheim orchestra as well. And my friends, who wouldn't have, given half the chance?

In general, Richter's symphonic music isn't nearly as adventurous as Stamitz's. And in general, Richter avoided the sort of extreme virtuosity and musical effects (like the crescendo) that were so closely associated with the Mannheim style. Nevertheless, he was considered one of the leading Mannheim composers, and his music swings just fine. Let's sample the first movement of his three-movement Symphony in G. We hear the exposition of this sonata-form movement.

[Musical example from the 1747 Symphony in G Major, Richter: I; Exposition]

Ignaz Holzbauer (1711-1783)

Elector Prince Carl Theodor was not just a connoisseur of orchestral and chamber music, but of opera as well. He built, according to Christian Schubart, "one of the greatest and most splendid opera theaters in all of Europe" for the performance of operas in Mannheim. Unlike the orchestra, which was filled with performers who were also composers, the elector did not employ an opera composer onsite, preferring to import productions from Milan, Rome and Vienna. Now that all changed on June 15, 1753, when an opera entitled *Il figlio delle selve* ("*The Son of the Forests*") was produced for the elector. Its composer was Ignaz Holzbauer, a native of Vienna and the music director to the Duke Carl von Württenberg in nearby Stuttgart. Elector Prince Carl Theodor decided on the spot that he must have this Holzbauer and have him he did. The Elector created the post of music director of the opera at Mannheim and installed Holzbauer within the month. It was a position that Holzbauer held for 25 years, until 1778, when the electoral court moved to Munich, which we'll discuss at the end of this lecture.

Who the heck is Ignaz Holzbauer? We'll let him tell us himself in a biographical sketch he wrote a few years before his death. "I was born in Vienna in 1711. My father was in the wholesale leather business. My mother died when I was barely seventeen years old. [My father wanted me to study law], but I always felt an irresistible inclination towards music." Now, Holzbauer goes on to describe how he learned to play a number of musical instruments and taught himself how to compose. He sought the advice of the Viennese Court Music Director, Johann Fux, the author of a very famous manual on counterpoint. Holzbauer described their meeting:

> I asked him to take me on as his pupil. "Well," he said, "but do you already know how to make a little music?" "Oh, yes," I answered. "I already know how to write a little music." "Good, take a little piece of paper lying on the piano, and write me a few lines of counterpoint." I did so and handed it him. He looked at it and said in complete astonishment, "You already know how to do that? Well then, I cannot teach you anything more. Go to Italy, so that you can rid your head of superfluous ideas. Then you will become a great man; you are a born genius."

Okay, yes, a bit self-serving that recollection, but Holzbauer did indeed go to Italy and study during the 1730s and in doing so, became an exponent of the new galant style. Holzbauer worked his way up the musical ladder until that good night when he met and was coveted by the elector, Prince Carl Theodor. Holzbauer's essential duties in Mannheim were to compose and produce operas and sacred music. But, you couldn't be and you wouldn't want to be a composer at Mannheim and not write for the orchestra, that incredible, superb, one-of-a-kind orchestra. Sixty-five symphonies of Holzbauer survive, most of them based on the three-movement scheme of the Italian opera overture We will sample the first movement of his Symphony in D Major, op. 3, no. 4, published in Paris in 1772 and most likely written the year before in 1771. Holzbauer begins the movement and symphony in a genuinely original way—*pianissimo*, very quiet—with a rising D-major scale, rather than a loud opening chord, the *premiere coup d'archet* so typical of most Mannheim symphonies. This rising opening sounds, virtually, like a rising curtain, and as it progresses—surprise—it gets louder! If it's Mannheim, we can never be far from a crescendo. We hear the exposition.

[Musical example from Symphony in D Major, Opus 3, No. 4; Holzbauer: I, exposition]

Johann Christian Cannabich (1731-1798)

No examination of the Mannheim group would be complete without the mention of Johann Christian Cannabich, who after his teacher Johann Stamitz, was the most talented and most important of the Mannheim composers. Christian Cannabich was born and raised at Mannheim, and he profited mightily from the musical education establishment created there by the elector, Carl Theodor. Cannabich was a violinist and became the prize student of Stamitz. At the age of 12, in 1743, he was allowed to enter the Mannheim orchestra as a special "scholar" with special permission from the elector. In 1750, at the age of 19, Cannabich traveled to Italy to study composition and violin in Rome and Milan at the elector's expense. It was money very well spent. When Stamitz died unexpectedly in 1757, Cannabich was recalled to Mannheim and was appointed concertmaster of the Mannheim orchestra. In 1774, Cannabich was appointed to Stamitz's old position of instrumental music director and became the sole director of what was called the "trainer" of the orchestra, which was then at the very height of its international fame.

Wolfgang Mozart had the opportunity to see Cannabich lead the orchestra from his concertmaster's seat, and he had this to say in a letter to his father, Leopold, dated July 9, 1778. "Cannabich, who is the best director I have ever seen, has the love and awe of those [musicians] under him." This is high praise indeed, from perhaps the greatest musician who ever lived.

Christian Cannabich was also a prolific composer and as an example of his work, we turn to his Symphony No. 50 in D Minor, op. 10, no. 5, published in Mannheim in 1778. We hear the first movement of this most uncharacteristic work—a Mannheim symphony that begins in minor. It is a stirring movement in sonata form, performed here without an exposition repeat.

[Musical example from Symphony No. 50 in D Minor, Opus 10, No. 5, Cannabich: I (circa 1778)]

Mozart visited Mannheim four times. The longest of his visits began in 1777, when on his way to Paris with his mother, he seriously considered settling down in Mannheim instead. Mozart stayed in the city for six months and during that time became excellent friends with Cannabich and his family. Cannabich showed Mozart around and introduced his to the orchestra. Mozart wrote his father, "I am with Cannabich every day. He has taken a great fancy to me…I cannot tell you what a good friend Cannabich is to me." Mozart composed and dedicated his Piano Sonata in D Major, K. 309 to Cannabich's daughter Rose, to whom he gave almost daily lessons during his stay.

The End of the Road

On December 31, 1778, the elector of Bavaria, seated in Munich, passed away. Prince Carl Theodor, Elector Palatine in Mannheim, inherited the title of Elector of Bavaria, and in August 1779, his electoral court was moved from Mannheim to Munich. The Mannheim court orchestra was merged with the existing Munich orchestra, and with the merger, it was the end of an era. The golden age of music at Mannheim came to an abrupt end. However, Carl Theodor's patronage of the arts did not.

Two years after the move to Munich, in 1780, Prince Carl Theodor commissioned the 24 year-old Wolfgang Mozart to compose an opera for the city of Munich. In January of 1781, that opera, *Idomeneo*, received its premiere at the Munich opera house, with the newly constituted Munich orchestra in the pit.

Thank you.

Lecture Five
Classical Masters

Scope: By the 1770s and 1780s, the number of first-rate symphonists working across Europe was astonishing. In this lecture, we will discuss the lives and music of five symphonic masters, all born within a nine-year period: Francois-Joseph Gossec (1734–1829), Michael Haydn (1737–1806), Carl Ditters von Dittersdorf (1739–1799), Johann Ignatius Vanhal (1739–1813), and Luigi Boccherini (1743–1805).

Outline

I. Ridolfo Luigi Boccherini was born on February 19, 1743, in Lucca, about 35 miles from Florence, into an artistic family.

    A. Luigi originally took up the 'cello, preparing to follow in his father's footsteps. He quickly developed into a superb 'cellist, made his public debut as a soloist at the age of 13, and was packed off to Rome for advanced study. Throughout his late teens, he commuted between Lucca and Vienna, playing in opera theater orchestras in both cities.

    B. In 1766, at the age of 23, Boccherini and his friend, the violinist Filippo Manfredi, embarked on a concert tour. The tour ended in Paris, where Boccherini had the pleasure of seeing some of his music published for the first time, a set of six string quartets and a set of trios for two violins and 'cello.

    C. In 1768, the 25-year-old Boccherini and Manfredi moved on to Madrid. The musical scene there was dominated by Italians, and Boccherini quickly made a place for himself in the community. Manfredi returned to Lucca in 1772, but Boccherini remained in Madrid for the rest of his life, the next 37 years.

    D. If we listen carefully, we can occasionally hear some Spanish influence in Boccherini's otherwise brilliantly Italianate, Classically styled music. For example, let's hear a bit of the third and final movement of his Symphony no. 15 in D Major, op. 35, no. 1, composed in 1782. Listen for the Spanish inflection in the second phrase of the opening theme. (**Musical selection:**

Boccherini, Symphony no. 15 in D Major, op. 35, no. 1, movement 3 [1782].)

E. Boccherini was an elegant, urbane, honorable, and thoroughly delightful man, and he won many friends and patrons in Madrid. He composed for the court, played the 'cello, and kept up his contacts in France and Germany, contacts that supplemented his income through commissions and publications of his music. Altogether, he wrote 29 symphonies, composing most of them after he settled in Madrid.

F. We hear all of Boccherini's fabled good humor and *joie de vivre* in his music. As an example, we turn to his Symphony no. 18 in F Major, composed in 1782 and scored for strings, two oboes, and two horns. It is a three-movement symphony, although we should not consider it a throwback to the old Italian-style overture, for reasons we will discover when we get to the third and final movement.

    1. The first movement begins with a quiet, compact, repeated musical idea that drives the entire movement, both melodically and rhythmically. This is an example of the most characteristic element of Boccherini's melodic style—the repetition of short, memorable musical phrases. (**Musical selection**: Boccherini, Symphony no. 18 in F Major, movement 1, exposition [1782].)

    2. The second movement of Boccherini's Eighteenth is a graceful and dancing andantino for strings alone. (**Musical selection**: Boccherini, Symphony no. 18 in F Major, movement 2, exposition.)

    3. The third and final movement is in three parts, and it is a fascinating composite, featuring fast, duple-meter music at the beginning and the end, with a triple-meter minuet inserted in the middle. In essence, this third movement is two movements in one, a minuet and a quick, upbeat final movement. We listen first to the beginning. (**Musical selection**: Boccherini, Symphony no. 18 in F Major, movement 3.)

    4. Again, the middle section is a stately and graceful minuet, the sort of music we would have expected to hear in the third movement of a four-movement symphony. (**Musical selection**: Boccherini, Symphony no. 18 in F Major, movement 3.)

5. Finally, the quick opening music—characteristic of a symphonic fourth movement—resumes and brings the symphony to its conclusion. (**Musical selection**: Boccherini, Symphony no. 18 in F Major, movement 3.)

G. We should note that even though Boccherini is not considered a first-rate composer, his work was admired by Haydn. Indeed, all the composers featured in this lecture are of the second tier, but their work was a part of a rich contemporary musical environment that influenced the likes of Haydn and Mozart.

II. No music could be more different from Boccherini's light, lyric, "Italianate" symphonic work than the broad, heroic, and magnificent music of Francois-Joseph Gossec (1734–1829). As an immediate example, we hear the opening of Gossec's Symphony in C Major of 1769. (**Musical selection**: Gossec, Symphony in C Major, Brook 85, movement 1 [c. 1769].)

A. Gossec was born in 1734 to farmers in the southern Netherlands. His extraordinary musical talent was cultivated in the Catholic churches of the Netherlands and Belgium. In 1751, at the age of 17, recommendations in hand, he arrived in Paris and would never leave.

B. The long-lived Gossec had two distinct musical careers. His first was as an establishment royalist, writing operas, symphonies, and ballets for the aristocracy of the *ancien regime*. His second career was as an anti-establishment revolutionary, a purveyor of stirring marches and revolutionary hymns, elder statesman of musical life in revolutionary and Napoleonic Paris.

C. We return to Gossec's Symphony in C Major, scored for flutes, oboes, bassoons, horns, trumpets, timpani, and strings. The symphony is a three-movement work, and everything about its three movements is expressively grand. The second movement, marked *larghetto*, is a C minor–dominated movement of depth and gravity. (**Musical selection**: Gossec, Symphony in C Major, Brook 85, movement 2, opening.)

D. The third and final movement of Gossec's Symphony in C is royal and celebratory and in sonata form. We hear the recapitulation and the conclusion of the movement and the symphony. (**Musical selection**: Gossec, Symphony in C Major, Brook 85, movement 3.)

III. Carl von Dittersdorf (born Carl Ditters; 1739–1799) was a native Viennese who wrote chamber music, keyboard music, church music, oratorios, and operas, but his symphonies (approximately 120 of them) are his greatest compositional achievement.

   A. Von Dittersdorf had a penchant for writing programmatic works, that is, instrumental music that described a literary story. Program music became popular in the 19th-century Romantic era, but von Dittersdorf was composing in the 18th century, and his descriptive symphonies stood as the best of the genre until Beethoven set a new standard with his programmatic Symphony no. 6, the "Pastoral," of 1808.

   B. Von Dittersdorf's most significant collection of symphonic program music is a set of 12 symphonies based on literary excerpts from Ovid's *Metamorphoses*. The 7th through 12th of these symphonies have been lost except in a piano arrangement, but the first six of the symphonies—composed around 1767—have survived.

   1. Ovid's *Metamorphoses* is a series of poems, written between 1 and 8 C.E., that describe transformation and change. Von Dittersdorf used various descriptive titles and phrases from Ovid as the inspiration for 12 four-movement symphonies.

   2. Book I of Ovid's *Metamorphoses* opens with poems entitled "The Creation" and "The Four Ages of Mankind." The first of von Dittersdorf's "Ovid" Symphonies—in C major—is based on Ovid's poem "The Four Ages of Mankind." According to Ovid, the first age was that of gold, when mankind: "With heart and soul, obedient to the law, gave honor to good faith and righteousness."

   3. The first movement of von Dittersdorf's "The Four Ages of Man" Symphony—the "gold" movement—is not the typical first-movement symphonic allegro. Rather, it is music appropriate to the spirit of Ovid's text: It is measured, lyric, and almost hymn-like in tone as von Dittersdorf seeks to invoke this ancient, golden time of honor, faith, and righteousness. (**Musical selection**: von Dittersdorf, Symphony in C Major ["The Four Ages of Mankind"], movement 1, opening.)

   4. The second movement evokes the second age of mankind, the age of silver, when, according to Ovid: "Saturn fell to the dark

Underworld and Jove reigned upon the earth, when Jove led the world through its four seasons." Here, in place of the traditional symphonic slow movement, von Dittersdorf supplies a shimmering allegro dominated by brass and drums, meant to evoke the regal splendor of Jove's reign on earth. (**Musical selection**: von Dittersdorf, Symphony in C Major ["The Four Ages of Mankind"], movement 2, opening.)

5. According to Ovid: "[Third] in succession came the race of bronze, of fiercer temperament, more readily disposed towards war, yet free from wickedness." In terms of its moderate tempo and triple meter, von Dittersdorf's "bronze" movement would seem to be the "expected" minuet and trio, but its mood and spirit have nothing to do with "dance"; rather, the music is strutting, martial, and militant, as befits Ovid's poem. (**Musical selection**: von Dittersdorf, Symphony in C Major ["The Four Ages of Mankind"], movement 3, opening.)

6. For Ovid, the final age of mankind is: "The race of iron. In that hard age of baser vein all evil broke out, and honor fled and truth and loyalty, replaced by fraud and deceit and treachery and violence and wicked greed for gain." Von Dittersdorf's fourth movement is an extended piece of "battle music," beginning with a quiet, ominous introduction; a call to arms in a trumpet; and explosions in the timpani, all followed by the "great battle for the soul of humankind." (**Musical selection**: von Dittersdorf, Symphony in C Major ["The Four Ages of Mankind"], movement 4, opening.)

C. Von Dittersdorf's "Ovid" symphonies offer an entirely different approach to the genre of symphony than we will find anywhere else in the 18th century—a fascinating and entirely effective reconciliation of Classical symphonic forms with a powerful programmatic impulse.

IV. Yet another Classical master of the symphony was the Bohemian-born Jan Ignatius Vanhal (1739–1813). The son of a bonded Czech peasant, Vanhal was a product of the extraordinary music education apparatus in Bohemia that turned out many of the greatest composers, instrumentalists, and singers in Europe.

A. Like so many talented young men from the provinces, Vanhal traveled to Vienna, where he became one of the city's leading musicians. Over the course of his career, Vanhal wrote more than 100 symphonies, 100 string quartets, 95 major religious compositions, and literally hundreds of other works, including concerti, chamber and keyboard compositions, and so forth.

B. As an example of Vanhal's music, we turn to the first movement of his Symphony in D Major, circa 1777. The symphony begins with a slow introduction, a typically Viennese symphonic device. (**Musical selection**: Vanhal, Symphony in D Major, Bryan D17, movement 1 [c. 1777].)

C. Roughly two minutes in, the introduction concludes and a wonderful allegro in sonata form explodes out of the orchestra. As we listen to the exposition, be aware of the contrast between the blaring, martial first theme and the gentle, lyric second theme, which is drawn from musical materials first heard in the introduction. (**Musical selection**: Vanhal, Symphony in D Major, Bryan D17, movement 1.)

D. This is music of great dramatic scope and intensity, and it was extremely popular in its time, known and respected by Wolfgang Mozart and Joseph Haydn.

V. Like many younger siblings, Michael Haydn (1737–1806), five years Joseph's junior, followed a path blazed by his older brother.

A. As a child, Michael had a beautiful and clear singing voice. Like his brother Joseph, Michael became a choir boy at St. Stephen's Cathedral in Vienna; like his brother, Michael was dismissed from the choir when his voice changed; and like his brother, Michael managed to eke out a living in Vienna in the years following his dismissal, during which he slowly taught himself how to compose.

B. In 1763, at the age of 26, Michael assumed the duties of concertmaster for Archbishop Sigismond Schrattenbach in Salzburg. The archbishop was a generous patron of the arts and a great friend to the Mozart family. Wolfgang Mozart was 7 years old when Michael Haydn assumed his post.

C. Despite the many job offers he received throughout his long career, including one to join Joseph in the service of the Esterhazy family in Hungary, Michael Haydn remained in Salzburg for the rest of his life. He lavished his attention on the children of Salzburg, giving countless lessons in composition, keyboard, and violin for free. Without a doubt, one of those children was Wolfgang Mozart.

D. Through the years, Mozart and Michael Haydn collaborated on concerts, alternated organ-playing duties at the archbishop's chapel, and even collaborated on a few compositions, which has caused some attribution problems.

    1. For example, Mozart's Symphony no. 37 in G Major, K. 444, scored for two oboes, two horns, and strings, was actually written as a three-movement symphony in May 1783 by Michael Haydn. A couple of months later, Mozart added a slow introduction to the first movement. For 150 years, the symphony was known as Mozart's 37th, which tells us that Michael Haydn's symphony was good enough to be mistaken for the work of Mozart at a time when Mozart was writing masterworks.

    2. Haydn's first movement—in sonata form—begins with a brisk and engaging first theme, followed by a scurrying modulating bridge and a light and playful second theme. We hear the exposition as Michael Haydn composed it. (**Musical selection**: Michael Haydn, Symphony in G Major, movement 1, exposition [1783].)

    3. Mozart's introduction, labeled "slow and majestic," grounds and gives depth to what follows. (**Musical selection**: Michael Haydn, Symphony in G Major, movement 1, introduction.)

Lecture Five—Transcript
Classical Masters

Welcome back to *The Symphony*. This is Lecture Five—it is entitled "Classical Masters." A confession: my friends, I am a frustrated disc jockey. I grew up in New Jersey listening to a lot of radio, and I must admit that from the dulcet tones of William B. Williams at WNEW (that's 1130 in New York), to the ravaged larynx of Wolfman Jack, to Philadelphia's own Jerry Blavett (the self-proclaimed "Geeter with the Heater"), I believe the best DJs to be urban heroes, whose world view passed directly through the lens of the music they played, whose verbal abilities to ad lib left me shaking my head with awe and wonder.

Well, there you go—T.M.I. (too much information)—all offered as an explanation for what is about to follow. I'm going to play "the DJ way" for this, our fifth lecture. You see, by the 1770s and 1780s, the number of first-rate symphonists working across Europe was just astonishing. By the end of this lecture, we will have discussed the lives and music of five symphonic masters, all born within a nine-year period: Francois-Joseph Gossec, born in 1734; Michael Haydn, born in 1737; Carl Ditters von Dittersdorf, born 1739; Johann Baptist [Jan Ignatius] Vanhal, born 1739; and Luigi Boccherini, born 1743. My DJ act will take us first to Italy and Madrid, then to Paris, Vienna and, finally, to Salzburg. Let's do it!

Italy and Madrid: Luigi Boccherini, (1743-1805)

Ridolfo Luigi Boccherini was born on February 19, 1743 in Lucca, about 35 miles from Florence. His entire family were artistic overachievers, from his father, Leopoldo, who was a professional cellist, to his brother, Giovan Gastone Boccherini, who wrote opera libretti for, among others, Antonio Salieri and Joseph Haydn, to his sister, Maria Ester Boccherini, who had a distinguished career as a ballet dancer in Vienna.

Young Luigi apparently never used the name Ridolfo, ashamed I think. Young Luigi took up the cello, prepared to follow in his father's footsteps. He quickly developed into a superb cellist, made his public debut as a soloist at the age of 13, and was packed off to Rome for advanced study. Throughout his late teens he commuted between Lucca and Vienna, playing in opera orchestras in both cities. In 1766, at the age of 23, Boccherini and his best pal, the violinist Filippo Manfredi, embarked on a concert tour.

They ended up in Paris, which is not a bad place to have to end up, where Boccherini had the pleasure of seeing his music published for the first time, a set of six string quartets and a set of trios for two violins and cello.

In 1768, the 25 year-old Boccherini and his bud Manfredi moved on to Madrid. The story goes that the Spanish ambassador in Paris made them an offer they simply couldn't refuse. The musical scene in Madrid was dominated by Italians, and Boccherini quickly made a place for himself in the community. Manfredi returned to Lucca in 1772, but Boccherini remained in Madrid for the rest of his life, the next 37 years. Every now and then, if we listen very carefully, we can hear some Spanish influence in Boccherini's otherwise brilliantly Italianate, Classically styled music. For example, let's hear a bit of the third and final movement of his Symphony no. 15 in D Major, op. 35, no. 1, composed in 1782. Let's listen for the Spanish inflection in the second phrase of the opening theme.

[Musical example from Symphony No. 15 in D Major, Opus 35, No. 1, Boccherini: III]

Luigi Boccherini was an elegant, urbane, honorable, and thoroughly delightful human being. According to the violinist Alexandre Boucher, who played in Madrid's court orchestra, Boccherini was, "gentle, patient and polite." Character traits that no doubt helped Boccherini win the many friends and patrons he had in Madrid. Boccherini composed for the Court, played the cello, and kept up his contacts in France and Germany, contacts that supplemented his income through commissions and publications of his music. Altogether, he wrote 29 symphonies, composing the great bulk of them, 26 of the 29, after he settled in Madrid. Of the 29, only one has failed to survive, although almost all of his handwritten manuscripts were destroyed in 1936 during the Spanish Civil War.

We hear all of Boccherini's fabled humor and his *joie de vivre* in his music. As an example, we turn to his Symphony no. 18 in F Major, composed in 1782 and scored for strings, two oboes, and two horns. It's a three-movement symphony, although we should not consider it a throwback to the old Italian-style overture, for reasons we will discover when we get to the third and final movement.

The first movement begins with a quiet, compact, repeated musical idea that drives the entire movement. This is an example of the single most characteristic element of Boccherini's melodic style—the repetition of short, memorable musical phrases. We hear the exposition.

[Musical example from Symphony No. 18 in F Major, Boccherini: I; Exposition; 1782]

The second movement of Boccherini's Eighteenth is a graceful and dancing andantino for strings alone.

[Musical example from Symphony No. 18 in F Major, Boccherini: II]

The third and final movement is in three parts, and it is a fascinating composite featuring fast, duple-meter music at its beginning and end, with a triple-meter minuet inserted into the middle. In essence, then, this third movement is two movements in one, a minuet and a quick, upbeat final movement. Cool. The movement begins this way:

[Musical example from Symphony No. 18 in F Major, Boccherini: III]

And now the middle section—the stately and graceful minuet—just the sort of music we would have expected to hear in the third movement of a four-movement symphony.

[Musical example from Symphony No. 18 in F Major, Boccherini: III]

And now the quick opening music—music characteristic of a symphonic finale—resumes and brings the symphony to its conclusion.

[Musical example from Symphony No. 18 in F Major, Boccherini: III]

David Wyn Jones writes: "[Boccherini's] melodic invention is always distinctive and memorable, his scoring imaginative and carefully crafted, and there is never an awkward moment in the unfolding of his music. Boccherini fully deserves his reputation as one of the very best composers of the second division."

Damned by faint praise? No, not really. We could say the same thing about all of the composers represented by this lecture. There aren't many Haydns and Mozarts out there, although we should be aware that Haydn knew and admired much of Boccherini's music. And that's really the important point: my friends, without the Boccherinis and Gossecs and von Dittersdorfs and Vanhals, Joseph Haydn and Wolfgang Mozart would not have developed as they did; these composers were all part of a rich, contemporary musical environment in which everyone listened to and stole from each other. Truly, it takes a village to make a composer.

Paris: Francois-Joseph Gossec, (1734-1829)

We cannot imagine music more different than Boccherini's and Francois-Joseph Gossec's even if we tried. Should their music ever come to blows, Boccherini's light, lyric, "Italianate" symphonic music would be annihilated by Gossec's broad, heroic, frequently overpowering and magnificent music; Bambi versus Godzilla, no contest. As an immediate example we hear the opening of Gossec's Symphony in C Major of 1769.

[Musical example from Symphony in C Major, Gossec: I]

Wow! That sounds like Beethoven, doesn't it? Except that Beethoven hadn't been born yet when that music was written. Gossec's beginnings were as humble as they get. He was born to a family of farmers in the southern part of the Netherlands, but Francois-Joseph's extraordinary musical talent was cultivated in the Catholic churches of the Netherlands and Belgium. In 1751, at the age of 17, recommendations firmly in hand, he arrived in Paris. He never left. Ates Orga writes:

> Gossec's subsequent appointments in Paris, in a professional life stretching to the 1820s, trace a career of starry magnitude, culminating in his office as Professor of Composition and Joint Inspector at the newly constituted Paris Conservatory. He was admitted to the Academie des Beaux-Arts of the Institut de France in 1799,... and he continued to attend the meetings of the academy until 1823.

In July of 1826, as a member of the Institut de France, Gossec gave a failing grade to a fugue submitted by a Conservatory student in support of his application for a Prix de Rome. The student's name was Hector Berlioz; Gossec was 92 at the time.

> Spanning the old and new from Pergolesi and Vivaldi to Franck and Wagner, outliving his contemporaries, bridging Voltaire's age of skepticism and Rousseau's one of sensibility, living through that era when, as [Luigi] Cherubini's wife put it, "the guillotine was busy in the morning, and one could not get a seat at the opera in the evening." Gossec was many things: composer, instrumentalist, conductor, administrator, academic, theorist, publisher, "democratizer of art," reformer, a survivor sailing with the wind.

Yes indeed, the long-lived Gossec had two distinct musical careers. His first was as an establishment loyalist, writing operas, symphonies and ballets for the aristocracy of the *ancien regime*. His second career was as an anti-establishment revolutionary, a purveyor of stirring marches and revolutionary hymns, elder statesman of musical life in a revolutionary and Napoleonic palace. Turncoat? Opportunist? No, a survivor. As a composer, he was the real deal, and his symphonies, around 45 in number, remain a high point in his output.

We've already heard the opening of Gossec's Symphony in C Major, composed around 1769, and we will stay with it. Scored for flutes, oboes, bassoons, horns, tympani, trumpets and strings, both the size of the orchestra and the magnificence of the music itself attest to the French predilection for grandiosity and magnificence in their musical art, a predilection that has hardly diminished to this day.

Gossec's C Major Symphony is a three-movement work, and expressively, everything about its three movements is grand. The second movement, marked *larghetto*, is a C minor-dominated movement of great depth and gravity. We hear its opening minute.

[Musical example from Symphony in C Major, Gossec: II]

The third and final movement of Gossec's Symphony in C is royal and celebratory and in sonata form. We hear the recapitulation and the conclusion of the movement, and with it, the symphony.

[Musical example from Symphony in C Major, Gossec: III]

Vienna: Carl Ditters von Dittersdorf, (1739-1799)

Born Carl Ditters (the von Dittersdorf part was added when he was given a Certificate of Nobility by the old lady herself, Empress Maria Theresa), Carl Ditters was a native Viennese who wrote a lot—we mean a lot—of music. Chamber music, keyboard music, church music, oratorios, and operas; you name it, he wrote them. But it was his symphonies, approximately 120 of them, that are his greatest accomplishment. In particular, von Dittersdorf had a penchant for writing programmatic works, that is, instrumental music that describes some kind of literary story. Real 19th-century Romantic era stuff, this program music, but no one bothered telling Ditters von Dittersdorf that he was an 18th-century composer, and the program music wasn't going to be the big thing for another 60 years. So, he went ahead and wrote his descriptive symphonies anyway, and they stand as the best of the genre until Beethoven came along and set an entirely new standard with his programmatic Symphony no. 6, the "Pastoral" of 1808.

Ditters von Dittersdorf's most significant chunk of symphonic program music is a collection of 12 symphonies based on literary excerpts from Ovid's *Metamorphoses*. The seventh through twelfth of these symphonies have been lost except in a piano arrangement, but the first six of the symphonies, composed around 1767, have indeed survived.

Ovid's *Metamorphoses* is a series of poems written between the years of 1 and 8 C.E. that describe transformation and change. Ditters von Dittersdorf took various descriptive titles and phrases from Ovid and used them as the inspiration for 12 four-movement symphonies. Book One of Ovid's *Metamorphoses* opens with the poems entitled "The Creation" and "The Four Ages of Mankind." The first of von Dittersdorf's "Ovid" Symphonies—in C major—is based on Ovid's poem "The Four Ages of Mankind." According to Ovid, the first age was that of gold, when mankind: "with heart and soul, obedient to the law, gave honor to good faith and righteousness."

The first movement of von Dittersdorf's symphony—the "gold" movement—is not your typical first movement symphonic allegro. Rather, it is music appropriate to the spirit of Ovid's poem: It is measured, lyric and almost hymn-like in tone as von Dittersdorf seeks to invoke this ancient golden time of honor, faith, and righteousness.

[Musical example from Ovid Symphony in C Major, von Dittersdorf: I; The Gold Movement]

The second movement evokes the second age of mankind, the age of silver when, according to Ovid: "Saturn fell to the dark Underworld and Jove reigned upon the earth, when Jove led the world through its four seasons."

Here, in place of the traditional symphonic slow movement, von Dittersdorf supplies a shimmering brass and drum dominated allegro, meant to evoke the regal splendor of Jove's reign on earth.

[Musical example from Ovid Symphony in C Major, von Dittersdorf: II; The Silver Movement]

According to Ovid: "[The third] in succession came the race of bronze, of a fiercer temperament, more readily disposed towards war, yet free from wickedness." Von Dittersdorf's third movement, the "bronze" movement is absolutely terrific in terms of its moderate tempo and its triple meter. The movement would seem to be the "expected" minuet and trio, but the mood and the spirit of this movement had nothing to do with "dance"; rather, the music is strutting, martial, and militant, as befits Ovid's poem.

[Musical example from Ovid Symphony in C Major, von Dittersdorf: III; The Bronze Movement]

According to Ovid, the fourth and final age of man is: "The race of iron. In that hard age of baser vein all evil broke out, and honor fled and truth and loyalty were replaced by fraud and deceit and treachery and violence and wicked greed for gain."

Von Dittersdorf's fourth movement is an extended piece of "battle music," beginning with a quiet and ominous introduction, then a call to arms in a trumpet, explosions in the tympani, all followed by the "great battle for the soul of mankind." We listen to the first half of the movement.

[Musical example from Ovid Symphony in C Major, von Dittersdorf: IV; The Iron Movement]

Carl Ditters von Dittersdorf's "Ovid" symphonies offer an entirely different approach to the genre of symphonies than we will find anywhere else in the 18th century—a fascinating and entirely effective reconciliation of Classic symphonic forms with a powerful programmatic impulse. My friends, seek them out!

Bohemia and Vienna: Johann Ignatius Vanhal, (1739-1813)

Yet another Classical master of the symphony was the Bohemian born Johann Vanhal. The son of a bonded Czech peasant, Vanhal was yet another product of the extraordinary music education apparatus of Bohemia that turned out many of the greatest composers, instrumentalists, and singers in Europe. Oh my goodness—Gluck, Stamitz, Richter, Smetana, Dvorak, Mahler—the list of major Bohemian talents goes on and on. When Charles Burney, around the year 1770, called Bohemia "Europe's Conservatory," he wasn't exaggerating; he was simply giving voice to something that had been common knowledge for 100 years—that the music schools, conservatories, and performance venues in Bohemia were among the very, very best in Europe, and that the number of really first-rate musicians that emerged from this relatively small geographical area was really nothing short of astonishing.

Back to Vanhal. He ended up in Vienna where he became one of the city's leading musicians and where he played in a pick-up string quartet in the 1780s with Joseph Haydn, Carl Ditters von Dittersdorf and Wolfgang Mozart. Would we have liked to record those sessions, or what?! Over the course of his career, Vanhal composed over 100 symphonies, 100 string quartets, 95 major religious compositions and literally hundreds of other works, including concerti, chamber and keyboard compositions, and so forth. Point in fact—Vanhal wrote so much music of such high quality that it's caused huge problems of authorship over the years. A lot of Vanhal's music has been misidentified as being by Joseph Haydn and vice versa. Joe Haydn, not a bad person to be confused with.

As an example of Vanhal's music, we turn to the first movement of his Symphony in D Major, circa 1777. The symphony begins with a slow introduction, a typically Viennese symphonic device. Vanhal's intro is a beauty, and according to Dr. Allan Badley: "Mozart, who knew Vanhal well, quotes part of it in both his Symphony no. 36 and no. 38." Let's hear the first half of Vanhal's first movement introduction.

[Musical example from Symphony in D Major, Vanhal: I]

Roughly two minutes into the movement, the introduction concludes and a wonderful allegro in sonata form just explodes out of the orchestra. Let's hear the exposition of this first movement and let's be particularly aware of the huge contrast between the blaring, martial first theme and the gentle, lyric second theme, a second theme drawn from musical materials first heard in the introduction.

[Musical example from Symphony in D Major, Vanhal: I; Exposition; circa 1777]

This is music of great dramatic scope and intensity, music that's extremely popular in its time, music that was known and respected by Wolfgang Mozart and Joseph Haydn. Now, speaking of Joseph Haydn, did we all know that he had a baby brother named Michael who was also a composer, and who, in his lifetime, was almost as famous as his big brother Joseph?

Salzburg: Michael Haydn, (1737-1806)

There must have been something in the drinking water in that little Austrian village of Rohrau, not too far from the Hungarian border. According to Joseph Haydn, there had never been a single literate musician in his family before himself and his brother Michael. Joseph and Michael's parents, Anna Maria and Mathias Haydn were proud, but they were flummoxed: Mikey and Joey, our boys? The professional composers? Who would have thunk it?

Like many younger siblings, Michael Haydn, five years Joseph's junior followed a path blazed by his older brother. As a child, Michael had a clear and beautiful singing voice like his brother Joseph. Michael became a choir boy at St. Stephen's Cathedral in Vienna; like his brother, Michael was rather unceremoniously bounced out of the choir when his voice changed; and like his brother, Michael managed to eke out a living in Vienna in the years following his dismissal during which he, like his brother before him, slowly taught himself how to compose.

In 1763, at the age of 26, Michael assumed the duties of concertmaster for Archbishop Sigismund Schrattenbach in Salzburg. The archbishop was a generous patron of the arts and a great friend to that most famous of all Salzburg clans, the Mozart family. The amazing little Wolfgang was seven years old when Michael Haydn assumed his post.

Despite the many job offers he received over the remainder of his long career, including one to join his brother Joseph in the service of the Esterhazy family in Hungary, Michael Haydn put down his roots and remained in Salzburg for the rest of his life. We read that he adored children, and as his only child, a daughter named Aloysia Josepha, died in infancy, he lavished his attention on the children in Salzburg instead, giving countless lessons in composition, keyboard and violin for free. Without a doubt, one of those children was Wolfgang Mozart.

Through the years, Haydn and Mozart collaborated on concerts, they alternated organ-playing duties at the archbishop's chapel, and even collaborated on a few compositions, which has caused some attribution problems as well. For example, there was Mozart's so-called Symphony no. 37 in G Major, K. 444, scored for two oboes, two horns and strings. "So-called" because the three-movement symphony was written in May of 1783 by Michael Haydn. A few months later, Mozart, while staying in nearby Linz, added a slow introduction to the first movement. For 150 years, the symphony was known as Mozart's 37th, which tells us that Michael Haydn's symphony was good enough to be mistaken for the work of Mozart at a time when Mozart was writing such masterworks as the opera *The Abduction from the Harem* and his greatest piano concerti.

Haydn's first movement—in sonata form—begins with a brisk and engaging first theme, followed by a scurrying modulating bridge and a light and playful second theme. Let's hear the exposition as Michael Haydn had composed it. It is delightful, even brilliant music.

[Musical example from Symphony in G Major, Michael Haydn: I; Exposition]

Mozart's introduction, labeled "slow and majestic," grounds and gives depth to what follows. Let's hear it.

[Musical example from Symphony in G Major, Michael Haydn: I; Introduction by Wolfgang Mozart]

The story behind this symphonic collaboration is worth telling if only because it demonstrates that Mozart was one great guy. Mozart and his wife Constanze went to visit Salzburg in late July of 1783. An early biography of Michael Haydn, published in 1808, relates what happened:

> Michael Haydn was supposed to compose duets for violin and viola [for Archbishop Colloredo]. But he fell ill. Because of the [subsequent] delay, he was threatened with cancellation of his salary, for his patron was presumably unaware of Haydn's state of health. Mozart, who visited Haydn every day, learned of this, sat down and composed for his distressed friend with such uninterrupted speed that the duets were quickly finished, and [were] delivered a few days later under Michael Haydn's name.

The great Haydn and Mozart scholar, H.C. Robbins Landon, finishes this story:

> Composing these [duets] for his Salzburg colleague was at once a kind deed and an act of homage. The archbishop never suspected that Mozart was behind the duets. [We are told that Michael Haydn "kept Mozart's original manuscripts as a sacred relic," as would we all.] Mozart thought highly of Michael Haydn's music; when he left Salzburg to go to Linz, Mozart took with him a new Symphony in G by Haydn, adding a slow introduction and performing the work, [there in Linz], in this guise.

Luigi Boccherini, Francois-Joseph Gossec, Carl Ditters von Dittersdorf, Johann Baptist [Jan Ignatius] Vanhal, and Michael Haydn—genuine, bona fide masters all. Names to respect and names to remember; composers to be heard and enjoyed!

Now, then to that "other" Haydn, Michael's big brother Joseph. Thank you.

Lecture Six
Franz Joseph Haydn, Part 1

Scope: Franz Joseph Haydn was the Babe Ruth of the symphony—a man who reinvented his field of endeavor and was admired by the public and fellow professionals alike. In this first of two lectures on Haydn, we take an in-depth look at his Symphony no. 1 in D Major, a relatively modest pre-Classic symphony, along with some later works that prefigure Haydn's development into an artist of genius in his mature compositions.

Outline

I. We begin this lecture by listening to the conclusion of Haydn's Symphony no. 96 in D Major, the so-called "Miracle" of 1791. (**Musical selection**: Haydn Symphony no. 96 in D Major ["Miracle"], movement 4, conclusion [1791].)

    A. Franz Joseph Haydn was born on March 31, 1732, in the Austrian town of Rohrau, not far from the Hungarian border. At the age of 6, he went to live with a relative named Johann Franck, a harsh man from whom Joseph received his first musical training.

    B. At age 8, Haydn became a choirboy at St. Stephen's Cathedral in Vienna, where his musical education was limited to the practical experience of singing and hearing a tremendous variety of music. At 17, he was dismissed from the choir, because his voice had changed with puberty.

    C. Alone and destitute, Haydn managed to eke out a living in Vienna by taking odd jobs and teaching music. He taught himself harmony and counterpoint from manuals he bought secondhand and managed to secure a number of composition lessons with the Italian opera composer and singing teacher Nicola Porpora.

    D. Finally, in 1758, the 26-year-old Haydn was hired by the Bohemian Count Karl Joseph Franz von Morzin to be his music director and court composer. The working conditions at Count Morzin's court were excellent; Haydn had an orchestra of 16 musicians to write for and experiment with. He wrote his first symphonies for this orchestra and was transformed from a composer of promise to a genuine professional.

E. When financial difficulties forced Count Morzin to disband his orchestra in 1761, Haydn was taken into the service of Prince Paul Anton Esterhazy, head of one of the wealthiest and most powerful noble families in Hungary and a man devoted to music and the arts. Haydn stayed in the service of the Esterhazy family for nearly 30 years under conditions that were ideal for his development as a composer.

F. When Prince Nicholas Esterhazy died in 1790, Haydn took up residence briefly in Vienna. He embarked on two extended visits to London, where he composed his last 12 symphonies. He returned to Vienna in 1795 and devoted himself to writing Masses, string quartets, and the monumental oratorios *The Creation* (1798) and *The Seasons* (1801). He died, an honored and beloved Austrian national hero, on May 31, 1809, at the age of 77.

II. Haydn wrote at least 108 symphonies, of which 104 have survived.

A. His symphonies are loosely grouped as follows:
Symphonies nos. 1–5, composed between 1759 and 1761 for performance by Count Morzin's orchestra.
Symphonies nos. 6–81, composed between 1761 and 1784 for the Esterhazy orchestra.
Symphonies nos. 82–87, composed in 1785 and 1786 for performance in Paris (the "Paris" Symphonies).
Symphonies nos. 88–92, composed between 1786 and 1789, commissioned by various individuals.
Symphonies nos. 93–104, composed between 1791 and 1795 for performance in London (the "London" Symphonies).

B. Our two-lecture survey of Haydn's symphonies will take a chronological approach. We will observe the manner in which the musical and expressive content of Haydn's symphonies developed, from the relatively modest pre-Classical symphonies he wrote for Count Morzin to those he composed for the cities of Paris and London, works that have been considered essential symphonic repertoire since they were first performed.

C. We will begin with Haydn's first efforts and musical influences, which were, by his own admission, Carl Philip Emanuel Bach and Georg Wagenseil.

  1. C. P. E. Bach (1714–1788) was the second surviving son of Johann Sebastian and his first wife, Barbara. He was the most famous of Sebastian Bach's sons and, as a composer, the one who stayed closest to his north German musical roots. He was an exponent of the *empfindsamer Stil* (the "sensitive" or "sentimental" style), a pre-Classical north German musical style that combined something of the new Italian galant style with the traditional seriousness and expressive depth of north German music.

  2. Through hearing and studying the symphonies of such Viennese composers as Georg Christoph Wagenseil (discussed in Lecture Three)—composers who had already adopted the techniques of the Italian galant style and the Mannheim school—Haydn also "received" and absorbed the influence of Sammartini and Stamitz. Haydn had no need to go to Italy, Bohemia, or Mannheim to hear and study the musical styles of those places; they were all to be found right in Vienna.

III. Composed in 1759, Haydn's Symphony no. 1 in D Major was almost certainly among the first piece he wrote after being hired by Count Morzin.

  A. Haydn's Symphony no. 1 is a three-movement work built along the lines of an Italian opera–style overture.

  1. It begins with a familiar device: an orchestral crescendo, an attempt by Haydn to capitalize on the popularity of the crescendo and its association with the Mannheim court orchestra. (**Musical selection**: Haydn, Symphony no. 1 in D Major, movement 1, theme 1 [1759].)

  2. Haydn's crescendo comes with a twist: The typical Mannheim crescendo doesn't usually occur until the transitional music that comes after the first theme. In Haydn's First Symphony, however, he employs the cliché—the crescendo—as an element of the opening theme itself, rather than as a transitional element heard only after the first theme.

B. Typical of its time, this movement is a hybrid of sonata form and binary form, in which the recapitulation and development of sonata form are repeated as the "b" section of a binary form.

   1. As Haydn understood it at the beginning of his career, sonata form had three main sections: the exposition, development, and recapitulation.

   2. In the exposition, two contrasting themes are introduced, separated by a modulating bridge—a transition that changes key, or *modulates.*

   3. During the development, the themes interact—they are broken down, juxtaposed, superimposed, and so forth—over an essentially dissonant or "unstable" harmonic accompaniment.

   4. In the recapitulation, the themes return in their original order but now in the home key, that is, the same key as theme 1. Later in the Classical era, a fourth section will be added to the sonata form, the *coda*—an extended closing section of music that serves to reinforce the conclusion.

C. We return to the beginning of the first movement of this symphony and listen to theme 1 and the modulating bridge that follows. Be aware of the presence, in our recording, of a harpsichord continuo part: This is, indeed, a galant-style piece of music, but one that has much in common with late Baroque practice. (**Musical selection**: Haydn, Symphony no. 1 in D Major, movement 1, theme 1 and modulating bridge.)

D. We now hear the remainder of the exposition, beginning with theme 2, which is as much a new "key area" as it is a truly memorable, contrasting theme. (**Musical selection**: Haydn, Symphony no. 1 in D Major, movement 1, theme 2 and cadence material.)

E. Next, the entire exposition is repeated. (**Musical selection**: Haydn, Symphony no. 1 in D Major, movement 1, exposition repeat.)

F. In the development section, we are reminded that this is not an ordinary pre-Classic symphony. Haydn's development section is an extremely substantial and harmonically sophisticated piece of music, relative to other development sections being written by other composers during the same period. (**Musical selection**: Haydn, Symphony no. 1 in D Major, movement 1, development.)

1. Note the unrelenting rhythm that drives the development from beginning to end and the open cadence, followed by a pause that concludes the development.
2. The tension is palpable; harmonically, we are suspended in midair, and only the resolution that will occur at the beginning of the recapitulation will bring us back to earth.

G. The recapitulation now begins and, with it, a reprise of theme 1, characterized by its Mannheim crescendo, but here, we find another Haydnesque touch. (**Musical selection**: Haydn, Symphony no. 1 in D Major, movement 1, recapitulation.)
1. Even this early in his compositional career, Haydn demonstrates something that will characterize his music to the end: his disdain for long-range repetition.
2. The formal standards of his time demanded that Haydn repeat the exposition verbatim, which he does. The standards of the time also demanded that he repeat the development and the recapitulation verbatim, and that he does, as well. But Haydn could not be forced to repeat the exposition verbatim in the recapitulation; thus, the recapitulation is substantially different from the exposition, not only in terms of the key of the second theme but also in terms of its overall length and the musical content of the modulating bridge.
3. Haydn's recapitulation is about one-third shorter than the exposition, which helps to even out the proportions of the large-scale binary structure, given that the repeated development and recapitulation are much longer than the repeated exposition.

H. In the repetition of the development and the recapitulation, we hear Haydn's "bow" to the formal ritual of the composite sonata/binary form. (**Musical selection**: Haydn, Symphony no. 1 in D Major, movement 1, development and recapitulation.)

I. Although most modern commentators generally refer to Haydn's early symphonies as "unspectacular and unoriginal," we must understand that these words are used relative to his later symphonies. Relative to its contemporaries, Haydn's First is excellent. Musicologist A. Peter Brown wrote that the second movement of Haydn's First "displays an imagination [that other] composers could not command." (**Musical selection**: Haydn, Symphony no. 1 in D Major, movement 2.)

J. The third and final movement, marked *presto*, displays any number of techniques that will become hallmarks of Haydn's mature compositional style.

   1. The first of these is a remarkably brief theme that is nevertheless ingratiating and memorable.

   2. The second is Haydn's non-stop manipulation of phrase lengths and cadences to create unexpected and sometimes genuinely humorous musical moments.

   3. Another technique is the chirping strings and barking horns that make this music smile without rendering it cheap or trivial.

K. This final movement is in rondo form, which means that the opening theme will return, nearly as it was first heard, after various contrasting or developmental episodes. We first listen to the rondo theme itself, a marvelously memorable tune filled with irregular and unpredictable phrases. (**Musical selection**: Haydn, Symphony no. 1 in D Major, movement 3, theme.)

L. We now listen to the entire movement. Note that the rondo theme will be played twice in succession at the outset of the movement to help us recognize it when it returns. (**Musical selection**: Haydn, Symphony no. 1 in D Major, movement 3.)

   1. A brief contrasting episode follows, which is followed by a reprise of the rondo theme in its entirety. Another contrasting episode ensues, followed by one last iteration of the rondo theme.

   2. The large-scale form of the movement, then, is A–A (the two A's representing the rondo theme and its immediate repetition), B–A–C–A.

   3. This modest movement is, in its brevity and simplicity of form, the most conventional in the symphony. Without a doubt, Joseph Haydn's Symphony no. 1 reveals a musical voice of great promise, a promise that Haydn will more than fulfill.

IV. Starting with his Symphony no. 3 in G Major of 1762, the four-movement symphony quickly became, for Haydn, the rule rather than the exception. The "new" movement, of course, was the third of the four—the minuet and trio.

A. From the beginning, Haydn's minuet and trio movements contained some of his most wonderful music; he was able to imbue this otherwise formulaic genre of dance music with ever-new melodic character, instrumental color, and harmonic invention. We listen to the minuet section from the third movement of Haydn's Symphony no. 3 in G Major (1762), his first symphonic minuet. (**Musical selection**: Haydn, Symphony no. 3 in G Major, movement 3 [1762].)

B. Wonderful as Haydn's third-movement minuets may be, it was the fourth and final movement that eventually came to be the "crowning glory" of Haydn's symphonies. According to music historian Donald Grout:

> He...developed a new type of closing movement...in duple meter, in sonata or rondo form, shorter than the first movement, compact, swiftly moving, overflowing with high spirits and nimble gaiety, abounding in little whimsical tricks of silence and all sort of impish surprises. (Grout, Donald and Claude Palisca, *A History of Western Music*. 4th Edition. New York: W.W. Norton, 1988.)

C. As an example, we turn to the fourth and final movement of Haydn's Symphony no. 77 of 1782, a brilliant and mature example of the sort of finale for which Haydn became famous. The movement is in a composite form, but not the composite sonata form/binary form we've observed to this point of the course. Rather, it is a composite of sonata form and binary form and rondo form.

1. As in sonata form, there is an exposition section, in which a first theme is introduced, followed by a modulating bridge, another thematic statement in a new key, and a closing, or cadential, section of music. As in sonata form (and binary form), this entire exposition is then repeated. As in sonata form, a development section is heard next, followed by a recapitulation. As in binary form, the development section and recapitulation are then immediately repeated in their entirety.

2. Now, the rondo part begins. Instead of stating a second, contrasting theme after the modulating bridge in the exposition and recapitulation—as we would expect in sonata form—Haydn instead restates the opening theme (theme 1). Thus, as in rondo form, a single principal theme keeps returning after variously contrasting material; in this movement, that "contrasting material" is the modulating bridge and the development section.

D. We work our way through this movement by first listening to "the theme," a wonderful, bouncing, folk-like tune. (**Musical selection**: Haydn, Symphony no. 77 in Bb Major, movement 4, theme [1782].)

    1. We now hear the modulating bridge that immediately follows the theme, which in terms of rondo form, constitutes the first contrasting episode. (**Musical selection**: Haydn, Symphony no. 77 in Bb Major, movement 4, modulating bridge.)

    2. Of course, what follows is not a contrasting theme in a new key (as in sonata form) but an abbreviated version of the original theme in a new key. We listen to this abbreviated theme, as well as the closing material that follows and brings this *faux* exposition to its close. (**Musical selection**: Haydn, Symphony no. 77 in Bb Major, movement 4, theme A1 and cadential material.)

    3. Next, the music goes back to the beginning and repeats this entire "exposition," as it would in sonata form and binary form. (**Musical selection**: Haydn, Symphony no. 77 in Bb Major, movement 4, exposition repeat.)

    4. Now begins the development section or, in terms of rondo form, the second contrasting episode. Haydn's development is a thrilling tour-de-force of polyphonic writing, as fragments of the theme overlap with each other in kaleidoscopic variety, all the while modulating through a non-stop series of keys. (**Musical selection**: Haydn, Symphony no. 77 in Bb Major, movement 4, development.)

    5. Then, Haydn glides back into the theme in its original key of Bb major. Let's hear the entire recapitulation. (**Musical selection**: Haydn, Symphony no. 77 in Bb Major, movement 4, recapitulation.)

    6. Fulfilling the demands of binary form, Haydn now goes back and repeats the development and recapitulation in their entirety. (**Musical selection**: Haydn, Symphony no. 77 in Bb Major, movement 4, recapitulation.)

E. The fourth movement of Haydn's Symphony no. 77 is an altogether fantastic combination of sonata, rondo, and binary form—a work of great breadth and substance.

Lecture Six—Transcript
Franz Joseph Haydn, Part 1

Welcome back to *The Symphony*. This is Lecture Six entitled "Franz Joseph Haydn, Part 1."

Innovation and longevity; professionalism and insolence; and yes, yes, genius. We search in our world, in our culture for individuals whose innovations entirely changed their professions, whose longevity guaranteed the creation of a body of work that became the standard against which other accomplishments in their field would be measured, someone whose professionalism was admired, even idolized, by not just the lay public but more importantly by his and her fellow professionals. Someone who, in his or her field, is a genius, however we define that subjective and all-too casually used word. We search in our word, in our culture, for our Franz Joseph Haydn.

The world of sports is the easiest because accomplishments are so easily quantifiable. Certainly, the first American person that comes to mind is Babe Ruth, who single-handedly changed the nature of baseball, from a game based on foot-speed, guile, and slap-hitting to what rooted in sheer, pure, spectacular power. For better or for worse, Ruth's career invented the game. And Ruth played long enough to create a statistical legacy. He set records—for most homeruns in a season, most homeruns in a career, most walks, highest slugging percentage and so forth—that stood for decades.

In dance, Vaslav Nijinsky redefined the very notion of what was physically possible on the dance floor and became a legend in his own time. Leonard Bernstein, passionate, articulate and photogenic, self-absorbed and egocentric to a point extraordinary even for a conductor—single-handedly created the image of the modern, post-war, jet-setting conductor.

We could each make our own list of the great re-inventors of the last 100 years, though I must mention one more person, a redefining innovator of great longevity, someone who has left a huge, profound body of work behind her, someone of unerring professionalism and yes, genius in her field—Julia Child. Joseph Haydn was the Babe Ruth, the Nijinsky, and yes, the Julia Child of the symphony. We hear the conclusion of Haydn's Symphony no. 96 in D Major, the so-called "Miracle," of 1791.

[Musical example from Symphony No. 96 in D Major, Joseph Haydn: IV]

As if all of Haydn's symphonies aren't "miracles!"

Background

Franz Joseph Haydn was born on March 31, 1732, in the Austrian town of Rohrau, not far from the Hungarian border. At the age of 6, he went to live with a relative named Johann Franck, from whom he received his first musical training, and, in Haydn's own words, from whom "I received more thrashings than food." At the age of 8, Haydn became a choirboy at St. Stephen's Cathedral in Vienna where his music education was limited to the practical experience of singing and hearing a tremendous variety of first-rate music, and second- and third-rate music, as well. At the age of 17, he was tossed out of the choir when his puberty-ravaged voice could no longer be disguised. The empress, Maria Theresa complained about Haydn's singing voice, declaring that he no longer could sing, but rather "crow like a rooster." Oh, Mama, to be singled out by the empress, truly a bad review from a major critic.

Alone and destitute, but young and determined, Haydn managed to eke out a living in Vienna by taking odd jobs and teaching music. He taught himself harmony and counterpoint from manuals he bought secondhand. And, as a result of the serendipitous meeting with the great and famous opera librettist Pietro Metastasio, managed to secure a number of composition lessons with the Italian opera composer and singing teacher Nicola Popora. Finally, in 1758, the 26 year-old Haydn caught a major break. He was hired by the Bohemian Count Karl Joseph Franz von Morzin to be his music director and court composer. The working conditions at Count Morzin's court were excellent. And most importantly, Haydn had at his disposal an orchestra of 16 musicians to write for, and really, to experiment with. It was for Count Morzin's orchestra that Haydn wrote his first symphonies.

We cannot underestimate the importance of the practical experience Haydn gleaned during his three years with Count Morzin's orchestra. In that brief period of time, he went from being a composer of promise to a genuine professional. And when bad finances forced Count Morzin to disband his orchestra in 1771, Haydn was ready for the big time. Opportunity knocked, and almost immediately Haydn was taken into the service of Prince Paul Anton Esterhazy, head of one of the wealthiest and most powerful noble families of all of Hungary, and a man devoted entirely to music and the arts.

Donald Grout and Claude Palisca describe Haydn's relationship with the Esterhazy family:

> In the service of Paul Anton and his brother Nicholas, who succeeded to the title in 1762, Haydn passed nearly thirty years under circumstances well-nigh ideal for his development as a composer. From 1766, Prince Nicholas lived most of the year on his country estate of Esterhaza, the palace and grounds of which had been constructed to rival the splendor of the French court of Versailles. Haydn was obligated to compose whatever music the Prince demanded, to conduct the performances, to train and supervise all the musical personnel, and to keep all the musical instruments in repair. He built up the orchestra from ten up to about twenty-five players; all the principal musicians were recruited from the best talent available in Austria, Italy, and elsewhere. Two operas and two long concerts were presented each week. In addition, there were special operas and concerts for notable visitors, as well as almost daily chamber music in the prince's private apartments, in which the Prince himself usually joined.

> Although Esterhaza was isolated, the constant stream of distinguished guests and artists, together with occasional trips to Vienna, enabled Haydn to keep abreast of the current developments in the word of music. He had the inestimable advantages of a devoted, highly skilled band of musicians, and a patron whose understanding and enthusiasm were an inspiration. As Haydn [himself] once said: "My prince was pleased with all my work; I was commended, and as conductor of an orchestra I could make experiments, observe what strengthened and weakened an effect and thereupon improve, substitute, omit and try new things. I was cut off from the world, there was no one around me to mislead or harass me, and so I was forced to become original."

When Prince Nicholas Esterhazy died in 1790, Haydn took up residence in Vienna, but not for long. Two extended visits to London followed one upon the other, from January 1791 to July 1792 and then again from 1794 to August 1795. It was during his residencies in London that Haydn composed his last 12 symphonies. He returned to Vienna in 1795 and devoted himself to writing Masses (six of them), quartets (spectacular ones, among the most important in the repertoire), and the monumental oratorios *The Creation* in

1798 and *The Seasons* in 1801. Haydn died an honored and beloved Austrian national hero on May 31, 1809, at age 77 years and 2 months.

Symphonies

Haydn wrote at least 108 symphonies of which 104 have survived to be counted. Grouped by the commissioning party, they lay out as follows:

> Symphonies nos. 1-5, composed between 1759 and 1761, were written for performance by Count Morzin's orchestra

> Symphonies nos. 6-81, composed between 1761 and 1784, were written for the Esterhazy orchestra

> Symphonies nos. 82-87 were composed between 1785 and 1786 for performances in Paris and are, appropriately, if not terribly cleverly, referred to collectively as the "Paris" Symphonies

> Symphonies nos. 88-92, composed between 1786 and 1789, were commissioned by various individuals, bless them all

> Symphonies nos. 93-104, Haydn's last 12 symphonies, were composed between 1791 and 1795. Each one of them is a consummate masterwork. They were written for performance in London and are thus referred to as the "London" Symphonies.

In our two-lecture survey of Haydn's symphonies, we will take a chronological route and observe the manner in which the musical and expressive content of Haydn's symphonies develop. From the relatively modest pre-Classical symphonies he wrote for Count Morzin to those he composed for the cities of Paris and London, works that have been considered essential symphonic repertoire since the moment they were first performed.

Influences and First Efforts

By his own admission, Haydn's two greatest musical influences were C. P. E. Bach and Georg Wagenseil. To refresh our memories, C. P. E. Bach—the so-called "Hamburg" Bach—was the second surviving son of Johann Sebastian Bach and his first wife Barbara. He was the outstanding exponent of the *empfindsamer Stil* (the "sensitive" or "sentimental" style), that pre-Classical north German musical style that combined something of the new Italian galant style with the traditional seriousness and expressive depth of north German music.

Haydn knew of C. P. E Bach from his keyboard music and later from his orchestral music, as well. Closer to home—meaning Vienna— was the music of Georg Christoph Wagenseil, who was born and died in Vienna. In his symphonies, Wagenseil combined the lyric grace of the Italian galante style, the discipline and expressive depth of the German *empfindsamer* style, and the orchestral techniques of the Manheim composers. It was through hearing and studying the symphonies of such Viennese composers as Wagenseil, composers who had already adapted the techniques of the Italian galant style and the Mannheim School, that Haydn himself "received" and then absorbed the influence of Sammartini and Stamitz. Haydn had no need to go to Italy, Bohemia, or Mannheim to hear and study the musical styles of all those places; they were all there to be found in Vienna, right in his own backyard.

Symphony no. 1 in D Major, 1759

Please, despite the chronological confusion that often surrounds a composer's early works because, you know, as often as not, early works get rewritten, they get lost, they're simply thrown away by the composer—"I'll do better next time." The symphony we refer to as "Haydn's First" is indeed probably Haydn's first symphony. Haydn himself designated it as numero uno in a catalog of his works that he prepared for his biographer Georg August Griesinger in the early 1800's. Composed in 1759, Haydn's First was almost certainly among one of the first pieces he wrote after being hired by Count Morzin and installed in Morzin's Bohemia estate at Lukavec.

Haydn's Symphony no. 1 is a three-movement work built along the lines of an Italian-opera style overture. It begins with a familiar device: an orchestral crescendo, an attempt by Haydn to cash in on the incredible popularity of the crescendo and its association with the Mannheim court orchestra. Let's hear the first thing, characterized as it is by a crescendo, although, a crescendo *mit a tvist* (with a twist).

[Musical example from Symphony No. 1 in D Major, Haydn: I; Theme I]

Here's the twist. Your typical Mannheim crescendo in your typical Stamitz symphony doesn't usually occur until the transitional music that comes after the first theme. In his first symphony, Haydn employs the cliché—the crescendo—but as an element of the opening theme itself, rather than as a transitional element heard only after the first theme.

Typical of its time, this first movement is a hybrid of sonata form and binary form in which the recapitulation and development of sonata form are repeated as the "b" section of a binary form.

By way of review, sonata form as Haydn understood it at the beginning of his career was three main sections: exposition, development, and recapitulation. In the exposition, two contrasting themes are introduced, separated by a modulating bridge—a transition that changes key, or *modulates*. During the development, the themes interact—they are broken down, juxtaposed, superimposed and so forth—over an essentially dissonant or "unstable" harmonic accompaniment. In the recapitulation, the themes return in their original order, but now in the same key, the home key, in the home key of theme 1. Later in the Classical era, a fourth section will be added; something called the *coda*—an extended closing section of music that serves to reinforce the conclusion. Exposition, development, recapitulation, coda. The fact that these terms were invented long after Haydn died in no way diminishes their value. Good useful terminology almost always follows practice.

Back then to the first movement of Haydn's Symphony no. 1 in D Major, structurally a hybrid of sonata form and binary form. Let's work our way through the movement one large section at a time. We'll return to the beginning, and we'll now listen to theme 1 and the modulating bridge that follows. Please be aware of the correct presence, in our recording, of a harpsichord continuo part: This is indeed a pre-Classical gallant-style piece of music, but one that shares much in common with late Baroque practice.

[Musical example from Symphony No. 1 in D Major, Haydn: I; Theme I and Modulating Bridge]

We'll now hear the remainder of the exposition, beginning with theme 2, which is frankly as much a new "key area" as it is a truly memorable contrasting theme.

[Musical example from Symphony No. 1 in D Major, Haydn: I; Theme II and Repetition of Entire Exposition]

Haydn's development section is an extremely substantial and harmonically sophisticated chunk of music relative to other development sections being written by other composers during the same time period. Let's hear it and let's note: 1) the unrelenting rhythm that drives the development from beginning to end; and 2) the open cadence followed by a pause that concludes the development. The tension is palpable. We're suspended in harmonic mid air and only the resolution that will occur at the beginning of the recapitulation will bring us back to harmonic terra firma.

[Musical example from Symphony No. 1 in D Major, Haydn: I; Development Section]

The recapitulation now begins and, with it, a reprise of theme 1, characterized by its crescendo. And then, another Haydnesque touch. Even here, early in his compositional career, in his first symphony, Haydn demonstrates something that will characterize his music to the end, and that is his distain for long-range repetition when something just a little different will do just as well. Yes, yes, the large-scale formal standards of his time demanded that Haydn repeat the exposition verbatim and then the development and the recapitulation verbatim; and this he does. But only laziness and or a lack of imagination could force Haydn to repeat the exposition verbatim here in the recapitulation, and Haydn was pretty much never lazy and always imaginative. So the recapitulation is substantially different from the exposition, not only in terms of the key of the second theme, which we would expect, but in terms of its overall length and the musical content of the modulating bridge. Haydn's recapitulation is about one-third shorter than the exposition, which helps to even out the proportions of the large-scale binary structure, which would otherwise be bottom-heavy, the repeated development and recapitulation being much longer than the repeated exposition. Let's listen to Haydn's foreshortened recapitulation.

[Musical example from Symphony No. 1 in D Major, Haydn: I; Recapitulation]

And now, Haydn's "bow" to the formal ritual of the composite sonata/ binary form—the repetition of the development and the recapitulation.

[Musical example from Symphony No. 1 in D Major, Haydn: I; Repetition of Development and Recapitulation]

And that's it; the first movement of Haydn's Symphony no. 1. Now, most modern commentators generally refer to Haydn's early symphonies as "unspectacular and unoriginal." We must understand that these are words used relative to Haydn's own later symphonies. Relative to his contemporaries, Haydn's First is an excellent symphony. The musicologist A. Peter Brown goes so far as to write that: "Whether its ancestor is the Mannheim symphony or an opera overture, Haydn's first symphony musters a drive unsurpassed by his predecessors and contemporaries. [As for the second movement], compared to slow [symphonic] movements by Wagenseil or Vanhal, [Haydn's First] displays an imagination those composers [simply] could not command."

We sample the opening minute of that second movement.

[Musical example from Symphony No. 1 in D Major, Haydn: II]

The third and final movement of Haydn's First Symphony, marked *presto*, displays any number of techniques that will become hallmarks of Haydn's mature compositional style: 1) a remarkably brief theme that is nevertheless ingratiating and memorable; 2) Haydn's non-stop manipulation of phrase lengths and cadences to create unexpected and sometimes generally humorous turns of musical events; 3) chirping strings and barking horns that make this music smile without ever rendering it cheap or trivial.

This final movement is in rondo form, which means that the opening theme will return, pretty much as first heard, after various contrasting or developmental episodes. Let's first sample the rondo theme itself, a marvelously memorable tune filled with irregular, and therefore, unpredictable phrases.

[Musical example from Symphony No. 1 in D Major, Haydn: III; Opening]

Now let's listen to the entire movement. Note that the rondo theme will be played twice in succession at the outset of the movement, the better to get it in our ears so that we'll recognize it when it returns. A brief contrasting episode follows, which is followed by a reprise of the rondo theme in its entirety. Another contrasting episode ensues, followed by one last iteration of the rondo theme. The large-scale form of the movement is, then, A-A (the two A's representing the rondo theme and its immediate repetition), B-A-C-A. Let's hear it.

[Musical example from Symphony No. 1 in D Major, Haydn: III]

This modest movement is, in its brevity and simplicity of form, the most conventional in the symphony. Without a doubt, Joseph Haydn's Symphony no. 1 reveals, for those disposed to look past its clichés, a musical voice of great promise. Yes, well Haydn will fulfill that promise rather nicely before he's through.

The Four-Movement Symphony

The first bit of pre-Classical symphonic baggage that Haydn left behind was the Italian overture-inspired three-movement scheme. Starting with his

Symphony no. 3 in G Major of 1762, the four-movement symphony for Haydn quickly became the rule rather than the exception. The "new" movement, of course, was the third movement—the minuet and trio. From the very beginning, Haydn's minuet and trio music contained some of his most wonderful music. Somehow, he was able to imbue this otherwise formulaic genre of dance music with ever new melodic character, instrumental color, and harmonic invention. Like a great blues performer, Haydn got maximum mileage out of an otherwise very predictable musical procedure. We listen to the opening minuet from the third movement of Haydn's Symphony no. 3 in G Major of 1762, his first symphonic minuet.

[Musical example from Symphony No. 3 in G Major, Haydn: III; Minuet]

Haydn once remarked that someone would "write a really new minuet." But, oh Papa, you succeeded in doing that pretty much every time you wrote one.

Haydn and the "Fourth Movement"

Wonderful as Haydn's third movement minuets may be, it was the fourth movement, the final movement that eventually became the "crowning glory" of his symphonies. According to music historian Donald Grout:

> The Classical symphony generally got through its more serious business in the first two movements. The [third-movement] minuet provided more relaxation; it was shorter than either of the two preceding movements, it was written in a more popular style, and had a form [that was easier] for the listener to follow. But the minuet does not make a satisfactory closing movement: it's too short to balance the preceding two, and moreover, the spirit of relaxation it induces needs to be balanced by a further climactic tension and release. Haydn soon came to realize that the [fast, triple meter] finales of his earliest symphonies were inadequate to accomplish this, being too light in form and content to produce a satisfying unity of effect in the symphony as a whole. He therefore developed a new type of closing movement, which begins to make its appearance in the late 1760s: [a fast movement] in duple meter, in sonata or rondo form, shorter than the first movement, compact, swiftly moving, overflowing with high spirits and nimble gaiety, abounding in little whimsical tricks of silence and all sorts of impish surprises.

As an example, we turn to the fourth and final movement of Haydn's Symphony no. 77 of 1782, admittedly a later symphony, but a brilliant and mature example of the sort of finale for which Haydn became famous.

The movement is in a composite form, but not the composite sonata form/binary form we have observed to this part of the course. Rather, it is a composite of sonata form and binary form and rondo form. Okay, this is how the rondo works. As in sonata form, there is an exposition in which a first theme is introduced, followed by a modulating bridge, another thematic statement in a new key, and a closing, or cadential section of music. As in sonata form (and binary form), this entire exposition is then repeated. As in sonata form, a development section is heard next, followed by a recapitulation. As in binary form, the development and recapitulation are then immediately repeated in their entirety. Okay. Now, the rondo part. Instead of stating a second, contrasting theme after the modulating bridge in the exposition and the recapitulation (as we would expect in sonata form), Haydn instead restates the opening theme (theme 1). And thus, as in rondo form, a single principle theme keeps returning after variously contrasting material. In the case of this movement, that "contrasting material" is the modulating bridge and the development section.

Did he do that? Yes, well, he's Haydn; he can do whatever he wants. Let's work through this wonderful movement, a perfect example of Haydn's brilliant use of form, and the structural and expressive "oomph" he built into the final movements of his mature symphonies. We listen first to "the theme." It's a bouncing, folk-like tune, the sort of melody that Haydn seemed to be able to write in endless number and variety in his sleep, for goodness sake.

[Musical example from Symphony No. 77, Haydn: IV; Rondo Theme]

Now the modulating bridge that immediately follows the theme, which, in terms of rondo form, constitutes the first contrasting episode.

[Musical example from Symphony No. 77, Haydn: IV; Rondo, Modulating Bridge]

What follows is not a contrasting theme in a new key (as in sonata form) but rather an abbreviated version of the original theme in a new key. We hear it, as well as the closing material that follows and which brings this *faux* exposition to its close.

[Musical example from Symphony No. 77, Haydn: IV; Rondo, Close of Exposition]

And now we go right to the beginning and repeat this "exposition," as we would in sonata form or binary form.

[Musical example from Symphony No. 77, Haydn: IV; Rondo, Repeat of Exposition]

Now begins the development section or, in terms of rondo form, the second contrasting episode. Haydn's development is a thrilling tour-de-force of polyphonic writing, as fragments of the theme overlap with each other in a kaleidoscopic variety of ways, all the while modulating through a non-stop series of keys.

[Musical example from Symphony No. 77, Haydn: IV; Rondo; Development]

Just like that, smooth as a peeled onion, Haydn glides back into the theme in its original key of Bb major. Let's hear the entire recapitulation.

[Musical example from Symphony No. 77, Haydn: IV; Rondo, Recapitulation]

And finally, fulfilling the demands of binary form, Haydn now goes back and repeats the development and recapitulation in their entirety.

[Musical example from Symphony No. 77, Haydn: IV; Rondo, Repeat of Development and Recapitulation]

An all-together fantastic movement of great breadth and substance. As to the former question—is it sonata form, is it rondo form, is it binary form? Well, it's all of them, the fourth and last movement of Symphony no. 77, and it works like a charm.

We take a moment and reflect my friends, to reflect on that lucky audience there in Esterhaza, that great estate built by the Esterhazy family, the opportunity this audience got to hear week after week, these new works by Haydn that were not just symphonies—chamber works, operas and other such works—all from the pen of this extraordinary composer, piece after piece. Did they know what they were hearing? Were they aware that these would become the seminal works of the repertoire, the symphonic repertoire, the chamber repertoire, and so forth? Yes, I do believe they were aware.

By the time that Haydn had created the 77th Symphony, he had created a body of work the likes of which stood by itself, despite his isolation out in the swamps of Hungary. Yes, he was appreciated and he was treated well. It would take the death of his patron to make him leave and seek his pastures somewhere else. But what a wonderful opportunity to sit on a nightly basis and hear this music fresh and ready, the ink still wet on its pages.

I thank you. When we return, we'll resume our exploration of Haydn and his symphonies.

Lecture Seven
Franz Joseph Haydn, Part 2

Scope: Haydn's later work was influenced by the *Sturm und Drang* movement, which emphasized emotional expression in art. As an example of this influence, we explore Haydn's "Farewell" Symphony, a unique composition that added an element of the theatrical to what had been a purely musical genre. We also listen to examples from Haydn's "Paris" and "London" Symphonies. Haydn's body of work elevated the symphony to its position as the most important genre of instrumental music, an art form that demanded repeat performances and concentrated listening.

Outline

I. During the early 1770s, an artistic movement called *Sturm und Drang* ("storm and stress") swept across Europe. At first, "storm and stress" was a literary movement meant to express personal feelings and emotions. Spearheaded by Jean Jacques Rousseau in France and Wolfgang von Goethe in Germany, the ideals of *Sturm und Drang* quickly passed on to other arts, including music.

A. Under the influence of *Sturm und Drang*, Haydn began experimenting with minor keys, abrupt changes of dynamics, and a greater degree of thematic contrast, all to create a higher and often darker level of expression in his music. Haydn's "*Sturm und Drang*" compositional period dates from roughly 1770–1774, when he began writing the music for which he is remembered today.

B. As an example of Haydn's *Sturm und Drang* symphonies, we turn to his Symphony no. 45 in F# Minor, the so-called "Farewell" Symphony of 1772. The choice of a minor key immediately tells us that this symphony will be far from ordinary.

1. We start by listening to the entire exposition and the beginning of the exposition repeat of the first movement. Note the dark, throbbing, angst-filled mood of this music, achieved by the minor key, the wide leaps in themes, the sudden changes in dynamics, the unexpected accents in the principal melodic parts, and the "off-the-beat" accompanimental parts.

2. In terms of expressive content, this symphonic music is unlike anything Haydn had written to this point of his career. (**Musical selection**: Haydn, Symphony no. 45 in F# Minor [Farewell], movement 1, exposition and beginning of repeat [1772].)

C. Haydn's 45th is known as the Farewell Symphony because of what happens in the fourth and final movement. As the story goes, the fourth movement was intended as a gentle but pointed suggestion to Prince Nicholas Esterhazy that it was time to pack up the summer palace at Esterhaza and return to Vienna for the winter.

1. The fourth movement begins dramatically enough, with a vigorous theme in the home key of F# minor. (**Musical selection**: Haydn, Symphony no. 45 in F# Minor [Farewell], movement 4, opening.)

2. As the movement moves towards its conclusion, this fast, driving, dramatic music unexpectedly gives way to a gentle *adagio*, during which, per Haydn's notated instructions, groups of players, having finished their parts, would put out their candles, stand up, and exit the stage. By the end of the movement, the orchestra has dwindled away to only two violins. (**Musical selection**: Haydn, Symphony no. 45 in F# Minor [Farewell], movement 4, final violin duet.)

3. Following this forlorn duet, the two violinists in the original performance, Haydn and the concertmaster Luigi Tomasini, blew out their candles and left the darkened stage. We are told that after an appropriate moment of silence, Prince Nicholas and his entourage went wild with excitement, and the symphony remained one of the prince's favorites. The prince also got the message; the musicians were back home in Vienna with their wives and children within a week.

4. The marvelous conclusion of Haydn's F# minor symphony does something that no symphony had done before: It adds an element of theater to what had been a purely musical genre. Although some musicologists still have difficulty dealing with this conclusion, it stands as an example of what we will observe throughout this course—the ever-expanding expressive content of this evolving orchestral genre.

D. The *Sturm und Drang* movement had essentially run its course for Haydn by 1774, but his compositional style had been forever transformed by it. The expressive elements of *Sturm und Drang* had embedded themselves in Haydn's musical psyche, where they would share equal billing with the charm and ease of his earlier, more galant style music.

    1. These "storm and stress" musical elements include occasional but pointed use of minor; driving rhythms and unexpected rhythmic accents; sudden changes of dynamics; increasing use of polyphony, particularly in development sections and transitions; and unusually wide melodic leaps.

    2. The mid-1770s mark the beginning of Haydn's musical maturity, the point at which his compositions became distinctly his own.

II. We leap forward to the years 1785–1786, a period that saw the composition of the "Paris" Symphonies.

    A. In the 13 years between the composition of the Farewell Symphony and the first of the Paris Symphonies, Haydn had composed at least 27 new symphonies. In these compositions, from 1772–1785, we observe a steady development in Haydn's use of the orchestra.

        1. Haydn began giving prominent roles to solo wind instruments in his scores; he combined various winds, brass, and strings in new and different ways; and rather than have one set of instruments play a particular theme from beginning to end—first violins and flutes, for example—he often varied his thematic orchestrations, feathering instruments in and out during the course of a theme, imbuing the themes with a sense of constantly shifting instrumental weight and color.

        2. Along with Haydn's evolving approach to orchestration were those aspects of his *Sturm und Drang* music that remained essential elements in his mature compositional style: an expressive gravity and a new degree of thematic contrast and development that became increasingly evident in the symphonies composed between 1772 and 1785.

        3. In these symphonies, Haydn created ever longer and more organic symphonic movements by expanding his development sections and avoiding any exact phrase repetitions, preferring to vary his ideas, no matter how slightly, when repeating them.

B. While Haydn's orchestrational technique and compositional voice were evolving, the ears of European music lovers were increasingly turned to him. Despite his geographical isolation at the palace at Esterhaza, Haydn's music began to circulate across the Continent, particularly after 1779, when Prince Nicholas gave him permission to freely publish and distribute his music.

C. His growing fame was particularly noteworthy in Paris and London, cities for which Haydn would ultimately compose some of his greatest symphonies.

III. Sometime in late 1784 or early 1785, Haydn received a commission from a young and wealthy Parisian aristocrat and patron of the arts, Claude-Francois-Marie Rigoley, the Count D'Ogny, who was a co-founder of one of the most celebrated of all Parisian concert societies, the Concerts de la Loge Olympique. Haydn was asked to compose six symphonies for the society.

A. The orchestra of the Concerts de la Loge Olympique was large and included 40 violins and 10 double basses, along with a large complement of wind, brass, and percussion instruments. While performing, all the members of the orchestra wore sky-blue dress coats and swords, and we are told that their playing was as "audacious and flamboyant" as their appearance. The symphonies that Haydn wrote for the Parisians are audacious and flamboyant, as well.

B. When he sat down to compose these Paris Symphonies, Haydn was well aware that he was no longer composing just to please Prince Nicholas Esterhazy, but rather, the varied, jaded, and highly critical Parisian audience. Most cleverly, Haydn filled his Paris Symphonies with devices and details intended to appeal to a wide range of listeners, from professional musicians to middle-class amateurs and, in particular, to Parisians.

C. For example, the first of the Paris Symphonies—no. 82 in C Major—begins with a celebratory, fanfarish opening that is sure to please and excite almost any audience, but particularly a Parisian one, with its special affection for the splendid and magnificent. (**Musical selection**: Haydn, Symphony no. 82 in C Major, movement 1, opening [1786].)

1. This symphony is often referred to as "The Bear" because of the rustic, plodding, "dancing bear"–style theme that begins the fourth and final movement. This is not the sort of music that Haydn would have written for Prince Nicolas Esterhazy and his court, but it is the kind of music that Parisian audiences adored. (**Musical selection**: Haydn, Symphony no. 82 in C Major, movement 4, opening.)

2. Similarly, Symphony no. 83 in G Minor was almost immediately dubbed "The Hen" as a result of the clucking second theme of the first movement. (**Musical selection**: Haydn, Symphony no. 83 in G Minor, movement 1, theme 2 [1785].)

D. The Symphonies nos. 84, 86, and 87 were written to appeal to the Parisian audience's predilection for the *grande symphonie*, but no piece pleased the Parisians more than no. 85 in Bb Major (1785). It was said to have been a special favorite of Marie Antoinette, and because of her affection for it, the symphony is referred to as "The Queen."

1. The first movement of "The Queen" opens with an introduction that evokes the great tradition of the French overture. (**Musical selection**: Haydn, Symphony no. 85 in Bb Major, movement 1, introduction [1785].)

2. The second movement, entitled "Romance," is a *gavotte*—a "dance"— based on a popular French song entitled "Young and Tender Lisette." (**Musical selection**: Haydn, Symphony no. 85 in Bb Major, movement 2, opening.)

3. The third movement is a rustic, engaging, occasionally even yodeling minuet of incredible charm, as only Haydn could write. We listen to its conclusion. (**Musical selection**: Haydn, Symphony no. 85 in Bb Major, movement 3, closing minuet.)

4. The bristling fourth movement has the character of a French contradance in rondo form. We hear the final statement of the dance theme and the conclusion of the movement and the symphony. (**Musical selection**: Haydn, Symphony no. 85 in Bb Major, movement 4, conclusion.)

IV. If Haydn's six Paris Symphonies were the only of his works to survive, he would still be celebrated as one of the great masters of the symphony. But, of course, they are not the only of his symphonies to survive, and they were, in many ways, just a warm-up to Symphonies nos. 88–92, commissioned by various private individuals, and the transcendent Symphonies nos. 93–104, the 12 "London" Symphonies, composed between 1791 and 1795.

A. In 1790, Prince Nicolas Esterhazy died, and after 29 years, Haydn was released from his employ with the Esterhazy family to pursue the international career he had long desired. Two extended stays in London followed one upon the other, during which Haydn composed his last 12 symphonies.

B. Haydn's London Symphonies were molded to what he perceived as "English" taste and style. In these works, Haydn generally avoided the over-the-top magnificence and overtly comic elements he provided for the Parisians. Instead, for the English, he composed music that struck an equal balance between intellect and feeling, between high rhythmic energy and gentle lyricism, music that would appeal to what Haydn perceived as both the aristocratic and middle-class English listener. What Haydn produced in his London Symphonies was the ultimate manifestation of what he had always sought to achieve: a perfect balance between head and heart, dance and song.

C. We will examine the last of Haydn's symphonies, no. 104 in D Major, composed in early 1795.

    1. In Lecture Six, we listened to Haydn's Symphony no. 1 in D Major of 1759. For all of its "promise" and its moments of originality, Haydn's "First" is a three movement, pre-Classical symphony built along the lines of an Italian opera overture. In its entirety, it runs a modest 11 minutes. Haydn's final symphony, no. 104 in D Major, composed 36 years after the First, could not be a more different work. Its four movements run a full half-hour in length, while its mood and spirit look forward to the 19th century, rather than backward to the beginning of the 18th century.

    2. The first movement begins with a royal and magnificent introduction, which starts with a fanfare played by the entire orchestra, consisting of two flutes, two oboes, two clarinets, two bassoons, two horns, two trumpets, timpani, and strings. (**Musical selection**: Haydn, Symphony no. 104 in D Major, movement 1, introduction.)

    3. This "fanfare"-like opening is performed as an *orchestral unison*, meaning that all the instruments of the orchestra simultaneously play the exact same pitch, in this case, D-D-D-

A, D-D-D-A, the bottom and top pitches of a D chord. However, they do not play the middle pitch of the chord, the one that would tell us whether this is in D major (as the symphony advertises itself) or D minor. This bit of tonal ambiguity is not resolved until the third measure of the introduction, when we hear an F natural sandwiched between the D and the A and we realize that we are in D minor! (**Musical selection**: Haydn, Symphony no. 104 in D Major, movement 1, introduction.)

4. This use of D minor—dark and dramatic, where we expected the light and brilliance of D major—imparts tremendous depth and metaphoric meaning to the music that follows. First, let us hear the remainder of the introduction, which is characterized by descending "sighing" motives and further fanfares. (**Musical selection**: Haydn, Symphony no. 104 in D Major, movement 1, introduction.)

5. A broad and lyric first theme now begins. But more than just a "theme in D major," this music takes on the character of an arrival, an accomplishment, the goal of a short but troubling journey through a dark-toned place. This D-major theme has a meaning and power that it would not have had without the D minor–inspired darkness of the introduction. (**Musical selection**: Haydn, Symphony no. 104 in D Major, movement 1, theme 1.)

6. Theme 1 in D major constitutes a brilliant, varied, and totally engaging passage of music, filled with expressive contrast and thematic development—and that's just the first theme of the sonata-form movement!

7. The second movement is a moderately paced duple-meter dance of great elegance and style. (**Musical selection**: Haydn, Symphony no. 104 in D Major, movement 2, opening.)

8. The third-movement minuet is yet another example of Haydn's incredible imagination, of how he could turn the clichéd genre of *minuet* into something truly individual and unique. We listen to the opening minuet section in its entirety; it bubbles over with life and energy! (**Musical selection**: Haydn, Symphony no. 104 in D Major, movement 3, minuet.)

9. The fourth and final movement of Haydn's 104th bristles with energy. The movement is in sonata form and features three distinct themes.
    a. The first is a rustic, utterly Haydnesque theme heard over a drone, or pedal-point. (**Musical selection**: Haydn, Symphony no. 104 in D Major, movement 4, theme 1.)
    b. Theme 2 is joyful and celebratory and is heard in the violins even as theme 1 continues to be played by the winds and second violins. The effect is stunning. (**Musical selection**: Haydn, Symphony no. 104 in D Major, movement 4, theme 2.)
    c. Theme 3 is a *cadence theme*, that is, a theme associated with the closing moments of a large section of music, like an exposition. Haydn's cadence theme is sustained and quiet and offers just about the only moment of respite in this otherwise dynamic exposition. (**Musical selection**: Haydn, Symphony no. 104 in D Major, movement 4, cadence theme.)
    d. We now listen to the entire exposition. (**Musical selection**: Haydn, Symphony no. 104 in D Major, movement 4, exposition.)
10. Finally, we hear the recapitulation and the coda. (**Musical selection**: Haydn, Symphony no. 104 in D Major, movement 4, recapitulation.)

V. At the time Haydn composed his First Symphony, in 1759, the genre was the province of the aristocracy, intended for princely entertainment. By the end of his career, Haydn's symphonies were being created for: "the concert milieu [and] for *concentrated* listening [emphasis added]" (Brown, 23).

   A. Haydn's symphonies constitute the first large body of orchestral music by a single composer that became a basic and essential repertoire. At a time when audiences were accustomed to hearing new works at every sitting, Haydn's symphonies—by dint of their beauty, orchestral brilliance, depth of expression, and content—demanded and received repeated performances. In creating such works as the Farewell Symphony, the Paris Symphonies, and the London Symphonies, Haydn almost single-handedly changed the way instrumental music was perceived and performed.

B. Beethoven began work on his First Symphony just three years after Haydn composed his last. We might wonder if Beethoven would have conceptualized the symphony as a vehicle for profound self-expression, as a piece of music that had to be heard a number of times to be understood, without Haydn's symphonies as his model.

C. Haydn's compositional career spanned a period that saw the audience for symphonic music begin to shift from the aristocracy to the middle class and saw, as well, the genre *symphony* grow to become the single most important and popular type of instrumental music.

D. An argument can be made that Haydn appeared on the scene at an opportune moment in history and that his symphonic output mirrored the ongoing rise of the symphony and its changing constituency. Of course, the argument can also be made that it was Haydn's symphonies themselves, more than any other factor, that elevated and popularized the genre to an extent that would not have otherwise occurred.

Lecture Seven—Transcript
Franz Joseph Haydn, Part 2

Welcome back to *The Symphony*. This is Lecture Seven entitled "Franz Joseph Haydn, Part 2."

Sturm und Drang.

During the early 1770s, an early artistic movement called *Sturm und Drang* ("storm and stress") swept across Europe. At first, *Sturm and Drang* was a literary movement, bent on expressing ever-greater personal feelings and emotions. Spearheaded by Jean Jacques Rousseau in France and Wolfgang von Goethe in Germany, the ideals of *Sturm and Drang* quickly passed on to the other arts, including music.

The *Sturm und Drang* movement hit Haydn's music, my friends, like a 60-pound schnitzel dropped from the roof of St. Stephen's. Under the influence of the expressive geshtalt of *Schmerz und Angst* that was *Sturm and Drang*, Haydn began experimenting with minor keys, abrupt changes in dynamics, and a greater degree of thematic contrast, all in his desire to create a higher and often darker level of expression in his music.

By the early 1700s, in his so-called "*Sturm and Drang*" works, his symphonies in particular, Haydn allowed himself to express a range of moods quite new to his music. Haydn's so-called "*Sturm und Drang*" compositional period dates from roughly 1770 to 1774. This is when Haydn wrote the music for which he is remembered today, a compositional period that represents the first great flowering of his symphonic craft.

As an example of Haydn's *Sturm und Drang* symphonies, we turn to his Symphony no. 45 in F# Minor, the so-called "Farewell" Symphony of 1772. The choice of a minor key for this symphony—F# minor—tells us by itself that this is not going to be "easy Classical listening" as usual. We start by listening to the entire exposition and the very beginning of the exposition repeat of the first movement. Please note the dark, throbbing angst-filled mood of this movement, achieved by being in minor, by the wide leaps in the themes, by the sudden changes in dynamics, the unexpected accents in the principle melodic parts, and the "off-the-beat" accompanimental parts. In terms of expressive content, this is symphonic music unlike anything Haydn had written to this point of his career.

[Musical example from Symphony No. 45 in F Sharp Minor, "Farewell," Haydn; I]

Haydn's 45th is known as the "Farewell" Symphony because of what happens in the final movement. As the story goes, the fourth movement was intended as a gentle but pointed suggestion to Prince Nicholas Esterhazy that it was time to pack up the summer place at Esterhaza and head back to Vienna for the winter. It seems that the Prince had dawdled that fall of 1772, and the men of the orchestra who lived together in a dormitory were anxious to get back to their own homes in Vienna to see their wives, sleep in their own beds, and you know the rest. The men of the orchestra went to Haydn—their leader, their benefactor, their friend, their "papa" as they called him out of respect—and asked him if he could maybe do something to foreshorten what had already been a long season at the palace. This fourth movement is the product of that request.

The fourth movement begins dramatically enough with a vigorous theme in the home key of F# minor.

[Musical example from Symphony No. 45 in F Sharp Minor, "Farewell," Haydn; IV]

As this movement moves towards its conclusion, this fast, driving, dramatic music quite unexpectedly gives way to a gentle *adagio*, during which, as per Haydn's notated instructions, groups of players having finished their parts, put out their candles, stand up and one after the other, exit the stage. By the end of the movement, the orchestra has dwindled away to only two violins. In the original performance, it was the *Kapellmeister* Joseph Haydn and the concertmaster Luigi Tomasini who remained on the stage playing their muted violins in the nearly darkened hall of Esterhaza. Let's hear the final minute of the movement, and with it, the final minute of the symphony.

[Musical example from Symphony No. 45 in F Sharp Minor, "Farewell," Haydn: IV]

Following this forlorn duet, Haydn and Tomasini blew out their candles and left the darkened stage. We are told that after an appropriate moment of silence, Prince Nicholas and his entourage went crazy with excitement, screaming and clapping and pounding the floor with their feet. The symphony remained one of the Prince's favorites for the rest of his life, and he got the message. The musicians were back at home in Vienna with their wives and children within a week.

The marvelous conclusion of Haydn's F# minor symphony does something that no symphony with which I am familiar had done before. It adds an element of theater to what had been a purely musical genre. It's something that some musicologists are still having trouble dealing with two-and-a-half centuries after the fact. One such observer, an estimable chap who chaired the musicology program at a major midwestern university huffs and puffs that: "the finale remains open-ended is an unfathomable gesture that requires further critical interpretation."

Earth to academia: no, it's not "unfathomable" and it doesn't "require further interpretation." The finale of Haydn's Symphony no. 45 in F# Minor is an example of exactly what we've observed and will continue to observe over the course of this study—and that is the ever-expanding expressive content of this evolving orchestral genre called "symphony."

Well, for Haydn, the *Sturm und Drang* movement had essentially run its course by 1774. His compositional style had been forever transformed. After 1774, Haydn would no longer compose, as his music was described in 1776, "merely charming, ingratiating, engaging, naturally humorous and enticing music." The expressive elements of *Sturm und Drang* had embedded themselves in Haydn's musical psyche where they would share equal billing with the charm and ease of his earlier, more galant style music. These "storm and stress" musical elements include occasional but pointed use of minor; driving rhythms and unexpected rhythmic accents; sudden changes of dramatics; increased use of polyphony, particularly in development sections and transitions; and unusually wide melodic leaps. The mid-1770s marked the beginning of Haydn's musical maturity, the point at which his compositions become distinctly "his own."

Development and Growth

Time demands that we jump forward to 1785 and 1786—two years that saw Haydn completely outdo himself and everyone around him in terms of symphonic composition. 1785 and 1786 saw the composition of the so-called "Paris" Symphonies, nos. 82-87. Now, in the 13 years between the competition of the Farewell Symphony and the first of the Paris Symphonies, between the years 1772 and 1785, Haydn had composed at least 27 new symphonies. We must say "at least" because in November of 1779, a fire in the theater at the Esterhazy Palace destroyed a large amount of stored music, including a number of Haydn's symphonies which were lost forever and about which we know nothing today.

Anyway, in the 27 known symphonies that Haydn composed between 1772 and 1785, we can observe a steady development in the use of the orchestra. Haydn began giving prominent roles to solo instruments in his scores. He combined various winds, brass, and strings in new and different ways. And rather than having one set of instruments play a particular theme from beginning to end—first violins and flutes, for example—he often his thematic orchestrations, feathering various instruments in and out during the course of the theme and imbuing the theme with a sense of constantly shifting instrumental weight and color.

Along with Haydn's evolving approach to orchestration, there were those aspects of his *Sturm and Drang* music that remained essential elements in his mature compositional style: an expressive gravity and a new degree of contrast in development that became increasingly evident in the symphonies composed between 1772 and 1785. In these symphonies, Haydn created ever longer and more organic symphonic movements by expanding his development sections and avoiding, at almost any cost, any exact phrase repetitions, preferring to vary his ideas, no matter how slightly, when repeating them.

While Haydn's orchestrational technique and compositional voice were thus evolving, the ears of music lovers were increasingly upon him. Despite his geographical isolation there at the palace of Esterhaza (let's face it my friends, the rural Hungarian marshlands were no one's idea of a happening place), despite his isolation, Haydn's music began to circulate across the continent, particularly after 1779, when Prince Nicholas gave him permission to freely publish and distribute his music. Haydn's growing pains were particularly noteworthy in those two most magnificent and wealthy European capitals, Paris and London, cities for which Haydn would ultimately compose some of his greatest symphonies.

The Paris Symphonies

Sometime in late 1784 or early 1785, Haydn received a commission from a very young aristocratic patron of the arts called Claude-Francois Marie-Rigoley, the Count D'Ogny, who was at the time the Postmaster-General of France. The count was also the co-founder of what had become the most celebrated of all Parisian concert societies, the Concerts de la Loge Olympique. Haydn was asked to compose six symphonies for the society, for which he was to be paid 25 *louis d'or* per symphony—as Haydn called it, *"un prix magnifique; un prix magnifique colossal"*—a magnificent, colossal price, the largest fee by far that he had ever received for his music.

The orchestra of the Concerts de la Loge Olympique was equally as colossal and included among its strings 40 violins and 10 double basses, along with a large complement of wind, brass, and percussion instruments. While performing, all the members of the orchestra wore sky-blue dress clothes and swords, and we are told their playing was as "audacious and flamboyant" as their appearance. And the symphonies that Haydn wrote for the Parisians are audacious and flamboyant, as well. When he sat down to compose these Paris Symphonies, Haydn was well aware that he was no longer composing to please just his boss, Prince Nicholas Esterhazy, but rather the varied, jaded, bitchy and highly critical Parisian audience. Most cleverly, Haydn filled his Paris Symphonies with devices and details intended to appeal to a wide range of listeners, from professional musicians to middle-class amateurs, and in particular, to Parisian audiences.

For example, the first of the Paris Symphonies—no. 82 in C Major—begins with just that sort of celebratory, fanfarish opening that is sure to please and excite just about any audience anywhere, but particularly a Parisian audience, with its special affection for the splendid and the magnificent. Please, the opening of the Symphony no. 82 in C Major of 1786.

[Musical example from Symphony No. 82 in C Major, Haydn: I; Opening]

This symphony is often referred to as "The Bear" because of the rustic, plodding, "dancing bear" style theme that begins the fourth and final movement. This is generally not the sort of music Haydn would have written for Prince Nicholas Esterhazy and his court, but it is the sort of music that Parisian audiences just adore, and Haydn knew it.

[Musical example from Symphony No. 82 in C Major, Haydn]

Speaking of animals, Symphony no. 83 in G Minor was almost immediately dubbed "The Hen" as a result of the clucking second theme of the first movement. Let's hear it.

[Musical example from Symphony No. 83 in G Minor, Haydn: I, Second Theme]

The Symphonies nos. 84, 86 and 87 were written to appeal to the Parisian audience's well-known predilection to the *grande symphonie*. But despite the "magnifique-ness" of Haydn's Paris Symphonies nos. 84, 86, and 87, no one of them appealed to the locals more than did no. 85 in Bb major. It was said to be a special favorite of the queen, Marie Antoinette, the daughter of Empress Maria Theresa and the sister of the Austrian Emperor Joseph II. Marie Antoinette frequently attended the Concerts de la Loge Olympique and as a result of her special affection for Haydn's Symphony No. 85, it has forever since been referred to as "The Queen."

The first movement of The Queen opens with an introduction that evokes the great and familiar tradition of the French overture.

[Musical example from Symphony No. 85 in Bb Major, Haydn: I; Opening]

The second movement, entitled "Romance," is a *gavotte* (a dance) based on a popular French song entitled "Young and Tender Lisette."

[Musical example from Symphony No. 85 in Bb Major, Haydn: II; Romance]

The third movement is a rustic, engaging, occasionally even yodeling minuet of incredible charm as only Haydn could have possibly written. We listen to its conclusion.

[Musical example from Symphony No. 85 in Bb Major, Haydn: III; Minuet, Conclusion]

Lastly, the energized fourth movement has the character of a French contradance in rondo form. We hear the final statement of the dance theme and the conclusion of the movement and the symphony.

[Musical example from Symphony No. 85 in Bb Major, Haydn: IV; Rondo, Conclusion]

In 1787, the following review of Haydn's Symphonies nos. 82-87 appeared in the *Mercure de France:*

> This past year symphonies of Haydn were performed at all concerts. Day by day the impression grows so that one admires more and more the products of this immense talent who, in each of his pieces, shaped so well, on a unique subject, drawing from it such rich and very developments, so different from those sterile composers who move constantly from one idea to another, without knowing how to present any in varied guising, piling up effects, without connection and without taste.

Leave it to a French reviewer to compliment by denigrating someone else.

The London Symphonies

My friends, we move on to those London symphonies, the capstones of Haydn's career. If Haydn's six Paris Symphonies were the only of his works to survive, he would still be celebrated today as one of the great masters of the symphony. But of course, they are not the only of his symphonies to survive, and they were, in many ways, but a warm-up—a *canapé* to what followed. Symphonies nos. 88-92, commissioned by various private individuals, and the transcendent and always incredible Symphonies nos. 93-104, the 12 so-called "London" Symphonies, composed between 1791 and 1795. Onward to those symphonies.

The particulars. On September 28, 1790, Prince Nicholas Esterhazy died, and after 29 years, Haydn was released from his employ with the Esterhazy family, free to pursue the sort of international career he had long desired. Two extended stays in London followed, one upon the other, during which Haydn composed his last 12 symphonies.

Presented and produced under the direction of the German violinist and impresario Johann Peter Salomon, Haydn's London Symphonies were molded to what Haydn perceived as "English" taste and style. In these symphonies, Haydn generally avoided the sort of over-the-top magnificence and overly comic elements he provided for the Parisians in his Paris Symphonies. Instead, he composed, for the English, music that struck an equal balance between intellect and feeling, between high rhythmic energy and gentle lyricism, music that would appeal to what Haydn perceived as both the aristocratic and middle-class English listener. What Haydn produced in his London Symphonies was the ultimate manifestation of what he had always sought to achieve: a perfect balance between head and heart, dance and song.

Haydn told his biographer, Georg Griesinger, that in his London Symphonies he was "interested in surprising the public with something new." And surprise them he did, with the most brilliant orchestral music ever heard in England. Time precludes us from exploring these masterworks in any detail. We will examine the Twelfth London Symphony, the last of Haydn's symphonies, no. 104 in D Major, composed in early 1795. Itself nicknamed the "London" Symphony, the premiere took place at the Haymarket Theater on May 4, 1795.

Back in Lecture Six, we took a look at and listened to Haydn's Symphony no. 1 in D Major of 1759. For all of its "promise," Haydn's "First" is a three movement, pre-Classical symphony built along the lines of an Italian overture. In its entirety, it runs a modest 11 minutes in total length. Haydn's final symphony, no. 104 in D Major, composed 36 years after the First, could not be a more different work. Its four incredible movements run a full half-hour in length, while it's mood and spirit look forward towards to the 19th century, rather than backwards to the beginning of the 18th century.

The first movement begins with royal and magnificent introduction, which begins with a fanfare played by the entire orchestra, an orchestra consisting of two flutes, two oboes, two clarinets, two bassoons, two horns, two trumpets, timpani, and strings. We hear that introduction to the first movement of Haydn's Symphony no. 104.

[Musical example from Symphony No. 104 in D Major, Haydn: I; Introduction]

This "fanfare"-like opening of the introduction is performed as an *orchestral unison*, meaning that all the instruments of the orchestra simultaneously play exactly the same pitch, in this case, D-D-D-A, D-D-D-A, the bottom and top pitches are the D chord. However, they do not play the middle pitch of this chord, the one that would tell us whether this was a D major (as the symphony advertises itself) or D minor chord. This bit of total ambiguity is not resolved until the third measure of the introduction when we hear an F natural sandwiched between the D and the A and we realize, to our shock, that we are, at least for now, in D minor.

[Musical example from Symphony No. 104 in D Major, Haydn: I; Introduction, D Minor Theme]

Now this use of D minor—darkly dramatic, where we expected the lightness and brilliance of D major—imparts tremendous depth and metaphoric meaning to the music that follows. First, let us hear the remainder of the introduction, characterized as it is by these descending "sighing" motives and further fanfares.

[Musical example from Symphony No. 104 in D Major, Haydn: I; Introduction, D Minor Theme]

The broad and lyric theme in D major now begins, but more than just a "theme in D major." This theme takes on the character of an arrival, an accomplishment, the goal of a short and troubling journey through a dark-toned place. This D major theme has a meaning, a depth, a power that it would not have had without the D-minor-created darkness of the introduction. Let's hear this opening theme in D major.

[Musical example from Symphony No. 104 in D Major, Haydn: I; Introduction, D Major Theme]

This theme 1 in D major constitutes a brilliant, lengthy, and totally engaging passage of music filled with expressive contrast and thematic development—and that's just the first theme of the sonata form movement! The second movement is a moderately paced duple-meter dance of great elegance and style.

[Musical example from Symphony No. 104 in D Major, Haydn: II]

The third movement minuet is just awesome, yet another example of Haydn's incredible imagination, of how he could turn the clichéd genre of minuet into something truly special, truly his own. We listen to the opening minuet section in its entirety; it veritably bubbles over with life and energy.

[Musical example from Symphony No. 104 in D Major, Haydn: III; Minuet Opening]

The fourth and final movement of Haydn's 104th bristles with energy. It sends off sparks; it snaps, crackles, and yes, it pops! The movement is in sonata form and features three distinct themes. The first theme is a rustic, utterly Haydnesque theme heard over a drone or a pedal-point.

[Musical example from Symphony No. 104 in D Major, Haydn: IV; Theme I]

Theme 2 is joyful and celebratory and is heard in the first violins even as theme one continues to be played by the winds and second violins. The effect is absolutely stunning. Let's hear it.

[Musical example from Symphony No. 104 in D Major, Haydn: IV; Theme II]

Theme 3 is a so-called *cadence theme*, that is, a theme associated with the closing moments of a large section of music like an exposition. Haydn's cadence theme is sustained and quiet and offers just about the only moment of respite in this otherwise booty-kicking exposition. Let's hear the exposition through the end of the exposition.

[Musical example from Symphony No. 104 in D Major, Haydn: IV; Conclusion of Exposition]

And now, start to finish, the entire exposition.

[Musical example from Symphony No. 104 in D Major, Haydn: IV; Exposition]

(I frankly cannot fathom how anyone can sit still while listening to this music. It makes us twitch and smile and dance in place; it makes us giddy; we forget who we are and we're the better for it. Oh, the power of music; and whoa, the music of Joseph Haydn!) The music rocks and rolls its way through the exposition repeat and the development section. We rejoin the action with the recapitulation. Let's hear the recapitulation and the coda, the last two minutes of this last movement of Haydn's last symphony.

Haydn was 64 years old when he composed this, his final symphony, and I don't need to tell you that 64 years old in 1796 was a lot older than 64 years is now. He had the consummate technical skill of an experienced master, but my goodness, with this music as the evidence, he still had the fire of youth in his belly.

The English adored Haydn as both a man and as a musician. Charles Burney, among many others, was at the Haymarket on the evening of May 4, 1795, where he heard the premiere of this last of Haydn's symphonies as well as a performance of Haydn's Symphony no. 100 in G major. Two days later, Burney wrote his friend Susan Philips and described the symphonies as works: "such as were never heard before any mortal's production; of what Apollo and the Muses compose we can only judge by such productions as these."

Conclusion

At the time Haydn composed his First Symphony, in 1759, the genre was the province of the aristocracy, intended for princely entertainment. By the end of his career, Haydn's symphonies were being created for: "the concert milieu [and] for concentrated listening."

Haydn's symphonies constitute the first large body of orchestral music by a single composer that became basic and essential repertoire. At a time when audiences were accustomed to hearing new works at every sitting, Haydn's symphonies—by dint of their beauty, their orchestral brilliance, their depth of expression, and content—Haydn's symphonies, my friends, demanded and received repeated performances, repeated listenings. We cannot overestimate the importance of this. In creating works like the Farewell Symphony, the Paris Symphonies, and the London Symphonies, Haydn almost single-handedly changed the way instrumental music was perceived and performed. As a result of Haydn's symphonies, according to musicologist A. Peter Brown: "The demand for new repertoire was broken, as a canon of first-rate compositions became, through repeated hearings, imprinted on the minds of the public."

Beethoven began work on his First Symphony just three years after Haydn composed his last. Food for thought: without Haydn's symphonies as his model, would Beethoven have conceptualized the symphony as he did? As a vehicle for profound self-expression, as a piece of music that had to be heard a number of times in order to be understood? And without Haydn's symphonies as a precedent, would Beethoven's audiences have been willing to listen to his strange and wonderful symphonies over and over again until they began to understand them? Interesting questions.

Haydn's compositional career spanned a period that saw the essential audience for symphonic music begin to shift from the aristocracy to the middle-class concertgoer, and saw as well the genre "symphony" grow to become the single most important and popular type of instrumental music. An argument could be made that Haydn appeared on the scene at an opportune moment in history and that his symphonic output mirrored the ongoing rise of the symphony and its changing constituency. Of course, the argument can also be made that it was Haydn's symphonies themselves, more than any other single factor, that elevated and popularized the genre to an extent that would not have otherwise occurred. Frankly, I vote for the later suggestion.

Thank you.

Lecture Eight
Mozart

Scope: In this lecture, we look at the all-too-brief career of probably the greatest composer who ever lived, Wolfgang Mozart. Although Mozart never completely realized his potential as a symphonist, and wrote only 10 symphonies in his mature period, he nevertheless produced masterpieces of the genre. We'll listen to excerpts from symphonies written across the span of Mozart's career, from his First, composed when he was eight, to his last three, the only symphonies he composed as a coherent set.

Outline

I. As mentioned in Lecture Seven, Joseph Haydn and Wolfgang Mozart, despite the 24-year age difference, were friends; the two met in Vienna, sometime in December of 1781, when Mozart would have been 25 and Haydn, 49.

   A. Mozart and Haydn participated in chamber music parties, during which they would play through music together. At one such party, a group had played through three of Mozart's six string quartets dedicated to Haydn. After the reading, Haydn, the guest of honor, pulled aside Mozart's father, Leopold, and told him that his son was the greatest composer he had ever known.

   B. Haydn was undeniably correct. Wolfgang Mozart possessed more pure, overwhelming technique and melodic and harmonic taste than almost any composer before or after him. It is an enduring tragedy that he died so pathetically young (at age 35) and that because of his foreshortened life, he never completely realized his potential as a symphonist.

   1. The statement that Mozart never realized his potential may seem ludicrous in light of the brilliant Symphony in A Major, K. 201, or the virtually perfect Symphony no. 39 in Eb Major, or the dark and tragic no. 40 in G Minor, or others.

   2. Of Mozart's 41 numbered symphonies, however, the first 30 were products of his youth; only the last 10 were written after 1775, when he had achieved his full musical maturity. And of those "mature" symphonies—composed in fits and starts between 1778 and 1788—only the final three (nos. 39, 40, and 41) were conceived as a coherent symphonic unit.

3. The writing of symphonies was never a priority for Mozart; if he were with us now, he'd tell us that he was an opera composer at heart who wrote piano concerti for a living and chamber music for his friends. For the most part, he wrote symphonies to earn some quick cash and to impress the locals wherever he happened to be.

4. Although we should be grateful for what we have of Mozart's symphonies, it is impossible not to wonder what Mozart might have done had he lived longer and taken the genre of symphony more seriously.

II. Mozart's First Symphony was composed when he was eight years old and living in London. The galant influence of Mozart's friend and mentor, Johann Christian Bach, is clear in this symphony, as is the hand of his father, Leopold, who undoubtedly critiqued and corrected every aspect of his son's work.

A. The First Symphony, scored for two oboes, two horns, strings, and continuo, is built on the three-movement scheme of an Italian-style overture. The first movement is a sonata-form/binary-form composite; we hear the exposition. (**Musical selection**: Mozart, Symphony no. 1 in Eb Major, K. 16, movement 1, exposition [1764].)

B. The second movement, which begins in C minor, is characterized more by its harmonic progressions than any particular melody. (**Musical selection**: Mozart, Symphony no. 1 in Eb Major, K. 16, movement 2, exposition.)

C. The third movement of Mozart's First Symphony is a dance-like movement in a fast triple meter, typical of the symphonic finales of its time. (**Musical selection**: Mozart, Symphony no. 1 in Eb Major, K. 16, movement 3.)

D. We must keep in mind that this First Symphony is somewhat derivative and not unusual for its time, but it is also brimming with energy and competence, and it is the product of an eight-year-old! More early symphonies followed, written for performance in London, The Hague, Vienna, Rome, Milan, and Bologna.

III. Between late 1771 and early 1775, Mozart indulged in an explosion of symphonic composition, writing at least 20 "Salzburg" Symphonies, including his first symphonic masterwork, the so-called "Little" G Minor Symphony, K. 183, in 1773.

    A. The first of these Salzburg Symphonies, no. 14 in A Major, K. 114 (1771), is pervaded by a gentle, Italian-style lyricism, which we will hear in the first-movement exposition. Note that instead of the usual loud symphonic opening, played by the entire orchestra, Mozart's Symphony no. 14 opens quietly and delicately, initially scored for violins only. Also note that this movement uses flutes instead of the standard oboes, which brightens the overall sound of the orchestra. (**Musical selection**: Mozart, Symphony no. 14 in A Major, K. 114, movement 1, exposition [1771].)

    B. Mozart was 17 years old when he completed his Symphony no. 25 in G Minor (1773). It is his first symphony in a minor key, and it was most likely conceived to appeal to the taste of the Viennese, who were under the spell of the *Sturm und Drang* movement. The Symphony in G Minor is generally considered Mozart's first symphonic masterwork, and it is the earliest of his symphonies that is performed regularly today. We will listen to the recapitulation of the first movement, during which we will hear both themes in G minor and a brief but powerful closing section, or coda. (**Musical selection**: Mozart, Symphony in G Minor, K. 183, movement 1, recapitulation [1773].)

    C. With the composition of the radiant Symphony no. 29 in A Major six months after the "Little" G Minor, Mozart had found his own compositional voice. From this point to the end of his life, his constant refinement of that voice put him in a musical class by himself.

IV. In October 1777, the 21-year-old Mozart left his post with the archbishop of Salzburg and traveled to Mannheim and Paris with his mother. The trip was a disaster, and Mozart returned to Salzburg and the employ of the archbishop in 1779.

    A. One of the few fruits of his stay in Paris was a symphony in D major, a three-movement work that Mozart composed for the Concert Spirituel. The ensemble available to him included two flutes, two oboes, two clarinets, two bassoons, two horns, two trumpets, and strings; this is Mozart's first "grand" symphony in terms of both its orchestral forces and its style.

B. We hear the royal first theme of the first movement, with its nod to the French overture. Note the complementary phrases of this opening theme, as blaring, drum-rolling machismo alternates with quiet lyricism. (**Musical selection**: Mozart, Symphony no. 31 in D Major, K. 297, movement 1 [1778].)

C. Mozart wrote to his father that the third and final movement of this symphony found particular favor with the Parisians. We hear the opening of the third-movement sonata form: theme 1 and the modulating bridge. (**Musical selection**: Mozart, Symphony no. 31 in D Major, movement 3.)

V. After his return to Salzburg, Mozart composed, among many other works, three stunning symphonies: nos. 32, 33, and 34.

A. We'll look at Mozart's Symphony no. 34 in C major, K. 338, a three-movement work completed in 1780. Because of the nature of the trumpets and timpani of Mozart's day, the key of C major was ideally suited for celebratory and martial music, which typically featured trumpets and drums. Beginning with the Symphony no. 34, three of Mozart's final seven symphonies are in C major (the others are no. 36, the "Linz," and no. 41, the "Jupiter.")

   1. Typical of the "C-major" symphonic style, no. 34 opens with a magnificent and fanfarish theme 1. (**Musical selection**: Mozart, Symphony no. 34 in C Major, movement 1 [1780].)

   2. Likewise, the final movement brims over with brilliance and energy. (**Musical selection**: Mozart, Symphony no. 34 in C Major, movement 3.)

B. Mozart's next three symphonies were composed between 1782 and 1786. The Symphony no. 35 in D Major dates from 1782 and is nicknamed the "Haffner" because Mozart wrote it in honor of his Salzburg friend Siegmund Haffner, on the occasion of his elevation to the nobility.

C. Mozart's next symphony—no. 36, in C major—was composed in just a few days at the end of October and beginning of November of 1783. Mozart and his wife, Constanze, were guests at the castle of a count in Linz. Mozart, having failed to bring the count a gift, quickly composed the symphony as his offering. It was premiered at the castle on November 4th and has since borne the nickname "Linz."

1. Typical of a C-major symphony, Mozart's Linz is filled with fanfares and flourishes. It also features a slow introduction, the first of Mozart's symphonies to do so. The opening few measures feature the long-short rhythms of a French overture, although the melodic leaps, the descending chromatic line in the bass, and the triple meter are certainly not characteristic of a French overture. (**Musical selection**: Mozart, Symphony no. 36 in C Major, movement 1, introduction [1783].)

2. The finale of Mozart's Linz Symphony is brilliant and festive, as befits a symphony in C major. We hear the first theme of this sonata-form movement. (**Musical selection**: Mozart, Symphony no. 36 in C Major, movement 4.)

D. Like the Linz, Mozart's next symphony—no. 38 in D Major ("Prague")—was named for the city of its premiere. Completed on December 6, 1786, the symphony was written almost immediately after Mozart finished *The Marriage of Figaro*.

VI. Eighteen months passed before Mozart completed another symphony. During that time, he composed and produced *Don Giovanni* to ecstatic audiences in Prague, but his personal life was in disarray. His finances were a mess; his health was bad; and on June 29, 1788, his six-month-old daughter died.

A. Under these terrible circumstances, Mozart composed his last three symphonies, one after the other, during the summer of 1788. Symphony no. 39 in Eb Major was completed on June 26. The G minor, dark and tragic in tone, was completed on July 25. The Symphony no. 41 in C Major, the "Jupiter"—martial and celebratory in tone—was completed roughly two weeks later, on August 10.

B. We still don't know exactly why Mozart wrote these symphonies, although he may have meant them to be performed in a series of subscription concerts. If that was his intention, the concerts were never produced, and to this day, we know of only one performance of one of the symphonies—probably the Jupiter—in Mozart's lifetime.

C. Mozart's Jupiter is the grandfather of all C-major symphonies—truly imperial in its scope and power and well deserving of the appellation of "Jupiter," the king of the gods.

D. The symphony opens with a theme that features the same alternation of martial bluster and lyric gentleness we heard in the first-movement opening of the Symphony no. 31 in D Major. (**Musical selection**: Mozart, Symphony no. 41 in C Major, movement 1, theme 1 [1788].)

E. As the exposition proceeds, Mozart continues to exploit the alternation between machismo and lyricism that characterizes theme 1. At the end of the exposition, Mozart suddenly introduces an entirely new theme so that he might have something to develop in the development section. He inserts the tune of a concert aria he had just finished entitled *"Un bacio di mano,"* "A Kiss on the Hand." (**Musical selections**: Mozart, *"Un bacio di mano,"* K. 541 [1788], and Symphony no. 41 in C Major, movement 1, *"Un bacio di mano."*)

F. The second movement is a lyric *andante* in sonata form, scored without the trumpet and drums that so dominated the first movement.

G. The third movement is a broad, courtly minuet. (**Musical selection**: Mozart, Symphony no. 41 in C Major, movement 3, minuet.)

H. The last movement is a tour-de-force of developmental and polyphonic writing, in which almost everything grows out of the superb first theme that begins the movement. (**Musical selection**: Mozart, Symphony no. 41 in C Major, movement 4, theme 1.)

I. At the end of this incredible movement, Mozart manages to combine virtually every thematic and transitional element heard in the movement in a breathtaking episode in five-part polyphony. That means that we hear five distinct strands of melodic material simultaneously. Let's hear this episode, followed by the conclusion of the movement and the symphony. (**Musical selection**: Mozart, Symphony no. 41 in C Major, movement 4, conclusion.)

Lecture Eight—Transcript
Mozart

Welcome back to *The Symphony*. This is Lecture Eight entitled "Mozart."

Papa and Wolfie

We don't know exactly when Wolfgang Mozart met Joseph Haydn, although obviously each of the composers was aware of the other's existence. Haydn would have first heard of Mozart as the *Wunderkind*, the child prodigy who blazed his first trail across Europe in the early 1760s. Mozart probably first became aware of Haydn a few years later, most likely through his contact with Haydn's brother Michael, who entered into the service of the Archbishop of Salzburg in 1763 when Mozart was 7 years old.

The two met in Vienna, sometime in 1781, the year Mozart rather unceremoniously left the service of the Archbishop Hieronymus Colloredo of Salzburg ("with a kick on my ass," as Mozart later recalled it) and settled in Vienna where he worked and lived as a freelance pianist and composer. Haydn kept a place in Vienna, where he stayed when he wasn't working at Esterhaza.

At the time they had met, Mozart would have been 25 years old and Haydn, 49 years old. The 24-year age disparity was the least of their differences. Mozart was a natural party animal. He ran with a very fast crowd and boogied all night. Haydn was an old-style musical functionary in the employ of an old-world aristocrat. He was a kind, considerate, peace-loving man of generally conservative temperament. And though it would be an overstatement to say that Mozart and Haydn became drinking buddies, it would be accurate to say that these two most different men became genuine friends, based first and foremost on their mutual respect for each other as musicians.

Sometime after they met, Mozart and Haydn began to participate together in "chamber music parties," during which they would play through music together. One such party was hosted by the English composer Steven Storace. There, in Storace's Viennese flat, a string quartet consisting of Joseph Haydn (1st violin), Carl Ditters von Dittersdorf (2nd violin), Wolfgang Mozart (viola) and Johann Baptist Vanhal (cello) read through Haydn's newly published string quartets, op. 33. According to the singer

Michael Kelly, who was among the guests that night, "the four played well enough, but by no means extraordinarily well." Well, so who's perfect? What a scene it must have been.

Inspired to the cockles by Haydn's string quartets, Mozart composed six of his own and dedicated them to Haydn. The title page of Mozart's quartets, published as a group in 1785, bears this inscription: "Six quartets for two violins, viola and cello, composed and dedicated to 'Signor Guiseppe Haydn,' Master of Music for the Prince of Esterhaz; '*dal suo amico*' [from his friend], W. A. Mozart."

In 1785, Mozart's father, Leopold, came to Vienna for an extended visit. While he was there, Leopold himself participated in a chamber music party held at Mozart's apartment. The quartet, which consisted of Wolfgang, Leopold, and brothers Anton and Bartholomaus Tinti, read through three of the string quartets Mozart had dedicated to Haydn. Joseph Haydn was himself there as the guest of honor, and after the reading, the most famous and respected composer in the German-speaking world (of course we're talking about Haydn here) took Leopold Mozart aside and told him: "Before God and as an honest man I tell you that your son is the greatest composer known to me either in person or by name. He has taste and, what is more, the most profound knowledge of composition."

Joseph Haydn, the person who for all intents and purposes created the Classical string quartet and the symphony, a man of great kindness, goodness of spirit, and humility, was also clearly one of the least self-delusional geniuses in history. Because he was right: Wolfgang Mozart brought more pure, overwhelming technique and melodic and harmonic taste to the compositional table than pretty much anyone before him or after him. It is one of the great and enduring tragedies that he died so pathetically young, aged 35 years, 10 months, and 8 days, and that, because of his foreshortened life, he never completely realized his potential as a symphonist.

What? Never really realized his potential as a symphonist? How about the brilliant Symphony in A Major, K. 201 which we sampled in the opening lecture? Or the wonderful Symphonies nos. 35 and 36, the "Haffner" and the "Linz?" How about the glowing Symphony no. 38, the "Prague?" Or the virtually perfect Symphony no. 39 in Eb Major? Or the dark and tragic no. 40 in G Minor? Or the Magisterial "Jupiter," no. 41? Well, what about them? They're great, they're fantastic no doubt, but of Mozart's 41 numbered symphonies, the first 30 were products of his youth. Only the last

10 were written after 1775, when he had achieved his full musical maturity. And of those 10 "mature" symphonies, composed in fits and starts between 1778 and 1788, only the final three (nos. 39, 40, and 41), written during the summer of 1788, only the final three were conceived as a coherent symphonic unit.

All in all, the writing of symphonies was never a priority for Mozart. If he were with us, here, now, he'd tell us that he was an opera composer at heart who wrote piano concerti for a living and chamber music for his friends. The symphonies? Well, the symphonies. He'd tell us that for the most part he wrote them on the run, usually to make a splash, earn some cash and to impress the locals wherever he was. Of course, Mozart would be the first one to tell us that had he lived long enough to be inspired by Haydn's London Symphonies or Beethoven's symphonies, well, who knows what would have happened?

So back to the point. Mozart never completely realized his potential as a symphonist. And while I know we should be grateful for what we have, it is, nevertheless, impossible not to wonder what Mozart might have done had he lived longer and taken the genre of symphony as seriously as he did those of opera, the piano concerto, and the string quartet.

Early Symphonies

Mozart's First Symphony was composed when he was 8 years old and living in London. The galant influence of Mozart's friend and mentor, Johann Christian Bach, is clear in the symphony, as is the hand of his father, Leopold, who undoubtedly critiqued and corrected every aspect of his young son's work. The symphony, scored for two oboes, two horns, strings and continuo, is built on the three-movement scheme of an Italian-style overture.

The first movement is a sonata-form/binary-form composite. We hear the exposition.

[Musical example from Symphony No. 1 in Eb Major, K. 16, Mozart: I; Exposition]

The second movement, which begins in C minor, is characterized more by its harmonic digressions than any particular melody.

[Musical example from Symphony No. 1 in Eb Major, K. 16, Mozart: II]

Finally, the third movement of Mozart's First is a dance-like movement in a fast triple meter, typical of the symphonic finales of its time.

[Musical example from Symphony No. 1 in Eb Major, K. 16, Mozart: III]

Mozart's First Symphony. Derivative? Yes. Typical of its time? Yes, but brimming with energy and competence—and the product of an 8-year old kid! If it's no better than thousands of other like symphonies, then it's simply no worse, either, and it bespeaks a precocity that is still hard for us to fathom. More early symphonies followed, written Mozart was on one or another of his youthful tours, symphonies written for performance in London, The Hague, Vienna, Rome, Milan and Bologna.

A Symphonic Explosion

On December 15, 1771, the Archbishop Sigismund Schrattenbach of Salzburg, a man who had been a great friend and patron of the Mozart family, died. His successor was Count Hieronymus von Colloredo, an exacting and difficult man who was elected to the post of archbishop on the forty-ninth ballot. It would seem that Count Colloredo's peers had reservations about him, reservations that the Mozart clan would soon enough come to share. But not at first. At first, Archbishop Colloredo continued to be a generous benefactor of the teenage Wolfgang Mozart. The hard evidence of which is the virtual explosion of symphonic composition Mozart indulged in between the last days of 1771 and early 1775, symphonies composed for performance at the archbishop's court. Never before and never again would Mozart write so many symphonies in such a short period of time, at least 20 of them, and very likely others that have since been lost. These "Salzburg" Symphonies include Mozart's first symphonic masterwork, the so-called "Little" G Minor Symphony, K. 183 of 1773. Look, the designation of "Little" is simply to designate this G Minor symphony from Mozart's later and more famous Symphony in G Minor of 1788.

The first of these Salzburg Symphonies, no. 14 in A Major, is dated December 30, 1771. A gentle, Italian lyricism pervades the entire piece; as an example of which we will hear the first exposition. Please note that instead of using the usual loud symphonic opening played by the entire orchestra, Mozart's Symphony No. 14 opens quietly and delicately, initially scored for violins alone. Note as well that this movement uses flutes instead of the standard oboes, which brightens substantially the overall sound of the orchestra.

[Musical example from Symphony No. 14 in A Major, Mozart: I; Exposition]

Symphony in G Minor, K. 183 (1773)

Mozart was 17 years old when he completed his Symphony no. 25 in G Minor, on October 5, 1773. It is Mozart's first symphony in a minor key, and it was almost without a doubt conceived to appeal to the taste of the Viennese, who were at the time under the spell of the *Sturm und Drang* movement. For reference, I would point out that Mozart's "Little" G Minor Symphony was composed less than a year after Haydn's Symphony no. 45 in F# Minor, the "Farewell." Mozart's "Little" Symphony in G Minor is generally considered his first symphonic masterwork, and it is today the earliest of his symphonies that's performed on a regular basis. We're going to listen to the recapitulation of the first movement, during which we will hear both themes in G minor and a brief, but powerful closing section, or coda, that comprises the final 24 seconds of this two-and-one-half minute excerpt.

[Musical example from Symphony in G Minor, K. 183, Mozart: I; Recapitulation]

According to Stanley Sadie writing in *The New Grove Dictionary of Music and Musicians*: "The 'Little' G Minor Symphony is music of a [new and] different temper. The urgent tone of the repeated syncopated notes at the start represents something new, and so do the...repeated thrusting phrases that follow. [This is the music of a new and different temper.]"

With the composition of the radiant Symphony no. 29 in A Major six months after the "Little" G Minor—if you recall we sampled its four movements back in Lecture One—Mozart had found his own compositional voice. From this point to the end of his life, his constant refinement of that voice put him increasingly in a musical place occupied by himself alone.

Paris and the Symphony no. 31 in D Major, K. 297

In October of 1777, the 21-year-old Mozart did what we are never supposed to do—he quit his day job for the archbishop, and with his mother in tow, left Salzburg to make his fame and fortune. The trip was a disaster. At first everything was great. Mozart and mom arrived in Mannheim where they stayed for 10 months. Mozart met Cannabich and heard the Mannheim Symphony. He made contacts and friends, wrote a lot of music, played a lot of concerts, and even fell in love with a knockout, beautiful 17-year-old blonde singer named Aloysia Weber. Mozart would have been quite happy to stay in Mannheim, but his father, back at home, had other plans. Writing from Salzburg, Leopold Mozart harangued his son, insisting that he leave whatever success he had achieved in Mannheim (Loserville!) and head immediately to Paris, wherefore was the real action and the real money.

So move on to Paris Mozart and his mother did, where things went really badly. Mozart hated the city. He hated the French. And then, as if not being able to get a decent schnitzel wasn't bad enough, his mother got sick and died (for which his father blamed him!) Heartbroken, Mozart headed home to Salzburg. On the way, he stopped in Mannheim to see his beloved Aloysia, who dropped him like a rock. Mozart arrived in Salzburg on January 15, 1779; there to return to his father and the despised archbishop, in whose employ he would remain until his famous emancipation in 1781.

One of the few genuine fruits of the stay in Paris was a symphony in D major, a three-movement work that Mozart composed for the Concert Spirituel. The ensemble available to him was a large one—two flutes, two oboes, two clarinets, two bassoons, two horns, two trumpets, and strings— and truly, this is Mozart's first "grand" symphony in terms of orchestral forces and its style. Mozart's father—with his eye, as always, on the bottom line—had begged his son to be conscious of prevailing French tastes. Leopold Mozart wrote: "I implore you, before you write for the French, listen and find out above all what pleases them. You should become a Frenchman and endeavor, I hope, to acquire the correct accent. Your object is to make a name for yourself and to get money."

Mozart, having just finished writing what we now refer to as his Symphony no. 31, wrote back: "I cannot say whether it will be popular, and to tell the truth I care very little, for who will not like it? [It will please] the few intelligent French people who may be [here], and as for the stupid ones, I shall not consider it a great misfortune if they are not pleased. I still hope, however, that even the asses find something in it to admire."

Well, admire the symphony the Parisians did—it was the single most successful premiere Mozart had in Paris, despite rehearsals that had gone so badly that he had seriously considered not attending the premiere performance at all. We hear the royal, French overture-ish first theme of the first movement. Note the complementary phrases of this opening theme, as blaring, drum-rolling machismo alternates with quiet lyricism.

[Musical example from Symphony No. 31 in G Major, Mozart: I. 1778]

Of the third and final movement, Mozart wrote his father:

> The last allegro [found particular favor] because, having observed that all final as well as first [movements] here begin with all the

instruments playing together, I began mine with only two violins, *piano*, for the first eight bars, followed instantly by a *forte*; the audience, as I'd expected, said 'hush' at the soft beginning, and when they heard the *forte*, began at once to clap their hands.

Let's hear that opening of the third movement sonata form, Theme I and the subsequent modulating bridge.

[Musical example from Symphony No. 31 in G Major, Mozart: III; Opening]

Mozart was thrilled with the premiere performance and reception of what is now referred to as his "Paris" Symphony. In a tone so eager-to- please that it makes us really want to gag, he immediately wrote his father:

I was so happy that as soon as the symphony was over, I went off to the Palais Royale, where I had a large ice, said the Rosary as I had vowed to do, and went home, for I always am and always will be happiest there, or else in the company of some good, honest German who, if he is a bachelor, lives alone like a good Christian, or, if married, loves his wife and brings his children up properly.

What Mozart failed to mention in his prim, post-concert letter is that his mother is lying dead in her bed, having died that very afternoon. Strange people these Mozarts.

Symphonies in C Major

So in January 1779, Mozart returned to Salzburg, without his mother, without a job, and without even a girlfriend. All his grief and frustration aside, Mozart managed to compose, among many other works, three stunning symphonies over the course of the next 18 months: nos. 32, 33, and 34. We turn to Mozart's Symphony no. 34 in C Major, a three-movement work completed on August 29, 1780. Because of the nature of the trumpets and timpani of Mozart's day, the key of C major was ideally suited for the sort of celebratory and martial music that typically featured trumpets and drums. Beginning with the Symphony no. 34, three of Mozart's final seven symphonies are in C Major (the others are nos. 36, the "Linz" and 41, the "Jupiter"). For the remainder of this lecture, these are the symphonies on which we shall focus.

Typical of the "C major" symphonic style, no. 34 opens with a magnificent and fanfarish theme 1.

[Musical example from Symphony No. 34 in C Major, Mozart: I; Opening]

Likewise, the final movement brims over with brilliance and energy.

[Musical example from Symphony No. 34 in C Major, Mozart: IV; Excerpt]

Mozart's next three symphonies were written between 1782 and 1786. The Symphony no. 35 in D Major dates from 1782 and is nicknamed the "Haffner" because Mozart wrote it in honor of his Salzburg friend Sigmund Haffner, on the occasion of his elevation to nobility. Mozart's next symphony—no. 36 in C Major—was composed in just a few days at the end of October and the beginning of November of 1783. Mozart and his wife Constanze were guests at the castle of Count Joseph Anton von Thun-Hohenstein at Linz, where they stopped off on the way back from a stay in Salzburg. The Thun-Hohenstein's were great patrons of the arts and they played a huge role in the careers of Joseph Haydn and Ludwig Beethoven, as well as Mozart's.

Mozart, having failed to bring the count a bottle of wine or some flowers, quickly composed the symphony as a gift. It was premiered at the castle on November 4 and has ever since borne the nickname "Linz." What Mozart did bring to Linz was a symphony, a new symphony in G Major, composed by his ailing friend Michael Haydn. It was there, in Linz, that Mozart added the first movement introduction to Michael Haydn's symphony, and in doing so created a question in ownership that lasted for the next hundred and fifty years. Mozart's "37th" indeed!

Typical of a C major symphony, Mozart's "Linz" (properly Mozart's 36th) is filled with "fanfares, ruffles and flourishes." It also features a slow introduction, the first of Mozart's symphonies to do so, which makes us wonder whether the introduction he wrote for Michael Haydn's symphony was a warm-up for one of his own. Let's hear the introduction to the first movement of the "Linz." The opening measures feature the long-short rhythms of a French overture, although the huge melodic leaps, the descending chromatic line in the bass, and the triple meter are certainly not characteristic of a French overture. Mozart here is invoking that genre, but not actually writing one.

[Musical example from Symphony No. 36 in C Major, Mozart: I; Introduction; 1783]

There is so much musical information present in just this introduction—not to mention the nine-minute long sonata form that follows it—that one modern writer finds himself in sympathy with Mozart's contemporaries:

"One can understand why many listeners, including Emperor Joseph II, found Mozart's music overloaded."

The finale of Mozart's Linz Symphony is brilliant and festive, as befits a symphony in C major. We hear the first theme of this sonata form movement.

[Musical example from Symphony No. 37 in C Major, The Linz, Mozart: I; Introduction]

Like the Linz, Mozart's next symphony—no. 38 in D Major, the "Prague"—was named for the city of its premiere. Completed on December 6, 1786, the symphony was written almost immediately after Mozart completed *The Marriage of Figaro*, which is only one of a handful of greatest operas of all time. By 1786, Mozart was at the very top of his game, and I cannot encourage you too much to listen to and to know his 38th symphony. As for us, time demands that we move forward.

The Final Three

Eighteen months past before Mozart completed another symphony. During that time, he composed and produced *Don Giovanni* to ecstatic audiences in Prague, and almost total indifference in Vienna. His finances, well, they were a big, gnarly mess. His health, which was never good, was particularly bad; he was plagued by infections, kidney ailments, viruses—you name it he got it, a walking petri dish. On June 17, 1788, Mozart's finances forced him to move to a less expensive flat outside the city walls of Vienna. Twelve days later, on June 29, 1788, his six-month-old infant daughter Theresia died of some unspecified childhood ailment.

It was under these terribly gloomy circumstances that Mozart composed his last three symphonies, one after the other, during that summer of 1788. Symphony no. 39 in Eb Major—according to Donald Frances Tovey "the locus classicus of Euphony"—was completed on June 26. The G Minor, dark and tragic in tone, was completed on July 25. The Symphony no. 41 in C Major, the "Jupiter,"—martial and celebratory in tone—was completed roughly two weeks later on August 10. We still don't know exactly why Mozart wrote these symphonies, although it is likely that he meant them to be performed at a series of special subscription concerts that he intended to produce. If that indeed was his intention, the concerts never happened, and until this day we only know of one performance of one of the symphonies—probably the "Jupiter"—in Mozart's own lifetime.

In language appropriately flowery for these amazing symphonies, the French musicologist Georges Saint-Foix writes:

> Never since he arrived at maturity had [Mozart] produced, at intervals of a few days only, a succession of compositions of the same caliber; the Eb Symphony represents the immense portico through which the composer reveals to us all the warm and poetic beauty thronging his mind, before surrendering himself before our eyes to a struggle of exalted passion, to be manifest in the Symphony in G Minor; and finally he invites our presence at a sort of apotheosis of his musical genius, freed from all shackles, in what has come to be known as the "Jupiter" Symphony. This imposing [trinity is] his symphonic testimony [which] sums up for us his inmost soul.

Mozart's Jupiter is the grandfather of all C-major symphonies—truly imperial in its scope and power—and well-deserving of the appellation "Jupiter," the king of the gods, that a grateful 19th century bestowed upon it.

The symphony opens with a theme that offers the same sort of alternation of martial bluster and lyric gentleness that we heard in the first movement opening of the Symphony no. 31 in D Major. Let's hear it.

[Musical example from Symphony No. 41 in C Major, Mozart: I; Theme I]

As the exposition proceeds, Mozart continues to develop theme 1. Theme 2 grows out of Theme 1 and then he continues this developmental process until as he arrives at the end of the exposition. Mozart realizes (I think) that he's already developed theme 1 as far as he can, so he suddenly introduces there at the end of the exposition an entirely new theme, a third theme, so that he might actually have something to develop in the development section. Kerplunk! He drops in the tune of a concert aria he had just finished composing, an aria entitled "*Un bacio di mano*," "A Kiss on the Hand." Please, let's just hear that concert aria a little bit. K. 501, Un Batu Domano.

[Musical example from Un Batu Domano]

And now let's hear that same tune as the third theme of the first movement of the Jupiter Symphony, the theme that Mozart will now develop in the development section.

[Musical example from Symphony No. 41 in C Major, Mozart: I; Development]

The second movement is a gorgeous and lyric *andante* in sonata form, scored without the trumpet and drums that so dominated the first movement. The third movement is a broad and courtly minuet.

[Musical example from Symphony No. 41 in C Major, Mozart: III; Minuet]

And the last movement, which deserves at least a lecture unto itself, is an absolute tour-de-force of developmental and polyphonic writing, in which almost everything grows out of the superb first theme that begins the movement.

[Musical example from Symphony No. 41 in C Major, Mozart: IV; Opening]

At the end of this incredible movement, Mozart, by some magical alchemy, manages to combine virtually every thematic and transitional element heard in the movement to this point, combine them together into an absolutely breathtaking episode in what we call five-part polyphony. That means simultaneously we are hearing five distinct melodic strands. Let's hear this episode followed by the conclusion of the movement, and with it, the conclusion of the symphony.

[Musical example from Symphony No. 41 in C Major, Mozart: IV; Conclusion]

Of the Jupiter Symphony, Mozart scholar David Johnson writes:

> Mozart did not give his last symphony its nickname. But for many of us it could hardly be bettered. The work resounds from one end to the other with a god-like pomp, a Roman splendor, a mastery of craft that the "thunderer" himself might envy. It is by no means experimental; on the contrary, it is reactionary compared to some of Haydn's [symphonies]. But it climaxes and fixes an age.

I would repeat that last line because it is an important one: "But it climaxes and fixes an age"—the age of Classicism, the age of elegance, the age of restraint.

When we return, we return to a different age just a few years later, but an age of revolution and an age of change, an age best represented by the music of Ludwig van Beethoven.

Until then, thank you.

Lecture Nine
Beethoven

Scope: Beethoven came of age during the era of the French Revolution, and to a great degree was inspired by the personal and political empowerment that the Revolution represented. Over the course of his lifetime, Beethoven reinvented himself as an artist twice, and, in doing so, his musical voice evolved into a highly personal and original style that revolutionized the symphonic genre. This lecture traces that evolution in Beethoven's nine symphonies and discusses the musical inheritance he left for the Romantic composers who were his successors.

Outline

I. Biographers have noted the progression in Beethoven's musical achievements from an extension of the Viennese Classical tradition to a wholly personal, original, and profoundly influential musical style. Nowhere is Beethoven's compositional development and his fabled popularity better illustrated than in his symphonies.

A. For an in-depth discussion of Beethoven's life and times, please refer to the eight-lecture Teaching Company biography of Beethoven in the "Great Masters" series (which also includes biographies of Haydn and Mozart). An in-depth exploration of Beethoven's symphonies can be found in The Teaching Company course entitled *The Symphonies of Beethoven*. In this lecture, we will examine Beethoven's nine symphonies as a musical diary, each one demonstrating his ongoing development as a composer.

B. As we will learn, Beethoven came to believe in self-expression and originality above all else. Each symphony, especially from the Third onward, was conceived as an entity unto itself, and Beethoven was not disposed to repeat himself stylistically from one piece to the next. Further, although Beethoven used the four-movement symphonic template of Classicism, he used it only to the point where he found it useful. To Beethoven's way of thinking, originality and expressive content always trumped ritual and tradition.

II. Compared to his string quartets, piano trios, and piano sonatas of the same period, Beethoven's "First" Symphony (no. 1 in C Major, op. 21 [1800]), is a relatively conservative composition, but we still see his trademark rhythmic drive, as well as his audacious use of harmony and other features that will mark his later work.

    A. We turn directly to the first-movement introduction. Note that the introduction begins on a dissonance in the key of F major, which is not the home key of this symphony. The opening of the introduction is, in fact, a series of dominant, or dissonant, chords that resolve upwards, creating a tonal ambiguity that is not resolved until the arrival of theme 1. (**Musical selection**: Beethoven, Symphony no.1 in C Major, op. 21, movement 1, introduction, opening.)

    B. As the movement continues, we discover that these introductory harmonies constitute, in reality, the harmonic underpinning of the first theme. Further, as the movement continues to unfold, we discover that the seemingly insignificant half-step rise represented by each of the resolutions of these introductory dissonances becomes an important thematic, transitional, and developmental aspect of the movement!

    C. Did Beethoven expect his audiences to notice all of this on their first hearing of the symphony? Of course not. Beethoven's conception of the symphony was, from the beginning, preconditioned by Haydn's late symphonies: that a symphony need not be understood entirely at its first hearing, that subsequent performances were to be expected, and that a symphony was no longer merely an aristocratic amusement but a multifaceted musical statement, that was operatic in its degree of contrast, conflict and resolution.

III. Beethoven's Second Symphony was composed between late 1801 and late 1802, which was, physically and spiritually, a bad time for the composer.

    A. By 1802, Beethoven had come to realize that his progressive hearing loss was probably incurable, and he was terribly depressed, even suicidal. He felt tremendous rage, an overpowering sense of isolation and alienation, frustration, and a sense of victimization. Despite his depression, we do not hear Beethoven's "personal issues" in his Second Symphony. Instead, we hear a brilliant work in D major, in which a number of the rituals of the Classical symphony begin to crumble under Beethoven's increasingly self-expressive onslaught.

B. Most notable of these is Beethoven's treatment of the third-movement minuet and trio. He had little patience for the musical tradition of the minuet, a stately, courtly dance invented in France in the 17th century and overused in the music of the 18th. By his Second Symphony, Beethoven's destruction of the Classical-era minuet was complete. He called his third movement a "*scherzo*," a term meaning, literally, "I'm joking."

C. In the third-movement scherzo of his Second Symphony, Beethoven creates a micro-miniature theme, consisting of three rising notes, that bounces around the orchestra like a ping-pong ball; each set of three notes is played by a different group of instruments. (**Musical selection**: Beethoven, Symphony no. 2 in D Major, op. 36, movement 3, minuet, opening.)

D. This is not a Classical minuet; it's not a minuet at all. It is, to paraphrase Napoleon Bonaparte, "the Revolution already in action," a musical revolution that will hit with full force in Beethoven's Symphony no. 3.

IV. In 1803, Beethoven dug himself out of his depression by reinventing himself as a Promethean hero. This bit of self-delusion allowed him to survive, and to create music that he likely would not have imagined otherwise.

A. The inspiration for Beethoven's heroic reinvention was twofold. The first part was the Greek legend of Prometheus, who stole fire from the gods, gave it to man, and roused the anger of Zeus. In 1801, Beethoven composed a ballet entitled *The Creatures of Prometheus*; certainly, the heroic Promethean ideal was in the forefront of his mind in 1802 and 1803. His other inspiration for his personal reinvention was Napoleon Bonaparte who, in 1803, was still perceived by many as the man who would free Europe from the ancient bondage of the monarchies.

B. Beethoven's Third Symphony, nicknamed "*Eroica*," or the "Heroic" Symphony, is autobiographical. The first movement is about a hero—undoubtedly Beethoven himself—who faces extraordinary adversity and, after death-defying struggles, portrayed by terrible dissonances, rhythmic ambiguities, and so forth, triumphs over that adversity.

1. At the heart of the extremely long first movement is its extremely long first theme, which personifies "the hero," warts and all. Following two explosive Eb-major chords, the theme begins. It is heard initially in the orchestral 'cellos, the baritone voice of the string section, and is, thus, immediately perceived as being a "male" voice.

2. As the theme progresses through its four component phrases, we hear a good deal of harmonic dissonance and rhythmic ambiguity; this is a theme or, perhaps, a personality with significant issues to be confronted and overcome.

3. The fourth and final phrase of the theme is triumphant and magnificent; from the beginning of the movement, we are aware of a musical character that aspires to the heroic ideal. (**Musical selection**: Beethoven, Symphony no. 3 in Eb Major, op. 55, movement 1, theme 1.)

V. Of the brilliant and engaging Fourth Symphony, we sample a marvelous moment in the fourth and final movement.

A. As the development is drawing to its conclusion, a solo bassoon bursts in—prematurely—with the scurrying first theme of the recapitulation, dominated, as it is, by 16th notes. The effect is entirely comic; has the bassoon gotten lost, or was it just a bit overenthusiastic?

B. This brief but intensely difficult bassoon solo is one of the most famous in the repertoire, and this moment is typical of a symphony that is filled with energy, joy, and wit. (**Musical selection**: Beethoven, Symphony no. 4 in Bb Major, op. 60, movement 4, theme 1.)

VI. Beethoven's Fifth Symphony is an icon of Western culture. Across the span of its four movements, Beethoven tells a tale of musical birth and growth, destruction, regrowth, and ultimately, triumph.

A. This catharsis from destruction to triumph, this struggle between despair and hope, is portrayed across the grand span of the symphony as a struggle between the keys of C minor and C major. During the third-movement scherzo, the key of C major triumphs over C minor, and thus, the fourth movement can begin in a blaze of C-major glory. (**Musical selection**: Beethoven, Symphony no. 5 in C Minor, op. 67, movement 4, theme 1.)

B. The third movement is pivotal. It begins in C minor and features a barking, blaring, and entirely ferocious theme in the same key. (**Musical selection**: Beethoven, Symphony no. 5 in C Minor, op. 67, movement 3, theme 1.)

C. This theme, featuring three fast, repeated notes and a fourth, longer note, grows directly out of the opening four notes of the first movement. (**Musical selection**: Beethoven, Symphony no. 5 in C Minor, op. 67, movement 1, theme 1.)

D. In the fourth movement, hope and triumph, as represented by C major, have won out over darkness and despair, represented by C minor, and the fourth movement bounces from one glory to the next. (**Musical selection**: Beethoven, Symphony no. 5 in C Minor, op. 67, movement 4, development conclusion and recapitulation opening.)

1. As the development section draws to its conclusion, a magnificent passage builds toward a huge climax. We await what will undoubtedly be an earth-shattering recapitulation when, instead, quietly ticking violins lead to a ghostly reappearance of the barking, blaring, third-movement theme in C minor!

2. The music is quiet, insidious, malevolent. Is this thematic reappearance real, an indication that we are returning to the "dark side" of C minor, or is it just a dream?

3. Before we can answer that question, the music transitions back to the long awaited and hoped for recapitulation in C major! The third-movement quote was not a harbinger of things to come but merely a memory of distance traversed, a last moment of melancholy before we give ourselves over to the cathartic joy of C major!

4. This sort of thematic quotation from an earlier movement is pure musical storytelling. From an analytic point of view, it has no place in the fourth movement, but expressively, it's a stroke of genius. With each symphonic step, the symphony becomes, for Beethoven, a more inclusive and expressively wide-ranging genre.

VII. Nowhere is Beethoven's proclivity toward symphonic "inclusivity" more explicitly apparent than in his Sixth Symphony, the so-called "Pastoral" Symphony.

    A. That Beethoven's Pastoral Symphony is a programmatic piece describing a day in the country has been understood since its premiere in 1808. What's remarkable about Beethoven's Sixth is how its composer elevated what was a pedestrian genre of music to a level of high art.

    B. The most famous moments in Beethoven's Sixth are those in which he explicitly evokes some aspect of nature in the orchestra. For example, as the second movement draws to its conclusion, we hear a series of woodwind cadenzas, each imitating a different bird and labeled in the score as follows: *Nachtigall* ("nightingale," in the flute); *Wachtel* ("quail," in the oboe); and *Kuckuck* ("cuckoo," in the clarinet). (**Musical selection**: Beethoven, Symphony no. 6 in F Major, op. 68, movement 2, coda, part 2.)

    C. The birdcalls are delightful but not extraordinary. The great strength of Beethoven's Sixth rests, instead, in its breathtaking subtlety. For example, the first movement begins with a rustic first theme heard over a bagpipe-like drone. This theme concludes with a simple, rising melodic idea that is repeated, with only slight variations, 13 times in succession. (**Musical selection**: Beethoven, Symphony no. 6 in F Major, op. 68, movement 1, theme 1.)

    D. Later, during the development section of the movement, Beethoven takes this "idea" of varied melodic repetition even further. (**Musical selection**: Beethoven, Symphony no. 6 in F Major, op. 68, movement 1, development, parts 2–5.)

    E. Beethoven entitled this first movement "The cheerful impressions excited by arriving in the country." His use of varied musical repetition throughout this first movement is a metaphor for what he perceives as the varied repetition of nature.

VIII. Beethoven's Seventh Symphony, begun in late 1811 and completed in April of 1812, is often referred to as his "dance" symphony.

    A. Beethoven designed each movement around a single, powerfully felt rhythmic pattern. (**Musical selection**: Beethoven, Symphony no. 7 in A Major, op. 92, movement 1.)

B. Richard Wagner described the fourth and final movement of Beethoven's Seventh as the "apotheosis of the dance." (**Musical selection**: Beethoven, Symphony no. 7 in A Major, op. 92, movement 4.)

IX. Beethoven's Eighth Symphony is, ostensibly, his "homage" to Classicism. Although in its broadest outline, the Eighth may resemble a Classically proportioned symphony, in its details, it is nothing of the sort. In reality, it is filled with the kinds of themes, phrase irregularities, harmonic surprises, rhythmic ambiguities, developmental devices, and slapstick musical humor that mark it as a work of Beethoven's maturity.

A. As an example, we turn to the second movement, which in a Classical symphony, we would expect to be slow. In Beethoven's Eighth, the second movement is a moderately fast-paced musical portrait of what was, for Beethoven, a high-tech device: the metronome!

B. The merciless ticking of the metronome is portrayed by staccato winds and horns. A simple theme in the first violins does its best to keep up, but it keeps falling slightly out of rhythm with the ticking winds and horns. Near the end of our excerpt, we "hear"—in the orchestra—the metronome being wound, not once, but twice. (**Musical selection**: Beethoven, Symphony no. 8 in F Major, op. 93, movement 2.)

C. The metronome portrayed here comes to a bad end. At the close of the movement, it begins to break down, and the orchestra, frustrated past its limits of endurance, does what every musician has fantasized about doing—it smashes the metronome.

X. After the Eighth, Beethoven did not complete his next symphony—the Ninth, which would be his last—for nearly 12 years. In those 11 years between the Eighth and the Ninth, from 1813–1824, Beethoven put himself and everyone around him through hell.

A. After 1815, Beethoven's music fell out of favor with the Viennese public; his patrons either died or became estranged from him; what was left of his hearing disintegrated; and he became embroiled in a terrible custody battle over his brother's son. Around 1819–1820, he reinvented himself and began to compose music of transcendent technical and expressive content.

B. The Ninth Symphony is a product of this late period of Beethoven's compositional life. For all of the gut-wrenching, soul-inspiring music we hear in the first, second, and third movements, it is the fourth movement of the Ninth that changed music history and the collective concept of what constituted a *symphony*.

C. As we observed in Lecture One, this historical landmark was Beethoven's inclusion of vocal texts in the fourth-movement finale. Beethoven didn't just cross the line between instrumental music and vocal music; he obliterated the distinction between the genre of symphony and the vocal genres of opera, cantata, and oratorio. (**Musical selection**: Beethoven, Symphony no. 9 in D Minor, op. 125, movement 4, first choral climax.)

D. The impact of Beethoven's Ninth Symphony rippled outward for the next 80 years. Like Haydn before him, Beethoven reinvented the genre.

    1. Earlier in his career, Beethoven's music had shown that existing musical forms, such as sonata form, minuet, and trio, were contextual; that is, one need use those forms only to the point that they serve the expressive context.

    2. With his Ninth Symphony, Beethoven said to the next generations of composers that genre was contextual as well; that the expressive needs of the composer must take precedence over any musical tradition, no matter how sacred and time-honored that tradition might be.

E. This message fell gratefully on the ears and minds of the next generation of composers, the so-called Romantics who, using Beethoven as their model, sought an ever freer, more self-expressive approach to composition.

Lecture Nine—Transcript
Beethoven

We return to The Symphony. This is Lecture Nine—it is entitled "Beethoven." We concluded Lecture Eight with words written in reference to Mozart's Symphony no. 41 in C Major, the "Jupiter," that it "climaxed and fixed an age." It was an age that saw the genre of symphony grow from a brief and entertaining three-section Italian opera overture to a musically and intellectually compelling four-movement symphony. Mozart's era was an age of elegance, of structural clarity and beautiful melody, of emotional restraint and good taste in all things. It was the age of Classicism, which found its highest musical expression in the so-called Viennese Classical Style and the music of Joseph Haydn and Wolfgang Mozart himself. It was the age of Enlightenment, that great 18th-century social evolution that saw a growing and increasingly empowered middle class enter the mainstream of European society for the first time. And it was an age that saw the beginning of the end of the great European monarchies and the aristocracy that fed the monarchies and profited from their existence.

On July 14, 1789, 11 months after Mozart finished his Jupiter Symphony, a predominantly middle-class Parisian mob stormed the city jail—the ancient fortress of the Bastille. The guards put up one hell of a fight, but they were hopelessly outnumbered. The victorious rioters freed a few prisoners, grabbed some weapons, beheaded the surviving guard and the warden, as well as the mayor of the city. Who says you can't beat City Hall? They paraded around Paris with the heads of their victims skewered on the ends of some pikes. Thus began the French Revolution and the subsequent age of Napoleon. Had the hotheads who marched on the Bastille that day had any idea of the world of hurt they were about to unleash on themselves and the planet, they might very well have spray-painted something clever on the limestone walls of the Bastille, something like "The middle class rules; aristocrats drool!" and would have gone home, had some brandy and tried to figured out a more peaceful way to address their admittedly, most legitimate grievances. But history has never worked that way and thus, the great social evolution of the Enlightenment became the revolution of the middle class, and the world has never been the same since.

Roughly 200 miles away in Bonn lived a young man named Ludwig van Beethoven. He was 17 years and 7 months old when the news from Paris reached him, and like so many of his generation he was frightened by the potential for anarchy implied by the revolution in France, and at the same time inspired by the personal and political empowerment that the Revolution represented. Joseph Kerman and Alan Tyson describe Beethoven's life and career:

> [Beethoven's] early [musical] achievements show him to be extending the Viennese Classical tradition that he had inherited from Mozart and Haydn. As personal affliction—deafness, the inability to enter into happy personal relationships—loomed [ever] larger, he began to compose in an increasingly individual musical style, and at the end of his life, he wrote his most sublime and profound works. From his success at combining tradition and exploration and personal expression, he came to be regarded as the dominant musical figure of the nineteenth century, and scarcely any significant composer since his time has escaped his influence or failed to acknowledge it. For the respect his works have commanded of musicians, and the popularity they have enjoyed among wider audiences, he is probably the most admired composer in the history of Western music.

Nowhere, my friends, is Beethoven's compositional development and his fabled popularity better demonstrated than in his symphonies. For an in-depth discussion of Beethoven's life and times, I would direct your attention to my eight-lecture Teaching Company biography of Beethoven in the "Great Master" series where you will also find biographies of Haydn and Mozart. For an in-depth exploration of Beethoven's symphonies, I would direct your attention to my 32-lecture Teaching Company super course: The Symphonies of Beethoven. So, what can we do here in one lecture that required a total of 40 lectures in other courses? Our very best.

Here's our game plan. Beethoven's symphonies are a musical diary composed across the span of his career, each one demonstrating in some way his ongoing development as a composer. There are only nine of them, as compared to Haydn's 104 or von Dittersdorf's 120. The reason there are only nine is that Beethoven came to believe in self-expression and originality above all else. Each symphony, especially from the Third onward, was conceived as an entity unto itself. It takes time to write a symphony, especially if one is disposed not to repeat oneself stylistically from one piece to the next. In his symphonies, Beethoven most assuredly does not repeat himself. And while Beethoven used the four-movement symphonic template of Classicism, he used it only to the point where he found it useful, and then he ignored it. By Beethoven's way of thinking, originality and expressive context always trumped ritual and tradition.

We are going to move through all nine of Beethoven's symphonies with shameful rapidity. We will briefly discuss each symphony and then identify each aspect that I consider the most striking, a really fool-hearty exercise admittedly. It's like focusing on but a single body part that is the cumulative perfection that is Sofia Loren. The point of the exercise though will be cumulative. Having noted these striking moments, we'll have a sense of just how far beyond the Classical standard Beethoven went during his symphonic lifetime.

Symphony no. 1 in C Major, op. 21, 1800; published 1801

You know, it's almost too convenient that the 18th century ended with the composition of Beethoven's "First" Symphony in 1800 and the 19th century began with its publication in 1801. Compared to his string quartets, piano trios, and piano sonatas of the same period, Beethoven's First is, all in all, a comparatively conservative composition, and that should come as no surprise. In his First, Beethoven was going head to head with the biggies my friends, with Haydn and Mozart, in what has become, by 1800, the most important of all instrumental genres—the symphony.

In his First Symphony, Beethoven chose over all to play it safe which is why Donald Francis Tovey chose to call the piece "a fitting farewell to the eighteenth century." Well, almost. Certainly Beethoven's trademark rhythmic drive is present throughout, as are his concise-bordering-on-atomic themes, his audacious use of harmony, and his pack rat-like mentality to never let a good musical idea go to waste.

We turn directly to the first movement, the introduction. There's nothing new or original in having an introduction. Of Haydn's final 21 symphonies, only three of them are without a first movement introduction. Let's hear the very opening of Beethoven's introduction.

[Musical example from Symphony no. 1 in C Major, Opus 21, Beethoven: I; Opening]

Nothing surprising here, a run of the mill introduction, yes? no. You see, the introduction to the first movement of Beethoven's First Symphony begins on a dissonance in the key of F major, which is not the home key of this symphony. The opening of the introduction is, in fact, a series of dominant or dissonant chords that resolve upwards, creating a tonal ambiguity that is not resolved until we arrive at the beginning of theme 1. Let's hear it again.

[Musical example from Symphony no. 1 in C Major, Opus 21, Beethoven: I; Opening]

In his a seminal study of Beethoven's symphonies published back in 1896, George Grove wrote, "The opening of [Beethoven's First] may not seem novel or original to us [here today], but at that time it was audacious and amply sufficient to justify the unfavorable reception with which it met from such established critics of the day as Preindl, the Abbe Stadler, and Dionys Weber."

But even more important than the shock value of these rising dissonances is what Beethoven actually does with them, what they mean, how they're integrated organically into the rest of the movement. As the movement continues, we discover that these introductory harmonies constitute, in reality, the harmonic underpinning of the first theme. As the movement continues to unfold, we discover that the tiny, seemingly insignificant little half-step rise represented by each of the resolutions of these introductory dissonances becomes a hugely important thematic, transitional, and developmental aspect of the music. That's Beethoven, my friends, already at his best, turning the seemingly insignificant, the often banal, into something surprising, shocking, profound and even sublime.

Did Beethoven expect his audience to notice all of this at their first hearing of the symphony? Of course not. But Beethoven's conception of the symphony was, from the very beginning, preconditioned by Haydn's late symphonies. That conception was that a symphony need not be entirely understood at its first hearing, that subsequent performances were to be expected, that a symphony was no longer an aristocratic amusement, but a multi-faceted musical statement, an instrumental genre, operatic in its degree of contrast, conflict, and resolution.

Symphony no. 2 in D Major, op. 36, 1802

Beethoven's Second Symphony was composed between 1801 and 1802—physically and spiritually a bad time for Beethoven. By 1802, he had come to realize that his progressive hearing loss wa probably incurable. The hearing loss had started around 1796, and though Beethoven would not be clinically deaf until 1818, by 1802 he was terribly depressed, even suicidal. The demons of his extremely dysfunctional upbringing came back full force and with them tremendous rage, overpowering feelings of isolation and alienation, frustration, powerlessness and a sense of victimization—why does all of this always happen to me? Beethoven would have been a great guest on the Jerry Springer Show: "Today: Composer/pianists Who Were Beaten as Children and then Go Deaf in their Young Adulthood! Who is van Beethoven? We have a surprise for you...Everybody put your hands together for the drunk putz who never spared the rod, Beethoven's father, Johann van Beethoven! C'mon out, Johann. Yeah, put down the bottle. C'mon, c'mon, sit down next to your Ludwig!" Oh my goodness, the fur would fly!

Anyway, depressed though he was, we do not hear Beethoven's "personal issues" in his Second Symphony although we will hear them in his Third of 1803. What we do hear is a brilliant work in D major, in which any number of the rituals of the Classical symphony are beginning to crumble under Beethoven's increasingly self-expressive onslaught. Most notable among these is Beethoven's treatment of the third movement minuet and trio. Please, even the most casual glance at virtually any picture of Beethoven will reveal that he was not a powdered wig sort of guy. Heck, he wasn't even a brush and comb sort of guy. He had zero tolerance for aristocratic pretensions, which meant that he had little patience for the musical tradition of the minuet, a stately, courtly dance invented in France back in the 17th century and done to death in the music of the 18th.

By his Second Symphony, Beethoven's destruction of the Classical-era minuet was complete. He called his third movement a scherzo, which means, literally, "I'm joking." In Beethoven's many subsequent scherzi, he generally retained the overall form and meter of the Classical minuet, but not the moderate tempo and certainly not the courtly mood. In the third-movement scherzo of his Second Symphony, Beethoven creates a micro-miniaturized theme consisting of three rising notes that bounce around the orchestra like a ping-pong ball, with each set of three notes being played by a different group of instruments—first low strings, then violins, then low strings, then horns, then violins, then horns, then everybody.

[Musical example from Symphony no. 2 in D Major, Opus 36, Beethoven: III]

This is not a Classical minuet. It's not a minuet at all. It is to paraphrase Napoleon B., "the revolution already in action," a musical revolution that will hit with full force in Beethoven's Symphony no. 3.

Symphony no. 3 in Eb Major, op. 55 ("Eroica"), 1803

Beethoven dug himself out of his hearing-loss inspired funk of 1802 by reinventing himself in 1803. We're well aware, my friends, that emotionally healthy people don't go around reinventing themselves, but Beethoven was certainly not an emotionally healthy person in 1802. Neither did he have the benefit of antidepressants, or even simple psychiatric therapy. For Beethoven, it was either the bottle or a pistol or self-delusion; so let us be grateful it was the latter. His new self-image, that of a Promethean hero conquering adversity by creating a music the likes of which no one had ever heard before, allowed him to tap a level of self-expression and to create a level of music that he could never have otherwise imagined.

The inspiration for Beethoven's heroic reinvention was twofold. The first was the Greek legend of Prometheus, who stole fire from the gods and gave it to man and in doing so roused the anger of Zeus, who had him chained to a mountain peak in the Caucasus. Better there than a weekend in New Jersey, but only by just a little. In 1801, Beethoven composed a ballet entitled The Creatures of Prometheus and the heroic Promethean ideal was therefore in the forefront of his mind in 1802 and 1803. Beethoven's other inspiration for his personal reinvention was none other than the man of the hour, Napoleon Bonaparte, who in 1803 was still perceived by many as the sword-arm of the French Revolution, the man who would free Europe from the ancient bondage of the monarchies.

Beethoven's Third Symphony—nicknamed the "Eroica," or the "Heroic" Symphony—is an autobiographical piece of music. The first movement is about a hero—Beethoven himself, without any doubt—who faces extraordinary adversity, and after death-defying struggles, portrayed by terrible dissonances, rhythmic ambiguities, and so forth, triumphs over those adversaries.

At the heart of this extremely long movement is its extremely long first theme, a theme that personifies "the hero," warts and all. Following two explosive Eb-major chords, the theme begins. It's heard initially in the orchestral cellos, the baritone voice of the string section, and is, thus, immediately perceived as being a "male" voice. As the theme progresses through its four component phrases, we hear all sorts of harmonic dissonance and rhythmic ambiguity. This is a theme, or personality, if you will, with major issues, issues to be confronted and overcome. The fourth and final phrase of this opening theme is triumphant and magnificent. From the beginning of the movement then, we're aware of a musical character that aspires to the heroic ideal.

[Musical example from Symphony no. 3 in Eb Major, Opus 55, "The Eroica," Beethoven: I]

Of Beethoven's Third Symphony, Joseph Kerman writes, "[The Third Symphony] is a watershed work, not only in terms of Beethoven's own music, but in terms of our whole musical tradition, considered as broadly as we please. [After the Third], there was no more chance of turning back to Viennese Classicism than there was to the ancien regime. After the Eroica, Beethoven's music breathes in a different world."

Symphony no. 4 in Bb Major, op. 60, 1806

From the brilliant and engaging Fourth Symphony we sample a marvelous moment in the fourth and final movement. As the development is drawing to its conclusion, a solo bassoon bursts in—prematurely—with the scurrying 16th-note dominated first theme of the recapitulation. The effect is entirely comic—has the bassoon gotten lost, or was it just a tad bit overenthusiastic? Whatever we want to call it, this brief but intensely difficult little bassoon solo is one of the most famous in the repertoire, and this moment is typical of this symphony that is filled with energy, joy, and great wit.

[Musical example from Symphony no. 4 in Bb Major, Opus 60, Beethoven: IV]

Symphony no. 5 in C Minor, op. 67, 1808

Beethoven's Fifth Symphony is simply the single most famous work in the orchestral repertoire. Like Da Vinci's Mona Lisa, Michelangelo's David, Eiffel's tower, it is a symbol, an icon of Western culture. Across the span of its four movements, Beethoven tells a tale of musical birth and growth, destruction, regrowth, and ultimately triumph. This catharsis from destruction to triumph, this journey from darkness to light, this struggle between despair and hope, is portrayed across the grand span of the symphony as a journey from a struggle between the keys of C minor and C major. It is during the third-movement scherzo that the key of C major finally triumphs over C minor, and thus the fourth movement can begin with a blaze of C-major glory. The fourth movement opening.

[Musical example from Symphony no. 5 in C Minor, Opus 67, Beethoven: IV]

Now back to the third movement, the pivotal movement. The third movement begins in C minor and features a barking, blaring, and entirely ferocious theme in C minor.

[Musical example from Symphony no. 5 in C Minor, Opus 67, Beethoven: III]

This theme, featuring three fast, repeated notes and a fourth, longer note, "da-da-da-DUM," grows as it does so much of this symphony directly out of the opening four notes of the first movement.

[Musical example from Symphony no. 5 in C Minor, Opus 67, Beethoven: I]

Back to the fourth and final movement: hope and triumph—as represented by C major—have triumphed over darkness and despair, as represented by C minor, and the fourth movement bounces from one glory to the next. As the development section draws towards its conclusion, a magnificent passage builds towards a huge climax. Trembling with anticipation we await what will undoubtedly be an earth-shattering recapitulation when…quietly ticking violins lead to…a ghostly, ghastly reappearance of the barking, blaring, third-movement theme in C minor! The music is quiet; it's insidious; it's oozing with malevolence. Is this thematic reappearance real? An indication that we are returning to the "dark side" of C minor? Or is it just a dream?

Before we can even answer that question, the music transitions back to the long awaited for and very much hoped for recapitulation in C major. No, the third-movement quote was not a harbinger of things to come but merely a memory of distance transversed, a last moment of melancholy before we give ourselves completely to the cathartic joy of C major. Let's hear this entire episode from the end of the development section, a huge build-up, the reappearance of the third-movement theme, and then the beginning of the recapitulation back in C major.

[Musical example from Symphony no. 5 in C Minor, Opus 67, Beethoven: IV]

This sort of thematic quotation from an earlier movement is pure musical storytelling. From a purely analytic point of view, it has no place in the fourth movement, whereas expressively, it's a stroke of genius. And that's the larger point. With each symphonic step, the symphony becomes, for Beethoven, a more inclusive, a more expressively wide-ranging genre.

Symphony no. 6 in F Major, op. 68 ("Pastoral"), 1808

Nowhere is Beethoven's proclivity towards symphonic "inclusivity" more explicitly apparent than in his Sixth Symphony, the so-called "Pastoral" Symphony. That Beethoven's Pastoral Symphony is a "program symphony" describing a day in the country has been understood since the moment of its premiere on December 22, 1808. It's certainly not the first, nor the last "Pastoral" composition. Instrumental music extolling and describing the wonders of nature is a veritable compositional cottage industry, and has been since the invention of musical instruments. What is remarkable about Beethoven's Sixth is how Beethoven elevated what is a pedestrian genre of music to a level of high art.

The most famous moments in Beethoven's Sixth are those in which he explicitly evokes some aspect of nature in the orchestra. For example, as the second movement draws to its conclusion, we hear a series of woodwind solos or cadenzas, each imitating a different bird and labeled in the score as follows: Nachtigall ("nightingale," in the flute); Wachtel ("quail," in the oboe); and Kuckuck ("cuckoo," in the clarinet).

[Musical example from Symphony no. 6 in F Major, Opus 68, "Pastoral," Beethoven: II; Conclusion]

The birdcalls are delightful, but anyone could have done that. No, the great strength of Beethoven's Sixth is its high art rests in its extraordinary subtlety. For example, the first movement begins with a rustic first theme heard over a bagpipe-like drone. This first theme concludes with a simple rising melodic idea that is repeated, with only the slightest variation, 13 times in succession.

[Musical example from Symphony no. 6 in F Major, Opus 68, "Pastoral," Beethoven: I]

Later, during the development section of this same first movement, Beethoven takes this "idea" of varied melodic repetition an order of magnitude further.

[Musical example from Symphony no. 6 in F Major, Opus 68, "Pastoral," Beethoven: I]

Beethoven entitled this first movement "The cheerful impressions excited by arriving in the country." And no, all the repetition in the movement is not a sign that Beethoven's musical well had run dry. On the contrary, Beethoven's use of varied musical repetition throughout this first movement is a metaphor for what he perceives as the varied repetition of nature. He sees both the forest and the trees. Very subtle, very effective, and my friends, very high art.

Symphony no. 7 in A Major, op. 92, 1812

Beethoven's Seventh Symphony, begun in late 1811 and completed in 1812, is often referred to as his "dance" symphony." Now this doesn't mean that the symphony was actually intended as a dance piece or a ballet. What it means is that Beethoven designed each movement around a single, powerfully felt rhythmic profile or pattern. For example, after a rather lengthy introduction, the first movement eases into a rhythmic groove that underlies the remainder of the movement from the exposition all the way through the development section and the recapitulation. Let's sample that groove as it grows out of the introduction and then settles in under theme 1 and the modulating bridge. I will tell you now that the groove goes something like this: Bum-ba-ba Bum-ba-ba Bum-ba-ba Bum-ba-ba Bum.

[Musical example from Symphony no. 7 in A Major, Opus 92, Beethoven: I; Introduction, Theme I and Modulating Bridge]

Richard Wagner described the fourth and final movement of Beethoven's Seventh as "the apotheosis of the Dance, the 'Dance' in its highest condition; the happiest realization of bodily movement in ideal form."

Please, let's sample a little of that fourth movement of Beethoven's Seventh.

[Musical example from Symphony no. 7 in A Major, Opus 92, Beethoven: IV]

Writes musicologist Antony Hopkins:

> The apotheosis of the dance...Thus spoke the master, reputedly carrying out his belief by improvising and himself dancing a balletic interpretation of the symphony to [his father in-law, Franz] Liszt's piano accompaniment. The scene would be greeted with incredulous hilarity were it to appear in a film biography of either composer, yet it seems that it [actually] happened.

Symphony no. 8 in F Major, op. 93, 1812

Beethoven's Eighth Symphony ostensibly is his "homage" to Classicism. Oh, isn't this nice of him really to pay his respects to a Viennese Classical style that he pretty much single-handedly destroyed? Well, in its broadest outline Beethoven's Eighth might resemble a Classically proportioned symphony. It is in its details nothing of the sort. In reality, Beethoven's Eighth is filled to brimming with just the sort of themes, phrase irregularities, harmonic surprises, rhythmic ambiguities, developmental devices, and frankly, slapstick humor, that mark it as a work of Beethoven's full maturity.

As an example, we turn to the second movement where, in a Classical symphony, we would expect a slow movement. In Beethoven's Eighth, we get a moderately fast-paced musical portrait of what was for Beethoven a new-fangled high tech device: the metronome! The merciless ticking of the metronome is portrayed by staccato winds and horns. A simple little theme in the first violins does its level best to keep up, but alas, it keeps falling out of rhythm with the ticking winds and horns. Near the end of our excerpt, we will actually "hear"—in the orchestra—the metronome being wound up—not once, but twice.

[Musical example from Symphony no. 8 in F Major, Opus 93, Beethoven: II]

The metronome portrayed here comes unfortunately to a bad end. At the end of the movement, it begins to break down, and the orchestra, frustrated way past its limits of endurance, does what every one of us has fantasized about doing—it smashes the metronome to smithereens. Anyway, the metronome is road kill. The symphony as theater. Haydn for one would have loved it.

Symphony no. 9 in D Minor, op. 125, 1824

Following the Eighth Symphony, Beethoven did not complete his next and last symphony, the Ninth, for nearly 12 years, almost the same amount of time that had elapsed between the composition between the First and the Eighth. In those 11 years between the Eighth and Ninth Symphonies, between 1813 and 1824, Beethoven put himself and everyone around him through bloody hell. After 1815, Beethoven's music fell out of popular favor with the Viennese public. His great patrons either died or became estranged from him. What was left of his hearing disintegrated, and he became involved in a terrible custody battle over his brother's son, a kid named Karl. Around 1819-1820, Beethoven reinvented himself again and began to compose music of such transcendent technical and expressive content that many of our most eloquent writers and commentators are rendered inarticulate when they attempt to describe it. Fortunately, I am not one of them.

The Ninth Symphony is a product of this late period of Beethoven's compositional life and for all the gut-wrenching, soul-inspiring music we hear in the first, second and third movements, it is the fourth movement of the Ninth that changed music history and the collective concept of what constituted a symphony. As we observed way back in Lecture One, that's because of the presence of words sung by singers in the fourth-movement finale. Beethoven didn't just cross the line between instrumental music and vocal music. Oh no, no, no, he obliterated the distinction between the genre of symphony and the vocal genres of opera, cantata, and oratorio. It was something that perhaps only Beethoven with his unimpeachable reputation as an innovator could have pulled off.

[Musical example from Symphony no. 9 in D Minor, Opus 125, Beethoven: IV]

The impact of Beethoven's Ninth Symphony rippled outwards for the next 80 years. Like Haydn before him, Beethoven reinvented the genre of symphony. Earlier in his career, Beethoven had said that—through the example of his music—that pre-existing musical forms like sonata form and trio were contextual, that is, one need use those forms only to the point that they serve the expressive context. With his Ninth Symphony, Beethoven said to the next generations of composers that the genre was contextual as well, that the expressive needs of the composer must take precedence over any musical tradition, no matter how sacred and time honored that tradition might be.

It was a message that fell gratefully on the ears and minds of the next generation of composers, the so-called Romantics who, using Beethoven as their model, sought an ever freer, more self-expressive approach to composition.

Nicholas Temperley writes:

> Like no one before, Beethoven seized the listener's attention and compelled him to follow the emotional conflicts in his music

through to their resolution. His symphonies have always conveyed an actual sense of struggle, though critics have differed as to what the struggle is about. Some have depicted it as the heroic struggle of man against faith; others have tried to see an expression of Beethoven's personal circumstances (his deafness, [or] his unhappy sexual and family relationships). Whether one sees the struggle on a symbolic, personal, or technical level, it is impossible to avoid being caught up in it, so imperious and intense is Beethoven's manner. This was a period of great change in society and in ideas, [and to the discomfort of many,] Beethoven chose to confront the personal, social, and ethical problems of his time in his music.

A couple of closing thoughts. Sometime during the first years of the 20th century, Claude Debussy imagined and described a heavenly conversation between Johann Sebastian Bach and Ludwig van Beethoven:

> [Beethoven's] unhappy spirit [now dwells] where only the music of the spheres is heard! His noble ancestor, Bach, must say to him with some severity:

> "My little Ludwig, I see by your somewhat rumpled soul that you have again been in disreputable places."

> But perhaps after all, they are not on speaking terms.

Perhaps not, but certainly Beethoven is on speaking terms with everyone who came after him.

And this would be my second closing thought, an interesting and frankly first person autobiographical story. As a grad student once sitting around a table with my fellow composers and our professor, we got into a discussion as to whom, for us, was the most important composer. Every student wanted to score points with his fellows and with the professor, so every student tried to be more clever in coming up with which composer was the most important to them. People said Stravinsky and Schoenberg and Berio, all 20th century composers they. But it took the professor, a very wise and experienced person who had nothing to prove to anyone at the table, to put the spike in the conversation and bring it to the point where it should have been. After everyone had their say, we turned to him and he simply said, "Beethoven," and slowly but surely, everyone else around the table, thinking we were such hot stuff, began to nod our heads in agreement.

Because without Beethoven's expressive revolution, without Beethoven's belief in expressing ourselves above all things, the 19th century could not have happened the way it did, and the 20th century could not have happened the way it did either, because truly the 20th century was an extension of the 19th century in terms of the basic importance of self-expression and emotion in one's art.

On those lines, we draw to our conclusion with the understanding that Beethoven's shadow will loom large over the remainder of this course.

Thank you.

Lecture Ten
Schubert

Scope: Today, of course, Beethoven's symphonies are rightly perceived as epitomizing the revolutionary spirit and growing middle-class empowerment of the early 19th century, but for his contemporaries, the early 19th century was about the discovery and study of Haydn's and Mozart's late symphonies. These contemporaries included, among others, Carl Friedrich Zelter, Jean-Paul Richter, Carl Maria von Weber, Ludwig Spohr, and Franz Peter Schubert, all but one of whom have fallen into obscurity. This lecture looks at Schubert, who managed to strike a balance between Classical lyricism and Beethoven's revolutionary expression.

Outline

I. Franz Peter Schubert was born in Vienna on January 31, 1797, and died there on November 19, 1828, at the age of 31. Of all the great masters of Viennese Classicism—Haydn, Mozart, and Beethoven—Schubert was the only native Viennese.

   A. Franz Schubert was the beloved pet of his family; a small, plump, and endearingly sweet child. Even fully grown, Schubert was only a little over five feet tall, and as his portraits attest, he never lost his cherubic appearance.

   B. At age 9, Schubert began formal music studies, and at age 11, he was admitted to the Imperial and Royal City College, a first-rate Viennese boarding school. Among those who auditioned him for admission was the music director for the Viennese court, Antonio Salieri, rival of Wolfgang Mozart.

   C. Schubert's first masterwork was the song *"Gretchen am Spinnrade,"* which he composed in 1814, when he was 17 years old. By writing songs, he learned to convey literary and expressive meaning with brevity and to exploit his amazing gifts as a melodist. As an example, we listen to the second theme from the first movement of Schubert's Symphony in B Minor. (**Musical selection**: Schubert, Symphony no. 8 in B Minor, D. 759, movement 1, theme 2.)

D. We cannot discuss Schubert's creative output in great detail, because he wrote a prodigious amount of music in his short lifetime. (He died of syphilis at age 31.) In the final 16 years of his life, Schubert produced, among other works, 9 symphonies, 10 orchestral overtures, 22 piano sonatas, 6 masses, 17 operas, more than 1,000 works for solo piano and piano four hands, 637 songs, 145 choral works, and 45 chamber works, including 13 string quartets and 1 string quintet.

II. Schubert's Symphonies nos. 1 through 5 were composed between 1813 and 1816, when he was between 16 and 19 years old. They are Classical symphonies in every sense, clearly influenced by Haydn and Mozart. Despite the fact that Schubert's First Symphony was composed after Beethoven completed his Eighth, there is scant evidence of Beethoven's influence in these early symphonies of Schubert.

    A. As an example, we turn to Schubert's Symphony no. 5 in Bb Major, completed on October 3, 1816.

        1. Scored for one flute, two oboes, two bassoons, two horns, and strings, the symphony was first played by a small orchestra that met and performed at the house of a merchant in Vienna. Following this private reading, Schubert's Fifth was forgotten and nearly lost, and it wasn't published until 56 years after his death.

        2. It is a polished and entirely charming work, undoubtedly better than any other Classically styled symphony being written at the same time by composers older and more famous than Schubert.

        3. We'll listen to the exposition of the first movement, which is characterized by elegant themes and marvelous and unexpected harmonic twists. For our information, the modulating bridge begins 44 seconds into the excerpt, and theme 2 begins 1 minute and 8 seconds into the excerpt. (**Musical selection**: Schubert, Symphony no. 5 in Bb Major, D. 485, movement 1, exposition.)

    B. Schubert's next symphony—his Sixth, in C major, completed in February 1818—illustrates his transition away from a purely Classical language and toward one that reflects the growing influence on his music of Gioacchino Rossini and Ludwig van Beethoven.

1. We listen to the most "Beethovenian" movement of Schubert's Sixth, the third movement, which is not entitled *minuet* (as Schubert had called the third movements of his Symphonies nos. 1–5) but, instead, *scherzo*, based on Beethoven's model.

2. Startling shifts in dynamics, unexpected accents, and thematic material based on short, crackling melodic ideas rather than long and complete tunes betray Beethoven's influence, yet the grace and humor here are Schubert's own. (**Musical selection**: Schubert, Symphony no. 6 in C Major, D. 589, movement 3, exposition.)

III. Schubert's symphonic output after the Sixth Symphony, which was completed in 1818, presents some numerical confusion.

A. After 1818, Schubert sketched a number of symphonic movements in D major, which ultimately came to nothing. In August of 1821, he began a draft of a symphony in E major. This one, he almost completed, but then, it, too, was abandoned. Many years later, after Schubert had died, this piece was called Schubert's Symphony no. 7.

B. On October 30, 1822, Schubert began yet another symphony, this one in B minor. He completed the first two movements of this symphony and arranged to have the score for those two movements presented to the Styrian Musical Society of Graz in gratitude for having been elected into the society.

C. Schubert then began composing the third-movement scherzo, sketching the opening 128 measures, of which he orchestrated the first 20 measures. He then left this symphony incomplete, as well, probably because of health problems. We take a brief detour into Schubert's biography to explain these problems.

D. Across the span of his all-too-short life, Schubert seems to have expressed genuine interest in only two women: the countess Karoline Esterhazy, a tall, gorgeous, intelligent, and rich piano student of Schubert's, and the soprano Therese Grob, with whom he had fallen in love when he was 18.

1. Maynard Solomon, biographer of both Mozart and Beethoven, offers compelling evidence that Schubert was bisexual, with homosexuality being his dominant sexual orientation. The stigma attached to homosexuality in Biedermeier Vienna

would help to explain many of Schubert's behavioral patterns, his mood swings and depression, and his almost complete dependence on male friends for housing and emotional and financial support.

2. Finances were another significant issue for Schubert. He could not land a job and was a terrible businessperson, naïve and inept when dealing with publishers and concert producers. Thus, many of his larger works languished in obscurity until well after his death, resulting in poverty in his lifetime and contributing to his depression and abuse of alcohol and tobacco.

3. Schubert contracted syphilis in late summer or early fall 1822, when he was 25 years old, most likely during one of his pleasure jaunts with his friend Franz von Schober. Von Schober was tall, good-looking, wealthy, and hedonistic. He frequented prostitutes of both sexes and probably fixed Schubert up with whoever gave him syphilis.

4. Unaware that he was infected, just a couple of weeks later, Schubert began composing what would be the first two movements of the Eighth Symphony, the "Unfinished" Symphony in B Minor.

5. The first symptoms of the disease began to manifest themselves in the late fall of 1822 and became pronounced by January of 1823. Schubert stopped working on his B-minor symphony.

6. Schubert was terrified as the syphilis took hold and began to chart its agonizing course. Periods of remission were followed by periods of painful lymphatic swelling, rashes, hair loss, lesions in the mouth and throat, debilitating muscle aches, and so forth. Depression and despair accompanied the periods of relapse. It soon became clear that Schubert's case was especially virulent and that he was unlikely to live for long.

E. We can understand, then, why Schubert had no heart to return to the B-minor symphony in October or November of 1822: It represented a time of his life that ended abruptly with his fatal diagnosis.

F. The two movements that today represent Schubert's Unfinished Symphony were discovered in 1865 in Graz and premiered in

Vienna on December 17, 1865, 43 years after their composition and 37 years after Schubert's death.

1. The first of the two movements is a dark and brooding sonata form of considerable length, about 15 minutes. Theme 1 consists of three distinct and memorable elements. The first element is a low, dark, funereal melody played without an introduction by the 'cellos and double basses. (**Musical selection**: Schubert, Symphony no. 8 in B Minor, D. 759, movement 1, opening.)

2. Out of the darkness cast by this opening emerges the second element of theme 1, an element that will soon fall back into the middle ground: quiet, twitching violins supported by pizzicato low string from below. (**Musical selection**: Schubert, Symphony no. 8 in B Minor, D. 759, movement 1, opening.)

3. The third element of the theme is a forlorn melody in B minor scored for oboe and clarinet, which seems to float above the twitching violin accompaniment. The theme builds to a climactic cadence in B minor, then simply ends. (**Musical selection**: Schubert, Symphony no. 8 in B Minor, D. 759, movement 1, theme 1.)

4. Schubert chose not to provide a modulating bridge. Instead, using a technique called a *pivot modulation*, he effects the briefest of transitions, and within six measures, he has slowed the action, changed the key, and begun theme 2.

    a. The effect of this sudden change of musical direction comes as a shock, and the lyric beauty of the theme that follows—theme 2, in G major—makes this turn of events that much more dislocating.

    b. Having said that, theme 2 is so innocent and memorable that we momentarily forget the dark musical place from which we so unexpectedly emerged, at least until theme 2 suddenly and unexpectedly stops in midphrase.

    c. Whatever lyric calm this second theme represents, it cannot yet be sustained. Let's listen from the cadence that concludes theme 1 through the pivot modulation that follows it, theme 2, and its sudden end. (**Musical selection**: Schubert, Symphony no. 8 in B Minor, D. 759, movement 1, theme 2.)

5. The darkness and pathos of theme 1 return with a series of vicious, trembling harmonies. (**Musical selection**: Schubert, Symphony no. 8 in B Minor, D. 759, movement 1, theme 2.)

6. Then, once again, the music transits back to theme 2, although now the theme is fragmented and presented imitatively, its tone darkened by movement into minor key areas. Theme 2 is still beautiful, but it has lost its veneer of innocence and simplicity; it has been made to "grow up" very quickly—perhaps too quickly. (**Musical selection**: Schubert, Symphony no. 8 in B Minor, D. 759, movement 1, theme 2.)

7. Finally, Schubert brings this exposition to its conclusion with a momentary return to theme 2 "as it once was," a lyric memory of youth and beauty before the crushing onslaught of the development section. (**Musical selection**: Schubert, Symphony no. 8 in B Minor, D. 759, movement 1, cadence material.)

8. In the second-movement *andante con moto* ("moderate but with motion"), Schubert again juxtaposes aching lyricism with explosively dramatic music. The movement is structured as a rondo; let's listen to the principal theme, the "rondo" theme. (**Musical selection**: Schubert, Symphony no. 8 in B Minor, D. 759, movement 2, opening.)

IV. Schubert himself designated his Symphony no. 9 in C Major *grosse*, meaning "grand" or "large"; it has since become known as "The Great."

A. Undoubtedly inspired by the model of Beethoven's Ninth, which received its premiere in 1824, Schubert's Ninth typically runs an hour in performance and is scored for a full orchestra, replete with trumpets, trombones, and timpani. Schubert, who had once considered Beethoven an "eccentric," had, by 1826, been won over entirely by Beethoven's music.

B. We turn to the fourth and final movement of this, Schubert's last symphony. The character of the movement is, according to one critic, "A conflation of the heroic and the frantic" (Brown, 638). At more than 1,150 measures in length, it is also huge and absolutely brilliant!

C. Schubert's orchestration is especially remarkable; the independence of the woodwind and brass writing is particularly striking. We hear the exposition of this final movement. For our information, theme 2 begins 1 minute and 47 seconds into this 4-minute exposition! (**Musical selection**: Schubert, Symphony no. 9 in C Major, D. 944, movement 4, opening.)

D. This last symphony showcases Schubert's ability to balance the Classical-era forms and an essentially Classical lyricism with the expanded expressive palette of the 19th century. The message for many composers of the post-Beethoven generation was that one didn't have to be angry and revolutionary in order to be current.

Lecture Ten—Transcript
Schubert

Welcome back to *The Symphony*. This is Lecture Ten entitled "Schubert." We again quote Napoleon Bonaparte: "What is history but a fable agreed upon?" That's a good question for a despot intent on creating his own fabled history, and one that applies as well to how we believe Beethoven's music was perceived in his own time. Today, of course, Beethoven's symphonies are rightly perceived as epitomizing the revolutionary spirit and the growing middle-class empowerment of the early 19th century. Our mistake—our "fable agreed upon"—occurs when we assume that Beethoven's contemporaries believed the same thing about his remarkable symphonies. They did not.

For Beethoven's symphonic contemporaries, the early 19th century was about the discovery of Haydn and Mozart's late symphonies. The musical style of such well-known, even famous, early 19th-century symphony composers as Carl Friedrich Zelter, Jean-Paul Richter, Carl Maria von Weber, Ludwig Sphor, Adalbert Gyrowetz, Ferdinand Ries, Andrea Romberg, and Peter Winter was firmly based on the Classical models of Mozart and Haydn. These composers and others like them "reached a [Classical] musical ideal to which Beethoven's mature art seemed an intrusive irrelevance."

Now of course, posterity—the fable that is history—has been unkind to the aforementioned composers whose symphonies—in their time—were played much more frequently than Beethoven's. Once Beethoven's symphonies came to be appreciated and understood for the masterworks that they are (and that's a process that took a generation), the symphonies of his more conservative, more classically-oriented contemporaries were relegated to almost total obscurity: the stuff of Ph.D. dissertations and scholarly papers, the surest indicators of total irrelevance.

With one exception…Franz Peter Schubert was born in Vienna on January 31, 1797. It was in Vienna that he died on November 19, 1828, aged 31 years, 9 months and 20 days. Of all the great masters of Viennese Classicism—Haydn, Mozart, Beethoven—Schubert was the only native Viennese. Franz Schubert was the beloved pet of his family, a small, plump, and endearingly sweet child from every account that has come down to us.

His growth spurt—well, his growth spurt hardly ever kicked in. The full-grown Schubert was 1.57 meters in height, about 5 foot 1 inch tall, and as his portraits attest, he never lost his cherubic appearance.

A wonderful description of the adult Schubert was written by his friend Anselm Hüttenbrenner:

> Schubert's outward appearance was anything but striking. He was short of stature, with a full, round face, and was rather stout. Because of his short sight, he always wore spectacles, which he never took off, even during sleep. Dress was a thing in which he took no interest whatsoever. He disliked bowing and scraping, and listening to flattering talk about himself he found downright nauseating.

Franz Schubert is your classic example of "big things come in small packages."

At the age of nine he began formal music studies with a local organist named Michael Holzer. Of his young charge Holtzer said, "If I wish to instruct him in anything fresh, he already knew it. Consequently, I eventually stopped giving him actual lessons but merely conversed with him and watched him with silent astonishment."

At the age of 11, in 1808, Schubert was admitted to the Imperial and Royal City College, a first-rate Viennese boarding school. Among those who auditioned him for admission was music director of the Viennese court, none other than Antonio Salieri. Yes my friends, that Salieri, pupil of the great Cristoph Willibald Gluck, friend of the great Joseph Haydn, rival of the incredible Wolfgang Mozart, vocal music tutor for the annoying and brash Ludwig van Beethoven, and future composition teacher of the extraordinary Franz Liszt. And, we might add, one of the most viciously libeled men in history. Salieri took personal charge of Schubert's musical education, a relationship that would extend beyond Schubert's college years.

Schubert's first masterwork was the song *"Gretchen am Spinnrade,"* which he composed on October 19, 1814, when he was 17 years old. It was the art song, songs for voice and piano, that brought Schubert to the compositional table. He cut his teeth writing songs. His first masterworks were songs. It was by writing songs that Schubert learned how to convey laser-like literary and expressive meaning with admirable brevity. It was through writing songs that Schubert learned how to exploit his amazing gifts as a melodist. For example, is there a better-known, more beloved tune in the entire symphonic repertoire than the second theme from the first movement of Schubert's Symphony in B Minor?

[Musical example from Symphony No. 9 in B Minor, Schubert: I; Second Theme]

Now obviously we can not discuss Schubert's creative output in any detail, even the most casual music fan should be aware that he wrote an unbelievable amount of good music in an unbelievably short amount of time. From the time Schubert composed "*Gretchen*" to the time he died was but 14 years. For the first three years of that period, from 1814 to 1817, Schubert taught elementary school. After 1817, he devoted himself entirely to composition.

"Without wide public recognition, sustained only by the love of a few friends and his family, constantly struggling against illness and poverty, Schubert composed ceaselessly." (Grout, 4th ed., 667-668)

In Schubert's own words, my friends, "I worked every morning. When I have finished one piece, I begin another." To which we might add: And another, and another, and another.

Schubert was, without a doubt, a workaholic, one that combined the amateur's pure joy of music making with a professional's discipline and technical abilities. In the final 16 years of his life, Schubert produced, among other works, 9 symphonies, 10 orchestral overtures, 22 piano sonatas, 6 masses, 17 operas, over 1,000 works for solo piano and piano four hands, 637 songs, around 145 choral works, and 45 chamber works, including 13 string quartets and one string quintet. When if ever did this guy sleep? We haven't a clue.

Schubert died of syphilis at he age of 31. On his tombstone was inscribed words written for him by his good friend the poet, Franz Grillparzer: "Music here has buried a rich treasure of still fairer hopes."

Early Symphonies

Schubert's Symphonies nos. 1 through 5 were composed between 1813 and 1816, when Schubert was between 16 and 19 years old. They are marvelous pieces in which Schubert makes up with sheer talent and imagination what he lacked in age and experience. They are also, my friends, Classical symphonies in every sense. The influence of Haydn and Mozart is as clear as can be. And despite the fact that Schubert's First Symphony was composed after Beethoven completed his Eighth Symphony, there is scant, if any, evidence of Beethoven's influence in these early symphonies of Schubert.

As an example, we turn to Schubert's Symphony no. 5 in Bb Major, completed on October 3, 1816. Scored for one flute, two oboes, two bassoons, two horns, and strings, the symphony was first played by a small pick-up orchestra that met and performed at the house of a merchant named Otto Hatwig in the Schottenhof district of Vienna. Following this modest, private reading, Schubert's Fifth was forgotten and nearly lost, and it wasn't published until 1885, 69 years after its composition and 56 years after Schubert's death, long after it could have done poor Schubert any good. For our sake, thank goodness it wasn't lost. It is a polished and entirely charming work, without a doubt better than any other Classically styled symphony being written at the same time by composers older, richer, or more famous than Schubert, which accounts for just about every other composer in Vienna.

We'll listen to the exposition of the first movement characterized by elegant themes and some marvelous and unexpected twists and turns. This is great stuff. For our information, the modulating bridge begins 44 seconds into the excerpt, and theme 2 begins 1 minute and 8 seconds into the excerpt.

[Musical example from Symphony No. 5 in Bb Major, Schubert: I; Exposition]

Schubert's next symphony—his Sixth, in C major, completed in February of 1818—is his breakaway symphony. In terms of transitioning away from a purely Classical language and towards one that reflects the growing influence on his music of Gioacchino Rossini and Ludwig van Beethoven.

We turn immediately to the most "Beethovenian" movement of Schubert's Sixth, the third movement, one entitled not *minuet* (as Schubert had entitled the third movements of his Symphonies 1 through 5), but, instead, *scherzo*, based on Beethoven's model. Startling shifts and dynamics, unexpected accents, and thematic material based on short, crackling melodic ideas rather than long and complete tunes betray Beethoven's influence in this movement, and yet, the grace and humor are Schubert's own.

[Musical example from Symphony No. 6 in C Major, Schubert: III]

Illness, Unfinished Symphonies, and Confusion!

First, the confusion. Numerical confusion, that is, and all Schubert's fault it was. Schubert completed his Sixth Symphony in 1818. Over the next couple of years he sketched a number of symphonic movements in D major, which ultimately came to nothing. In August of 1812, Schubert began a draft of yet another symphony, this one in E major. He almost completed the sketch and then abandoned this "child of his imagination" as well, left it sitting on a turnstile for abandoned compositions, either too bored to finish it or, more likely, suffering from a crisis of compositional language: "Hmmm, should I continue to compose symphonies along the tasteful, Classically inspired, Biedermeier lines of my Fifth, or should I grasp the Beethovenian expressive gestalt that I began to explore in my Sixth or squeeze it for all its worth? Hmmm, or should I try to find some Schubertian medium within the extremes?"

Well, Schubert couldn't decide, and thus he left his E Major Symphony incomplete. Many years later, after Schubert had died and had subsequently been deified (don't we love how that works?), the cataloguers moved in and decided to call the piece Schubert's Symphony no. 7. Well, in reality, there is no "Schubert's Seventh." It doesn't exist in playable form. So like Santa Claus, the Tooth Fairy, and a winning lottery ticket, we just sort of "pretend" that Schubert's Seventh is out there. We shouldn't wait up for it.

On October 30, 1822, Schubert began yet another symphony, this one in B minor. He actually completed the first two movements of this symphony, and he arranged to have the scores for these two movements presented for the Styrian Musical Society of Graz in gratitude for having been elected into the society. (It was a presentation that, unbeknownst to Schubert, never took place; which we'll explain in a minute.) Schubert then began composing the third-movement scherzo, sketching the opening 128 measures, of which he orchestrated the first 20 measures and then he stopped and left this symphony incomplete, unfinished as well. While there is no definitive explanation for Schubert's having abandoned this B Minor Symphony, the reason likely lies with his health, which took a terrible turn for the worse at just the time he quit the symphony, a symphony that otherwise had been going so very well. A little background material is now called for.

Getting To Know You

Schubert never married. Across the span of this all too short life, Schubert seems to have expressed genuine interest in only two women: the Countess Karoline Esterhazy and the soprano Therese Grob. Countess Karoline was a piano student of Schubert's for many years. She was tall, gorgeous, witty, charming, intelligent, and fabulously rich, and Schubert was, according to his friends, completely smitten with her. According to Baron Karl von Schonstein, a civil servant and a friend of Schubert's:

> A poetic flame sprang up in his heart [for Countess Karoline]. This flame continued to burn until his death. Karoline had the greatest regard for him and for his talent but she did not [nor could she] return his love; perhaps she had no idea of the degree to which it existed. That he loved her must surely have been clear to her from the remark of Schubert's—his only declaration in words. Once, namely, when she reproached Schubert in fun for having dedicated no composition to her, he replied, "What's the point? Everything is dedicated to you anyway."

The only other woman in Schubert's life was a soprano named Therese Grob. Schubert fell in love with her when he was 18, in 1815. According to Schubert's friend and early biographer Anselm Hüttenbrenner:

> During a walk which I took with Schubert, I asked him if he had never been in love. As he was always so cold towards [women] at parties, I was inclined to think that he had a complete aversion to them. "Oh no," he said. "I loved someone very dearly and she loved me too. She was a schoolmaster's daughter, somewhat younger than myself, and she sang most beautifully and with deep feeling. She was not exactly pretty; but she had a heart of gold. For years she hoped that I would marry her, but I could not find a position that would have provided for us both. She married someone else, which hurt me very much."

Now, according to Maynard Solomon, the essential biographer of both Mozart and Beethoven, Schubert was bisexual with homosexuality being his dominant sexual orientation. We won't go through Solomon's evidence, but suffice it to say that it is certainly compelling. Certainly, the stigma attached to homosexuality in Biedermeier Vienna would help to explain many of Schubert's behavioral patterns, his mood swings, his depression, and his almost complete dependence on male friends for housing and emotional, and financial support.

Financial support. Talk about a guy who simply could not land a job to save his life. When Schubert told his friend Anselm Hüttenbrenner that: "For years [Therese] hoped that I would marry her, but I could not find a position which would have provided for us both"—he wasn't kidding. Early in his career, Schubert developed a reputation as someone who was never on time. And while this might not have been a handicap in Italy or Spain, among the Viennese it was fatal. Truth be told, Schubert was one of those "artistic types" who couldn't be bothered with schedules. He wanted to be left alone to compose. It almost goes without saying that he was a terrible businessperson, naïve and inept when dealing with publishers and concert producers.

For Schubert, composing the next piece was much more important than having the last one performed, so his music, especially his larger works, languished in obscurity until after his death. As Schubert got older (or less young as the case may be), he became increasingly aware of all of this. His poverty and obscurity made him angry and depressed. By his mid-20s he was abusing both alcohol and tobacco. By the time he was 30 he had grown so fat that one contemporary attributed his death at the age of 31 to obesity. But it wasn't obesity that killed Schubert; it was syphilis, syphilis contracted in 1822 when he was 25 years old, most likely during one of his pleasure jaunts with his friend Franz von Schober.

A few words about every parent's worst nightmare, Schubert's friend Franz von Schober. Von Schober had been a friend and supporter of Schubert's since 1814, when they were both 17 years old. Where Schubert was short, and plump, and poor, and socially introverted, von Schober was tallish, good-looking, had family money in his pocket, and was a genuine party boy. His vices of choice (along with Schubert's music) were poetry, alcohol, and prostitutes of both sexes. It was von Schober who was blamed by Schubert's other friends for leading Schubert down the path of perdition and fixing him up with whomever gave him syphilis.

Schubert's friend, Joseph Kenner, wrote this after Schubert's death:

> Anyone who knew Schubert knows how he was made of two natures, foreign to each other, how powerfully the craving for pleasure dragged his soul down the [sewer] of moral degradation, and how highly he valued the utterances of friends he respected.

Schubert attracted, among other friends, a seductively amiable and brilliant young man, who won a lasting and pernicious influence over Schubert's honest susceptibility.

By Schubert's seducer, I mean Franz von Schober, whom I had known, and known intimately, since 1808. Under the guise of the most amiable sociability, and even engaging affection, there reigned in this whole [Schober] family a deep moral depravity.... He was willing to tolerate no religion, no morals, no restraint.

With marvelous English understatement, Schubert biographer Brian Newbould concludes, "Schober was a work-shy hedonist, notable for sensual rather than intellectual pursuits, who settled in no employment." In other words my friends, von Schober was a bum, a jobless dilettante sex-freak. Bad news.

Sometime during the late summer or early fall of 1822, Schubert caught syphilis, most likely during one of his outings with Franz von Schober. Just a couple of weeks later, unaware that he was infected, he began composing what would be the first two movements of his next symphony, the Eighth Symphony, the "Unfinished" Symphony in B Minor.

The first symptoms of the disease began to manifest themselves in the late fall of 1822 and became pronounced by January of 1823. No wonder Schubert stopped working on his B minor symphony—he was 25 years old, had VD, and he knew it. In those days, my friends, it was like being told that he had AIDS—not HIV—but AIDS. The question wasn't "will" the disease kill you, but when? He was terrified as the syphilis took hold and began to chart a rather agonizing course. Periods of remission were followed by periods of painful lymphatic swelling, pustules, rashes, hair loss, lesions in the mouth and throat, debilitating muscle aches and so forth. Depression and despair accompanied these periods of relapse. It soon became clear to pretty much everyone involved—Schubert, doctors, and his friends—that his particular case was especially virulent and it was unlikely he'd live for very long.

In March of 1825, a despondent Schubert wrote his friend Leopold Kupelweiser:

I feel myself to be the most unhappy and wretched creature in the world. Imagine a man whose health will never be right again; imagine a man, I say, whose most brilliant hopes had perished, to whom the felicity of love and friendship have nothing to offer but pain, at best, whose enthusiasms for all things beautiful [is gone], and I ask you, is he not a miserable, unhappy being? "My peace is gone, my heart is sore, I shall find it never and nevermore." I may well sing every day now, for each night, on retiring to bed, I hope I may not wake up again, and each morning but recalls yesterday's grief.

Back, then, to October and November of 1822, during which Schubert composed the two plus symphonic movements that would forever be known as his Symphony no. 8, the "Unfinished" Symphony in B Minor. Of course Schubert stopped working on the B minor symphony during the late fall of 1822, and of course he had no heart to return to it once the initial shock of his condition had worn off. It represented "before"—a time of his life that ended abruptly with his fatal diagnosis.

The two movements that today represent Schubert's Unfinished Symphony were discovered in 1865 in Graz. Back in 1823, Schubert had given the manuscripts to his friend Josef Hüttenbrenner to deliver to the Styrian Music Society in Graz. Hüttenbrenner, a genuine Schubert groupy, had no such intention of turning such a treasure over to the Society, so—without Schubert's knowledge—he kept the scores. At some point Josef turned the music over to his brother Anselm for safekeeping and thank goodness he did. In 1848, Josef Hüttenbrenner's maid used the manuscript of the second and third acts of Schubert's opera *Claudine von Villa Bella* as kindling. It was the only extant copy of the opera, and so the second and third acts were lost forever up Josef Hüttenbrenner's chimney in Graz. In 1865, the manuscript for the first two movements of a B minor symphony was found in a chest of drawers in Anselm Hüttenbrenner's house by the Viennese conductor Johann von Herbeck. Herbeck premiered the "symphony" (or "symphonic torso" as it were), in Vienna in a concert sponsored by the "Society for the Friends of Music" on December 17, 1865, 43 years after these movements were composed and 37 years after Schubert's death.

The first of the two movements is a dark and brooding sonata form of considerable length, about 15 minutes. Theme 1 consists of three distinct and memorable elements. The first element is a low, dark, funereal melody played without introduction on the cellos and double basses.

[Musical example from Symphony No. 8 in B minor, "The Unfinished Symphony," Schubert: I, Theme I, i]

Out of the darkness cast by this opening emerges the second element of theme 1, an element that will soon fall back into the middle ground: quiet, twitching violins supported by pizzicato low strings from below.

[Musical example from Symphony No. 8 in B minor, "The Unfinished Symphony," Schubert: I, Theme I, ii]

And then the third element of the theme, a forlorn melody in B minor scored for oboe and clarinet, which seems to float above the twitching violin accompaniment. The theme builds to a climactic cadence in B minor and then, simply, it ends.

[Musical example from Symphony No. 8 in B minor, "The Unfinished Symphony," Schubert: I, Theme I, iii]

Schubert chose not to provide a modulating bridge. Instead, using a technique called *pivot modulation*, he effects the briefest of transitions, and within six measures, he has slowed the action, changed the key, and begun theme 2. The effect of this sudden change of musical direction comes as a genuine shock and the lyric beauty of the theme that follows—theme 2, in G major—makes this turn of events that much more dislocating. Having said that, theme 2 is so innocent, so memorable that we momentarily forget the dark musical place we just so unexpectedly emerged from, at least until theme 2 suddenly and unexpectedly stops in midphrase. Whatever lyric calm this second theme represents, it simply cannot be sustained. Let's listen from the cadence that concludes theme 1 through the pivot modulation that follows it, theme 2, and its sudden end.

[Musical example from Symphony No. 8 in B minor, "The Unfinished Symphony," Schubert: I; End of Theme I through Theme II]

Yes, and all together we say, "Uh oh." Uh oh indeed, like a railroad spike drilled through our collective foreheads, the darkness and pathos of theme 1 suddenly return with a series of vicious, trembling harmonies.

[Musical example from Symphony No. 8 in B minor, "The Unfinished Symphony," Schubert: I]

And then, once again the music transits back to theme 2, although now the theme is fragmented and presented imitatively, its tone darkened by movement into minor key areas. Theme 2 is still beautiful, but it's lost its veneer of innocence and simplicity; it's been made to "grow up" very quickly—perhaps too quickly.

[Musical example from Symphony No. 8 in B minor, "The Unfinished Symphony," Schubert: I, Theme II]

Finally, Schubert brings this exposition to its conclusion with a momentary return to theme 2 "as it once was," a lyric memory of youth and beauty before the absolutely crushing onslaught of the development section.

[Musical example from Symphony No. 8 in B minor, "The Unfinished Symphony," Schubert: I, Theme II]

In the second-movement *andante con moto*, which means "moderate but with motion," Schubert again juxtaposes aching lyricism with explosively dramatic music. The movement is structured as a rondo. Let's hear the principal theme, the "rondo" theme, the sort of melody for which the term "Schubertian" was invented.

[Musical example from Symphony No. 8 in B minor, "The Unfinished Symphony," Schubert: II, Rondo Theme]

And there they are, the two movements that comprise Schubert's Symphony no. 8 in B Minor, the Unfinished, the most beautiful and elegant torso this side of the Venus di Milo.

Of the premiere of the B minor symphony, which occurred in Vienna in 1865, the famed critic Eduard Hanslick wrote:

> The tonal beauty of the two movements is fascinating. Schubert achieves, with the most simple, basic orchestra, tonal effects which no refinement of Wagnerian instrumentation can capture. This symphonic fragment can be counted among Schubert's most beautiful instrumental works, and I am especially happy to say so here because I have permitted myself to speak more than once warningly of over-zealous Schubert worship and the adulation of Schubert relics.

Symphony no. 9 in C Major ("The Great"), 1826

Every now and again, the folly of such a survey as this, become apparent. Schubert's Ninth, the C Major, in a few hundred words and a single musical example? Hah. I'm so ashamed. First of all, the designation "The Great," which Schubert himself assigned this symphony even though it turned out to be an accurate appraisal of the symphony, rather, Schubert called it a *"grosse"* Symphony, meaning a "grand" or "large" symphony. And that it is. Undoubtedly inspired by the model of Beethoven's Ninth, which received its premiere in 1824, Schubert's Ninth typically runs a full hour in performance and is scored for the fullest of full orchestras—replete with trumpets, trombones and timpani.

Schubert, who in his musical youth had considered Beethoven an "eccentric," had, by 1826 at the age of 29, been won over entirely by Beethoven's music. Schubert's Ninth is his Beethoven Symphony and we can only cry the bitterest tears that he, Schubert, did not live long enough to build upon the model. The history of the symphony would have been very different had he had the opportunity to do so.

We turn to the fourth and final movement of this, Schubert's last symphony. The character of the movement is, according to one critic, "A conflation of the heroic and the frantic." At more than 1,150 measures in length, not counting the exposition repeat, it's also huge and absolutely brilliant. Schubert's orchestration is especially remarkable; the independence of the woodwind and brass writing is particularly striking. We hear the exposition of this final movement. For our information, theme 2 begins 1 minute and 47 seconds into this four-minute exposition.

[Musical example from Symphony No. 9 in C Major, "The Great," Schubert: IV; Exposition]

That's just fabulous music, my friends, monumentally conceived. The eminent musicologist. A. Peter Brown writes:

> "Schubert's 'Unfinished' [B Minor] and 'Great' C Major Symphonies are landmarks in the history of the genre, just as Beethoven's 'Eroica' was twenty years earlier. Whereas the 'Eroica' expanded the Classical symphony to its dramatic maximum, the Schubert works additionally demonstrate the possibilities of the lyric and the colorful, whether tonally or orchestrally, for a different symphonic tradition. When these works received their first public performances in the mid-19th century, they provided a viable alternative to Beethoven's dominance of the symphonic landscape."

The "viable alternative" to which Professor Brown refers has to do with Schubert's ability – in his final two symphonies – to balance the Classical era forms and an essentially Classical lyricism with the expanded expressive palette of the 19th century. The message for many composers of the post-Beethoven generation was that you didn't have to be angry and revolutionary – a la Beethoven – in order to be current. It was a message that was gratefully received by, among others, Robert Schumann and Johannes Brahms, whose symphonies we will encounter soon enough.

Thank you.

Lecture Eleven

Berlioz and the *Symphonie fantastique*

Scope: Hector Berlioz, a late-blooming, anti-academic, self-indulgent radical, was a controversial man and an equally controversial composer. In this lecture, we examine his *Symphonie fantastique*, an avant-garde autobiographical work that explores the full gamut of emotions associated with love, from ecstasy to despair. The *Symphonie fantastique* was a puzzle for most of its original listeners, but it served as a spark for a new generation of Romantic radicals, including Liszt and Wagner.

Outline

I. Hector Berlioz's father, Louis Berlioz, was a well-known and well-to-do doctor, and from the beginning, it was understood that Hector would become a physician. What Hector wanted, however, more than anything else in the world, was to become a composer.

A. Nevertheless, having graduated from high school, Berlioz was sent to Paris at the age of 18 to study medicine, which he detested. Within two years, he dropped out of medical school and became estranged from his parents. He survived by giving music lessons, singing in choruses, and writing reviews for anyone who would hire him to do so.

B. He attended the opera, in standing room; took private lessons in composition when he could afford them; and studied scores in the library of the Paris Conservatory. Berlioz longed to be a student at the Conservatory, but his resources didn't permit it and his first encounter with the director of the Conservatory apparently ended in a ridiculous chase scene around the library.

C. In early 1826, at the age of 23, Berlioz's finances forced him to move back to his parents' home. After a short time, his father agreed to let him return to Paris to study music, but Hector could remain there only if he was successful. According to Berlioz's memoirs, his mother cursed his decision and his father warned him against becoming a second-rate artist, the likes of whom he considered to be "useless members of society."

D. Under these circumstances, Hector Berlioz entered the first year class of the Paris Conservatory in the fall of 1826. For the next four years, he immersed himself in his studies; in the Parisian theaters, concert halls, and opera houses; and in composing and writing reviews; in the process, he proved himself to be one of the greatest late bloomers in the history of Western music.

II. Like Mozart before him, Berlioz was, in his heart, an opera composer. He fed on the emotional extremes and dramatic conflicts of opera, embracing in particular the grand operas of Gluck and the experimental operas of such German Romantics as Carl Maria von Weber.

   A. Berlioz was a radical person in many ways. He lived at the extreme edge of his emotions almost all the time. Today, we would consider Berlioz's endless outbursts and emotional self-indulgence as the tiresome marks of an adolescent personality, but in the 1820s and 1830s, his affectations were the marks of the *artiste*. In a 19th-century artistic environment that celebrated individuality, originality, and extremes of expression, Berlioz was the quintessential Romantic artist, and the *Symphonie fantastique*, the quintessential Romantic symphony.

   B. Despite his operatic predisposition, Berlioz wrote four works that he described as "symphonies": the *Symphonie fantastique* (1830), *Harold in Italy* (1834), *Romeo and Juliet* (1839), and the *Grand Funeral and Triumphal Symphony* (1840). The only one of these works that is a symphony by the standards of this course is the first, the *Symphonie fantastique*. It is also the most influential 19th-century symphony written after Beethoven's Ninth.

   C. What makes the *Symphonie fantastique* so important is Berlioz's success in uniting, within the framework of a "symphony," virtually all of his personal, musical, and literary priorities as they existed when he composed it: the magnified and intensified emotions and conflicts of the opera house; the explicit narrative storyline of a Shakespearean play; the Faustian concept of man as deeply flawed but worthy of redemption; and perhaps most important, intimate autobiographical confession.

   D. Like Beethoven's Symphony no. 6, the *Symphonie fantastique* is a program symphony in that it seeks to tell a single story across the span of its multiple movements. However, Berlioz goes far beyond Beethoven's Sixth in the degree to which he personalizes the expressive content of his symphony and renders explicit the imagery contained in it. The *Symphonie fantastique* would seem to include within its five movements almost everything Berlioz knew and understood about music and himself at the time he wrote it.

E. The *Symphonie fantastique*, then, is a frankly bizarre, experimental, all-inclusive piece of over-the-top autobiographical art, composed at a time when bizarre, experimental, inclusive, and over-the-top art was increasingly thought to hold the keys to higher experience and self-knowledge.

F. Three revelations—all experienced between 1827 and 1828— provided Berlioz the grist that he milled into the *Symphonie fantastique*: his discovery of Shakespeare and his subsequent crush on a Shakespearean actress; his discovery of Beethoven's symphonies; and his reading of Goethe's *Faust*.

1. On September 11, 1827, Berlioz went to the theater to see an English-language play called *Hamlet*. He had to follow the action from a crudely written synopsis, because he spoke no English, but the events of that evening marked the rest of his life. He fell in love with both the actress playing Ophelia, Harriet Smithson, and the poetry of the play itself.

2. The second revelation occurred in early 1828, when Berlioz read Goethe's *Faust*, which had just been published in a French translation. In a letter written later in 1828, Berlioz described Shakespeare and Goethe as "[t]he silent confidants of my suffering; they hold the key to my life."

3. Finally, on March 9, 1828, just a few weeks after having read *Faust* and almost six months to the day after having first seen Harriet Smithson as Ophelia in Shakespeare's *Hamlet*, Berlioz attended the first public concert of the newly created Conservatory Concert Society, conducted by its founder, François-Antoine Habeneck, who single-handedly introduced and championed Beethoven's symphonies in France.

4. Many members of the Parisian audience reacted to Beethoven's music the same way they reacted to Berlioz's: that is, with amazed incomprehension. Berlioz, though, was thunderstruck. He had always assumed that only opera could express the full gamut of human emotions. Suddenly, he was faced with the evidence that instrumental music had an

expressive power that was, for him, even greater than that of vocal music.

III. The event that forged all of these influences into the *Symphonie fantastique* occurred sometime in early 1830, when Berlioz heard a rumor that Harriet Smithson was having an affair with her manager, which unhinged him completely.

   A. The *Symphonie fantastique* is an autobiographical work, in which Berlioz portrays an artist who is hopelessly in love with a woman who doesn't care that he exists. We know this because Berlioz himself prepared a program note describing the meaning of each of the five movements and handed it out to his opening-night audience!

   B. The five movements of the symphony explore a progression of emotional states, from the roller coaster of passion and depression of the first movement, to denial in the second, to hope and despair in the third.

      1. According to Berlioz, the fourth movement depicts the artist's suicide attempt when he becomes convinced that his love is unappreciated. The dose of narcotic he takes does not kill him but thrusts him into a nightmare, in which he witnesses his own execution. The theme that accompanies the trip to the guillotine is perhaps the most famous Berlioz ever composed. (**Musical selection**: Berlioz, *Symphonie fantastique*, movement 4, "Scaffold March" theme [1830].)

      2. The fifth movement is even stranger; in it, the artist witnesses his own funeral during the course of a witches' sabbath..

      3. For an in-depth examination of these last two movements, I direct your attention to Lectures Thirty-Five and Thirty-Six of The Teaching Company super course *How to Listen to and Understand Great Music*.

   C. For now, we will examine the first movement of the *Symphonie fantastique*, entitled "Reveries—Passions." It's a strange and wonderful movement that undoubtedly left Berlioz's audience confused. It is also pure Berlioz, and it exhibits exactly those characteristics that make the *fantastique* so compelling and original, avant-garde and controversial.

      1. Berlioz's program notes identify the most important element of the *Symphonie fantastique*, the element that binds its five movements together and allows the programmatic content of the piece to make sense. This element is the theme that represents the beloved in the artist's mind, which appears, in some guise, in each of the five movements of the symphony. Let's hear it as it first appears, as theme 1 of the first-movement sonata form. (**Musical selection**: Berlioz, *Symphonie fantastique*, movement 1, *idée fixe*.)

2. The tune aches with emotion and passion, ecstatically climbing, higher and higher, until it finally reaches its peak, from where it gradually descends in a series of sigh-like motives. We listen to it again. (**Musical selection**: Berlioz, *Symphonie fantastique*, movement 1, *idée fixe*.)

3. According to the program notes, the subject of the first movement is "the passage from [a] state of melancholy reverie...to one of frenzied passion." The first movement begins with a long, almost sniveling introduction, during which Berlioz seeks to invoke the "ache of passions" he describes in his program. We listen to the beginning of the introduction and the wheezing, weakly throbbing winds and strings that set a mood of dismal, pained longing. (**Musical selection**: Berlioz, *Symphonie fantastique*, movement 1, introduction, opening.)

4. This introduction wanders through a series of episodes, until finally, the orchestra converges on a dramatic tremolo, which is followed by an explosive series of "heartbeats," followed by the first appearance of the *idée fixe* ("fixed idea"). We listen from the dramatic tremolo through the beginning of theme 1, the *idée fixe*. (**Musical selection**: Berlioz, *Symphonie fantastique*, movement 1, introduction, conclusion.)

5. Berlioz structures the movement as a sonata form, complete with an exposition repeat. If we try to follow it, we will become lost and confused. However, if we ignore the sonata form—as Berlioz ultimately did—and hear the movement as an expressionistic artwork, with its constant shifts of expressive content and mood, reflecting inner emotional experience, we realize that the movement is not "about" sonata form but, rather, the conscious and unconscious flow of emotions triggered by the beloved image—which was Berlioz's intent all along!

6. Let's hear the remainder of the exposition, the music that follows theme 1. Immediately following the invocation of "her," the strings launch into a "paroxysm of ecstasy," as the artist's hopes soar; only to be followed by a quiet, shy, cautious bit of music, then another "paroxysm of ecstasy," followed by a brief modulating bridge. Last, in place of a second theme, an alternating episode is heard, as winds invoke theme 1, followed by explosive strings. (**Musical selection**: Berlioz, *Symphonie fantastique*, movement 1, exposition, conclusion.)

7. The development is also rather "idiosyncratic." It is less about fragmenting, reassembling, and metamorphosing the thematic material over an essentially unstable harmonic underpinning than it is an almost stream-of-consciousness series of musical/emotional responses to theme 1, the fixed idea. Despite the opinions of some scholars and critics, this development is entirely appropriate for the stated expressive goal of the movement.

8. We conclude our examination of this first movement with the recapitulation and the coda. When theme 1 returns at the beginning of the recapitulation, it is manic with excitement. The mood swings between this passion and quiet doubt, until the last minute of the movement. In the end, we hear theme 1 set as a hymn. Marked *religiosomente* ("religiously"), the passage is a worshipful paean to the beloved image, as well as a prayer for peace, even sanity. Let's hear the remainder of the movement from the beginning of the recapitulation. (**Musical selection**: Berlioz, *Symphonie fantastique*, movement 1, recapitulation and coda.)

D. The *Symphonie fantastique* received its premiere on December 5, 1830, performed by the Conservatory Concert Society. We can well imagine the reaction of the opening-night attendees, who must have been particularly confused about Berlioz's treatment of the large orchestra he had called for.

1. Berlioz "played" the orchestra the way other composers "play" the piano or the violin. From the very first, Berlioz "thought" orchestrally, and in an era of great orchestrators, he outdid almost all of them in terms of special effects and experimental daring.

2. Most composers begin their lives as pianists. They conceive an orchestral work, first, as a piano piece; then, they orchestrate it. Of course, for many of his contemporaries, Berlioz's orchestration was as incomprehensible as his music.

E. The *Symphonie fantastique*—composed just six years after the premiere of Beethoven's Ninth Symphony—again redefined the genre of symphony. The radical fringe of the time, represented by Franz Liszt, understood its importance, though many important musicians and critics initially wrote Berlioz off as a crackpot. Now, he is seen as one of the seminal figures of Romanticism, and his *Symphonie fantastique* is viewed as perhaps the most remarkable "First" symphony in the repertoire.

Lecture Eleven—Transcript
Berlioz and the *Symphonie fantastique*

Welcome back to *The Symphony*. This is Lecture Eleven—it is entitled "Berlioz and the *Symphonie fantastique*." A radical in his own words, we read from page one, paragraph one of Hector Berlioz's autobiography:

> I was born on the 11th of December, 1803, at La Côte-Saint-André, a very small town in France, situated between Grenoble and Lyons. During the month that preceded my birth, my mother never dreamt, as Virgil's [mother] did, that she was about to bring forth a branch of laurel. However painful to my mother this confession may be, I ought to add that neither did she imagine like Olympius, the mother of Alexander, that she bore within her a fiery brand. Strange, I admit, but true. I came into the world quite naturally, unheralded by any of the signs which, in poetic ages, preceded the advent of remarkable personages.

Don't you just love this guy already? Berlioz's father, Luis Berlioz, was a well-known and well-to-do doctor, and from the beginning it was understood that Hector would follow in his father's footsteps and become a physician. Of course, no one asked Hector about this. He was an indulged, pampered, oversensitive, overstimulated, first-born son. What he wanted to be more than anything else in the world was a composer. Nevertheless, having graduated from high school, he was sent to Paris at the age of 18 to study medicine. His passport contained the following physical description: "About five-foot three or five-foot four inches in height; red hair; red eyebrows; beginning to grow a beard; forehead ordinary, eyes gray; complexion high."

Berlioz later wrote:

> [I was being forced] to become a doctor! Study anatomy! Dissect! Take part in horrible operations—instead of giving myself body and soul to music, sublime art whose grandeur I was beginning to perceive! Forsaking the highest heavens for the wretchedest regions of the earth, the immortal spirits of poetry and love and their divinely inspired strains for dirty hospital orderlies, dreadful dissecting-room attendants, hideous corpses, the screams of the patients, the groans and rattling death of the dying! No! It seemed

to me the reversal of the whole natural order of my existence. It was monstrous! It could not happen! Yet it did.

But not for long. Within two years Berlioz had dropped out of medical school and in the process became estranged from his parents. He survived by giving music lessons, singing in choruses, and writing reviews for anyone who would hire him to do so. He attended the opera, in the standing room; he took private lessons in composition when he could afford them and he composed; he studied scores at the library of the Paris Conservatory. Oh, what Berlioz wanted more than anything in the world was to be a student at the Conservatory, but his resources simply didn't permit it. Nevertheless, in 1825, Berlioz finally had the opportunity to meet and chat with the new director of the Conservatory, the Italian composer and pedant, Luigi Cherubini. We'll let Berlioz describe their meeting:

> No sooner was Cherubini appointed director, than he introduced all sorts of restrictions. [For example], in order to prevent the intermingling of the two sexes, except in the presence of professors, he issued an order that the men were to enter by the door in the Fauberg Poisonniere, and the woman by that in the Rue Bergère; the two [doors] being at opposite ends of the building.

> Wholly ignorant of this decree, I betook myself one morning to the library, entering as usual by the Rue Bergère, the female door, and was making my way to the library when I found myself confronted by a servant, who stopped me in the middle of the courtyard, and told me to go back and return to the very same spot by the other entrance. I thought this so absurd that I sent the [dog] about his business, and went on my way. The rascal went on to report [me]. I had been absorbed in [a score of Gluck's] *Alceste* for a quarter of an hour when Cherubini entered the reading room, his face more cadaverous, his hair more bristling, his eyes more wicked, and his step more abrupt than ever. He and my accuser made their way around the table, examining several unconscious students, until the servant stopped in front of me and cried, "Here he is!" Cherubini was in such a passion that he could not utter a word. "Ah! Ah, ah, ah!" he cried at last, his Italian accent comically intensified in his anger. "And so you are the man who dares come in by the door by which I forbid you to enter?" "I was not aware, sir, of your order, and another time I will obey it." "Another time! Another time! What, what, what are you doing here?" "As you see, sir, I am

studying Gluck's scores." "And what, what, what are Gluck's scores to you? And who allows you to, to, to enter the library?" "Sir?" (I was now getting angry.) "Gluck is the grandest dramatic music composer I know, and I need no one's permission to come here and study him. The Conservatory library is open to the public from 10 till 3, and I have the right to use it." "The, the, the right?" "Yes, sir." "I don't think you could come here." "Nevertheless, I will return." "What, what, what's your name?" he cried, trembling with passion. I was, by this time, white with anger too. "Sir, perhaps you may hear my name some day, but you will not hear it now." "Sei-sei-seize him!" [he cried to the servant]. "Seize him and take him to prison!" Then, to the astonishment of everyone, master and servant pursued me around the table, knocking over stools and reading desks in the vain attempt to catch me, until at last I escaped calling out with a laugh as I vanished: "You shall neither have me nor my name, and I shall soon be back studying Gluck's scores again!"

This was my first interview with Cherubini.

In early 1826, at the age of 23, Berlioz's finances forced him to move back to his parent's home.

I met with a chilling reception, and was left for some days to my own reflections. Then my parents called upon me to choose some other profession, since I did not choose to be a doctor. I replied that my sole desire was to be a musician, and that I could not believe they would refuse to let me return and pursue my career in Paris.

One morning early, I was awakened by my father. "Get up," he said, "and when you are dressed, come into my study. I want to speak to you." I obeyed. My father was grave. "I stood expecting another attack, when these words fell on my startled ears: "After several sleepless nights I have made up my mind. You shall go to Paris and study music; but only for a time. If you fail, you will choose some other career. You know what I think of second-rate poets; second-rate artists are no different, and it would be a deep sorrow and profound humiliation to me to see you numbered among these useless members of society."

My father, it may be remarked, was far less intolerant of second-rate doctors, who are not only quite as numerous as bad poets and artists, but are not merely as useless, but positively dangerous.

I threw myself into my father's arms, and promised all he asked. "Seeing how radically different your mother's and my ideas are on this subject," he continued, "I have thought it better not to inform her of my decision."

But of course, Berlioz's mother did discover what was going on. And a great darkness came over the land. Her fury knew no bounds.

[My mother] was convinced that, in adopting music as a career, I was pursuing a path which leads to discredit in this world and damnation in the next. The moment I saw her face, I knew that she knew, and tried to avoid her until my departure. But I had scarcely found a hiding place when she discovered me, and with flashing eyes and furious gestures, she exclaimed, addressing me as 'vous', not 'tu': "Your father has been weak enough to allow you to return to Paris, and to encourage your wild and wicked plans; but I will not have this guilt on my soul, and, once and for all, I forbid your departure!" "Mother!" "Yes, I forbid it, and I beg you not to persist in your folly, Hector. See, I your mother, kneel to you, and beg you humbly to renounce it!" "Good heavens, mother. do not kneel to me! Stand up, I beg you!" "No, I will kneel." After a moment's pause: "Wretched boy! You refuse? You can stand, unmoved, with your mother kneeling at your feet? Well then, go! Go and wallow in the filth of Paris, sully your name, and kill your father and me with sorrow and shame! I will not re-enter the house until you have left it. You are my son no longer. I curse you!"

These then are the circumstances under which Hector Berlioz, age 23, entered the freshman class of the Paris Conservatory in the fall of 1826. Soon enough, Luigi Cherubini would discover who had been admitted. But by then, it was too late to do anything about it. For the next four years, Berlioz, with a passion bordering on the pathological, immersed himself in his studies; in the Parisian theaters, concert halls, opera houses; in composing and writing reviews; and in the process of all of this, he proved himself to be one of the greatest late bloomers in the history of Western music.

Berlioz's Symphonies

Like Mozart before him, Berlioz was, in his heart-of-hearts, an opera composer. Like blood to a vampire, Berlioz fed on the emotional extremes and dramatic conflicts of opera; like a roller coaster freak, the greater the operatic thrill, the more Berlioz liked it. Needless to say, his operatic tastes leaned towards the radical. He rejected contemporary *bel canto* Italian opera, which he groused was light weight and merely "entertaining," and embraced, instead, the grand operas of Gluck and the experimental operas of German Romantics like Carl Maria von Weber.

Truth be told, Berlioz was a radical person in many ways. He lived at the extreme edge of his emotions it would seem all the time. And he was the sort of person who was great in small doses but could be terribly vexatious for those who spent any amount of time in his company. Frankly, today, we consider Berlioz's endless passions, his outbursts, his emotional self-indulgence as being the tiresome marks of an over-engaged and over-caffeinated adolescent personality. But in the 1820s and 1830s, his affectations were the marks of the *artiste*—the post-Byron, post-Beethoven, post-Napoleon middle-class creator who answered only to his own drum, communed only with his own muses, followed his own star. In a 19th-century artistic environment that celebrated individuality, originality, and extremes of expression, well, Hector Berlioz was the quintessential Romantic artist, and the *Symphonie fantastique* the quintessential Romantic symphony.

Berlioz wrote four works that at one time or another he described as symphonies. The *Symphonie fantastique* of 1830; *Harold In Italy*, 1834; *Romeo and Juliet*, 1839, and the *Grand Funeral and Triumphal Symphony* of 1840. However, the only one of these works that is a "symphony" by the standards of this course is the first, the *Symphonie fantastique*. It is, without a doubt, the most influential 19th-century symphony written after Beethoven's Ninth. Here in his first attempt at writing a symphony, Berlioz hit the bulls-eye on his first shot.

Revelations

What makes the *Symphonie fantastique* so important a work is Berlioz's success in uniting, within the framework of a "symphony," virtually all of his personal, musical and literary priorities as they existed when he composed the piece: the magnified and intensified emotions and conflicts of the opera house; the explicit narrative story line of a Shakespearean play; the Faustian concept of man as deeply flawed but worthy of redemption, as expressed specifically in Goethe's *Faust*; and lastly, perhaps most importantly, intimate autobiographical confession. Like Beethoven's Symphony no. 6, the *Symphonie fantastique* is a program symphony in that it seeks to tell a single story across the span of its multiple movements. However, Berlioz goes far beyond Beethoven's Sixth in terms of the degree to which he personalizes the expressive content within the symphony and of course renders explicit the imagery contained within this symphony. The *Symphonie fantastique* would seem to include within its five movements just about everything Berlioz knew and understood about music and himself at the time he wrote it.

The *Symphonie fantastique,* then, is a frankly bizarre, experimental, all-inclusive bit of over-the-top autobiographical art, composed at a time when bizarre, experimental, inclusive and over-the-top art was increasingly thought to hold the keys to higher experience and knowledge. Three blinding revelations—all experienced between 1827 and 1828—provided Berlioz the grist that he milled into the *Symphonie fantastique*: The discovery of Shakespeare and his subsequent crush on a Shakespearean actress; his discovery of Beethoven's symphonies; and his reading of Goethe's *Faust.*

Revelation number one: On September 11, 1827, Berlioz went to the theater to see an English language play called *Hamlet* by a playwright named William Shakespeare. Berlioz had to follow the action from a crudely written synopsis, as he spoke not a jot of English, although later in his life, he learned to both read and speak English quite well. The events of that evening marked the rest of his life. Again, Berlioz himself tells us the story:

> I now come to the supreme drama of my life. I shall not recount all its sad vicissitudes. I will say only this: an English company came over to Paris to give a season of Shakespeare at the Odeon, with a repertory of plays then quite unknown in France. I was at the first night of *Hamlet*. In the role of Ophelia I saw Henriette Smithson. The impression made on my heart and mind by her extraordinary talent, nay, her dramatic genius, was equaled only by the havoc wrought in me by the poet she so nobly interpreted. That is all I can say.

Berlioz refers here to Harriet (not "Henriette") Smithson, a 27 year-old Anglo-Irish actress who was then at the height of her fame. For Berlioz, it was insane, unquenchable love at first sight, and he went off the deep end. For the next two years, he did everything he could to bring himself to her attention. He pursued her relentlessly and in the process made a total fool of himself. When Smithson left Paris to return to England two years later, she had yet to actually meet her deranged young admirer. But Berlioz continued to nourish his passion. On February 6, 1830, almost two-and-a-half years after he first saw Smithson, Berlioz wrote his friend Humbert Ferrand:

> After a period of calm, I have just been plunged again into all the tortures of an endless and unquenchable passion without cause, without purpose. She is still in London and yet I seem to feel her all around me; I hear my heart pounding and its beats set me going like the piston strokes of a steam engine. Each muscle in my body trembles with pain. Useless! Frightening!

> Oh! Unhappy woman! If she could only for one moment conceive all the poetry, all the infinity of such a love, she would fly to my arms, even if she must die for my embrace!

Revelation number two occurred sometime in very early 1828, when Berlioz read Goethe's *Faust*, which had just been published in a French translation. In a letter written later in 1828, Berlioz described Shakespeare and Goethe as "the silent confidants of my sufferings; they hold the key to my life."

Revelation number three: On March 9, 1828, just a few weeks after reading Goethe's Faust and almost six months to the day after having first seen Henriette Smithson as Ophelia in Shakespeare's *Hamlet*, Berlioz attended the first public concert of the newly created Conservatory Concert Society, which was conducted by its founder, François-Antoine Habeneck. Habeneck is one of those movers and shakers whose actions change their world, but who are often forgotten when the histories are told. Well, not in this history. What Habeneck did was single-handedly introduce and then champion Beethoven's symphonies in France through the venue of his Conservatory Concert Society. On that first concert of 1828, the Society performed Beethoven's Third Symphony. On their third concert they introduced Beethoven's Fifth Symphony, and soon after, the Ninth Symphony.

Many of the Parisian audience reacted to Beethoven's music the same way they reacted to Berlioz's music—with amazed comprehension. Berlioz, though, was thunderstruck. He had always assumed that only opera could express the full gamut of human emotions. Suddenly, he was faced with the evidence that instrumental music had an expressive power that was, for him, even greater than vocal music. He was entirely won over and he later wrote that "Beethoven opened before me a new world of music, as Shakespeare had revealed a new universe of poetry."

Putting it all together

The event that forged all of these various influences into the *Symphonie fantastique* occurred sometime in early 1830, when Berlioz heard a rumor circulating that Harriet Smithson—his adored and perfect Harriet (or "Henriette" as he insisted on calling her, even after they were married in 1832, much to her endless frustration), that his adored and perfect Mademoiselle H. was having an affair with her manager. The rumor regarding her illicit behavior unhinged Berlioz completely. Writes Berlioz scholar Hugh MacDonald: "When in 1830 it seemed that [Berlioz's] love for [Smithson] had turned sour [as a result of the rumors concerning her affair], the accumulation of nervous tension broke out in the *Symphonie fantastique* which describes and transmutes into [music] the artist's passions, dreams, and frustrations."

The *Symphonie fantastique* then, is an autobiographical work, in which Berlioz portrays an artist who is hopelessly in love with a woman who does not know (or care) that he exists. And how do we know this? We know it because Berlioz himself prepared a program note describing the meaning of each of the five movements and handed this program note out to his opening-night audience. That's how we know it.

The five movements of the symphony explore a progressive series of emotional states, from the emotional roller coaster of passion and depression of the first movement to denial in the second movement, to hope and despair in the third movement, and then, then things get weird. We read Berlioz's own description of the fourth movement: "Convinced that his love is unappreciated, the artist poisons himself with opium. The dose of the narcotic, too weak to kill him, plunges him into a sleep accompanied by the most horrible visions. He dreams that he has killed his beloved, that he is condemned and led to the scaffold, and that he is witnessing his own execution."

Well, there you go. Timothy Leary, plus a scene from revolutionary France equals the fourth movement of Berlioz's *Symphonie fantastique*. The theme that accompanies the trip to the guillotine is perhaps the most famous that Berlioz ever composed.

[Musical example from *Symphonie fantastique*, Berlioz: IV]

This fourth movement ends with an extremely explicit musical depiction of the head of the artist being chopped off by the guillotine and falling into a basket. If you think that's weird, well I'll tell you, the fifth movement's even stranger. Berlioz's description in part: "Dream of a Witches' Sabbath. He sees himself at the Sabbath, in the midst of a frightful group of ghosts, sorcerers, monsters of every kind, come together for his funeral. Strange noises, groans, bursts of laughter, distant cries which other cries seem to answer. A devilish orgy!"

Please, for an in-depth examination of these last two extraordinary movements, I would direct your attention to Lectures Thirty-five and Thirty-six of my Teaching Company super course, *How to Listen and Understand Great Music*. For now, we will examine the first movement of the *Symphonie fantastique*, a movement entitled "Reveries—Passions." It's a strange and wonderful movement that undoubtedly left Berlioz's audiences scratching their heads in confusion. But it is also the purest of pure Berlioz, and it exhibits exactly those characteristics that make the *fantastique* so compelling and so original, so avant-garde and yes, so controversial.

First, Berlioz's program:

> Reveries—Passions. The author imagines that a young musician, afflicted with that moral disease that a well known writer calls the "ache of passion," sees for the first time a woman who embodies all the charms of the ideal being he has imagined in his dreams and he falls desperately in love with her. Through an odd whim, whenever the beloved image appears before the mind's eye of the artist, it is linked with a musical thought whose character, passionate but at the same time noble and shy, he finds similar to the one he attributes to his beloved.

> This melodic image and the model it represents pursue him incessantly like a double *idée fixe* [a "fixed idea"]. That is the reason for the constant appearance, in every movement of the symphony, of the melody that begins the first allegro.

My friends, Berlioz has just identified the single most important musical element of the *Symphonie fantastique*—the element that binds its five movements together and allows the programmatic content of the piece to actually make sense: "A musical thought whose character, passionate but at the same time noble and shy, he finds similar to the one he attributes to his beloved."

What Berlioz refers to here is a theme, a melody, that represents *her*, the beloved image—Harriet Smithson, if you will—a theme that will appear in each of the five movements of the symphony in some guise or another. Let's hear this theme, this *idée fixe*, this fixed idea, this theme that represents *her* as it first appears as theme 1 of the first-movement sonata form.

[Musical example from *Symphonie fantastique*, Berlioz: I; Theme I]

On the printed page, Berlioz has filled this theme—this manifestation of the ideal "she"—with enough articulation and dynamic marks to choke a coloratura soprano. The tune veritably aches with emotion and passion, ecstatically climbing, higher and higher, until it finally reaches its peak, from where it gradually descends in a series of sigh-like motives. Please, let's hear it one more time.

[Musical example from *Symphonie fantastique*, Berlioz: I; Theme I]

The fact that Berlioz had originally used this melody in 1828, in a cantata entitled *Herminie,* in no way diminishes its impact here, in the *Symphonie fantastique.* We cannot imagine a tune better suited to fit Berlioz's expressive needs and obviously, neither could Berlioz.

We continue and complete Berlioz's description, his program note for this first movement: "The passage from [a] state of melancholy reverie, interrupted by a few fits of groundless joy, to one of frenzied passion, with its moments of jealousy, fury, its return of tenderness, its tears, its religious consolations—this is the subject of the first movement."

Please, a brief important sidebar. There is a school of thought that claims that any such program note as we've been reading, is in reality a post-facto apologia designed to cover the flaws and weaknesses of whatever music it purports to "describe"; an after-hours declaration of purpose when, in fact, the composer hadn't a clue as to what he was doing while he was actually writing the music; a verbal band-aid placed over a bleeding, bone-splintered stump of badly written music. In reference to the *Symphonie fantastique*, we say, "wrong." Berlioz did indeed have a most vivid imagination. He was a great raconteur, as our brief quotes from his memoirs attest. He was an opera maven, meaning dramatic narrative was the first of his musical priorities. And he was a person of extraordinary emotional excess, and was prepared to indulge that excess at the drop of a beret. Berlioz's program notes should therefore not be perceived as a cover for poor composition as has been suggested by some less than charitable critics, but rather as an intrinsic part of the symphony, an "invisible libretto," if you will.

The first movement begins with a long, drooping, almost sniveling introduction, an introduction that precedes the theme we just heard, during which Berlioz seeks to invoke the "ache of passions" he describes in his program. We'll listen to the very beginning of the introduction and the wheezing, weakly throbbing winds and strings that set a mood of dismal, pained longing.

[Musical example from *Symphonie fantastique*, Berlioz: I; Introduction]

My goodness, this dismal introduction wanders through a series of episodes until finally the orchestra converges on a dramatic tremolo followed by an explosive series of "heart-beats" ("Be still my heart! Be still, the beloved image is nigh!), followed by the first appearance of the *idée fixe*, the fixed idea, the theme that represents her, the first theme of the sonata form movement. We listen from the dramatic tremolo through the beginning of theme 1, the fixed idea.

[Musical example from *Symphonie fantastique*, Berlioz: I]

Berlioz structures this first movement as a sonata form, complete with an exposition repeat. If we try to follow the sonata form, I guarantee we will become lost and confused. However, if we ignore the sonata form (as Berlioz in reality did) and hear the movement as an expressionistic artwork, with its constant rise and fall and shifts on a dime of expressive content and mood, reflecting inner emotional experience, well, then we'll realize that the movement is not about sonata form, not about contrasting themes and their development, but rather the conscious and unconscious flow of emotions triggered by the beloved image, which is Berlioz's intent all along.

Let's hear the remainder of the exposition, the music that follows theme 1, the fixed idea. Immediately following the invocation of "her," the strings launch into a "paroxysm of ecstasy," if you'll excuse me, as the artist's hopes soar; only to be followed by a quiet, shy, cautious bit of music. Could she really love me? And then, another "paroxysm of ecstasy" followed by a brief modulating bridge. Lastly, in place of a genuine second theme, an alternating episode is heard as winds invoke theme 1, followed by explosive strings, as if to say that any reference to her in our minds will be followed by the most extraordinary emotional explosion. Please, let's hear the conclusion of the so-called exposition of the first movement of Berlioz's *Symphonie fantastique.*

[Musical example from *Symphonie fantastique*, Berlioz: I; Exposition]

Oh really, sonata form be damned my friends. This music only makes sense if we understand the conscious and the unconscious flow and the motion Berlioz is attempting to express. The development section is also rather "idiosyncratic" (if we might put it again charitably.) It is less about fragmenting, reassembling and metamorphosing the thematic material over an essentially unstable harmonic underpinning than it is an almost stream-of-consciousness series of musical/emotional responses to theme 1, to the fixed idea, to the image of her. Does this mean that Berlioz, at this point of his career, could not write a proper development section? Well, according to some scholars and critics, yes. But to belabor Berlioz's technical shortcomings in the *Symphonie fantastique* is to entirely miss the piece. The point is that Berlioz did with the development section precisely what he wanted to do. And what he does is fascinating and entirely appropriate for his stated expressive goal of the movement.

We conclude our examination of this first movement with the recapitulation and the coda. When theme 1 returns at the onset of the recapitulation, it is manic, crazy with excitement. The mood continues to swing between the sort of irrepressible mania and quiet doubt until the last minute of the movement. In the end, we hear theme 1 set as a hymn. Marked *religiosomente* ("religiously"), the passage is a worshipful paean to the beloved image, as well as a prayer, a prayer for peace, even sanity. Let's hear the remainder of the movement beginning with the manic opening of the recapitulation.

[Musical example from *Symphonie fantastique*, Berlioz: I; Recapitulation and Coda]

The *Symphonie fantastique* received its premier on December 5, 1830, performed by the Conservatory Concert Society, the aforementioned François-Antoine Habeneck conducting. My friends, we can well imagine the reaction of the opening night audience. As the last explosive chords of the fifth movement dissipated, the audience must have looked shell-shocked, mouths hanging open, eyes glazed, an occasional twitch under an eye as if they'd just been forced to watch Kevin Costner play Othello. Except for Berlioz's new friend, Franz Liszt, who was there in the audience and who would have been bouncing up and down in his seat, hooting and hollering around, the cigar in his mouth, clapping his hands and stomping his feet. That opening night audience had a lot to be confused about, including Berlioz's treatment of the very large orchestra he had called for.

Berlioz "played" the orchestra the way other composers "play" the piano or the violin. From the very first, it would seem that Berlioz "thought" orchestrally, and in an era of great orchestrators, he outdid every one of them in terms of special effects and experimental daring. Please, most composers begin their musical lives as piano players, and they spend much of their musical lives hearing music through their fingers and through the piano. It was not, and still is not, atypical to this day for composers first to write a piece of music as a piece of piano music, or perhaps arrange it for two pianos and then orchestrate this piano score into an orchestral score. What this means is they conceived of an orchestral piece first pianistically, then orchestrally.

Berlioz couldn't play piano to save his soul. He played guitar and a little flute. Berlioz did not conceive of an orchestral piece as a piano piece that had been orchestrated, but rather Berlioz immediately went to the orchestra. He heard the orchestra in his ear. It was part and parcel of the concept as he composed. And in doing so, Berlioz wrote for the orchestra in a very different way than someone who is actually arranging a piano score for orchestra. Berlioz called for an orchestra that was huge and used his resources in an utterly idiosyncratic way, and in doing so revolutionized the art of orchestration. Of course, for many of his contemporaries, Berlioz's orchestration was as incomprehensible as his music. Unfortunately, radical innovators are rarely understood by their contemporaries.

Hector Berlioz, essentially self-taught and proud of it, was going to do things his own way. A late-blooming, anti-academic, extraordinarily self-indulgent radical from the start, he was by his very nature a very controversial man and an equally controversial composer. And he became a poster child for the new generation of post-Beethoven Romantic radicals, who numbered among their ranks Berlioz's good friends Franz Liszt, and Liszt's son-in-law, Richard Wagner.

The *Symphonie fantastique*—composed just six years after Beethoven's Ninth—further redefined the genre of symphony. Whether or not Berlioz's contemporaries were aware of the revolutionary importance of the *fantastique* depended on the individual. Certainly the radical fringe, as represented by Franz Liszt, understood the importance, but many good and important musicians and critics initially wrote Berlioz off as a total crackpot. For example, Gioachino Rossini, recently retired from the opera stage at the time the *fantastique* was premiered, remarked while he was examining the score, "What a good thing that this young man has not taken up music! He'd certainly be very bad at it!"

But time has been good to Berlioz. We see him now as one of the seminal figures of Romanticism and his *Symphonie fantastique* is perhaps the single most remarkable "First" symphony in the repertoire. We give the last word to the great 20th century composer Darius Milhaud, who concluded an interview regarding Richard Wagner by saying, "Whew! Give me some fresh air! I would give up all of Wagner for one page of Berlioz."

And thank you.

Lecture Twelve
Mendelssohn and Schumann

Scope: The symphonies of Felix Mendelssohn and Robert Schumann reflect Classical tradition, acknowledge Beethoven's contributions to the genre, and offer a personal, innovative voice. This lecture explores Mendelssohn's "Italian" Symphony, the epitome of his "conservative Romanticism," and two of Schumann's four symphonies. In both artists, we see the necessity, in the 19th century, to reconcile their own work, in some way, with the legacy of Beethoven.

Outline

I. Nineteenth-century composers of symphonies, living and writing after Beethoven, had some tough choices to make.

    A. They could, first of all, try to pick up the musical/expressive gauntlet defined by Beethoven, but almost no one chose that option. Beethoven was an entirely unique "radical Classicist" who pushed the genre so far that he rendered any imitation of his personal musical "style" nearly impossible.

    B. The second choice was to use the expressive model of Beethoven's symphonies as a point of departure for ever more programmatic works—works that built on but did not compete with Beethoven's own symphonies, such as Berlioz's *Symphonie fantastique.*

    C. The third choice was to pretend that Beethoven had never existed, as Schubert did in his Symphonies nos. 1–5 and as Ludwig Spohr, Carl Maria von Weber, and other composers did who are less well known today.

    D. The fourth choice available to those composers of symphonies who followed Beethoven was to take a flexible approach to the Classical symphonic template; acknowledge, not ignore, Beethoven's innovations; and cultivate a personal expressive voice. Whether a composer chose the radical route, as Berlioz did, or this more conservative route, as Mendelssohn and Schumann did, Beethoven's contribution to the genre of symphony had to be acknowledged by those composers who followed him.

E. Our approach for the remainder of our discussion of the 19th-century symphony will focus on composers who chose, somehow, to reconcile their work with the symphonic legacy of Beethoven.

II. Along with Wolfgang Mozart, Felix Mendelssohn (1809–1847) was the greatest child prodigy in the history of Western performing arts.

    A. He was born in Hamburg on February 1, 1809. His grandfather was Moses Mendelssohn, the great Jewish philosopher. His father, Abraham, was a successful banker. Mendelssohn's mother, Leah, came from Berlin, where her father, Levy Salomon, was the court jeweler. Like Abraham Mendelssohn, Leah Salomon grew up in a well-to-do household in which a premium was placed on education, culture, and assimilation.

    B. When Felix was three years old, the family moved to Berlin; there, his parents supervised his education and fostered what Harold Schonberg called "an atmosphere of grim culture" in the household.

    C. Felix Mendelssohn was an extraordinary prodigy as a pianist, composer, painter, and linguist. Between the ages of 12 and 14, he composed, among other works, 13 symphonies for string orchestra, all of which were performed at the Mendelssohns' Berlin home.

    D. These symphonies are conservative pieces that explore a wide range of Baroque and Classical styles and techniques, but they are, by no means, "student" works. They were written under the supervision of Felix's teacher, Carl Friedrich Zelter, the director of the Berlin Singakademie. Zelter put Mendelssohn through a rigorous, Bach-dominated course of musical study.

    E. Mendelssohn's Symphony no. 1 in C Minor was completed on March 31, 1824, just a month after he turned 15 years old. It capped his education with Zelter, although it should not be considered a mature work. Maturity—and the clear influence of Beethoven—arrived the following year, when Mendelssohn composed his first great masterwork, the Octet in Eb Major, for strings. A year later, at age 17, he composed one of the most enduring and popular orchestral works in the repertoire, the *Overture to a Midsummer Night's Dream.*

F. All together, Mendelssohn composed four mature symphonies. Two of them are religious works: no. 5, the so-called "Reformation" Symphony, and no. 2, the "Lobgesang," which Mendelssohn called a "symphony-cantata." Mendelssohn's other two symphonies have programmatic titles: no. 3 is known as the "Scotch" and no. 4, the "Italian." (Note that numbers were assigned to Mendelssohn's symphonies in the order in which the symphonies were published, not the order in which they were composed.)

G. The pre-eminent symphonic example of Mendelssohn's "conservative Romanticism" is his Symphony no. 4 in A Major, op. 90, the "Italian."

1. The symphony was completed on March 13, 1833, and premiered two months later. Mendelssohn began work on the symphony during an extended trip through Italy in 1830–1831, and it is, essentially, an impressionistic work based on the sights, smells, and emotions inspired by this Italian jaunt.

2. The first theme of the first-movement sonata form is one of the most memorable in the repertoire. Chirping winds introduce a buoyant theme in the violins that Mendelssohn almost immediately begins to develop. We hear the theme and the modulating bridge that follows it. (**Musical selection**: Mendelssohn, Symphony no. 4 in A Major, op. 90 [Italian], movement 1, theme 1.)

3. Theme 2, graceful and lyric, is initially heard in the clarinets and bassoons. After a series of wonderful episodes inspired by theme 2 and featuring the winds, theme 1 briefly returns and the exposition comes to its conclusion. Let's hear the remainder of the exposition, beginning with the second theme. (**Musical selection**: Mendelssohn, Symphony no. 4 in A Major, op. 90 [Italian], movement 1, theme 2.)

4. The second-movement andante is a quiet and melancholy march, inspired, perhaps, by the religious processionals Mendelssohn witnessed during his stay in Italy. We hear the opening theme first in the winds, accompanied by steady, pizzicato low strings. (**Musical selection**: Mendelssohn, Symphony no. 4 in A Major, op. 90 [Italian], movement 2, opening.)

5. The third movement is as lyric and lovely—and as "Italian"— a minuet as we'll ever hear. (**Musical selection**: Mendelssohn, Symphony no. 4 in A Major, op. 90 [Italian], movement 3, opening.)

6. The last movement is a bit of a rarity, a minor-mode finale for a major-mode symphony. It is also the most outwardly "Italian" of the four movements, evoking the peasant dance music of southern Italy. Mendelssohn labeled the movement "*saltarello*," which is a fast, energized dance of Italian origin. Despite its minor mode, like any good symphonic finale of the Classical era, this one leaves us with a bounce in our steps. (**Musical selection**: Mendelssohn, Symphony no. 4 in A Major, op. 90 [Italian], movement 4, opening.)

III. Robert Schumann (1810–1856) was a quintessential artist of his time, a Romantic-era composer who believed utterly that art was a vehicle for personal confession and self-revelation. Like Berlioz, Schumann thought that the future of music was tied to merging music with literature and, in doing so, creating a composite art form, the whole greater than the parts.

A. Schumann's father, August, was an author, translator, and bookseller who passed on his passion for literature to his son. An avid reader, Schumann began writing poems around the age of 10 and, throughout his teens, fancied himself a genuine poet.

B. Concurrent with the development of the "literary" Schumann was the development of the musical Schumann. At the age of seven, he began piano lessons, and within a year, he had written his first compositions, a set of dances for the piano.

C. According to a boyhood friend, Schumann was convinced that he would become famous. All that remained to be determined was what profession he would distinguish himself in, no small detail considering his early accomplishments as both a writer and a musician.

D. An in-depth examination of the music, life, and times of Robert Schumann can be found in The Teaching Company's "Great Masters" series. A few brief highlights of his life follow here.

1. As a young man, Schumann was sent to Leipzig to learn the law but began studying with a piano teacher named Friedrick Wieck instead. Within a few months, Schumann started to experience numbness in one of the fingers of his right hand, a condition most likely caused by repetitive stress from practicing exercises at the piano for more than eight hours at a time. Within a couple of years, Schumann's injured finger was almost unusable.

2. Schumann, who had been composing all the while, shifted his musical emphasis to composition and, between 1830 and 1840, produced a large number of extraordinary and avant-garde compositions for solo piano.

3. At the same time, Schumann fell in love with his former piano teacher's daughter, the young and beautiful Clara Wieck. In December of 1835, Robert (25 years old) and Clara (16 years old) pledged themselves to each other and began a five-year battle to convince Clara's father to allow them to be married. In the meantime, Clara began to perform Schumann's music publicly, even though it confused her and her audiences.

4. Aside from his own compositional ambitions, it was Schumann's marriage to Clara and her overwhelming confidence in him that gave him the push he needed to write his first mature symphony. He also benefited from the incredibly stimulating environment in Leipzig, one of the major musical centers in Germany. At the center of the city's musical life stood Felix Mendelssohn, the conductor of Leipzig's Gewandhaus Orchestra.

5. Under Mendelssohn's baton, the Gewandhaus became a musical shrine at which the faithful gathered to hear the masterpieces of the past, including Beethoven, Schubert, and Bach. Schumann was awed by Mendelssohn's intellect and musical talents. Without a doubt, it was Felix Mendelssohn and the Gewandhaus Orchestra, along with Clara, that gave Robert Schumann the impetus to compose his first complete "symphony" in 1841.

IV. When Schumann sat down to write a symphony in 1841, he was faced with the question of how to build on the model of Beethoven's symphonies and still be original. For Schumann, the answer lay in writing a piece that walked the fine line between absolute and program music, between Classical-era structural integrity and Romantic-era musical storytelling.

A. Schumann sketched his Symphony no. 1 in just four sleepless days and nights, between January 23 and 26, 1841. He called the symphony "Spring," explaining that it was inspired by a poem of the same name by Adolph Bottger. The horn and trumpet fanfare at the beginning of the symphony is a wordless setting of the last lines of Bottger's poem:

> O turn from this, your present course,
> Springtime blossoms in the valley!

> *O wende, wende deinen Lauf,*
> *Im Tale blüht der Frühling auf!*

(**Musical selection**: Schumann, Symphony in Bb Major, op. 38, movement 1 opening fanfare [1841].)

B. The slow, solemn introduction that follows this opening fanfare leads to a brilliant exposition, consisting of an energized and propulsive first theme, followed by a delicate, lyric, woodwind-dominated second theme. Let's hear the exposition as it follows the slow introduction. (**Musical selection**: Schumann, Symphony in Bb Major, op. 38, movement 1, themes 1 and 2.)

C. Compared to Schumann's earlier works, this is very conservative music. In particular, its programmatic content is much less important than its use of the traditional, Classical-era musical forms, sonata form most notably, forms that Schumann had rarely used before composing the Spring Symphony.

D. The symphony was premiered under the baton of Felix Mendelssohn at the Gewandhaus on March 31, 1841. The concert was a great success, and the premiere of his First Symphony gave Schumann one of the few unadulterated triumphs he would experience during his career. His last such triumph was also a symphony: his third and most famous, the "Rhine" Symphony, or simply, the "Rhenish."

V. On March 31, 1850, Schumann formally accepted an offer to become the music director for the city of Düsseldorf. When he arrived on September 2, 1850, to take the job, both he and Clara were welcomed warmly. Schumann, however, was not the equal to the conducting duties he had taken on, and within three years, he was forced to resign his position.

A. Unfortunately, a far worse fate awaited him just a short time later. The victim of tertiary syphilis, he went mad and tried to commit suicide by throwing himself into the Rhine River in February, 1854. He died in an asylum outside of Bonn on July 29, 1856.

B. Schumann had never spent any appreciable time in the Rhineland before his move to Düsseldorf in 1850, but the Rhine River and its surrounding landscape captivated him. His third symphony reflects his fascination with the Rhenish landscape and its history, as well as the optimism he felt during those first heady months in Düsseldorf, when the symphony was composed.

C. The first movement begins with one of Schumann's greatest themes; its breadth and magnificence are meant to invoke the grandeur of the Rhine itself. (**Musical selection**: Schumann, Symphony no. 3 in Eb Major, op. 97, movement 1, theme 1 [1850].)

D. The second-movement scherzo is an engaging, rough-hewn *landler* (a rustic German three-step), a movement that Schumann had originally entitled "Morning on the Rhine." Like the first, this second movement invokes the majestic sweep of the Rhine River. (**Musical selection**: Schumann, Symphony no. 3 in Eb Major, op. 97, movement 2, opening.)

E. The third movement is a charming, delicately scored intermezzo. (**Musical selection**: Schumann, Symphony no. 3 in Eb Major, op. 97, movement 3, opening.)

F. Four weeks after they had arrived in Düsseldorf, Robert and Clara took a trip on the new railway line to Cologne, where they visited the Cathedral of Cologne, the largest Gothic building in northern Europe. Schumann was awed by the cathedral and the majestic ritual he witnessed there. Taken together, the cathedral and its Catholic ritual were the inspiration for the fourth movement of the Rhenish Symphony. Schumann indicated that the movement be played: "In the character of an accompaniment to a solemn processional."

G. Only now, in this fourth movement, do the trombones begin to play, heightening and intensifying the majesty and dignity of the music. We hear the opening minutes of the magnificent fourth movement of Schumann's Third Symphony. (**Musical selection**:

Schumann, Symphony no. 3 in Eb Major, op. 97, movement 4, opening.)

H. The fifth movement is a dancing and sweeping return to the sunshine and bustle of life on and by the river Rhine. (**Musical selection**: Schumann, Symphony no. 3 in Eb Major, op. 97, movement 5, opening.)

Lecture Twelve—Transcript
Mendelssohn and Schumann

Welcome back to *The Symphony*. This is Lecture Twelve and it is entitled "Mendelssohn and Schumann." No series on the symphony would be complete without a mention of Ludwig Spohr (1784-1859). Spohr was one of the leading composers of instrumental music in the first half of the 19th century and his symphonies were among the most popular of his time.

Good. We mentioned Ludwig Spohr. We should also mention Carl Maria von Weber (1786-1826), who wrote two extremely popular symphonies in C Major between 1806 and 1808. Done.

Now I know I'm being flip. But for a reason. Nineteenth-century composers of symphonies, living and writing after Beethoven, had some tough choices to make. Choice number one: you could try to "be like Ludwig"; pick up the expressive/musical gauntlet as defined by "The Man from Bonn," and run with it for all you were worth. But that didn't happen, because Beethoven was one in a gazillion, a "radical Classicist" (talk about an otherwise self-canceling phrase!) who pushed the genre so far that he rendered any imitation of his "style" pretty much impossible. Choice number two: you could radicalize the radical, and use the expressive model of Beethoven's symphonies as a point of departure for evermore programmatic works, works that built on but did not compete with Beethoven's own symphonies, like, for example, Berlioz's *Symphonie fantastique*. Choice number three: you could pretend, as best you could, that Beethoven had never happened, like Schubert in his Symphonies nos. 1-5. And yes, like Carl Maria von Weber and Ludwig Spohr. The English musicologist Clive Brown writes:

> Spohr's and Weber's musical proclivities had been essentially determined before they were exposed to the music of Beethoven's second and third periods [his Symphonies nos. 3-9]. Any reactions to Beethoven's later works, positive or negative, were largely superficial; The fundamental characteristics of their styles were not significantly affected by Beethoven's example.

And please, it wasn't just that Weber and Spohr had developed their musical styles before they were exposed to Beethoven's more radical works, oh no, they were also, like so many of their contemporaries, deeply ambivalent about Beethoven's symphonies, starting with the Third on out. For example, in 1810, Weber wrote:

> The passionate, almost incredible inventive powers inspiring [Beethoven] are accompanied by such a chaotic arrangement of his ideas that only his earlier compositions appeal to me; the latter ones seem to me hopeless chaos, an incomparable struggle for novelty, out of which breaks a few heavenly flashes of genius, proving how great he could be if he would tame his rich fantasy.

Spohr was rather more succinct in his criticism of Beethoven's Symphonies writing that they were: "Wanting in aesthetic feeling and a sense of the beautiful."

The fourth choice available to those composers of symphonies who followed Beethoven was to take a flexible approach to the Classical symphonic template; acknowledge, not ignore, Beethoven's innovations; and at the same time cultivate a personal expressive voice of their own. A difficult balancing act, but not impossible. It's precisely what Schubert managed to do in his Eighth and Ninth Symphonies. Whether a composer chose the radical route (like Berlioz), or the more conservative route (like Mendelssohn and Schumann), Beethoven's contribution to the genre of symphony had to be acknowledged by those composers that followed him. One simply couldn't pretend that he wasn't there; thus, my unseemly treatment of Weber and Spohr. By ignoring Beethoven's symphonies, they rendered their symphonies historically irrelevant. A harsh judgment, but those are the breaks. Our game plan for the remainder of our discussion for the 19th century will focus on composers who chose, somehow, to reconcile their symphonies with the symphonic legacy of Beethoven.

Felix Mendelssohn (1809-1847)

Along with Wolfgang Mozart and perhaps Gary Coleman, Felix Mendelssohn was perhaps the greatest child prodigy in the history of Western performing arts. He was born in Hamburg on February 1, 1809. His grandfather was Moses Mendelssohn, the great Jewish philosopher. His father, Abraham, was a successful banker, banking being one of the few professions open to Jews at the time. Mendelssohn's mother, Leah, came from Berlin where her father, Levy Salomon (Felix's grandfather), was the court jeweler. Like Abraham Mendelssohn, Leah Salomon grew up in a well-to-do household in which a premium was placed on education, culture, and assimilation. Leah's brother, Jacob, converted to Lutheranism;

subsequently he took the name Bartholdy. The kids were given that name as well, Felix and Fanny, and they were baptized in 1816, as if by calling them Mendelssohn-Bartholdy, they were actually going to be able to avoid the rampant anti-Semitism of the time.

When Felix was three, his family moved to Berlin and it was there that according to Harold Schonberg:

> [Mendelssohn] grew up in an atmosphere of grim culture. Grim because both parents were determined to see that their children had every advantage money and position could provide. Leah was an amateur musician and artist, a student of English, French and Italian literature, and she could read Homer in the original. Abraham loved music and was a cultured and literate man. He and Leah not only supervised their children's education, but were also determined that the children should be serious about it. That meant a great deal of work. Felix would be up at 5 a.m., ready to work on his music, his history, his Greek and Latin, his natural science, his contemporary literature and his drawing and painting. (He was to retain that early rising hour for the rest of his life.) He thrived on the regimen.

Felix Mendelssohn was an extraordinary prodigy. As a pianist, composer, painter, linguist, you name it, he mastered it. Between 1821 and 1823, between the ages of 12 and 14, he composed, among other works, 13 symphonies for string orchestra, all of which were performed in the Mendelssohn's Berlin home. They are conservative pieces that explore a wide range of Baroque and Classical styles and techniques. Having said that, it would be a mistake to call them "student" works because Mendelssohn was no ordinary student. They were written under the supervision of his teacher, Carl Friedrich Zelter, the director of the Berlin Singakademie. Zelter put Mendelssohn through a rigorous, Bach-dominated course of musical study. Of the modern composers, Zelter emphasized C. P. E. Bach and Mozart. According to our Larry Todd: "By the third of February, 1824, [Felix's] fifteenth birthday, Zelter could proclaim him a member of the brotherhood of Mozart, Haydn, and Bach. Beethoven, conspicuously absent in the list, was just beginning to influence Mendelssohn significantly."

Mendelssohn's Symphony no. 1 in C Minor was completed on March 31, 1824, just a month after he turned 15 years old. It capped his education with Zelter, although it should not be considered a mature work. That maturity and the clear influence of Beethoven arrived the following year when, at the age of 16, Mendelssohn composed his first great masterwork—the Octet in Eb Major, for strings. A year later, at the age of 17, he composed one of the most enduring and popular works of the repertoire, the *Overture to a Midsummer Night's Dream* for orchestra, at 17.

All together, Mendelssohn composed four mature symphonies, nos. 2 through 5. Two of them are religious works: no. 5, the so-called "Reformation" Symphony, and no. 2, the "Lobgesang," which Mendelssohn called a "symphony-cantata." Mendelssohn's other two symphonies have programmatic titles: no. 3 is known as the "Scottish" and no. 4, the "Italian." For our information, the numbers given to Mendelssohn's symphonies have nothing to do with the order in which they were composed, but rather the order in which they were published. Of his four mature symphonies, the first to be composed, in 1832, was the "Reformation," which bears the number "5." The second to be composed, dating from 1833, is the "Italian," which bears the number "4." Next came what is now called the Symphony no. 2 in 1840, and lastly, the "Scotch" Symphony completed in 1842, which bears the number "3." (Yes, you heard me correctly, the "Scotch" Symphony. Today of course, we only use the word "Scotch" to designate whiskey. People and places are, according to contemporary PC, designated as "Scots" and "Scottish." But this differentiation did not exist in Mendelssohn's time and the symphony was called the "Scotch" without objection until well into the 20th century.)

The pre-eminent symphonic example of Mendelssohn's "conservative Romanticism," if we may call it that, is his Symphony no. 4 in A Major, op. 90, the "Italian." My friends, if you can find someone who doesn't like this symphony, you have found someone for whom joy, beauty, song, and dance are meaningless, someone who can neither enjoy, nor deserves the Italian experience, which is at its essence what Mendelssohn's form is all about.

The symphony was completed on March 13, 1833 and premiered two months later on May 13, 1833 in London, in the same Hanover Square Rooms where Haydn premiered so many of his London Symphonies back in the 1790s. Mendelssohn began work on the symphony during an extended trip through Italy in 1830 and 1831. At its essence, the symphony is an impressionistic work based on the sights, smells and emotions inspired by Mendelssohn's Italian jaunt. It must have been a great trip because the music is among the most brilliant Mendelssohn ever wrote. Even he remarked that the symphony "was the most cheerful piece I had yet composed."

The first theme of movement one, which is the sonata-form movement, has got to be one of the most memorable in the entire repertoire. Chirping winds introduce a buoyant theme in the violins that Mendelssohn almost immediately begins to develop. Let's hear the theme and the modulating bridge that follows it.

[Musical example from Symphony No. 4 in A Major, Opus 90, "The Italian," Mendelssohn: I; Theme I to Modulating Bridge]

Theme 2, graceful and lyric, is initially heard in the clarinets and bassoons. After a series of wonderful theme 2-inspired episodes featuring the winds, theme 1 briefly returns and the exposition comes to its conclusion. Let's hear the remainder of the exposition beginning with the second theme.

[Musical example from Symphony No. 4 in A Major, Opus 90, "The Italian," Mendelssohn: I; Theme II to Conclusion of Exposition]

The second-movement andante is a quiet and melancholy march, inspired, perhaps, by the religious processionals Mendelssohn witnessed during his stay in Italy. We hear the opening theme first in the winds, accompanied by steady, pizzicato (or plucked) low strings.

[Musical example from Symphony No. 4 in A Major, Opus 90, "The Italian," Mendelssohn: II; Opening Theme]

The third movement is an absolutely gorgeous minuet, as lyric and lovely— and as "Italian"—a minuet as we'll ever hear.

[Musical example from Symphony No. 4 in A Major, Opus 90, "The Italian," Mendelssohn: III]

The last movement of Mendelssohn's Fourth is a bit of a rarity, a minor-mode finale for what otherwise is a major-mode symphony. It is also the most outwardly "Italian" of the four movements of the symphony, evoking as it does the peasant dance music of Southern Italy. Mendelssohn labeled the movement "*saltarello*," a *saltarello* being a fast, energized dance of Italian origin that features lots of hoping and leaping, the sort of ants-in-your-pants dance, sure to put a smile on everyone's face. Minor mode or not, my friends, this movement absolutely rocks. And like any good finale of the Classical Era, it leaves us with a big-time bounce in our steps.

[Musical example from Symphony No. 4 in A Major, Opus 90, "The Italian," Mendelssohn: IV; Opening]

Mendelssohn and Berlioz

Mendelssohn's unbelievable talent and his unbelievable intelligence, combined with his incredible musical training, his innate conservatism, and his privileged upbringing, invested him, well it invested him with an air of superiority and downright priggishness that many people found just a little hard to take. (That he was a converted Jew who married one of the most beautiful Christian women in all of Europe, a woman named Cecile Jeanrenaud, gave his detractors that much more reason to dislike him.) Hector Berlioz, whose own musical education was as spotty as Mendelssohn's was complete, found Mendelssohn prissy and arrogant. In reference to Mendelssohn's musical conservatism, Berlioz was quoted as having said that Mendelssohn was "rather too fond of the dead," although, to his great credit, Berlioz was crazy about the Italian symphony, which he called: "admirable, magnifique!"

Mendelssohn for his part found Berlioz the man rather affected, writing: "This purely external enthusiasm, this desperation in the presence of women, this assumption of GENIUS in capital letters, is intolerable to me."

As for Berlioz's music, in a letter to the pianist, Ignaz Moscheles, Mendelssohn wrote:

> I quite agree with you [as to his noisy orchestration and barbarous counterpoint]. His orchestration is so utterly slovenly and haphazard that one ought to wash one's hands after [handling] a score of his. I am sorry, for Berlioz is intelligent, cool and sensible in his judgments, and always thoughtful. But he does not see how much absurdity there is in his works.

Nevertheless, and it's a credit to both Berlioz and Mendelssohn, that as conductors they championed each other's music. In early 1843, having not seen each other for 12 years, Berlioz visited Mendelssohn in Leipzig where Mendelssohn was conducting the Gewandhaus Orchestra. At Berlioz's suggestion, the two exchanged conductor's batons as a symbol of their newfound friendship. Mendelssohn came out the total loser in the deal; he gave up a costly whalebone baton covered in leather and received in exchange a painted piece of wood that Berlioz referred to as a "heavy oaken staff." At the time of the trade, Berlioz was reading James Fenimore Cooper's *Leatherstocking Tales*. Inspired, he enclosed the following note with his "heavy oaken" baton:

To the Chief Mendelssohn! Great Chief! We have promised to exchange tomahawks. Mine is a rough one. Only squaws and pale-faces are fond of ornate weapons. Be my brother! And when the Great Spirit shall have sent us to hunt in the land of souls, may our warriors hang up their tomahawks together at the door of the council chamber!

Mendelssohn can only have shaken his head and looked at the ceiling, but he and Berlioz made their peace, and Berlioz later wrote in his memoirs: "Mendelssohn was a wonderful man in every respect. We exchanged our batons as a sign of friendship. He is truly a great master. [During my stay in Leipzig,] he helped me like a brother. His patience was inexhaustible."

Berlioz grieved long when Mendelssohn died of a stroke just four years later at the age of 38, but no one grieved harder or longer for Mendelssohn than his friend and colleague, the pianist and composer Robert Schumann.

Robert Schumann (1810-1856)

In June of 1848, seven months after Mendelssohn's death, the great and famous Franz Liszt paid a visit to the home of Robert and Clara Schumann. Clara went to great pains to arrange a dinner in Liszt's honor, inviting among others, Richard Wagner. The guest of honor, Maestro Liszt, well, he wandered in two hours late, just in time to hear a performance of Schumann's Piano Quintet, about which he proceeded to make a tactless remark, calling it "Leipzig-like," meaning provincial and over-intellectual. Schumann, a quiet, withdrawn man, overheard Liszt's comment, made himself a quadruple bourbon straight up, and said nothing.

After dinner, the group began discussing opera and the relative merits of the recently deceased Felix Mendelssohn and Giacomo Meyerbeer. Liszt, unaware of the very thin ice he'd been treading on since his tardy arrival and tactless remarks, praised Meyerbeer at Mendelssohn's expense. Well, Schumann went ballistic. A big, bear-like man, he grabbed Liszt by the shoulders and screamed in his face, "Who are you that you dare to speak in such a way about a musician like Mendelssohn?" Breathing fire, Schumann turned heel, stomped out of the room, slamming the door behind him. The room turned to ice. You could hear the proverbial pin drop. Liszt, without a doubt the single greatest musical showman of the 19th century, a man that put the cool in cucumber, gathered himself up, turned to Schumann's wife Clara, bowed his head with respect and said, "Madame, please tell your husband that he is the only man in the world from whom I would take so calmly the words just offered me."

Robert Schumann was a quintessential artist of his time, a Romantic-era composer who believed utterly that art was a vehicle for personal confession and self-revelation. Like Berlioz, Schumann believed that the future of music was tied to merging music with literature, and in doing so, creating a composite art form, the whole greater than the parts. Schumann's father, August, was an author, translator, and bookseller who passed on his passion for literature to his son. An avid reader, Schumann began writing poems around the age of 10, and throughout his teens, fancied himself a genuine poet.

Concurrent with the development of the "literary" Schumann was the development of the musical Schumann. At the age of seven, he began piano lessons, and within a year, at the age of eight, he had written his first compositions, a set of dances for the piano.

According to Schumann's boyhood friend, Emil Flechsig: "Schumann was absolutely convinced [as a teenager] that he would eventually become a famous man." Of course all that remained to be determined was what profession he would distinguish himself in, no small detail considering Schumann's early accomplishments as both a writer and a musician.

For an in-depth examination of the music, life, and times of Robert Schumann, I would direct your attention to my Teaching Company "Great Masters" biography. I will tell you by way of "highlights," or should we say "life-lights," that Schumann was sent at his mother's insistence to the University of Leipzig to study law. Well, he never went to a single class. Instead, he found a piano teacher by the name of Friedrich Wieck, who told both Robert and his mother that he, Wieck, would make Schumann one of the greatest pianists in Europe within three years. It didn't work out that way. Within a few months, Schumann was experiencing numbness in what was probably the ring finger of his right hand, a condition most likely caused by repetitive stress from practicing exercises at the piano for upwards of eight hours at a time. Within a couple of years, Schumann's injured finger was almost unusable. Schumann, who had been composing all the while, shifted his musical emphasis to composition and, between 1830 and 1840, produced a large number of really extraordinary and avant-garde compositions for solo piano.

At the same time, Schumann was falling in love with his former piano teacher's daughter, the young and beautiful piano prodigy, Clara Wieck. In November of 1835, Robert, then 25 years old and Clara, 16 years old, shared their first kiss. Within a month, they had pledged themselves to each other and thus began a five-year battle to convince Clara's father, Friedrich, to allow them to be married. In the meantime, Clara began to perform Schumann's music publicly even though it confused her and her audiences. Clara's reaction to Schumann's *Kreisleriana* for solo piano is a case in point. She wrote him, "Robert, sometimes your music actually frightens me, and I wonder: is it really true that the creator of such things is going to be my husband?"

Clara's ambitions for Schumann only grew once they were married in September of 1841. She wrote him, "Dear Robert, don't take it amiss if I tell you that I've been seized by the desire to encourage you to write for orchestra. Your imagination and your spirit are too great for the piano."

Aside from his own compositional ambitions, it was Schumann's marriage to Clara and her overwhelming confidence in him that gave him the push he needed to write his first mature symphony. That, and the incredibly stimulating environment in which the Schumanns were living at the time: Leipzig, one of the major music centers in Germany. And at the center of the city's musical life stood Felix Mendelssohn, the conductor of Leipzig's Gewandhaus Orchestra.

Under Mendelssohn's baton, the Gewandhaus became a musical shrine at which the faithful, and that includes Robert and Clara Schumann, gathered to hear the masterpieces of the past—Beethoven, Schubert, and Bach. Schumann was awed by Mendelssohn's intellect and musical talents, going so far as to call Mendelssohn "the Mozart of the nineteenth century." Without a doubt it was Felix Mendelssohn and the Gewandhaus Orchestra, along with Clara's insistence that he think big and write a symphony, that gave Robert Schumann the nerve and the impetus to compose his first complete "symphony" in 1841.

Symphony no. 1 in Bb Major, op. 38, the "Spring" Symphony

When Schumann sat down to write a symphony in 1841, he was faced with the question of how to build on the model of Beethoven's symphonies and still be original. For Schumann, the answer lay in writing a piece that walked the fine line between absolute and program music, between Classical-era inspired structural integrity and Romantic-era inspired storytelling. Schumann sketched his Symphony no. 1 in just four sleepless days and nights, between January 23 and 26, 1841. Schumann called the symphony "Spring," explaining that it was inspired by a poem of the same name by Adolph Bottger. The horn and trumpet fanfare at the beginning of the symphony is a wordless setting of the last lines of Bottger's poem. In English, those lines go like this:

> O turn from this, your present course,
> Springtime blossoms in the valley!

In German:

> *O wende, wende deinen Lauf,*
> *Im Tale blüht der Fruhling auf!*

[Musical example from Symphony No. 1 in Bb Major, Opus 38, "The Spring Symphony," Schumann: I; Opening]

The slow, solemn introduction that follows this opening fanfare leads to a brilliant exposition, consisting of an energized and propulsive first theme, followed by a delicate, lyric, woodwind-dominated second theme. Let's hear the exposition as it follows the slow introduction.

[Musical example from Symphony No. 1 in Bb Major, Opus 38, "The Spring Symphony," Schumann: I]

This is fabulous music. Relative to Schumann's earlier works, it is also very conservative music in that its programmatic content is much less important than his use of the traditional, Classical-era musical forms, sonata form most notably, forms he had never used before composing the Spring Symphony.

The symphony was premiered under the baton of Felix Mendelssohn of the Gewandhaus on March 31, 1841. Clara, four months pregnant with their first child, also performed. She played the first two movements of Chopin's Piano Concerto in F Minor, a piano duet with Mendelssohn, and a few solo piano pieces by Domenico Scarlatti, Sigmund Thalberg, and yes, Robert Schumann. It must have been quite a concert.

Certainly the audience and critics thought so. The concert was a smash and the premiere of his First Symphony provided Schumann with the first of his very few unadulterated triumphs that he would experience during his career. His last such triumph was also a symphony: his third and most famous symphony, the "Rhine" Symphony, or simply, the "Rhenish."

Symphony no. 3 in Eb Major, op. 97 (1850)

On March 31, 1850, Schumann formally accepted an offer to become the music director for the city of Düsseldorf. When he arrived on September 2,

1850 to take the job, both he and Clara were welcomed like conquering heroes. We could only hope that they enjoyed it while they could, because as it turned out, Schumann was not the equal to the conducting duties he had taken on and within 3 years he was forced to resign his position. But a far worse fate awaited him just a short time later. Plagued by a bipolar order his entire life, Schumann ultimately went mad while living there in Düsseldorf, the victim of tertiary syphilis. He was hospitalized after he tried to commit suicide by throwing himself into the Rhine River in February 1854, and he died in an asylum outside of Bonn two-and-one-half years later on July 29, 1856.

The Rhine, yes, the Rhine. Schumann had never spent any appreciable time in the Rhineland before his move to Düsseldorf in 1850. Well, the Rhine River and its surrounding landscape captivated him. Schumann's third and last symphony, his Rhine Symphony, reflects his fascination with the Rhenish landscape and its history, as well as the optimism he felt during those first heady moments in Düsseldorf, when the symphony was composed. (For our information, the work we know today as Schumann's Symphony no. 4, was actually composed back in 1841 and only revised in 1851. Schumann's Third, the Rhenish, is indeed his "last" symphony.)

The first movement begins with one of Schumann's greatest themes; its breadth and magnificence are meant to invoke the grandeur of the Rhine River itself.

[Musical example from Symphony No. 3 in Eb Major, Opus 97, "The Rhenish," Schumann: I]

The second-movement scherzo is an engaging rough-hewn *Ländler*, which means a rustic German three-step, a movement that Schumann had originally entitled, "Morning on the Rhine." Like the first movement, this second movement invokes the majestic sweep of the Rhine River.

[Musical example from Symphony No. 3 in Eb Major, Opus 97, "The Rhenish," Schumann: II]

The third movement is a charming, delicately scored intermezzo.

[Musical example from Symphony No. 3 in Eb Major, Opus 97, "The Rhenish," Schumann: III]

On September 30, 1850, four weeks after they had arrived in Düsseldorf, Robert and Clara took the 30-mile trip on the brand new railway line to Cologne, where they visited the Cathedral of Cologne, the largest

Gothic building in northern Europe. Schumann was absolutely floored by the cathedral and the majestic ritual he witnessed there. Taken together, the cathedral and its Catholic ritual were the inspiration for the fourth movement of the Rhenish Symphony. Schumann indicated that the movement be played "in the character of an accompaniment to a solemn processional."

Only now in this fourth movement do the trombones begin to play, heightening and intensifying, considerably, the majesty and the dignity of the music. (My friends, the same thing happens in Beethoven's Fifth Symphony, where the trombonists have to cool their collective heels through the first three movements, only to enter, finally, in the fourth movement. Asking trombonists to sit still and behave is difficult under the best of circumstances. Asking them to sit still and behave for three entire movements with nothing to amuse them but their spit valves and the exposed necks of the oboe players in front of them is well nigh impossible. Best to keep them leashed and caged until the last possible moment.)

We hear the opening minutes of the magnificent fourth movement of Schumann's Third Symphony.

[Musical example from Symphony No. 3 in Eb Major, Opus 97, "The Rhenish," Schumann: IV]

Two contemporary reviews of this really wonderful work are worth quoting. A reviewer known only as "J. C. H.," writing in February of 1851, called this fourth movement "a halo floating over the whole symphony." And Theodore Uhlig, writing in the *Neue Zeitschrift für Musik* in March 1852, opined that this fourth movement Schumann had "entered the delicate sphere of aesthetic speculation."

The fifth movement is a dancing and sweeping return to the sunshine and bustle of life on and by the River Rhine.

[Musical example from Symphony No. 3 in Eb Major, Opus 97, "The Rhenish," Schumann: V]

Felix Mendelssohn and Robert Schumann, composers whose symphonies reflect Classical tradition, Beethoven's contributions, and a personal, even innovative voice, a formula for 19th-century symphonic success, provided you've got the right stuff.

When we return we will journey back to France, Camille Saint-Saens, César Franck and the symphony in France. Thank you.

Lecture Thirteen
Franck, Saint-Saens, and the Symphony in France

Scope: The genre of symphony fell out of favor in France after the Revolution, but it was revitalized in the 1860s–1870s with the work of César Franck and Camille Saint-Saens. Franck wrote only one symphony, one that stands as a shining example of the balance between Classical structure and Romantic expression that we spoke about in the last lecture. Saint-Saens was a prodigy for whom music came easily. His work illustrates the 19th-century tendency toward cyclic themes, which offered some structure to symphonies that no longer adhered to Classical-era forms.

Outline

I. For some, the fact that this course does not deal with a single Italian composer of symphonies after Boccherini, who died in 1805, might be perceived as a flaw. But during the 19th century, the musical genius of the Italian nation was devoted almost entirely to opera. The same statement can almost be made of France.

   A. We could point to a number of mid-19th–century French symphonic works as evidence of the genre's continued life and viability in France, including Charles Gounod's two symphonies of 1855, Georges Bizet's Symphony in C of 1855, and other works by some little known composers. For the most part, however, these symphonies existed on the periphery of French musical culture.

   B. According to musicologist Ralph P. Locke, France had been "the land of symphonies" in the late 18th century, but with the Revolution and the decline of the aristocracy, this genre fell from popularity. Periodic revivals of the symphony as a genre took place, for example, with the founding of the Societe des Concerts du Conservatoire by François-Antoine Habeneck. But with the exception of Berlioz's *Symphonie fantastique*, Habeneck made almost no effort to promote and perform contemporary French symphonies.

   C. Thus, the symphony languished in France until the 1860s and 1870s, when a group of French composers reestablished a tradition of orchestral music in Paris. The leaders of this "new school" of

French music were César Franck (1822–1890) and Camille Saint-Saens (1835–1921).

D. We must also mention Jules Etienne Pasdeloup (1819–1887), the conductor who was responsible for the renaissance of French orchestral music in the late 19th century. In 1871, he founded the National Society of Music, an orchestra that performed the works of Berlioz and German Classical- and Romantic-era composers, and provided an outlet for contemporary French composers, as well.

E. Before we begin with the life and "symphony" of César Franck, let us first trace the musical-genetic line from Berlioz to Franck and, after him, Camille Saint-Saens.

    1. As you recall, Berlioz revolutionized even Beethoven's revolutionary model, taking program music and Romantic-era self-expression to a new level. Among his few imitators was the influential Hungarian-born pianist and composer Franz Liszt.

    2. Liszt, who lived a substantial portion of his life in Paris, wrote two program symphonies, *Faust* and *Dante*. Liszt's *Faust Symphony*, based on Goethe's telling of the Faust legend, is by far, the more successful of the two. It was Berlioz who introduced Liszt to Goethe's *Faust*, and Liszt dedicated the symphony to Berlioz. Through the influence of Franz Liszt and Liszt's protégé, Richard Wagner, Berlioz's symphonic legacy was finally felt in France, two generations after the composition of the *Symphonie fantastique*.

    3. The two most important, lasting, and influential symphonies written during France's late 19th-century symphonic renaissance were César Franck's Symphony in D Minor of 1888 and Camille Saint-Saens's Symphony no. 3 in C Minor, op. 78, the so-called "Organ" Symphony, of 1885. Both Franck's Symphony and Saint-Saens's Third owe a lasting debt to Berlioz's *Symphonie fantastique*.

II. César Franck (1822–1890) completed his only symphony, the Symphony in D Minor, in 1888, when he was 66 years old, 19 years after Berlioz's death and just 2 years before his own. His symphony was the culmination of his life as a musician and the capstone of a strange, circuitous career.

A. Franck's life was a struggle from the beginning. He was a musically precocious child whose childhood was dominated by his father's ruthless ambition. He was enrolled at the Liege Conservatory at the age of 7; he began performing publicly as a pianist at the age of 12; and later that same year, in 1835, he was taken to Paris to take his place among the greats.

B. He entered the Conservatory in 1837, where he won first prize in both piano (1838) and counterpoint (1840). Later, César's father, Nicholas-Joseph Franck, decided that his son wasn't receiving a proper education or his due as a student from the pedants at the Conservatory. In 1842, Nicholas-Joseph withdrew his 19-year-old son from the Conservatory, with the intention of turning him into a touring keyboard virtuoso, a plan that didn't work out.

C. Despite some early successes, by 1844, when he was 21, César's career as a performer was already in a tailspin. He had neither the heart nor the physical constitution to be a touring performer. The pressure, the traveling, the tyranny of his father, and his growing rage at not having a life of his own all took their toll. César became ill and made what turned out to be his last public appearance on January 1, 1846. Later that month, he walked out of his parents' Paris home and never returned.

D. Franck earned his living as a teacher at public and religious schools and by playing the organ at churches in and around Paris. He composed as well, mainly music for organ and for the religious celebrations at the churches where he played. Slowly, Franck began to be recognized, partly as a result of his music but mostly because many of his students grew up to become important players in the French musical scene.

E. In 1871, the now 48-year-old Franck finally got his break: A group of former students brought him to the attention of a man named Alexis de Castillon, who would become the first secretary of the National Society of Music. The society performed a number of Franck's works in Paris, which led, almost immediately, to Franck being offered the job of professor of organ at the Paris Conservatory.

F. Franck assumed his post at the Paris Conservatory in September of 1873, at the age of 50, and began his second career, the one for which he is known; he embarked on a creative phase that would continue until the end of his life 17 years later.

G. Franck's compositional style is an eclectic mix of influences: the musical forms of the Classical era; the complex counterpoint of Baroque-era organ music; a predisposition toward rich, often thick instrumental textures (undoubtedly an outgrowth of his experience as an organist); and his natural emotional/expressive leanings as a Romantic artist.

    1. We know a good deal about Franck's priorities because he communicated them constantly to his students, and his students communicated them to the world.

    2. Franck believed that the best music combined the compositional genres of the Classical era with the concision and expressive power of Beethoven and the harmonic language of late Romanticism. Such a musical balance is, as we discussed in Lecture Twelve, a difficult one to achieve. Nevertheless, this was Franck's artistic ideal, and it is well demonstrated in his Symphony in D Minor.

III. The large-scale storyline of the symphony, that is, "conquering adversity" or "victory through struggle," is a familiar one; we hear it in Beethoven's Fifth and Ninth and Brahms's First, as well.

A. As in Beethoven's Fifth and Ninth, Franck's symphony opens in a dark, minor key and aspires, ultimately, to an apotheosis in major. Unlike Beethoven's Fifth and Ninth, however, which begin in minor and only convincingly arrive in major during the last movement, each of the three movements of Franck's Symphony progresses from minor to major.

B. The first movement starts in D minor and ends in D major; the second movement starts in Bb minor and ends in Bb major; and the third movement starts in D major, goes to D minor, then concludes, triumphantly, in D major. We will base our listening on these "cathartic" changes of mode and the ongoing musical struggle they represent.

C. The first-movement sonata form opens with a brooding theme 1 in D minor, heard first in the low strings, then in the violins. (**Musical selection**: Franck, Symphony in D Minor, movement 1, theme 1.)

D. A lengthy transitional passage follows, which is then followed by an explosive, violent, and faster version of theme 1. Then, another slow, lengthy transitional passage is heard, followed by yet another explosive and violent version of theme 1.

E. Clearly, Franck is attempting to cast a dark, tragic pall over the symphony from the beginning, the better to magnify the impact of the catharsis to come. However, the repetitive, almost obsessive use of the same material for the opening six minutes of the movement has suggested to some critics an almost Wagnerian disregard for "real time" at best and a lack of imagination on Franck's part at worst.

F. Whether or not we accept that criticism, it does take a long time for Franck to get to theme 2. When the F-major theme finally arrives, it is lush and lyrical. (**Musical selection**: Franck, Symphony in D Minor, movement 1, theme 2, part 1.)

G. The moment we have all been waiting for comes in the second half of theme 2, the so-called "faith motive," triumphantly played by violins, woodwinds, and trumpets. (**Musical selection**: Franck, Symphony in D Minor, movement 1, theme 2, part 2.)

    1. Franck's student, the composer Vincent d'Indy, dubbed this marvelous bit of melody the "faith motive," and it is, indeed, the most memorable thematic element in the symphony. An extended version of the faith motive is heard in the recapitulation. (**Musical selection**: Franck, Symphony in D Minor, movement 1, recapitulation, theme 2, part 2, "faith motive.")

    2. This "faith motive" "inspires" the movement to fight against the repetitive darkness of theme 1 and D minor; Franck concludes the movement by placing a powerful reprise of theme 1 in D minor back-to-back with a series of blaring D-major chords.

    3. This conclusion is ambiguous; we know only that the struggle between minor and major, between darkness and light, has not yet been won by either major or minor and that it will continue in the subsequent movements. We hear the conclusion of the first movement. (**Musical selection**: Franck, Symphony in D Minor, movement 1, conclusion.)

H. The second movement, the gem of the symphony, begins with quiet, pizzicato strings in Bb minor. (**Musical selection**: Franck, Symphony in D Minor, movement 2, opening.) It ends with rich, organ-like sonorities in Bb major. (**Musical selection**: Franck, Symphony in D Minor, movement 2, conclusion.)

I. The third and final movement reflects the symphony's cyclic nature, meaning that themes from earlier movements now return to be heard again.

    1. Of this last movement, Franck wrote: ""The finale, just as in Beethoven's Ninth, recalls all the themes, but in my work, they do not make their appearance as mere quotations. I have adopted another plan, and made each of them play an entirely new part in the music" (Chesky, Annette and Jeffrey, *Franck—Symphonic Music of César Franck*. Program Note. Chesky CD CD87, 1993.)

    2. During the last minute of the finale, the faith motive returns, and as it is repeated, it morphs, note by note, into the main theme of this third movement. That's what Franck meant when he said that he doesn't merely quote his earlier themes; rather, he uses them developmentally, to great effect. Let's hear this last triumphant minute of the symphony. (**Musical selection**: Franck, Symphony in D Minor, movement 3, conclusion.)

J. Over the years, some critics have voiced the opinion that Franck's Symphony in D Minor is "emotionally strong but structurally weak." I would suggest that if there are structural weaknesses in Franck's symphony, they are perceived as such only if we judge the piece against the Classical-era template. Judged against Berlioz's *Symphonie fantastique*, the symphonies of Liszt, and the music dramas of Wagner, we realize that Franck's treatment of sonata form is not flawed but entirely of its time.

IV. Born in Paris, Camille Saint-Saens (1835–1921) composed his first music a few days after his third birthday and made his formal concert debut at the age of 10 with a program that included piano concerti by Beethoven and Mozart. He entered the Paris Conservatory in 1848 and created a sensation.

    A. Like Felix Mendelssohn, Saint-Saens's intellectual gifts were equal to his musical gifts. Like Mendelssohn, Saint-Saens's fluency has been held against him, the logic being that music came so easy for him that he rarely felt the need to indulge in self-criticism. Like Mendelssohn, Saint-Saens has been accused of writing music that is too polished and too technically perfect. However, his intellect and virtuosity also won him patrons, friends, and admirers, including such musicians as Charles Gounod, Gioacchino Rossini, Hector Berlioz, and Franz Liszt.

B. As an adult, Saint-Saens championed the music of Richard Wagner, Franz Liszt (to whom he dedicated his Third Symphony), and Robert Schumann. He was also famous for his performances of J. S. Bach, Mozart, and Handel and helped to reestablish all three composers in the Parisian musical mainstream.

C. We turn to Saint-Saens's Symphony no. 3, the "Organ" Symphony, so-called because of its organ part.

    1. Much has been made of the fact that Saint-Saens's Symphony no. 3 is written in two movements, but this is a classic red herring. In reality, each of the movements is two-movements-in-one; the first movement is an allegro plus an adagio, played without a pause, and the so-called "second movement" is a scherzo plus a *maestoso*, again, played without a pause. In reality, then, Saint-Saens's Third is a four-movement symphony, with only one break, between the second and third movements.

    2. Like Franck's Symphony in D Minor, Saint-Saens's Third is a "catharsis" or "struggle" symphony, in that it achieves the triumph of the fourth movement only after the rigors of the earlier movements, dominated, as they are, by the minor mode.

    3. The principal theme of the first movement is a quivering tune that clearly recalls the opening of the first movement of Schubert's Unfinished Symphony in B Minor. (**Musical selection**: Saint-Saens, Symphony no. 3 in C Minor, op. 78 [Organ].)

    4. The second movement (or the second half of the first movement) is a lush and gorgeous meditation that opens with the organ and strings. (**Musical selection**: Saint-Saens, Symphony no. 3 in C Minor, op. 78 [Organ].)

    5. The third movement (or the beginning of the second "half" of the symphony) is a rousing scherzo; we hear its opening moments. (**Musical selection**: Saint-Saens, Symphony no. 3 in C Minor, op. 78 [Organ].)

   6. This music winds down to a gentle conclusion, which acts as a perfect setup for the majestic, rippling, triumphal C-major opening of the fourth movement (or the second half of the second movement). (**Musical selection**: Saint-Saens, Symphony no. 3 in C Minor, op. 78 [Organ].)

D. Like so many 19th-century instrumental compositions, Saint-Saens's Third is a cyclic work; that is, themes from earlier movements "cycle back" into later movements.

   1. We first noted this in Beethoven's Fifth Symphony, where the blaring, C-minor theme of the third movement makes its ghostly return in the fourth movement. Berlioz's *Symphonie fantastique* is also a cyclic work, because the *idée fixe*—the tune that represents "her"—is heard, in some guise or another, in each movement.

   2. Cyclic organization ensured a measure of large-scale coherence and development, from movement to movement, in a Romantic era that could no longer count on the rituals of the Classical era to provide coherence on their own. We have not pointed out the cyclic elements in Saint-Saens's Third, but if you listen carefully, you will notice a number of connections between the earlier movements and the last.

Lecture Thirteen—Transcript
Franck, Saint-Saens, and the Symphony in France

Welcome back to *The Symphony*. This is Lecture Thirteen entitled "Franck, Saint-Saens, and the Symphony in France." We return to France, that great and vibrant nation that gave Western civilization a measure of culture and the *"je ne sais quoi"* it could never have achieved without her. It has been said that Italy gave us the Renaissance and France just about everything else, a statement that Guiseppe Verdi, for one—arch-Italian nationalist that he was—would have agreed with entirely. Verdi watched with horror the progress of the war between France and Prussia in 1870. In a letter written on September 30, 1870, immediately after the French defeat at Sedan, Verdi said that it was hard for him to adequately describe "the desolation in my heart over France. France has given liberty and civilization to the modern world. Let us not deceive ourselves. If she falls, our civilization will fall."

There's a message here, an important one, and I know you'll forgive me a rare bit of non-musical sermonizing. Like Verdi, I would respectfully suggest that we all keep in mind that much of the best of what we are today, as a civilization, we owe, and will always owe, to France. Many Americans remember the year 1917 as the year the United States entered the First World War and "bailed the French out." In the process, those individuals forget that for three years, in defending Western Europe, the French and the British had been bled dry, fighting off an enemy—Germany—that had over twice the population of France. That war claimed the lives of more than 1,721,000 French combatants, roughly the same number as all the wars ever fought by the United States—from the Revolution through the Gulf—combined, times three. Many Americans recall the year 1944 as the year that the United States (and the British, and the Canadians, and the Australians, New Zealanders, Free French, Free Polish and so forth) invaded Europe and liberated France. In the process, they forget that in 1781 it was a French fleet under the command of Admiral de Grasse, that blockaded the Chesapeake Bay, defeated the British naval forces under Admiral Graves, and thus allowed a Franco-American army under the joint command of General George Washington and Marshall Vimeur, Count of Rochambeau, to defeat Cornwallis at Yorktown a month later, and in doing so, end the Revolutionary War. 1944, 1781—hey, I'd say we were even.

Meanwhile, the French have created a civilization—a standard of food and drink, urban design, fashion, a standard for life—that is still the envy of the planet. They have created a capital city—Paris—that is by whatever standard you choose to measure cities, without equal. Let's face it, without France and Italy, we in the West would still be barbarians. The English writer Charles Morgan wrote, "France is an idea necessary for civilization." And if the French still feel that they've some right to assert their national will in a global community that they, as much as any other single nation, helped to civilize, well, that's their right as well. *Vive la France*!

Opera in France and Italy

To some, the fact that this course does not deal with a single Italian composer of symphonies after Boccherini (who, after all, died way back in 1805), might be perceived as a flaw. To those who feel that way, I would say, "Show us the symphonies!" During the 19th century, the musical genius of the Italian nation was devoted almost entirely to opera, and the same statement can almost be made of France. Paul Henry Lang writes in his *Music in Western Civilization*:

> In the [middle] of the 19th century the musical despot in France was the opera, the *genre national* so auspiciously launched by Meyerbeer. "*Musique*" was synonymous with the lyric stage, and no one paid serious attention to anything else. The century saw the ascent of the middle class. This middle class became accustomed to well-being and luxury, and exercised the right of a ruling class; it demanded [of its operas] caressing melodies, pleasant stories and plots which would help to obliviate the worries of daily existence.

Now I suppose that one could argue that these words are far too black and white. In support of that argument one could point to a number of mid-19th-century French symphonic works as evidence of the genre's continued life and viability in France. Like Charles Gounod's two symphonies of 1855, George Bizet's Symphony in C of 1855, and other works by such non-household name composers as Adolphe Blanc, Theodore Gouvy, Louis Wely, Henri Reber, Scipion Rousselot, and Celestien Tingry. But with the exception of the Gounod and Bizet symphonies, these are obscure works by forgotten composers, composers who had to copy their own parts by hand, rent their own halls, hire their own performers, pay for and place their own ads in the newspapers, and, often as not, conduct their own premieres and hope to God that they didn't lose their frock coats in the bargain, which they usually did.

This music, these symphonies, only existed on the far periphery of French musical culture. Taken together they were a musical Oort cloud—

that spherical cloud of objects that surrounds the solar system beyond the orbit of Pluto—music that existed so far outside the French musical mainstream as to be essentially invisible to the naked eye (or ear, as the case may be). And to think France, of all places, according to musicologist Ralph P. Locke:

> In the late eighteenth century, France had been the land of symphonies, such as the symphonies of Francois Gossec, as well as works by Haydn and the Mannheim composers, which could be heard at several concert series and were put on sale by the many prominent musical publishers of Paris. The Revolution of 1789 put the breaks on much of this activity, which had been patronized to a large extent by the aristocracy.

Periodic revivals of the symphony as a genre did take place, for example, with the founding of the Societie des Concerts du Conservatoire by François-Antoine Habeneck, the orchestra and conductor that introduced Beethoven's symphonies to Paris and premiered Berlioz's *Symphonie fantastique* in 1830. But excepting Berlioz's *fantastique*, Habeneck made almost no effort to promote and perform contemporary French symphonies. And so, the symphony languished in France until the 1860s and 1870s, when a group of French composers reestablished a tradition of orchestral music in Paris. The leaders of this "new school" of French music were César Franck and Camille Saint-Saens. (Before the Belgians among us have a oiseaux, please, upfront: César Franck was born to a German mother and a Belgian father in the city of Liège, which is today part of Belgian, but was, at the time of Franck's birth, controlled by France. French was his native language; he was educated in Paris, he taught in France, he achieved his lasting fame in Paris and became a naturalized French citizen in 1873. César Franck was, de facto, a French composer. Sorry, Belgium.)

Another name must be mentioned here, and once again, it is a testament to the fact that without enlightened orchestral conductors and good orchestras, symphonic music cannot happen. The name is Jules Etienne Pasdeloup, 1819 to 1887. Pasdeloup was the conductor who was responsible for the renaissance of French orchestral music in the late 19th century. In 1871, he founded the National Society of Music, an orchestra that performed the works of Berlioz and German Classical- and Romantic-era composers, and provided, finally, an outlet for contemporary French composers as well— like Serge Koussevitsky, Paul Sacher, and Leonard Bernstein are the 20th century. Pasdeloup was an essential patron for an entire generation of composers. César Franck is a perfect example of Pasdeloup's benevolence. After laboring in obscurity for 50 years, a series of performances by Pasdeloup's National Society of Music vaulted Franck into national prominence. He was subsequently hired to teach at the Paris Conservatory and his creativity took off like a sugar fiend after a Twinkie.

Before we jump into the life and "symphony" (singular) of César Franck, let us first trace the musical-genetic line that gets us from Berlioz to Franck and, after him, Camille Saint-Saens. By way of review, we read from Nicholas Temperley's article on "Symphony" in the *New Grove Dictionary of Music and Musicians*:

> Alone among composers of his generation in any country, Berlioz accepted Beethoven's symphonies, not as incredible demonstrations of musical power which none could equal, but as models for immediate imitation and further development. He set at once to work to build a symphony that would stand on the shoulders of Beethoven's. Beethoven in his Sixth Symphony had written a programme; Berlioz wrote a more explicit one, embodying the wild and most sensational Romantic ideas of the day, as well as much of his personal emotional experience. Berlioz's model attracted few imitators.

Yes, but among those imitators was the unbelievably influential Hungarian-born virtuoso-turned-composer Franz Liszt. Liszt, who lived a substantial part of his life in Paris wrote two symphonies, both of them program symphonies, titled *Faust* and *Dante*. Liszt's *Faust Symphony*, based on Goethe's telling of the Faust legend, is by far, the more successful of his two symphonies. It was Berlioz himself who introduced Liszt to Goethe's *Faust*, and it was to Berlioz that Liszt dedicated his *Faust Symphony*. Through the influence of Franz Liszt and Liszt's own protégé, Richard Wagner, Berlioz's symphonic legacy was finally felt in France, two generations after the composition of the *Symphonie fantastique*. We will observe the same phenomenon when we discuss the symphonies of Charles Ives, symphonies that remained shrouded in obscurity for two generations before they were discovered and their influence was finally felt.

The two most important, most lasting, and most influential symphonies written during France's late 19th-century symphonic renaissance were César Franck's Symphony in D Minor of 1888 and Camille Saint-Saens's Symphony no. 3 in C Minor, op. 78, the so-called "Organ" Symphony of

1885. Both Franck's Symphony and Saint-Saen's Third owe a lasting debt to Berlioz's *Symphonie fantastique.*

César Auguste Jean Guillaume Hubert Franck (1822-1890).

César Franck was born in 1822, four years before Hector Berlioz was admitted to the Paris Conservatory. He completed his one and only symphony, the Symphony in D Minor, in 1888, when he was 66 years old, 19 years after Berlioz's death and just two years before his own. His symphony was the culmination of his life as a musician and the capstone of a strange, circuitous career that almost didn't happen.

Franck's life was a struggle from the very beginning. He was a musically precocious child who was exploited from the start by his father. Franck's childhood was not marred by the violence that we see in Beethoven's early life, nor the incessant touring and illness that we see in Mozart's. Nevertheless, it was dominated by his father's ruthless ambition. He was enrolled in the Liege Conservatory at the age of 7. He began performing publicly as a pianist at the age of 12; and later that same year, 1835, he was taken to Paris, there to take his place among the greats. He entered the Conservatory in 1837, where he won the first prize in both piano (1838) and counterpoint (1840). And then, well then everything began to fall apart. His father, Nicholas-Joseph Franck, decided that César wasn't receiving a proper education or his due as a student from the pedants in the Conservatory, the evidence being the mere second prize César received in organ in 1841. In 1842, Nicholas-Joseph withdrew his 19-year-old son from the Conservatory with the intention of turning him into a touring keyboard virtuoso. It didn't work out that way.

Despite some early successes, by 1844, at the age of 21, César's career as a performer was already in a tailspin. He had neither the heart, nor the physical constitution to be a touring performer. The pressure, the travel, the tyranny of his father, his growing rage, not having a life of his own—well, that all took their toll. César got very sick and made what turned out to be his last public appearance on January 1, 1846. It was later that month that finally, at 23 years of age, he mustered the nerve to tell his parents "where to put all of it" and he walked out of their Paris home, never to return.

So began Franck's long journey, the "years in between." He earned his living as a teacher at public and religious schools, and by playing the organ at churches in and around Paris. He composed as well, much of the music being for organ and for the religious celebrations at the churches where he played. With glacial slowness, Franck began to be recognized partly as a result of his music, but mostly because so many of his students, who adored their teacher, grew up to become important players of the French musical scene.

In 1871, the now 48-year-old Franck finally caught his break. A group of former students brought him to the attention of a man named Alexis de Castillon, someone who was to become the first secretary of the National Society of Music. The Society performed a number of Franck's works in Paris, which led almost immediately to Franck being offered the job of professor of organ at the Paris Conservatory. In one of those ironic twists of fate, the person he was to replace at the Conservatory, Francois Benoist, was the same man who had awarded him the second prize in organ back in 1841, the second prize that had so enraged Franck's father and led to his departure from the Conservatory. Franck assumed his post at the Paris Conservatory in September of 1873, at the age of 50, and so began his second career, the one for which he is known. He embarked on a creative jag which was to continue until the end of his life, 17 years later.

Franck's compositional style is made up of an eclectic mix of influences: the musical forms of the Classical era; the complex counterpoint of the Baroque-era organ music; a predisposition towards rich, often thick instrumental textures (undoubtedly an outgrowth of his experience as an organist); and his natural emotional/expressive leanings as a Romantic-era artist.

We know a lot about Franck's priorities because he communicated them constantly to his students, and his students communicated them to the world. Franck believed that the best music was one that combined the compositional genres of the Classical era with the precision and expressive power of Beethoven and the harmonic language of late Romanticism. Now, such a musical balance is, as we discussed, a difficult one to achieve. Nevertheless, this is Franck's artistic ideal, and it is well demonstrated in his Symphony in D Minor.

The large-scale storyline of the symphony—"conquering adversary" or "victory through struggle"—is a familiar one: We hear it in Beethoven's Fifth and Ninth, for example. Though, given his own life experience, Franck had every right to compose such a symphony, as well. As in Beethoven's Fifth and Ninth, Franck's Symphony is "about" starting in a dark, minor key and aspiring, ultimately, to an apotheosis in major. Unlike Beethoven's Fifth and Ninth, which begin in minor and only convincingly arrive in major during the last movements of the symphonies, each of the three movements of Franck's symphony progresses from minor to major. The first movement starts in D minor and ends in D major; the second movement starts in Bb minor and ends in Bb major; and the third movement starts in D major, goes to D minor, and then concludes triumphantly in D major. We will do our listening based on these "cathartic" changes of mode and the ongoing musical struggle that they represent.

The first-movement sonata form opens with a brooding theme 1 in D minor, heard first in the low strings and then in the violins.

[Musical example from Symphony in D Minor, Franck: I; Opening]

A lengthy transitional passage follows, which is then followed by an explosive, violent, and faster version of theme 1. Then, another slow, lengthy transitional passage is heard, followed by yet another explosive and violent version of theme 1. Clearly, Franck is attempting, quite successfully we would suggest, to cast a dark, tragic pall over the symphony from the get-go, the better to magnify the impact of the catharsis to come. However, the repetitive, almost excessive use of the same material, over and over again, for the opening six minutes of the movement has suggested to some critics an almost Wagnerian disregard for "real time" at best and a lack of imagination on Franck's part at worst. Charles Gounod was quoting as having said a apropos of Franck's symphony that it was: "The affirmation of incompetence pushed to dogmatic limits!"

Well, we might suggest that this is less a valid criticism and more an example of the sort of thing one living composer says about another. Nevertheless, it does take a long time for Franck to get to theme 2, and by the time he does, the opening six minutes of his movement have made us close to suicidal. The opening of the long awaited theme 2 is lush, lyric, and in F major.

[Musical example from Symphony in D Minor, Franck: I; Theme II, Part I]

And now my friends, the moment we have been waiting for, the second half of theme 2, the so-called "faith motive," triumphantly played by the violins, woodwinds, and trumpets.

[Musical example from Symphony in D Minor, Franck: I; Theme II, Part II]

It was Franck's student, the composer Vincent d'Indy who dubbed this marvelous bit of melody the "faith motive," and it is, indeed, the most memorable thematic element in the symphony. It is also typical of Franck's best melodies, observes John Manduell, "One of Franck's [favorite melodic devices] is the way his themes rock to and fro on a central note from which the tune never moves very far. A Franck melody seldom contains any wide [leaps]; it essentially uncoils." An extended version of the faith motive is heard in the recapitulation.

[Musical example from Symphony in D Minor, Franck: I; Recapitulation]

This "faith motive" does indeed "inspire" the movement to fight the good fight against the repetitive darkness of theme 1 in D minor. Franck concludes the movement by placing back-to-back a powerful reprise of theme 1 in D minor, followed by a series of blaring D-major chords, an ambiguous conclusion to be sure. One that suggests and assures us that this struggle between minor and major, between darkness and light, has not yet been won by either major or minor, and that the struggle will continue in the subsequent movements. We hear the conclusion of the first movement.

[Musical example from Symphony in D Minor, Franck: I; Conclusion]

The second movement, the gem of the symphony in my humble opinion, begins with quiet, pizzicato strings in Bb minor.

[Musical example from Symphony in D Minor, Franck: II; Opening]

This second movement ends with rich organ-like sonorities in Bb major.

[Musical example from Symphony in D Minor, Franck: II; Conclusion]

The third and final movement reflects the symphony's "cyclic" nature, meaning that themes from earlier movements now return to be heard again. Of the "cyclical" nature of the last movement, Franck himself wrote, "The finale, just as in Beethoven's Ninth, recalls all the themes, but in my work, they do not make their appearances mere quotations. I have adopted another plan, and made each of them play an entirely new part in the music. It seems to me successful."

During the last minute of the finale, the faith motive returns, and as it is repeated, it morphs note by note into the main theme of this third movement. That's what Franck meant when he said that he doesn't merely quote his earlier themes; rather, he uses them developmentally to great effect. Let's hear this last triumphant minute of the symphony.

[Musical example from Symphony in D Minor, Franck: III; Conclusion]

Harold Schonberg writes:

> Franck was the dominating musical force of the period in France, both as composer and as teacher, and he gathered unto himself a group of pupils [including Vincent d'Indy and Emmanuel Chabrier] who did everything but put a halo over him. There was something in the man that encouraged worship. He was kind to a point of saintliness; serene, otherworldly. Never did a harsh word pass his lips, never a derogatory remark. He was not interested in honors or money. People compared him to Fra Angelico. It was to Franck that the younger generation turned, much to the distress of such "Members of the Establishment" as Saint-Saens and Massenet.

Over the years, some critics have voiced the opinion that Franck's Symphony in D Minor is "emotionally strong but structurally weak." Oh, that's just the sort of easy, aphoristic critical statement that critics love to write, allowing them both to denigrate and dismiss the object of their criticism without any necessity for further explanation. I would suggest that if there are structural weaknesses in Franck's symphony, they're only perceived as such if we judge the piece against the Classical-era template. Judged against Berlioz's *Symphonie fantastique*, and the symphonies of Liszt, and the music dramas of Wagner, we realize that Franck's treatment of sonata form is not flawed, but of its time. One thing is for certain and that is, along with Camille Saint-Saens's Symphony no. 3, Franck's Symphony in D Minor has turned out to be the most lasting and popular late 19th-century French symphony in the repertoire, and it well deserves our attention and respect.

Camille Saint-Saens (1835-1921)

Born in Paris, Camille Saint-Saens exhibited what musicologist James Harding calls "Mozartian precocity," composing his first music a few days after his third birthday. He made his formal concert debut at the age of ten with a program that included piano concerti by Mozart and Beethoven, and as an encore, the little shaver offered to play any one of Beethoven's 32 piano sonatas from memory.

He entered the Paris Conservatory in 1848, 11 years after Franck, and created a sensation. Saint-Saens attended Francois Benoist's organ class (the same organist that César Franck eventually succeeded to the

Conservatory), and unlike Franck, he scored a first prize, numero uno, at the age of 13.

Like Felix Mendelssohn, Saint-Saens's intellectual gifts were equal to his musical gifts. Like Mendelssohn, Saint-Saens's fluency has been held against him, the logic being that music came so easy for him that he rarely felt the need to indulge in self-criticism. Like Mendelssohn, Saint-Saens has been accused of writing music that is too polished, too technically perfect. To those critics we quote Max Bialystock, "If ya got it, flaunt it, baby. Flaunt it!" In a reference to his own facility, Saint-Saens combined metaphors, both marine and terrestrial, saying, "I live in music like a fish in water; I compose as an apple tree produces apples."

His virtuosity won him patrons and friends from the very beginning, including such friends as Charles Gounod, Giocchino Rossini, and Hector Berlioz, who said of Saint-Saens that, "He knows everything but lacks in experience." Franz Liszt heard Saint-Saens improving on the organ in Paris's *Madeleine* (where Saint-Saens was the house organist for 19 years), and hailed him as the greatest organist in the world. As an adult, Saint-Saens championed the music of Richard Wagner, Franz Liszt (to whom he dedicated his Third Symphony), and Robert Schumann. He was also famous for his performances of J. S. Bach, Mozart, and Handel, and helped to re-establish all three composers into the Parisian musical mainstream.

Saint-Saens cut a strange figure. He was a small, dandified, bitchy man, "and a dangerous one to cross despite his foppish looks. Pierre Lalo described him: 'He was short, and always strangely resembled a parrot: the same sharply-curved profile; a beak-like nose; lively, restless, piercing eyes. He strutted like a bird and talked rapidly, precipitously, with a curiously affected lisp.'" (Saint-Saens was almost as famous for his nose as Beethoven was for his hair. When he concertized in the United States during the 1906-1907 season, Philip Hale wrote in the Boston Symphony program book, "His eyes are almost level with his nose. His eagle-beak would have excited the admiration of Sir Charles Napier, who once exclaimed, 'Give me a man with plenty of nose!'")

We turn to Saint-Saens Symphony no. 3, the "Organ" Symphony, so-called because of its organ part. I would tell you it could also be called the "Piano" Symphony or the "Keyboard" Symphony because it also calls for a piano, played alternately by two and four hands. Now, much has been made of the fact that Saint-Saens Symphony no. 3 is written in two movements, but this is a classic red herring. In reality, each of the movements is two-movements-in-one. The first-movement allegro, plus an adagio, played without a pause; and the so-called "second movement," well, it's a scherzo plus a *maestoso*, again, played without a pause. In reality, then, Saint-Saens's Third is a four-movement symphony, with only one break, between the second and third movements.

Like César Franck's Symphony in D Minor, Saint-Saens's Third is a "catharsis" or "struggle" symphony, in that it achieves the triumph of the fourth movement only after the minor-mode dominated rigors of the earlier movements.

The principal theme of the first movement is a quivering tune that clearly recalls the opening of the first movement of Schubert's Unfinished Symphony in B Minor.

[Musical example from Symphony No. 3 in C Minor, The "Organ Symphony", Saint-Saens: I; Opening]

The second movement (or the second half of the first movement) is a lush and gorgeous meditation that opens with the organ and strings. Let's hear it.

[Musical example from Symphony No. 3 in C Minor, The "Organ Symphony", Saint-Saens: II; Opening]

The third movement of Saint-Saens's Symphony no. 3 (or should we say the beginning of the second "half" of the symphony—you take your pick) is a rousing scherzo. We hear its opening moments.

[Musical example from Symphony No. 3 in C Minor, The "Organ Symphony", Saint-Saens: III; Opening]

This music, this third-movement scherzo winds down to a gentle conclusion, which acts as a perfect set-up for the majestic, rippling, triumphal, C-major opening of the fourth movement (or the second half of the second movement.) My friends, if you're feeling down and out, if the world has been hard on you, if mail has been received from the IRS or bad words from whomever bosses you around, then put on this fourth movement (or second half of the second movement) of Camille Saint-Saens's Organ Symphony. This is music that will uplift almost any emotional condition, of that, I guarantee.

[Musical example from Symphony No. 3 in C Minor, The "Organ Symphony", Saint-Saens: IV]

Now doesn't that just make us feel good? Like so many 19th-century instrumental compositions, Saint-Saens's work is what we call a cyclic work, that is, themes from earlier movements "cycle back" into later movements. We first noted this in Beethoven's Fifth Symphony, where the blaring C-minor theme of the third-movement scherzo makes its ghostly return in the fourth movement. Berlioz's *Symphonie fantastique* is a cyclic work in that the *idée fixe*—the tune that represents "her"—is heard in some guise or another in each movement of the symphony. Cyclic organization ensured a measure of large-scale coherence and development from movement to movement in a Romantic era that could no longer count on the rituals of the Classical era to provide coherence on their own.

We have not pointed out the cyclic elements here in Saint-Saens's Third, but should you, while listening to the symphony on your own, and I hope you have the opportunity, notice all sorts of connections between the earlier movements and this last one, I would assure you that you are not imaging things.

Conclusions

Saint-Saens had the good fortune to be born a genius and a native Parisian. Above all, he was a composer of extraordinary, truly classical elegance. He is, I believe, a composer whose music awaits serious revival.

We leave the last word on Saint-Saens to his teacher, Charles Gounod, and we quote Gounod: "He is a musician armed with every weapon. He is a master of his art as no other composer is; he knows the classics by heart. He is not finicky, violent or emphatic. He has no system, belongs to no party or clique; he does not pose as a conformer of anything; he writes as he feels and he makes use of what he knows."

Thank you.

Lecture Fourteen
Nationalism and the Symphony

Scope: Although Tchaikovsky and Dvorak were very different as men, they both serve as examples of *musical nationalism*, which emphasized references to a composer's heritage as another form of Romantic self-expression. In this lecture, we explore the Bohemian nationalist sentiments in Dvorak's Seventh Symphony and the distinctly Russian elements in Tchaikovsky's Second Symphony. Both composers represent a new approach to reconciling the Classical-era genre of "symphony" with the melodic and harmonic language of Romanticism.

Outline

I. We turn to two composers who might seem an odd couple to share a lecture, Peter Tchaikovsky (1840–1893) and Antonin Dvorak (1841–1904).

   A. We could not possibly have chosen two more different men. Tchaikovsky was a hypersensitive homosexual, terribly unhappy, tortured by his sexual proclivities, and terrified that he would be exposed. Antonin Dvorak, on the other hand, had a long, stable, and happy marriage and eight children, who were the joys of his life.

   B. Tchaikovsky grew up in St. Petersburg and had a privileged, upper middle–class upbringing. Dvorak was born and raised in the village of Nelahozeves, a Bohemian backwater, where he was taken out of school and apprenticed as a butcher at the age of 11.

   C. Tchaikovsky grew up in Russia, where the genre of symphony played no part at all in national musical life until the mid-19th century. Bohemian composers, such as Dvorak, had been major players in the symphonic tradition since the birth of the genre.

   D. For all their differences, Tchaikovsky and Dvorak were cut from the same musical cloth. They were both "conservative Romantics" in that they constrained their Romantic-era expressive impulses in Classical-era forms. They were both master melodists, and they were both nationalist composers, drawing on the music of their respective homelands for substance and inspiration.

E. By the 1850s and 1860s, such musical nationalism had become an essential self-expressive element for many composers living and working outside of the Austrian, German, or Italian mainstream. For such composers, references to the music of their ethnic or national heritage was just another form of self-expression in the age of Romanticism.

F. As much as it was a self-expressive phenomenon, musical nationalism was also a political phenomenon. Before we begin to listen to the symphonies of Tchaikovsky and Dvorak, we take a moment to explore this strange relationship between music and politics.

II. One of the legacies of the Enlightenment in the 18th century was the desire on the part of a growing European middle class for social justice and political freedom in the 19th century.

A. By the turn of the 19th century, Napoleon Bonaparte had come to power, with his dream of creating a "Continental system"—a pan-European community. Napoleon might have been a tyrant, but the administrative and legal reforms he brought to the regions he occupied were a revelation for populations long accustomed to the arbitrary and despotic rule of hereditary monarchies. He destabilized the old order and changed the map of Europe. In doing so, he created the preconditions necessary for the development of national movements across 19th-century Europe.

B. Napoleon's banishment in 1815 did nothing to quell the spirit of revolution he had so effectively exported across Europe. That simmering spirit came to a boil in 1848, when revolutions broke out across the Continent. Every one of the revolutionary movements was crushed, but this so-called "year of failed revolutions" helped give rise to a musical movement called *nationalism*. Musical nationalism saw the incorporation of indigenous folk music or folk-like music into the concert works of non-German and non-Austrian composers.

C. Nowhere was musical nationalism cultivated more fervently than in Bohemia, the "conservatory of Europe." Dominated for centuries by Austria and Germany, a genuine "Czech" national school of composition—informed by the rhythmic power and melodic lilt of Slavic folk music—began to emerge in the 1860s and 1870s.

1. The essential proponents of this new "Czech" music were the Bohemian composers Bedrich Smetana (1824–1884) and Antonin Dvorak. Of the two, Smetana was by far the more radical; he wrote no symphonies, claiming that the genre was an antiquated holdover from the Classical era and one that would be forever associated with the oppression of the Austrian Habsburgs.

2. Dvorak, a less stridently politicized and frankly more capable composer, had no problem with writing symphonies, and he composed nine of them.

D. Musically, Dvorak was a "conservative Romantic." He managed to reconcile his love for the melodic elegance and formal clarity of Classicism with the harmonic language, emotional content, and nationalistic accent of post-1848 Romanticism, and he managed to please almost everyone.

E. Dvorak developed his style—his vaguely Slavic, Czech "sound"— effortlessly; it was the natural "accent" with which his music spoke. The nationalist elements of his style include his use of characteristic Czech dance rhythms; his tendency to immediately repeat the first motivic idea of a melody before continuing and completing the phrase (which is a stock characteristic of much Czech folk music); and his direct, genuinely "popular" melodic language. All these elements combine to give his music a Bohemian veneer that rides effortlessly atop his Germanic craft and formal structures derived from the Classical era.

F. Dvorak composed nine symphonies, and despite the fame of his Symphony no. 9 in E Minor, the so-called "New World" Symphony, written during his residency in the United States in 1893, his greatest symphony is his Symphony no. 7 in D Minor, composed between December 13, 1884, and March 17, 1885. It was first performed in London on April 22, 1885, where Dvorak enjoyed the same fame and reverence that earlier generations of English music lovers had lavished on Handel, Haydn, and Mendelssohn.

III. The symphony that we, today, call Dvorak's "Seventh" (Symphony no. 7 in D Minor, op. 70 [1885]) was known as his "Second" until 1955.

Of Dvorak's nine symphonies, only five were published in his lifetime. In 1955, with the appearance of a complete edition of Dvorak's works, all nine symphonies were accounted for and numbered in their order of composition.

A. Dvorak's immediate inspiration for his Seventh Symphony was Brahms's Third, a piece that Dvorak heard in Berlin in January of 1884. Further, Dvorak was inspired by Brahms's prediction that Dvorak's next symphony would be quite different from his Sixth. Indeed, Dvorak's Seventh Symphony is as dark and powerful as his Sixth was brilliant and ingratiating.

B. As we would expect from a Classicist like Dvorak, the first movement of his Seventh is in sonata form. The dark, rumbling, vaguely Slavic-sounding first theme, based on an old Hussite folksong, was conceived at the Prague railway station.

    1. An arriving train there held almost 450 anti-Habsburg Czech and Hungarian nationalists who had come to Prague to attend a special event at the National Theater.

    2. Their presence in Prague was viewed by both the citizens and the Habsburg government as a provocation, a de facto demand for independence and nationhood, just the sort of event that would stir Dvorak's nationalist sentiment. Let's hear the opening of this theme. (**Musical selection**: Dvorak, Symphony no. 7 in D Minor, op. 70, movement 1, theme 1 opening [1885].)

C. We listen to the long first theme—or theme group, to be accurate—as it unfolds at the beginning of the first movement. Dvorak scholar Michael Beckerman writes: "[A]ll the musical metaphors for battle are there, including the darkened military key [of D Minor], the quasi military fanfares, [and so forth]." We will listen through the modulating bridge and up to theme 2. Be aware of the variety of music exhibited by the theme itself, which rivals Beethoven's Symphony no. 3 for internal conflict. (**Musical selection**: Dvorak, Symphony no. 7 in D Minor, op. 70, movement 1, theme 1.)

D. After this terrifically dramatic music, the lyric second theme in Bb major comes as a great relief. Let's hear the rest of the exposition: theme 2 and the subsequent cadence material, which effects a return to "the dark side." (**Musical selection**: Dvorak, Symphony no. 7 in D Minor, op. 70, movement 1, theme 2 and exposition conclusion.)

E. The second movement opens with a chorale-like theme of great elegance and gravity, played by a clarinet and delicately accompanied by other winds and pizzicato strings. (**Musical selection**: Dvorak, Symphony no. 7 in D Minor, op. 70, movement 2, opening.)

F. The third-movement scherzo is a genuine duet between a Bohemian dance, a *furiant*—heard on top, in the violins—and a Viennese waltz—heard below, in the bassoons and 'cellos. One commentator has suggested that this "duet" is a "staged brawl...between the Czech and Viennese impulses in the composer's artistic personality." (**Musical selection**: Dvorak, Symphony no. 7 in D Minor, op. 70, movement 3, scherzo, opening.)

G. The fourth and final movement—in sonata form—is impassioned and tragic. We listen to the conclusion of the symphony. (**Musical selection**: Dvorak, Symphony no. 7 in D Minor, op. 70, movement 4, conclusion.)

H. Until 1935, 30 years after his death, Dvorak was generally considered, by audiences outside of Czechoslovakia, to be a composer of tertiary importance. Aside from the "New World" Symphony, the *Carnival Overture*, and his *Slavonic Dances*, his work had fallen into almost total obscurity.

1. Today, the ease and nationalistic flavor of his melodic language are no longer perceived as evidence of a composer lacking in gravitas but, rather, as the natural exuberance and accent of a Bohemian composer whose music is as lyric and well adjusted as the man who wrote it.

2. Dvorak is a not just a great melodist; he is also a technically brilliant composer who could, when he chose to, write music of great pathos and depth, such as his Seventh Symphony.

IV. More than anything else, 19ᵗʰ-century Russian composers were concerned with creating an identifiably "Russian" concert music. Having said that, of all the important Russian composers to emerge during the 19ᵗʰ century, none was less dogmatically "nationalistic" than Piotr (Peter) Ilyich Tchaikovsky.

A. An identifiably "Russian nationalist school" of music composition did not begin to evolve until the 1830s and 1840s.

    1. Unlike Bohemian music nationalism, which was largely a response to the failed revolutions of 1848, the development of a Russian national "musical school" was not triggered by any particular event.

    2. Rather, there was a growing perception in the years after the defeat of Napoleon in 1812 that Russian artistic products were not inferior, but as "legitimate" as anything created in the West.

    3. This new sense of pride in things Russian took many forms; among them was the opening of the St. Petersburg Conservatory in 1862, the first Western European–style music education institution in Russia.

B. In 1862, Peter Tchaikovsky was among the first students to enroll at the newly opened Conservatory, and after graduation, he became a professor at the new Moscow Conservatory. Tchaikovsky was a rare compositional combination: a Russian composer well schooled in both the craft of music composition and the Western repertoire.

C. Despite his training, however, Tchaikovsky was still a Russian, and his music—rhythmically, expressively, and melodically—sounds and acts Russian. Although Tchaikovsky never embraced the politicized, dogmatic Russian nationalism of so many of his contemporaries, his music is, nevertheless, quintessentially Russian—from its melodic flavor to its expressive sensibility.

D. For an in-depth investigation of Tchaikovsky and his music, including all six of his symphonies, see The Teaching Company's "Great Masters" series. For now, we will listen to and discuss Tchaikovsky's most explicitly Russian symphony, the Symphony no. 2 in C Minor, op. 17 (1872), subtitled "Little Russian."

V. Tchaikovsky sketched his Second Symphony while vacationing at his sister's dacha near Kiev during the summer of 1872. The symphony was completed by late November and premiered in Moscow three months later.

    A. A friend and colleague of Tchaikovsky's at the Moscow Conservatory suggested the symphony's nickname, "Little Russian." The phrase refers specifically to Ukraine, where

Tchaikovsky's sister's estate was located, and it also refers to the fact that Tchaikovsky uses four Russian folksongs in the symphony, one in each of the four movements. These folksongs effectively makes Tchaikovsky's Second a genuinely nationalist folk symphony, the likes of which he never attempted again.

B. For example, the first movement is a sonata form that uses as its first theme a Ukrainian version of a Russian folksong entitled "Down by Mother Volga." The song was associated with the Cossack rebel Stenka Razin and was a favorite among students. No Russian who heard this opening melody, played by a solo horn, would have failed to recognize it or, with it, Tchaikovsky's nationalist intent. (**Musical selection**: Tchaikovsky, Symphony no. 2 in C Minor, op. 17 [Little Russian], movement 1, opening [1872].)

C. The second movement of Tchaikovsky's Second Symphony is written in rondo form. The main theme is a gentle march. At the center of the movement, in the position of the second contrasting episode, is another Russian folksong, this one entitled "Spun, O my spinner." Starting quietly, the tune builds in intensity as it is repeated, over and over again, a particularly Russian technique called *varied repetition* that Tchaikovsky will use again in the fourth and final movement. (**Musical selection**: Tchaikovsky, Symphony no. 2 in C Minor, op. 17 [Little Russian], movement 2, "C.")

D. The middle section of the third-movement scherzo uses a theme that sounds like a Russian folksong, though the "experts" have not yet identified it as such. (**Musical selection**: Tchaikovsky, Symphony no. 2 in C Minor, op. 17 [Little Russian], movement 3, trio.)

E. The fourth and final movement was reportedly Tchaikovsky's favorite. The movement is based almost entirely on an extremely popular Ukrainian folksong and dance tune called "Let the Crane Soar," or simply, "The Crane." (**Musical selection**: Tchaikovsky, Symphony no. 2 in C Minor, op. 17 [Little Russian], movement 4, theme.)

F. This brief and straightforward version of "The Crane" appears about a minute into the movement, following a grand and magnificent introduction. Following this statement of the theme, it is repeated with slight variations over and over again.

1. This movement of the Second Symphony might be the purest "Russian music" Tchaikovsky ever composed for a symphony, in that the buildup achieved over the span of the movement is not a result of such Western European compositional techniques as contrast and development, but rather, of varied repetition, which is typical of Russian folk music.

2. As the movement progresses, the theme is played by more and more instruments and becomes louder and louder, though it's still the same tune, heard again and again. (**Musical selection**: Tchaikovsky, Symphony no. 2 in C Minor, op. 17 [Little Russian], movement 4, opening.)

G. In retrospect, Tchaikovsky was the odd man out in 19th-century Russian music. For the most part, arch-nationalist composers, such as the "Russian Five" (Balakirev, Cui, Borodin, Mussorgsky, and Rimsky-Korsakov), saw Tchaikovsky as a sellout to Western European music. And, of course, many Western European critics dismissed Tchaikovsky as an arch-Russian, whose veneer of "Western sophistication" did little to mask his barbarity.

1. Today, some critics are too concerned with the Classical elements of Tchaikovsky's symphonic art; they bemoan what is often described as his "clumsy" adherence to the old forms as pedantic and unimaginative.

2. This judgment, however, is too harsh. Wittingly or unwittingly, in his symphonies, Tchaikovsky was attempting to do what Dvorak, Brahms, Mendelssohn, Schubert, and other composers of the 19th century were attempting to do: reconcile an 18th-century musical genre with the innovations of Beethoven and the expressive, melodic, and harmonic language of the 19th century.

3. We also read that there are "structural" flaws in Tchaikovsky's symphonies. From a purely Classical-era point of view, there are indeed structural flaws in the Romantic-era symphonies of Tchaikovsky. But if they are flaws at all—and we noted the same thing apropos of Franck's Symphony in D Minor—Tchaikovsky's are the result of a 19th-century composer attempting to shoehorn a Romantic-era expressive

impulse into an 18th-century, Classical-era structure, specifically, sonata form.

4. Since the invention of the genre, sonata form had been a defining element of the symphony, and the struggle to use it as a "template," to "modernize it," or to do away with it altogether will remain a continuing challenge for symphonic composers through the 20th century.

Lecture Fourteen—Transcript
Nationalism and the Symphony

Welcome back to *The Symphony*. This is Lecture Fourteen—it is entitled "Nationalism and the Symphony." We turn now to two composers who might seem an odd couple to share a lecture, Peter Tchaikovsky, 1840 to 1893, and Antonin Dvorak, 1801 to 1894, an odd couple because we could not possibly have chosen two more different men. Tchaikovsky was a hypersensitive, cross-dressing homosexual with a penchant for pederasty, whose sham marriage to a nymphomaniacal former student of his named Antonina Milyukova lasted but 11 weeks and drove him nearly to suicide. Judgments aside, my friends, Tchaikovsky was a good but terribly unhappy man, tortured by his sexual proclivity and terrified that he would be exposed.

Antonin Dvorak, on the other hand, was as regular a Joe as ever put a pen to manuscript paper. He had a long, stabile and happy marriage to a woman named Anna Cermakova. He had six daughters: Anna, Josefa, Marenka, Otilka, Ruzena, and Zinda; and two sons: Antonin Jr. and Otakar; who were, as Dvorak would tell anyone who would listen, the great joys of his life. His hobby was trains, not women's underclothing. His favorite store was Prague Hardware and Garden Supplies, not Frederick's of Petersburg.

Tchaikovsky grew up in St. Petersburg and had a privileged upper middle class upbringing. Dvorak was born and raised in the village of Nelahozeves, a Bohemian backwater near Kralupy (as if that really helps) where he was taken out of school and apprenticed as a butcher at the age of 11, so that he might follow his father and grandfather's bloody footsteps in that trade. Tchaikovsky grew up in Russia, a country in which the genre of symphony played no part whatsoever in national life until the mid-19th century. Dvorak, once his musical talent had been recognized and he had traded his butcher's apron for concert blacks, knew, as does any Bohemian musician worth his crystal, that Bohemian composers had been major players in the symphonic tradition since the very birth of the genre.

For all their differences, Tchaikovsky and Dvorak were cut from the same musical cloth. They were both "conservative Romantics" in that they constrained their Romantic-era expressive impulses within the Classical-era forms. They were both master melodists. And both Tchaikovsky and

Dvorak were nationalist composers, drawing on the music of their respective homelands for substance and inspiration.

By the 1850s and 1860s, such musical nationalism had become an essential self-expressive element for many composers living and working outside of the Austrian/German/Italian mainstream. For such composers, references to the music of their ethnic and/or national heritage was but another way of being self-expressive, in that self-expression crazed environment that was the age of Romanticism.

As much as it was a self-expressive phenomenon, musical nationalism was also a political phenomenon. Strange bedfellows always, music and politics, and no more so than in the 19th century. So please, as we navigate the road to the symphonies of Peter Tchaikovsky and Antonin Dvorak, a brief but necessary detour.

Nationalism

One of the legacies of the Enlightenment of the 18th century was the desire, on the part of a growing European middle class, for social justice and political freedom in the 19th century. As I'm sure we're all aware, the so-called "age of revolutions" began in the late 18th century, first in North America and then in France.

In January 1793, the French king, Louis XVI, had a bit more than just "a little" taken off the top, an event of such magnitude, particularly for Louis himself, that those of us who still have our heads shake them in wonder. By the turn of the 19th century, Napoleon Bonaparte had come to power with his dream of creating a "Continental system," a pan-European community headquartered there in Paris. Napoleon might have been a megalomaniacal tyrant, but the administrative and legal reforms he brought to those regions he occupied were a revelation for populations long accustomed to the arbitrary despotic rule of hereditary monarchs. Napoleon destabilized the old order and changed the map of Europe. And by doing so created the preconditions necessary for the development of national movements across 19th-century Europe.

Napoleon's "make bye-bye" in 1815 did nothing to quell the spirit of revolution he had so effectively exported across Europe. The simmering spirit of revolution came to the big boil in 1848, when revolutions broke out across Europe, from Paris and Vienna to Scandinavia, from Budapest to Prague to Palermo. A messy year, this 1848, during which every one of the revolutionary movements was crushed. 1848, this so-called "year of failed revolutions," helped to give rise to a musical movement called *nationalism*. Musical nationalism saw the incorporation of indigenous folk music, or folk-like music into the concert works of non-German and non-Austrian composers.

Nowhere was musical nationalism cultivated more fervently than in Bohemia, the erstwhile "conservatory of Europe." Dominated for centuries by Austria and Germany, a genuine "Czech" national school of composition—informed by the rhythmic power and melodic lilt of Slavic music—began to emerge in the 1860s and the 1870s. The essential proponents of this new "Czech" music were the Bohemian composers Bedrich Smetana and Antonin Dvorak. Of the two, Smetana was by far the most radical. He wrote no symphonies, claiming that the genre was an antiquated holdover from the Classical era, one that would be forever associated with the oppression of the Austrian Habsburgs. Dvorak, a less stridently politicized and frankly more capable composer, had no problems whatsoever with writing symphonies, and he composed nine of them.

As it is said, "Smetana was the one who founded Czech music, but Antonin Dvorak was the one who popularized it." Musically, Dvorak was a "conservative Romantic." He managed to reconcile his love for the melodic elegance and formal clarity of Classicism with the harmonic language, the emotional content, and the nationalistic accent of post-1848 Romanticism. And unlike so many such middle-of-the-roaders who are often assailed by conservatives on one side and radicals on the other, Dvorak seems to have been able to please just about everyone. We might envy him that, if this music wasn't so self-conscious, so lyric, so well created, well crafted, and exciting. And there you have it. There's something in Dvorak's music for everyone, and that was as true in his day as it is in ours.

Dvorak developed his style—his vaguely Slavic, Czech "sound"—quite effortlessly. It was the natural "accent" with which his music spoke. The nationalist elements of his style include his use of characteristic Czech dance rhythms; his tendency to immediately repeat the first motivic idea of a melody before going on to continue and repeat the phrase (which is a stock characteristic of most Czech music); and his direct, genuinely "popular" melodic language. All of these combine to give his music a Bohemian veneer that rides effortlessly atop his Germanic craft and Classical era-derived formal structures.

There was never any doubt in Dvorak's mind that he would compose symphonies. All of his favorite composers—his friend and mentor,

Johannes Brahms, Mozart, Beethoven and Schubert—wrote them. All together Dvorak composed nine symphonies and despite the great and deserved fame of his Symphony no. 9 in E Minor, the so-called "New World" Symphony, written during his residency in the United States in 1893, his greatest symphony is his Seventh, in D Minor, composed between December 13, 1884 and March 17, 1885. It was first performed in London on April 22, 1885, where Dvorak enjoyed the same sort of fame and reverence that earlier generations of English music lovers had lavished on Handel, Haydn and Mendelssohn.

Antonin Dvorak, Symphony no. 7 in D Minor, op. 70 (1885)

Writing in his "Essays in Musical Analysis," first published back in 1935, the eminent English musicologist, Sir Donald Francis Tovey, begins his analysis of Dvorak's Seventh Symphony with these words: "I have no hesitation in setting Dvorak's Symphony along with the C Major Symphony of Schubert and the four symphonies of Brahms as among the greatest and purest examples of the art-form since Beethoven. There should be no difficulties at this time of day in recognizing its greatness."

High praise my friends, from one of the toughest and most critical musicians of the first half of the 20th century. For our information, the symphony that we call today Dvorak's "Seventh" was, in 1935, when Tovey wrote those words, known as the "Second." Of Dvorak's nine symphonies, only five of them were published in his lifetime. It wasn't until 1955, with the appearance of a complete edition of Dvorak's works, that all nine symphonies were accounted for and numbered in the order of their composition.

Dvorak's immediate inspiration for his Seventh Symphony was Brahms's most recent symphony, his Third, a piece that Dvorak heard in Berlin in January of 1884 and which we will discuss in Lecture Fifteen. In February of 1885, while at work on his symphony, Dvorak wrote a letter to his publisher, a gentleman named Simrock, in which Dvorak made it clear that Brahms's inspiration was not just musical but verbal as well. We quote Dvorak's letter: "I've been engaged in a new symphony for a long time; after all, it must be something really worthwhile, for I don't want Brahms's words to me, 'I imagine your [next] symphony [will really be] quite different from [the last]' to remain unfulfilled."

Brahms had nothing to worry about here; Dvorak's Seventh Symphony is as dark and as powerful as his Sixth was brilliant and ingratiating.

A sidebar: Seven years before, in 1878, Brahms had insisted that Simrock publish something—anything—by an unknown Czech composer named Dvorak who had come to Brahms's attention as a result of a composition competition. Simrock took Brahms's advice and overnight Antonin Dvorak's local reputation went international. Brahms made Dvorak, and Dvorak adored and revered Brahms for the rest of his life. As for the thorny and irascible Johannes Brahms, it's safe to say that no other living composer enjoyed the affection and respect he lavished on Dvorak, who he came to consider both his protégé and his great friend.

As we would expect from a diehard Classicist like Dvorak, the first movement of the Seventh is in sonata form. The dark, rumbling, vaguely Slavic-sounding first theme, based on an old Hussite folksong, was conceived at the Prague railway station. Yes. We knew before that Dvorak loved trains. He used to visit the Franz-Josef Station in Prague every day. He memorized all the timetables and the identification numbers and the specifications of the locomotives. Dvorak himself wrote on the manuscript of the score of his Seventh Symphony, "This main theme occurred to me during the arrival of the ceremonial train from Pest to the National Station in 1884." Onboard that special train were 442 anti-Habsburg Czech and Hungarian nationalists who had come to Prague to attend a special event at the National Theater. Their presence in Prague was viewed by both the citizens and the Habsburg government as a provocation, a de facto demand for independence and nationhood, just the sort of thing that would get Dvorak's nationalist juices flowing. Let's hear the opening of this theme, which we might accurately, if dramatically, call the "Freedom Train Theme".

[Musical example from Symphony No. 7 in D Minor, Opus 70, Dvorak: I]

Of this theme, the Dvorak scholar Michael Beckerman writes:

> It is of course impossible to explain fully the connection between Dvorak's musical imagination and his patriotic sense, but in light of [his patriotism], it seems clear that he decided on at least two things for the Seventh: that he would write a dramatic symphony and that he would populate it with nationalist symbols. Most potent of these was the embedding of the Hussite melody in the heart of his main theme as an ominous symbol of national struggle. Whatever else is true for the symphony, it is somehow concerned with struggle; all the musical metaphors for battle are there,

including the darkened military key [of D minor], the quasi-military fanfares, [and so forth].

We listen to this long first theme (or theme group as it should be more accurately called), as it unfolds at the beginning of the first movement. We will listen through the modulating bridge and right up to, but not including, theme 2. Be aware of the variety of music exhibited by the theme itself. We haven't heard a theme this ripe with internal conflict since the first theme of the first movement of Beethoven's Symphony no. 3.

[Musical example from Symphony No. 7 in D Minor, Opus 70, Dvorak: I; Opening through Modulating Bridge]

After this lengthy and terrifically dramatic theme, the lyric second theme in Bb major comes as a huge relief. Let's hear the rest of the exposition: theme 2 and the subsequent cadence material that effects a return to "the dark side." This is some of the finest music Dvorak ever wrote.

[Musical example from Symphony No. 7 in D Minor, Opus 70, Dvorak: I; Exposition, Theme II, Cadence]

The second movement opens with a chorale-like theme, played by a clarinet and delicately accompanied by other winds and pizzicato strings. We hear the opening of this second movement.

[Musical example from Symphony No. 7 in D Minor, Opus 70, Dvorak: II; Opening]

The third-movement scherzo is just too good. It's a genuine duet between a Bohemian dance, a *furiant*—heard on top, in the violins; and a Viennese waltz—heard below in the bassoons and cellos.

[Musical example from Symphony No. 7 in D Minor, Opus 70, Dvorak: III]

In regards to this "duet," one commentator has gone so far as to suggest that, "The battle between the two themes is a staged brawl between a furiant and a waltz, that is, between the Czech and Viennese impulses in the composer's artistic personality." You know, taking this a step further, between Bohemian nationalism and the Austrian status quo—a Battle Royale! Whatever we choose to call it, duet or brawl, Dvorak's scherzo is a wonderful and, yes, a nationally schizophrenic combination of two very different sorts of dance music. Great stuff.

The fourth and final movement—in sonata form—is impassioned and tragic. We listen to the conclusion of this symphony about which Tovey writes, "The solemn tone of the close is amply justified by every theme and every note of this great work, which never once falls below the highest plane of tragic music, nor contains a line which could have been written by any composer but Dvorak."

[Musical example from Symphony No. 7 in D Minor, Opus 70, Dvorak: IV; Conclusion]

A last word about Dvorak. When Donald Tovey's most laudatory appraisal of Dvorak's Seventh appeared in 1935—30 years after Dvorak's death—it came as something of a surprise to the larger international community. You see, outside of Czechoslovakia, audiences generally considered Dvorak a composer of tertiary importance (when he was considered at all). Aside from the "New World" Symphony, the *Carnival Overture*, and his *Slavonic Dances* (music considered most appropriate for "pops" concerts), his work had fallen into almost total obscurity.

Thankfully, this is no longer the case. The ease and nationalistic flavor of his melodic language are no longer perceived as evidence of a composer lacking in gravitas, as was believed in 1910s, '20s, and '30s. But rather, as the national exuberance and accent of the Bohemian composer whose music is as lyric and well adjusted as the man who had wrote it. Dvorak is not just a great melodist, he's also a technically brilliant composer who could, when he chose to, write music of great pathos and depth like his Seventh Symphony. Look, I'm sure it's out there; I'm sure I've simply not yet heard it, but thusfar in my musical life, I have not yet encountered any bad Dvorak. And despite the fact that as a composition it lies outside the purview of this course, I would suggest that anyone who hasn't heard Dvorak's Cello Concerto in B minor is missing one of the most extraordinary experiences life has to offer.

Peter Tchaikovsky (1840-1893)

More than anything else, 19th-century composers were concerned—my friends, they were obsessed—with creating an identifiably "Russian" concert music. Having said that, of all the important Russian composers to emerge during the 19th century, Glinka, Alexander Dargomyzhsky, Mili Balakirev, Alexander Borodin, Modest Mussorgsky, Cesar Cui, Nicolai Rimsky-Korsakov—none was less dogmatically "nationalistic" than Peter Ilyich Tchaikovsky.

Some background information and then to the point. An identifiably "Russian nationalist school" of music did not begin to evolve until the

1830s and 1840s. Unlike Bohemian musical nationalism, which was to a great extent a response to the failed revolutions of 1848, the development of a Russian national "music school" was not triggered by any particular event. Rather, there was a growing perception in the years after the defeat of Napoleon in 1812 in Moscow that artistic things Russian were not inferior, but as "legitimate" as anything created in the West. This new sense of pride in things Russian took many forms; among them was the opening of the St. Petersburg Conservatory in 1862, the first Western-style education institution in Russia. Founded by the Russian-born but Western European-trained pianist Anton Rubinstein. Its avowed mission was to create and "To encourage indigenous talent by offering formal education in music, and to develop a taste for music in Russians."

In 1862, Peter Tchaikovsky was among the first students to enroll at the newly opened Conservatory, and immediately after graduating, he became a professor at the brand new Moscow Conservatory. Tchaikovsky was that rare compositional bird: a Russian composer well schooled in the craft of musical composition and the Western repertoire, a genuine cosmopolitan. To quote Donald Grout: "In [Tchaikovsky], Slavic temperament and German training were leavened by lyrical genius and a lively appreciation of Italian opera and French ballet."

"Slavic temperament." Grout is right on the button here, because despite his training, Tchaikovsky was still a Russian, and his music—rhythmically, expressively and melodically—sounds and acts Russian. For those who did not hear Tchaikovsky's music as being "explicitly" Russian, the great Russian composer Igor Stravinsky wrote: "[On the contrary, Tchaikovsky's music is] more often profoundly Russian than music which has long since been awarded the facile label of Muscovite picturesqueness." Referring to Tchaikovsky's ballet, *The Sleeping Beauty*, Stravinsky continues: "This music is quite as Russian as Pushkin's verse or Glinka's song. While not specifically cultivating in his art 'the soul of the Russian peasant' [like Mussorgsky], Tchaikovsky drew unconsciously from the true, popular sources of our race."

Stravinsky's point is extremely well taken. While Tchaikovsky never embraced the politicized and dogmatic nationalism of so many of his contemporaries, his music is, nevertheless, quintessentially Russian—from its melodic flavor to its expressive sensibility.

For an in depth investigation of Tchaikovsky and his music, including all six of his symphonies, I would refer you to my Teaching Company biography of Tchaikovsky in the "Great Masters" series. For now, we will listen to and discuss Tchaikovsky's most explicitly Russian symphony, his Symphony no. 2 in C minor, op. 17, subtitled "Little Russian."

Symphony no. 2 in C Minor (1872)

Tchaikovsky sketched his Second Symphony while vacationing at his sister Sasha's (or Alexandra's) dacha at Kamenka, near Kiev, during a three-week stay in the summer of 1872. He was 32 years old at the time. The symphony was completed by late November and premiered in Moscow three months later, on February 7, 1873. A friend named Nickolay Kashkin, a colleague of Tchaikovsky's at the Moscow Conservatory, suggested the symphony's nickname, "Little Russian." The phrase "Little Russia" refers specifically to Ukraine, where his sister's estate was located. But the title also, and rather more importantly, makes a musical reference. It refers to the fact that Tchaikovsky uses four Russian folksongs in the symphony, one folksong in each of the four movements. The presence of these folksongs effectively makes Tchaikovsky's Second a genuinely nationalist folk symphony, the likes of which he never attempted again.

For example, the first movement is a sonata form that uses as its theme 1 a Ukrainian version of a Russian folksong entitled "Down by Mother Volga." The song was associated with the Cossack rebel Stenka Razin and was a favorite among students. No Russian who heard this opening melody, played by a solo horn, would have failed to recognize it or, with it, Tchaikovsky's nationalist intent.

[Musical example from Symphony No. 2 in C Minor, Opus 17, Tchaikovsky: I]

The second movement of Tchaikovsky's Second Symphony is written in rondo form. The main theme is a gentle march. At the very center of the movement, in the position of the second contrasting episode, is another Russian folksong, this one entitled "Spun, O my spinner." Starting quietly, the tune builds and builds in intensity as it is repeated, over and over again, a technique called *varied repetition*, a particularly Russian technique that Tchaikovsky will use again in the fourth and final movement of this symphony. But first, movement two at the very center, the appearance of the second of the four Russian folksongs.

[Musical example from Symphony No. 2 in C Minor, Opus 17, Tchaikovsky: II]

The middle section of the third-movement scherzo uses a theme that sounds very much like a Russian folksong, although we should note that the "experts" have not yet identified it as such. Let's hear it.

[Musical example from Symphony No. 2 in C Minor, Opus 17, Tchaikovsky: III]

The fourth and final movement was reportedly Tchaikovsky's favorite. The movement is based almost entirely on an extremely popular Ukrainian folksong and dance tune called "Let the Crane Soar," or just simply, "The Crane." The tune goes like this.

[Musical example from Symphony No. 2 in C Minor, Opus 17, Tchaikovsky: IV; The Crane Theme]

Now this brief and straightforward version of "The Crane" appears about a minute into the movement, following a grand and magnificent introduction. Following this statement of the theme, it is more or less repeated over and over again. To tell you the truth, this movement of this Second Symphony might be the purest "Russian music" Tchaikovsky ever composed for a symphony, in that the buildup achieved over the span of the movement is not a result of such Western European compositional techniques as contrast and development, but rather, by varied repetition, a sort of repetition very typical of Russian folk music. As the movement progresses, the theme is played by more and more instruments and gets louder and louder as it goes, though it is still the same tune, heard again and again.

[Musical example from Symphony No. 2 in C Minor, Opus 17, Tchaikovsky: IV]

A great story: In December of 1872, just a month after having completed this Second Symphony, Tchaikovsky was in St. Petersburg, where he was the guest of honor at the dinner party at the home of the composer Nicolai Rimsky-Korsakov. He played this last movement of this new symphony on the piano for the guests who included the members of the so-called "Russian Five"—about whom we'll speak at length in Lecture Eighteen—the composers Balakirev, Cui, Borodin, Mussorgsky, and Rimsky-Korsakov himself. According to Tchaikovsky: "They almost tore me to bits with rapture [and Rimsky's wife, Nadezhda], begged me in tears to let her arrange the movement for piano duet." One suspects, based on their reaction to this folk-infused movement, that the members of the five were convinced that Tchaikovsky was about to foreswear his Germanic training, quit his job at the Conservatory and become one of them. No such luck, gentlemen! No such luck.

In retrospect, Tchaikovsky was the odd-man-out in 19th-century Russian music, and we're not talking here about his cross-dressing. He wasn't comfortable with such overtly nationalist composers as the "Five," whom he considered technically raw and expressively uncouth. According to Tchaikovsky's brother and early biographer, Modest Tchaikovsky: "My brother laughed at [the Five's] ultra-radical tendencies, and was contemptuous of their naïve and crude efforts, especially those of Mussorgsky. Peter's relationship with the Five was like that between two neighboring states…cautiously prepared to meet on common ground, but jealously guarding their separate interests."

For the most part, arch-nationalist composers like the Five saw Tchaikovsky as a sell-out to Western European music. And, of course, it's one of those easily anticipated ironies that many Western European critics dismissed Tchaikovsky as an arch-Russian, whose veneer of "Western sophistication" did little to mask his Russian barbarity. For example, when Tchaikovsky's Violin Concerto in D Major, a piece that today is considered one of the cornerstones of the repertoire, when the concerto premiered in Vienna in 1881, the important and influential critic, Eduard Hanslick, wrote this in the *New Free Press*:

> The Russian composer Tchaikovsky is an inflated [talent], with a genius-obsession without discrimination or taste. Such is also his latest, long, and pretentious Violin Concerto. The violin is no longer played; it is pulled, torn, shredded. Friedrich Vischer once observed, speaking of obscene pictures, that they stink to the eye. Tchaikovsky's Violin Concerto gives us for the first time the hideous notion that there could be music that stinks to the ear.

Today, some critics are, I think, too concerned with the Classical elements of Tchaikovsky's symphonic art. They bemoan what is often described as his "clumsy" adherence to the old forms as pedantic and unimaginative, new wine in old bottles. For example, in the article on "Symphony" in the *New Grove Dictionary of Music and Musicians*, we read:

> Tchaikovsky's [symphonies have gained a] lasting fame, founded on their expressive melodies, brilliant orchestration, and piquant harmony. So firmly was the Classical ideal of the symphony fixed in his mind that he used the forms quite rigidly without any

apparent effort to mold them to suit his materials. There is no better example of a Romantic composer treating the Classical forms as textbook models, mere skeletons on which any music could be hung.

This, my friends, is simply much too hard an appraisal. In his symphonies, Tchaikovsky was attempting to do what Dvorak, Brahms, Franck, Saint-Saens, Schumann, Berlioz, Mendelssohn, Schubert and gaggle of other somewhat less notable composers of the 19th century were trying to do. That was to reconcile an 18th-century Classical-era music genre with the innovations of Beethoven and the expressive, harmonic, and melodic language of the 19th century. It was not an easy task and many 19th-century composers chose not to even attempt it, composing works called "symphonic poems" or "tone poems" instead.

But back to the criticism, one voiced so often, that there are "structural" flaws in Tchaikovsky's symphonies. From a purely Classical-era point of view, there are indeed structural flaws in the Romantic-era symphonies of Tchaikovsky, and Berlioz, and Franck for that matter. But if they are indeed flaws at all—and we noted the same thing apropos of Franck's Symphony in D Minor—Tchaikovsky's are the result of a 19th-century composer attempting to shoehorn a Romantic-era expressive impulse into an 18th-century Classical-era structure, specifically sonata form. Since the invention of the genre, sonata form has been a defining element of the symphony, and the struggle to use it as a "template," to "modernize it," or do away with it all together will remain a continuing challenge for symphonic composers through the 20th century. Let the challenge continue! Next up: Bruckner and Brahms.

Thank you.

Lecture Fifteen
Brahms, Bruckner, and the Viennese Symphony

Scope: Brahms and Bruckner may also be an odd pairing, but they were both children of Beethoven; they both held Beethoven's Ninth Symphony to be: "the unapproachable ideal, the standard against which all music had to be measured." Bruckner rose from obscurity in middle age and, influenced by Wagner, wrote nine symphonies, all controversial and complex. Brahms was "discovered" at the age of 20 by Robert Schumann but did not complete a symphony until he was 43. When he finally did, it was a masterpiece of synthesis, combining the best elements of the past with the new language of modern music.

Outline

I. Anton Bruckner (1824–1896) was born in the Austrian town of Ansfelden, near Linz.

   A. His father was the town schoolmaster and church organist, and Anton was educated in the churches and monasteries of his native upper Austria. Indeed, the church was his spiritual refuge for his entire life. He once remarked to Gustav Mahler that he (Bruckner) had to finish his tenth symphony before he passed before God; otherwise, God would be disappointed in his use of his gifts.

   B. As an aside, we might note that in the 19th century, nine symphonies seemed to be a mystical number past which no composer was capable of going. Beethoven, Schubert, and Dvorak all died before completing their tenth symphonies, as did Bruckner. Johannes Brahms never worried about his tenth symphony, because he completed his fourth and final symphony in 1855, at the age of 52.

   C. Bruckner, it seems, believed in everything except himself. At 18 years of age, despite his training, talent, and the many musical opportunities available to him in mid-19th–century Austria, he had neither the confidence nor the grit to brave the hazards of a musical career. Instead, he sought out the safety of the same jobs his father held, provincial schoolteacher and part-time organist.

D. Bruckner lived and worked in total obscurity, taking correspondence courses in harmony and counterpoint with Simon Sechter, a professor at the Vienna Conservatory. Bruckner often worked seven hours a day on the exercises, and even Sechter, who was a notoriously hard taskmaster, was taken aback by Bruckner's obsessive dedication to his studies.

E. Sechter demanded that his students, Bruckner included, do no free composing while taking his course. Thus, for six years, from the age of 31 to 37, Bruckner composed nothing. Finally, in 1861, Bruckner finished the course and traveled to Vienna to apply for a certificate that would allow him to teach harmony and counterpoint in music schools.

F. The climax of Bruckner's examination in Vienna was his improvisation of an organ fugue based on a theme submitted by the examining committee. After Bruckner had finished, a member of the committee, Joseph Herbeck, conductor of the concerts of the Viennese Friends of Music and a faculty member at the Vienna Conservatory, remarked that Bruckner should have been examining the committee.

G. Bruckner returned home, where he continued to take correspondence courses in orchestration and musical form. He might have been content to live out his life as a provincial teacher and correspondence student except for an event that occurred in February of 1863, when he was 38 years old: He attended a performance of Richard Wagner's *Tannhäuser* and was awed, by both the opera and his own realization that what made it great was that it broke so many of the rules of harmony and counterpoint that he had so studiously mastered!

H. From that moment on, Bruckner embraced Wagner's music with a religious fervor. Unfortunately, when he moved to Vienna in 1868, his Wagner-mania was considered impolitic at best. When Bruckner decided to call his Third Symphony the "Wagner" Symphony, the Brahms faction attacked him.

I. With the inspiration of his new god, Richard Wagner, Bruckner's extensive musical training finally began to pay off.

    1. In 1866, he completed his Symphony no. 1 in C Minor. It was premiered in Linz in 1868, a year that saw Bruckner's life change completely.

2. In 1867, Simon Sechter, Bruckner's correspondence course teacher, died, and in 1868, to Bruckner's amazement, he was offered Sechter's post at the Vienna Conservatory!

3. Filled with misgivings, he accepted the position and moved to Vienna, where he would live out the remaining 28 years of his life.

J. Bruckner cut a strange figure in Vienna. He maintained his simple rural manners but was plagued by compulsions, such as the need to count things. He never had a serious relationship with a woman and probably never had a sexual relationship. Despite his extensive training, he was obsessed with gaining certificates and diplomas and had no confidence in his own musical mastery.

II. Bruckner's rise from obscurity sounds similar to César Franck's, but Franck composed only one mature symphony, and Bruckner composed nine of them—all long, dense, complicated, Wagnerian, and controversial.

A. Bruckner's First was initially rejected by the Vienna Philharmonic Orchestra for its "wildness and daring"; the same organization dismissed Bruckner's Second as "nonsense." In 1875, the Philharmonic dismissed the Third as "unplayable" but was forced to perform it when a cabinet minister who was a patron of Bruckner's intervened. Bruckner conducted the premiere, which was a disaster.

B. It wasn't until the premiere of his Seventh Symphony, in 1884, when Bruckner was 60 years old, that he began to taste success, although not in Vienna. The Seventh was premiered in Leipzig, at the Gewandhaus, under the baton of the famous Artur Nikisch, who afterwards declared that Bruckner's work approached that of Beethoven.

C. Not everyone shared Nikisch's enthusiasm. When the symphony was performed in Vienna, Eduard Hanslick's review gave voice to critical issues in Bruckner's music that trouble many listeners to this day. Acknowledging the symphony's moments of "ingenious inspiration," Hanslick criticized the work for its "interminable stretches of darkness, leaden boredom, and feverish over-excitement."

D. Even more than César Franck, Bruckner's experience as an organist colored his symphonic music. His love for huge, multicolored sonorities came from his experience as an organist, as did his predilection for slow, sometimes plodding, hymn-like sections of music. His rather "leisurely" sense of development was, for some, an object of scorn. Finally, influenced by his great affection for Wagner and the time-scale of Wagner's music, Bruckner's symphonies are of a length that would seem, at times, not necessarily justified by their musical materials.

E.   The Symphony no. 4 in Eb Major, subtitled "The Romantic," is an example of Bruckner at his best. It is also an example of the fate of so much of Bruckner's music.

1.   At the time the Fourth was initially completed, in 1874, Bruckner's friends and students decided that their beloved master's symphonies were not being acclaimed as they should be because of their length and orchestration. Bruckner, always insecure, allowed these well-meaning but misguided friends to cut and reorchestrate his symphonies.

2.   The first published edition of the Fourth Symphony was a massacre; the cuts destroyed the symphony's formal balance, and almost every measure was reorchestrated in some way.

3.   Bruckner contributed to the confusion by constantly revising his own works. For example, he first completed the Fourth in 1874. In 1877-1878, he rewrote entirely the first, second, and fourth movements and discarded and replaced the third-movement scherzo. Then, in 1880, he discarded and replaced the fourth and final movement.

4.   This 1880 version is the one usually heard today. It is an excellent but long symphony, running about an hour and a quarter in length.

F.   Bruckner's Fourth begins with his most famous symphonic opening: A quiet tremolo in the strings evokes the dawn beneath a broad and regal theme—the "wake-up call" in the solo horn. (**Musical selection**: Bruckner Symphony no. 4 in Eb Major [Romantic], movement 1, opening.)

1.   Despite Bruckner's programmatic rationale for this opening (the symphony begins at dawn in a medieval city), we should note that this is how most of Bruckner's symphonies begin: with a quiet tremolo in the strings beneath what the Germans call an *Urthema*, a "primordial, elemental theme."

2. This *Urthema*—which is also the first theme of a sonata-form structure—continues to unwind and build up until theme 2 is heard, itself a typically Brucknerian explosion of magnificence dominated by the brass. Perhaps this second theme is meant to represent "the knights on their proud steeds" described by Bruckner's program. (**Musical selection**: Bruckner Symphony no. 4 in Eb Major [Romantic], movement 1, theme 2.)

3. This sort of monumental magnificence, to which Bruckner builds and builds again, is a staple of Bruckner's style, as it was a staple of Wagner's.

G. The development section of this first movement reaches its climax with a grand and majestic chorale for brass. This is music of genuinely religious impact, a cathedral in sound, timeless and heroic. (**Musical selection**: Bruckner Symphony no. 4 in Eb Major [Romantic], movement 1, development climax.)

H. The second-movement andante of Bruckner's Fourth is cast in sonata form, as well. We hear the opening of the first theme, scored primarily for 'cellos. (**Musical selection**: Bruckner Symphony no. 4 in Eb Major [Romantic], movement 2, opening.)

I. Bruckner himself referred to his third-movement scherzo as "hunting" music, and it is. Starting with a rustic, open-fifth drone in the strings, hunting horn–like fanfares build to a huge and typically Brucknerian climax. Note that the principal rhythm here—two eighth notes followed by an eighth-note triplet—was one of Bruckner's favorite rhythmic profiles, and it characterized the rhythm of theme 2 in the first movement, as well. (**Musical selection**: Bruckner Symphony no. 4 in Eb Major [Romantic], scherzo opening.)

J. The fourth and final movement is a huge, sprawling affair in sonata form, which begins much as the first movement began: An *Urthema*, played initially by a solo horn, is heard over quietly thrumming strings and a repeated melodic pattern in the second violins. Over the course of the first minute and 20 seconds, the music builds from quiet mystery to explosive drama. (**Musical selection**: Bruckner Symphony no. 4 in Eb Major [Romantic], movement 4 opening.)

III. Johannes Brahms (1833–1897) managed to synthesize the discipline of the Classical-era symphonic forms and procedures with the expressive drama of Beethoven and the harmonic and melodic language of late Romanticism more convincingly, more artistically, and more effectively than any other 19th-century composer.

A. A composer of impeccable craft and technique—perhaps the most technically complete composer since Beethoven—Brahms created a body of work that was modern, yet still recognized and affirmed his debt to the musical past.

B. Brahms was a thorny and complex man, whose life and personality are described in The Teaching Company's "Great Masters" biography. In the interest of time, after one brief detour, we'll move directly on to his symphonies.

C. On September 30, 1853, Johannes Brahms, 20 years old, tiny, slim, blonde-haired, and blue-eyed, showed up at the door of Robert and Clara Schumann's house in Düsseldorf.

    1. Brahms had been on tour with a violinist named Eduard Rimenyi, who had left when Brahms behaved poorly toward the great Franz Liszt in Weimar. Brahms, now in Düsseldorf, was hoping for an audience with the Schumanns.

    2. He ended up staying for the next three months. Robert Schumann, absolutely astonished by Brahms's early piano music, not only saw to its immediate publication but also wrote an article that ran in the influential magazine *Neue Zeitschrift für Musik*, in which he introduced Brahms as the new German messiah of music.

    3. In essence, Schumann told the musical community that Johannes Brahms would one day compose a symphony that would be the worthy successor to Beethoven's Ninth. Of course, Brahms was terrified by Schumann's prediction and was unable to complete a symphony for the next 23 years. When his First was finally released, friends and foes alike immediately referred to it as "Beethoven's Tenth."

    4. For Brahms, the act of completing and releasing the First had a cathartic effect; his three remaining symphonies followed rather quickly: The Second was completed one year later, in 1877; the Third, in 1883; and the Fourth, in 1885. We will focus on Brahms's Third, which like all four of his symphonies, is a masterpiece of synthesis—the best of the old and new, woven into a deeply moving and admirably compact whole.

IV. Brahms' Third Symphony is his "heroic" symphony, his own *Eroica*.

    A. The opening of the first movement is one of the most sensational in the symphonic repertoire, a free mix of F major and F minor built atop a titanic rising motive: F–Ab–F, heard first in the upper winds and brass, then, as the magnificent, descending first theme begins in the upper strings, in the bass line. (**Musical selection**: Brahms, Symphony no. 3 in F Major, op. 90, movement 1 opening [1883].)

    B. Brahms composed most of the Third during the summer of 1883, while he was staying in the resort town of Wiesbaden, within sight of the Rhine River. He was inspired by both the magnificent setting and by the memory of his friend and mentor, Robert Schumann, and the Rhenish Symphony of 1850.

        1. Brahms went so far as to base his own magnificent first movement/first theme on Schumann's first-movement "Rhine" theme. A back-to-back comparison will be most revealing. First, we hear a bit of Schumann's theme, from the blaring conclusion of the first movement of the Rhenish. (**Musical selection**: Schumann, Symphony no. 3 in Eb Major, op. 97, movement 1, conclusion [1850].)

        2. Now, we listen to Brahms's swirling and magnificent first theme in its entirety. (**Musical selection**: Brahms, Symphony no. 3 in F Major, op. 90, movement 1, theme 1.)

    C. Brahms's first movement plumbs an extraordinary range of expression, from heroic majesty to delicate, intimate lyricism. Throughout the first movement, the rising three-note motive, or *motto*, that began the movement is a constant presence: here, a foreground melody; there, an accompanimental line; here, a cadential figure; there, a bass line; everywhere, unifying, relating, and organizing the diverse but always interrelated elements of the movement.

    D. The second movement is a gorgeous, vaguely rustic movement in C major that opens with a luminous, clarinet-dominated theme, sounding more like a serenade than a symphony. (**Musical selection**: Brahms, Symphony no. 3 in F Major, op. 90, movement 2, opening.)

E. The third movement in C minor contrasts with the second movement, featuring an opening theme that is as melodically sophisticated and "urban," as haunting and melancholy, as the second-movement opening was gentle and rustic. (**Musical selection**: Brahms, Symphony no. 3 in F Major, op. 90, movement 3, opening.)

F. The fourth and final movement is one of the most inspired and exciting symphonic movements ever composed.

  1. The movement begins quietly and mysteriously in the key of F minor, a key that was implicitly implied, if not explicitly stated, by the rising F–Ab–F motto of the first-movement opening. (**Musical selection**: Brahms, Symphony no. 3 in F Major, op. 90, movement 4, opening.)

  2. This restrained, almost furtive opening theme, which contains virtually all the basic melodic material Brahms needs to construct the remainder of the movement, gives way to a chorale of great beauty and gravity. (**Musical selection**: Brahms, Symphony no. 3 in F Major, op. 90, movement 4, chorale.)

  3. This, in turn, gives way to an explosive return of the formerly "mysterious" first theme, which is now followed immediately by the modulating bridge. (**Musical selection**: Brahms, Symphony no. 3 in F Major, op. 90, movement 4.)

  4. This bridge powers directly into a fabulous second theme, a strutting and wonderful tune played initially by the 'cellos and horns. We listen through to the conclusion of the exposition. (**Musical selection**: Brahms, Symphony no. 3 in F Major, op. 90, movement 4, theme 2.)

  5. The glories of this movement continue to build, one upon the next. It ends with a sublime and shimmering coda, during which the opening moments of the first movement return with a serenity and nobility that defies easy description. (**Musical selection**: Brahms, Symphony no. 3 in F Major, op. 90, movement 4, theme 2.)

G. Brahms's Third Symphony is Brahms at his best: majestic, passionate, intimate; as always, reconciling the clarity and concision of Classicism with the expressive palette of Romanticism.

Lecture Fifteen—Transcript
Brahms, Bruckner, and the Viennese Symphony

Welcome back to *The Symphony*. This is Lecture Fifteen—it is entitled "Brahms, Bruckner and the Viennese Symphony." As if pairing Dvorak and Tchaikovsky in Lecture Fourteen wasn't strange enough, here we paired Brahms and Bruckner. We can list what they have in common in five sentences. They are both presently dead. They were both native German speakers. They both wrote symphonies. They both achieved lasting fame in their adopted city of Vienna. Sentence number five is the clincher, the reason why we've paired them together. Symphonically, both Brahms and Bruckner were the "children of Beethoven." Specifically, they both held Beethoven's Ninth Symphony to be "the unapproachable ideal, the standard against which all music had to be measured."

Anton Bruckner (1824-1896)

Bruckner was born in the Austrian town of Ansfelden, near Linz. His father, Anton Sr., was the town schoolmaster and church organist, and it was at the local Catholic Church that Bruckner sang as a choirboy and learned to play the violin and organ. Bruckner was educated in the churches and monasteries of his native upper Austria. Truly, the church was Bruckner's spiritual refuge for the rest of his life. He was as religiously devout a man as you will ever find outside a monastery or a foxhole. As an elderly man, Bruckner once told the young Gustav Mahler:

> Yes, my dear, now I have to work very hard so at least [my] Tenth Symphony will be finished. Otherwise, I will not pass before God, before whom I shall soon stand. He will say, "Why else have I given you talent, you son of a bitch, that you should sing My praise in glory? But [no], you have accomplished much too little."

You know, one can only hope that when Bruckner did pass before God, having completed nine symphonies was deemed good enough, because he died before he finished his Tenth.

This "nine" symphony thing was a big deal in the 19th century, a mystical number past which no one seemed capable of going. Beethoven wrote his Ninth, began his Tenth, and died. Schubert—nine symphonies, dead. Dvorak—nine symphonies and kaput. Gustav Mahler, whose neuroses made Ted Bundy look like a mentally healthy man, completed his Ninth

Symphony, then crossed out the designation 'Nine' and retitled the work *Das Lied von der Erde*, (*The Song of the Earth*). He then composed his next symphony and told his wife Alma: "Actually, of course, it's the Tenth, because *Das Lied von der Erde* was really the Ninth. [But] now the danger is past."

A classic instance of speaking too soon. Mahler started work on what would have been known as his Tenth Symphony, got sick and died having never finished it. Arnold Schönberg, a great friend of Mahler's, was convinced, as were many of Mahler's friends, that by attempting to cheat fate and compose a Tenth symphony, he had tampered with forces beyond his comprehension. In 1913, two years after Mahler's death, Schönberg wrote: "It seems that the Ninth is the limit. He who wants to go beyond it has to leave [life]. Those who had written a Ninth symphony were too close to the beyond."

Johannes Brahms never had to worry about what to do "about" his Tenth symphony. He completed his Fourth and final symphony in 1885, at the age of 52. In later years, in an entirely Brahmsian dig at the competition, Brahms liked to say that with the exception of the "great one" (referring not to Jackie Gleason, but to Beethoven), "no one should have more than four symphonies in him."

Spiritually, Brahms could not have been more different than Bruckner. He was a non-believer and he said so with an ease that caused his more devout friends to fear for his soul. Dvorak, a deeply religious man was appalled by Brahms's atheism, and he is quoted as having said with tears in his eyes, "Such a great man! Such a great soul! And [yet], he believes in nothing!"

Back to Bruckner, who would seem to have believed in everything except himself. At 18 years of age, despite his musical training and talent (which was quite considerable) and the many musical opportunities available to him in mid-19th century Austria, he had neither the confidence nor the grit to brave the hazards of a musical career. Instead, he sought out the safety of the same jobs his father held, provincial schoolteacher and part-time organist. So, Bruckner lived and worked in total obscurity, taking correspondence courses in harmony and counterpoint with Simon Sechter, a professor at the Vienna Conservatory. Bruckner often worked seven hours a day on the exercises, and even Sechter, who was a notoriously hard taskmaster, was taken aback by Bruckner's obsessive dedication to his correspondence course. One day, Sechter received from Bruckner 17 music manuscript books absolutely crammed with various solutions, prompting

Sechter to write him a letter in which he told him that he was endangering his mental and physical health by driving himself so hard.

Sechter demanded that his musical students, Bruckner included, do no free composing while taking his course. So for six years—from the age of 31 to 37—Bruckner, obedient to a fault, composed nothing. Finally, in 1861, Bruckner finished the course and traveled to Vienna to apply for a certificate that would allow him to teach harmony and counterpoint in music schools.

The climax of Bruckner's examination in Vienna was his improvisation of an organ fugue based on a theme submitted by the examining committee. After Bruckner had finished, a member of the committee, Joseph Herbeck, the conductor of the concerts of the Viennese Friends of Music and a faculty member of the Vienna Conservatory said, for the record, "He should have examined us! If I knew one-tenth of what he knows, I'd be happy!"

Teaching certificate in hand, Bruckner headed back home where he continued to take correspondence courses in orchestration and musical form. Bruckner might have been content to live out his life as a provincial music teacher and correspondence student except for an event that occurred in February 1863, when he was 38 years old. He attended a performance in Linz of Richard Wagner's *Tännhauser*. It is no exaggeration to say that Bruckner was blown away by *Tännhauser* and his realization of what made *Tännhauser* so great was that it broke so many of the rules of harmony and counterpoint he had so studiously mastered.

From that moment on, Bruckner embraced Wagner's music with a genuinely religious fervor, a fervor which might have been endearing had he not moved to Vienna in 1868 where his Wagner-mania was considered impolitic at best. When Bruckner decided to call his Third Symphony the "Wagner" Symphony, the Brahms faction attacked like wolves on a crippled lamb. In the words of Erwin Doernberg: "Bruckner strayed into the battlefield and became the only casualty!" (The Viennese critic Eduard Hanslick—a confirmed Brahmsian—described Bruckner's Third as: "Beethoven's Ninth meets Wagner's *Walküre* and is trampled under her hooves."

Anyway, inspired by his new god—Richard Wagner—Bruckner's extensive musical training finally began to pay off. In 1866, he completed his Symphony no. 1 in C Minor. It was premiered in Linz in 1868, a year that saw Bruckner's life change completely. The year before, 1867, Simon Sechter, Bruckner's correspondence teacher, had died in Vienna. And in

1868, to Bruckner's absolute amazement, he was offered Sechter's post at the Vienna Conservatory. Well, filled with misgivings, he accepted the position, and thus, at the age of 44, Bruckner took up his duties in Vienna where he would live out the remaining 28 years of his life.

Never was there a major composer who struck a stranger figure than Anton Bruckner. Deryck Cooke writes:

> Bruckner's character, as a man and as an artist, was fundamentally formed by his origins in one of the most primitive and lowly strata of European society—the Austrian peasantry, rooted to the land, unquestioningly obedient to the state and the Roman Catholic Church.

> Bruckner was as simple, naïve, trustful, deferential and pious a man as any man could be who had grown up in a small village in Metternich's his time, ruled by a conservative and authoritarian government.

> What remained puzzling about Bruckner was he did not change with the changing times or with his changing environment. When he arrived in Vienna, he still adhered to his old-fashioned rural manners and customs. His inability to acquire even a little sophistication may to some indicate a retarded psychological development, caused by having spent his youth [and early adulthood] in monastic settings. It certainly had something to do with an unworldliness arising from his religious faith. But in addition to the understandably gaucherie of a simple and pious villager in a big city, there was a fundamental, entirely personal sense of insecurity of Bruckner's character.

> This insecurity was basic to Bruckner's life, and explains certain strange, unconsciously motivated features of his personality. His neuromania, the counting of things, was a compulsion. His attitude towards women must [also] be mentioned, which neatly ensured that he should never have to enter into a real relationship, with its possible threats to what little security he did possess. So pious a man could not contemplate any sexual relationship not sanctified by marriage [and Bruckner never married. You do the math.] Another aspect of Bruckner's insecurity was his mania for taking examinations and gaining diplomas and testimonials. For all of his technical mastery he could never be convinced that his knowledge was sufficient without the official confirmation of some expert or authority.

Bruckner Symphonies

Bruckner's rise from obscurity sounds a lot like César Franck's. But where Franck composed only one mature symphony, Bruckner composed the big number—nine of them. And they were big symphonies—long, dense, complicated, and well, Wagnerian, and controversial from the beginning. Bruckner's First was initially rejected by the Vienna Philharmonic Orchestra for its "wildness and daring." I would tell you that the VPO is a thorny lot now and they were a thorny lot then. They dismissed Bruckner's Second as "nonsense." In 1875, they dismissed the Third as "unplayable," and were only forced to perform it when a cabinet minister, who was a patron of Bruckner's, intervened.

Bruckner conducted that premiere and it was a disaster. The orchestra butchered the piece. The audience booed and whistled and then walked out during the performance. By the end of the symphony, only 25 members of the audience remained. Among them, a 17-year old conservatory student named Gustav Mahler.

It wasn't until the premiere of his Seventh Symphony in 1884, when Bruckner was 60 years old, that he began to taste success, although not in Vienna. The Seventh was premiered, in Leipzig at the Gewandhaus, under the baton of the great and famous Artur Nikish, who afterwards declared that: "Since Beethoven there has been nothing that can even approach it. From this moment I regard it my duty to work for the recognition of Bruckner."

While we respect Heir Nikish's enthusiasm, not everyone shared it with him. When the symphony was performed in Vienna, Eduard Hanslick's review gave voice to critical issues in Bruckner's music that trouble many listeners to this day: "Like every one of Bruckner's works, the symphony contains ingenious inspirations, interesting details—here [for] six, [for] eight measures—but in between are interminable stretches of darkness, leaden boredom, and feverish over-excitement."

Even more than César Franck, Bruckner's experience as an organist colored his symphonic music, his love for huge, multicolored sonorities—not a bad thing if done with discretion—came from his experience as an organist. His predilection for slow, sometimes plodding, hymn-like sections of music, likewise, came from his experience as an organist. Bruckner's music is rarely fast or even moderately paced. His rather "leisurely" sense of development, though his fans would call it his "deliberately meditative musical spirit," was for some the object of scorn. The Viennese called him the "*adagio-Komponist,*" (the "adagio composer"), because even his fast movements felt slow. And of course, reinforced by his great affection for Wagner and the huge timescale of Wagner's music, Bruckner's symphonies are of a length that would seem, at times, not necessarily justified by their musical materials.

Bruckner's Symphony no. 4 in Eb Major, subtitled by Bruckner "The Romantic," is an example of Bruckner at his very best. It's also an example of the fate of so much of Bruckner's music. At the time the Fourth was initially completed, in 1874, Bruckner's friends and students got it into their heads that the reason that their divine master's symphonies were not being acclaimed as they should be was because of their length and orchestration. Bruckner, insecure to a fault, allowed these well meaning but misguided friends and students to cut and reorchestrate his symphonies. The first published edition of the Fourth Symphony is a massacre; the cuts destroyed his symphony's formal balance, and almost every measure was reorchestrated in some way. Bruckner also contributed to the confusion by constantly revising his works. For example, he first completed the Fourth in 1874. In 1877 and 1878, he rewrote entirely the first, second and fourth movements and discarded and replaced the third-movement scherzo. Then, in 1880, he discarded and replaced the fourth and final movement as well. It is Bruckner's own 1880 version that is usually heard today. It's an excellent but long symphony running about an hour and a quarter in length.

One must be relaxed with no pressing engagements or phone calls to make to appreciate the kind of symphonic experience Bruckner has to offer. Let us turn off our phones then, and proceed. Bruckner provided a brief but telling program note for the opening of the first movement of this symphony. It reads:

> Medieval city—Dawn—From the city towers issue morning-waking calls—The gates open—The knights spring forth on proud steeds into the open air; the magic of the forest surrounds them—Forest murmurings—And thus, the Romantic image unfolds.

Bruckner's Fourth begins with what is his most famous symphonic opening: a quiet tremolo in the strings evokes the dawn beneath a broad and regal theme—the "wake-up" call in the solo horn.

[Musical example from Symphony No. 4 in Eb Major, Bruckner; I; Opening]

Despite Bruckner's programmatic rationale for this opening: "Medieval city—Dawn—From the city towers issue morning wake-up calls"—we should note that this is how most of Bruckner's symphonies begin: with a quiet tremolo in the strings beneath what the Germans call an *Urthema*, a "primordial, elemental theme." (One is reminded here of one anonymous wag's nasty statement that: "[Bruckner] composed not nine symphonies, but one symphony nine times.")

In any case, this *Urthema*—which is also the first theme of a sonata-form structure—continues to unwind and build up until theme 2 is heard, itself a typically Brucknerian explosion of magnificence dominated by the brass. Perhaps this second theme is meant to represent "the knights on their proud steeds," as described by Bruckner's program.

[Musical example from Symphony No. 4 in Eb Major, Bruckner; I]

This sort of monumental magnificence, to which Bruckner builds and builds again like successive waves building from quiet troughs into huge peaks, is a staple of Bruckner's symphonic style, as it was a staple of Wagner's. In many ways, Bruckner was the symphonic equivalent to Richard Wagner. And like Wagner's music dramas, Bruckner's symphonies express the most fundamental human impulses with an extraordinary purity and grandeur of expression. Like Wagner's music dramas, Bruckner's symphonies are on a monumental scale, which despite many internal subtleties and complexities has a shattering simplicity of outline.

The development section of this first movement reaches its climax with a grand and majestic chorale for brass. This is music of genuinely religious impact, a cathedral in sound, timeless and heroic. Let's hear it.

[Musical example from Symphony No. 4 in Eb Major, Bruckner: I; development climax]

Now I trust we've all noticed the pipe organ-like sensibility of what we've just heard. These huge sonorities sound like a pipe organ with all of its stops pulled out. And the leisurely pace of this music is reflective of the kind of hymns Bruckner spent the first half of his life playing in large spaces on a pipe organ. The second-movement andante in Bruckner's Fourth is cast in sonata form, as is the first. We hear the opening of the first theme scored primarily for cellos.

[Musical example from Symphony No. 4 in Eb Major, Bruckner: II; Opening]

Bruckner himself referred to his third-movement scherzo as "hunting" music. And so it is. Starting with a rustic open-fifth drone in the strings, hunting horn-like fanfares build to a huge and typically Brucknerian climax. Note that the principal rhythm here—two eighth notes followed by an eighth-note triplet (ta ta Ta-ta-ta, ta ta Ta-ta-ta)—was one of Bruckner's favorite rhythmic profiles, and it characterized the rhythm of theme 2 in the first movement as well. Please, we sample the beginning of the third movement of Bruckner's Symphony no. 4.

[Musical example from Symphony No. 4 in Eb Major, Bruckner: III; Opening]

The fourth and final movement of Bruckner's Fourth is a huge and sprawling affair in sonata form, which begins much as the first movement began: an *Urthema*, played initially by a solo horn, is heard over quietly strumming strings and a repeated melodic pattern in the second violins. Of the course, of the first minute and twenty seconds, the music builds from quiet mystery to explosive gut-wrenching drama. Please, the opening of the fourth movement of Bruckner's Symphony No. 4.

[Musical example from Symphony No. 4 in Eb Major, Bruckner: IV; Opening]

Not bad for someone who behaved more like Jethro Bodine than a great artist. At the final rehearsal before the premiere of this, his Fourth Symphony, Bruckner went up to the conductor—the world famous and very wealthy Franz Richter—and tipped him. I kid you not! "'Take this', [he said,] pressing a [coin] into [the great] Richter's hand, 'and drink a mug of beer to my health.' The dumbfounded conductor looked at the coin, put it in his pocket, and later had it put on his watch chain." That's quite a story, my friends.

Preston Steadman writes:

> [Composing his] symphonies over a period of about thirty years, Bruckner attempted to create a balance between the classic and romantic traditions of the symphony. Bruckner arrived at a solution influenced [particularly] by Wagner, by expanding the length of all the movements, by employing a much larger orchestra, and by scoring powerfully for the brass. Early in his symphonic output, he settled upon a style that remained constant in all his symphonies, a fact that caused a variety of comments.

Brahms, [who likewise attempted to create a balance between the classic and romantic traditions of the symphony], developed a style that was more concise, more integrated, and more involved intellectually, yet it was designed to stress the lyric and continuous nature of late nineteenth century music.

Johannes Brahms (1833-1897)

It was Johannes Brahms, a native of Hamburg, who moved permanently to Vienna in 1862, who stayed the course and pulled it off. It was Brahms in his four symphonies who managed to synthesize the discipline of the Classical-era symphonic forms and procedures with the expressive "oomph" of Beethoven, and the harmonic and melodic language of late Romanticism more convincingly, more artistically, and more effectively than any other 19th-century composer. A composer of impeccable craft and technique—perhaps, my friends, the most technically complete composer since Beethoven—Brahms created a body of work that was modern (as "modern" as anything Wagner or Bruckner composed), and yet still recognized and affirmed his debt to the musical past. In the eloquent words of the English musicologist Julius Harrison:

> In [our] age of turmoil and iconoclasm, Brahms's symphonies still stand four-square to the world: pillars of classical architecture on whose firm, consonant foundation nineteenth century Romantic sounds soar upwards in a preconceived plan mindful of every detail however small. Nothing is left to chance; [as in Beethoven], each movement has its course determined from the very first note. Imaginative and original themes, individual harmonies, rhythms and phrases set in unusual metrical patterns, complete mastery over counterpoint, orchestration consistently serving the spirit of the music without flamboyant rhetoric, all are to be found within a classical framework controlling everything.

> Brahms was certainly one of music's paradoxes, from [the beginning], carrying an old philosopher's head on young athletic shoulders; playing something of a lone hand in the age of change—the age of Berlioz, Liszt, and Wagner. Within [his] thoroughly German concept of art, within the limits of which he saddled himself, he succeeded mightily in his efforts to unite Classical forms and nineteenth century Romantic expression.

Brahms was a thorny and complex man, whose life and personality are well described in my Teaching Company "Great Masters" biography. In the necessary interest of time then, after one brief detour, we'll move directly on to his symphonies, symphonies that almost didn't happen. On September 30, 1853, Johannes Brahms, 20 years old, tiny, slim, blonde-haired, and blue-eyed, with nary a whisker to be seen on what would become his famously bearded face, showed up at the door of Robert and Clara Schumann's house in Düsseldorf. Brahms had been on tour with a violinist named Eduard Remenyi. Remenyi had dropped him like a hot knockwurst when Brahms behaved poorly towards the great Liszt back in Weimar. And Brahms, now in Düsseldorf, was hoping for an audience with the Schumanns. He got a bit more than just that. He ended up staying for the next three months, and Robert Schumann was absolutely floored by Brahms's early piano music—not only saw to its immediate publication, but wrote an article which ran in the influential magazine the *Neue Zeitschrift für Musik*, in which he introduced Brahms as the new, German messiah of music who would someday: "[aim] his magic wand where the massed might of choir and orchestra can lend it strength, [and so present] still more wonderful glimpses into the mysteries of the spirit world."

What Schumann said in essence, and this is how Brahms and the musical community of Germany took it, was that Johannes Brahms was the anointed one who would one day compose the worthy successor to Beethoven's Ninth. Of course, what Schumann actually did was scare the living bejeezus out of the 20-year-old Brahms and induce a symphonic writers block that lasted for the next 23 years. That's right. With the lofty expectations of Schumann and the derisive snickers of the moderns like Wagner ringing in his ears, it took Brahms 21 years to complete his First Symphony once he began it, a work he began around 1855, and one not finally finished and released until 1876. And, true to form, friends and foes alike immediately referred to it as "Beethoven's Tenth."

For Brahms, the act of finally completing and releasing the First had an amazingly cathartic effect. With the symphonic cat finally out of the bag, his three remaining symphonies followed rather quickly. The Second was completed one year later, in 1877; the Third, in 1883; and the Fourth, in 1885. In the brief time we have remaining, we'll focus on Brahms's Third, which like all four of his symphonies, is a masterpiece of synthesis—the best of the old and the best of the new, woven seamlessly together into a deeply moving and admirably compact whole.

Johannes Brahms, Symphony no. 3 in F Major, op. 90 (1883)

Brahms's Third Symphony is his "heroic" symphony, his own *Eroica.* Certainly the opening of the first movement is one of the most sensational in the symphonic repertoire, a free mix of F major and F minor built atop a titanic rising melodic idea, a motive: F–Ab–F, heard first in the upper winds and brass, and then, as the magnificent, descending first theme begins in the upper strings, in the bass line.

[Musical example from Symphony No. 3 in F Major, Opus 90, Brahms: I; Opening]

Brahms composed the great bulk of the Third Symphony during the summer of 1883, while he was staying in the resort town of Wiesbaden, within sight of the Rhine River. He was inspired by both the magnificent setting and by the memory of his friend and mentor, Robert Schumann, and Schumann's own symphony, the Rhenish Symphony of 1850. Brahms went so far as to base his own magnificent first movement/first theme on Schumann's first movement "Rhine" theme. A back-to-back comparison will be most revealing. First, a bit of Schumann's theme from, the blaring conclusion of the first movement of his Rhenish Symphony.

[Musical example from Symphony No. 3 in Eb Major, Opus 97, "The Rhenish", Schumann: I; Conclusion]

Now, Brahms's swirling and magnificent first theme in its entirety.

[Musical example from Symphony No. 3 in F Major, Opus 90, Brahms: I; Theme I]

Throughout Brahms's first movement, which plumbs a magnificent range of expression, from heroic majesty to intimate, delicate realism, the rising three-note motive, or *motto,* that began the movement is a constant presence: here, a foreground melody; there, an accompanimental line; here, a cadential figure; there, a bass line; everywhere unifying, relating, and organizing the diverse but always interrelated elements of the movement in a way, well, in a way that would have made Beethoven proud.

The second movement is a gorgeous, vaguely rustic movement in C major that opens with a luminous, clarinet-dominated theme, a theme sounding more like a serenade than a symphony.

[Musical example from Symphony No. 3 in F Major, Opus 90, Brahms: II; Opening]

The third movement in C minor is the "omega" to the second movement's "alpha," featuring an opening theme that is as melodically sophisticated and "urban," as haunting and melancholy as the second movement opening was gentle and rustic and serenade-like.

[Musical example from Symphony No. 3 in F Major, Opus 90, Brahms: III; Opening]

The fourth and final movement of Brahms's Third is for me one of the most inspired and exciting symphonic movements ever composed. The movement begins quietly and mysteriously in the key of F minor, a key that was implicitly implied, if not explicitly stated, by the rising F–Ab–F motto of the first movement opening.

[Musical example from Symphony No. 3 in F Major, Opus 90, Brahms: IV; Opening]

This restrained, almost furtive opening theme, which contains within it basically all the melodic material Brahms needs to construct the remainder of the movement, gives way to a chorale of great beauty and gravity.

[Musical example from Symphony No. 3 in F Major, Opus 90, Brahms: IV; Chorale]

This now gives way to the explosive return of the formerly "mysterious" first theme, which is now followed immediately by the modulating bridge.

[Musical example from Symphony No. 3 in F Major, Opus 90, Brahms: IV; Reprise of Theme I and Modulating Bridge]

This powers directly into a fabulous second theme, a strutting and a wonderful tune played initially by the cellos and horns. Let's hear this second theme through to the conclusion of the exposition.

[Musical example from Symphony No. 3 in F Major, Opus 90, Brahms: IV; Theme II and Exposition]

Wow. The glories of this movement just continue to build, one upon the next. It ends with a sublime and shimmering coda, during which the opening moments of the first movement return with a serenity and nobility that defy easy description.

[Musical example from Symphony No. 3 in F Major, Opus 90, Brahms: IV; Conclusion]

Brahms's Third Symphony is Brahms at his best: majestic, passionate, intimate; as always, reconciling the clarity and concision of Classicism with the expressive palette of Romanticism.

Thank you.

Lecture Sixteen
Gustav Mahler

Scope: In the late Romantic era, many composers believed that form must follow expressive function and, thus, turned away from the symphony as a genre. Gustav Mahler managed to reconcile the multi-movement symphony of the Classical era and Beethoven, dominated by the sonata form, with the explicit literary and over-the-top expressive content of the period. What's more, he did so without either sacrificing musical integrity or skimping on emotional content. In this lecture, we take an in-depth look at Mahler's Second Symphony, a tour-de-force of compositional technique and individual expression.

Outline

I. We cap the 19th century with an investigation of a Gustav Mahler's Symphony no. 2 in C Minor ("Resurrection") of 1895, an almost perfect bookend to Beethoven's Ninth. This symphony picks up the expressive and constructive innovation of Beethoven's Ninth and brings it to a point that would seem to encompass almost every musical trend and spiritual belief of 19th-century Romanticism.

   A. For the most part, Mahler composed only songs and symphonies. He completed nine numbered symphonies, plus the symphonic song-cycle *Das Lied von der Erde*, ("The Song of the Earth") and the torso of a tenth symphony, left incomplete at his death. Mahler's "symphonies" would seem to "embrace everything"; they are philosophical tracts, spiritual musings, and musical reflections on the great unanswered questions of human existence.

   B. Mahler was born in a Bohemian village not far from the Austrian border on July 7, 1860. He grew up in a Jewish, German-speaking household that followed a distinctly Austrian cultural orbit. Someone else might have felt enriched by such a varied cultural background, but Mahler was left with a sense of never really "belonging" anywhere. He felt that he was alone in the world, with only his talent, strength, and imagination to sustain him.

C. One of the reasons behind Mahler's sense of loneliness and alienation was the situation in his household, which scarred the young Mahler's hypersensitive psyche.

    1. Of Bernard and Marie Mahler's 14 children, 8 died in infancy and childhood, including Mahler's brother Ernst, who was Gustav's best friend and died, literally, in his arms, at the age of 14. A surviving sister died of a brain tumor at 26, and a brother committed suicide at 21.

    2. Further, Mahler's father, Bernard, was a tyrannical and brutal man for whom domestic violence was an outlet for his rage and frustration. Mahler's mother, Marie, was clubfooted, sickly, and wretchedly unhappy.

    3. It would seem that Mahler inherited the worst characteristics of both his parents: from his mother, severe hypochondria and an overwhelming sense of victimization and, from his father, a pitiless, tyrannical nature that allowed him to drive those around him mercilessly.

D. After graduating from the Vienna Conservatory, circumstances conspired to "force" Mahler into a career as an opera conductor. He became one of the greatest conductors of his time—brilliant, passionate, electrifying, and utterly terrifying.

E. Details of his life and career can be found in The Teaching Company's "Great Masters" biography of Mahler. For now, suffice it to say that Gustav Mahler was a deeply troubled man and an extraordinarily gifted composer and conductor who spent his life searching for answers to questions about life and death; the nature of the universe; and the nature of love, God, redemption, and resignation. He was a genuine philosopher, who used the medium of the symphony to explore a realm of ideas that others might write about, preach about, and teach about.

II. Mahler's earliest compositions were songs for voice and piano, many of which he then arranged for voice and orchestra.

A. These early songs—with texts drawn most notably from a poetic anthology called *Des Knaben Wunderhorn*, or "*The Youth's Magic Horn*"—became a source of material that Mahler used in his symphonies. Mahler's Symphonies nos. 2, 3, and 4 are often referred to as the "*Wunderhorn*" Symphonies, because each one of them contains songs and melodies taken from songs that were set to poems drawn from *Des Knaben Wunderhorn.*

B. The music Mahler composed for his songs became iconographic for him. For example, if a poem about loneliness and resignation inspired Mahler to compose a certain melody, then that melody became symbolic, for Mahler, of loneliness and resignation. For Mahler, that melody, alone, without its words, could be plugged into a symphony to evoke loneliness and resignation. This is what Wagner called a *leitmotif,* a musical idea that represents a person, place, emotion, or thing; Mahler took the concept a step further.

C. Mahler had three great influences. The first of these was Beethoven, particularly Beethoven's Ninth Symphony, that most perfect symphonic construct that included music and words, instruments and voices, a work that for Mahler, "embraced the world." The second influence was the music dramas of Richard Wagner, and the third was Berlioz's *Symphonie fantastique,* the work, along with Beethoven's Ninth, that showed Mahler how to write a multi-movement program symphony.

III. We will examine Mahler's Second Symphony, composed between 1888 and 1894, because this symphony best demonstrates Mahler's debt to Beethoven's Ninth and to the *Symphonie fantastique.* It is a perfect example of the Mahler symphony as a religious, spiritual, and philosophical tract and the last 19th-century symphony we will examine before we move on to the 20th century.

A. Mahler's Second was a long time in the making. He composed what eventually became the first movement in 1888 as a self-standing *symphonic poem,* that is, a piece of orchestral program music, and entitled it "Funeral Rites."

1. Then, after having composed almost nothing for five years, Mahler returned to his "Funeral Rites" during the summer of 1893, determined to turn it into the first movement of a grand symphony. He quickly composed the second and third movements.

2. For the fourth movement, Mahler wanted to follow the model of Beethoven's Ninth and have a choral finale, but he needed a text, one appropriate to the spirit of death and life explored in the other movements. He searched the Bible, European and

Eastern poetry, and Eastern mystical and philosophical texts, but to no avail.

3. Then, on March 29, 1894, at the funeral of the conductor and pianist Hans von Bülow, Mahler heard a setting of Theodor Klopstock's poetic ode "Resurrection" and knew he'd found his solution.

4. The finale was composed during the summer of 1894, and later that same year, Mahler inserted another movement immediately before the finale, bringing the symphony's total to five. The "new" movement is the song *"Urlicht"* ("Primordial Light"), which Mahler had originally composed in 1892 based on a text from *Des Knaben Wunderhorn*.

B. Mahler disliked providing his audiences with written programs that described the storyline of his symphonies, but at the request of King Albert of Saxony, he did so for a performance of the Second that took place in Dresden in 1901. He later revised the program for his bride, Alma, and it is from this revision that we follow the symphony.

IV. Like his Symphonies nos. 5, 6, and 7, Mahler's Second begins with a funeral march, which serves as the first theme of a massive sonata-form movement with three main themes. According to Mahler's program: "We are standing beside the coffin of a man beloved."

A. The movement begins with a violent introduction consisting of a shivering upper-string tremolo and a dark, explosive tune in the low strings that features a series of vicious downward gestures. Death seems real, present, and unavoidable. (**Musical selection**: Mahler, Symphony no. 2 in C Minor, movement 1, introduction.)

B. The first-theme funeral march follows. It represents Mahler's "man beloved," and it is angry and defiant in tone. Starting quietly, it builds to a climax, then descends, which is understood as being representative of death. The theme concludes with a stark fanfare, as if to say, "Death is victorious this day." (**Musical selection**: Mahler, Symphony no. 2, movement 1, theme 1 [funeral march].)

C. Theme 2 follows immediately. It is brief and forlorn in tone and represents the grief of the living. (**Musical selection**: Mahler, Symphony no. 2, movement 1, theme 2.)

D. Suddenly, we hear the last thing we would expect in this gloomy environment: a gentle, ascending, heavenly theme in E major.

(**Musical selection**: Mahler, Symphony no. 2, movement 1, theme 3.)

1. The theme emerges as if in a dream, throwing a shaft of light across this dark, funereal landscape. It represents the hope that death is not the end, after all.

2. This third theme will become the "resurrection" theme of the fifth and final movement, although for now, the blissful, dreamlike mood it creates is crushed by an outburst in the brass and strings as the violent introduction begins again. Here, in the first movement, death is the reality, and resurrection will not be achieved without a struggle.

E. Immediately following this reprise of the introduction, an extraordinary thing happens: Inspired by the fleeting vision of heaven represented by theme 3, the soul of the "man beloved," represented by the opening five notes of the funeral march, becomes emboldened.

1. The reanimated soul is portrayed by a rising fanfare in Eb major, the key of *Eroica*, the heroic key. This rising "hero's fanfare" immediately begins to struggle with various downward moving musical elements, which represent death and nothingness.

2. The meaning is clear: For Mahler, this passage represents the soul's struggle for something beyond death, a struggle for wisdom and revelation, for transfiguration and resurrection. This passage—and the exposition—ends quietly, with the return of the opening funereal march. We listen, from the advent of the "hero's fanfare" through the end of the exposition. (**Musical selection**: Mahler, Symphony no. 2, movement 1, "hero's fanfare" to exposition end.)

F. In his program notes, Mahler describes the ongoing action of this first movement:

> For the last time, his battles, his suffering, and his purpose pass before the mind's eye. And now, at this moment, when we are released from the paltry distractions of everyday life, our hearts are gripped by a voice of awe-inspiring solemnity, which we seldom or never hear above the deafening traffic of mundane affairs. What next? it says. What is life—and what is death? Have we any continuing existence?

G. The movement ends with a terrifying descent, as the coffin of the man beloved is lowered into the grave. (**Musical selection**: Mahler, Symphony no. 2, movement 1, conclusion.)

H. Mahler continues: "Is it all an empty dream, or has this life of ours, and our death, a meaning? If we are to go on living, we must answer this question."

V. The second and third movements look back over the life of the man. Of the second movement, Mahler writes: "A blissful moment in his life and a mournful memory of youth and lost innocence." (**Musical selection**: Mahler, Symphony no. 2, movement 2, opening theme [A only].)

VI. Mahler continues his description: "The spirit of disbelief and negation has taken possession of him. He despairs of himself and God. The world and life become a witches' brew; disgust of existence in every form strikes him with an iron fist and drives him to despair."

A. For this third movement, Mahler turned to a song for voice and piano he had composed in early 1893, "St. Anthony of Padua Preaches to the Fishes." The comic and ironic text, from *Des Knaben Wunderhorn*, uses fish as a metaphor for people, depicting the fish as spiritless, gluttonous, stupid, hypocritical, and amoral creatures who swim aimlessly and mindlessly through everyday life. (**Musical selection**: Mahler, "St. Anthony of Padua Preaches to the Fishes," first verse, original composition for voice and piano.)

> When it's time for his sermon
> Anthony finds the church empty.
> He goes to the river
> And preaches to the fishes!
> They clap with tails that
> Gleam in the sunshine.
>
> The carps with roe
> Are all gathered here;
> Their mouths agape,
> They listen intently;
> No sermon has ever
> Pleased the fish more!

Pointy-nosed pike,
That are always fighting,
Swim up in a hurry,
To hear the saint!
And those visionaries
Who constantly fast:
The cod, I mean,
Appear for the sermon.
No sermon has ever
Pleased the cod as much.

Fine eels and sturgeons
That feast like lords,
Deign to hear,
The sermon!
Even crabs. And turtles,
Usually slowpokes,
Climb up from the bottom,
To hear the talker!
No sermon has ever
Pleased the crabs more!

Big fish and small fish,
Noble and common,
Raise their heads
Like intelligent creatures,
At God's command,
To listen to the sermon.

The sermon over,
Each one wanders away.
The pikes remain thieves,
The eels, big lovers;
They liked the sermon, but
They don't change their ways!

The crabs still walk backwards,
The cod are still fat,
The carp are still guzzlers,

The sermon forgotten!
They all liked the sermon, but
They don't change their ways!

(trans. Maggie Lyons)

B. In Mahler's mind, the comic, perpetual-motion music he created for this song fit perfectly the expressive message he wanted for the third movement of his Second Symphony: an image of people drifting through their lives, riding mindlessly the currents and eddies of their days, unaware of the terrible inevitability of death and the questions it poses. Mahler created an extended orchestral version of the song for this third movement. (**Musical selection**: Mahler, Symphony no. 2, movement 3, opening.)

VII. We return to Mahler's program: "The mourning voice of ingenuous belief sounds in our ears. I am from God and will return to God! God will give me a candle to light my way to the bliss of eternal life."

A. This fourth movement brings us back to the "present" and back to the presence of death and the questions of redemption and resurrection brought to the fore by death. This fourth movement also brings something new to the symphony, a human voice; with that voice and the words that are sung, the expressive content of the symphony changes from implicit to explicit.

B. As we previously observed, this fourth movement is a song on a text from *Des Knaben Wunderhorn* entitled "*Urlicht.*" The movement is scored for alto or mezzo-soprano and an exquisite, chamber-like orchestral accompaniment.

    1. The text describes a strange twilight world between death and rebirth. The first verse reads as follows:

O Röschen rot!	O rosebud red!
Der Mensch liegt in grosster Not,	Man lies in greatest need,
Der Mensch liegt in grosser Pein.	Man lies in greatest pain.
Ja lieber möcht ich im Himmel sein.	I'd much rather be in heaven.

    2. The first line of this poem, "O rosebud red," evokes purity, naiveté, and goodness. The solemn brass and bassoon chorale that immediately follows that first line creates a profound sense of quietude, unlimited space, and religious contemplation. (**Musical selection**: Mahler, Symphony no. 2, movement 4, verse 1.)

C.   Mahler introduces the second verse of the poem with traveling music at a walking tempo. "The path" from death to rebirth has been encountered:

Da kam ich auf einen breiten Weg,	Then I came upon a broad road;
Da kam ein Englein und wollt' mich abweisen.	an angel came and wanted to turn me away.
Ach nein? Ich liess mich nicht abweisen.	Oh no, I would not be turned away!

D.   That last line, sung with resolve and conviction, leads immediately to the third and climactic verse of the song, which introduces the central dramatic point of the next and last movement, resurrection. The third verse begins with anguish and ends with a profound sense of peace and tranquility:

Ich bin von Gott und will wieder zu Gott!	I am of God and will return to God!
Der liebe Gott wird mir ein Lichtlein geben,	Dear God will give me a light,
Wird leuchten mir in das ewig selig' Leben!	Will light my way into eternal, blissful life!

(**Musical selection**: Mahler, Symphony no. 2, movement 4, verse 3.)

VIII. The virtually perfect sense of peace we feel at the conclusion of the fourth movement is instantly shattered by the gut-wrenching eruption that begins the fifth and final movement. Clearly, redemption and resurrection will not be achieved without struggle.

A.   Here, Mahler has created his own version of the "from the chaos" opening that begins the final choral movement of Beethoven's Ninth Symphony. Mahler writes: "We are again confronted by terrifying questions!" (**Musical selection**: Mahler, Symphony no. 2, movement 5, ms. 1–26.)

B.   We continue with Mahler: "A voice is heard crying aloud: 'The end of all living things is come—the Last Judgment is at hand and the horror of the day of days has broken forth.' The earth quakes, the graves burst open, and the dead arise and stream on in endless procession."

C. A grisly, gruesome death march ensues that quotes liberally the melody of the "*Dies irae*," the Catholic prayer for the dead that describes the Day of Judgment. We listen from the quaking earth and the bursting graves. (**Musical selection**: Mahler, Symphony no. 2, movement 5, development, opening.)

D. From the program notes:

> The great and the little ones of the earth—kings and beggars, righteous and godless—all press on; the cry for mercy and forgiveness strikes fearfully on our ears. The wailing rises higher—our senses desert us; consciousness dies at the approach of the eternal spirit, the 'Last Trumpet' is heard— the trumpets of the apocalypse ring out; in the eerie silence that follows, we can just catch the distant, barely audible song of the nightingale, a last tremulous echo of earthly life!

(**Musical selection**: Mahler, Symphony no. 2, movement 5, ms 448–471.)

E. Next, Mahler writes: "A chorus of saints and heavenly beings softly breaks forth: 'Thou shalt arise, surely thou shalt arise.'" Their voices emerging as if from the ether, the chorus enters, singing the first words of Theodor Klopstock's ode, "Resurrection": "*Aufersteh'n, ja aufersteh'n*," "Arise, yea, arise." (**Musical selection**: Mahler, Symphony no. 2, movement 5, verse 1.)

F. Through an additional 14 minutes and a total of eight verses (of which only the first two are by Klopstock; the rest are by Mahler), the chorus and orchestra work their way to the breathtaking conclusion of the symphony.

G. Mahler completes his description: "Then appears the glory of God! A wondrous, soft light penetrates us to the heart—all is holy calm! And behold—there is no judgment. There are no sinners, no just. None is great, none is small. There is no punishment and no reward. An overwhelming love lightens our being. We know and are." The chorus sings:

Aufersteh'n, ja aufersteh'n wirst du,	Arisen, yea, arisen you shall be
Mein Herz in einem Nu!	My heart in an instant!
Was du geshlagen	What you have overcome
Zu Gott wird es dich tragen.	Will carry you to God.

(**Musical selection**: Mahler, Symphony no. 2, movement 5, verse 8, ms. 712–end.)

H. Mahler said of these final moments: "The increasing tension, working up to the final climax, is so tremendous that I don't know myself, now that it is over, how I ever came to write it" (Cardus).

Lecture Sixteen—Transcript
Gustav Mahler

Welcome back to *The Symphony*. This is Lecture Sixteen—it is entitled "Gustav Mahler." It's time to cap for now the 19th century with an investigation of a symphony that makes it almost a perfect bookend to Beethoven's Ninth, a symphony that picks up the expressive and constructive gauntlet of Beethoven's Ninth and drives it to a point that would seem to encompass almost every musical trend and spiritual belief of 19th-century Romanticism. We refer here to Gustav Mahler's Symphony no. 2 in C Minor, the so-called "Resurrection" Symphony of 1895.

"The symphony must be like the world; it must embrace everything." Thus *sprach* Gustav Mahler, and it is as accurate a case statement for his creative output as any we could imagine. For all intents and purposes, Mahler only composed songs and symphonies. He completed nine numbered symphonies, plus the symphonic song cycle *Das Lied von der Erde*, ("The Song of the Earth") and the torso of a tenth symphony, left incomplete at his death. Mahler's "symphonies" would seem to "embrace everything"; they are veritable philosophical tracts, spiritual musings, and musical reflections on the great unanswered questions. Collectively, they are his Bible, his Talmud, his worldview, the essence of his intellectual and spiritual existence.

Gustav Mahler was born in the Bohemian village of Kaliste, about 70 miles South of Prague, not far from the Austrian border, on July 7, 1860. He grew up in a Jewish, German-speaking household that followed a distinctly Austrian cultural orbit. While somebody else might have felt enriched by such a varied cultural background, for Mahler it was quite the opposite. Like the strange hybrid creature from the *Island of Doctor Moreau*, who rhetorically asked, "Are we not man? Are we not beast? Half man, half beast!" Well, so Mahler's sense of "half-ness," of never really "belonging," conditioned his psyche from the beginning. When as an adult he complained: "I am thrice homeless, as a Bohemian in Austria, as an Austrian among Germans, as a Jew throughout the world, everywhere an intruder, never welcomed." He was expressing a basic, if rather self-pitying, article of faith: that he was alone in the world with only his strength, his talent, and his imagination to sustain him.

One of the reasons behind Mahler's sense of loneliness and alienation was the morbidity rate of the Mahler household, a morbidity rate that irreparably scarred Mahler's hypersensitive psyche—and I will tell you, a morbidity rate far above even the rates of the day. Of Bernard and Marie Mahler's 14 children, 8 died in infancy and childhood, including Mahler's closest and best friend, his younger brother Ernst, a year younger than Gustav, who died, literally, in his arms at the age of 14. A surviving sister named Leopoldine died of a brain tumor at 26. A brother named Otto committed suicide at 21. If all of this wasn't bad enough, Mahler's father, Bernard, was a tyrannical and brutal man for whom domestic violence was an outlet for his rage and frustration. Mahler's mother, Marie, clubfooted and sickly, was wretchedly unhappy. And it would seem that Mahler inherited the worst characteristics of both his parents: from his mother, severe hypochondria and an overwhelming sense of victimization; from his father: a pitiless, tyrannical nature that allowed him to drive those around him mercilessly.

A quick sidebar here, just in case we should think that Mahler was the craziest musician running around central Europe at the time. While a student at the Vienna Conservatory, Mahler roomed with three other students: Hugo Wolf, who went on to become one of the greatest songwriters who ever lived; Hans Rott, a composer of tremendous promise; the violinist and conductor, Rudolph Krzyzanowki. Mahler died at home and in bed, surrounded by weeping friends and relatives. Wolf, Rott and Krzyzanowki all died alone and clinically insane. Mahler was the most normal of the bunch. It would seem that the phrase "mental health" was an oxymoron in those days.

After graduating from the Vienna Conservatory, circumstances conspired to "force" Mahler into a career as an opera conductor (at least that's how he saw it, referring always to his "damnable life in the theater"). He developed into one of the greatest conductors of his time—brilliant, passionate, electrifying, and utterly terrifying. We are told that Mahler was "a small, pale tyrant with a merciless tongue who gave [the unfortunate singers and instrumentalists under his baton] no quarter. They loathed him."

For the details of his life and career, I would direct your attention to my Teaching Company "Great Masters" biography of Mahler. For now, suffice it to say that Gustav Mahler was a deeply troubled man and an extraordinarily gifted composer and conductor who spent his life searching for answers to the big questions, questions regarding the purpose of life and death; the nature of the universe; the nature of love, of God, of redemption, of resignation. He was a genuine philosopher, who used the medium of the symphony to explore a realm of ideas that others might write about, preach about, and teach about.

Mahler as Symphonist

Mahler's earliest compositions were songs for voice and piano many of which he arranged later for voice and orchestra. His early songs—with texts drawn most notably from a poetic anthology called *Des Knaben Wunderhorn*, or "The Youth's Magic Horn"—became a source of material that Mahler used in his symphonies, particularly his first four symphonies. Mahler's Symphonies nos. 2, 3 and 4 are often referred to as his "*Wunderhorn*" Symphonies, because each one of them contains songs and melodies taken from songs that were set to texts drawn from *Des Knaben Wunderhorn*.

We explain: The music Mahler composed for his songs became iconographic, became symbolic for him. For example, if a poem about loneliness and resignation inspired Mahler to compose a certain melody, that melody became, for Mahler, symbolic, iconographic, of loneliness and resignation. For Mahler, that melody—alone, without its words—could be plugged into a symphony in order to evoke loneliness and resignation. This is what Wagner called a *leitmotif*, a musical idea that represents a person, a place, an emotion, or thing. And Mahler took the concept a step further.

Mahler's great influences are three in number. Number one: Beethoven, particularly Beethoven's Ninth Symphony, that most perfect symphonic construct that included both music and words, instruments and voices, a work that for Mahler "embraced the world." Influence number two: the music dramas of Richard Wagner. It might seem curious that Mahler, the greatest opera conductor of his time, certainly one of the greatest Wagner conductors of all time, never wrote an opera. But Mahler found a way to combine the dramatic storytelling of opera with the multi-movement symphony of Beethoven and was satisfied that this genre of program symphony gave him what he needed to make his expressive points. Mahler's third great influence was Berlioz's *Symphonie fantastique*, the work, along with Beethoven's Ninth, that showed Mahler how to do it, how to write a multi-movement program symphony.

It should come as no surprise to us then that Mahler, as a conductor, was famous for his Beethoven, his Wagner and his *Symphonie fantastique*. Regarding the later, we read from a review that appeared in the *New York Post* on January 7, 1910, a review of a performance of *Symphonie fantastique* performed at Carnegie Hall by the New York Philharmonic and its newly-hired conductor, Gustav Mahler:

> The Philharmonic audience at Carnegie Hall last night enjoyed a conductor who has no superior anywhere: Gustav Mahler, [who conducted among other works] Berlioz's *Fantastic Symphony*. The Berlioz Symphony has been interpreted here by nearly every noted conductor of the time, but not one of them succeeded in rousing a sober Philharmonic audience to such a state of frenzied excitement as Mahler did with his fourth and fifth movements. Mr. Mahler has worked a miracle—no other word seems strong enough to describe what he's done in making this [orchestra] the equivalent of the Boston Symphony Orchestra, if not its superior. No wonder the Mahlerites are growing so fast in numbers!

Symphony no. 2 in C Minor

We will examine Mahler's Second Symphony, composed between 1888 and 1894, because it is that symphony of Mahler's that best demonstrates his debt to Beethoven's Ninth and the *Symphonie fantastique*. It's a perfect example of the Mahler symphony as a religious, spiritual, and philosophical tract. Mahler's Second was a long time in the making. He composed what eventually became the first movement in 1888 as a self-standing *symphonic poem*, that is, a piece of orchestra program music, and entitled it "Funeral Rites." Then, after having composed almost nothing for five years, Mahler returned to his "Funeral Rites" during the summer of 1893, determined to turn it into the first movement of a grand symphony. He quickly composed the second and third movements and then, my friends, he hit the wall. You see for the fourth movement, Mahler wanted to follow the model of Beethoven's Ninth and have a choral finale, but he needed a text, one appropriate to the spirit of death and life explored in the other movements. By his own admission, he ransacked the Bible, European and Eastern poetry, Eastern mystical and philosophical texts, but to no avail.

Yet, on March 29, 1894, at the funeral of the conductor and pianist Hans von Bülow, Mahler heard a setting of Theodore Klopstock's poetic ode "Resurrection." He saw the light! Mahler described his moment of illumination:

> For a long time I've been considering the idea of introducing a chorus into the last movement, and only the fear that this might be interpreted as a servile imitation of Beethoven made me hesitate. Then Bülow died and I attended his funeral. The atmosphere in

which I found myself and the thoughts I dedicated to the dead man were very much in the spirit of the work I was then carrying within me. All of a sudden the choir, accompanied by an organ, intoned a setting of Klopstock's "Resurrection." It was as if I'd been struck by lightening; everything suddenly rose before me clearly! Such is the flash for which the creator waits, such is sacred inspiration!

The finale was composed during the summer of 1894, and later that same year, Mahler inserted another movement before the finale, bringing the symphony's total to five. The "new" movement, the second to last movement as it is now, is the song "*Urlicht,* ("Primordial Light"), a song Mahler had originally composed in 1892, one based on a text drawn from *Des Knaben Wunderhorn.*

Mahler hated providing his audiences with written program notes. His attitude was that if you couldn't figure out on your own what's going on in a piece of music—well, you had no right listening to it! However, at the request of King Albert of Saxony, Mahler did provide a written program for a performance of the Second that took place in Dresden in 1901. Mahler rather uncharitably described that program as "a crutch for a cripple." At the request of his new bride, Alma, Mahler revised the program—the "crutch"—that he'd prepared for Albert of Saxony, and he gave her a copy. Alma saved it, and it is from this program that we will now read.

Movement I

Like his Symphonies nos. 5, 6 and 7, Mahler's Second begins with a funeral march, a march that is the first theme of a massive three-main-theme sonata-form first movement. According to Mahler's program: "We are standing beside the coffin of a man beloved."

The movement begins with a violent introduction consisting of a shivering upper string tremolo and a dark and explosive tune in the low strings that features a series of vicious, deathly, downward gestures. This is "in your face" music; it is death, real and present and as unavoidable as Texas and Barbara Walters.

[Musical example from Symphony No. 2 in C Minor, Mahler: I; Opening]

The first-theme funeral march now follows. It represents Mahler's "man beloved," and it is angry and defiant in tone. Starting quietly, it builds to a climax, and then descends, which is understood as being representative as death. The theme concludes with a stark fanfare, as if to say, "death is victorious this day."

[Musical example from Symphony No. 2 in C Minor, Mahler: I; Theme I]

Theme 2 follows immediately. It is brief and forlorn in tone. It represents the grief of the living, standing there beside the coffin of the man departed.

[Musical example from Symphony No. 2 in C Minor, Mahler: I; Theme II]

And now, suddenly, out of the blue, the last thing we expect to hear in this gloomy environment: a gentle, ascending, genuinely heavenly theme in E Major. It emerges as if in a dream, throwing a shaft of light across this dark, funereal landscape. It represents the hope, the possibility that death is perhaps not the end after all. This third theme will become the "resurrection" theme of the fifth and final movement, although for now, the blissful, dreamlike mood it creates is crushed by a violent outburst in the brass and strings as the violent introduction begins again. Here, in the first movement, death is the reality, and resurrection will not be achieved without a struggle. Theme III:

[Musical example from Symphony No. 2 in C Minor, Mahler: I; Theme III]

Immediately following this reprise of the introduction, an extraordinary thing happens: Inspired by the fleeting version of heaven represented by theme 3, the soul of the "man beloved," as represented by the opening five notes of the funeral march of theme 1, becomes emboldened. His reanimated soul is portrayed by a rising fanfare in Eb major, the key of *Eroica*, the heroic key. This rising fanfare immediately begins to struggle with various downward-moving elements which represent death and nothingness. The meaning of all of this is crystal clear. For Mahler, this passage represents the soul's struggle for something beyond death, a struggle for wisdom and revelation, for transfiguration and resurrection. This passage—and the exposition—ends quietly, with the return of the opening funeral march. We listen, from the advent of the "hero's fanfare" through the end of the exposition.

[Musical example from Symphony No. 2 in C Minor, Mahler: I; Hero's Fanfare through Exposition]

Mahler describes the ongoing action of this first movement:

> For the last time his battles, his suffering, and his purpose pass before the mind's eye. And now, at this moment, when we are released from the paltry distractions of everyday life, our hearts are

gripped by a voice of awe-inspiring solemnity, which we seldom or never hear above the deafening traffic of mundane affairs. What next? it says. What is life—and what is death? Have we any continuing existence?

The movement ends with a terrifying descent as the coffin of the man beloved is lowered into the grave.

[Musical example from Symphony No. 2 in C Minor, Mahler: I; Conclusion]

Mahler continues his description: "Is it all an empty dream, or has this life of ours, and our death, a meaning? If we are to go on living, we must answer this question."

Movement II

The second—and I would tell you the third movement as well—the second movement looks back over the life of the man. Of the second movement, Mahler writes: "A blissful moment in his life and a mournful memory of youth and lost innocence." Please let us sample the opening of the second movement of Mahler's Symphony no. 2. This looks back to youth and the past.

[Musical example from Symphony No. 2 in C Minor, Mahler: II; Opening]

Movement III

Mahler continues his description: "The spirit of disbelief and negation has taken possession of him. He despairs of himself and God. The world and life become a witches' brew; disgust of existence in every form strikes him with an iron fist and drives him to despair."

For this third movement, Mahler turned to a song for voice and piano he had composed in early 1893, "St. Anthony of Padua Preaches to the Fishes." The comic and ironic text, from *Des Knaben Wunderhorn* uses fish as a metaphor for people, depicting the fish as spiritless, gluttonous, stupid, hypocritical, and amoral creatures who swim aimlessly and mindlessly through everyday life. Here's the text:

When it's time for his sermon
Anthony finds the church empty.
He goes to the river
And preaches to the fishes!

They clap with tails that
Gleam in the sunshine.

The carps with roe
Are all gathered here;
Their mouths agape,
They listen intently;
No sermon has ever
Pleased the fish more!

Pointy-nosed pike,
That are always fighting,
Swim up in a hurry,
To hear the saint!
And those visionaries
Who constantly fast:
The cod, I mean,
Appear for the sermon.
No sermon has ever
Pleased the cod as much.

Fine eels and sturgeons
That feast like lords,
Deign to hear,
The sermon!
Even crabs. And turtles,
Usually slowpokes,
Climb up from the bottom,
To hear the talker!
No sermon has ever
Pleased the crabs more!

Big fish and small fish,
noble and common,
raise their heads
like intelligent creatures,
at God's command,
to listen to the sermon.

The sermon over,
Each one wanders away.
The pikes remain thieves,
The eels, big lovers;
They liked the sermon, but
They don't change their ways!

The crabs still walk backwards,
The cod are still fat,
The carp are still guzzlers,
The sermon forgotten!
They all liked the sermon, but
They don't change their ways!

My friends, let's hear the first verse of the song as originally written for voice and piano.

[Musical example from Saint Anthony of Padua Preaches to the Fishes, Mahler; First Verse]

Now in Mahler's mind, the comic, perpetual-motion music he created for this song fit perfectly the expressive message he wanted for the third movement of the Second Symphony: A message, an image of people drifting through their lives, riding mindlessly the currents and eddies of their days, unaware of the great and terrible inevitability of death and the questions it poses. Mahler created an extended orchestral version of the song, and viola, the third movement was in place.

[Musical example from Symphony No. 2 in C Minor, Mahler: III]

Movement IV

We return to Mahler's program: "The mourning voice of ingenuous beliefs sounds in our ears. I am from God and will return to God! God will give me a candle to light my way to the bliss of eternal life." This fourth movement brings us back to the "present" and back to the presence of death and the questions of redemption and resurrection brought to the fore by death. This fourth movement also brings something new to the symphony—a human voice. And with that voice and the words that are sung, the expressive content of the symphony changes from implicit to explicit. As we previously observed, this fourth movement song is based on a text from *Des Knaben Wunderhorn*; it is a text entitled "*Urlicht*", or "Primordial Light." The movement is scored for alto or mezzo-soprano and an exquisite, genuinely chamber-like orchestral accompaniment. In my humble opinion, this movement is simply one of the most transcendentally beautiful and moving pieces of music ever written. The text describes a strange twilight world, one between death and rebirth. The first verse reads this way:

> O rosebud red!
> Man lies in greatest need,
> Man lies in greatest pain.
> I'd much rather be in heaven.

"O rosebud red," like Citizen Kane's sled, "Rosebud," the first line of this poem evokes purity, naiveté, and goodness. The solemn brass and bassoon chorale that immediately follows that first line creates a great sense of quietude, of unlimited space, of religious contemplation.

[Musical example from Symphony No. 2 in C Minor, Mahler: IV; Opening]

Mahler introduces the second verse of the poem with traveling music at a walking tempo. "The path" from death to rebirth has been encountered. The text reads:

> Then I came upon a broad road;
> an angel came
> and wanted to turn me away.
> Oh no, I would not be turned away!

Indeed not! That last line, sung with resolve and conviction leads immediately to the third and climactic verse of the song, a verse that introduces the central dramatic point of the next and last movement— "Resurrection." The third verse begins with anguish and ends with a profound sense of peace and tranquility. It reads:

> I am of God and will return to God!
> Dear God will give me a light,
> Will light my way into eternal, blissful life!

[Musical example from Symphony No. 2 in C Minor, Mahler: IV; Verse III]

Movement V

The virtually perfect sense of peace we feel at the conclusion of the fourth movement is instantly blown to bits by the gut-wrenching eruption, the death shriek that begins the fifth and final movement. Clearly, redemption and resurrection will not be achieved without struggle. Here,

Mahler has created his own version of the "from the chaos" opening that begins the choral movement of Beethoven's Ninth Symphony. Mahler writes: "We are again confronted by terrifying questions!" And thus, the last movement begins.

[Musical example from Symphony No. 2 in C Minor, Mahler: V; Opening]

"We are again confronted by terrifying questions. A voice is heard crying aloud, 'The end of all living things is come—the Last Judgment is at hand and the horror of the day of days has broken forth.' The earth quakes, the graves burst open and the dead arise and stream on in endless procession."

A grisly, gruesome, and entirely over the top death march ensues which quotes liberally the melody of the "*Dies irae*," the Catholic prayer for the dead that describes the Day of Judgment. We listen from the quaking earth and the bursting of the graves.

[Musical example from Symphony No. 2 in C Minor, Mahler: V]

Mahler's description continues:

> The great and the little ones of the earth—kings and beggars, righteous and godless—all press on; the cry for mercy and forgiveness strikes fearfully on our ears. The wailing rises higher—our senses desert us; consciousness dies at the approach of the eternal spirit, the "Last Trumpet" is heard—the trumpets of the apocalypse ring out; in the eerie silence that follows, we can just catch the distant, barely audible sound of the nightingale, a last tremulous echo of earthly life!

[Musical example from Symphony No. 2 in C Minor, Mahler: V]

And now Mahler writes: "A chorus of saints and heavenly beings softly breaks forth: 'Thou shalt arise, surely thou shalt arise.'" Their voices emerging as if from the ether, the chorus enters, singing the first words to Theodor Klopstock's ode, "Resurrection": "*Aufersteh'n, ja aufersteh'n*," "Arise, yea, arise."

[Musical example from Symphony No. 2 in C Minor, Mahler: V; Entrance of Chorus]

Through an additional 14 minutes, through a total of eight verses (of which only the first two are by Klopstock; the rest are by Mahler), the chorus and the orchestra work their way to the breathtaking conclusion of the symphony. Mahler completes his description: "Then appears the glory of

God! A wondrous, soft light penetrates us to the heart—all is holy calm! And behold—there is no judgment. There are no sinners, no just. None is great, none is small. There is no punishment and no reward. An overwhelming love lightens our being. We know and are."

And the chorus sings:

> Arisen, yea, arisen you shall be
> My heart in an instant!
> What you have overcome
> Will carry you to God.

[Musical example from Symphony No. 2 in C Minor, Mahler: V; Conclusion]

Mahler said of these final moments, "The increase in tension, working up to the final climax, is so tremendous that I don't know myself, now that it's over, how I ever came to write it."

Conclusion

In an era that believed increasingly that form must follow expressive function, in an era that saw many late Romantic composers turn away from the symphony as a genre, preferring instead to compose such structurally self-determined orchestral genres as the *symphonic poem* and the *tone poem*, Gustav Mahler managed to have his symphonic Linzer torte and eat it too. In his Second Symphony—to tell you the truth, in all of his symphonies—he manages to reconcile the multi-movement, sonata form-dominated symphony of the Classical era and Beethoven with the explicit literary and over the top self-expressive content of late Romanticism without sacrificing, my friends, either musical integrity or having to skimp unexpressive content. Mahler's Second Symphony, like all his symphonies, is a tour de force of incredible compositional technique and utterly individual expressive content.

Thank you.

Lecture Seventeen
Nielsen and Sibelius

Scope: Thus far, we have spent most of this course in the "land of the symphony," central and west-central Europe: Bohemia, Austria, and Germany. The composers of central Europe dominated the genre of symphony for 150 years or more. As we move into the late 19th and early 20th centuries, however, that dominance gives way, and the symphony becomes, increasingly, a global musical phenomenon. The remainder of this survey will take us out of central Europe to France, Russia, England, the United States, and Scandinavia. In this lecture, we explore the work of two Scandinavian composers, Carl Nielsen and Jean Sibelius, which is distinguished, in both, by a strong sense of place.

Outline

I.   Scandinavia is a huge area of great physical variety, and this region has produced a significant artistic community that seems out of proportion to its relatively small population. As we'll see, the Scandinavian environment has had a direct impact on the music created there.

   A. Scandinavia consists of the countries of Iceland, Norway, Sweden, Finland, and Denmark.
   1. Iceland is the westernmost European state, an island nation with a total population of around 266,000.
   2. Denmark is the southernmost of the Scandinavian countries, with a current population of 5.2 million people. It shares a 50-mile border with Germany and is more influenced by German art and culture than any other Scandinavian country.
   3. Norway lies northwest of Denmark; it has a current population of approximately 4.5 million people. Despite being 10 times the size of Denmark, Norway remained predominantly Danish (and, therefore, German) in cultural sympathy through the beginning of the 19th century.
   4. Sweden, immediately to the east of Norway, is both the largest and the most populous Scandinavian country. At 173,648 square miles, it's more than 20,000 square miles larger than California, and with about 8.5 million people, its total

population is about the size of the greater Bay Area. Sweden was a great power in the 17th and 18th centuries, but it cultivated no concert music tradition of its own.

5. Finland, the northeastern-most of the Scandinavian countries, with a current population of about 5.2 million, shares a 400-mile border with Russia. Over the centuries, Finland's cultural orbit has vacillated between Sweden and Russia, depending on who the occupying power was at any given period.

6. Altogether, the Scandinavian countries boast a landmass 10 times larger than New York State and a total population about the size of the New York City metropolitan area; needless to say, there is a good deal of empty space in Scandinavia.

B. We can easily list the preeminent Scandinavian composers of symphonies during the late 18th and early 19th centuries: Johan Agrel, Johan Berlin, and Joseph Kraus in the 18th century; the Norwegian Niels Gade, the Danes Johan Hartmann and Johan Svendsen, and the Swedes Adolf Lindblad and Franz Berwald in the 19th century. What all these composers have in common is that their music sounds like their Austrian models.

C. The spirit of nationalism that swept through much of Europe in the years after 1848 swept through Scandinavia as well. Four Scandinavian composers emerged, each of whom is now recognized as the "father" of his respective national tradition: in Norway, Edvard Grieg (1843–1907); in Sweden, Hugo Alfven (1872–1960); in Denmark, Carl Nielsen (1865–1931); and in Finland, Jean Sibelius (1865–1957).

D. The Norwegian Edvard Grieg wrote no symphonies of consequence and will not be discussed in this course. Hugo Alfven wrote five symphonies, but because they have not become part of the international repertoire, we will move past him as well. Carl Nielsen and Jean Sibelius, however, are both major symphonic composers whose symphonies are part of the international repertoire.

II. Carl Nielsen is the central figure in Danish music from the late 19th and early 20th centuries. His music and his writings about music exert a decisive influence over Danish music to this day and have been a source of inspiration for composers across Scandinavia. Among his most important and representative works are his six symphonies.

A. If Nielsen had worked in a major symphonic market, such as Vienna, his symphonies would be celebrated as being among the greatest in the repertoire. But he was born in a small village and worked in Copenhagen, and it wasn't until the 1950s, when the Danish State Radio Orchestra began touring with and recording his music, that his symphonies truly began to be heard outside of Denmark.

B. Nielsen's humble beginnings, as the 7th in a family of 12 children born to a housepainter, play a major part in his work. His concept of the "simple original," or what he also called "expressive simplicity," is the key to his music.

    1. The clarity, concision, and directness of expression Nielsen heard in the straightforward village music of his youth and in the music of Bach, Mozart, and Haydn remained the essential underpinning of all his work.

    2. We might think of him as a Danish Brahms, but without the unhappiness. Like Brahms, Nielsen generally disliked the excess that marked so much late Romantic music.

C. Nielsen's promise as a composer won him a scholarship through the Copenhagen Conservatory, where he studied from 1884–1886, and from which he received a strict, German-style schooling in harmony, counterpoint, and musical form.

    1. After graduating, he took various jobs as a violinist while he continued to compose on the side. In 1901, having completed his First Symphony and first opera, entitled *Saul and David*, he was granted an annual state pension so that he might have more time to compose.

    2. His Second Symphony followed in 1902; his Third, in 1911; the Fourth, in 1916; the Fifth, in 1922; and the Sixth, in 1925. Nielsen died six years later, in October of 1931, at the age of 66.

D. We turn to Nielsen's Symphony no. 4, op. 29, "The Inextinguishable" (1916), his most famous work.

    1. The symphony was composed between 1914 and 1916 against the backdrop of the First World War. The vicious, dehumanizing horror of the war profoundly affected Nielsen and prompted him to conceive a symphony that affirmed and celebrated the creative spirit of life.

2. In trying to capture the essence of the "life force" in one word, Nielsen came up with *inextinguishable*. He attempted to explain what he meant by *inextinguishable* in a preface appended to the score: "Under this title the composer has endeavored to indicate in one word what music alone is capable of expressing to the full: *the elemental will of life*."

E. The four movements of Nielsen's Fourth Symphony are played without a break. The opening allegro, in sonata form, begins explosively, with a brilliant effusion of rhythms, melodic lines, and harmonic areas. (For a moment, we hear D minor and C major simultaneously, superimposed one atop the other!) The opening is a wonderful musical metaphor for the explosive profusion and elemental force of life. Slowly, the energy dissipates. We listen to this opening, which taken together, constitutes theme 1 of the sonata-form structure. (**Musical selection**: Nielsen, Symphony no. 4 [The Inextinguishable], movement 1, theme 1.)

F. With the beginning of the bridge, more lyric elements come to the fore, consisting of a series of alternating statements between low strings, medium strings, and winds. (**Musical selection**: Nielsen, Symphony no. 4 [The Inextinguishable], movement 1, bridge.)

G. Theme 2 now begins. A sweet, rustic melody, heard initially in the winds, betrays, for just a moment, Nielsen's affection for Dvorak's music. As the theme proceeds, it develops, creating the impression of something lush and mysterious slowly unwinding or unfolding. (**Musical selection**: Nielsen, Symphony no. 4 [The Inextinguishable], movement 1, theme 2.)

H. As the exposition draws to its conclusion, the brilliant and exuberant spirit of theme 1 returns, then dissipates, in preparation for the development section. We hear the conclusion of the exposition. (**Musical selection**: Nielsen, Symphony no. 4 [The Inextinguishable], movement 1, exposition, conclusion.)

I. Obviously, this is not sonata form as we've encountered it before, where the delineation between themes, modulating bridges, development sections, recapitulations, and codas is relatively clear.
1. Nielsen's themes are longer and less clearly articulated than what we generally associate with sonata form in the Classical-era style.

2. Nielsen is subscribing to a process, not following a template. His expressive aim in this movement is to depict the ebb and flow of life itself, interpreted as a continuous progression of musical transformations and developments, a constant unfolding of materials; it's organized to follow sonata form but not dogmatically so.

J. The second movement (or the second large section of this otherwise continuous symphony) is marked *poco allegretto* (literally, "a little moderately fast"). It's a charming, woodwind-dominated intermezzo of extraordinary delicacy. (**Musical selection**: Nielsen, Symphony no. 4 [The Inextinguishable], movement 2, opening.)

K. The third and slow movement begins with a broad and dramatic theme for the violins, which are accompanied by pizzicato lower strings and drums in the style of an operatic recitative. (**Musical selection**: Nielsen, Symphony no. 4 [The Inextinguishable], movement 3, opening.)
  1. Originally, Nielsen had intended to seat all the violinists spread across the front of the stage, rather than bunch them together on the left, as has been the standard since the late 19th century.
  2. The effect, particularly at the onset of the third movement, would have had the sound of the violins coming from virtually every direction of the hall, enveloping the listeners.

L. In terms of Nielsen's avowed purpose to portray the "inextinguishable" force of life, the fourth movement is the most explicitly programmatic in the symphony.
  1. The movement opens with a driving, powerful theme in the strings. This theme represents "life"; its rhythmic drive and power are the "elemental will of life." The theme wants to run free, and it does so, until a gunshot-like explosion in the timpani brings it up short. (**Musical selection**: Nielsen, Symphony no. 4 [The Inextinguishable], movement 4, opening.)
  2. The four timpani, played by two timpanists and tuned to the extremely dissonant interval of a *tritone*, represent the forces of destruction over which life will triumph. That Nielsen chose the drums to play this role is no accident: Their

explosive, canon-like articulation evoked for him the terrible sounds of battle.

3. The battle between life and destruction is waged across the span of the movement. We listen to the last third of the movement, during which the powers of destruction are vanquished and the "will of life" proves itself victorious. (**Musical selection**: Nielsen, Symphony no. 4 [The Inextinguishable], movement 4, conclusion.)

III. Jean Sibelius (1865–1957) was born a few months after the end of the American Civil War, at a time when Berlioz and Liszt were actively concertizing and Brahms had not yet completed his First Symphony; he died two weeks before the launch of Sputnik I, when the ultramodern music of Babbitt, Stockhausen, and Boulez was all the rage and Romanticism and nationalism were nothing but chapter titles in music history books.

A. Sibelius was born in the small town of Hameenlinna in south-central Finland. He studied violin as a teenager and, for a time, aspired to a career as a violin virtuoso. His family, however, had other plans for him, and in 1885, at the age of 20, he was enrolled as a student of law at the University of Helsinki.

B. Within a year, Sibelius had abandoned any pretense to a legal career and become a serious student of music composition. Two years of study abroad, in Berlin and Vienna, rounded out his education, and he returned to Finland in 1891, at the age of 26. At the time of his return, Finland was in the midst of great political turmoil, which would shape Sibelius's artistic vision forever.

C. Sibelius was born into an ethnically Swedish family in south-central Finland. It wasn't until he was 11 years old that Sibelius was enrolled in a Finnish-speaking grammar school, and he didn't master the Finnish language until he was a young man. Considering that Sibelius was a great Finnish patriot, this might seem odd, but not when we consider the imperial realities of Europe over the centuries.

1. For example, Bedrich Smetana, the so-called "father of Czech music," was born in Bohemia, then part of the Austrian Empire. Smetana grew up speaking German and only learned to speak Czech as an adult. Gustav Mahler and Sigmund Freud, two other famous native Bohemians, grew up speaking

German and considered themselves culturally German; neither of them ever learned to speak Czech, and, ultimately, both of them settled in Vienna, not in Prague. Finland, which had been part of the Swedish Empire since the 13th century, was culturally in orbit around Sweden, just as Bohemia was in orbit around Austria.

2. That situation changed in 1807, when Napoleon Bonaparte and Czar Alexander signed the Treaty of Tilsit, freeing Russia to invade Finland. The following year, Russia did just that, effectively ending the 600-year relationship between Sweden and Finland. Finland became an autonomous duchy of the Russian Empire.

3. For most of the 19th century, the Russians left the Finns alone. However, during the 1870s and 1880s, a Finnish nationalist movement slowly gathered strength, and by the 1890s, the tsarist authorities felt compelled to crush the movement. Censorship and political repression followed. Sibelius returned to this environment in 1891, prepared to do battle for Finnish nationalism and the Finnish language.

D. In 1892, Sibelius composed a huge cantata for chorus and orchestra entitled *Kullervo*, based on the Finnish national epic *Kalevala*. Such patriotic works as *Karelia* and *Finlandia* followed, which cemented Sibelius's status as Finland's leading composer, as well as his reputation as a great Finnish patriot and an artist of international celebrity, someone untouchable by the Russian authorities.

E. Sibelius composed the first of his seven symphonies in 1899, immediately after completing *Finlandia*. He completed his Seventh Symphony in 1924, and his last major work, the symphonic poem *Tapiola*, in 1926. After that, we have nothing.

1. It appears that Sibelius composed an Eighth Symphony in 1929, but he destroyed it sometime in the 1930s, apparently terrified that it would diminish the extraordinary international reputation he had at the time. Though Sibelius lived for almost another 30 years, he never composed again.

2. We do not know why Sibelius chose to give up composing; perhaps he lived so long that the world he knew and understood had simply ceased to exist. Time passed him by, and his only defense was to retreat into what became known

as the "silence from Järvenpää," "Järvenpää" being the name of the town outside Helsinki where Sibelius lived.

IV. As an example of Sibelius's symphonic craft, we turn to his Symphony no. 5 in Eb Major, which was completed just months before Nielsen completed his Fourth.

A. In 1919, Sibelius revised his Fifth, merging what had been the first two movements—a first-movement sonata form and a second-movement scherzo—into a single movement. This "composite" first movement begins with characteristically Sibelian clarity and brevity, with a "daybreak-type opening" consisting of three gently rising horns heard over quietly rolling timpani, followed by a dialogue between the horns and birdlike flutes and oboes. (**Musical selection**: Sibelius, Symphony no. 5 in Eb Major, op. 82, movement 1, opening.)

B. The "second half" of this first movement (originally, the second movement) begins with the same theme that opened the symphony. Slowly but steadily, the music speeds up, and as it does, it is transformed into a dance. (**Musical selection**: Sibelius, Symphony no. 5 in Eb Major, op. 82, movement 1 [2], second half, opening.)

C. The second movement in G major has been described as a series of "variations on a five-note rhythm." It does, indeed, consist of a series of variations on a gentle and elegant theme initially presented by a flute and pizzicato strings.

D. The incredible third and final movement starts in the home key of Eb major with an agitated theme in the strings and winds. The rhythmic energy of this music is shocking after the relative quiet and stasis of the second-movement intermezzo. (**Musical selection**: Sibelius, Symphony no. 5 in Eb Major, op. 82, movement 3, opening.)

E. Sibelius begins to stack new material on top of the scurrying opening theme. Next comes a magnificent, rocking theme in the horns, a melody that had first been heard as a bass line back in the second movement. On top of that, he adds a woodwind line, as the rocking theme moves into the bass and begins to sound as if it is breathing life into the layers of music above. (**Musical selection**: Sibelius, Symphony no. 5 in Eb Major, op. 82, movement 3.)

F. The remainder of the movement consists of alternating, juxtaposing, and stacking these various thematic elements, even as they are developed and metamorphosed until, nearing the end, the music becomes blaringly dissonant. Michael Steinberg describes what happens next:

> There is an imperious command for silence. Then, four chords and two [orchestral] unisons enforce order, six sharp reports that, as the English writer Harold Truscott puts it, 'carry without effort the weight of the whole work.' No matter how often we hear [Sibelius's] Fifth Symphony, their sound and their timing can never cease to stun. (Steinberg, 601)

(**Musical selection**: Sibelius, Symphony no. 5 in Eb Major, op. 82, movement 3.)

Lecture Seventeen—Transcript
Nielsen and Sibelius

Welcome back to *The Symphony*. This is Lecture Seventeen—it is entitled "Nielsen and Sibelius." Except for a few excursions to France and Italy, and a couple of quick stopovers in Madrid and Russia, we have thus far spent the great bulk of this course in the "land of the symphony"—central and west-central Europe, Bohemia, Austria, and Germany. The composers of central Europe dominated the genre of symphony for 150 years or more. But as we move into the late 19th and early 20th centuries, that dominance gives way, and the symphony becomes, increasingly, a genuinely global musical phenomenon. The remainder of this survey will take us to places we have thus far visited briefly or not at all—France, Russia, England, the United States and Scandinavia.

Scandinavia is a huge climate-challenged area of great physical variety, a region that has produced an artistic community the breadth and depth of which is way out of proportion with its relatively small population. One might suggest that in such northern climes where it is so dark and so cold, and you have to stay indoors for so much of the year, there are just so many things that you can do after you've eaten, slept, and reproduced—and playing around with golf in February is not one of them. Certainly, the Scandinavian environment has had a direct impact on the sort of music created there, and that is something we'll talk about in due time. But first, the countries themselves.

Scandinavia consists of five countries: Norway, Sweden, Finland, Denmark, and Iceland. Iceland is the westernmost European state, an island nation with a total population of around 266,000; about 10,000 people fewer than Newark, New Jersey. Denmark is the southernmost of the Scandinavian countries with a current population of 5.2 million people. It shares a roughly 50-mile border with Germany and is, as a result, that Scandinavian country most influenced by German art and culture. Norway lies northwest of Denmark. It has a current population of approximately 4.5 million people. Despite being ten times the size of Denmark, Norway remained predominantly Danish (and therefore, German) in cultural sympathy through the beginning of the 19th century.

Sweden, immediately to the east of Norway, is both the largest and most populous Scandinavian country. At 173,648 square miles, it's more than 20,000 square miles larger than California. With about 8.5 million people, its total population is about the size of the Greater Bay area. Sweden was a great power in the 17th and 18th century, but it cultivated no music of its own. Finland, the northeastern most of the Scandinavian countries, with a current population of about 5.2 million, shares a roughly 400-mile border with Russia. Over the centuries, Finland's cultural orbit has vacillated back and forth between Sweden and Russia, depending on who the occupying power was at any given period.

Altogether, the Scandinavian countries boast a landmass ten times the size of New York State and a total population about the size of the New York City metropolitan area. It goes without saying that there's a lot of empty space in Scandinavia.

It's easy enough for us to list the preeminent Scandinavian composers of symphonies during the late 18th and early 19th symphonies, such names as Johan Agrel, Johan Berlin, Josef Kraus in the 18th century; the Norwegian Niels Gade, the Danes Johan Hartmann and Johan Svendson; and the Swedes Adolf Linblad and Franz Berwald in the 19th century. What all these composers have in common is that their music sounds like their Austrian models, only not as good. Hey, the truth hurts.

The spirit of nationalism that swept through most of Europe in the years after 1848 swept through Scandinavia as well. This is where our story really begins. Four Scandinavian composers emerged, each of whom is now recognized as the "father" of his respective national tradition: in Norway, Edvard Grieg, 1843-1907; in Sweden, Hugo Alfven, 1872-1960; in Denmark, Carl Nielsen, 1865-1931; and in Finland, Jean Sibelius, 1865-1957.

The Norwegian Edvard Grieg wrote no symphonies of consequence and thus is spared the indignity of having his music all too briefly discussed in this survey. Hugo Alfven wrote five symphonies, but because his symphonies have not become part of the international repertoire, we will move past him as well. (Although we must quote the self-effacing Alfven, who said of the first movement of his Fifth and final symphony that it was, "The least bad thing I have written.") With Carl Nielsen and Jean Sibelius, we have hit symphonic pay dirt. They are both major symphonic composers whose symphonies are, indeed, part of the international repertoire.

Carl Nielsen (1865-1931)

Carl Nielsen is the central figure in Danish music in the late 19th and early 20th centuries. His music and his writings about music exert a decisive influence over Danish music to this very day and have been a source of inspiration for composers across Scandinavia as well. Among his most important and representative works are his six symphonies, symphonies that I believe are among the very best out there and which should be much better known than they are.

Look, there's no doubt, had Nielsen worked in a major symphonic market like Vienna, for example, his symphonies would be celebrated as being among the greatest in the repertoire. But he was born in the boonies. He worked in Copenhagen, and it wasn't until the 1950s when the Danish State Radio Orchestra began touring with and recording his music, that his symphonies truly began to be heard outside of Denmark. Together, they constitute an indispensable portion of the symphonic repertoire.

Nielsen's rise to fame is a classic success story, a Scandinavian Horatio Alger yarn of a nice guy finishing first:

> From the seventh of twelve children born in 1865 to a village housepainter, to Denmark's national composer, and now to internationally acclaimed symphonist, is some story. And whatever the risk of fairytale cliché, the importance of Nielsen's humble background has to be stressed. [His] mother's singing, [his] father's violin and coronet playing in the village band, the four-year-old Nielsen's makeshift xylophone [made out of different sized logs from the woodpile]; the eleven year old's improvised [songs] at wedding feasts, all these, combined with the sights, sounds and personalities of [his home] island of Funen, implanted a reverence for the "simple original," which was to become a lifelong artistic creed.

Nielsen's concept of the "simple original," or what he also called "expressive simplicity," is the key to his music. He grew up on a diet of village music and Bach, Mozart, and Haydn. The clarity, concision, and directness of expression Nielsen heard in the straightforward village music of his youth and in the music of Bach, Mozart, and Haydn remained the central underpinning of all his music. We might think of Nielsen as a Danish Brahms, but without the schmerz, without the unhappiness, without the melancholy. And like Brahms, Nielsen generally disliked the sort of musical and expressive excess that marked so much late Romantic music. For example, commenting on Wagner's *Ring*, Nielsen wrote: "It is [Wagner's] taste that is intolerable. Reckless gorging [on every musical interval all the time] undermines the health [of his music]. We thus see how necessary it is to preserve contact with the simple original."

Nielsen's promise as a composer got him a free ride with the Copenhagen Conservatory where he studied from 1884 to 1886, and from which he received a strict, German-style schooling in harmony, counterpoint, and musical form. After graduating, he took various jobs as a violinist—ranging from the Royal Chapel to dance bands at the Tivoli Gardens—while he continued, always, to compose on the side. In 1901, having completed his first symphony and his first opera, the latter entitled *Saul and David*, he was granted an annual state pension so that he might have more time to compose. You've just got to love those state pensions! His second symphony followed in 1902, his third in 1911, the fourth in 1916, the fifth in 1922, and the sixth in 1925. Nielsen died six years later, in October of 1931, at the age of 66.

As a sidebar, we would note that Nielsen was not just a composer of symphonies, operas, and concerti. He was a general musical citizen of his country and his adopted city Copenhagen, as well. He composed a cantata for the 100th anniversary of the founding of the Copenhagen Polytechnic High School. He composed a cantata for the opening of the Copenhagen Municipal Swimming Pool. He composed cantatas for the 50th anniversaries of the Young Merchants' Education Association and, my personal favorite, for the Danish Cremation Union. We bet that piece was a real barn-burner, most assuredly. And he worked on educational and patriotic projects like the *Piano Album for the Young and Old* and the patriotic songbook, *Danmark*.

Symphony no. 4, op. 29, "The Inextinguishable" (1916)

We turn to Nielsen's Fourth Symphony, his most famous work. His symphony was composed between 1914 and 1916, against the backdrop of the First World War. The vicious, dehumanizing horror of the war profoundly affected Nielsen, as it did any right-thinking person, and thus affected he conceived a symphony that confirmed and celebrated the creative spirit of life. In 1914, he wrote a letter to his wife, the sculptress Anne Marie Brodersen: "I have an idea for a new work which has no program, but which is to express what we understand as the 'Life Urge' or

'Life Expression"— that is, everything that has the will to live. I must have a word or a short title that says this; that will be enough."

The "word" that Nielsen ultimately came up with is "inextinguishable." Please, let's immediately get the permutations out of our systems now, shall we? The undistinguished, the unexplainable, the unbearable, the indescribable, the ineluctable, the unelectable, the inexplicable, the incoherent, the unincredible, the un-indelible, and so forth. Nielsen attempted to explain what he meant by "inextinguishable" in a somewhat-less-than-coherent preface that he appended to the score:

> Under this title the composer has endeavored to indicate in one word what music alone is capable of expressing to the full: the elemental will of life. Music is life and, like it, inextinguishable. The title given by the composer to this musical work might therefore seem superfluous; the composer, however, has employed the word in order to underline the strictly musical character of his past. It is not a program, only a suggestion as to the way into this, music's own territory.

He was a bit more lucid in a letter written in 1920, four years after having completed the symphony:

> The title *The Inextinguishable* is not a program but a pointer. It is meant to express the appearance of the most elemental forces among human beings, animals, and even plants. We can say: in case the world were to be devastated, and all things destroyed, then nature would still begin to breed new life again, begin to push forward again with all the fine things inherent in matter. These forces, which are "inextinguishable," are what I have tried to present.

The four movements of Nielsen's Fourth Symphony are played without a break. The opening allegro, in sonata form, begins explosively, with a brilliant effusion of rhythms, melodic lines, and harmonic areas (for a moment we are hearing D minor and C major simultaneously, superimposed one on top of the other!), an altogether wonderful music metaphor for the explosive profusion—and elemental force—of life. Slowly, the energy dissipates. Let's hear this marvelous opening which taken together constitutes theme 1 of the sonata-form structure.

[Musical example from Symphony No. 4, Opus 29, Nielsen: I; Opening, Theme I]

With the beginning of the bridge, more lyric elements come to the fore, consisting of a series of alternating statements between low strings, medium strings, and winds.

[Musical example from Symphony No. 4, Opus 29, Nielsen: I; Bridge]

Theme 2 now begins. A sweet, rustic melody, initially heard in the winds. It betrays for the briefest of moments Nielsen's great affection for Dvorak's music. As the theme proceeds, it develops as it goes, creating the impression of something lush and mysterious, slowly "unwinding" or "unfolding."

[Musical example from Symphony No. 4, Opus 29, Nielsen: I; Theme II]

As the exposition draws to its conclusion, the brilliant and exuberant spirit of theme 1 returns and then dissipates in preparation for the development section. Let's hear the conclusion of the exposition.

[Musical example from Symphony No. 4, Opus 29, Nielsen: I; Exposition]

Now obviously, this is not sonata form as we've encountered it before, where the delineation of themes, modulating bridges, development sections, recapitulations, and codas is relatively clear. Nielsen's themes are longer and less clearly articulated than what we generally associate with Classical-era style sonata form. We should be aware that he is subscribing to a process, but not following a template. His expressive aim in this movement is to depict the ebb and flow of life itself, which he depicts as a continuous progression of musical transformations and developments, a constant unfolding of materials organized to follow sonata form, but not dogmatically so.

The second movement (or the second large section of this otherwise continuous symphony) is marked *poco allegretto*, meaning literally, "a little moderately fast." It's a charming woodwind-dominated intermezzo of extraordinary delicacy, and it begins this way.

[Musical example from Symphony No. 4, Opus 29, Nielsen: II; Opening]

The third and slow movement begins with a broad and dramatic theme for the violins, which are accompanied—or should we say "punctuated"—by plucked lower strings and drums in the style of an operatic recitative. Originally, Nielsen had intended to seat all the violinists—first and second—spread across the front of the stage, rather than bunch them together on the left, as had been the standard since the late 19th century. The effect, particularly here, at the onset of the third movement, would have had the sound of the violins coming from virtually every direction of the hall, enveloping the listeners like some great sonic cloud.

[Musical example from Symphony No. 4, Opus 29, Nielsen: III; Opening]

In terms of Nielsen's avowed purpose to portray the "inextinguishable" force of life, the fourth movement is the most explicitly programmatic in the symphony. The movement opens with a driving, locomotive power theme in the strings. This theme represents "life"; its rhythmic drive and power are the "elemental will of life." It is a theme that wants to run free, and it does so, until a gunshot-like explosion in the timpani brings it up short.

[Musical example from Symphony No. 4, Opus 29, Nielsen: IV; Opening]

The four timpani, played by two tympanists and tuned to the extreme dissonant interval of a *tritone*, represent the forces of destruction over which life will triumph. That Nielsen chose the drums to play this role is no accident: their explosive gun-like, cannon-like articulation evoke for him, literally, the terrible sounds of battle, battles fought even as he composed. The battle between life and destruction is waged across the span of this final movement. We listen to the last third of this movement during which time the powers of destruction are vanquished and the "will of life" proves itself victorious.

[Musical example from Symphony No. 4, Opus 29, Nielsen: IV Conclusion]

This, my friends, is incredible, uncompromising, breath-taking music, and there's nothing else like it in the entire repertoire.

Jean Sibelius (1865-1957)

Hey, who says the good die young? Jean Sibelius was born a few months after the end of the American Civil War, at a time when Berlioz and Liszt were actively concertizing and Brahms had not yet completed his First Symphony. He died during Eisenhower's second term of office, two weeks before the launch of Sputnik I, at a time when the ultramodern music of Babbitt, Stockhausen, and Boulez was all the rage, and Romanticism and nationalism were nothing but chapter titles in music history books.

Sibelius was born in the small town of Hameenlinna in south-central Finland. He studied violin as a teenager and, for a time, aspired to a career as a violin virtuoso. However, his family had other plans for him, and in 1885, at the age of 20, he was enrolled as a student of law at the University of Helsinki. That law school thing didn't last for very long. Within a year, he had abandoned any pretense of a legal career and had become a serious student of music composition. Two years of study abroad in Berlin and then in Vienna rounded out his education and he returned to Finland in 1891, at the age of 26. He returned to a Finland in the midst of great political turmoil and that turmoil was to shape forever Sibelius's artistic reason-to-be.

Some background. Sibelius was born into an ethnically Swedish family in south-central Finland. The family name, Sibelius, is of Swedish origin and the family spoke Swedish at home. It wasn't until he was 11 years old that Sibelius was enrolled in a Finnish-speaking grammar school, and he didn't master the Finnish language until he was a young man. Considering that Sibelius was a great Finnish patriot, this might seem rather odd, but not when we consider the imperial realities of Europe during the 19th century. For example, Bedrich Smetana, the so-called "father of Czech music," was born in Bohemia, then part of the Austrian Empire. Smetana grew up speaking German and only learned to speak Czech, poorly, as an adult. Gustav Mahler and Sigmund Freud, two other rather famous native Bohemians, grew up speaking German and considered themselves culturally German. It's significant that neither of them ever learned to speak Czech, and, ultimately, both of them settled in Vienna, not in Prague. Finland, which had been part of the Swedish Empire since the 13th century, was culturally in orbit around Sweden, just as Bohemia was around Austria.

Politically at least, that all changed thanks to Napoleon Bonaparte and those greedy Russians. In 1807, Napoleon and Czar Alexander signed the Treaty of Tilsit, freeing Russia to invade Finland, which it did the following year, in 1808, effectively ending the 600-year old relationship between Sweden and Finland. Finland became an autonomous duchy of the Russian Empire.

For most of the 19th century, the Russians left the Finns essentially alone. But during the 1870s and 1880s, the Finnish nationalist movement slowly but surely gathered strength, and by the 1890s, the czarist authorities—then and forever rather humorless about revolutionary movements—felt compelled to crush the Finnish upstarts and in doing so, make an example of them with their own domestic trouble-makers. Censorship and political repression followed, and it was back into this environment that Sibelius returned in 1891, prepared to do battle for Finnish nationalism and the Finnish language, which more than anything else, had come to represent Finnish nationalism.

In 1892, Sibelius composed a huge cantata for chorus and orchestra entitled *Kullervo*, based on the Finnish national epic, *Kalevala*. Such patriotic works as *Karelia* and *Finlandia* followed, which cemented not just Sibelius's status as Finland's leading composer, but his reputation as a great Finnish patriot and an artist of international celebrity, someone untouchable by the Russian authorities.

Sibelius composed the first of his seven symphonies in 1899, immediately after having completed *Finlandia*. He completed his Seventh Symphony in 1924, and his last major work, the orchestral poem *Tapiola* in 1926. And then, silence. It appears that Sibelius did compose an Eight Symphony in 1929, but he destroyed it in the 1930s, apparently terrified that it would only diminish what was at that time an extraordinary international reputation. Though Sibelius lived for another 30 years, he never composed again. Was he written out? Had he lost his gift? Who knows? What we do know is that Sibelius lived so long that the world he knew and understood simply ceased to exist. Time passed him by and his only defense was to retreat into what became known as the silence from Järvenpää—the town outside of Helsinki where Sibelius lived.

Symphony no. 5 in Eb Major, op. 82 (1915; revised 1916, 1919)

As an example of Sibelius's symphonic craft, we turn to his Symphony no. 5 in Eb Major, a symphony exactly contemporary with Nielsen's no. 4, completed just months before Nielsen completed his Fourth. In 1919, Sibelius revised his Fifth, merging what had been the first two movements—a first-movement sonata form and a second-movement scherzo—into a second movement. As such, the first movement of Sibelius's Fifth is in reality two movements zippered together. This "composite" first movement begins with a characteristically Sibelian tune, clear and brief with a "daybreak-type opening" consisting of three gently rising horns heard over quietly rolling timpani, followed by a dialogue between the horns and birdlike flutes and oboes.

[Musical example from Symphony No. 5 in Eb Major, Opus 82, Sibelius: I; Opening]

This terribly brief excerpt gives little indication of the charms and glories of this first movement. *C'est la vie*; if I could say it in Finnish, I would. The "second half" of this first movement begins with the same theme that opened the symphony. Slowly but steadily the music speeds up, and as it does, it is transformed, before our very ears, into a dance.

[Musical example from Symphony No. 5 in Eb Major, Opus 82, Sibelius: I]

Isn't that wonderful? The second movement in G major has been described as a series of "variations on a five-note rhythm." It does, indeed, consist of a series of variations on a gentle and elegant theme initially presented by a flute and pizzicato (or plucked) strings. Time precludes us from sampling this interlude-like movement. We move forward to tackle and be tackled by the incredible third and final movement.

Well, bang! The movement starts back in the home key of Eb major with the most agitated theme in the strings and winds. The rhythmic energy in this music literally takes our legs out from underneath us after the relative quiet and stasis of the second-movement intermezzo.

[Musical example from Symphony No. 5 in Eb Major, Opus 82, Sibelius: III, Opening]

And now Sibelius really goes to work. He begins to stack new material on top of the scurrying opening theme. Next comes a magnificent, rocking theme in the horns, a melody that had first been heard as a bass line back in the second movement. Then on top of that he adds a woodwind line, as the magnificent rocking theme moves into the bass, sounding just like a gigantic pair of lungs, slowly and deeply breathing in and out, oxygenating the layers of music above. Let's hear it.

[Musical example from Symphony No. 5 in Eb Major, Opus 82, Sibelius: III]

The remainder of the movement consists of alternating, juxtaposing, and stacking these various thematic elements, even as they are developed and metamorphosed until, nearing the end, the music becomes blaringly dissonant. Michael Steinberg describes what happens next: "There is an imperious command for silence. Then, four chords and two [orchestral] unisons enforce order, six sharp reports that, as the English writer Harold Truscott puts it, 'carry without effort the weight of the whole work.' No matter how often we hear [Sibelius's] Fifth Symphony, their sound and their timing can never cease to stun." Let's hear this extraordinary conclusion.

[Musical example from Symphony No. 5 in Eb Major, Opus 82, Sibelius: III; Conclusion]

Conclusion

According to music historian Robert Layton:

> What distinguishes [the music of Nielsen and Sibelius] is a strong sense of place. The open textures of Nielsen's [music] seem to spring naturally from the Nordic landscape, just as the string [and

woodwind] writing that Sibelius made so completely his own seemed to [grow from] "the air" [of Scandinavia]. Their music could be conceived in no other latitude, for it is the quality of light one finds in the north, the dark winters, and the long, white summer nights that condition their imagination. This pale, short-lived summer is central to the Scandinavian sensibility, and the sense of heightened awareness of the evanescence of light that it brings reinforces the gentle but intense feeling present in so much Nordic music.

But it is not only the natural landscape they inhabited that determined their musical physiognomy. Nielsen's musical language was enriched by the [nature] of Danish folk melody, [as well as] the broader symphonic tradition of Brahms and Dvorak. [And] Sibelius dominates because his musical inspiration sprang from the very soil of Finland, its rich and wholly individual repertory of myth and its speech rhythms.

Thank you.

Lecture Eighteen
The Symphony in Russia

Scope: In Lecture Fourteen, we discussed the fact that before the mid-19th century, Russia did not have any appreciable symphonic tradition or, indeed, any appreciable concert music tradition. Before that time, concert music in Russia's urban centers consisted largely of Italian-language opera and Italian and Viennese instrumental music. This situation began to change in the 1830s and 1840s, when a powerful sense of Russian musical nationalism developed. Early Russian nationalist composers turned to folksong, dance, and the Russian language itself for their melodic and rhythmic inspiration. As we noted in an earlier lecture, Tchaikovsky was an "inadvertent" nationalist; in this lecture, we discuss Russian composers of the 19th and early 20th centuries who proudly and purposely cultivated a specifically "Russian" music and whose impact was felt well into the 20th century.

Outline

I. Mikhail Glinka (1804–1857) was the godfather of Russian music. Born to a wealthy, land-owning family, he joined the civil service at the age of 20 and worked in the Ministry of Ways and Communication in St. Petersburg. His private wealth allowed him time to dabble in his hobby of choice, music. In 1828, at the age of 24, he quit his job and moved to Milan for three years, then Berlin for a year, all the while taking music lessons and listening to opera.

   A. Glinka was an amateur in the truest sense, a "lover of art" whose passion for music was never blunted by the necessity of having to make a living at it. As a composer, his training was spotty; certainly, by the time he returned to St. Petersburg in 1832 at the age of 28, he was not aware of how much he did not yet know.

      1. Glinka got the idea to write an opera based on a Russian theme in the Russian language. Inspired by the nationalist writings of his friends Pushkin and Gogol and working with only a rudimentary knowledge of musical composition, he turned out an opera entitled *A Life for the Czar*, which was premiered in 1836.

2. This was the first opera on a Russian subject and the first to explicitly quote Russian folk music. *A Life for the Czar* and Glinka's subsequent opera, *Ruslan and Ludmilla* of 1842, sparked a musical revolution in Russia; they became the textbook examples for other composers who wanted their music to be proudly and distinctly Russian.

B. In 1834, at just about the same time he began work on *A Life for the Czar*, Glinka decided to write a symphony. He used two Russian folksongs as themes 1 and 2 of the first-movement sonata form, then abandoned the piece after completing the first movement. Eighteen years later, in 1852, he tried and failed again to write a symphony and quit forever. In his memoirs, he wrote: "Not having the strength to get out of the German rut in the development, I rejected my effort." (Layton, 262).

C. Glinka actually says two important things in this quote. The first is that he had never properly learned and was unable to master the compositional craft required to write a convincing development section—thematic fragmentation and metamorphosis, polyphonic manipulation, modulation, and so forth. Second, Glinka is saying that he doesn't want to write a "Germanic-style" development of his themes, that doing so goes against his musical grain.

1. As we are well aware by now, sonata form lies at the heart of the 18th- and 19th-century symphony. And at the heart of sonata form is "the argument," that is, the development section, with its manipulation, fragmentation, and metamorphosis of previously stated materials.

2. By its nature, a development section represents a process of dissecting and reworking thematic material already presented whole in the exposition. It is a process that grew out of the Germanic predilection for analysis, introspection, argument, and investigation, a process that could not be further from the Russian psyche.

3. The point is that most 19th-century Russian symphonic music is "about" its thematic material, not "about" developing that thematic material.

D. Glinka died in February of 1857 and was all but canonized as the patron saint of Russian music. Among those who believed most fervently in Glinka's musical sainthood was a 20-year-old pianist and composer living in St. Petersburg named Mili Alekseyevich Balakirev (1837–1910).

1. Balakirev had even less musical training than his hero, but that didn't stop him from setting himself up in St. Petersburg as a music teacher and critic. Balakirev gathered around himself a group of young musicians who were to become known as the "Russian Five," the "Mighty Handful," or the "*Moguchay Kuchka*" (meaning, literally, "the mighty little heap").

2. This group of self-taught hobbyists included Cesar Antonovich Cui, an army engineer; Modest Petrovich Mussorgsky, an army ensign and postal worker; Nicolai Rimsky-Korsakov, a naval officer; and Alexander Porfiryevich Borodin, a physician and a chemist.

3. With Balakirev at their head, "The Five" were unabashed Russian nationalists. Their "gods" were the Russian language, Russian folksong, the poet Pushkin, and of course, Mikhail Glinka. Self-taught and proud of it, they made a virtue of their technical ignorance and raised the flag of their dogmatic Russian nationalism (and anti-Germanism!) at every opportunity.

E. Balakirev wrote two symphonies that do not deserve even the slightest presence in the repertoire, but their influence was tremendous, and for that reason, they merit discussion and some listening. He began his First Symphony in 1864 and finally finished it 33 years later, in 1897. He began his Second Symphony in 1900 and finished it in 8 years. We turn to the First Symphony, by far the more influential of the two.

1. The first movement begins with a lengthy introduction that spells out the principal theme. We hear the theme as it appears following the introduction, about three minutes into the movement. (**Musical selection**: Balakirev, Symphony no. 1 in C Major, movement 1.)

2. We next listen to the second-movement scherzo. (**Musical selection**: Balakirev, Symphony no. 1 in C Major, movement 2.)

3. The slow third movement is a nocturne with the melodic flavor of a sophisticated folksong. (**Musical selection**: Balakirev, Symphony no. 1 in C Major, movement 3.)

4. The fourth movement is based on three Russian folksongs, heard almost one after the other. We hear the beginning of the movement, with the first of these three folksongs. (**Musical selection**: Balakirev, Symphony no. 1 in C Major, movement 4.)

5. So far, we have a monothematic first movement in which Balakirev abandons any pretense to sonata form, a movement characterized, instead, by thematic repetition, variation, and extension. The other three movements feature even less "development" than the first, consisting almost entirely of alternating folk and folk-like melodies.

6. This lack of sonata form, however, represents the nature of Balakirev's enduring influence. His message was: "Be yourself, be Russian, be proud, and celebrate Russian cultural values without fear."

II. Alexander Porfiryevich Borodin (1833–1887) was a big man and, by every account, a wonderful person. He returned to St. Petersburg from medical school in Germany and was immediately given a faculty position at the Academy of Medicine. He once said, "Science is my work and music is my fun."

    A. In late 1862, immediately after Borodin had joined Balakirev's group, Balakirev decided that Borodin should compose a symphony. Given that Borodin knew nothing about large-scale composition or orchestration, Balakirev sent him home with scores of Beethoven's and Schumann's symphonies and told him to look them over and compose one of his own.

        1. Incredibly, Borodin managed to turn out a symphony of sorts, a testament to the power of determination, talent, and Balakirev's measure-by-measure oversight.

        2. Even with the example of his first, we would never anticipate that Borodin's Second Symphony would be a genuine masterwork, yet it had all hallmarks of such music: great breadth of conception, wonderful and memorable themes, a superb and advanced harmonic palette, and dramatic contrasts, all swept along with a palpably physical rhythmic power.

    B. Borodin began his Second Symphony almost immediately after the premiere of the First, in 1869, and finished it 1876. Along with his opera, *Prince Igor*, it is one of Borodin's finest compositions. We hear the opening two minutes—what amounts to the exposition—of the brilliant fourth and final movement. (**Musical selection**: Borodin, Symphony no. 2 in B Minor, movement 4.)

C. Borodin began a Third Symphony but completed only the first two movements before he died of a heart attack on February 27, 1887, at the age of 53. In 1906, Sir Henry Hadow wrote of Borodin: "No [composer] has ever claimed immortality with so slender an offering."

    1. This appraisal still stands. Borodin's best music, including his opera, *Prince Igor*; his orchestral tone poem, *In the Steppes of Central Asia*; his second string quartet; and his Second Symphony are a slender offering indeed, but they are superb works, and the Second Symphony deserves our attention.

    2. The consensus today is that, excepting Mussorgsky, Borodin was the most gifted of The Five. He was also, in terms of his profession outside of music, the most successful of The Five, and his career as a doctor, chemist, and professor precluded him from creating the body of work that might have made him a mainstay of the repertoire.

III. Of all the members of The Five, only Nicolai Rimsky-Korsakov (1844–1908) managed to make a career as a composer. In doing so, he became one of the most influential composers in the history of Russian music.

A. Rimsky-Korsakov came from a family of distinguished naval and military officers, and there was never any question that he would follow in their footsteps, despite his love for music.

B. Sometime in 1861, Rimsky-Korsakov, a 17-year-old cadet at the Naval Institute in St. Petersburg, decided to write a symphony.

    1. Given that he knew next to nothing about music theory, he sought out Balakirev, who as we are now aware, hardly knew any more than Rimsky. It made no difference; Rimsky-Korsakov, enthralled to be in the company of a "known" composer, did what Balakirev told him to do, which was to continue working on the symphony during Rimsky's two-and-a-half year cruise on the clipper *Almaz*.

    2. On his return to St. Petersburg, Rimsky-Korsakov became the fifth member of The Five. Under Balakirev's direction, he turned out a number of serviceable works, including his

Second Symphony, subtitled "*Antar*," the symphonic poem *Sadko*, and the opera *The Maid of Pskov*. This output was pretty impressive for someone who knew nothing about the craft of musical composition, which became painfully clear when Rimsky-Korsakov was invited to join the faculty of the St. Petersburg Conservatory as a professor of practical composition and instrumentation.

3. Somehow, the new professor, studying day and night, managed to stay a week ahead of his students. Eventually, Rimsky learned his craft, and as if to prove to himself that he had mastered the art of counterpoint, he composed his third and final symphony, in which, according to the composer himself, "I tried to cram into it as much counterpoint as possible!"

C. Written in the unusual meter of 5/4 (an uneven, asymmetrical meter that is more characteristic of Eastern European music than Western), the second movement of the symphony bubbles over with energy and life. We listen to its opening two minutes. (**Musical selection**: Rimsky-Korsakov, Symphony no. 3 in C Major, op. 32, movement 2 [1873; revised 1886].)

D. Rimsky-Korsakov's appointment at the St. Petersburg Conservatory went a long way toward breaking up The Five. Modest Mussorgsky, in particular, was furious about it, believing that Rimsky-Korsakov had sold out to the German enemy to compose fugues and sonatas.

E. For both Rimsky-Korsakov and the history of music, however, his move to the Conservatory was about the best thing that could have happened.

1. By being forced to teach theory and orchestration, Rimsky-Korsakov finally learned the subjects himself.

2. His position also allowed him to bridge the gap between the nationalist music and dogma of The Five and the traditional Western European musical establishment. He became an influential teacher, taking the nationalist message of The Five to the next generation of Russian composers, who were, unlike The Five, properly trained. Among Rimsky-Korsakov's students were: Igor Stravinsky, Sergei Prokofiev, and Alexander Glazunov, who himself became an important mentor of Dmitri Shostakovich.

IV. A prodigious talent, Alexander Glazunov (1865–1936) was often referred to as the "Mendelssohn of Russian music."

    A. Glazunov completed his First Symphony when he was 16; his First String Quartet (of seven) was completed at age 17. In 1899, he was appointed professor at the St. Petersburg Conservatory and, in 1905, at the age of 40, was appointed director of the Conservatory, a post he held for 25 years.

    B. Today, Glazunov is recognized as the composer who reconciled 19th-century Russian musical nationalism with the craft and developmental techniques of German compositional style.

    C. As an example of Glazunov's symphonic style, we turn to his Symphony no. 5 in Bb Major, op. 55, of 1895. We hear the conclusion of its ringing, chirping, and altogether wonderful second-movement scherzo. (**Musical selection**: Alexander Glazunov, Symphony no. 5 in Bb Major, op. 55, movement 2.)

V. Of the many other composers of pre-Revolution Russian symphonies and post-Revolution Soviet symphonies, we have time for only the briefest mention.

    A. Such composers as Mikhail Ippolitov-Ivanov, Reinhold Gliere, Sergei Lyapunov, Anton Arensky, Vasily Kalinnikov, Sergei Taneyev, and Alexander Scriabin all composed symphonies, none of which have entered into the international repertoire.

    B. A more familiar name is Sergei Rachmaninoff (1873–1943) who, despite having written three symphonies, is justifiably much more famous as a composer of piano concerti.

    C. Less well known but much more influential as a symphonist was Nikolai Myaskovsky, whose 27 symphonies, written between 1908 and 1950, spanned from the reign of Czar Nicholas II almost through to the end of Stalin's life.

    D. We can continue to name other mid-20th–century Soviet composers of symphonies, from Maximilian Steinberg and Vladimir Shcherbachev to Dmitri Kabelevsky and Aram Khachaturian, but their symphonies have not entered the international repertoire. Two masters of the mid-20th–century Soviet symphony eclipsed their contemporaries in much the same way that Haydn and Mozart eclipsed theirs in the late 18th century. We refer to Sergei Prokofiev and Dmitri Shostakovich. Lecture

Twenty-Four is devoted to Shostakovich and his Symphony no. 10, and here, we briefly highlight the work of Prokofiev.

VI. Not counting two student works, Sergei Sergeyevich Prokofiev (1891–1953) composed seven symphonies between 1917 and 1952. To this day, Prokofiev's most popular symphony is his First Symphony in D Major, op. 25, the so-called "Classical" Symphony.

  A. At the time he composed it, in 1916–1917, Prokofiev was already known as a steel-fisted modernist and anti-Romantic, a "musical Cubist and Futurist"; thus, a Classically proportioned First Symphony was the last thing the musical community expected.

  B. Prokofiev's First is a wonderful example of what would soon come to be called *Neo-Classicism*: the "New Classicism," in which Classical-era formal and melodic structures were layered like veneer over harmonic materials and orchestrational techniques that were otherwise very much of the 20th century. In the hands of a master like Prokofiev, the results can be delightful: wry, humorous, ironic, and engaging. As an example, we hear the exposition section that opens the first movement. (**Musical selection**: Prokofiev, Symphony no. 1 in C Major, op. 25, movement 1, exposition.)

  C. Prokofiev was born in Ukraine and entered the St. Petersburg Conservatory in 1904, at the age of 13. A brilliant pianist, he treated the piano like a percussion instrument, and he transferred his explosive, percussive vision of the piano to the orchestra, as well. When the Revolution came to Russia in 1917, the 26-year-old Prokofiev sailed for the United States by way of Japan.

  D. Prokofiev left the United States in 1923 and moved to Paris, which remained his base of operations for 13 years. During the late 1920s and early 1930s, Prokofiev was invited to concertize a number of times in the Soviet Union. The success of these tours convinced the naïve Prokofiev to return to Russia. In 1936, he renounced his "émigré" status, moved to Moscow, and became a Soviet citizen.

  E. Prokofiev initially had success in the Soviet Union, but he was censured by the Soviet government in 1948 and died a frightened, broken man on March 5, 1953, about one hour before Joseph Stalin died.

F. We close with the opening of the second-movement scherzo of Prokofiev's Symphony no. 5, composed in 1944 and perhaps the most successful of all the pieces he wrote after his return to the Soviet Union. (**Musical selection**: Prokofiev, Symphony no. 5 in Bb Major, op. 100, movement 2.)

G. That bit of scherzo from the Fifth Symphony sounds like the "old" Prokofiev: the wry, idiosyncratic humorist, the composer he was before he returned to the Soviet Union and, for the sake of survival, wrote music that satisfied the Soviet state. We'll discuss this issue of music and "the state" at greater length when we return to the Soviet Union and Shostakovich's Symphony no. 10 in Lecture Twenty-Four.

Lecture Eighteen—Transcript
The Symphony in Russia

Welcome back to *The Symphony*. This is Lecture Eighteen—it is entitled "The Symphony in Russia." Back in Lecture Fourteen, we discussed the fact that before the mid-19th century, Russia had not had any appreciable symphonic tradition. Well, to be perfectly accurate, before the 19th century, Russia didn't have any appreciable concert music tradition. Before then, if you heard concert music in one of Russia's principle urban centers—St. Petersburg, Moscow, and to a lesser extent Kiev—you were probably hearing Italian-language opera or Italian or Viennese instrumental music.

This all began to change in the 1830s and 1840s, when a powerful sense of Russian music nationalism began to develop. The early Russian nationalist composers turned, as do musical nationalists by definition, to Russian folk songs, dance, and the Russian language itself for their melodic and rhythmic inspiration. Now, back in Lecture Fourteen we discussed Tchaikovsky as an "inadvertent" nationalist. Rigorously trained in German compositional technique, Tchaikovsky's music sounds Russian because he was, well, Russian. Not because he adhered to a dogmatic nationalist agenda. It's time now to talk about the advertent Russian nationalists, those 19th century composers who proudly and purposefully cultivated a specifically "Russian" music and whose impact was felt well into the 20th century.

Beginnings

Mikhail Glinka, 1804-1857 was literally the godfather of Russian music. Born to a wealthy land-owning family, he joined the civil service at the age of 20 and worked in the Ministry of Ways and Communication in St. Petersburg. His private wealth allowed him lots of time to dabble in his hobby of choice, which was music. In 1828, at the age of 24, he figured, what the heck. He quit his day job and moved to Milan for three years and then Berlin for one year, all the while taking music lessons and listening to opera. Glinka was an amateur in the truest sense, a "lover of art" whose passion for music was never blunted by the necessity of actually having to make a living at it. As a composer, his training was spotty; certainly, by the time he returned to St. Petersburg in 1832, at the age of 28, he was not yet aware of how much he did not yet know. But perhaps he just didn't care. Whatever.

He got it into his head to write an opera based on a Russian theme in the Russian language, something that at that time just wasn't done. Inspired by the nationalist writings of his friends, Pushkin and Gogol, working with only a rudimentary knowledge of music composition, he turned out an opera entitled *A Life for the Czar*, which was premiered in 1836. It was the first opera on a Russian subject and the first to explicitly quote Russian folk music. *A Life for the Czar* and Glinka's subsequent opera, *Ruslan and Ludmilla* of 1842, sparked—well, they sparked a musical revolution in Russia. They became the textbook examples for other composers who wanted their music to be proudly and distinctly Russian.

In 1834, at just about the same time he began work on *A Life for the Czar*, Glinka decided to write a symphony. He used two Russian folksongs as themes 1 and 2 of the first-movement sonata form and that's as far as he got, abandoning the piece after completing just the first movement. Eighteen years later, in 1852, he tried and failed again to write a symphony. Glinka never tried again to write a symphony. In his memoirs Glinka wrote: "Not having the strength to get out of the German rut in the development, I rejected my effort."

Now Glinka is actually saying two very important things here despite his surly anti-German mode of expression. One, he's saying that the composition craft required to write a convincing development section— thematic fragmentation and metamorphosis, polyphonic manipulation, modulation and so forth—they were techniques he had never properly learned and was unable to master. Two, Glinka is saying that he does not want to write a "Germanic-style" development of his themes, that doing so goes against his very musical grain. And that's really the nub of the issue.

As we should all be aware of now, sonata form lies at the heart of the 18th- and 19th- century symphony. And at the heart of sonata form is "the argument"—the development section—the manipulation, fragmentation, and metamorphosis of previously stated themes. By its very nature, a development section represents a process of dissecting and reworking thematic material already presented wholly in the exposition. It is a process that in its 19th-century manifestation grew out of the Germanic predilection for analysis, introspection, argument and investigation, a process that could not be further from the Russian psyche. The great Modest Mussorgsky, who chose never to write a symphony, said exactly so much in a very famous letter written to his friend Nicolai Rimsky-Korsakov, dated August 15, 1868. Mussorgsky wrote:

And another thing about symphonic development: it is just like German philosophy—all worked out and systematized. When a German thinks, he reasons his way to a conclusion. Our Russian brother, on the other hand, starts with the conclusion and then might amuse himself with some reasoning. Just keep one thing in mind: the artist is a law unto himself. When an artist revises, it means he is dissatisfied. When he adds to [or develops] what already satisfies, he is Germanizing, chewing over what has [already] been said. We [Russians] are not cud-chewers, [we are] omnivores.

What all of this means is that most 19th-century Russian music would be "about" its thematic material, not "about" developing that thematic material.

Glinka died in February of 1857. He was all but canonized as the patron saint of Russian music. And among those who believed most fervently in Glinka's musical sainthood was a young 20-year-old pianist and composer living in St. Petersburg by the name of Mili Alekseyevich Balakirev, 1837-1910. According to Harold Schonberg, Balakirev was: "A short, squat, Asiatic-looking, largely self-taught composer. His friend, the violinist Peter Baborikin, attested to the fact that Balakirev owned not a single book on harmony, orchestration, or theory."

So Balakirev had even less musical training than his hero, Glinka. It didn't stop him from setting himself up in St. Petersburg as a music teacher and as a critic. In the musical vacuum that was Russia in the 1850s, such a thing was actually possible, whereas no one could have taken Balakirev seriously had he tried to pass himself off as a musician in Western Europe.

Eventually—and incredibly—Balakirev gathered around himself a group of young musicians who would become known as the "Russian Five," the "Mighty Handful," the *Moguchay Kuchka* (meaning, literally, the "mighty little heap", a termed coined by the writer Vladimir Stasov)—a group of self-taught hobbyists whose day jobs had nothing to do with music. Cesar Cui was an army engineer; Modest Petrovich Mussorgsky was an army ensign and then a postal worker; Nicolai Andreyevich Rimsky-Korsakov was a naval officer; and Alexander Porfiryevich Borodin was a physician and a chemist.

With Balakirev at their head, "The Five" were unabashed Russian nationalists. Their "gods" were the Russian language, Russian folksong, the poet Alexander Sergeyevich Pushkin, and of course, Mikhail Glinka. Self-taught and proud of it, they made a virtue of their technical ignorance and they raised the flag of their dogmatic Russian nationalism (and anti-Germanism!) at every opportunity.

Balakirev wrote two symphonies. We cannot pretend that they deserve even the slightest tippy-toehold in the repertoire. However, their influence was tremendous. And for that reason, they merit discussion and even some listening.

An understatement: Balakirev had some trouble completing large musical compositions. He began his First Symphony in 1864 and finally finished it 33 years later in 1897. He began his Second Symphony in 1900 and finished it in what was for him record time, in just 8 years, in 1908. We turn to the First Symphony, by far the more influential of the two.

The first movement begins with a lengthy introduction that spells out the principle theme—theme, singular—of the movement. We hear the theme as it appears following the introduction about three minutes into the movement.

[Musical example from Symphony No. 1 in C Major, Balakirev: I, Theme]

The second-movement scherzo opens this way.

[Musical example from Symphony No. 1 in C Major, Balakirev: II, Opening]

The slow third movement is a nocturne with the melodic flavor of a sophisticated folksong.

[Musical example from Symphony No. 1 in C Major, Balakirev: III]

The fourth movement is based on three Russian folksongs, heard pretty much one after the other. We hear the beginning of the movement, with the first of these three folksongs.

[Musical example from Symphony No. 1 in C Major, Balakirev: IV]

What have we got? A monothematic first movement in which Balakirev abandoned any pretense of sonata form, a movement characterized, instead, by thematic repetition, variation, and extension. And the other three movements feature even less "development" than the first, consisting entirely of alternating various folk and folk-like melodies.

My friends, this course's "musical purple prose award" goes to Edward Garden, the author of the book *Balakirev: A Critical Study of His Life and*

Music, St. Martin's Press, NY, NY, 1967. In his attempt to rationalize the absence of sonata form in the first movement, he writes:

> While ostensibly in sonata form, the continuous development of the scintillating material is a feature of Balakirev's style, and the mosaic patterns burgeon in all directions without adhering to strict formal rigidities, culminating in a final apotheosis in the guise of an augmentation of all the parts, accompanied by fresco-like diminutions of themselves.

One wonders what Mr. Garden was smoking when he wrote that. The fact is, there's not a single sonata form in Balakirev's First Symphony, "ostensible" or not. Balakirev couldn't have written one if he tried, although he wouldn't have tried to write one because the process was foreign to his psyche and culture. And there it is: the nature of Balakirev's enduring influence on not just the boys in his little composer's club, but on so many Russian artists of every stripe. His influence, his message: Be yourself! Be who you are! Be Russian, be proud, and celebrate those cultural values that are Russian without fear, without caution, and without any sense of inferiority vis-à-vis Western music.

A powerful message, one that fell like creamy borscht on the ears of Alexander Borodin, chemist and physician by day and rabid Balakirev groupie and composer in his spare time.

Alexander Porfiryevich Borodin (1833-1887)

Borodin was a big man, and by every account, a super guy. He returned to St. Petersburg from medical school in Germany and was immediately given a faculty position at the Academy of Medicine, which provided him an apartment on the grounds of the academy. We read that:

> There he lived for the rest of his life with his wife, innumerable cats, and the equally innumerable relatives, in a state of happy and maniacal disorder. He was an easy-going, kind-hearted man, one of the most respected [scientists] in Europe, loved by his pupils. How he found time to compose anything remains a mystery. Students, friends, scientists, musicians, and in-laws were constantly wandering through the rooms of the Borodin apartment. The samovar was at a perpetual boil. Often he found a relative or visitor in his own bed, and with a resigned shrug he would camp on the sofa for the night. He described himself as a "Sunday composer." "Science is my work and music is my fun."

In late 1862, immediately after Borodin had joined Balakirev's group, Balakirev decided that Borodin should compose a symphony. As Borodin didn't know anything about large-scale composition or orchestration, Balakirev sent Borodin home with scores of Beethoven's and Schumann's symphonies and told him to look them over and then compose one of his own, which is pretty much the same as handing someone books on aerodynamics and then expecting her to land an FA-18 Hornet on an aircraft carrier at night. Incredibly, Borodin managed to turn out a symphony of sorts, a testament to the power of determination, talent, and Balakirev's measure-by-measure oversight. Still, who could have anticipated that his Second Symphony would be a genuine symphonic masterwork, with all the hallmarks of such a masterwork: great breadth of conception, wonderful and memorable themes, a superb and advanced harmonic palette, and big dramatic contrast, all of it swept along with a palpably physical rhythmic power?

Borodin began his Second Symphony almost immediately after the premiere of the First, in 1869, and completed it in 1876. Along with his opera, *Prince Igor*, it is Borodin's finest single composition. We hear the opening two minutes—what amounts to the exposition of the brilliant fourth and final movement.

[Musical example from Symphony No. 2 in B Minor, Borodin: II; Opening]

My friends, if that doesn't whet your appetite for more, I do not know what will. Borodin began a Third Symphony of which he completed only the first two movements before he died of a heart attack on February 27, 1887, at the age of 53. It was one of those so-called "widow-makers." One second, Borodin was laughing and joking at a costume ball organized by the Medical Academy of St. Petersburg, and the next second he keeled over, dead before he hit the ground.

In 1906, Sir Henry Hadow wrote of Borodin that: "No [composer] has ever claimed immortality with so slender an offering." It's an appraisal that still stands. Borodin's best music—his opera, *Prince Igor*; his orchestral tone poem, *In the Steppes of Central Asia*; his second string quartet; and his Second Symphony—is a slender offering indeed, but they are superb works, and the Second Symphony deserves our attention. (Claude Debussy considered it the greatest of all Russian symphonies, ranking it above those of even Tchaikovsky!) The general consensus today is that excepting Mussorgsky, Borodin was by far the most gifted of The Five. He was also, in terms of his profession, outside of music by far the most successful of any member of The Five, although his career as a doctor, chemist, and professor precluded him from creating the sort of body of work that might have made him a mainstay of the repertoire. Along with Carlo Gesualdo before him, and Mr. Charles Edward Ives of Danbury, Connecticut after him, Alexander Borodin must go down in history as the greatest non-professional composer in the history of Western music.

Nicolai Rimsky-Korsakov (1844-1908)

Of all the members of The Five, only Nicolai Andreyevich Rimsky-Korsakov actually managed to make a career as a composer. In doing so, he became one of the most influential composers in the history of Russian music.

Rimsky-Korsakov came from a family of distinguished naval and military officers, and there was never any question that he would follow in their footsteps, despite his love for music. Sometime in 1861, Rimsky-Korsakov, then a 17-year-old cadet at the Naval Institute of St. Petersburg, decided to write a symphony. As he knew next to nothing about music theory, he sought out Balakirev who, as we are now aware, hardly knew any more than Rimsky. It made no difference. Rimsky-Korsakov, enthralled to be in the company of a "known" composer, did what Balakirev told him to do. And Balakirev told him to "continue working on the symphony" during Rimsky's two-and-a-half year cruise on the clipper *Almaz*. Rimsky-Korsakov later recalled that the slow movement was composed while the ship sat for months in the River Thames waiting for repairs. He claimed to have first played the movement through on a piano in a restaurant in Gravesend, in Kent, about 25 miles east of London.

On his return to St. Petersburg, Rimsky-Korsakov became the fifth member of The Five. Under Balakirev's direction, he turned out a number of serviceable works including his Second Symphony subtitled *"Antar"*; the symphonic poem, *Sadko*; and the opera, *The Maid of Pskov*. Pretty good for someone who didn't know squat about the craft of musical composition, something that became painfully clear when Rimsky-Korsakov was invited to join the faculty of the St. Petersburg Conservatory as a professor of practical composition and instrumentation. Harold Schonberg tells us: "He spent sleepless nights worrying about the invitation, as well he might. He already had a reputation as a composer, but only he knew how little he knew. Balakirev's teaching had not included even the most elementary aspects of the art of music."

Writing many years later in his autobiography, Rimsky confessed:

> It was not merely that I could not have harmonized a chorale properly, I'd never written a single [counterpoint] exercise in my life; I didn't even know the names of the chords. My grasp of musical forms was hazy. I had no real knowledge of string technique or the practical possibilities [of the other instruments]. As for conducting, I had never led an orchestra in my life.

Somehow, the new professor—studying day and night—managed to stay a week ahead of his students. When he began teaching he was still in the Navy, so he taught in his officer's uniform, which must have earned him a degree of cache from students who might have otherwise seen right through him. Eventually, Rimsky learned his stuff, and as if to prove to himself that he had mastered the art of counterpoint, he composed his Third Symphony in which, according to Rimsky himself: "I tried to cram into it as much counterpoint as possible." One source goes so far as to declare that Rimsky's Third and final symphony is: "the clearest evidence of his desperate determination to prove himself worthy of his Conservatory position."

Say what you will, it's an excellent symphony and it was well received when it was premiered in 1874. Tchaikovsky, who heard it in Moscow, wrote that: "The [second movement] scherzo is a real jewel."

Well, you know what? We agree. Written in the unusual meter of 5/4 (an uneven, asymmetrical meter that is much more characteristic of Eastern European music than Western), it bubbles over with energy and life. Let's hear its opening two minutes.

[Musical example from Symphony No. 3 in C Major, Opus 32, Rimsky-Korsakov: II; Opening]

Rimsky-Korsakov's appointment at the St. Petersburg Conservatory went a long way towards breaking up The Five. Modest Mussorgsky, in particular, was furious about it. According to Mussorgsky, Rimsky-Korsakov was a renegade, a sell-out; he had defected to the German enemy to compose fugues and sonatas. Mussorgsky wrote: "The Mighty Five have hatched into a horde of soulless traitors."

Calm down, Modest, just chill out. The break-up of The Five was inevitable. Alexander Borodin, not just talented but smart, understood what was happening perfectly well. He wrote:

So far as I see, this is nothing but a natural situation. As long as we were in the position of eggs under a sitting hen [and of course here he refers to Balakirev], we were all more or less alike. As soon as the fledglings broke out of their shells, they grew feathers. And when their wings grew, each flew to wherever his nature drew him.

As it turned out, for both Rimsky-Korsakov and the history of music as we know it, his move to the Conservatory was a very good thing. By being forced to teach theory and orchestration, Rimsky-Korsakov finally learned theory and orchestration. His position allowed him to bridge the gap between the nationalist music and dogma of The Five and the traditional Western music establishment. He became an incredibly influential teacher, taking the nationalist message of The Five to the next generation of Russian composers, composers who, unlike The Five, were properly trained. Among Rimsky-Korsakov's students were: Igor Stravinsky, Sergei Prokofiev, and Alexander Glazunov, who himself became an important mentor of Dmitri Shostakovich.

Alexander Glazunov (1865-1936)

Alexander Konstantinovich Glazunov was born in St. Petersburg in 1865 and died in Paris in 1936. A prodigious talent, he was often referred to as the "Mendelssohn of Russian music." At 14, he became the protégé of Nicolai Rimsky-Korsakov. Rimsky later said of Glazunov that he progressed: "not from day-to-day but from hour to hour."

Glazunov completed his First Symphony (of an eventual eight; a ninth was abandoned and remained unfinished) when he was 16. His First String Quartet (of seven) was completed at the age of 17. In 1899, he was appointed professor at the St. Petersburg Conservatory and at 1905, at the age of 40, was appointed Director of the Conservatory, a post he held for 25 years, until 1930. During his directorship, the Conservatory had three different names: the St. Petersburg Conservatory, the Petrograd Conservatory, and the Leningrad Conservatory. We cannot help but think that he would be pleased to know that it is today, once again, called the St. Petersburg Conservatory.

Today, Glazunov is recognized as the composer who reconciled 19th-century Russian music nationalism with the craft and developmental techniques of German compositional style. As an example of Glazunov's symphonic style, we turn to his Symphony no. 5 in Bb Major, op. 55 of

1895. We hear the conclusion of its ringing, chirping, and altogether wonderful second-movement scherzo.

[Musical example from Symphony No. 5 in Bb Major, Opus 55, Glazunov: II; Conclusion]

Of the many other composers of pre-Revolution Russian symphonies and post-Revolution Soviet symphonies, we have time only for the briefest mention. Such composers as Mikhail Ipolitov-Ivanov, Reinhold Gliere, Sergei Lyapunov, Anton Arensky, Vasily Kalinnikov, Sergei Taneyev (to whom, by the way, Glazunov dedicated his Fifth Symphony), and Alexander Scriabin all composed symphonies, none of which have entered into the international repertoire. A more familiar name is Sergei Rachmaninoff, 1873-1943, who, despite having written three symphonies, is more justifiably famous as a composer of piano concerti. Less well known, but much more influential as a symphonist was Nikolai Myaskovsky, whose 27 symphonies, written between 1908 and 1950, spanned from the reign of Czar Nicholas II almost through to the end of Stalin's life.

We can continue to name names of other mid-20th century Soviet composers of symphonies from Maximilian Steinberg and Vladimir Shcherbachev to Dmitri Kabalevsky and Aram Khachaturian, but I'd be pushing my luck in pronouncing their marvelous names and besides, their symphonies have not entered the repertoire. The larger point is that two masters of the mid-20th-century Soviet symphony eclipse their contemporaries much in the same way that Haydn and Mozart eclipsed theirs in the late 18th century. We refer to Sergei Prokofiev and Dmitri Shostakovich. We will devote an entire lecture—Lecture Twenty-Four—to Shostakovich and his Symphony no. 10. We will devote but 900 words to Prokofiev, a sin for which I will eventually be called to task.

Sergei Sergeyevich Prokofiev (1891-1953)

Not counting two student works, Prokofiev composed seven symphonies between 1917 and 1952. To this day, and much to his unhappiness while he was still alive, Prokofiev's most popular symphony was his First, in D major, op. 25, the so-called "Classical" Symphony. At the time he composed it, in 1915-1916, Prokofiev was already known as a steel-fisted modernist and anti-Romantic, a "musical Cubist and Futurist"; so a Classically proportioned First Symphony was the last thing the musical community expected. Of his First Symphony, Prokofiev wrote:

It seemed to me that had Haydn lived in our day he would have retained his same style while accepting something of the new at the same time. That was the type of symphony I wanted to write: a symphony in the Classical style. And when I saw [while composing it] that the idea was beginning to work, I called it the "Classical Symphony"; in the first place, because that was simpler, and secondly, for the fun of it, and in the secret hope that I would prove to be right if the symphony really did turn out to be a piece of Classical music.

Prokofiev's First is a wonderful example of what would soon enough come to be called *Neo-Classicism*: the "New Classicism" whereby Classical-era formal and melodic structures were layered like veneer over otherwise very 20th century harmonic materials and orchestration techniques. The results, in the hands of a real pro like Prokofiev, can be delightful: wry, humorous, ironic, and engaging, all at the same time. As an example, we hear the exposition section that opens the first movement.

[Musical example from Symphony No. 1 in D Major, Opus 25, "The Classical", Prokofiev: I; Exposition]

Of course, this was not the sort of music with which Prokofiev made his reputation. And the word "delightful," which fits his First Symphony so nicely, would be the very last word one would use to describe Prokofiev the person:

He was stubborn, ill-tempered, obstinate, and surly. Everything about him attracted attention, including his looks. His head was set on a pipe-stem neck; he had [white blond hair] and pink skin that would turn red when he was in a rage (which was often); piercing blue eyes, and thick protruding lips. He disturbed everybody with [his] irritating chuckle and celebrated leer.

Prokofiev was born in Ukraine and entered the St. Petersburg Conservatory at the age of 13, in 1904. A brilliant pianist, he treated the piano like a percussive instrument and transferred his explosive, percussive vision of the piano to the orchestra, as well. When the Revolution came to Russia in 1917, the 26-year-old Prokofiev, deciding that discretion was the better part of valor, sailed to the United States by way of Japan. When he arrived in San Francisco, he was detained on Angel Island for three days by immigration officials who suspected him of being a Bolshevik spy. Prokofiev recounted his interrogation: "Have you ever been imprisoned?"

"Yes I have." "That's bad. Where?" "Here, on your island." "So, you like to make jokes do you?"

In the United States, Prokofiev was discussed, admired, but not liked. One reviewer said of his compositions and piano playing: "Steel fingers, steel biceps, steel triceps—he is a tonal steel trust."

Prokofiev left the United States in 1923 and moved to Paris, which remained his base of operations for 13 years. During the late 1920s and early 1930s, Prokofiev was invited to concertize a number of times in the Soviet Union. The success of these tours convinced the unbelievably naïve Prokofiev to move back to Russia. In 1936, to the amazement of everybody, he renounced his "émigré" status, moved to Moscow, and became a Soviet citizen. Igor Stravinsky, for one, was disgusted with Prokofiev's return to mother Russia and later wrote that it was:

> A sacrifice to the bitch goddess [of greed] and nothing else. He had no success in the United States or Europe for several seasons, while his visits to Russia had been triumphs. When I saw him for the last time, he was despondent about his material fate in France. He returned to Russia, and when he finally understood his position there, it was too late.

Yes, it was way too late. Prokofiev was censured by the Soviet government in 1948, and he died a frightened, broken man on March 5, 1953, about one hour before Joseph Stalin died.

We close with the opening of the second-movement scherzo of Prokofiev's Symphony no. 5, composed in 1944 and perhaps the most successful of all the pieces of work he wrote after his return to the Soviet Union.

[Musical example from Symphony No. 5, Bb Major, Opus 100, Prokofiev: II; Opening]

That bit of scherzo from the Fifth Symphony sounds to my ears like the "old" Prokofiev: the wry, idiosyncratic humorist, the composer he was before he sold his soul, relinquished his true personality, and, for the sake of survival, wrote music that satisfied the Soviet state. An artistic tragedy, really, and a fate shared by so many Soviet artists. We'll discuss this issue of music and "the state" at greater length when we return to the Soviet Union and Shostakovich's Symphony no. 10 in Lecture Twenty-Four.

Thank you.

Lecture Nineteen
Charles Ives

Scope: America did not develop a concert music infrastructure until the 19th century, or an indigenous concert music tradition until the early 20th century. With Charles Ives, America could finally claim a distinctly American composer, one who acknowledged and represented the diversity of the nation in his music. Ives freely used quotations from the popular music of his youth and technical experimentation to create a musical language all his own.

Outline

I. America did not develop an indigenous concert music tradition until the beginning of the 20th century.

   A. There are any number of reasons for this, chief among them are economics and machismo. At the heart of the "American dream" is the concept of economic Darwinism, that is, survival of the economic fittest. In a freely competitive, merit-oriented marketplace, survival goes to those enterprises that can turn a profit and create something of value.

   B. The arts exist uncomfortably in an environment where intrinsic value is measured in dollars and cents. Further, although a painting or a book can have intrinsic value, what "value" does a piece of concert music have? Concert music "exists" only in the air. What is the hard value of a symphony or string quartet? How do we measure its intrinsic worth?

   C. In 18th- and 19th-century America, in a developing nation where success was measured by financial advancement and security, composers of concert music ranked exceedingly low on the social scale. In his book *Music in the United States: A Historical Introduction*, H. Wiley Hitchcock notes that music was considered "the most intangible and 'useless' [of] the arts," and it was left as the province of women or "immigrant 'professors'" (45–46).

   D. More than any other single group, it was the Germans who created what is now the American concert music infrastructure.

1. Massive crop failures in the 1840s, the failed revolutions of 1848, and the California gold rush of 1849 brought huge numbers of German-speaking immigrants to the United States in the mid-19th century. These immigrants brought with them their musical tastes and habits, and it was largely through their efforts and influence that German-style musical education institutions, concert halls, and performing organizations were born and funded.

2. Between 1860 and 1900, the American musical infrastructure virtually came into existence. Education institutions were founded, including the Peabody Conservatory in 1860 and the Institute of Musical Art (later renamed the Juilliard School) in 1904. Concert halls were built, including Carnegie Hall in 1891 and Boston's Symphony Hall in 1900. By the first decades of the 20th century, the Boston Symphony Orchestra, the Philadelphia Orchestra, and the New York Philharmonic rivaled any orchestra in Europe.

3. The "American" musical infrastructure exhibited a built-in German bias from the beginning. For example, the first full professor of music at any American university was the American-born composer John Knowles Paine (1839–1906), who studied in Berlin before returning to teach at Harvard. Paine was a famous composer in his day and a highly influential teacher, whose music has a distinctly German sound. (**Musical selection**: Paine, Symphony no. 1 in C Minor, op. 23, movement 1, opening [1876].)

E. Building a musical infrastructure was only half the battle. If an "indigenous" concert music tradition was to evolve in the United States, American composers also had to develop an awareness that their music must celebrate the American experience and reflect the diversity of the nation. Today, we recognize that an American music is only "American," if, like American society itself, it somehow synthesizes diverse musical elements into a whole greater than its parts.

1. Jazz, for example, is a quintessentially "American" music: a synthesis of West African rhythmic constructs and microtonal scales with European instruments and harmonic practice.

2. In other words, if the soul of American society is its rich ethnic and racial diversity, then no one racial or ethnic

tradition can, by itself, create a genuine American music. The first American-born composer of genius to intellectually and musically recognize this fact was a Connecticut Yankee, Charles Edward Ives.

II. Charles Ives (1874–1954) was born and raised in Danbury, Connecticut, where he lived the perfect New England childhood.

A. Aside from the New England environment of his youth, which he memorialized in his music, the great formative influence of Ives's life was his father, George Edward Ives, a Civil War veteran and a cornet player of some talent.

1. George Ives was Danbury's bandmaster and its music teacher. He conducted the local theater orchestras and was music director at the Methodist Church. He was also something of a rebel, being the only one of four siblings not to follow his father into a respectable job in business.

2. George's rebellious streak played itself out in his music and made a significant impression on his son Charlie. George was one of those individuals for whom the phrase "Yankee ingenuity" was coined; he was constantly building all sorts of musical inventions and creating musical exercises for his children.

3. George also imparted a traditional music curriculum to his children. According to one of Charles's biographers: "George Ives repudiated conformity, but he believed in discipline. [His] main departures from the academic standards were—one—that sound was a world of infinite possibilities to be explored and—two—that music was to be most valued when related to human events." (Gilbert Chase, *America's Music from the Pilgrim's to the Present*, 3rd ed., p. 430. Urbana and Chicago: University of Illinois Press.)

B. Ives's own music is a unique synthesis of his classical training, his love for American music of every kind, the New England of his childhood, experimentation, and his abject belief that music was the common language that bound together all humanity in all places at all times.

C. Ives's attitudes toward music were formed early, and they were bound to cause problems when he came in contact with the German-educated pedants that dominated the American musical scene at the end of the 19th century. At Yale, Ives studied composition with Professor Horatio Parker, who had studied in Munich. Ives later said that Parker was "governed too much by the German rule" to allow Ives to try out any of his father's experimental ideas.

D. Ives also worked with Parker on a symphony as a sort of "undergraduate thesis," a work now known as his "First" Symphony. Later, Ives chose not to revise his First Symphony because during its original composition, Parker had forced him to make changes in it that he didn't want to make. In the end, he had a technically polished, perfectly "nice" symphony that he saw as a bundle of compromises, more Parker's than his own, a monument to the futility of trying to please anyone but himself.

III. Ives graduated from Yale in 1898; took a weekend job as church organist and choir director in Bloomfield, New Jersey; and went to work as a clerk in the actuarial department of the Mutual Life Insurance Company. He also composed in every spare minute he had; his Symphony no. 2, composed between 1900 and 1902, is a product of this period.

A. We turn to the recapitulation and coda of the fifth and final movement of Ives's Second, because the central issue surrounding the symphony is best demonstrated in its last minutes.

1. That "issue" involves Ives's use of quotations, which are not momentary references to his musical heroes, but direct, often substantial quotations woven together to create a genuine American quilt. The musical references fly by, like momentary impressions seen from the window of a speeding train; together, they create an extraordinary sense of time and place.

2. We will hear the following: an energetic, almost Dvorak-like theme 1, followed by a bit of "Camptown Races" in the brass; a delicate version of theme 1 in the winds, followed by a Yankee drum-and-fife corps, with "Camptown Races" in the trombones, followed by a bit of "Turkey in the Straw"; a modulating bridge that uses material from themes 1 and 2, "Camptown Races," and other tunes, all of which coalesces into the patriotic march "Columbia, the Gem of the Ocean" in the brass; a buildup, a pause, a quiet transition in the strings…and then, theme 2.

3. Gentle and folk-like, theme 2 is punctuated by a brief bit of the song "Far, Far Away," heard in the oboe. Another bridge-like passage follows, combining almost everything we've heard so far; a snare drum then calls everyone to order; reveille is sounded in the trumpets, and a glorious, triumphant version of "Columbia, the Gem of the Ocean" blazes forth, followed by one last reveille call! (**Musical selection**: Ives, Symphony no. 2, movement 5, recapitulation and coda.)

4. Charles Ives developed a truly American artistic tenet based on pluralism, inclusivity, and the absolute necessity for diversity in an artist's outlook.

5. Ives's belief in the interrelation of all things was based on his Methodist spirituality and the New England Transcendental belief of the great uniting "over-soul" of the universe. For this reason, Ives freely juxtaposed different sorts of music as his imagination saw fit. The necessity of cultivating and celebrating musical diversity was seen by Ives as an essentially American principle.

B. The reason Ives was free to put his beliefs into his music and write what he wanted to write was that he made his living in the insurance business, not as a musician. Ives was a liberal idealist, and he viewed insurance as a great social equalizer that offered financial security for the "common person" decades before the creation of Social Security. Ives went on to make a fortune as a principal partner at Mutual Life.

C. He composed compulsively and continuously, but he refused to copyright his music, claiming that all music belonged to all people. He also refused to take royalties for his published works and donated the money to charity. He used his wealth to help other composers and musical enterprises; indeed, Ives's generosity kept many musicians and musical organizations in business through the Depression.

D. Ives rarely sought out performances. As a result, his musical impact on his own generation of composers was almost nonexistent. It took decades for the world to discover Ives's music. His Second Symphony, for example, largely completed by 1902, when Ives was 28 years old, didn't receive its premiere until 1951, when he was 77 years old. Ives didn't attend the premiere but listened to it on the maid's radio in his kitchen when it was broadcast a few days later.

E. Ives's refusal to be a professional musician and his reserve about having his music performed may also reflect an attitude symptomatic of America at the time; that is, that "real men are not professional musicians." Ives could not bring himself to be "merely" a professional composer, answering only to his own imagination, his main purpose in life to wallow in artistic self-indulgence.

F. As was most of his generation, Ives was also virulently homophobic and terrified that his musical interests would be interpreted as a sign of effeminacy. Ives's cultivation of startling, often violent dissonance can be traced, partially, to his desire to shock the genteel and, in his mind, "effeminate" concert music community. We listen, once again, to the amazing conclusion of the Second Symphony. (**Musical selection**: Ives, Symphony no. 2, movement 5, conclusion.)

IV. Ives composed very little after the mid-1920s, when a series of heart attacks left him a coronary invalid. He lived until 1954, long enough to witness the belated success of his music.

A. Ives's third symphony was begun in 1902, first completed in 1904, and further revised in 1909. It received its premiere in 1946, 37 years later, under the baton of Lou Harrison in Carnegie Chamber Music Hall. The following year, it was awarded the Pulitzer Prize in Music.

B. The symphony, called by Ives *The Camp Meeting*, is a three-movement work based on the revival meetings he attended as a boy in the Connecticut countryside.

    1. Each movement is an extended polyphonic fantasy based on the popular tunes and hymns he remembered from his youth. It is a gorgeous and, for Ives, a conservative work; one in which, true to form, the various quotations are subsumed into a deeply moving and lyric whole.

    2. The power and purity of Ives's childhood memories—the New England summer, his father, and the communal religious ecstasy of the occasion—create a symphony that is profoundly spiritual.

3. We hear the opening two and a half minutes of the first movement, subtitled "Old Folks Gatherin'," based largely on Lowell Mason's hymn "Azmon" and Charles Converse's hymn "What a Friend We Have in Jesus." (**Musical selection**: Ives, Symphony no. 3, movement 1 opening.)

V. The "cumulative" buildup we heard in the first movement of the Third Symphony characterizes Ives's fourth and last symphony to an overwhelming degree, although the musical language of the Fourth is very different from that of the Third.

    A. Ives began his Fourth Symphony in either 1909 or 1910 and finished it in 1916. It was first performed on April 26, 1965, at Carnegie Hall, by the American Symphony Orchestra, Leopold Stokowski conducting.

    B. Ives's Fourth is his crowning symphonic achievement; in it, he uses every device in his incredible compositional bag of tricks, treating this Fourth Symphony as a sort of personal retrospective. We turn, in closing, to the fourth and final movement. Slow in tempo, grand and somber in mood, the fourth movement is based almost entirely on the hymn "Nearer My God to Thee."

    C. The movement begins with a percussion *ostinato*, a repeated rhythmic pattern, that continues throughout at a tempo different from the rest of the orchestra. It represents "the constant," whatever we choose the constant to be. It is a constant against which the other musics are layered, musics that represent both the sacred and secular spirit that Ives perceived in humankind. (**Musical selection**: Ives, Symphony no. 4, movement 4, opening.)

    D. Certainly, Ives was an astonishing innovator: His use of polytonality, polyrhythm, atonality, quotations, and musical collage, along with his assumption that any sound was potentially "musical" were all far ahead of his time. Indeed, Ives's innovations had to be reinvented by others in the 1950s and 1960s, when the larger musical community was prepared to deal with them. Ultimately, however, Ives's music is not about his technical innovations but, rather, his unique expressive voice and the power of that voice.

Lecture Nineteen—Transcript
Charles Ives

Welcome back to *The Symphony*. This is Lecture Nineteen—it is entitled "Charles Ives." We've waited a long time to get to the "New World" and with good reason. Like Scandinavia, a genuine "American" concert tradition didn't even start to develop until the very end of the 19th century.

There is any number of reasons for this, chief among them: economics and machismo, or should we say the economics *of* machismo—the great American economic meritocracy. My friends, one of the great attractions of America is the article of faith that hard work will be rewarded, that anyone can make a buck if they're willing to work for it. At the heart of the "American dream" is the concept of economic Darwinism, survival of the economic fittest. In a freely competitive, merit-oriented marketplace, survival goes to those enterprises that can turn a profit and create something of value.

The arts exist most uncomfortably in an environment where intrinsic value is measured in dollars and cents. Granted, a painting or a book of poetry can have intrinsic value—these are objects that exist in space, you can hold them, buy them, sell them, trade them. A painting by a dead master or the first edition of Walt Whitman's *Leaves of Grass*, well, it's like money in the bank. And what "value" does a piece of concert music have, lacking as it does broad popular appeal and any genuine physical substance? Concert music "exists" in the air, in the ether. What is the hard value of a symphony or a string quartet? How do we measure its intrinsic worth?

Well, we can't. In 18th- and 19th-century America, in a developing nation where success was measured by financial advancement and security, composers of concert music rank as low as you can get on the social scale. In his book, *Music in the United States: A Historical Introduction*, H. Wiley Hitchcock writes:

> [Most 19th-century Americans, many of them] only one step removed from pioneering, viewed any time spent on non-productive, [non-useful] art as wasteful and effete. Land and money needed cultivation, not their sensibilities. Music, the most intangible and "useless" [of] the arts, had their special distain and hostility. Leave music to the women, or to the immigrant

"professors." Thus crystallized an American view of fine-art music as essentially the province of females, foreigners, or effeminates, a view still held common in the twentieth century until World War One.

It makes us reflect, doesn't it? Thank heaven the admittedly imperialistic, phallocentric European ruling class didn't feel that way. They were born with money into established cultures and could indulge themselves in what they considered the finer things in life. Without them, Haydn would have spent his life teaching piano. Mozart would have survived by writing jingles for chains of unpainted furniture stores, and Beethoven would have ended up in the service economy wearing a little paper hat and barking at his customers, "Pepsi!" "No, Coke!" "Pepsi!" "No, Coke!"

More than any other single group, it was the Germans who created what is now the American concert music infrastructure. Massive crop failures in the 1840s, the failed revolutions of 1848, and the California gold rush of 1849 brought huge numbers of German-speaking immigrants to the United States in the mid-19th century. These immigrants brought with them their musical tastes and habits, and it was largely through their taste and influence that German-style musical education institutions, concert halls, and performing organizations were born and funded. Between 1860 and 1900, the American musical infrastructure virtually came into existence. Educational institutions were founded: The Peabody Conservatory in 1860; the Oberlin Conservatory in 1865; the New England Conservatory and the Cincinnati Conservatory in 1867; the Institute of Musical Art (later renamed the Julliard School) in 1904. Concert halls were built, including the Academy of Music in Philadelphia in 1857; Cincinnati's Music Hall in 1878; Chicago's Auditorium in 1889; Carnegie Hall in 1891; and Boston's Symphony Hall in 1900. By the first decades of the 20th century, the Boston Symphony Orchestra, the Philadelphia Orchestra and the New York Philharmonic rivaled any orchestra in Europe.

And that's the good news. The bad news is that this "American" musical infrastructure exhibited a built-in German bias from the very beginning. Take, for example, the American-born composer John Knowles Payne, 1839-1906. Born in Portland, Maine, Payne studied in Berlin. He returned to the United States where he taught at Harvard, becoming, in 1875, the first full professor of music at any American University. Payne was a very famous composer in his day, a highly influential teacher whose music is as German sounding as German can be. Let's sample please, John Knowles

Paine's Symphony no. 1 in C Minor, op. 23, the beginning of movement one, a piece that dates from 1876.

[Musical example from Symphony No. 1 in C Minor, Opus 23, Paine: I; Opening]

As German as German can be, yes, building a musical infrastructure was only half the battle. If an "indigenous" concert music tradition was to evolve in the United States. Something else had to develop—an awareness that to be American, American music had to somehow celebrate the American experience. More easily said than done, because the first step was to realize what constituted the "American experience." It wasn't until the first decades of the 20th century that it came to be understood that for any music to be uniquely American, it had to somehow reflect the diversity of the American experience. Today we recognize that American music is only "American," if, like American society itself, it somehow synthesizes diverse musical elements into a whole greater than its parts. Jazz, for example, is a quintessentially "American" music: a synthesis of West African rhythms and microtonal scales, and European instruments and harmonic practice.

All together then: If the soul of American society is its rich ethnic and racial diversity, then no one racial or ethnic tradition can, by itself, create a genuine American music. Only music that somehow synthesizes some aspects of this diversity can be called uniquely American. The first American born composer of genius to intellectually and musically recognize this was a Connecticut Yankee, Charles Edward Ives.

Charles Ives (1874-1954)

Charles Ives was your basic, all-American kid. He was born and raised in Danbury, Connecticut where he lived, by his own admission, the perfect New England childhood. He played varsity football and baseball in high school and went on to pitch for the varsity team at Yale. Aside from the New England environment of his youth, which he spent the rest of his life memorializing in his music, the great formative influence of Ives's life was his father, George Edward Ives, a Civil War veteran and one hell of a coronet player. Charles Ives liked to say that when it came to music, "Pa taught me what I know."

George Ives was Danbury's bandmaster and its music teacher. He conducted the local theater orchestras and was the music director of the Methodist Church. George Ives's position in his community was not unlike Johann Sebastian Bach's in Leipzig, or for that matter, any one of the countless music masters in Europe and North America who directed the municipal and sacred activities for their communities. George Ives was something of a rebel, as well, being the only one of four siblings not to follow his father into a real job, a respectable job, a job in business. George's rebelliousness played itself out in his music and made an impression on his son Charlie that could only be called elemental.

George Ives was one of those individuals for whom the phrase "Yankee ingenuity" was coined. He was constantly building and futzing around with all kinds of musical inventions and gadgets. For example, he created a device capable of producing quartertones—the pitches in between the ones we're accustomed to hearing—and loved to experiment with it. Many years later Charles Ives remembered:

> [My father] rigged up a contrivance to stretch 24 or more violin strings and tune them up to suit the dictates of his own curiosity. He would pick out quarter-tone tunes and try to get the family to sing them, but I remember he gave that up except as a form of punishment. A little later on he did some experimenting with glasses and bells, and got some sounds as beautiful as they were funny.

George Ives also invented exercises that were intended, according to Charles: "to stretch our ears and strengthen our musical minds. [For example], he would occasionally have us sing a tune like *Swanee River* in the key of Eb, but play the accompaniment in C." But George didn't stint on the real stuff either; again, Charles Ives recalled: "Father kept me on Bach and taught me harmony from [the time I was] a child until I went to college."

Yes, according to the music historian Gilbert Chase:

> George Ives repudiated conformity, but he believed in discipline. [His] main departures from the academic standards were—one—that sound was a world full of infinite possibilities to be explored and—two—that music was to be most valued when related to human events.

> In later life Charles Ives reacted strongly to the criticism of "routine-minded professors" who told him that gospel hymns and [popular tunes] should have no place in a composer's music—certainly not in a symphony!

For Ives, human experience was the basis of all creativity. He wrote in retrospect: 'I remember when I was a boy—at the outdoor Camp Meeting services in Redding [Connecticut], all the farmers, their families and field hands, from miles around, would come afoot or in their wagons. I remember how the great waves of sound used to come through the trees—when [hymns] like *Beulah Land*, *Nearer My God to Thee*, *In the Sweet Bye and Bye* were sung by thousands of souls. Father, who led the singing, would encourage the people to sing their own way. Most of them knew the words and music by heart, and sang it that way. If they threw the poet and the composer around a bit, so much the better for the poetry and the music. There was power and exultation in these great conclaves of sound from humanity.'

Ives's own music is a unique synthesis of: 1) his classical training; 2) his love for American music of every kind, from patriotic march music and spirituals to ragtime and folksongs; 3) the New England of his childhood; 4) experimentation; and 5) his abject belief that music was the common language that bound together all humanity in all times and all places.

Ives's attitudes towards music were formed early, and they were bound to cause him problems when he came in contact with the German-educated pedants that dominated the American musical scene at the end of the 19th century. At Yale, Ives studied composition with Professor Horatio Parker who had studied at the *Hochschule für Musik* in Munich under Joseph Rheinberger—a German guy if you hadn't guessed. Of these lessons with Parker, Ives claimed: "I didn't bother him with any of the experimental ideas father had been willing for me to think about, discuss, and try out. Parker was governed too much by the German rule."

Ives is not being entirely honest here. In 1894, when he was 20 years old, he did indeed show Parker a composition of his entitled "Song for the Harvest Season," scored for voice, clarinet, trombone, and organ—in which each instrument plays in a different key. Parker's famous response was, "Ives! Must you always hog all the keys?"

Ives also worked with Parker on a symphony that he, Ives, envisioned as a sort of "undergraduate thesis," a work now known as his "First" Symphony. It's a work Ives never looked at twice after leaving Yale, which is odd because Ives was an inveterate reviser, who tended to see his compositions as "works in progress." Ives chose not to revisit and revise his First Symphony, a product of three long years of work because of the emotions associated with its creation. Ives would bring his work to Parker, Parker would tear it to shreds, Ives would make revisions he did not want to make. In the end, he had a technically polished, perfectly "nice" little symphony that he saw as a bundle of compromises, more Parker's than his own, a monument to the futility of trying to please anyone but himself. That was the essential lesson Ives took away from the composition of his First Symphony.

Symphony no. 2.

Ives graduated from Yale in 1898. He took a weekend job as church organist and choir director in Bloomfield, New Jersey, and for a day gig he went to work as a clerk in the actuarial department of the Mutual Life Insurance Company in Lower Manhattan, at a salary of five dollars a week. He also became the star pitcher on Mutual's baseball team. They should have paid him more, my friends. Anyway, he composed. In every spare minute, he composed. Ives's Symphony no. 2, composed between 1900 and 1902 is a product of just this period, although we should point out that Ives continued to rewrite and reorchestrate and revise it on and on through 1950.

We turn to the recapitulation and coda of the fifth and final movement of Ives's Second, because the central issue surrounding the symphony is best demonstrated in its last minutes. That "issue" has to do with Ives's use of quotations. We're not talking here about momentary references to his musical heroes, like Stephen Foster, and Antonin Dvorak, and Johannes Brahms. No, we're talking about the use of direct, often substantial quotations, woven together to create a symphonic barn door collage, a genuine American quilt. The musical references fly by, like momentary impressions seen from a speeding train window; together, they create an extraordinary sense of time and place.

This is what we're going to hear in our excerpt: the energetic, almost Dvorak-like theme 1, followed by a brief bit of "Camptown Races" in the brass; a delicate version of theme 1 in the winds, followed by a Yankee drum and fife corps, with "Camptown Races" in the trombones, followed by a brief bit of "Turkey in the Straw"; a modulating bridge that uses material from themes 1 and 2, "Camptown Races," and other tunes, all of which coalesces into the patriotic march "Columbia, the Gem of the Ocean" in the brass; a buildup, a pause, a quiet transition in the strings, and then theme 2. Gentle and folk-like, theme 2 is punctuated by a brief bit of the song "Far, Far Away," heard in the oboe. Another bridge-like passage follows, combining almost everything we heard so far; a snare drum then calls everyone to order; reveille is sounded in the trumpets, and the glorious, triumphant version of "Columbia, the Gem of the Ocean" blazes forth followed by one last reveille call and then, and then—and then my friends—yikes! Let's listen.

[Musical example from Symphony No. 2, Ives, I]

We'll discuss the musical Bronx cheer that concludes the movement in just a moment. But first, we must address the issue of all these musical quotations. Gilbert Chase quite brilliantly writes:

> Ives's use of borrowed material is both evocative and structural, both symbolic and functional. Far from relying mainly on literal quotations, it is an evocation by allusion and association, stirring roots of memory and recalling the collective experiences of Americans through remembrances creatively reinterpreted and transformed, not a medley but a melding.

Charles Ives developed a truly "American" artistic tenet. Based on pluralism, inclusivity, and the absolute necessity of diversity for the artist's outlook. In the epilogue of his famous "Essays Before a Sonata," Ives wrote this:

> If a man finds that the cadences of an Apache war-dance come nearest to his soul—provided that he has taken the pains to know enough other cadences, for eclecticism is part of his duty—let him assimilate whatever he finds highest in the [Apache] ideal, so that he can use it, fervently, transcendentally, inevitably, furiously, in his symphonies, in his operas, in his whistlings on the way to work, so that he can paint his house with them, make them a part of his prayer-book—this is all possible and necessary if he is confident that they have a part in his spiritual consciousness. With this assurance, his music will have everything it should of sincerity, nobility, strength, and beauty, no matter how it "sounds"; and if, with this, he is true to none but the highest of American ideals (that is, the ideals that coincide with his spiritual consciousness), his music will be true to itself and American, and it will be so even after it is proved that all our Indians came from Asia.

Ives's belief in the interrelation of all things was based on his Methodist spirituality and the New England Transcendental belief, as espoused by Ralph Waldo Emerson, of the great uniting "over-soul" of the universe.

That's why Ives had no problem or compunction with juxtaposing all different sources of music as his imagination saw fit, the willingness to accept that sort of musical diversity. Indeed, the necessity of cultivating it, of indulging it, of celebrating it, was seen by Ives as an essentially American thing. The reason why Ives was free to put his beliefs into his music and write whatever sort of music he wanted to write was because he could. He was that rare bird—a composer of genius who didn't make his living as a musician. He went into the insurance business. Ives was a liberal idealist, and he viewed insurance not with our jaded 21st-century eyes, but rather as a great social equalizer, one that offered financial security for the "common person" decades before the creation of Social Security. Ives went on to make a fortune as a principal partner at Mutual Life, putting in 60-hour workweeks in New York, and commuting by train from his home in Connecticut.

As for his music, which he composed compulsively and continuously, well, he refused to copyright it, claiming that all music belonged to all people. He refused to take royalties for his published works, donating the money to charity. He used his wealth to help other composers and musical enterprises, almost always giving his gifts anonymously through a third party. Ives's generosity kept any number of musicians and musical organizations in business through the Depression. Ives maintained his individuality, his privacy, and his creative freedom by heeding the words of one of his heroes, Henry David Thoreau, who wrote, "Instead of studying how to make it worth other men's while to buy my baskets, I studied rather how to avoid the necessity of selling them."

Ives rarely sought out performances. And sadly, as a result, his musical impact on his own generation of composers was almost non-existent. It took decades for the world to discover Ives's music and to realize that he was the real deal. The story of the premiere of Ives's Second Symphony is a perfect example of what we're talking about. This wonderful piece, composed largely in 1902, when Ives was 28 years old, received its premiere in 1951, when he was 77 years old.

> The news that the Second Symphony was at last to be performed by the New York Philharmonic and in Carnegie Hall (where Ives had attended many concerts in his younger days, and must— despite his aloofness and ironic turn of mind—often have dreamed of hearing his own music performed), caused considerable stir in the Ives household. But, through some complexity of emotion that perhaps can never be fully explained, the 77-year-old composer

grew more and more upset at the idea of attending this first performance of a work so closely connected with his youth. Although Leonard Bernstein offered to conduct a private performance for Ives in the darkened hall where he could confront this long-neglected child of his brain intimately and alone, the composer was unable to bring himself to go.

And thus it was Mrs. Ives, sitting in a box by the stage, who accepted the great waves of applause by which the Carnegie Hall audience signaled their delight with the Second Symphony.

Ives's biographers, Henry and Sidney Cowell, describe what happened next:

At the end of the performance, Bernstein applauded the players and then turned towards the Ives box to join in the wild and prolonged applause. Realizing that Mrs. Ives was not grasping its extent, a guest touched her arm to suggest she turn away from the stage and see the cheering audience below her. The warmth and excitement suddenly reached her and she said in a heart-breaking tone of pure surprise, "Why, they like it, don't they?"

A few days later, when the symphony was broadcast, Ives took the bull by the horn and went into the kitchen of his home in Redding, Connecticut, and listened to [it] on the maid's radio. He was so happy with the quality of the performance that he emerged from the kitchen doing an awkward little jig of pleasure and vindication. This seems to be the only unqualified pleasure in an orchestra performance that Ives ever had.

There's another element in Ives's refusal to be a professional musician and his reticence to have his music performed, and it reflects a rather darker reality, an attitude symptomatic of his time and his America, that being "real men are not professional musicians." Yes, his father was a bandmaster, but that was one thing. As the town musician, George Ives served a useful role in the community. He was one with his community. But to be a professional composer answering only to his own imagination, his main purpose in life to wallow in artistic self-indulgence, divorced from the community, from the world? No. This, Ives could not bring himself to do. And he decried other composers whose musical effeminacy he perceived to be a product of a soft mind and a soft body. Of Claude Debussy, for example, Ives wrote: "We might offer the suggestion that Debussy's [musical] content would have been worthier if he had hoed corn, dug potatoes, or sold newspapers for a living, for in this way he might have gained deeper vitality and truer theme."

As was most of his generation, Ives was virulently homophobic. According to the musicologist Philip Brett, Ives was: "thoroughly saturated in homosexual panic." And he was terrified that his musical interests would be interpreted as a sign of effeminacy. Ives's cultivation of startling, often violent dissonance can be traced, partially, to his desire to shock the genteel, and in his mind, the "effeminate" concert music community, as he believed it existed at the turn of the century. We listen, once again, to the amazing conclusion of the Second Symphony.

[Musical example from Symphony No. 2, Ives; Conclusion]

Yes, a musical Bronx cheer! According to Ives, that was a "Take that, Rollo!" moment. Ives created an imaginary person, someone he called "Rollo Finke," who was the object of his greatest disdain. "Rollo" was the earnest, ignorant young man of Horatio Alger fame; according to Ives, he was a mindless dink, representative of mindless dinks everywhere. Henry Theophileus Finke was the anti-American, anti-new music critic whom Ives regarded as a sissy, someone unable to take his dissonance like a man!

Yes, indeed, for Ives, "dissonance" equaled manhood. On January 10, 1931, he intended a concert that included not only the first performance of his own *Three Places in New England*, but works by his friends, the American composers Carl Ruggles and Henry Cowell as well. Ives later described what happened at the concert in third person. Ives wrote:

> At this concert [Ives] sat quietly through the "boos" and jeers of his own music, but when that wonderful orchestral work *Men and Mountains* [by] Carl Ruggles was played, a hiss was heard near him. Ives got up and shouted [at the offending party]: "You goddamned sissy-eared molly-coddle, when you hear strong masculine music like this, stand up and use your ears like a man!"

Symphony no. 3

Ives composed very little after the mid-1920s, when a series of heart attacks left him a coronary invalid. He lived until 1954, at the age of 80, long enough to witness and enjoy—we could only hope—the belated success of his music.

Ives's Third Symphony was begun in 1902, first completed in 1904, and then further revised in 1909. It received its premiere 37 years later under the baton of Lou Harrison in Carnegie Chamber Music Hall. The following year, 1947, it was awarded the Pulitzer Prize in Music. Better late than never, we suppose.

The symphony, called by Ives *The Camp Meeting*, is a three-movement work based on the revival meetings he attended as a boy in the Connecticut countryside. Each movement is an extended polyphonic fantasy based on the popular and hymn tunes he remembered having been sung. It is a gorgeous, and for us, a conservative work; one in which, true to form, the various quotations are subsumed into a deeply moving and lyric whole. The power and purity of Ives's childhood memories—the New England summer, his father, and the communal religious ecstasy of the occasion— together create a symphony that is profoundly spiritual and very, very beautiful. We hear the opening two-and-a-half minutes of the first movement, a movement subtitled "Old Folks Gatherin'," based largely on Lowell Mason's hymn, "Azmon," and Charles Converse's hymn, "What a Friend We Have in Jesus."

[Musical example from Symphony No. 3, Ives: I; Opening]

Symphony no. 4

The sort of "cumulative" buildup we just heard in the first movement of the Third Symphony characterizes Ives's Fourth and last symphony to an overwhelming degree, although the musical language of the Fourth is very different from that of the Third.

Ives began his Fourth Symphony in either 1909 or 1910, and sorta/kinda finished it in 1916. It was first performed in its entirety on April 26, 1965, at Carnegie Hall, by the American Symphony Orchestra, Leopold Stokowski conducting.

Ives's Fourth is his crowning symphonic achievement; in it, he uses every device in his incredible compositional bag of tricks, treating this Fourth Symphony as a source of personal retrospective. Writes Paul Echols:

> Portions and even whole torsos of earlier pieces—some fifteen in all—found their way into the work, the earliest of them dating back to Ives's years at Yale. The compositional techniques represent a stylistic synthesis of Ives's most far-reaching and arresting musical ideas, developed over two decades of experimentation. Densely layered textures are formed by superimposing two, three, and even four different ensembles, centered on different tonalities and proceeding in different meters and tempi, constantly shifting in and

out of sync. This polytonal, polyrhythmic fabric is [itself] made from fantastically intricate webs of [melody lines] moving in different rhythmic patterns and often at different dynamic levels— now prominently in the foreground, then receding into the middle or barely audible background. The individual melodic lines are frequently derived from the familiar Ivesian mix of hymn tunes and popular and patriotic songs (over thirty of which have been identified to date in the work). The borrowed material is sometimes directly quoted, but just as often, the tunes are fragmented. As these melodic [fragments] undergo [further] transformation, they skitter in a dream-like fashion, back and forth across the threshold of perceptibility.

We turn, in closing, to the fourth and final movement, which, according to Ives: "is an apotheosis of the previous [movements], in terms that have something to do with the reality of existence and its religious experience."

Slow in tempo, grand and somber in mood, the fourth movement is based almost entirely on the hymn "Nearer My God to Thee." The movement begins with a percussion *ostinato*, a repeated rhythmic pattern, that continues throughout, at a tempo different from the rest of the orchestra. It represents, my friends, "the constant"—whatever we choose the constant to be—God, the speed of light, the music of the rotating spheres, or the background hum of the big bang—whatever, you pick. It is a constant against which the other musics of this movement are layered, musics that represent both the sacred and secular spirit Ives perceived in humankind. According to Mark Vignal: "This finale represents the supreme aesthetic achievement of Ives's transcendentalist ideal."

We hear the opening minute and a half of the movement.

Certainly, Ives was an astonishing innovator: his use of polytonality (which means many keys heard simultaneously), polyrhythm (meaning many rhythmic lines heard simultaneously), and atonality; of quotations and musical collage; his assumption that any sound was a potentially "musical" sound were all far ahead of his time. Like Leonardo da Vinci's bicycle and contact lenses, Ives's innovations had to be reinvented by others in the 1950s and 1960s, when the larger musical community was prepared, finally, to deal with it. Ultimately, however, Ives's music is not about his technical innovations, but rather about his unique expressive voice and the power, the sheer power of that voice.

We leave the final words to the great Arnold Schoenberg, himself a composer whose innovations changed forever Western concert music. Schoenberg wrote: "There is a great man living in this country—a composer. He has solved the problem of how to preserve one's self and learn. He responds to negligence [with] contempt. His name is Ives."

Thank you.

Lecture Twenty
Aaron Copland and Samuel Barber

Scope: The American concert music tradition began to emerge in the 1920s, and the American spirit of the time was captured in the work of Aaron Copland. Copland studied in France but returned to the United States with a spare and angular compositional style that was heavily influenced by jazz. Other American composers followed Copland, notably Samuel Barber, who is most well known for his *Adagio for Strings*. Barber wrote only two symphonies, but his work elevated the art form in America to a new level of beauty, design, and elegance.

Outline

I. An identifiably "American" concert music finally emerged in the 1920s, brought on by four changes in society.

   A. First, by the 1920s, the frontier expansion that had consumed so much of the creative energy of 19th-century America was complete. From coast to coast, particularly in the rapidly expanding urban centers, people could begin to focus on quality of life and quality of culture.

   B. Also by the 1920s, the music education institutions of the United States were turning out significant numbers of instrumentalists, singers, and composers who had been born in the United States and worked here.

   C. Third, the sinking of the *Lusitania* in 1915 resulted in a rejection of all things German and Austrian by both the American public and the professional music community. This rejection became almost universal when the United States entered the First World War against Germany and Austria in 1917.

   D. Finally, the emergence of American concert music was spurred by the isolationist attitude of the 1920s, during which time the American nation turned inward and began to shed its cultural inferiority complex. In the process, the public and professional musical community alike began to recognize and even embrace such quintessentially American musics as blues, ragtime, and jazz and the incredibly rich regional musical heritage of America, from folksong to Tex-Mex, from bluegrass to zydecko.

E. No composer better epitomized the new "pan-American" musical spirit of the 1920s–1940s than Aaron Copland. For the American public and professional community alike, Copland remains the most representative "American" composer of the 20th century.

II. Aaron Copland (1900–1990) was in Brooklyn, New York, the son of Polish/Lithuanian Jewish immigrants. His father, Morris, was a successful merchant, and Aaron, the pet of the family, grew up comfortably ensconced in the middle class.

A. Charles Ives and Aaron Copland could not have come from more opposite backgrounds, yet they had much more in common than not. They both grew up in large, loving, and religious households. Both Ives and Copland had strong father figures, who believed in America and the value of hard work.

B. Unlike Charles Ives, Aaron Copland was not a musical prodigy. He was a talented piano player whose love of music befuddled his family. What made Copland special was the initiative he took in his own music education. He found his own piano teachers, arranged for his own lessons, and took correspondence courses in harmony and theory; in early 1917, a few months after his 16th birthday, he began taking harmony, counterpoint, and composition lessons with Rubin Goldmark. Copland studied with Goldmark for four years and received a solid grounding in the basics of music composition and theory.

C. In 1921, Copland left for Europe to study music, but instead of going to Vienna or Berlin or Hamburg, as had previous generations of aspiring American composers, he ended up in Fontainebleau, just outside of Paris, at the New School of Music for Americans, as a student of Nadia Boulanger.

   1. It was said that Nadia Boulanger taught music theory and composition to so many Americans that by the 1940s, every American town had two things: a five-and-ten-cent store and a former student of Nadia Boulanger.

   2. As an educator, Boulanger was just as familiar with the music of Mussorgsky and Stravinsky as she was that of the dead Germans, and she was fascinated by the experimental trends of the time.

3. Through Boulanger, Copland got to meet the artistic movers and shakers of Paris, including Stravinsky, Ravel, Prokofiev, Francois Poulenc, Darius Milhaud, Diaghilev, Picasso, Hemingway, Gertrude Stein, and James Joyce.

D. Copland returned to the United States in 1924 with a compositional technique profoundly influenced by the Parisian scene, particularly Igor Stravinsky, and a burning desire to be "as recognizably American as Mussorgsky and Stravinsky were Russian."

E. Aaron Copland wrote three symphonies. The first was composed immediately after he returned to the United States, at the request of Boulanger, who had been invited to appear as an organ soloist at the Boston Symphony Orchestra. Boulanger insisted that her star student, Copland, write a piece for her to perform with the orchestra; the result was Copland's First Symphony, the "Organ" Symphony.

F. Copland's compositional style was firmly in place by 1927 and is characterized by a spare, angular, open sound and a rhythmic impulse influenced equally by the asymmetrical rhythms of Igor Stravinsky and the explosive polyrhythms of jazz. The dual rhythmic influences of Stravinsky and jazz are joined wonderfully in Copland's Symphony no. 2, the so-called "Short Symphony," of 1933.

G. Most listeners are familiar with the "populist" Aaron Copland, who composed such works as *Appalachian Spring*, *Fanfare for the Common Man*, and the grandiose Third Symphony of 1946. The other Aaron Copland is uncompromising, abstract, and "modernist," the composer of the *Variations for Piano* in 1930; the *Fantasy for Piano* in 1957; the orchestral works *Connotations* and *Inscape* in 1962 and 1967, respectively; and the "Short Symphony" in 1933; among other works. Many believe that this Aaron Copland is a much more interesting and original composer than the populist one.

H. We take our cue for the first movement from Copland's own alternative title for the piece: *The Bounding Line*; it is a movement conceived as a single, leaping, uninterrupted melody line. As we listen, be aware of the following three points:

1. For the most part, at any given moment, we will hear only one pitch at a time and almost never more than two at a time. This texture is spare, tidy, and "thrifty."

2. Also note the explosive manner in which the notes are articulated and the unpredictable, "herky-jerky" rhythmic profile of these explosive articulations. This rhythmic asymmetry is a product of the combined influence of Stravinsky and jazz on Copland's compositional language.

3. Finally, Copland makes no attempt to work within the confines of any existing form. This music develops as it goes, following its own interior logic. It is also music of tremendous charm, filled with life; music that is both playful and frantic; and music that is identifiably "American." (**Musical selection**: Copland, Symphony no. 2 [Short Symphony], movement 1, opening [1933].)

I. One reason this music is as supple and light as it is has to do with Copland's orchestration. The piece is scored for a full wind section, including a rarely heard bass oboe, an instrument called a *heckelphone*. The brass section consists of four horns and two trumpets only; there are no trombones or tubas to weigh the piece down. There is a full string section but, in lieu of any percussion, a piano.

J. The second movement is achingly beautiful and utterly original. We'll hear the first of the movement's three parts. (**Musical selection**: Copland, Symphony no. 2 [Short], movement 2, part 1.)

K. The third and final movement melds together the sprightly rhythmic profile of the first movement with the thematic material and denser harmonic structure of the second. It is an entirely thrilling movement, one that anticipates Copland's orchestral work *El Salon Mexico*, composed between 1933 and 1936. (**Musical selection**: Copland, Symphony no. 2 [Short Symphony], movement 3, opening.)

III. Fast on the heels of Aaron Copland, a bevy of American symphonists emerged in the 1930s and 1940s, composers whose music spanned a wide variety of styles and who were, in their own ways, each identifiably American.

A. For the remainder of this lecture and the entirety of the next, we will discuss three of these composers: Samuel Barber, Roy Harris, and William Schuman. Before we begin with Samuel Barber, however, the following is a short list of mid-century American symphonists and Dr. Greenberg's favorites among the symphonies of each of them.

B. Howard Hanson (1896–1981) was born in Wahoo, Nebraska, and was a genuine Romantic. He wrote seven symphonies between 1922 and 1977 and was the first president of the Eastman School of Music. Dr. Greenberg recommends his Second Symphony of 1930, subtitled "The Romantic," in particular the second movement, which John Williams adapted for his music for the bicycle chase scene in the movie *E.T.*

C. Walter Piston (1894–1976) was a professor of composition at Harvard, the author of textbooks on harmony and orchestration, and the composer of eight symphonies. His music combines great clarity and workmanship with a marvelous melodic sensibility, a genuinely American rhythmic energy, and an utter lack of pretension. Dr. Greenberg recommends Piston's Sixth Symphony of 1955.

D. Roger Sessions (1896–1985) was a professor of music composition at Princeton University and the University of California at Berkeley and a legend as both a teacher and a composer. He wrote nine symphonies, complex works of extraordinary craft and expressive power. For those prepared to do battle with a great but challenging piece of music, Dr. Greenberg recommends Sessions's Fourth of 1958.

E. Henry Cowell (1897–1965) composed 21 symphonies. He was an experimenter and teacher; as a music publisher and conductor, he was a great friend to other composers and the man responsible for bringing the music of Charles Ives to the attention of the world. His Symphony no. 11 of 1954, entitled *The Seven Rituals of Music*, is a compendium of the musical styles and techniques he spent a lifetime developing.

F. Peter Mennin (1923–1983) was the composer of nine symphonies and president of the Peabody Conservatory in Baltimore and of the Juilliard School from 1962 until his death in 1983. His music is filled with energy and edge, very "New York" in its power and intensity. His Seventh Symphony of 1963 is one of Dr. Greenberg's favorites.

G. David Diamond (b. 1915) has composed 11 symphonies that are marked by extraordinary refinement, craftsmanship, and expressive power. Dr. Greenberg suggests Diamond's Fourth Symphony of 1945 as a starting place.

H. Vincent Persichetti (1915–1987) composed nine symphonies; Dr. Greenberg recommends his Symphony no. 5 (*Symphony for Strings*) of 1954.

I. Alan Hovhaness (1911–2000) composed 67 numbered symphonies, many of them colored by his Armenian heritage and his fascination with Eastern mysticism. The piece that put him on the symphonic map is his Symphony no. 2, subtitled "Mysterious Mountain."

IV. Samuel Osborne Barber (1910–1981) was born in West Chester, Pennsylvania, the son of a well-known doctor and a mother with a passionate interest in music.

A. Barber wrote his first piece at age 7 and tried writing his first opera at 10. When he was 14, he was among the first students to enter the new Curtis Institute of Music in Philadelphia, where he studied voice, piano, composition, and conducting with the great Fritz Reiner.

B. Barber composed only two symphonies, the first while he was in residence at the American Academy in Rome. Barber was 26 years old when it was premiered in Rome in May of 1936. The piece was awarded a Pulitzer Traveling Scholarship in 1936; because Barber had also won the Pulitzer Scholarship in 1935, he became the first composer to win the award in back-to-back years.

C. Barber's Second Symphony was composed in 1944 when he was a corporal in the Army Air Force; it was commissioned by and dedicated to the U.S. Army Air Force. Barber was never satisfied with it. In 1964, he extracted a single movement from the symphony and entitled it "Night Flight." Four years later, in 1968, 24 years after its composition, he withdrew the entire symphony and destroyed his manuscript score. Nevertheless, recordings are available.

D. We return to Barber's Symphony no. 1, op. 9, of 1936, revised in 1943. Although the four sections of the symphony are played without a break, they trace the familiar pattern of the traditional symphonic template: a first-movement allegro in sonata form, a second-movement scherzo, a third-movement andante, and a somewhat faster and dramatic fourth movement that sums up and extends what has gone before it.

1. The four continuous sections of Barber's First are unified by a single thematic idea, a *motto* theme, that's heard at the very beginning of the first movement. (**Musical selection**: Barber, Symphony no. 1, motto theme, opening.)

2. As the development section approaches its climax, this motto theme is heard three times in the brass. (**Musical selection**: Barber, Symphony no. 1, motto theme, development.)

E. As the development section comes to its shattering, drum-dominated climax, instead of the expected return to the motto theme at the beginning of what we expect will be the recapitulation, we hear, instead, the motto theme in an entirely different guise, as the opening of the scherzo. Thus, the run-on sections here are actually bridged over; the motto theme acts both as a recapitulatory statement of the sonata form and an opening thematic statement of the scherzo.

1. First, we hear the motto theme as it initiates the scherzo, quick, chipper, and full of repeated notes. (**Musical selection**: Barber, Symphony no. 1, scherzo, opening.)

2. Next, we hear the connection between the truncated sonata form and the scherzo. We listen from the statement of the motto theme in the development section of sonata form through the first third or so of the scherzo. (**Musical selection**: Barber, Symphony no. 1, motto theme, development through scherzo opening.)

F. The andante is Barber at his lyric best: music of great beauty and expressive power. The music begins quietly, with an aria-like theme played by a solo oboe accompanied by muted strings, building to an amazing climax. We will listen to the entire andante so that we might hear it as a single magnificent melodic line powered, ultimately, by a single huge crescendo. (**Musical selection**: Barber, Symphony no. 1, andante.)

G. The fourth and final section is a *passacaglia*, meaning that the theme heard at the very beginning in the 'cellos and basses is repeated over and over, while the music heard above that theme is ever changing. The passacaglia theme—the opening melody heard

in the 'cellos and basses on which the entire movement is based—
is another version of the motto theme heard at the beginning of the
symphony.

1.   By way of review, we listen to the motto theme as it first
appeared at the beginning of the symphony, followed
immediately by the passacaglia theme at the beginning of the
fourth section. (**Musical selections**: Barber, Symphony no. 1,
section 1, motto theme, and section 4, passacaglia theme.)

2.   This passacaglia—and the symphony—concludes with blaring
brass reiterating the motto theme, followed by a forceful
ending. (**Musical selection**: Barber, Symphony no. 1,
movement 4, conclusion.)

Lecture Twenty—Transcript
Aaron Copland and Samuel Barber

Welcome back to *The Symphony*. This is Lecture Twenty—it is entitled "Aaron Copland and Samuel Barber." An identifiably "American" concert music finally did emerge in the late 1920s. We'd like to be able to give the credit to Charles Ives, but you know what? We can't. And neither can we credit the American born but German-trained composers who are the backbone of the American concert scene during the late 19th and early 20th centuries. According to Aaron Copland: "My own generation found very little interest in the work of [our] elders, Macdowell, Chadwick, [Parker and Payne]; and their influence on our music was nil. And we had only an inkling of the music of Charles Ives in the 1920s."

So, what happened in the 1920's to finally bring about the creation of an identifiably American tradition? Four things. One: By the 1920's, the processes of frontier expansion that had consumed so much of the creative energy of 19th-century America was complete. From coast to coast, particularly in the rapidly expanding urban centers, people could focus on issues concerning quality of life and quality of culture. Two: By the 1920s, the music education institutions of the United States were turning out a critical mass of instrumentalists, singers, and composers who were born in the United States and who found work in the United States. Call it the "Americanization" of a workforce formerly dominated by Europeans, principally Germans. Item three that brought about an identifiably "American" music tradition had a lot to do with the rejection of things German and Austrian by both the American public and professional community, a rejection that began with the torpedoing of the passenger liner the *Lusitania* in 1915, and which became universal when the United States entered the First World War against Germany and Austria in 1917. Fourth and last was the isolationist attitude of the 1920s, during which time the American nation turned inwards and began to shed its cultural inferiority complex vis-à-vis Europe and celebrate things "American." In the process, the public and professional musical community alike began to recognize and even embrace such quintessentially American musics as blues, ragtime, jazz, and the incredibly rich regional music heritage of America, from folksong to Tex-Mex, from bluegrass to zydeco.

No composer better epitomized the new "pan-American" musical spirit of the 1920s, '30s and '40s better than Aaron Copland. For the American public and professional community alike, Copland remains the most representative "American" composer of the 20th century.

Aaron Copland (1900-1990)

Copland was born on November 14, 1900, in Brooklyn, New York. The son of Polish/Lithuanian Jewish immigrants, the family name Copland was an Anglicization of "Kaplan," which explains why there is no "E" after the first three letters "C-o-p." Copland's father, Morris, was a successful merchant, and Aaron grew up the fifth and youngest child, the pet of the family, comfortably ensconced in the middle class. Copland recalled:

> My father was a strong figure in the eyes of both his family and his employees. Father was justifiably proud of what he had accomplished in the business world. But above all, he never let us forget that it was America that made all this possible. A long time member of the local Democratic Club, he voted a straight Democratic ticket at every election. Moreover, he depended on the club for his principle diversion: playing pinochle on many an evening with his fellow members.

Charles Ives and Aaron Copland could not have come from more opposite backgrounds. The Ives family arrived in North America from England in 1653. The Coplands were new immigrants, Eastern European Jews for whom English was not their first language. Yet Charles Ives and Aaron Copland had much more in common than not. They both grew up in large, loving households. Both families were religious. The Ives's were, as we know, deeply involved in the Protestant communities in and around Danbury, Connecticut. And the Coplands belonged to Brooklyn's oldest synagogue, congregation Beth Israel—at Kane and Court Streets in downtown Brooklyn—where Aaron was Bar Mitzvahed in 1913 (and where Copland's father, Morris, was president of the congregation for many years). Both Ives and Copland had strong father figures, fathers who believed in the value of hard work and believed in America, and who taught their sons to work hard and believe as well.

Unlike Charles Ives, Aaron Copland was not a musical prodigy. He was a talented piano player whose love of music otherwise befuddled his nonmusical family. What did make Copland special was the initiative he took in his own music education. Despite, or perhaps because of the indifference of his family, he found his own piano teachers, arranged for his own lessons, took correspondence courses in harmony and theory until, in early 1917, a few months shy of his 16th birthday, he began taking harmony, counterpoint, and composition lessons with Rubin Goldmark, the nephew of the famous Viennese composer, Karl Goldmark. Copland studied with Rubin Goldmark for four years, until 1921, and from Goldmark he received a solid grounding in the basics of music composition and music theory. Copland later recalled: If a student made a real boner [of a mistake], he was invited by Goldmark, with a twinkle in his eye, to become a member of his 'Schlemiel' Club."

The problem with Goldmark—a problem that ultimately drove Copland away from Goldmark and the Austrian/Germanic party line that he espoused—was his musical conservatism. Again, Copland recalled:

> [Goldmark] had little if any sympathy for the advanced musical idioms of the day. I remember seeing on his piano in 1921 a copy of Charles Ives's extraordinary *"Concord" Sonata*. I immediately asked if I could borrow the music, but Goldmark said, "You stay away from it. I don't want you to be contaminated by stuff like that." I never remember him discussing the subject of nationalism or folklorism and he certainly never suggested them to me as possible influences.

In 1921, Copland left for Europe to study music, but instead of going to Vienna or Berlin or Hamburg to study, as had previous generations of aspiring American composers, Copland ended up in Fontainebleau, just outside of Paris, at the New School of Music for Americans, as a student of Nadia Boulanger. It was said that Nadia Boulanger taught musical theory and composition to so many Americans that by the 1940s every American town had two things, a five-and-ten-cent store, and a former student of Nadia Boulanger. Boulanger was hip and she was French, *not* German, no small thing in those post-war years. As an educator, she was just as familiar with the music of Mussorgsky and Stravinsky as she was with the dead Germans, and she was fascinated by experimental trends. Through Boulanger, Copland got to meet the artistic movers and shakers of Paris. And my goodness, movers and shakers they were—Stravinsky, Ravel, Prokofiev, Francois Poulenc, Darius Milhaud, Diaghilev, Picasso, Hemingway, Gertrude Stein, James Joyce. Hey, who was not living in Paris in the 1920's? What a town!

Copland returned to the United States in 1924 with a compositional technique profoundly influenced by the Parisian scene, particularly Igor Stravinsky and a burning desire to be "as recognizably American as

Mussorgsky and Stravinsky were Russian." Copland's biographer Vivian Perlis writes:

> Copland had gone to Europe to learn how to compose and had "found" America while viewing it from abroad. He saw European composers take up American jazz and thought if composers like Debussy and Ravel, Stravinsky and Milhaud could use ragtime and jazz rhythms, the way might be open for American composers [to do so as well]. Perhaps, he thought, here finally was a music an American might write better than a European. [In particular], Darius Milhaud's [jazz-influenced work], the *Creation of the World*, caused a sensation when premiered in Paris in 1923. The only American piece that came close to the notoriety of Milhaud's was Gershwin's *Rhapsody in Blue*, commissioned by Paul Whiteman and first played on Lincoln's birthday in 1924 in a concert called, "An Experiment in Modern Music." Jazz was considered a new discovery, as though it had just happened on the scene in time for white composers to use its lively danceable rhythms in their concert music. Only black Americans puzzled over this, including the question of how a [white] bandleader with the incredible name of Whiteman had come to be called "The King of Jazz."

Aaron Copland wrote three symphonies. The first was composed immediately after he returned to the United States, and thereby hangs a tale that is a testament to having group connections. In 1824, the year Copland returned to the United States, the Russian-double-bass-virtuoso-turned-conductor, Serge Koussevitzky, began his long tenure as conductor of the Boston Symphony Orchestra. Koussevitzky invited Nadia Boulanger to appear as an organ soloist, in his first season there in Boston. And Boulanger insisted that her star student, Aaron Copland, write a piece for her to perform with the orchestra. Koussevitzky, a passionate believer in new music and new talent, bless him, was thrilled, and the result was Copland's First Symphony, the so-called "Organ" Symphony. The piece was played in Boston and in New York in 1925, and Copland's success was, as they say, assured.

Copland's compositional style was firmly in place by 1927. One: a spare angular open sound. (Copland was your basic minimalist, in that he believed in saying what he had to say with as little fuss as possible. He liked to refer to himself as being musically "thrifty.") Two: a rhythmic impulse influenced equally by the asymmetrical rhythms of Igor Stravinsky and the explosive polyrhythms of jazz. The dual rhythmic influences of Stravinsky and jazz are joined wonderfully in Copland's Symphony no. 2, the so-called "Short" Symphony, of 1933.

Copland dedicated his Second Symphony to his great friend, the Mexican composer and conductor, Carlos Chavez, who conducted the first performance in Mexico City on November 23, 1924.

A sidebar, my friends. Carlos Antonio de Padua Chavez y Ramirez was born in Mexico City in 1899 and died there in 1978. Chavez was one of the great composers of the 20th century. He composed seven symphonies between 1933 and 1961, and we're not looking at a single one of them. He is one of the many, many worthy and notable 20th-century symphonists we simply don't have time to discuss. But that should not preclude you from acquiring, listening to, and reveling in his symphonies, of which I would recommend you begin with the Second, the so-called "Sinfonia India," or "Indian (as in Aztec) Symphony."

A word of warning before we begin listening to Copland's Symphony no. 2. The "Aaron Copland" with whom most listeners are familiar is the "populist" Aaron Copland—you know, the composer of such nationalistic and accessible chestnuts as *Appalachian Spring, Rodeo, Billy the Kid*, the *Fanfare for the Common Man*, and the grandiose and rather overblown Third Symphony of 1946, a work that incorporates the *Fanfare for the Common Man* into its monumental finale. But there's another Aaron Copland, the one who composed the *Variations for Piano* in 1930, the *Fantasy for Piano* in 1957, the orchestral works *Connotations* and *Inscape*, in 1962 and 1967 respectively, and the "Short" Symphony in 1933, among other works. This is the uncompromising, abstract "modernist" Aaron Copland, a much more interesting and original composer than the well-known "populist" one. Forewarned is forearmed.

With brevity equal to the 15-minute duration of the entire symphony, Copland described his "Short" Symphony this way:

> The work is in three movements (fast, slow, fast), played without a pause. The first movement is scherzo-like in character. Once, I toyed with the idea of naming the piece *The Bounding Line* because of the [bouncing melodic] nature of the first [movement]. The second movement is in three brief sections. The final is once again bright in color and rhythmically intricate.

We take our cue for the first movement from Copland's own description of the music: *The Bounding Line;* this movement is a movement conceived as a single, leaping, uninterrupted melody line. We'll hear the opening two minutes of this first movement, this "bounding line." Please be aware of the following three things. First, for the most part, at any given moment, we will hear only one pitch at a time, and almost never more than two at a time. Talk about a spare, tidy, and "thrifty" texture. Second, be aware of the explosive way the notes are articulated and the unpredictable, "herky-jerky" rhythmic profile of these explosive articulations. This rhythmic asymmetry is a product of the combined influence of Stravinsky and jazz on Copland's compositional language. Third, Copland makes no attempt to work within the confines of any pre-existing form. This is music that develops as it goes, written "by ear" as we say; music that follows its own interior logic. It is also music of tremendous charm; it's filled with life; music that is both playful and frantic, music as identifiably "American" as that proverbial "apple pie." Symphony no. 2; 1933.

[Musical example from Symphony No. 2, Copland: I; Opening]

One reason that this music is as sinewy and supple and light as it is has to do with Copland's orchestration. The piece is scored for a full wind section, including a rarely heard bass oboe, an instrument called a *heckelphone.* The brass section consists of four horns and two trumpets only; there are no trombones or tubas to weigh things down. There is a full string section, but in lieu of any percussion, a piano.

The second movement is achingly beautiful and utterly original. There's just no other music that sounds like this. We'll hear the first of the movement's three parts.

[Musical example from Symphony No. 2, Copland: II; Part I of III]

The third and final movement melds together this brightly rhythmic profile of the first movement with the thematic material and denser harmonic structure of the second. It is an entirely thrilling movement, one that anticipates Copland's orchestral work, *El Salon Mexico*, which was composed between 1933 and 1936.

[Musical example from Symphony No. 2, Copland: III]

Despite its spareness and its brevity, music like Copland's Symphony no. 2 is not written quickly; it's just too darned different. Many years after it was composed, Copland recalled: "Although the performance time is only fifteen minutes, it took me almost two years to complete it. On other occasions I've written fifteen minutes of music in two weeks: if I expended so much time and effort on the Short Symphony, it was because I wanted to write as perfect a piece as I could." Copland succeeded. His Second Symphony is one of the great and underappreciated masterworks of the 20th century.

The American Symphony Comes of Age

Fast on the heels of Aaron Copland, a bevy of American symphonists emerged in the 1930s and 1940s, composers whose music spanned a wide variety of styles and were each, in his own way, identifiably American. For the remainder of this lecture and the entirety of the next, we're going to study three of them: Samuel Barber, Roy Harris and William Schuman, which of course leaves out some wonderful composers and their symphonies. So, as a public service, before moving on to Samuel Barber, a short list of mid-century American symphonists and my personal favorite symphony of each of them.

Howard Hansen, 1896-1981. Born in Wahoo, Nebraska, Hansen was a genuine romantic. He wrote seven symphonies between 1922 and 1977, and he was the first president of the Eastman School of Music. Check out his Second Symphony of 1930, subtitled "The Romantic," particularly the second movement, which John Williams gracelessly ripped off for his music to the bicycle chase scene in the movie *E.T.*

Walter Piston, 1894-1976, professor of composition at Harvard and the author of ubiquitous textbooks on harmony and orchestration. Piston composed eight symphonies. His music combines great clarity and workmanship with a marvelous melodic sensibility, a genuine American rhythmic energy, and an utter lack of pretension. I am crazy about Piston's Sixth Symphony of 1955.

Rodger Sessions, 1896-1985, professor of music composition at Princeton University and the University of California at Berkeley. Sessions was the teacher of my teachers, a legend as both a teacher and as a composer. He wrote nine symphonies, and they are complex works of extraordinary craft and expressive power. For those prepared to do battle with a great but challenging piece of music, I recommend Sessions's Fourth of 1958.

Henry Cowell, 1897-1965, composed 21 symphonies. Cowell was a great experimenter and teacher; as a music publisher and conductor, he was also a great friend to other composers, and the man responsible for bringing the music of Charles Ives to the attention of the world. His Symphony no. 11 of

1954, entitled *The Seven Rituals of Music*, is a compendium of the musical styles and techniques he spent a lifetime developing.

Peter Mennin, 1923-1983, the composer of nine symphonies, Mennin was the president of the Peabody Conservatory in Baltimore and then the president of the Julliard School from 1962 until his death in 1983. His music is filled with energy and edge, very "New York" in its power and intensity. His Seventh Symphony of 1963 is one of my all-time favorite pieces.

David Diamond, born 1915, has composed 11 symphonies, and they are marked by extraordinary refinement, craftsmanship, and real expressive power. I suggest Diamond's Fourth Symphony of 1945 as a starting point.

Vincent Persichetti, 1950 to 1987, composed nine symphonies; I recommend his Symphony no. 5 for strings of 1954.

And finally, for the sake of completeness, we mention Allen Hovhaness, 1911-2000, who composed 67 numbered symphonies, many of them colored by his Armenian heritage and his fascination with Eastern mysticism. The piece that put him on the symphonic map is his Symphony no. 2, subtitled "Mysterious Mountain." My enthusiasm for this music is, unfortunately, muted—my loss.

Samuel Barber (1910-1981)

Well, we should have no trouble generating a great amount of enthusiasm for the music of Samuel Barber. And we're not just talking here about his *Adagio for Strings*, originally the slow movement of his String Quartet op. 11 of 1936, a piece of music so ubiquitous that it can be rightly called the "Pachelbel's Canon" of the 20th century.

Samuel Osborne Barber was born on March 19, 1910 in Westchester, Pennsylvania, the son of a well-known doctor and a music-fiend mother. Barber wrote his first piece at age 7 and took a shot at writing his first opera at the age of 10. When he was 14, he was among the very first students to enter the brand new Curtis Institute of Music in Philadelphia, where he studied voice, piano, composition, and conducting with the great Fritz Reiner.

Samuel Barber was, my friends, a phenom. While Barber composed but two symphonies, they are important works and they are worthy of our time. The First, on which we will focus, was composed while he was in residence at the American Academy in Rome. Barber was 26 years old when it premiered in Rome in May 1936 by the Augusteo Orchestra, under the baton of Bernardino Molinari. After the premiere, an elderly Italian princess remarked rather loudly as she toddled out of the hall, "That young man should have been strangled at birth." Not a terribly charitable remark, one that leaves us concerned for the health and safety of the princess's own children and grandchildren.

In any case, most auditors of Barber's First did not agree with her. The piece was awarded a Pulitzer Traveling Scholarship in 1936, and as Barber had also won the Pulitzer Traveling Scholarship in 1935, he thus became the first composer to win the award in back-to-back years. (For our information, the actual "Pulitzer Prize in Music" wasn't established until 1943. The first winner was William Schuman, who we will discuss in our next lecture. Barber would win two Pulitzer Prizes in Music, one in 1953 and another in 1963.)

Barber's Second Symphony was composed in 1944 when he was a corporal in the Army Air Force. Commissioned by and dedicated to the United States Army Air Force, it is the only symphony that I know that's dedicated to an arm of the American military. Barber was never satisfied with this Second Symphony. In 1964, he extracted a single movement from the symphony, entitled it "Night Flight"; and four years later, in 1968, 24 years after its composition, he withdrew the entire symphony and destroyed his manuscript score. Nevertheless, there are recordings available of the entire symphony and they reveal a fine and taut work.

We return to Barber's Symphony no. 1, op. 9, of 1936, revised in 1943. While the four sections of the symphony are played without a break, they trace what should now be for us a very familiar pattern, the pattern of the traditional symphonic template: a first-movement allegro in sonata form, a second-movement scherzo, a third-movement andante, and a somewhat faster and very dramatic fourth movement which sums up and extends what has gone before. The four continuous sections of Barber's First are unified by a single thematic idea—a so-called *motto* theme—that's heard at the very beginning of the first movement. Let's hear it as it first appears.

[Musical example from Symphony No. 1, Opus 9, Barber: I; Opening]

This is a proud magnificent theme. It's one that demands a second listening. Again!

[Musical example from Symphony No. 1, Opus 9, Barber: I Opening]

As the development section approaches its climax, this first theme, this motto theme is heard three times in the brass.

[Musical example from Symphony No. 1, Opus 9, Barber: I; Development Section; Motto Theme]

And here Barber does something that's really neat-o. As the development section comes to its shattering, drum-dominated climax, instead of the expected return to the motto theme at the beginning of what we expect will be the recapitulation, we hear, instead, the motto theme in an entirely different guise, as the opening of the scherzo. Thus, the run-on sections here are actually bridged over, as the motto theme acts both as a recapitulatory statement of the sonata form first movement, and as an opening thematic statement of the scherzo. First, we hear the motto theme as it initiates the scherzo—quick, chipper, and full of repeated notes.

[Musical example from Symphony No. 1, Opus 9, Barber: II; Motto Theme]

Now, let's hear the connection between the truncated sonata form and the scherzo. We listen for the statement of the motto theme in the development section of the sonata form through the first third or so of the scherzo.

[Musical example from Symphony No. 1, Opus 9, Barber: II; Motto Theme and Scherzo]

The andante is Barber at his lyric best: music of great beauty and expressive power. The music begins quietly, with an aria-like theme played by a solo oboe accompanied by muted strings, building eventually to an amazing climax. We're going to listen to the entire andante, all four plus minutes of it, so that we may hear it as it really is, a single magnificent melody line powered, ultimately, by a single huge crescendo.

[Musical example from Symphony No. 1, Opus 9, Barber: III; Andante]

Absolutely breathtaking. The fourth and final section or movement is a *passacaglia*, meaning the theme heard at the very beginning in the cellos and basses is repeated over and over, while the music above that theme is ever changing. The passacaglia theme—the opening melody heard in the cellos and basses on which the entire movement is based—is, as I'm sure you've anticipated, another version of the motto theme heard at the very beginning of the symphony. By way of review, let's hear the motto theme as it first appeared at the beginning of the symphony, followed immediately by the passacaglia theme here at the beginning of the fourth movement. First, movement one.

[Musical example from Symphony No. 1, Opus 9, Barber: I; Motto Theme]

And now the passacaglia theme as it initiates the fourth movement.

[Musical example from Symphony No. 1, Opus 9, Barber: IV; Passacaglia Theme]

This passacaglia—and the symphony—concludes with blaring brass reiterating the motto theme, followed by a crash and bang, take no prisoners ending. It's great stuff! Let's hear it.

[Musical example from Symphony No. 1, Opus 9, Barber: IV; Conclusion]

In 1943, the critic and music writer Robert Horan published this appraisal of Barber's music in the journal *Modern Music*:

> Barber's music is of particular importance because of its concentration on the beauty and possibility of design; because of its alive and moving personality and its entirely musical integrity.
>
> It is absurdly Romantic in an age when romanticism is the catchword of fools and prophets. It is cerebral, [but] only in the perspective of its craft, its logic, and its form. It lacks casualness and often spontaneity. But it is composed. On paper and in the ear, its design and articulateness reveal a profound elegance of style, and a personal melancholy.

Thank you.

Lecture Twenty-One
Roy Harris and William Schuman

Scope: During the heyday of the American symphony, the 1930s–1950s, Roy Harris and William Schuman were considered the preeminent symphonic composers of their time, and they remain among the most important symphonists of the 20th century. Harris wrote 15 symphonies, and his work, like that of Ives, makes use of distinctly American sounds, including folksongs and hymns, combined with a rustic musical voice. Schuman composed 10 symphonies; we will examine his Third, which embodies the optimistic and aggressive spirit of America during this period.

Outline

I. The life of Roy Harris (1898–1979) reads almost like a storybook.

    A. "Leroy" Harris was born in a log cabin on Abraham Lincoln's birthday in Lincoln County, Oklahoma. He grew up on a hardscrabble farm, the child of genuine pioneers.

        1. In 1904, when Harris was 6 years old, the family moved to California, where Harris's father, Elmer, bought a small piece of grazing pasture just east of Pasadena and started a farm.

        2. The country changed dramatically over the next few years, as the orange groves and ranch lands of Los Angeles County were swallowed up by growth and development, but the simple pioneer environment in which Harris came of age was the foundation of his artistic makeup.

        3. Like Charles Ives, Roy Harris was profoundly influenced by the folksongs and patriotic anthems he heard and sang while he was growing up, and like Ives, Harris associated that music with the physical environment of his childhood, in his case, the open spaces of the American West.

    B. Harris's musical education was nothing out of the ordinary. He took piano lessons as a child and played clarinet in the Covina Public High School band. Because his interest in music was considered effeminate by his peers, he tried out for football. While playing, he broke his nose and arm and injured one of his fingers, thus ending his chances of becoming a pianist.

C. During the First World War, Harris served in the heavy artillery. After being discharged, he spent a year bumming around the country. He returned to southern California and got a job driving a truck for a local dairy.

    1. Harris also began attending concerts of the Los Angeles Philharmonic; because he couldn't afford to buy tickets, he got in as an usher. His interest in music rekindled, Harris took some private lessons, then applied and was accepted at the University of California at Berkeley, where in his mid-20s, he finally began his formal training in music.

    2. He stayed at Berkeley for two years, then returned to Los Angeles for private study with Arthur Farwell, a local composer, and his career began to take shape.

    3. Harris composed a piece for orchestra entitled *Andante*. The piece fell into the hands of Howard Hanson, who agreed to perform it in Rochester, New York, where he conducted the orchestra and directed the Eastman School of Music. Hanson invited Harris to come out for the performance, and Harris scraped together the train fare for what was supposed to be a two-week trip. He didn't return to California for five years.

D. While in New York, Harris was offered a residency at the Macdowell artists' colony. There, he met Aaron Copland, recently returned from France and already a rising star, who told Harris that he should study with Nadia Boulanger at Fontainebleau.

    1. Almost immediately, Harris managed to secure the first of two Guggenheim grants that made it possible for him to travel to Paris to study with Boulanger.

    2. At first, Harris engaged in a kind of independent study with Boulanger, exploring Beethoven's string quartets on his own. They were the revelation that changed his artistic life.

    3. Ultimately, Harris stayed in France for four years and was exposed to the culture there. Boulanger understood that it was best to stay out of Harris's way, to remain in the background, from where she directed his education without stifling his enthusiasm or personal initiative. Harris—gregarious, enthusiastic, and filled with energy—was one of those people who had to learn things on his own, through a process of self-discovery and trial and error.

E. The music Harris wrote while in Paris betrayed a certain rusticity that never entirely left his musical voice. As Harris learned how to compose, he cultivated this rusticity as an essential element of his compositional style.

    1. Compositionally, Harris was what we might call a highly sophisticated primitive. He was a composer who always sought the "broad stroke," the most direct expressive path, and the most brilliant coloration he could create.

    2. His "primitivism," based on American folksong, fiddling, and Protestant hymns, honed and polished in Fontainebleau and Paris, made his music quintessentially American for a generation in search of an American "sound."

    3. As we listen to Harris's Symphony no. 3, his greatest and most famous symphony, we will define and describe just those elements of Harris's style that make his music seem so American.

F. Having returned to the United States from France and with his music in increasing demand, Harris's success was just around the corner. His First Symphony, composed in 1933, was commissioned by Serge Koussevitzky and the Boston Symphony Orchestra. Harris's Second Symphony, of 1935, was also commissioned and premiered by the Boston Symphony Orchestra, as was the Third Symphony of 1937, which received its premiere on February 24, 1939.

II. Harris's Symphony no. 3 is a one-movement work consisting of five continuous parts that outline a history of music, from its Gregorian chant–like opening through its tragic, Romantic conclusion.

    A. Part 1 opens with a long, unaccompanied melody, reminiscent of a plain chant, in the 'cellos, that evokes the wide open spaces of the American countryside. (**Musical selection**: Harris, Symphony no. 3, part 1, opening.)

    B. The violas now join the 'cellos in playing the "chant" tune in parallel fourths and fifths, evoking the music—called *parallel organum*—of the 9th and 10th centuries C.E. (**Musical selection**: Harris, Symphony no. 3, part 1, continued.)

    C. More instruments now join in, thickening and intensifying the purposely "primitive" counterpoint until, with the entry of the French horns, the richly lyric part 2 begins. Here, the harmonic and melodic language has "progressed" to include major and minor elements, and this section is filled with "major-then-minor" harmonic shifts that are an essential part of Harris's mature compositional language. (**Musical selection**: Harris, Symphony no. 3, part 2, opening.)

D. Part 3 exhibits another step forward in the "musical evolution" that marks the symphony. About one-third of the way through, the music coalesces into a strikingly beautiful passage, as shimmering, muted string arpeggios outline shifting harmonies, while solo wind instruments float above, playing varied fragments of the opening "chant" melody. (**Musical selection**: Harris, Symphony no. 3, part 3.)

E. This section builds in intensity and reaches its climax with the beginning of part 4, entitled "Fugue." It's a rather unconventional and very much American fugue; its theme has the short melodic phrases and foot-stomping rhythmic power of a barn dance! (**Musical selection**: Harris, Symphony no. 3, part 4 [Fugue], opening.)

F. The fugue builds to a brilliant climax, which leads directly into part 5. Part 5 begins as a dialogue among blaring brass, explosive timpani, and sustained strings. We listen from the last moments of the fugue, which are scored for brass, winds, and timpani only. Part 5 "officially" begins with the entrance of the strings. It is a terrific passage, which eventually gives way to a bold but tragic march, initiated by the timpani. (**Musical selection**: Harris, Symphony no. 3, part 4, conclusion and part 5, opening.)

G. The symphony concludes about two minutes later, monumentally, magnificently, and tragically, recalling the opening chant theme in the brass. (**Musical selection**: Harris, Symphony no. 3, part 5, conclusion.)

H. This music is powerful but also concise; like the quintessential American hero—the "strong, silent type"—this is bold, stark, frankly masculine music that says what it needs to say with a minimum of fuss. Harris's penchant for simple melodic and harmonic intervals—fourths and fifths—imbues his music with both an open sound and a certain "primitive simplicity," but underlying this simplicity is great emotional depth and expressive sophistication.

I. Serge Koussevitzky's believed that Harris's Third represented a level of symphonic accomplishment that was new to the American scene, and this belief was shared by many of his contemporaries. During the 1941–1942 concert season alone, Harris's Third was performed by 33 orchestras in just the United States, a record for a contemporary work that stands to this day.

III. William Howard Schuman (1910–1992) was born in New York City, on the upper West Side, and grew up happily in a middle-class household.

    A. When he was 12 years old, he learned to play the violin, mostly by ear, in order to play in the school band. Through his teens, his interest was in popular music; he organized his high school's dance band and wrote melodies for more than 200 songs, but he was, for all intents and purposes, a musical illiterate.

    B. After high school graduation, Schuman enrolled at the School of Commerce at New York University, which he attended for two years. Pestered by his mother, he allowed himself to be dragged to Carnegie Hall, where he heard Arturo Toscanini conduct the New York Philharmonic in a program of music by Robert Schumann, Richard Wagner, and Zoltan Kodaly. Bill Schuman was enthralled and, within days, had taken up the study of harmony to become a composer.

    C. According to Schuman, for the next five years he "ate, slept, and lived" at Carnegie Hall and Town Hall, typically attending both matinee and evening concerts on the same day. In 1933, Schuman enrolled at Teachers College at Columbia University, where he received his B.S. in 1935 and M.A. in 1937. In 1936, while Schuman was attending Columbia, he heard a performance of Roy Harris's Symphony no. 1 and was stunned.

    D. To his huge surprise and delight, Schuman discovered that Harris was teaching at the Juilliard School, which was, at the time, just across the street from Columbia University. Schuman wasted no time in seeking Harris out, and for the next two years, from 1936–1938, he studied privately with Harris. Harris's direct, extroverted, muscular style of composition found an eager disciple in Schuman.

IV. For all of his fine music, the core of Schuman's output is his orchestral music, of which his 10 symphonies hold pride of place.

A. With Harris's guidance, Schuman wrote his Second Symphony in 1937, which then came to the attention of Aaron Copland. In an article in the influential journal *Modern Music*, Copland called Schuman "the musical discovery of the year." Copland also contacted his friend Serge Koussevitzky about Schuman. The result was a series of performances and commissions from Koussevitzky and the Boston Symphony Orchestra, capped by the commission and premiere of Schuman's Symphony no. 3 of 1941, dedicated to Serge Koussevitzky.

B. Schuman's Third Symphony is cast in two movements, each of which is divided into two parts. The titles of the two movements indicate that, structurally, Schuman's Third pays homage to the Baroque era: Movement one is entitled "Passacaglia and Fugue," and movement two is entitled "Chorale and Toccata."

   1. A *passacaglia* is a Baroque variations procedure in which a bass line is presented and repeated, as the material above that bass line changes constantly. The first iteration of the bass line—the passacaglia theme—is referred to as the *theme*, and each reiteration, with the changing materials above, is called a *variation.*

   2. Schuman's passacaglia is usual in two ways. First, the theme is initially presented not by the basses and 'cellos but by the violas, which makes it sound like a genuine "tune," not just a bass line. As we listen to it, be aware of Schuman's typical melodic style, in which the passacaglia theme, though pensive and lyric, is filled with leaps and wide-open melodic spaces. (**Musical selection**: Schuman, Symphony no. 3, movement 1, passacaglia theme.)

   3. The second reason that Schuman's passacaglia is unusual is that each successive entry of the theme is stated a half-step higher than the last, imbuing the music with a sense of rising tension that is "sensed" if not consciously "heard." We listen from the beginning to the theme and the first five variations. Note how the texture thickens as each variation adds a new melodic line. (**Musical selection**: Schuman, Symphony no. 3, movement 1, passacaglia theme and first five variations.)

   4. This is powerful and expansive music. About halfway through the passacaglia, we hear a variation for brass alone. The block-like brass writing here is typical of the mature

Schuman. (**Musical selection**: Schuman, Symphony no. 3, movement 1, passacaglia, brass variation.)

C. The fugue almost spills out of the conclusion of the passacaglia. The fugue subject—initially played by four horns and pizzicato violas and 'cellos—is terse and spiky and offers a perfect contrast to the broad passacaglia theme that went before it. (**Musical selection**: Schuman, Symphony no. 3, movement 1, fugue subject.)

D. Like the passacaglia, the fugue builds in intensity, as more and more instrumental lines are layered, one atop the other. The conclusion of the fugue—and of this huge first movement—is fabulous: raucous, brilliant, blaring, and energized. (**Musical selection**: Schuman, Symphony no. 3, movement 1, fugue conclusion.)

E. The second-movement "chorale" opens with a gentle, undulating prelude scored for violas and 'cellos. (**Musical selection**: Schuman, Symphony no. 3, movement 2, opening.)

F. About a minute later, a solo trumpet, then a solo flute, enter; each sings a typically Schuman melody of extraordinary beauty and breadth. (**Musical selection**: Schuman, Symphony no. 3, movement 2, chorale, trumpet entry.)

G. The chorale eventually gives way to a very low Bb, played by the bassoon and a contrabassoon, which indicates that the final section—the toccata—has begun. A snare drum taps out the rhythm of the toccata's main theme, which is then played by a solo bass-clarinet. The theme is an incredibly virtuosic tour-de-force for the bass clarinet. (**Musical selection**: Schuman, Symphony no. 3, movement 2, toccata, opening.)

H. As we would expect, the symphony ends with a bang! (**Musical selection**: Schuman, Symphony no. 3, movement 2, conclusion.)

I. Schuman was not just a great composer, but a great educator and arts administrator, as well.

    1. He virtually created the music program at Sarah Lawrence College, where he taught from 1935–1945. He was president of the Juilliard School from 1945–1962, then became the first president of Lincoln Center, from 1962–1969. He formed the Juilliard String Quartet, which became the model for quartets-in-residence throughout the world. He founded the Lincoln

Center Student Program, the Lincoln Center Chamber Music Society, and many other performance programs.

2. Somehow, he also found time to compose. His Third Symphony received the first New York Critics' Circle Award, in 1941, and he was awarded the first Pulitzer Prize given in musical composition, in 1943. Schuman was awarded a second Pulitzer in 1985 for his lifetime achievements in composition, teaching, and administration.

Lecture Twenty-One—Transcript
Roy Harris and William Schuman

Welcome back to *The Symphony*. This is Lecture Twenty-One—it is entitled "Roy Harris and William Schuman." Roy Harris and William Schuman, real household names, yes? During the great days of the American symphony—the 1930s, '40s and '50s—they were considered the preeminent symphonic composers of their time. So why are their names so unfamiliar to most concertgoers? Were they just symphonic flashes-in-the-pan, composers who had their 20 minutes of fame and have since fallen into well-deserved obscurity, eclipsed by greater talents and a musical language that passed them by? Most assuredly not. Would we be spending an entire lecture on these guys if they were mere blips on the symphonic radar screen? No, we wouldn't.

Roy Harris (who wrote 15 symphonies) and William Harris (who wrote 10) are among the most important symphonists of the 20th century, and their Third Symphonies are among their very best work. Both Harris and Schuman are major composers, and if they're relatively unknown today—just a few years after their deaths (Harris in 1979 and Schuman in 1992)—well, then it speaks rather more poorly of us as a listening public than it does of Roy Harris and William Schuman who were the two greatest symphonists the United States has yet to produce.

Roy Harris (1898-1979)

Harris's life story reads like a classic American success story. Harris himself was not above doctoring up his rags-to-fame story of his whenever it was to his advantage to do so. To tell you the truth, the facts surrounding his early life are already so storybook that they don't already require any exaggeration.

"Leroy" Harris was born in a log cabin on Abraham Lincoln's birthday—February 12, 1898—in Lincoln County, Oklahoma. A confluence of time and place that prompted Harris to remark many years later that: "Ever since [my birth], the shadow of Abe Lincoln has remained with me."

Well, okay, whatever. Roy Harris was born in Oklahoma nine years before it became a state. He did indeed grow up on a hardscrabble farm, the child of genuine pioneers. In 1904, when Harris was 6 years old, the family pulled up stakes and headed to California where Harris's father Elmer—yes, you heard that correctly, Elmer Harris—bought a small piece of grazing pasture in the San Gabriel Valley, just east of Pasadena, and started a farm. It was country that changed dramatically as Harris grew up, as the orange groves and ranch lands of Los Angeles County were swallowed up by growth and development.

Harris later said that he witnessed, "The end of the pioneer days and the beginning of commercial, standardized America." But truly, we're not romanticizing here, just telling it like it is—it was the simple, open, pioneer environment in which Harris grew up that most influenced his artistic makeup. Like Charles Ives, Roy Harris was profoundly influenced by the folksongs and patriotic anthems he heard and sang while he was growing up. And like Ives, Harris associated that music with the physical environment in which he grew up, in his case, the open spaces of the American West.

Harris's musical education was nothing out of the ordinary. He took piano lessons as a kid and played clarinet in the Covina Public High School Band. His interest in music was an interest not looked upon kindly by his peers. In a profile written in 1952, Madeleine Goss observed:

> [Harris's] fellow pupils were inclined to look down on his musical accomplishments. In those days, people were apt to consider the 'long-haired arts' as they called them, effeminate. Roy, anxious to prove his virility, decided it would be better to give up music and go in for athletics. In the process, as a football player, he broke his nose and arm and ended all possibility of a pianist's career by badly injuring one of his fingers.

During the First World War, Harris served in the heavy artillery. After being discharged, he spent a year bumming around the country and found himself in 1920, at the age of 22, with "neither money nor connections."

He returned to southern California and got a job driving a truck for a local dairy and for the next few years he made his living delivering milk, butter, and eggs to the locals. But Harris also began attending concerts at the Los Angeles Philharmonic. Since he couldn't afford to buy tickets, he got in as an usher. His interest in music rekindled, Harris took some private lessons and then applied and was accepted at the University of California at Berkeley, where in his mid 20's he finally began to get some formal training in music. He stayed at Berkeley for two years, went back to Los Angeles for private study with a well-known local composer named Arthur

Farwell, and then things started to happen. He composed a piece for orchestra entitled *Andante*—I know, what a wild man; what a wild title!—and the piece ended up in the hands of Howard Hanson, who agreed to perform it in Rochester, New York where he conducted the orchestra and directed the Eastman School of Music. Hanson invited Harris to come out for the performance, and Harris scraped together the train fare for what was supposed to be a two-week trip. He didn't return to California for five years.

Here's what happened. In the early summer of 1926, Harris arrived in New York. The orchestra piece, *Andante*, goes really well. Who is this guy, everyone asks? A Californian? They write music in California? Cool. Harris, perceived as an exotic, is offered a residency at the Macdowell artists' colony that very summer. He meets a young Aaron Copland, recently returned from France, and already a rising star, who tells Harris that he should study with Nadia Boulanger at Fontainebleau, "She's like, really great man. You'll love her. She's great."

Harris manages to almost immediately secure the first of what will be two Guggenheim grants, which makes it possible for him to travel to France to study with Madame herself. But, at first, he doesn't really study with her. Boulanger warmly refers to him as her "autodidact," which is the same thing as saying, "I'll take his money and then he goes off and does his own thing." What Harris was "doing on his own" was studying Beethoven's string quartets and they were the revelation that changed his artistic life. He later wrote: "Beethoven became a wise teacher. I learned about the passion and discipline of uninterrupted eloquence. In short, I became a profound believer in discipline and form."

Ultimately, Roy Harris—this self-professed hick from the Oklahoma territory and Covina, California—stayed in France for four years where he got himself some high culture. Nadia Boulanger understood that it was best to stay out of Harris's way, to remain in the background from where she directed his education without stifling his enthusiasm or personal initiative. Harris—gregarious and enthusiastic, filled with energy—was apparently one of those people who had to learn things on his own, through a process of self-discovery and trial and error. And as a late bloomer, he was, like Hector Berlioz for example, going to have to learn things on the job. There wasn't time for the sort of long apprenticeship that Samuel Barber, for example, had been able to enjoy.

The music Harris wrote while in Paris betrayed a certain rusticity, a rusticity that never entirely left his musical voice. As Harris learned how to compose, it was a rusticity that he affected, that he cultivated as an essential element of his cultural style. Aaron Copland could not have been more correct when he wrote: "[Roy Harris's] late start in his musical education was at first held responsible for a certain awkwardness, both in manipulating materials and in writing for instruments. But gradually, as if in spite of himself, this awkwardness became part and parcel his style, taking on a charm of its own."

Compositionally, then, Roy Harris was a highly sophisticated primitive, an entirely oxymoronic phrase, but an accurate one nonetheless. He was a composer who always sought the "broad stroke," the most direct expressive path, and the most brilliant coloration he could create. His "primitivism," based on American folksong, fiddling, and Protestant hymns, honed and polished into the something-less-than-rough-and-tumble wilds of the Fontainebleau in Paris, made his music quintessentially American for a generation of Americans in search of an American music and an American "sound."

Writing in the journal, *The International Musician*, Serge Koussevitzky said exactly so much: "I think that nobody has expressed with such genius the American life, the vitality, the greatness, the strength of this country. Roy Harris seems to be the answer to our desire for the essential American."

In 1967, the English musicologist Peter Jona Korn wrote:

> Harris's [musical] language is perhaps more characteristically American than that of any other symphony composer; it is "American" music as Brahms is German, Debussy French, or Vaughn Williams English, not because of an occasional use of folk material, but because of an inherent national flavor that defies description.

Defies description? No; where there's an adjective, there's a way. As we listen to Harris's Symphony no. 3, his greatest and most famous symphony, we will define and describe just those elements of Harris's style that make his music seem so essentially American.

Having returned to the United States from France with two Guggenheims under his belt and his music in increasing demand, Harris's success was just around the corner. His First Symphony, composed in 1933, was commissioned by Serge Koussevitzky and the Boston Symphony Orchestra. Koussevitzky, who debuted the premiere on January 26, 1934 called it, "The first truly tragic symphony by an American." Harris's Second

Symphony of 1935 was also commissioned and premiered by the BSO, as was the Third Symphony of 1937, which received its premiere under the baton of Maestro Koussevitzky on February 24, 1939.

Harris's Symphony no. 3 is a one-movement work consisting of five continuous parts that outline a virtual history of music, from its Gregorian chant-like opening through to its tragic, Romantic conclusion. Part 1 evokes Gregorian chant with a long, unaccompanied melody that, characteristic of Harris's style, is filled with leaps and open musical space. It's the sort of melody that's immediately evocative of the wide open spaces of the American West, a plain chant filtered through the kidneys of the San Gabriel Valley, as it were.

[Musical example from Symphony No. 3, Harris: Part I; Opening]

The violas now join the cellos in playing the "chant" tune in parallel fourths and fifths, evoking the music—called *parallel organum*—of the 9th and 10th centuries C.E.

[Musical example from Symphony No. 3, Harris: Part I]

More and more instruments now join in, thickening and intensifying the purposefully "primitive" counterpoint until, with the entry of the French horns, part 2 of the symphony begins. Part 2 is richly lyrical in content. Here, the harmonic and melodic language has "progressed" to include major and minor elements, and this section is filled with the sort of "major-then-minor" harmonic shifts, striking and bold harmonic shifts that are an essential part of Harris's mature compositional language.

[Musical example from Symphony No. 3, Harris: Part II; Opening]

Part 3 exhibits another step forward in the "musical evolution" that marks the symphony. About one-third of the way through, the music coalesces into a strikingly beautiful passage, as its shimmering, muted string arpeggios outline shifting harmonies, while solo wind instruments float above, playing varied fragments of the opening Gregorian "chant" melody.

[Musical example from Symphony No. 3, Harris: Part III]

This section builds in intensity and reaches its climax with the beginning of part 4, entitled "Fugue." It's a rather unconventional fugue, and it's very much an American fugue, as its theme—its subject—has the short melodic phrases and foot-stomping rhythmic power of a barn dance.

[Musical example from Symphony No. 3, Harris: Part IV; Fugue]

The fugue builds up to a brilliant climax, which leads directly into part 5. Part 5 begins as an explosive dialogue between blaring brass, explosive timpani, and sustained strings. We listen from the last moments of the fugue, which are scored for brass, winds, and timpani only. Part 5 "officially" begins with the entrance of the strings. It's a terrific passage, which eventually gives way to a bold but tragic march, initiated by the timpani.

[Musical example from Symphony No. 3, Harris: V; Opening]

The symphony concludes about two minutes later—monumentally, magnificently, and tragically, recalling as it does, the opening chant theme in the brass.

[Musical example from Symphony No. 3, Harris: V; Conclusion]

This is very powerful music. It is also very concise music. Like the quintessential American hero—the "strong, silent type," be he Gary Cooper or Clint Eastwood—this is bold, stark, frankly masculine music that says what it means to say with a minimum of fuss and bother. Harris's proclivity for simple melodic and harmonic intervals—fourths and fifths—imbues his music with both an open sound and a certain "primitive simplicity." But like Gary Cooper in *Sergeant York* or *High Noon,* like Clint Eastwood in *The Unforgiven*, it is a primitive simplicity underlain by great emotional depth and expressive sophistication.

At the time of its premiere, Serge Koussevitzky, in a fit of well-meaning hyperbole, said of Harris's Third that is was: "the first truly great orchestral work produced in America." My friends, knowing as we do Ives's Second, Third and Fourth Symphonies, Aaron Copland's Second Symphony, Howard Hanson's Symphony no. 2, Barber's Symphony no. 1, and Carl Ruggles's *Sun Treader* (which we have not discussed as it is technically not a symphony), we would not agree with Maestro Koussevitzky. Nevertheless, his belief that Harris's Third represented a level of symphonic accomplishment moved to the American scene was one shared by many, if not most, of his contemporaries. During the 1941-1942 concert series alone, Harris's Third was performed by 33 different orchestras in just the United States; that's a record for a contemporary work that stands to this day.

[Madeleine Goss wrote:] "The final seal of popular approval came to Harris in a letter from the manager of a baseball team: 'If I had pitchers who could pitch as strongly as you do in your symphony, my worries would be over.'"

Lawrence Gillman wrote in the New York Herald Tribune:

> Certainly, Mr. Harris would qualify as the hero of an American success story. Yet Harris's success story differs from many others because it has been achieved without any sacrifice of the ideals and standards of the singularly high-minded, sincere, and uncompromising artist. The melodies, the harmonies, the rhythms, the counterpoint, have lived their own way with an independence and a power that bespoke the presence of that rarest thing in art, a genuinely individual voice.

William Schuman (1910-1992)

William Howard Schuman, known as "Bill" to everyone, was born to parents of German-Jewish heritage in New York City on the upper West Side on August 4, 1910. He grew up in a middle-class household, by his own account a happy, regular kid. When he was 12 years old he learned to play the violin, mostly by ear, in order to play in the school band. Through his teens, his interest was in popular music—dancing music and jazz. Like the rock and rollers of my generation, who learned to strum the few chords necessary to play "Proud Mary" and "Indagadavida"; who played great air guitar while lying in bed dreaming of glory and girls (admittedly, mostly girls); who organized bands with names like "The Scammers" and "Cold Sun" and "Hot Borscht" (I kid you not, I played in all three of those bands, I swear); who played hackneyed versions of Top 40 Songs as well as their own, usually awful "originals"; like the rock and rollers of my generation, Bill Schuman was a heavy-duty musical hobbyist. He was the kid who organized the Washington High School dance band, which was properly called "Billy Schuman and his Alamo Society Orchestra," who wrote melodies for songs—over 200 of them—and who was, for all intents and purposes, a musical illiterate.

After high school graduation, Schuman enrolled in the School of Commerce at New York University, which he attended for two years. Had he completed his course of study, he would have undoubtedly have followed his father into a career in business. However, he did not complete his degree because of a single, epiphanous event that completely changed the course of his life. The story goes like this: For years, Schuman's mother had been trying to get her son to listen to some legitimate music; you know, the classics, something other than that horrible, noisy dance music. Finally, according to Schuman, she put it to him as a challenge: "I can't imagine anyone so lacking in curiosity as to not be willing to listen, at least once, to some serious music." Just to shut his mother up, Schuman allowed himself to be dragged to Carnegie Hall where he heard Arturo Toscanini conduct the New York Philharmonic in a program of music by the other Schumann (that is Robert), Richard Wagner, and Zoltan Kodaly. Well, he was enthralled and fascinated too. By his own admission, he was really impressed by the way the strings all bowed in the same direction at the same time and the fact that the drums didn't play continuously through an entire piece as they did in a dance band. Well, that was it, the epiphany.

Within a day or two, according to Michael Steinberg:

> He stopped in at the Malkin School of Music and said, "I want to be a composer. Tell me what I have to do." He was told to study harmony, which would be $1.00 per class or $3.00 for a private lesson. The next thing, he was a pupil of Max Persin, who had studied with [Anton] Arensky at the Moscow Conservatory and whom Schuman described as "something of a visionary, a wonderful influence and a marvelous teacher."

According to Schuman, for the next five years he "ate, slept, and lived" at Carnegie Hall and at Town Hall, typically attending both matinee and evening concerts on the same day. Of course, going to two concerts a day could get really expensive, really fast, so Schuman would buy a ticket to an afternoon show and then, armed with a book and a sandwich, retire undisturbed to a stall in the men's room, there to await the next concert, at which he would take whichever seat was available.

In 1933, Schuman enrolled at Teachers College at Columbia University, where he received his B.S. in 1935 and an M.A. in 1937. It was in 1936, while Schuman was attending Columbia by day and Carnegie Hall by night, that he had yet another epiphany. He heard a performance of Roy Harris's Symphony no. 1. Schuman was stunned; he thought it was: "the most exciting piece of new music I had ever encountered." To his huge surprise and delight, Schuman discovered that Harris was teaching at the Julliard School, which was then, literally, just across the street from Columbia University. Schuman wasted no time in seeking Harris out, and for the next two years, from 1936 to 1938, he studied privately with Roy Harris. Harris's direct, extroverted, muscular style of composition found an eager disciple in Schuman, who, according to one source, had been leaning: "in just those directions, and he came away from his lessons with a vocabulary, the beginnings of a technique, and the validation of his own expressive stance." The men became lifelong friends, and Schuman gave full credit to

Harris for helping him to develop as a composer, saying later that: "Harris helped me formulate my point of view. Basically, our aesthetic springs from the same direction."

For all of his fine music, the core of Schuman's output is his orchestral music of which his 10 symphonies hold pride of place. With Harris's guidance, Schuman wrote his Second Symphony in 1937, the first had been written a couple of years before in 1935. Schuman's Second came to the attention of Aaron Copland, who liked it a lot. In an article in the influential journal *Modern Music*, Copland called Schuman "the musical discovery of the year." And Copland, bless him, did more than just talk the talk; he walked. He contacted his friend Serge Koussevitzky and suggested that he check out this Billy Schuman guy. The result was a series of performances and commissions for Koussevitzky and the Boston Symphony Orchestra, capped by the commission and premiere of Schuman's Symphony no. 3 of 1941, dedicated to Serge Koussevitzky.

Shuman's Third Symphony is cast in two movements, each of which is divided into two parts. The titles of the two movements indicate that structurally Schuman's Third pays homage to the Baroque era. Movement one is entitled "Passacaglia and Fugue," and movement two is entitled "Chorale and Toccata."

A *passacaglia* is a Baroque variations procedure in which a bass line is presented and then repeated, as the material above that bass line changes constantly. The first iteration of the bass line—the passacaglia theme—is referred to as the *theme*, and each reiteration, with the change in materials above, is called a *variation*.

Schuman's passacaglia is unusual in two ways. First, the theme is initially presented not by the basses and cellos but by the violas, which makes it sound much more like a genuine "tune," and not just a bass line. Let's hear it, and let's be aware that typical of Schuman's melodic style, the passacaglia theme, though pensive and lyric, is also as broad as the Hudson at Tapan Zee, filled with leaps and wide-open melodic spaces.

[Musical example from Symphony No. 3, Schuman: I; Passacaglia Theme]

We said that Schuman's passacaglia was unusual for two reasons. The second is that each successive entry of the theme is stated a half-step higher than the last one, imbuing the music with a sense of rising tension that is "sensed" if not consciously "heard." We listen from the beginning to the theme and the first five variations. Note how the texture thickens as each variation adds a new melodic line.

[Musical example from Symphony No. 3, Schuman: I; Passacaglia Theme and First Five Variations]

This is powerful and expansive music. About halfway through the passacaglia, we hear a variation for brass alone. The block-like brass writing is very typical of a mature Schuman, and we should hear it.

[Musical example from Symphony No. 3, Schuman: I; Passacaglia and Brass Variation]

The fugue just sort of spills out of the conclusion of the passacaglia. The fugue subject, the fugue theme—initially played by four horns and pizzicato (or plucked) violas and cellos—is terse and spiky, just the sort of melody that's the product of someone raised on jazz and offers a perfect contrast to the broad passacaglia theme that went before it.

[Musical example from Symphony No. 3, Schuman: I; Fugue Subject]

Like the passacaglia, the fugue builds and builds in intensity, as more and more instrumental lines are layered, one on top of the other. The conclusion of the fugue—and of this huge first movement—is absolutely fabulous. It's raucous; it's brilliant; and it's blaring and energized. Let's hear it.

[Musical example from Symphony No. 3, Schuman: I; Conclusion]

Oh, man. That's really music. The second movement "chorale" opens with a gentle, undulating prelude scored for violas and cellos.

[Musical example from Symphony No. 3, Schuman: II; Chorale Opening]

About a minute or so later, a solo trumpet and then a solo flute enter; each sings a typically Bill Schuman melody of extraordinary beauty and breadth.

[Musical example from Symphony No. 3, Schuman: II; Chorale]

My friends, this is music of ethereal beauty, and it's magnificently scored. The chorale eventually gives way to a very, very low Bb, played by the bassoon and the contrabassoon, which indicates that the final section of the symphony—the toccata—has begun. A snare drum taps out a rhythm that as we soon discover is the rhythm of the toccata's main theme, which is then played by a solo-bass clarinet. The theme is an incredibly virtuosic tour-de-force for the bass clarinet, written especially for the Boston Symphony

Orchestra's all-star clarinetist Rosario Mazzeo, who played with the orchestra for 33 years, 27 of them as the bass clarinetist. Let's listen.

[Musical example from Symphony No. 3, Schuman: II; Toccata Opening]

As we would expect from a symphonist as energized as Bill Schuman, the symphony ends with a bang. Let's hear its conclusion.

[Musical example from Symphony No. 3, Schuman: II; Conclusion]

The conductor John Canorina writes:

> Though composed during the early stages of World War II, William Schuman's Third Symphony is a work of unbridled optimism and exhilaration. As such, it is an expression of its time in so far as American music is concerned, for it heralded a period when American composers became accepted, performed and appreciated in their own country to a previously unprecedented degree.

My friends, William Schuman was not just a great composer, but a great educator and arts administrator, as well. He virtually created the music program at Sarah Lawrence College where he taught from 1935 to 1945. He was the president of the Julliard School from 1945 to 1962, for 17 years, and then became the first president of Lincoln Center from 1962 to 1969. He formed the Julliard String Quartet, which became the model for quartets-in-residence throughout the world. He created curricular designs that are still in use today. He founded the Lincoln Center Student Program, the Lincoln Center Chamber Music Society, and many other like performance programs, as well. And somehow, he found time to compose. Yes indeed, typical of someone like himself, summer was for composing. But how he managed to compose so much high quality music, just in his summers, well, it leaves us all shaking our head. This is the life of the American academic composer incidentally, teach all year and try to shoehorn your work into the summertime. Sometimes it works, and sometimes it does not. For Bill Schuman, it worked.

His Third Symphony received the first New York Critics' Circle Award, in 1941, and it received the first Pulitzer Prize awarded in music composition in 1943. Schuman was awarded a second Pulitzer in 1985 for his lifetime achievements in composition, teaching, and administration. My friends, if we haven't heard of William Schuman or Roy Harris, might I suggest that it's not their fault. Thank you.

Lecture Twenty-Two
The 20th-Century British Symphony

Scope: Even more than America, Britain was dominated by German
musical influences, producing not a single major compositional
figure of its own between 1700 and 1850. That situation changed
with Edward Elgar, whose work mirrored the Victorian elegance,
Edwardian propriety and nobility, and an exuberance that mirrored
the British Empire itself at its peak. Following Elgar, Ralph
Vaughn Williams wrote symphonies that offer a different picture
of Britain, one that makes substantial use of native British folk
influences. In doing so, Vaughan Williams almost single-handedly
re-established an English vernacular and, along with Elgar,
established a genuinely English symphonic tradition.

Outline

I.   With some exceptions, England produced few major compositional
     figures until the birth of Edward William Elgar.

   A.   The late 1500s and early 1600s saw a brilliant group of composers
          working in London, including William Byrd, Orlando Gibbons,
          Thomas Morley, John Dowland, John Wilbye, and Thomas
          Weelkes. The English Baroque reached its zenith with the music of
          Henry Purcell, whose opera, *Dido and Aeneas* (1689) is still
          considered one of the great masterworks of the 17th century. From
          that point until the birth of Elgar in 1857, however, England's
          musical output was unremarkable.

   B.   This is not to say that England didn't have an appetite for new
          music, but that appetite was fed, for the most part, by German
          composers.

      1.   The English appetite for German music began with the arrival
             of the Saxon-born, Italian-trained George Frederick Handel in
             London in 1711. Handel lived and composed in England until
             his death in 1759, and his music was revered to the extent that
             native English music ceased to be cultivated.

      2.   A hundred years later, at a time when English literature was
             flourishing, the German-born Felix Mendelssohn became the
             musical hero to another generation of English audiences.

3. England became known in Germany as "*Das Land ohne Musik*," "the country without music," although what the Germans meant was that England was "the country without composers." Nineteenth-century England did indeed produce some native-born composers, such as William Bennett, Charles Hubert Parry, Alexander Mackenzie, Charles Stanford, and Arthur Sullivan, but there were no major compositional figures in England until the appearance of Elgar.

II. Edward William Elgar (1857–1934) was born in Broadheath, in the southwest of Manchester, the fourth of seven children of Anne Greening and William Henry Elgar.

A. Elgar's father was a competent organist and violinist who made his living as a piano tuner. Despite the musical environment in which he grew up, Elgar was almost entirely self-taught as a musician, having had only a few lessons on the violin and virtually no training as a composer. Nevertheless, he began writing music at around the age of 10, and after working briefly in a lawyer's office, he decided at the age of 16 to make a career in music.

B. At first, he was just another provincial hack, fiddling away in theaters and taverns and writing forgettable salon compositions for the amusement of "the ladies." His working life, however, became his classroom. He held down a number of jobs, including organist at St. George's Church in Worcester, director of the Worcester Instrumental Society, and conductor of the Worcester Philharmonic. He also played bassoon in a wind quintet, established a studio as a violin teacher, and from 1879–1884, conducted the staff orchestra at the county lunatic asylum at Powick. All the while, Elgar composed music of every sort.

C. In 1890, recently married and burning with ambition, the 32-year-old Elgar and his bride moved to London. Without realizing it, Elgar had everything going against him. He was a self-taught provincial trying to make a career in what was, at the time, the most cosmopolitan city in the world. He had no academic degrees, and he arrived without recommendations or connections. Almost predictably, Elgar failed miserably; he felt himself degraded and returned to the English Midlands, depressed and humiliated.

D. Back in Worcestershire, embittered by his experience in London, Elgar continued to compose and conduct, and slowly his reputation grew. In 1899, at the age of 42, he completed the orchestral work that would make him famous: the *Variations on an Original Theme*, op. 36, a piece of music known today as the *Enigma Variations*.

E. Elgar's Symphony no. 1 in Ab Major was completed in 1908, and his Symphony no. 2 in Eb Major, completed in 1911, was premiered in London that same year. The following year, Elgar and his wife moved back to London, arriving, this time, in triumph. Elgar was made Master of the King's Music; he was knighted and made First Baronet of Broadheath; he was commissioned to write the coronation music for King Edward VII; he was awarded no less than 10 honorary degrees by universities; and among his many awards, he received the Gold Medal of the Royal Philharmonic Society in 1925.

III. Elgar's Second Symphony, based on materials sketched as early as 1903–1904, was begun in 1909 and completed on February 28, 1911. Elgar dedicated the symphony to the memory of King Edward VII, who had died on May 6, 1910, during its composition.

A. The first of its four movements opens with a grand and spacious theme that is typical of Elgar's mature music: He wrote in a big way; his phrases are long; he called for a gigantic orchestra and filled his scores with a tremendous amount of orchestrational detail. (**Musical selection**: Elgar, Symphony no. 2 in Eb Major, op. 63, movement 1, opening, theme 1.)

B. In his second movement, Elgar pays tribute to Beethoven's own Eb symphony, the *Eroica*. Like Beethoven's Third, Elgar's Second features a second-movement dirge, one associated by the public with the death of the king. (**Musical selection**: Elgar, Symphony no. 2 in Eb Major, op. 63, movement 2, opening.)

C. The third-movement scherzo is a brilliant tour-de-force of rhythmic energy and orchestration. We will listen to the very beginning and the very end of this movement. (**Musical selection**: Elgar, Symphony no. 2 in Eb Major, op. 63, movement 3, opening and conclusion.)

D. Like the first movement, the fourth movement opens with a long and spacious theme, played by the brass. (**Musical selection**:

Elgar, Symphony no. 2 in Eb Major, op. 63, movement 4, opening.)

E. While Elgar's First Symphony of 1908 was a triumph, his Second was not. It was a bit too long and complicated for listeners at first, but ultimately, the English music-loving public embraced Elgar's Second.

F. Elgar's reputation changed dramatically between the time he completed his Second Symphony in 1911 and his death 23 years later, in 1934.

   1. Incredibly popular at the time he composed his Second Symphony, he watched in horror as he became a musical dinosaur in his own lifetime. During the period of modernism, he was viewed as a throwback to the Edwardian era.

   2. Elgar's music has, rightfully, come a long way back since the mid-20th century. It is not explicitly "nationalistic" music, although it is implicitly of its time and place. It displays a Victorian elegance, an Edwardian propriety and nobility, and a broadness and exuberance of conception that mirrors the British Empire itself at the time of its greatest breadth.

IV. Ralph Vaughn Williams (1872–1958) was an English composer of symphonies who looked to the folk heritage of England for musical inspiration.

   A. Vaughn Williams had all the musical and educational opportunities that Edward Elgar did not. He came from a well-to-do family, and as a child, he studied the violin, piano, and organ. In 1890, he embarked on an 11-year stint in academia, studying at the Royal College of Music, Trinity College at Cambridge, and in Berlin.

   B. Academically, Vaughn Williams was as pedigreed as they come, but the turning point of his life didn't occur until after he got his doctorate, when he joined the English Folk Music Society. Along with his good friend, the composer Gustav Holst, Vaughn Williams traveled the English countryside, collecting native folk music in as pure a state as it could be found.

   C. Vaughn Williams immersed himself in the folk music he collected; its spirit entered his heart and mind and became the essential substance of his musical language. Ultimately, Vaughn Williams became a rabid musical nationalist, and he rejected the German musical influence that had been so pervasive in English music since at least the time of Handel, 200 years earlier.

V. Altogether, Ralph Vaughn Williams wrote nine symphonies, although he didn't begin numbering them until the Fourth. Many of Vaughn Williams's symphonies bear programmatic titles, and two of them, the First and the Seventh, are scored for vocal soloists and chorus and could just as easily be called *oratorios* as symphonies.

    A. The following is a chronological list of Vaughn Williams's symphonies:

> Symphony no. 1 (1909) is known as *A Sea Symphony.*
> Symphony no. 2 (1913) is known as *A London Symphony.*
> Symphony no. 3 (1921) is known as the *Pastoral Symphony.*
> Symphonies nos. 4, 5, and 6 (1934, 1943, and 1947, respectively) have no programmatic titles and were, thus, numbered.
> Symphony no. 7 (1952) is known as *Sinfonia Antarctica.*
> Symphonies nos. 8 and 9 (1955 and 1957, respectively) also have no programmatic titles.

    B. We turn to Vaughn Williams's Symphony no. 6 in E Minor. The symphony was begun in 1944, completed in 1947, and premiered in 1948 by the BBC Symphony Orchestra.

        1. The dates of this symphony are significant. Vaughn Williams began the symphony in 1944, during the second-to-last year of the Second World War, and completed it three years later, in 1947, at a time when a Third World War appeared increasingly likely.

        2. I've chosen this symphony because it is the first work we have encountered in this course that reflects the experience of World War II, the birth of the atomic age, and the terrible fears that another war, one between the Communist East and the Democratic West, was inevitable.

    C. Vaughn Williams's Sixth is a compelling, powerful, often anguished work, and it was perceived as being all the more so by audiences who were accustomed to his generally more cheerful expressive palette. The first movement begins explosively; it is not difficult to hear the massed brass and the explosive attacks and rolls in the bass drum as a reference to war. (**Musical selection:**

Vaughn Williams, Symphony no. 6 in E Minor, movement 1, opening.)

D. Vaughn Williams introduces a pastoral episode in D major, influenced by English folksong, during the development section and recapitulates this pastoral music near the close of the movement. These two episodes are as close to "the old, familiar" Vaughn Williams as we will hear in the Sixth Symphony. We hear the closing version of this pastoral music, followed by one last iteration of the dramatic and explosive opening theme. (**Musical selection**: Vaughn Williams, Symphony no. 6 in E Minor, movement 1, conclusion.)

E. We should not expect any slow, lyric relief in the second movement. Labeled "*moderato*," it is as dark and funereal in tone as anything Vaughn Williams ever wrote. The movement is in three parts; we listen to the beginning of the third part, where an obsessive, nagging rhythm, reminiscent of a funeral march and consisting of three notes—short–short–long—works the orchestra into a state of rage and despair. (**Musical selection**: Vaughn Williams, Symphony no. 6 in E Minor, movement 2, part 3, opening.)

F. A bitter, ironic, Shostakovich-like third-movement scherzo follows. (**Musical selection**: Vaughn Williams, Symphony no. 6 in E Minor, movement 3, opening.)

G. The music of the fourth movement, entitled simply "Epilogue," is so unexpected that it takes the listener's breath away. During its almost 10-minute length, the movement never rises above a *pianissimo*. In 1948, at the time of the symphony's premiere, the quiet desolation of this final movement was interpreted by many as being a depiction of a world laid to waste by nuclear war. (**Musical selection**: Vaughn Williams, Symphony no. 6 in E Minor, movement 4, opening.)

H. Vaughn Williams's Sixth Symphony is, in many ways, atypical of his overall output. Its four-movement design is more Classical than much of his mature music, and the relatively few episodes of folk-like material, in favor of the relatively modern, post-Romantic idiom that characterizes the piece, are also unusual in his mature music. If anything, the Sixth shows that Vaughn Williams could quite comfortably go beyond his Tudor England–inspired musical language and write a first-class postwar symphony.

I. Through the strength of his example, Vaughn Williams almost single-handedly reestablished an English musical vernacular. Along with Edward Elgar, he also established, almost from scratch, a genuine English symphonic tradition.

Lecture Twenty-Two—Transcript
The 20th-Century British Symphony

Welcome back to *The Symphony*. This is Lecture Twenty-Two—it is entitled "The 20th Century British Symphony." I know it's a cheap shot to talk about the food of Great Britain, but we must do so if for just a moment. We ask: Why should such a sophisticated and culturally diverse nation—one just a few miles away from France—be, by comparison, so gastronomically bereft? How many of us would honestly prefer an English kidney pudding to a French cassoulet; a Scottish Cock-a-Leekie Stew to a fine French bouillabaisse; boiled beef to a medium rare Chateaubriand? The names alone of much traditional English fare are enough to spoil the heartiest appetite: there's Likky Pie, which is leeks and pork in a puffed pastry; there's syllabub, a drink that originated in the 17th century, when a milkmaid would squirt a stream of warm milk directly from a cow into a bowl of spiced cider or ale, creating a curd on the top. Oh, yum. There's Welsh faggots—pig's liver made into meatballs with onion, beef suet, bread crumbs and sometimes a chopped apple; and of course, spotted dick, a dessert the ingredients of which will remain our little secret for the nonce, perhaps even two nonces.

Why do we bring all of this up? Because, as it goes with British food, so it went with English music. Oh, this is not to say that England was always bereft of tasty composers. In particular, the late 1500s and early 1600s, the latter part of the reign of Queen Elizabeth I, saw a brilliant group of composers working in London: William Byrd, Orlando Gibbons, Thomas Morley, John Dowland, John Wilbye, and Thomas Weelkes head the top of a long list. These composers were contemporaries of, and often collaborated with, an amazing group of writers, poets and playwrights including William Shakespeare, Christopher Marlowe, Ben Johnson, John Donne, and Robert Herrick. Talk about a star-studded environment!

The English Baroque reached its zenith with the music of Henry Purcell, a first-class genius whose opera, *Dido and Aeneas* of 1689 is still considered one of the great masterworks of the 16th century. Purcell died in 1695, at the terribly young age of 36 and, from the point of view of English music, that was it until the birth of Edward Elgar in Broadheath, southwest of Manchester, on June 2, 1857. Oh, this was not to say that there wasn't a huge appetite for new music in England, perhaps it was even greater than the English appetite for mulligatawny soup, but that appetite was fed, by and large, by German composers.

The English appetite for German music began with the arrival of the Saxon-born, Italian-trained George Frederick Handel in London in 1711. Handel lived and composed in London until his death in 1759, and the music consuming English aristocracy and the public could not get enough of the big man from Germany, to the point that a native English music ceased to be cultivated. A hundred years later, at the time when English literature again flourished in the works of Byron, Keats, Shelley and Wordsworth, it was the German-born Felix Mendelssohn who became the musical hero to yet another generation of English audiences.

England became known in Germany as *"Das Land ohne Musik,"* "the country without music," although what the Germans really meant was that England was "the country without composers." We forgive the Germans their overstatement as there were native-born composers in 19th-century England—William Bennett, Charles Hubert Parry, Alexander Mackenzie, Charles Stanford, Arthur Sullivan—to name a few. But truly, there were no major, even slightly major compositional figures in England, this otherwise extraordinarily powerful and creative nation, until the appearance of Edward William Elgar.

Edward William Elgar (1857-1934)

Elgar was the fourth of seven children born to Anne Greening and William Henry Elgar. Elgar's father was a competent organist and a violinist who made his living as a piano tuner. Despite the musical environment in which he grew up, Elgar was almost entirely self-taught as a musician, having had only a very few lessons on the violin and virtually no training as a composer. Nevertheless, he began writing music at the age of 10, and after working briefly in a lawyer's office, he decided at the age of 16 to make his career in music. And thus he began, at first, just another provincial hack, fiddling away at taverns and writing forgettable salon compositions for the amusement of "the ladies."

And that's how it was, at first. Elgar was your classic freelance musician. He never said no to a gig. His working life began at the tender age of 16 and became his classroom. He learned on the job, and he did hold down a lot of jobs. He succeeded his father as organist at St. George's Church in Worcester. In 1877, at the age of 20, he became the director of the Worcester Instrumental Society. In 1879, he began conducting the Worcester Philharmonic and became the accompanist and conductor of the

Worcester Glee Club. He played bassoon in a wind quintet and established a studio as a violin teacher. In 1882, he became the conductor of the Worcester Amateur Instrumental Society. And between 1879 and 1884, he conducted the staff orchestra at the county lunatic asylum at Powick. So much for the romance of a career in music.

All the while, Elgar composed music of every sort. According to musicologist Diana McVeaghy: "His school was the sharp one of performance; if he lacked guidance, he suffered no false influence; and he acquired craft and speed. Though some of [his] early music is personal, none is exceptional, and Elgar must have been sustained at this time by an inward sense of [belief in himself]."

In 1890, recently married and burning with ambition, the not quite 33-year old Elgar and his bride, a lady named Alice, moved to London, there to make a go at it. Without realizing it, Elgar had everything going against him. He was a self-taught provincial, trying to make a career in what was, at the time, the most cosmopolitan city in the world. He had no academic degrees, and he arrived without recommendations or connections. He was a Catholic in an overwhelmingly Protestant and generally anti-Catholic city. So, what happened? Elgar failed miserably. He felt himself degraded, mistreated, and found almost no work whatsoever. He went home to the English Midlands, depressed and humiliated. David Cairns describes Elgar at this time as: "a hypersensitive, moody, at times suicidally unhappy genius with small, nervous hands: an English eccentric who loved fishing, dogs, recondite information [that's trivia], and bonfires, who practiced chemistry and patented the Elgar sulfurated hydrogen apparatus, and who nursed within him a wound that never healed."

Back in Worcestershire, embittered by his experience in London—"that wound that never healed"—Elgar continued to compose and conduct, and slowly his reputation grew. In 1899, at the age of 42, he completed the orchestral work that would make him famous: the *Variations on an Original Theme*, op. 36, a piece of music known today as the *Enigma Variations*. According to the *New Groves Dictionary of Music and Musicians*, "[the piece was] quite simply, the most distinguished British orchestral work [composed] to that date."

Elgar's Symphony no. 1 in Ab Major was completed in 1908, and his Symphony no. 2 in Eb Major was completed in 1911, and was premiered in London on May 14, 1911. The following year, 1912, Elgar and his wife Alice moved back to London, arriving this time in triumph. The provincial and his wife were now treated like royalty. Elgar was made Master of the King's Music. He was knighted and made First Baronet of Broadheath. He was commissioned to write the coronation music for King Edward VII. He was awarded no less than 10 honorary degrees by universities old and new. And among his many awards, he received the Gold Medal of the Royal Philharmonic Society. Did Elgar feel vindicated? Perhaps, but his bitterness never left him. He once turned down an important invitation by writing his hostess that: "You would not wish your [table] to be disgraced by the presence of a piano-tuner's son and his wife."

Symphony no. 2 in Eb Major, op. 63

Elgar's Second Symphony, based on material sketched as early as 1903 and 1904, was begun in 1909 and completed on February 28, 1911. In a letter, Elgar described the process of composing the piece as: "weaving strange and wonderful memories into very poor music." Elgar dedicated the symphony to the memory of King Edward VII, who had died on May 6, 1910, during its composition.

The first of its four movements opens with a grand and spacious theme that is typical of Elgar's mature music: he wrote big; his phrases are long; he called for a gigantic orchestra and filled his scores with a tremendous amount of orchestrational detail.

[Musical example from Symphony No. 2 in Eb Major, Opus 63, Elgar: I; Opening]

And my friends, all of that music constitutes only the first theme of that long sonata-form first movement. In his second movement, Elgar pays tribute to Beethoven's own Eb symphony, Beethoven's *Eroica*. Like Beethoven's Third, the *Eroica*, Elgar's Second features a second-movement dirge, one associated by the public with the death of the king, Edward VII.

[Musical example from Symphony No. 2 in Eb Major, Opus 63, Elgar: II; Opening]

Regarding this second-movement dirge, the truth be told, Elgar actually sketched that theme way back in 1904 after the death of his friend Alfred E. Rodewald, long before the death of Edward VII. The public's association of the movement with a dead king was rather more politically and monetarily advantageous to Elgar than that of his departed friend, a textile merchant by trade. So he kept mum on the origin of the movement.

The third-movement scherzo is a brilliant tour-de-force of rhythmic energy and orchestration. I'd like us to hear the very beginning and then the very end of this third movement. First, the beginning:

[Musical example from Symphony No. 2 in Eb Major, Opus 63, Elgar: III; Opening]

And now the energized conclusion:

[Musical example from Symphony No. 2 in Eb Major, Opus 63, Elgar: III; Conclusion]

Like the first movement, the fourth movement opens with a long and spacious theme, played by the brass.

[Musical example from Symphony No. 2 in Eb Major, Opus 63, Elgar: IV; Opening]

While Elgar's First Symphony of 1908 was a triumph, Elgar's Second, the work we've just sampled, was not, at least not at first. It was a bit too long, a bit too complicated. Perplexed and angry, Elgar, who conducted the premiere, gestured towards the audience and asked the concertmaster of the Queens Hall Orchestra, William Reed, "What's the matter with them, Billy? They [just] sit there like a lot of stuffed pigs."

Well, not everyone sat there like a stuffed pig, and it didn't take long for Elgar's Second to be embraced by the English music-loving public. Neville Cardus, who would go on to a long career as a writer on music and cricket, was 19 years old when he attended the premiere of Elgar's Second. He later described the experience from his point of view: "Those of us who were students were excited to hear, at last, an English composer addressing us in a spacious way, speaking a language which was European and not provincial. No English symphony existed then, at least not [one] big enough [to be compared] with a symphony by Beethoven or Brahms, and not be dwarfed at once into insignificance."

Elgar's reputation changed dramatically between the time he completed his Second Symphony in 1911, and his death 23 years later in 1934. Incredibly popular at the time he composed his Second Symphony, Elgar watched in absolute horror as he became a musical dinosaur in his own lifetime. Writes Schonberg:

> During the modernism of the 1920-1940 period, the great days of Stravinsky, Bartok, Prokofiev, and Milhaud, most musicians ridiculed the very idea of Elgar being a very important composer.

He was considered an inflated provincial, popular in his day only because England was so desperate to claim an important composer for her own. He was Edwardian, stuffy, a relic of Colonel Blimp and the Empire. What else could be expected of a man who indulged in foxhunting, golf, fishing and kite flying? Even Elgar's very appearance was held against him. He was tall, straight, heavily mustachioed, with a hooked nose and flaring nostrils; he carried his umbrella at the furl; his entire bearing was military; his clothes were proper; he [would seem to have been, although we know that he was not] the very model of an English clubman. It followed that he was a musical wallah who composed vulgar and jingoistic music. His music, [so it went] could no more be listened to than the poet, Rudyard Kipling, could be read. And so mounted the catalogue of [his] sins.

Elgar's music has, rightfully, come a long way back since the mid-20th century. It's not explicitly "nationalistic" music, although it is implicitly of its time and place. It displays a Victorian elegance, an Edwardian propriety and nobility, and a broadness and exuberance of conception that mirrors the British Empire itself at this time of its greatest breadth, the empire on which "the sun never set."

Ralph Vaughn Williams (1872-1958)

That English composer of symphonies who did look to the folk heritage of England for musical inspiration was Ralph Vaughn Williams. Yes, his first name is spelled Ralph, but please, pronounced "Rafe"; any other pronunciation used to infuriate him. Vaughn Williams was born in Gloucestershire in 1872 and died in London in 1958. We might add that he holds the record for the longest professional compositional career in the history of Western music. He was first published when he was 19-years old, and he completed his Ninth and last symphony shortly before his death, giving him a total professional career length of 65 years.

Ralph Vaughn Williams had all of the musical educational opportunities that Edward Elgar did not. He came from a well-to-do family, and as a child played the violin, piano, and organ. In 1890, at the age of 18, he moved to London where he attended the Royal College of Music for two years. Vaughn Williams then moved on to Trinity College in Cambridge, where he received a Bachelor of Music degree in 1894 and a B.A. in History in 1895. Then it was back to the Royal College of Music to study composition with two of the leading English composers of the time, Charles Parry and

Charles Stanford. And then, after a brief bit of study in Berlin, it was back to Cambridge where he received the degree of Doctor of Music in 1901. Academically, Ralph Vaughn Williams was as pedigreed as they come, but by his own admission, the turning point of his life, his epiphany, didn't occur until after his doctorate, when he joined the English Folk Music Society. Along with his great and good friend, the composer Gustav Holst (This is the composer of *The Planets* fame; the two of them met in the Royal College of Music back in 1895), Vaughn Williams traveled the English countryside, collecting native folk music in as pure a state as it could be found. Now in this, Vaughn Williams and Holst were doing exactly what their contemporaries, Bela Bartok and Zoltan Kodaly were doing in Hungary and Bulgaria.

Like Bela Bartok, Vaughn Williams immersed himself in the folk music he collected and the spirit and substance of this English folk music entered into his heart, his mind, his blood and became the essential substance of his musical language. In a lecture delivered many years later, many years after he did his collecting, Vaughn Williams described the impact of English folk music on his own compositions:

> In days when Elgar formed his style [in the 1880s], English folk song was not "in the air," but [rather it] was consciously revised and made popular only [during the first decade of this, the 20th century]. Now, what does this revival mean to the composer? It means several of us found here in its simplest form the musical idiom which we were unconsciously cultivating ourselves. It gave a point [of departure] to our imagination. The knowledge of our folk songs did not so much for us discover something new, but uncovered something which had been hidden by foreign [musical influence and] matter.

Ultimately, Vaughn Williams became a rabid musical nationalist— as rabid a musical nationalist as has ever existed—and he rejected, in particular, the German musical influence that had been so pervasive in England since at least the time of Handel, 200 years earlier. Vaughn Williams wrote, "As long as composers persist in serving up at second hand the externals of the music of other nations, they must not be surprised if audiences prefer the real Brahms, the real Wagner, the real Debussy, the real Stravinsky to their pale reflections. Every composer cannot expect to have a world-wide message, but he may reasonably expect to have a message for his own people."

A great anecdote before we tackle Vaughn Williams's symphonies. Vaughn Williams began to attract some serious attention with the composition of such explicitly nationalist works as *In the Fen Country* of 1904, and *Norfolk Rhapsodies* of 1906. Still, he felt his compositional technique was not what it could or should be, and he decided to study with the French composer Maurice Ravel, of all people. Of this decision, Vaughn Williams wrote: "In 1908 I came to the conclusion that I was being stodgy. I'd come to a dead end and a little French polish would be of use to me."

Well, Harold Schonberg picks up this story:

> Off he went to Paris, a big, stout, bear-like man, dressed with cheerful sloppiness (someone once remarked that Vaughn Williams always dressed "as though stalking the folksong to its lair"), [and he headed to Paris, there] to confront the tiny, dandified Ravel, who did not know exactly what to make of the [English] invader. [Ravel] looked at some of Vaughn Williams's music and told him to write a little minuet in the style of Mozart. Vaughn Williams met this head on, thundering, "Look here, I've given up my time, my work, my friends and my career to come here and learn from you, and I am not going to write a little minuet in the style of Mozart."

So much for Paris. After a most brief stint with Ravel, Vaughn Williams decided, finally and rightly, that his music education was complete.

We would observe that Vaughn Williams was one of those big, gruff, fearless people who seemed to believe everything he felt and said was true. He also apparently believed that discretion was the last refuge of the coward and scoundrel. Partly because he liked to say outrageous things, and partly because, in his mind at least, his own mind, he needed to separate himself from composers and traditions he felt hindered the development of a genuine "English" music. Vaughn Williams said some pretty nasty things about some pretty good composers. For example, he said that Mahler was: "A tolerable imitation of a composer." Of Beethoven's symphonies, Vaughn Williams wrote late in his life: "to this day the Beethoven idiom repels me." Vaughn Williams claimed that: "Stravinsky [is] merely a clever and fashionable composer who relies on a sophisticated bag of tricks." and went on to say: "[Arnold] Schoenberg [has] meant nothing to me, but as apparently he meant a lot to other people, I dare say it is all my own fault." Well, Vaughn Williams was nothing if not quotable.

Ralph Vaughn Williams's Symphonies

Altogether, Ralph Vaughn Williams wrote nine symphonies, although he didn't begin numbering them until the Fourth. This was not out of some Mahler-like paranoia of writing nine and then dropping dead (although that is exactly what happened to Vaughn Williams). Rather, many of Vaughn Williams's symphonies bear programmatic titles, and two of them, the First and the Seventh, are scored for vocal soloists and chorus and could just as easily be called "oratorios" as symphonies. As a public service, we offer a chronological list of Vaughn Williams's symphonies: Symphony no. 1, more commonly known as *A Sea Symphony*, was completed in 1909; Symphony no. 2, known as *A London Symphony*, was completed in 1913; Vaughn Williams's Symphony no. 3, known as the *Pastoral Symphony*, was finished in 1921; Symphonies nos. 4, 5, and 6, dating respectively from 1934, and 1943, and 1947 have no programmatic titles, and were indeed just numbered; Symphony no. 7 of 1952 is known as *Sinfonia Antarctica*; and the Symphonies nos. 8 and 9 of 1955 and 1957 are known as…Symphonies nos. 8 and 9! There we have it.

We turn now to Symphony no. 6 in E Minor. The symphony was begun in 1944, and completed in 1947, and was premiered on April 21, 1948 by the BBC Orchestra, under the baton of Sir Adrian Boult at London's Royal Albert Hall. These dates are very significant. Vaughn Williams began the symphony in 1944, during the second-to-last year of the Second World War, and completed it three years later, in 1947, at a time that a Third World War appeared increasingly likely. I've chosen this symphony because it is the first work we will have encountered in this course that reflects the experience of World War II, the birth of the atomic age, and the terrible fears that another war, a Third World War, one between the Communist East and the Democratic West, appeared inevitable.

Vaughn Williams's Sixth is a compelling, powerful, often anguished work, and it was perceived as being all the more so by audiences accustomed to his generally more cheerful expressive palette. The first movement begins explosively, and it's frankly difficult not to hear the masked brass and the explosive attacks and rolls in the bass drum as a reference to war.

[Musical example from Symphony No. 6 in E Minor, Vaughn Williams: I; Opening]

Following the premiere of the Sixth, Frank Howes, the music critic of *The Times of London*, referred to the symphony as Vaughn Williams's "War" Symphony. Well, true to form, Vaughn Williams—at 76 years of age, as crusty, cantankerous and curmudgeonly an old coot as you'll ever meet—was furious, claiming that the symphony had no programmatic meaning whatsoever.

In regards to the Sixth Symphony and the sort of discussion it engendered, Vaughn Williams told his friend Roy Douglas: "It never seems to occur to people that a man just might want to write a piece of music." Well, me thinks Vaughn Williams protesteth much too much; whether it's explicitly "programmatic" or not, this is music utterly of its time and the temper of its time, to say nothing for the "temper" of its composer.

We shouldn't think that the entire movement, the entire first movement, consists of such overtly dramatic music. Vaughn Williams introduces a wonderfully pastoral English folksong influence episode in D major during the development section, and recapitulates this pastoral music near the close of the first movement. These two episodes are as close to "the old, familiar" Vaughn Williams as we will hear in the Sixth Symphony. Let's listen to the closing version of this pastoral music, followed as it is by one last iteration of the dramatic and explosive opening theme.

[Musical example from Symphony No. 6 in E Minor, Vaughn Williams: I; Conclusion]

We should not expect any slow, lyric relief in the second movement. Labeled "*moderato*," it is as dark and funereal in tone as anything Vaughn Williams ever wrote. The movement is in three parts. We'll listen to the beginning of the third part where an obsessive, nagging, funeral march-like rhythm—consisting of three notes, short-short-long—ba-ba bum, ba-ba bum—works the orchestra up into a veritable tizzy of rage and despair.

[Musical example from Symphony No. 6 in E Minor, Vaughn Williams: II; Opening]

A bitter, ironic, Shostakovich-like third-movement scherzo follows.

[Musical example from Symphony No. 6 in E Minor, Vaughn Williams: III]

And now, my friends, the truly awesome fourth movement, entitled simply "Epilogue." It is music so unexpected that it takes our breaths away. During its almost 10-minute length, the movement never rises above a *pianissimo*, meaning very, very quiet. It is hushed and whispered with, in Vaughn Williams's words: "Whiffs of theme drifting about." Look, after all the "in your face" drama of the first three movements, we have to lean forward to hear this fourth movement. And if we expect to be suddenly assaulted by something that recalls the angst of the earlier movements—well, it never comes. While we listen to the first couple of minutes of this sublime movement, I want us to ask ourselves this most important question: Coming as it does at the end of a long, dark, dramatic and often tragic-tinged symphony, a symphony composed between 1944 and 1947, what might this hushed and whispered music mean?

[Musical example from Symphony No. 6 in E Minor, Vaughn Williams: IV; Opening]

In 1948, at the time of his symphony's premiere, the quiet desolation of this first movement was interpreted by many as being a depiction of a world laid to waste by nuclear war. In a letter dated January 22, 1956, Vaughn Williams wrote his biographer, Michael Kennedy, that in fact: "With regard to the last movement of my no. 6, I do not believe in meanings and mottos, as you know, but I think words nearest to the substance of my last movement [are]: 'We are such stuff as dreams are made on, and our little life is rounded with asleep.'" Michael Kennedy, the biographer, points out that: "These are lines from Prospero's farewell in Shakespeare's *The Tempest*; and they are the correct clue to the whole work's emotional climate. The storms of life, of which war is but one, end in the greatest mystery of all, the eternal 'sleep' which rounds it off."

Vaughn Williams Sixth Symphony is in many ways atypical of his overall output. Its four-movement design is frankly more Classical than much of his mature music, and the relatively few episodes of folk-like material, in favor of the relatively modern, post-Romantic idiom that characterizes the piece are, again, unusual in his mature music. If anything the Sixth shows that Vaughn Williams could quite comfortably go beyond his Tudor England-inspired musical language and write a first class post-war symphony.

Through the strength of his example, Vaughn Williams almost single-handedly reestablished an English musical vernacular. Along with Edward Elgar, he also established—almost from scratch—a genuine English symphonic tradition. As for the other English symphonists of the early and mid-20th century, Havergal Brian, who composed an astonishing 32 symphonies; Rutland Boughton, Arnold Bax, William Walton, Michael Tippett, Edmund Rubbra, Lennox Berkeley, and William Alwyn—as for these other English symphonists of the early and mid-20th century, I must leave you to your own devices. But for now, at the very least, we can say that these more than deserving composers did indeed merit a mention—albeit a brief and unsatisfactory one—in this course. On that note, I thank you.

Lecture Twenty-Three
Olivier Messiaen and *Turangalila!*

Scope: Olivier Messiaen's *Turangalila Symphony* is a magnificent achievement; it is among the first masterworks of the postwar era and among the first of Messiaen's storied career. The *Turangalila Symphony* is completely different from any other piece of music by any other composer. Like his Gallic predecessors, Hector Berlioz and Claude Debussy, Messiaen was a true original, whose music and teaching continue to exert an incredible degree of influence. In this lecture, we take an in-depth look at the *Turangalila Symphony*, which is meant to encompass the movement and rhythm of the universe and finds joy in the cycle of life and death.

Outline

I.   Olivier Messiaen, born on December 10, 1908, was 36 years old when the war in Europe ended in May of 1945. As they had been for so many of his fellow French citizens, the previous five years had been difficult and extremely dangerous for Messiaen.

   A.   Messiaen joined the French army when war broke out in 1939 and was taken prisoner in 1940. He spent the next two years in Stalag VIII in Gorlitz, in Silesia. Messiaen was freed and repatriated in 1942. He returned to Paris, where he was appointed professor of harmony at the Paris Conservatory.

   B.   On top of his duties at the Conservatory, Messiaen began teaching private composition classes in 1943 at the home of a friend. Among the students who attended these private classes was the pianist Yvonne Loriod, who would eventually become Messiaen's wife and play a pivotal role in the creation of the *Turangalila Symphony*, and a young Pierre Boulez, who is one of the most important musicians of the 20th and early 21st centuries.

   C.   On April 1, 1945, about eight months after the liberation of Paris and a month before the end of the war in Europe, Messiaen, still working in relative obscurity, premiered a work for orchestra and chorus entitled *Three Small Liturgies of the Divine Presence*. The piece unleashed a storm of controversy and attention.

D. A short time after the premiere of *Three Small Liturgies of the Divine Presence*, Serge Koussevitzky contacted Messiaen and commissioned him to write a symphony of any length, using any instrumentation he pleased, to be delivered whenever he finished it.

E. Messiaen dedicated more than two years of his life to writing this symphony. It was a summation of virtually everything he loved and believed in at that time: Eastern religions and a personal, pantheistic spirituality; Gregorian chant; birdsong; ancient Greek scales; and ancient Hindu rhythmic constructs. The result was a 10-movement symphony, running 1 hour and 15 minutes, for orchestra, piano, and an early electronic keyboard instrument called an *ondes martenot*.

F. Messiaen called his sprawling, unique work the *Turangalila Symphony*. The title is derived from two Sanskrit words: *turanga* and *lila*. *Turanga* means "time" and, by extension, "movement" and "rhythm," activities marked by physical movement that take place in time. *Lila* means, literally, "play," "sport," or "amusement" in terms of divine activity in the cosmos, such as the act of creation. It can also mean transcendent "love" and "joy."

G. That dazzling and abandoned joy is perfectly expressed in the fifth of the symphony's 10 movements. The fifth movement, a scherzo, is entitled "Joy of the Blood of the Stars," and it brings the first half of the symphony to its close. It is a brilliant, visceral, and perfect representation of what Messiaen means by the word-construction *Turangalila*. We listen to the first two minutes of this movement. Messiaen creates here an overpowering sense of euphoric, energized abandon. (**Musical selection**: Messiaen, *Turangalila Symphony*, movement 5 ["Joy of the Blood of the Stars"], opening.)

H. The *Turangalila Symphony* was premiered by the Boston Symphony Orchestra on December 2, 1949, under the baton of Serge Koussevitzky's 31-year-old protégé, Leonard Bernstein. In the program note he prepared for the premiere, Messiaen wrote that the symphony embodies love such as "is symbolized by Tristan and Isolde."

    1. The *Turangalila Symphony* was the second of three works by Messiaen inspired by the legend of Tristan and Isolde. The first is a song-cycle entitled *Harawi*, for soprano and piano, composed in 1945, and the third is a work entitled *Cinq rechants* ("*Five Songs Sung Again*"), for small chorus, composed in 1950.

2. Unlike its companions, the *Turangalila Symphony* is an entirely instrumental piece; its only "words" are the descriptive titles of each of the 10 movements, which suggest how the movements may be related to the legend of Tristan and Isolde.

3. Soon after his symphony's incredibly successful premiere, Messiaen began to regret his program note, the titles he had given to each movement, and even the title he had given to the entire work. His regrets were the result of the endless questions and "interpretations" of what the symphony was "really" about. Messiaen later claimed that he had chosen the title for the symphony merely because he liked the sound of the word.

II. *Turangalila* remains Messiaen's only symphony, and it is a work that capped his early compositional efforts.

A. Messiaen was born in Avignon, France, on December 10, 1908. His mother, Cecile Sauvage, was a well-respected poet, and his father, Pierre Messiaen, taught English. Among Pierre Messiaen's accomplishments was having translated the complete works of Shakespeare into French.

B. In such a highly cultured household, Olivier's musical precocity was recognized early and carefully cultivated. He began composing at the age of 7. When he was 10, his harmony teacher gave Olivier a score of Claude Debussy's only opera, *Pelleas and Melisande*, which was, for Messiaen, a revelation. Debussy's extraordinary and original treatment of harmony, tonality, and rhythm inspired Messiaen to even greater tonal and rhythmic freedom in his own works. If any single composer can be said to be the successor of Debussy in terms of both musical syntax and sheer originality, it would have to be Messiaen.

C. The year after he received the score of *Pelleas and Melisande*, the 11-year-old Messiaen entered the Paris Conservatory. His tenure there was marked by one amazing success after another. In 1926, at the age of 18, he won first prize in harmony, counterpoint, and fugue. In 1928, he won first prize in piano accompaniment. In 1929, he won first prize in music history. And in 1930, the year he graduated, he won the prize he most coveted, first prize in composition.

D. Immediately after graduating, Messiaen was appointed organist at La Trinité in Paris, a post he held for 40 years. In 1936, at the age of 28, he joined the faculty of the Ecole Normale de Musique in Paris, and in 1939, he joined the French army after Germany invaded Poland and France subsequently declared war on Germany.

III. Messiaen organized the 10 movements of the *Turangalila Symphony* around a number of "cyclic" themes, that is, themes that cycle back from movement to movement.

A. The two most important of these cyclic themes are polar opposites. The first, what we will call the *earth theme*, is heavy, monumental, and craggy in character. This earth theme represents the corporeal, that which is real and solid, permanent and unchanging. When we first hear this theme, about 30 seconds into the first movement, it is played by trombones and tuba. We listen to the first two iterations of this earth theme. (**Musical selection**: Messiaen, *Turangalila Symphony*, movement 1 [Introduction], earth theme.)

B. We now listen from the beginning of the first movement, which Messiaen calls simply "Introduction." The movement begins dramatically and with a sense of great anticipation, anticipation that is well satisfied by the appearance of the earth theme about 30 seconds in. (**Musical selection**: Messiaen, *Turangalila Symphony*, movement 1 [Introduction], opening.)

C. The second of the cyclic themes presented in the first movement could not be more different from the first. In his program note, Messiaen refers to this theme as the "flower" theme, because of its gentle, supple, curving contour. We hear this second theme, which makes its first appearance about two and a half minutes into the first movement. (**Musical section**: Messiaen, *Turangalila Symphony*, movement 1 [Introduction], spirit theme.)

D. As the flowers evoked by Messiaen's program note grow from the earth, so this second theme grows out of the earth theme. We will refer to this second theme as the *spirit theme*, because for Messiaen, it represents the ineffable, the beautiful, that which changes and metamorphoses, the life cycle of death and rebirth. We listen to it again. (**Musical selection**: Messiaen, *Turangalila Symphony*, movement 1 [Introduction], spirit theme.)

E. What we have called the earth theme has also been referred to in the literature as the *masculine* or *phallic theme*, and what we are calling the spirit theme has also been referred to as the *feminine* or *blossom theme*. Whatever we choose to call them, these two themes represent the complementary opposites of the universe.

F. The meeting of these two themes occurs at the beginning of the second half of the symphony—during the beginning of the sixth movement—when the harmonic elements of the earth theme are mated and merged with the melodic element of the spirit theme.

　1. The offspring of the two is a long, slow melody that represents idealized love, a theme that will be heard cyclically during the second half of the symphony.

　2. We listen to this idealized love theme as it appears at the beginning of the sixth movement, which is entitled "Garden of Love's Sleep." The theme, shimmering and otherworldly, is played by an electronic keyboard instrument called an *ondes martenot*, accompanied by strings and decorated by the piano and percussion instruments. (**Musical selection**: Messiaen, *Turangalila Symphony*, movement 6 [Garden of Love's Sleep].)

G. The *ondes martenot* was invented by a Parisian pianist and composer named Maurice Martenot and was first heard publicly in 1928.

　1. It resembles a small electric organ with a big speaker attached to it, and the keyboard is played using the right hand, while the left hand controls the various dials and slides that modify its tone color and volume.

　2. During the late 1920s and 1930s, the *ondes martenot* was perceived by many as "an instrument of the future," and many of France's leading composers wrote music for it.

　3. Along with the *theremin*, the *ondes martenot* was the most popular electronic instrument developed before the synthesizer, and Messiaen uses it with superb effect in the *Turangalila Symphony*.

IV. We return to the first movement of the *Turangalila Symphony*, entitled "Introduction."

    A. The first half of this first movement is "about" the introduction of the earth and spirit themes. After a brief piano cadenza, the second half of the movement is given over to an amazing passage in which four different rhythmic patters are superimposed one atop the other. Using Hindu rhythmic patterns called *tala*, Messiaen creates an incredibly energized passage characterized by constantly shifting rhythmic relationships, as different rhythmic patterns go in and out of phase with each other. (**Musical selection**: Messiaen, *Turangalila Symphony*, movement 1 [Introduction].)

    B. During the course of the second movement, entitled "Love Song I," explosive passages of music characterized by superimposed rhythmic patterns alternate with calm, static, and extremely lyric passages. Like Hector Berlioz in the first movement of the *Symphonie fantastique*, Messiaen is depicting the emotional extremes of love: intense pleasure and intense pain, clarity and disorientation. We hear the opening of the movement. (**Musical selection**: Messiaen, *Turangalila Symphony*, movement 2 [Love Song I].)

    C. The third movement is entitled "Turangalila I." It opens with a ghostly solo for clarinet, accompanied by the *ondes martenot*. (**Musical selection**: Messiaen, *Turangalila Symphony*, movement 3 [Turangalila I].)

    D. Messiaen entitled the fourth movement "Love Song II." It is, like so much of the symphony, a tour-de-force of layering and superimposition.

        1. The movement begins, simply enough, as a duet between a piccolo and a bassoon, accompanied by a ringing *ondes martenot*. Soon enough, a woodblock enters, followed by low pizzicato strings and a rustling piano, with each new part characterized by its own melodic material and its own rhythmic profile.

        2. By the time the opening section of the movement comes to its conclusion, the texture consists of five distinctly different, yet amazingly unified parts. (**Musical selection**: Messiaen, *Turangalila Symphony*, movement 4 [Love Song II].)

E. The fifth movement, entitled "Joy of the Blood of the Stars,"
    brings the first half of the symphony to its conclusion. Movement
    six, "Garden of Love's Sleep," begins with the gorgeous and
    dreamlike idealized love theme that is itself a product of the
    "mating" of the earth theme and the spirit theme. This sixth
    movement is the symphony's adagio. It is a magical movement,
    with its lush harmonies and birdsongs heard in the piano based on
    the actual songs of the nightingale, blackbird, and garden warbler.

F. The seventh movement, entitled "Turangalila II," is the shortest of
    the symphony. It features a bristling, birdsong-dominated piano
    part; it's as if the quiet and relaxed nightingale, blackbird, and
    garden warbler of the previous movement have all been
    transformed into much more animated creatures. We hear the
    piano solo that initiates this seventh movement. (**Musical
    selection**: Messiaen, *Turangalila Symphony*, movement 7, opening
    [Turangalila II].)

G. The eighth movement is the longest of the symphony. Entitled
    "Development of Love," this movement is exactly what it says it
    is—a huge development section, during which all of the major
    themes heard thus far in the symphony appear.
    1. The ongoing developmental process that occurs during this
        eighth movement is interrupted three times by increasingly
        longer and more ecstatic versions of the idealized love theme.
    2. Messiaen refers to these moments as the "explosions" of the
        love theme, and their appearance marks the climax of the
        symphony. We listen to the third and last of these
        "explosions" and the gradual subsidence that follows.
        (**Musical selection**: Messiaen, *Turangalila Symphony*,
        movement 8, [Development of Love].)

H. The ninth movement, entitled "Turangalila III," is a brief series of
    variations on the earth theme. The tenth movement, entitled simply
    "Finale," is the only one of the movements written in sonata form.
    1. The spirit of this final movement is joyful and dancing, a
        return to the frenetic mood of the fifth movement. Messiaen
        indicates that this finale should be performed "very fast, and
        with great joy."
    2. We listen to the recapitulation and conclusion of the
        movement and the symphony. Please note, about 1 minute and
        22 seconds into the excerpt, we will hear the idealized love

theme, which has, in this movement, been used as theme 2 of the sonata form. (**Musical selection**: Messiaen, *Turangalila Symphony*, movement 10 [Finale].)

Lecture Twenty-Three—Transcript
Olivier Messiaen and *Turangalila*!

Welcome back to *The Symphony*. This is Lecture Twenty-three—it is entitled "Oliver Messiaen and *Turangalila!*"

The Commission

Talk about a dream come true—instant validation and recognition, to say nothing for dollars and francs raining directly from heaven. Here's what happened: Olivier Messiaen, born on December 10, 1908, was 36 years, 5 months old when the war in Europe ended in May of 1945. Like so many of his fellow French citizens, the previous five years had been very difficult and extremely dangerous. Messiaen joined the French army when war broke out in 1939 and was taken prisoner in 1940. He spent the next two years in Stalag VIII in Gorlitz, in Silesia, and it was there, as a prisoner of war in Stalag VIII, that Messiaen composed his *Quartet for the End of Time* for clarinet, violin, cello and piano. It was first performed at the camp on January 15, 1941, where it was heard by over 5,000 prisoners.

Messiaen was freed and repatriated in 1942. He returned to Paris where he was appointed professor of harmony at the Paris Conservatory. On top of his duties at the Conservatory, he began teaching private composition classes in 1943 at the home of a friend named Guy Delapierre. Among the students who attended these private classes was the pianist Yvonne Loriod, who would eventually become Messiaen's wife, and who would play a pivotal role in the creation of the *Turangalila Symphony*, and a very young Pierre Boulez, who today would make just about everyone's short list of most important musicians of the 20th and early 21st centuries.

On April 1, 1945, roughly eight months after the liberation of Paris, and a month before the end of the war in Europe, Messiaen, still working in relative obscurity, premiered a work for orchestra and chorus entitled *Three Small Liturgies of the Divine Presence*. Well, so much for relative obscurity. The piece unleashed a veritable *merde* storm of controversy. According to Messiaen's biographer, Robert Sherlaw Johnson:

> Overnight, Messiaen was condemned, on one hand, for his vulgarity and lack of good taste, and praised, on the other, for [having] a vivid imagination and true genius. The work was disliked by the avant-garde for what they regarded as his [19th

century] harmonies, and it shocked the conservatives because of [its] peculiar dissonances which had become a feature of Messiaen's style. The non-Christian was out of sympathy for the religious sentiments expressed, while the traditional Catholic was [disgusted] by the apparently vulgar treatment of sacred ideas.

My friends, this sort of controversy attracts attention, and thus, the manna from heaven about which I waxed so mysteriously at the beginning of this lecture. A short time after the premiere of the *Three Small Liturgies of the Divine Presence*, out of the blue came the commission. Serge Koussevitzky, conductor of the Boston Symphony Orchestra, the same Serge Koussevitzky who commissioned key early symphonies from Aaron Copland, Roy Harris, and William Schuman, among literally hundreds of others, who founded the Tanglewood Festival, who created the Koussevitzky Foundation, who took on the young and brash Leonard Bernstein as his assistant and gave him the break that made his career. Serge Koussevitzky contacted this Olivier Messiaen and made him an offer no one could possibly refuse. The offer? A commission, carte blanche, to write a symphony of any length, using any instrumentation he pleased, to be delivered whenever he finished it, with no deadline. Messiaen, of course, turned it down.

I'm joking. It was an incredible offer to which Messiaen dedicated the next two years of his life, from 1946 to 1948. Never having even considered writing a symphony, Messiaen wrote a symphony that was a summation of virtually everything he loved and believed in at the time: Eastern religions and a very personal sort of pantheistic spirituality; Gregorian chant; bird song; ancient Greek scales; and ancient Hindu rhythmic constructs. The result was a 10-movement, one-and-one-quarter hour symphony for orchestra, piano (an extremely virtuosic piano part I would tell you; there are portions of the piece that more closely resemble a piano concerto than a symphony), and an early electronic keyboard instrument called the *ondes martenot*, which we will discuss in detail when we actually start listening to the symphony.

Messiaen called his sprawling, utterly unique new work the *Turangalila Symphony*. "Turangalila": it's quite a word, and it is derived from two Sanskrit words, *Turanga* and *Lila*. *Turanga* means "time" and, by extension, "movement" and "rhythm," activities marked by physical movements that take place in time. *Lila* means, literally, "play," "sport," or "amusement." According to Robert Sherlaw Johnson:

["Lila" means] "play" in the sense of divine action on the cosmos; that is, the acts of construction, reconstruction and the play of life and death. It can also mean "love." ["Turangalila"], therefore, means "a song of love," "a hymn to joy," time, movement, rhythm, life and death. When Messiaen speaks of joy in connection with *Turangalila*, he describes it as a superhuman, overflowing, dazzling and abandoned joy; and the joy, signified by "Lila," is an irresistible love, transcending all things.

That dazzling and abandoned joy is perfectly expressed in the fifth of the symphony's 10 movements. The fifth movement—the scherzo—is entitled "Joy of the Blood of the Stars," and it brings the first half of the symphony to its conclusion. It is a dazzling, visceral and always perfect representation of what Messiaen means by the word-construction *Turangalila*. Let us listen to the first two minutes of this movement, the capstone of the first half of this symphony. Messiaen creates here an overpowering sense of euphoric, energized abandon that we'd be hard put to find anywhere else in the symphonic repertoire.

[Musical example from *Turangalila Symphony*, Messiaen: V]

The *Turangalila Symphony* was premiered by the Boston Symphony Orchestra on December 2, 1949, under the baton of Serge Koussevitzky's 31-year-old protégé, Leonard Bernstein. In the program note he prepared for the premiere, Messiaen wrote: "The *Turangalila Symphony* is a hymn to joy, a joy that is overflowing, blinding, unlimited. Love is present here in the same manner: this is a love that's fatal, irresistible, suppressing everything outside of itself, a love such as is symbolized by Tristan and Isolde."

The Tristan and Isolde reference requires an explanation. The *Turangalila Symphony* was the second of three works by Messiaen inspired by the legend of Tristan and Isolde. The first is a song-cycle entitled *Harawi*, for soprano and piano, which was composed in 1945. The third is a work entitled *Cinq rechants*, or "*Five Songs Sung Again*," for small chorus, composed in 1950. Unlike its companions, the *Turangalila Symphony* is an entirely instrumental piece; its only "words" are the descriptive titles of each of the 10 movements, titles which suggest, although only barely, how the movements may be related to the legend of Tristan and Isolde.

Soon after its incredibly successful premiere, Messiaen began to regret his program note with its sincere, but admittedly overblown references to love, joy, and Tristan and Isolde. He began to regret the titles he gave to each of the movements. Apparently, he even began to regret the title he gave to the entire work—*Turangalila Symphony*. His regrets were the result, the inevitable result it would seem of the endless questions, comments, inferences and interpretations of what he really meant and what the symphony was "really" all about. So Messiaen picked up his pen again and wrote: "Some people have seen in the word 'Turangalila' the name of a young girl, while others [have] thought that my symphony was based on the Hindu rhythm of the same name. This is not so. I chose the word for its sonority [its sound] alone, for its melodious qualities—simply because I liked the sound of it, because it fell agreeably on the ear."

Isn't it amazing, my friends, how so many composers feel the need to fib about the meaning of a composition in order to avoid talking about it? In our previous lecture, we observed Ralph Vaughn Williams's entirely bogus claim that his Sixth Symphony had nothing to do with World War II. And here, well after the fact, Messiaen claimed that he gave his symphony the name "Turangalila" just "because I like the sound of the word." Well, why not the word "smidgen" then? Smidgen Symphony; that's a fun-sounding word, isn't it? How about the word "wombat," or "lalaleelou," or perhaps "Schwarzenegger"? To Monsieur Messiaen we cry: Take responsibility, man, for the meaning of your piece, so perfectly described by the title you so well crafted!

Composers. On one hand, they cry out to be loved and understood, and on the other hand, they do everything they can to deny the meaning of what they've done, out of some strangely misplaced belief that they'll only look foolish if they admit to what they intended. My friends, between you and me, in general, the very last person you want to hear describing a piece of music is the person who actually wrote it. In general, they either distance themselves from their own music by hiding behind some intellectual polemic that has little or nothing to do with the piece itself, or they simply deny any expressive meaning so as not to expose themselves to the ridicule of critics and other such self-important and cynical protectors-of-art, those delightful individuals who live to embarrass and humiliate anyone foolish enough to express some genuine personal sentiment. Do I sound just a little bit sensitive here? You bet. Enough said.

Olivier Messiaen, Early Years

Turangalila remains Messiaen's one and only symphony, and it is a work that capped his early compositional efforts. Olivier Messiaen was born in Avignon, France on December 10, 1908. His mother, Cecile Sauvage, was a well-respected poet, and his father, Pierre Messiaen, taught English. Among Messiaen's père's accomplishments was having translated the complete works of Shakespeare into French. In such a highly cultured household, Olivier's musical precocity was recognized early and carefully cultivated. He began composing at the age of 7. When he was 10 years old, his harmony teacher gave Olivier a score of the then just-deceased Claude Debussy's one and only opera, *Pelleas et Melisande*. It was, for Messiaen, a revelation. He later wrote that having received and studied the score was, "probably the most decisive influence in my life." Without a doubt, it was Debussy's extraordinary and completely original treatment of harmony, tonality, and rhythm—rhythm liberated from the tyrannical and predictable pulse of the steady beat and regular bar lines—that inspired Messiaen to even greater tonal and rhythmic freedom in his own works. Truly, if any single composer could be said to be the successor of Debussy, in terms of both musical syntax and sheer originality, it would have to be Messiaen.

The year after he received that oh-so-important score of *Pelleas and Melisande*, 11-year-old Messiaen entered the Paris Conservatory. He put the place on its ear; you know, they still talk about him to this day, that his tenure there was marked by one amazing success after another. In 1926, at the age of 18, he received first place in counterpoint, harmony and fugue. In 1928, he won first prize in piano accompaniment. In 1929, he won first prize in music history. And in 1930, the year he graduated, he won the prize he most coveted, first prize in composition.

Immediately after graduating in 1930, Messiaen was appointed organist at La Trinité in Paris, a post he held for 40 years, until 1970. In 1936, at the age of 28, he joined the faculty of the Ecole Normale de Musique in Paris. In 1939, he joined the French army after Germany invaded Poland and France subsequently declared war on Germany. And that's where we began our biography earlier in this lecture.

Turangalila Symphony

Messiaen organized the 10 movements of the *Turangalila Symphony* around a number of "cyclic themes," that is, things that return, that cycle back from movement to movement. The two most important of these cyclic things are polar opposites—the alpha-omega, the yin and yang of the symphony. The first, what we will call the *earth theme* is heavy, monumental, and craggy in character. This earth theme represents the corporeal, that which is real and solid, permanent and unchanging. When we first hear this theme, about 30 seconds into the first movement, it is played by trombones and tuba. For starters, let's just hear the first two iterations of this earth theme that appear 30 seconds or so into the first movement.

[Musical example from *Turangalila Symphony*, Messiaen: I; Earth Theme]

Now, let's listen from the beginning of this first movement, a movement Messiaen simply calls "Introduction." The movement begins emphatically and with a sense of great anticipation, anticipation that is well-satisfied by the appearance of the earth theme about 30 seconds in.

[Musical example from *Turangalila Symphony*, Messiaen: I; Opening]

The second of the cyclic themes presented here in the first movement could not be more different from the first. In his program note, Messiaen refers to this theme as the "flower" theme, because of its gentle, supple, curving contour like: "the tender orchid, the ornamental fuchsia, the red gladiolas, the supple corn-lily."

Let's hear this second theme, which makes its first appearance about two-and-a-half minutes into this first movement.

[Musical example from *Turangalila Symphony*, Messiaen: I; Flower Theme]

As the flowers evoked by Messiaen's program note grow from the earth, so this second theme grows out of the earth theme. We are going to refer to this second theme as the *spirit theme*, because for Messiaen, it represents the ineffable, the beautiful, that which changes and metamorphoses, the life cycle of death and rebirth. Let's hear it again.

[Musical example from *Turangalila Symphony*, Messiaen: I; Flower Theme]

What we have called the earth theme has also been referred to in the literature as the *masculine theme* or *phallic theme*, and what we are calling the spirit theme, has also been referred to as the *feminine theme* or *blossom theme*. Whatever we choose to call them—earth and spirit, masculine and feminine, Tristan and Isolde, plug and socket—they represent the complementary opposites of the universe. And when they combine, that is, when they meet and mate in the middle of the symphony, the musical sparks will surely fly.

That most noteworthy event, the great mating, occurs at the beginning of the second half of the *Turangalila Symphony*—during the beginning of the sixth movement—when the harmonic elements of the earth theme are mated and merged with the melodic element of the spirit theme.

The offspring of the two is a long, slow melody that represents idealized love, a theme that will be heard cyclically during the second half of the symphony. Let's hear this idealized love theme as it appears at the beginning of the sixth movement, a movement entitled "Garden of Love's Sleep." The idealized love theme, shimmering and otherworldly, is played by an electronic keyboard instrument called an *ondes martenot* (which we'll talk more about after we've heard the theme), accompanied by strings, and decorated by the piano and percussion instruments.

[Musical example from *Turangalila Symphony*, Messiaen: VI; "Garden of Love's Sleep"; Opening]

The *ondes martenot* was invented by a Parisian pianist and composer named Maurice Martenot. It was first heard publicly on April 20, 1928. Looking like a small electric organ with a big speaker attached to it, the keyboard is played using the right hand while the left hand controlled the various dials and slides that modify its tone-color and volume. During the late 1920s and 1930s, the *ondes martenot* was perceived by many as "an instrument of the future," and many of France's leading composers wrote music for it— including Darius Milhaud, Arthur Honegger, André Jolivet, Jacques Ibert, and the great French-composer-transplanted-to-the-United-States, Edgard Varèse. Along with the "theremin," the *ondes martenot* was the most popular electronic instrument before the synthesizer, and Messiaen uses it with superb effect in the *Turangalila Symphony*. My friends, we must be eternally grateful that Messiaen did not choose to use the theremin, a device invented in 1920 by Leon Theremin, a Russian scientist of French descent. Today, we know its gooey, slippery, swooping, and sliding sound from the soundtracks of all those fabulously awful post-World War II, apocalyptic science fiction and giant radioactive mantis/spider/crab/rabbit movies that are now the essential grist of Mystery Science Theater.

So anyway, we're going to hear the *ondes martenot* throughout the *Turangalila Symphony* and it's to Messiaen's great credit that the music he wrote for it sounds neither silly nor dated at this point in time.

Back to the Top

The first movement of the *Turangalila Symphony* is called "Introduction." The first half of this first movement is "about" the introduction of the earth and spirit themes. After a brief piano solo—a cadenza—the second half of this first movement is given over to an amazing passage in which four different rhythmic patterns are superimposed one atop each other, creating an effect that is, for me, like four individual gamelan orchestras simultaneously performing different parts of Stravinsky's *The Rite of Spring* after having consumed quadruple espressos spiked with Bacardi 151 and way too much sugar. I'm not going to even attempt to explain what Messiaen does. Suffice it to say that using Hindu rhythmic patterns called *tala*, he creates an incredibly energized passage characterized by constantly shifting rhythmic relationships, as different rhythmic patterns go in and out of phase with each other. "The total impression [here] is one of relentless power, brought about by the inner complexity of rhythmic superimpositions, and the effect is that of a ritual incantation, preparing for the play of life and death which is to follow." Let's hear it.

[Musical example from *Turangalila Symphony*, Messiaen: I, Part II; Introduction]

During the course of the second movement, entitled "Love Song I," explosive passages of music characterized by the same sort of superimposed rhythmic patterns or *tala*, alternate with calm, static, extremely lyric passages. Like Hector Berlioz in the first movement of the *Symphonie fantastique*, Messiaen is here depicting the emotional extremes of extreme love: intense pleasure and intense pain, clarity and disorientation, rapture and rupture, if you'll excuse me. We hear the beginning of the movement, beginning with "rupture" (as in "disruption").

[Musical example from *Turangalila Symphony*, Messiaen: II; "Love Song I," Opening]

The third movement is entitled, "Turangalila I." It opens with a ghostly solo for clarinet, accompanied by, or should we say more properly, shadowed by, the *ondes martenot*.

[Musical example from *Turangalila Symphony*, Messiaen: III; "Turangalila I," Opening]

Messiaen entitled the fourth movement "Love Song II." It is, like so much of the symphony, a tour-de-force of layering and superimposition. The movement begins simply enough, as a duet between a piccolo and a bassoon, accompanied by a ringing *ondes martenot*. Soon enough, a woodblock enters, followed by low plucked or pizzicato strings, and then a rustling piano, with each new part characterized by its own melodic material and its own rhythmic profile. By the time the opening section of the movement comes to its conclusion, the texture consists of five distinctly different, and yet, amazingly unified parts. Let's hear it.

[Musical example from *Turangalila Symphony*, Messiaen: IV; "Love Song II"]

We've already sampled movements five and six. The fifth movement, entitled "Joy of the Blood of Stars," brings the first half of the symphony to its conclusion. Movement six, "Garden of Love's Sleep," begins with a gorgeous and dreamlike idealized love theme, a theme that itself is a product of the joining, the "mating" of the earth theme and the spirit theme. The sixth movement is the symphony's slow movement—the adagio—and heaven knows, we need a break after the absolutely manic fifth movement. Messiaen's description of the sixth movement sounds like a description of a painting by Henri Rousseau:

> The two lovers are immersed in the sleep of love. A landscape has emanated from them. The garden that surrounds them is called "Tristan"; the garden that surrounds them is called "Isolde." The garden is full of light and shade, of plants and new flowers, of brightly colored and melodious birds. Time flows on, forgotten, the lovers are outside time, let us not wake them.

It is a magical movement with its lush harmonies and birdsongs heard in the piano, musical birdsongs based on the actual songs of the nightingale, blackbird, and garden warbler.

The seventh movement, entitled "Turangalila II," is the shortest movement of the symphony. It features a bristling, energized, birdsong-dominated piano part. It's as if the quiet and relaxed nightingale, blackbird, and garden warbler of the previous movement have here all been transformed into Rockin' Robin or some reasonable imitation thereof. We hear the piano solo that initiates this seventh movement.

[Musical example from *Turangalila Symphony*, Messiaen: VII; "Turangalila II," Opening]

The eighth movement is the longest of the symphony. Entitled "Development of Love," this movement is exactly what it claims to be—a huge development section during, which all of the major themes heard thusfar in the symphony appear. The ongoing developmental process that occurs during this eighth movement is interrupted three times by increasingly longer and more ecstatic versions of the idealized love theme.

Messiaen refers to these moments as the "explosions" of the love theme, and their appearances mark the climax of the entire symphony. We listen to the third and last of these explosions of the idealized love theme and the gradual subsidence that follows. Movement eight.

[Musical example from *Turangalila Symphony*, Messiaen: VIII; Third version of "idealized love theme"]

The ninth movement, entitled "Turangalila III," is a brief series of variations on the earth theme. The tenth movement, entitled simply "Finale," is the only one of the ten movements written in sonata form. Now we're not going to analyze it as such, but I thought that you'd like to know that a procedure developed way back in the 1730s and 1740s was still of great use to an avant-garde composer working in the late 1940s. The spirit of this tenth and final movement is joyful and dancing, and in this, we return to the frenetic mood of the fifth movement, "Joy of the Blood of Stars," the first of the symphony's two finales, as it was.

Messiaen indicates that this tenth movement finale should be performed "very fast and with great joy." We listen to the recapitulation and conclusion of the movement and the symphony. Please note about one minute and twenty-two seconds into the excerpt (give or take), we will hear the idealized love theme, which has, in this movement, been used as theme 2 of the sonata form.

[Musical example from *Turangalila Symphony*, Messiaen: X; Finale, Recapitulation and Conclusion]

Conclusions

In January of 1950, after its New York premiere, the critic for the journal *Music America* offered as short-sighted a statement as any we are liable to read when he said of the *Turangalila Symphony* that: "Messiaen has produced a work of a vulgarity scarcely paralleled in the entire history of serious music." Oh, please. The *Turangalila Symphony* is a magnificent achievement. It is among the first masterworks of the post-war era and among the first masterworks of what would become Messiaen's storied career. It remained his only symphony, though, and for that we must treasure it all the more, because it is unique in Messiaen's output.

"Vulgar" Messiaen's *Turangalila Symphony* is not, but it is different, completely and totally different from any other piece of music by any other composer. And frankly, we could say just the same thing for just about any piece of music Messiaen ever composed. Like his great French predecessors, Hector Berlioz and Claude Debussy, Olivier Messiaen was a true original. He belonged to no "school." He spouted no polemic. He pushed no personal or political agenda. As a person he bore no grudges and hid no skeletons in his emotional closet. He was a genuinely good and kind man who, it seems, was loved and respected by everyone who knew him. He was a complete original, whose music and teaching exerted, and will continue to exert, an incredible degree of influence.

Forward then, to our final lecture, and the Tenth Symphony of Dmitri Dmitriyevich Shostakovich.

Thank you.

Lecture Twenty-Four
Dmitri Shostakovich and His Tenth Symphony

Scope: It is entirely appropriate that we conclude this survey with Dmitri
Shostakovich. What Haydn was for the 18th century, what
Beethoven was for the 19th century, so Shostakovich was for the
20th—the preeminent composer of symphonies in his century. Like
Haydn and Beethoven before him, Shostakovich wrote
symphonies throughout his compositional career and wrote a large
enough number of symphonies to constitute a major body of work.
Like Haydn and Beethoven, Shostakovich's symphonies constitute
a virtual diary of his life and evolving compositional style. And
like Haydn and Beethoven, Shostakovich's symphonies are a true
and unapologetic mirror of his times and his environment. We can
only wonder which composers history will choose as
representative of our time, but we can be sure that the symphonic
genre will play a major role in helping to make that determination.

Outline

I. To understand the life and music of Dmitri Shostakovich (1906–1975),
    we must take a clear, honest, and unemotional view of the events that
    shaped him.

   A. Shostakovich was the greatest composer produced by the Soviet
       Union. Propaganda of the time tells us that he was a model for the
       superior Soviet way of life and a hero of the Soviet Union. In
       reality, Shostakovich was abused, deceived, manipulated, and
       frightened by his government to a degree that threatened his sanity.
       That Shostakovich survived without being imprisoned or
       "liquidated" is a miracle. He survived because he was considered
       by the authorities to be a *yurodivy*, a "village idiot" or "holy fool";
       by Russian tradition, one of the chosen few allowed to speak out.

   B. After Shostakovich's death in August of 1975 and his subsequent
       "posthumous rehabilitation," the Soviet authorities declared him to
       be "Soviet Russia's most loyal musical son." Again, in reality, the
       "public" Shostakovich said and did what he was told. He joined
       the Communist party when Khrushchev told him to do so in 1960,
       at the age of 54; he sat on official state committees and attended

their meetings religiously; and he allowed his name to be signed to anti-Western rants and editorials.

C. Very few people outside the Soviet Union were clever enough to see the truth about Shostakovich. One of those people was the composer Nicholas Nabokov, an émigré to the United States and a cousin of the writer Vladimir Nabokov, who met Shostakovich in New York in 1949 and made some extraordinary observations at the time.

   1. In 1948, Shostakovich was officially censured and nearly purged by the Soviet authorities, despite the fact that just seven years before, he had been proclaimed "a hero of the Soviet people" for having stayed in Leningrad during the siege and composed his Symphony no. 7, the so-called "Leningrad" Symphony.

   2. At the time, Stalin had decided to bring to heel those members of the military and government, as well as artists and intellectuals, who had become emboldened by contact with the West during the war and by the Soviet victory over the Nazis. Thus, Shostakovich was fired from his teaching jobs at the Moscow and Leningrad Conservatories and his music was banned. He waited at night, awake and terrified, to be arrested. This "threat of arrest" had happened once before to Shostakovich, in 1936–1937, and he knew the taste of fear. As he had in 1936–1937, Shostakovich also considered suicide in 1948.

   3. Then, in late February 1949, Stalin called Shostakovich and "asked" him to travel to the United States as a member of the Soviet delegation to the Congress of Peace and Culture. Shostakovich replied that the trip might seem odd, given that his works were freely played in America but had been forbidden in the Soviet Union. Stalin ordered that the ban on Shostakovich's music be lifted, and in March of 1949, the composer left for the United States during the iciest days of the Cold War.

   4. During the trip, hostile, strident, anti-Western, anti-American speeches were read—in English, by interpreters—while Shostakovich looked on in misery; gullible Westerners believed that these speeches were written by Shostakovich himself.

5. Nicholas Nabokov, however, knew that the remarks attributed to Shostakovich had been written in the standard style of Soviet propaganda, and he saw clearly that Shostakovich was being punished—he was publicly humiliated by having to express his gratitude to the Communist Party for helping him recognize flaws in his work!

II. We take a brief detour from this period in Shostakovich's life—the years 1948–1953, which saw the gestation and composition of the Tenth Symphony—to discuss the book that exposed the truth behind the carefully crafted, Soviet version of "Shostakovich" and ignited a debate about the composer and his music that goes on to this day.

    A. The book, entitled *Testimony: The Memoirs of Dmitri Shostakovich*, consists of a series of interviews that Shostakovich gave near the end of his life. Sick and embittered, he poured out his heart and soul, his hostility and hatred toward the Soviet regime, and discussed the true meaning of his music.

        1. The interviews—conducted at Shostakovich's flat by a young Soviet musicologist named Solomon Volkov—were transcribed; Shostakovich signed the transcripts; and they were smuggled out of the Soviet Union with the promise that they would not be published until after the composer's death.

        2. Shostakovich died in 1975; when the Soviet government learned of the existence of the interviews, it did everything possible to prevent publication, but the memoirs were published by Harper and Row, in New York in 1979.

        3. The Soviet government decried the book as another example of the West defaming a Soviet hero. The last thing the Soviets wanted in 1979 was to have Shostakovich—so recently rehabilitated—reconstrued as a closet dissident.

        4. In the United States, Volkov was vilified and accused of having fabricated portions of the memoir; of using Shostakovich's words to push his own personal agenda; and of trying to make money off the memory of a revered composer. The debate between "pro-Testimony" and "con-Testimony" writers and academics raged on.

    B. In 1991 came the fall of the Soviet Union and, with it, the truth. We learned that what actually went on in the Soviet Union was much worse than what we in the West had thought possible.

C. Should we now believe *Testimony*? The answer is yes. Shostakovich's friends and associates—speaking freely in interviews since 1991 or speaking from the grave in newly discovered and translated material—tell us repeatedly that the words and stories in *Testimony* are Shostakovich's own. In the post-Soviet world, as the truth comes out, the dark tales contained in *Testimony* are now being corroborated. Finally, the Shostakovich we meet in *Testimony*—furious, embittered, humorous, and blackly ironic—is seen as a man who squares with his music.

III. Shostakovich, unlike many of his contemporaries, neither wept nor celebrated when he heard about Stalin's death on March 5, 1953, but he did arrange for the release and premiere of the many masterworks he had composed and hidden since 1948.

A. A veritable flood of "new" Shostakovich works was heard in the months after Stalin's death, including the Fourth String Quartet, the Fifth String Quartet, the Violin Concerto No. 1, and the song cycle *From Jewish Poetry*. The big premiere of this post-Stalin period, however, was that of the Symphony no. 10 in E Minor, op. 93, composed during the summer after Stalin's death.

B. Shostakovich's Tenth immediately became the most talked-about and influential piece of music in the Eastern Block. In those heady days after the death of Stalin, a period known as the "Thaw," Shostakovich's Tenth became a model for what the "new," post-Stalin Soviet music might aspire to be: a more personally expressive, less explicitly programmatic work, one that both engaged and challenged its listeners.

C. Structurally, Shostakovich was very much a Classicist: We will observe in his music the now quite familiar Classical-era formal structures of sonata form, scherzo, and rondo. Harmonically, Shostakovich never abandoned traditional tonality, and his melodic language grows directly out of 19th-century Russian nationalism. If all of this would seem to indicate that Shostakovich was a musical conservative, we must remember that he had to walk a fine line between the doctrine of Soviet Socialist Musical Realism, that is, to compose music accessible to the Soviet masses, and his own compositional muse.

IV. The first of the four movements of Shostakovich's Tenth is epic in terms of both expressive content and length, running around 25 minutes in performance. Structurally, it is a gigantic sonata form with three distinct themes.

  A. The movement opens with a familiar "Russian" device: massed low strings, the deep, masculine, "Russian" voice of the bass singer. Familiar as this device may be, it is nowhere used to better effect than here, imbuing this opening with tremendous gravity and a hint of the tragic. (**Musical selection**: Shostakovich, Symphony no. 10 in E Minor, op. 93, movement 1, opening, theme 1.)

  B. This magnificent and contemplative music now gives way to an exquisitely melancholy theme initially played by a clarinet. This constitutes the second of the three thematic elements that make up the exposition. (**Musical selection**: Shostakovich, Symphony no. 10 in E Minor, op. 93, movement 1, theme 2.)

  C. This "second theme" music builds to a huge climax, which is then followed by a reprise of the clarinet theme. Finally, six minutes into the movement, the third and final thematic element is heard: a slightly nervous, slightly dancing theme initially heard in a solo flute accompanied by pizzicato strings. (**Musical selection**: Shostakovich, Symphony no. 10 in E Minor, op. 93, movement 1, theme 3.)

  D. Not one of this movement's three principal themes is magnificent, heroic, or otherwise dramatic when it makes its first appearance. In fact, the impression we get during this first movement has been described as "the quality of absence—of emptiness." Yes, the thematic ideas develop, but in their primal state, they are all quiet, melancholy, restrained; the anticipated "bombast" of a typical symphonic first movement is replaced with introspection and uneasy quiet, a perfect metaphor for the mood in the Soviet Union after the death of the "leader and teacher."

V. The second movement cannot be said to have a mood of introspection or uneasy quiet. It is a raw, brutal, and vicious piece of music— Shostakovich's famous musical portrait of Stalin. It starts fortissimo and, from there, features 50 crescendos and only 2 decrescendos! (**Musical selection**: Shostakovich, Symphony no. 10 in E Minor, op. 93, movement 2, entirety.)

VI. Throughout both the third and fourth movements, Shostakovich repeatedly uses a particular melodic idea consisting of four pitches.

    A. These pitches, D–Eb–C–B, are quite significant, in that they constitute Shostakovich's musical signature: D–S–C–H. In German, the pitch names are D–S(Eb)–C–H(B)—D S C H, as in D. Shostakovich.

    B. This musical signature is first heard about 1 minute and 10 seconds into the third movement. When it first appears, it is rather shrilly played by winds and accompanied by a triangle. This is cartoon-like music, a herky-jerky puppet's dance, and it is a clear statement on Shostakovich's part. He often said that "we are all marionettes." That he would portray himself—with his own musical signature—in the guise of a puppet is typical of his cynical, ironic sense of humor. (**Musical selection**: Shostakovich, Symphony no. 10 in E Minor, op. 93, movement 3, D–S–C–H appearance.)

VII. The fourth movement begins with a slow introduction that itself begins with a pensive melody for 'cellos and double basses, a clear reference to the beginning of the first movement of the symphony. (**Musical selection**: Shostakovich, Symphony no. 10 in E Minor, op. 93, movement 4, introduction, opening.)

    A. When this long and bleak introduction finally ends, the fast, chipper and upbeat music that follows it seems ridiculously incongruous, as if Shostakovich is saying, "Smile! Smile! We're supposed to be happy! The leader and teacher says so! Smile!" (**Musical selection**: Shostakovich, Symphony no. 10 in E Minor, op. 93, movement 4, introduction, opening.)

    B. Given the spirit of the first three movements of this symphony, the mock gaiety of this movement becomes more and more forced, until the music metamorphoses into something very dark; the "smile" disappears, and the frenzied viciousness of the second movement returns, followed by a huge and howling appearance of the D–S–C–H motive. It is as if Shostakovich is saying to us, "I have danced the dance and smiled the smile, and now Stalin is dead and I will do it no longer!" (**Musical selection**: Shostakovich, Symphony no. 10 in E Minor, op. 93, movement 4.)

    C. The final minutes of the symphony are deeply moving. The "smile" is gone; the music becomes lyric and introspective, punctuated throughout by the D–S–C–H motive. Finally, the fast, upbeat music returns, but it seems less incongruous, as if perhaps, now, there is a genuine reason to smile. Certainly, the celebratory conclusion of the movement would seem to reinforce that interpretation; the reiterated D–S–C–H motive heard among blaring brass is a clear and personal statement: "I am here; I am alive; and I can still write!" (**Musical selection**: Shostakovich, Symphony no. 10 in E Minor, op. 93, movement 4, conclusion.)

D. It was just this sort of movement that confused Western commentators for years. Thanks to *Testimony* and the work of such scholars as David Fanning, we now understand that irony is the key to understanding Shostakovich's music.

E. A few months after the premiere of the Tenth, Shostakovich wrote a truly absurd apology for the symphony that helped him "play it safe" with the authorities. He gave the official critics the negative comments they required and, at the same time, distracted them from thinking too deeply about the "true" meaning of the symphony. Nonetheless, Shostakovich's Tenth became an instant classic, and the composer emerged from his censure with his reputation enhanced. The sheer quality of his Tenth Symphony was a testament to Shostakovich's incredible artistic integrity and imagination.

Lecture Twenty-Four—Transcript
Dmitri Shostakovich and His Tenth Symphony

We return to *The Symphony*. This is our final lecture, Lecture Twenty-Four—it is entitled "Dmitri Shostakovich and His Tenth Symphony."

A Necessary Diversion Here, at the Onset of Our Final Lecture

Before we begin our discussion of Shostakovich, a few words about the many worthy composers and symphonies that have gone, and will go, unexamined and unexcerpted in this course. As is always the case in the survey, what is omitted says as much about a course as what is included.

While I was planning the course, I spoke to and emailed a whole lot of my friends and colleagues and asked for their opinions regarding which symphonies should, and should not, be included in a survey like this one. Well, their responses were wonderful, and almost every one of them had some personal favorite that simply had to be discussed. For example, one friend absolutely insisted that I discuss the two symphonies of the Czech composer Josef Suk, who lived from 1874 to 1935. I fear I have disappointed this lovely and loyal person. Another friend, who was a huge fan of Havergal Brian's massive Symphony no. 2, the so-called "Gothic" Symphony, told me that without its inclusion, my course would, sadly, be insignificant (that's his word, admittedly, said in the heat of passion). A former colleague of mine, an expert on early music, recommended that I simply survey all of Haydn's symphonies and stop there, as, "No symphony of consequence has been written since 1796." Not very useful, that one. And of course, my composer friends weighed in on all the contemporary symphonies I should include, works by such composers as Peter Maxwell Davies, Witold Lutoslawski, Christopher Rouse, John Corigliano, Henryk Gorecki, and so forth.

As it turns out, there are no living composers represented in this survey. Shostakovich's Tenth is the most "recent" symphony we'll examine, and it was composed in 1953, over half a century ago. You'll pardon me a self-congratulatory statement: this "50-year" cutoff is one of the best decisions I made in preparing this course. My friends, it's virtually impossible to know what contemporary repertoire will be both representative of our time and will mange to serve the test of time. Sure, we can guess, but as often as not, we guess wrong; and by including guesswork repertoire, we would have had to leave out music that was genuinely worthy of inclusion. That there are no living composers here is an act of genuine hypocrisy on my part; as a "living" composer (at least last I checked), I'm always whining about how living composers are ignored in their own lifetimes. But there you go; we need the perspective provided by a complete creative lifetime to understand the place of a particular symphony within that lifetime; and we need to be far enough away from the events that shaped that lifetime to see them clearly and honestly and unemotionally.

Dmitri Dmitriyevich Shostakovich (1906-1975)

Clear and honest and unemotional. If we are to understand the life and music of Dmitri Shostakovich, then, more than any other composer I can think of, a clear and honest and unemotional view of the events that shaped his life is an absolute necessity. A task more easily said than done. You see, Shostakovich was the single greatest composer produced by the Soviet Union. He was the poster child for the new and superior Soviet way of life, a model for the new species of man called the "Homo Sovieticus" (on this I kid you not). A hero of the Soviet Union; that's what the propagandists told us. In reality, Shostakovich was used and abused, lied to and lied about, stroked, manipulated, and scared out of his wits to a degree that he went just a little bit crazy. That Shostakovich survived without being imprisoned or "liquidated," is itself a small miracle, although not so small for Shostakovich himself. He survived because he was considered by the authorities to be a *yuridivy*, a "village idiot," by Russian tradition one of the chosen few allowed to speak out, a "holy fool," a sort of societal safety valve in a culture otherwise almost entirely lacking in anything resembling free and honest speech.

After Shostakovich's death in August of 1975, after his subsequent "posthumous rehabilitation" (do you love that phrase as much as I do, "posthumous rehabilitation"?) the Soviet authorities declared that their dear, departed, Dmitri Dmitriyevich was: "Soviet Russia's most loyal musical son." To which we say—"right." But really, who could argue with them? The "public" Shostakovich, the Shostakovich we read about in the newspapers and saw on his rare trips outside the Soviet Union, said whatever he was told to say and did whatever he was told to do. He joined the Communist Party when Khrushchev told him to do so in 1960, at the age of 54; he sat on official state committees and attended their endless brain-addling meetings religiously; he allowed his name to be signed at the bottom of anti-Western rants and editorials, while he fidgeted, twitched, and literally smoked himself to death.

Very few people outside of the Soviet Union were clever or smart enough to see what was really going on with Shostakovich. One of those people was the composer Nicholas Nabokov, an émigré to the United States and a cousin of the writer Vladimir Nabokov, who met Shostakovich in New York in 1949 and had some extraordinarily accurate observations to make. Some background: In 1948, Shostakovich was officially censured and nearly purged by the Soviet authorities, despite the fact, or perhaps *because* of the fact, that just seven years before, during the siege of Leningrad, he had been proclaimed "a hero of the Soviet people" for having stayed in Leningrad during the beginning of the siege and having composed his Symphony no. 7, the so-called "Leningrad" Symphony. Anyway, in 1948, Stalin decided it was time to bring to heel those members of the military, the government, artists, and intellectuals who had become emboldened by contact with the West during the war and by the Soviet victory over the Nazis. So Shostakovich, among many others, was made an example of. He was fired from his teaching jobs at the Moscow and Leningrad Conservatories, his music was banned, the water was cut off to his apartment, he waited at night, awake and terrified for thugs to come and arrest him. He kept a small bag packed and a toothbrush and toothpaste in his jacket pocket. This "threat of arrest" had happened once before to Shostakovich, in 1936 and 1937, and so he knew the taste of fear. And like 1936 and 1937, in 1948, Shostakovich considered suicide.

In order to survive, Shostakovich wrote scores for industrial films and the occasional feature film. Yes, that's right, one of the greatest composers of all time, reduced to doing hackwork to survive. It's incredible. And then, in late February of 1949, during a visit from his friend and former student, Yuri Levitin, the phone rang at the Shostakovich flat. Here's Levitin's account of what happened:

> Dmitri Dmitriyevich wasn't feeling very well. I sat talking to him. The telephone rang, and Dmitri Dmitriyevich picked up the receiver. A second later he said helplessly: "Stalin is about to come on the line."

> I froze in position on the sofa. For the next moments, naturally, I all I heard was Dmitri Dmitriyevich's answers, but from them I could clearly deduce the nature of the talk. Stalin was evidently inquiring after Shostakovich's health. Dmitri Dmitriyevich answered disconsolately: "Thank you, everything is fine. I am only suffering somewhat from a stomach ache."

Stalin asked if he needed a doctor or any medicine. "No, no thank you. I don't need anything. I have everything I need."

Then there was a long pause while Stalin spoke. It transpired that he was asking Shostakovich to travel to the United States for the Congress of Peace and Culture. "Of course I will go, if it's really necessary, but I am in a fairly difficult position. Over there, almost all of my symphonies are played, whereas over here, they are forbidden. How am I to behave in this situation?'

And then, as has been recounted many times since, Stalin said with his strong Georgian accent, "How do you mean forbidden? Forbidden by whom?" "By the State Commission for Repertoire," answered Dmitri Dmitriyevich.

Well, Stalin assured Shostakovich that this was a mistake, which would be corrected; none of Dmitri Dmitriyevich's had been forbidden; they could be freely performed.

Well, within a few weeks, Stalin personally ordered that the ban on Shostakovich's music be lifted. A few days after that, on March 20, 1949, Shostakovich left for the United States as a member of the Soviet delegation to the Congress of Peace and Culture, during the iciest, most frigid days of the Cold War. During the trip, Shostakovich said what he was told to say. Hostile, strident, anti-Western, anti-American speeches were read in English by interpreters—while Shostakovich looked on in misery, speeches that gullible Westerners believed were written by Shostakovich himself.

Back now to Nicholas Nabokov, who met and observed Shostakovich during his stay in the United States. Nabokov, a Russian émigré, saw directly through the charade. He wrote:

In March of 1949, still bruised from the thrashing he had received, Shostakovich was picked out of the clothes hamper like dirty laundry. He was washed, ironed out, and sent to America. He arrived in New York in company with five other gentlemen in blue serge suits with oversized-sleeves a la Stalin, and was exhibited as the biggest publicity and public attraction of that Communist-inspired performance.

Shostakovich's speech, written in the standard style of agitation/propaganda [or agitprop] speeches, was quite obviously prepared by the "party organs" in charge of the conference. In it, the mouthpiece Shostakovich condemned most Western music as decadent bourgeois and admitted that he himself had often erred and sinned against the decrees of the Party.

I sat in my seat petrified at a spectacle of human misery and degradation. It was crystal clear to me that this whole speech of his, this whole "peace-making mission," was part of a punishment, part of a ritual redemption he had to go through before he could be pardoned again. He was to tell, in person, to all the Western dupes at the conference and to the whole decadent bourgeois world that he, Shostakovich, the famous Russian composer, is not a free man but an obedient tool of his government. He told us, in effect, that every time the Party found flaws in his art, the Party was right, and every time the Party put him on ice, he was grateful to the Party, because it helped him to recognize his flaws and mistakes.

Testimony

Now we're going to pick up at exactly this point of time in just a couple of minutes because these are the years, between 1948 and 1953, that saw the gestation and composition of what is one of Shostakovich's greatest symphonies, his Tenth. But before we can talk about the Tenth and its true meaning, we must first discuss the book that blew the lid off the carefully crafted, Soviet version of "Shostakovich" and ignited a debate regarding both Shostakovich and his music that goes on to this day.

The book, entitled *Testimony: The Memoirs of Dmitri Shostakovich*, consists of a series of interviews that Shostakovich gave near the end of his life when, sick and embittered, he poured out his soul, his hostility and hatred towards the Soviet regime, and discussed the true meaning of his music. The interviews—conducted at Shostakovich's flat by a young Soviet musicologist named Solomon Volkov—were transcribed; Shostakovich signed the transcriptions, and they were smuggled out of the Soviet Union with the promise that they would not be published until after Shostakovich's death. Shostakovich died in 1975, and when the Soviet government learned of these interviews and their impending publication, they did everything they could to keep them from being published. But published they were, by Harper and Rowe, in New York in 1979.

Such a "*Shrei*" from the Soviet government! "Lies, all lies, just another example of the West defaming a Soviet hero!" The last thing the Soviets wanted in 1979 was to have Shostakovich—so recently rehabilitated—reconstrued as a closet dissident.

In the United States, Volkov was vilified and accused of having fabricated portions of the memoir, of using Shostakovich's words to push forth a personal agenda of unspecified content, of making money off the memory of a revered composer who, because he was dead, could no longer defend himself or the "true" meaning of his words. The debate between "pro-*Testimony*" and "con-*Testimony*" writers and academics rages on.

And then, in 1991, came the fall of the Soviet Union and, with it, the truth. The truth, my friends, first in dribs and drabs, and now today, a veritable torrent. And what is the truth? That what actually went on in the Soviet Union was in actuality much, much worse than what we in the West had ever thought possible. So why should we believe *Testimony*? Because Shostakovich's friends and associates, speaking freely in interviews since 1991, or speaking from the grave in newly discovered and translated material, tell us repeatedly that the words and stories in *Testimony* are Shostakovich's own. Because the composer's sons and daughter have both endorsed the book. Because Mstislav Rostropovich, for whom Shostakovich wrote two cello concertos, was informed by Shostakovich that his 15 symphonies were, essentially, a coded history. Because in the post-Soviet world, as the truth comes out, the dark tales and stories contained in *Testimony* are now being corroborated left and right. And most importantly, it is because the Shostakovich we meet in *Testimony*—furious, outraged, embittered, blackly ironic, the real Shostakovich—is a man that squares finally with his music.

The Thaw and the Tenth

Joseph Stalin, the great leader and teacher, died at 11:50 pm on March 5, 1953. Shostakovich, unlike many of his contemporaries, neither wept nor went around giving flying high-five's when he heard about Stalin's death. When asked by his student, the composer Edison Denisov, if he thought there would now be changes for the better, Shostakovich replied, "Edik, the times are new, but the informers are old."

Nevertheless, we know that Shostakovich breathed a big sigh of relief when Stalin died, because his immediate preoccupation following Stalin's death was to arrange for the release and premiere of the many works he had composed and then hidden since his censure in 1948. Shostakovich might have been a small, frail, frightened, seemingly timid man, but he had a creative force measurable in megatonnage. Between 1948 and 1953, he wrote many works, many masterworks that discretion required he keep out of sight. So a veritable flood of new Shostakovich works were heard in the months following Stalin's death, including the Fourth String Quartet, the Fifth String Quartet, the Violin Concerto no. 1, and the song cycle, *From Jewish Poetry*. But the big premiere of this post-Stalin period was that of Shostakovich's Symphony no. 10 in E Minor, op. 93, composed during the summer of 1953, immediately after Stalin's death.

Shostakovich's Tenth was first performed in December of 1953. According to music historian Boris Schwarz: "The accumulation of sorrow that Shostakovich experienced [between 1948 and 1953] came out with elemental, explosive force in his Tenth Symphony. The great work that heralded the [post-Stalin] liberalization of the human spirit."

Shostakovich's Tenth immediately became the most talked-about and influential piece of music in the entire Eastern Block. In those heady days after the death of Stalin, a period known as the "Thaw," Shostakovich's Tenth became a model for what the "new," post-Stalin Soviet music might aspire to be: a more personally expressive, less explicitly programmatic work, one that both engaged and challenged its listeners.

A word about Shostakovich's compositional style before we start listening. Structurally, Shostakovich was very much a Classicist: We will observe his music the now quite familiar Classical-era formal structures of sonata form, scherzo, and rondo. Harmonically, Shostakovich never abandoned traditional tonality, and his melodic language grows directly out of 19th-century Russian nationalism. If all of this would seem to indicate that Shostakovich was a musical conservative, we must remember that he had to walk a fine and almost impossibly difficult line between the doctrine of Soviet Socialist Musical Realism—that is, to compose music accessible to the Soviet masses—and his own, amazing, compositional muse. Having said this, Shostakovich had a compositional technique that was second-to-none, and he had what Arnold Schoenberg called: "the breath of the symphonist," meaning the natural dramatic inclination to make the grand statement in this grandest of all instrumental genres—the symphony.

Movement One

The first of the four movements of Shostakovich's Tenth is epic in terms of both expressive content and sheer length, running about 25 minutes in performance. Structurally, it's a gigantic sonata form movement with three distinct themes. The movement opens with a familiar "Russian" device: massed low strings, the deep masculine "Russian" voice of the bass singer. Familiar as this device may be, it is nowhere used to better effect than right here, and it imbues this opening with tremendous gravity and a hit of the tragic. We hear the opening thematic material, what amounts to theme 1, roughly the first two minutes of the movement.

[Musical example from Symphony No. 10 in E Minor, Shostakovich: I; Theme I, Opening]

This magnificent and completive music now gives way to an exquisitely melancholy theme initially played by a clarinet. This constitutes the second of the three thematic elements that make up the exposition. Let's hear it.

[Musical example from Symphony No. 10 in E Minor, Shostakovich: I; Theme II]

This "second theme" music builds up to a huge climax, which is then followed by a reprise of the clarinet theme. Finally, six minutes in the movement, the third and final thematic element is heard: a slightly nervous, slightly dancing theme initially heard in the solo flute accompanied by pizzicato (or plucked) strings. Let's hear this third thematic entity.

[Musical example from Symphony No. 10 in E Minor, Shostakovich: I; Theme III]

Now to point out the obvious, not one of this movement's three principle themes is magnificent, heroic, or otherwise dramatic when it makes its first appearance. In fact, the overwhelming impression we get during this first movement, despite its climactic moments, is what has been referred to as the "quality of absence—of emptiness." Yes, the thematic ideas develop, but in their primal state, they are all quiet, melancholy, restrained in nature, and the anticipated "bombast" of a typical symphonic first movement is here replaced with introspection and uneasy quiet, a perfect metaphor for the mood in the Soviet Union after the death of the "leader and teacher."

Movement Two

Introspection and an uneasy quiet. Well, the same can certainly not be said of the second movement, Shostakovich's famous musical portrait of Stalin. Near the end of his life, Shostakovich told Solomon Volkov:

> [In my Ninth Symphony in 1945], I couldn't write an apotheosis for Stalin, I simply couldn't [even though that was what was expected of me]. But I did depict Stalin in music in my next symphony, the Tenth. I wrote it right after Stalin's death and no one guessed what the symphony was about. It's about Stalin and the Stalin years. The second movement, the scherzo, is a musical portrait of Stalin, roughly speaking.

Now this second movement of Shostakovich's Tenth is as brutal a piece of music as he ever wrote: raw, vicious, and loud, pretty much from beginning to end. I would tell you that it starts fortissimo (very loud), and then from there features 50 crescendos and only two decrescendos. We hear this remarkable second movement in its entirety.

[Musical example from Symphony No. 10 in E Minor, Shostakovich: II]

Movement Three

Throughout both the third and fourth movements, Shostakovich uses a particular melodic idea over and over again. It consists of four pitches: D–Eb–C–B. These four pitches are incredibly significant. They constitute Shostakovich's musical signature: D–Eb–C–B. In German, the pitches are "D"; they don't say "Eb," they say "S"; "C"; and they don't say "B," they say "H." In German, these four pitches are: D–S–C–H (as in Dmitri Shostakovich). This musical signature is first heard about one minute and ten seconds into the third movement. When it first appears, it is rather shrilly played by winds and accompanied by a triangle. This, my friends, is cartoon-like music, a herky-jerky puppet's dance, and it's a clear statement on Shostakovich's part. He often said that, "we are all marionettes." That he would portray himself—with his own musical signature—in the guise of a puppet is typical of his cynical, ironic sense of humor. Let's hear this moment in the third movement.

[Musical example from Symphony No. 10 in E Minor, Shostakovich: III; Shostakovich Signature Theme]

Shostakovich first used this four-pitch musical signature in his Second Piano Sonata of 1943 and then again in his Violin Concerto no. 1 of 1948. Increasingly, this melodic idea—this musical signature—became a feature in Shostakovich's music, a musical code, a way for him to say, "Yes, yes, it is I, Dmitri Dmitriyevich Shostakovich, who has thought these thoughts and felt these feelings."

Movement Four

The fourth movement begins with a slow introduction that itself begins with a pensive melody for cellos and double basses. It's a clear reference to the beginning of the first movement of the symphony. Let's hear this fourth movement introduction.

[Musical example from Symphony No. 10 in E Minor, Shostakovich: IV; Introduction]

When this long and bleak introduction finally ends, the fast, chipper and upbeat music that follows it seems ridiculously incongruous, as if Shostakovich is saying, "Smile! Smile! We're all supposed to be happy! The leader and teacher say so! Smile!" Let's hear this incongruous tune that follows this dark introduction.

[Musical example from Symphony No. 10 in E Minor, Shostakovich: IV]

My friends, given the spirit of the first three movements of this symphony, the mood of this music here in the fourth movement is completely out of whack. This mock gaiety here in the fourth movement becomes increasingly forced until the music indeed metamorphoses into something very dark. The "smile" disappears, and the frenzied viciousness of the second movement, the Stalin portrait, returns, followed by a huge and howling appearance of the D–S–C–H motive. It is as if Shostakovich himself is saying to us, "Here and now I have danced the dance, I have smiled the smile demanded by the leader and teacher, and now the bastard is dead and I will do it no longer!" Again, this is what we're going to hear, this gay and flippant tune metamorphoses into the Stalin theme and the Stalin theme finally gives way to a huge statement of Shostakovich's own signature. The gaiety is forced; it's all an object of the leader's will.

[Musical example from Symphony No. 10 in E Minor, Shostakovich: IV; Stalin Theme and Shostakovich Signature Theme]

The final minutes of the symphony are deeply moving. The "smile" is gone; the music becomes lyric and introspective, punctuated throughout by the D–S–C–H or D–Eb–C–B natural motive, Shostakovich's signature. Finally, the fast, upbeat music returns, but it seems less incongruous now, as if perhaps now there is actually a genuine reason to smile. Certainly, the celebratory conclusion of that movement would seem to reinforce that interpretation; the reiterated D–S–C–H or Shostakovich motive heard among blaring brass is a clear and personal statement: "I am here; I am alive; and I can still write!" Let's hear this fourth movement conclusion.

[Musical example from Symphony No. 10 in E Minor, Shostakovich: IV; Conclusion]

It was just the sort of movement that for years drove Western commentators absolutely wild with confusion. "What does it mean?" they cried. They, we, thought that we "knew" what Shostakovich was all about, and we just didn't get it. The English Shostakovich scholar David Fanning writes:

In recent years, there has been an increasing willingness among Western commentators, bolstered by remarks in *Testimony*, to admit the possibility of ironic intention [in Shostakovich's music], that in ostensibly fulfilling the demands of Socialist Realism by outward cheerfulness, Shostakovich lets the authorities have a poisoned cake [to] eat.

So Fanning is suggesting that irony lies at the heart of Shostakovich's music, that irony is the key to understanding Shostakovich's music, and in this he could not be more correct. David Remnick, who witnessed the fall of the Soviet Union as a Moscow-based reporter for *The Washington Post*, writes in his superb and indispensable book, *Lenin's Tomb*:

[The Soviet Union] was Oz, the world's longest running and most colossal mistake, and the only way to endure it all was the perfection of irony. There was no other way to live. Even the sweetest sounding grandmother, her hair in a babushka and her bulk packed into a housecoat, even she was possessed of a sense of irony that would chill the spine of any "absurdist" at the Café Flore.

A few months after the premiere of the Tenth, Shostakovich wrote a truly absurd apology for the symphony—"I wrote it too fast, the first movement isn't 'a proper sonata form,' the second movement is too short, the third movement this, the fourth movement that." Shostakovich was playing it safe: by making these ridiculous statements, he wanted to hand the official critics all the negative grist that they required and, at the same time, distract them from thinking too deeply about the "true" meaning of the symphony. And critics there were.

"Pavel Apostolov accused Shostakovich of the sin of 'modernism' and 'a gloomy, introverted psychological outlook.' Boris Yarustovsky objected to the lack of 'an active struggle for the good' and [asked], 'Where are the positive ideas of this symphony?'"

But for once, my friends, the critics were in the minority, and in the post-Stalin atmosphere of the "Thaw," these critiques carried little weight. Shostakovich's Tenth became an instant classic. For Shostakovich, after five years of disgrace following his censure in 1948, he emerged with his reputation actually enhanced. The sheer quality of his Tenth Symphony was a testament to his incredible artistic integrity and imagination.

Conclusion

It is entirely appropriate that we conclude this survey with Dmitri Shostakovich. What Haydn was for the 18th century, what Beethoven was for the 19th century, so Shostakovich was for the 20th—the preeminent composer of symphonies in his century. Like Haydn and Beethoven before him, Shostakovich composed symphonies across the entire span of his compositional career, composing his First in 1925, at the age of 19, and completing his Fifteenth and last symphony 46 years later, in 1971. Like Haydn and Beethoven before him, Shostakovich wrote a large enough number of symphonies—15 in all—to constitute a major body of work unto themselves. Like Haydn and Beethoven before him, Shostakovich's symphonies constitute a virtual diary of his life and evolving compositional style. And like Haydn and Beethoven, Shostakovich's symphonies are a true and unapologetic mirror of his times and his environment, and what an environment Shostakovich lived and worked in.

We can only wonder what composers history will choose as representatives of our time—here, today. Whoever it will be, we can be sure that the genre of symphony will play a major role in helping to make that determination. I'll see you then in 50 years for our update.

Thank you.

Timeline of Works

1826	Franz Schubert, Symphony no. 9 in C Major, D. 944
1830	Hector Berlioz, *Symphonie fantastique*
1833	Felix Mendelssohn, Symphony no. 4 in A Major, op. 90, "Italian"
1841	Robert Schumann, Symphony in Bb Major, op. 38, "Spring"
1850	Robert Schumann, Symphony no. 3 in Eb Major, op. 97, "Rhenish"
1872	Peter Tchaikovsky, Symphony no. 2 in C Minor, op. 17, "Little Russian"
1873	Nicolai Rimsky Korsakov, Symphony no. 3 in C Major, op. 32
1876	Alexander Borodin, Symphony no. 2 in B Minor
1876	John Knowles Paine, Symphony no. 1 in C Minor, op. 23
1880	Anton Bruckner, Symphony no. 4 in Eb Major, "Romantic"
1883	Johannes Brahms, Symphony no. 3 in F Major, op. 90
1885	Antonin Dvorak, Symphony no. 7 in D Minor, op. 70
1886	Camille Saint-Saens, Symphony no. 3 in C Minor, op. 78, "Organ"
1888	César Franck, Symphony in D Minor
1894	Gustav Mahler, Symphony no. 2 in C Minor
1895	Alexander Glazunov, Symphony no. 5 in Bb Major, op. 55

Glossary

academy: Public concert in 18th-century Vienna, Austria.

adagio: Slow.

allegretto (It.): Fast but not as fast as *allegro*.

allegro: (It.): Lively, somewhat fast.

andante: Walking speed.

andantino: Slower than walking speed.

arpeggio: Chord broken up into consecutively played notes.

augmented: (1) Major or perfect interval extended by a semi-tone, e.g., augmented sixth: C-A sharp. (2) Notes that are doubled in value; e.g., a quarter note becomes a half note. Augmentation is a device for heightening the drama of a musical section by extenuating the note values of the melody.

Baroque: Sixteenth- and seventeenth-century artistic style characterized by extreme elaboration. In music, the style was marked by the complex interplay of melodies, as manifest, for example, in a fugue.

bridge: Musical passage linking one section or theme to another. (See **transition**.)

Brook: Cataloging identification, as for works of Gossec, systematically cataloged by musicologist Barry S. Brook.

Bryan: Cataloging identification, as for works by Vanhal, systematically cataloged by musicologist Paul Bryan.

cadence: Short harmonic formulas that close a musical section or movement. The most common formula is dominant–tonic (V–I). (1) A *closed* (or *perfect*) *cadence* fully resolves: The dominant is followed by the expected tonic. (2) An *open* (or *imperfect*) *cadence* is a temporary point of rest, usually on an unresolved dominant. (3) A *deceptive* (or *interrupted*) *cadence* is one in which the dominant resolves to some chord other than the expected tonic.

cadenza: Passage for solo instrument in an orchestral work, usually a concerto, designed to showcase the player's skills.

chromatic: Scale in which all the pitches are present. On a keyboard, this translates as moving consecutively from white notes to black notes.

classical: Designation given to works of art of the 17th and 18th centuries, characterized by clear lines and balanced form.

coda: Section of music that brings a sonata-allegro movement to a close.

concertmaster: In early terminology, conductor; in modern terminology, the principal first violinist.

consonance: Stable and resolved interval or chord; a state of musical rest.

crescendo: Getting louder.

da capo: Back to the top or beginning (instruction in a score).

development: Section in a classical sonata-allegro movement in which the main themes are developed.

diminished: Minor or perfect interval that is reduced by one semi-tone; e.g., minor seventh, C-B flat, becomes diminished when the minor is reduced by one semi-tone to become C sharp-B flat. Diminished sevenths are extremely unstable harmonies that can lead in a variety of harmonic directions.

dissonance: Unresolved and unstable interval or chord; a state of musical tension.

dominant: Fifth note of a scale and the key of that note; e.g., G is the dominant of C. The second theme in a classical sonata-allegro exposition first appears in the dominant.

double fugue: Complex fugue with two subjects, or themes.

drone: Note or notes, usually in the bass, sustained throughout a musical section or composition; characteristic of bagpipe music.

dynamics: Degrees of loudness, e.g., *piano* ("quiet"), *forte* ("loud"), indicated in a musical score.

Empfindsam: Pre-Classical, mid-18th–century German musical style, characterized by melodic tunefulness, simplicity of utterance, and directness of expression.

enharmonic: Notes that are identical in sound but with different spellings depending on the key context, e.g., C sharp and D flat.

Enlightenment: Eighteenth-century philosophical movement characterized by rationalism and positing that individuals are responsible for their own destinies and all men are born equal.

eroica: Sobriquet, literally meaning "heroic," given to Beethoven's Symphony No. 3.

exposition: Section in a classical sonata-allegro movement in which the main themes are exposed, or introduced.

fermata: Pause.

flat: Note that has been lowered by one half-tone in pitch; symbolized by ♭.

forte (It.): Loud.

fortissimo (It.): Very loud.

French overture: Invented by the French composer Jean-Baptiste Lully, court composer to King Louis XIV. The French overture was played at the theater to welcome the king and to set the mood for the action on the stage. It is characterized by its grandiose themes; slow, stately tempo; dotted rhythms; and sweeping scales.

fugato: Truncated fugue in which the exposition is not followed by true development.

fugue: Major, complex Baroque musical form, distantly related to the round, in which a theme (or subject) is repeated at different pitch levels in succession and is developed by means of various contrapuntal techniques.

Galant: Pre-Classical, mid-18th–century Italian musical style, characterized by melodic tunefulness, simplicity of utterance, and directness of expression.

Gesamtkunstwerk: All-inclusive artwork or art form, containing music, drama, poetry, dance, and so on; term coined by Richard Wagner.

Heiligenstadt Testament: Confessional document penned by Beethoven at a time of extreme psychological crisis. In it, he despairs over his realization that he is going deaf but determines to soldier on.

hemiola: Temporary use of a displaced accent to produce a feeling of changed meter. Beethoven uses it to effect an apparent change from triple (3/4) meter to duple (2/4) meter, without actually changing the meter.

home key: Main key of a movement or composition.

homophonic: Musical passage or piece that has one main melody and everything else is accompaniment.

interval: Distance in pitch between two tones, e.g., C-G (upwards) = a fifth.

inversion: Loosely applied to indicate a reversal in direction; e.g., a melody that goes up, goes down in inversion and vice versa. Its strict definitions are as follows: (1) Harmonic inversion: The bottom note of an interval, or chord, is transferred to its higher octave, or its higher note is transferred to its lower octave; e.g., C-E-G (played together) becomes E-G-C or E-C-G. (2) Melodic inversion: An ascending interval (one note played after the other) is changed to its corresponding descending interval and vice versa; e.g., C-D-E becomes C-B-A.

K. numbers: Koechel numbers, named after L. von Koechel, are a cataloging identification attached to works by Mozart.

Kapellmeister (Ger.): Orchestra director/composer.

key: Central tonality, named after the main note of that tonality.

largo (It.): Broad, slow.

major/minor key system: Two essential *modes*, or "pitch palettes," of European tonal music; *major* is generally perceived as being the brighter sounding of the two, and *minor*, the darker sounding of the two.

Mannheim School: Composers, orchestra, and teaching institutions of the court of Mannheim between 1741 and 1778.

measure (abbr. ms.): Metric unit; space between two bar lines.

melisma: Tightly wound, elaborate melodic line.

meter: Rhythmic measure, e.g., triple meter (3/4), in which there are three beats to the bar, or duple meter (2/4), in which there are two beats to the bar.

metric modulation: Main beat remains the same while the rhythmic subdivisions change. This alters the meter without disturbing the tempo.

minuet: Seventeenth- and eighteenth-century graceful and dignified dance in moderately slow three-quarter time.

minuet and trio: Form of a movement (usually the third) in a classical symphony. The movement is in ternary (ABA) form, with the first minuet repeated after the trio and each section itself repeated.

modal ambiguity: Harmonic ambiguity, in which the main key is not clearly identified.

mode: Major or minor key (in modern Western usage).

modulation: Change from one key to another.

motive: Short musical phrase that can be used as a building block in compositional development.

movement: Independent section within a larger work.

musette: (1) Bagpipe common in Europe in the 17th and 18th centuries. (2) Piece of music in rustic style with a drone bass.

musical form: Overall formulaic structure of a composition, e.g., sonata form; also the smaller divisions of the overall structure, such as the development section.

nationalism: Incorporation of folk or folk-like music into concert works and operas.

Ostinato: Motive that is repeated over and over again.

overture: Music that precedes an opera or play.

pedal note: Pitch sustained for a long period of time against which other changing material is played. A pedal harmony is a sustained chord serving the same purpose.

pianissimo (It.): Very quiet.

piano (It.): Soft or quiet.

piano trio: Composition for piano, violin, and cello.

pivot modulation: A tone common to two chords is used to effect a smooth change of key. For example, F sharp-A-C sharp (F sharp-minor triad) and F-A-C (F-major triad) have A in common. This note can serve as a pivot to swing the mode from F sharp minor to F major.

pizzicato (It.): Very short (plucked) notes.

polyphony: Dominant compositional style of the Pre-Classical era, in which multiple melodies are played together (linear development), as opposed to one melody played with harmonic accompaniment.

polyrhythm: Simultaneous use of contrasting rhythms.

polytonality: Simultaneous use of two or more different keys (major and/or minor) or modes.

presto: Fast.

quartet: (1) Ensemble of four instruments. (2) Piece for four instruments.

recapitulation: Section following the development in a sonata-allegro movement, in which the main themes return in their original form.

recitative: Operatic convention in which the lines are half-sung, half-spoken.

retrograde: Backwards.

retrograde inversion: Backwards and upside down.

ripieno (It.): Passage played by the whole orchestra as opposed to a passage played by solo instruments (*concertante*).

ritardando (It.): Gradually getting slower (abbreviation: *ritard*).

ritornello (It.): Refrain.

Romanticism: Nineteenth-century artistic movement that stressed emotion over intellect and celebrated the boundlessness, the fantastic, and the extremes of experience.

rondo (It.): Musical form in which a principal theme returns—like a refrain—after various contrasting episodes.

scherzando (It.): In a joking manner.

scherzo (It.): "Joke"; name given by Beethoven and his successors to designate a whimsical, often witty, fast movement in triple time.

semi-tone: Smallest interval in Western music; on the keyboard, the distance between a black note and a white note; also, B-C and E-F.

sequence: Successive repetitions of a motive at different pitches. A compositional technique for extending melodic ideas.

sharp: Note that has been raised one half-tone in pitch; symbolized by #.

sonata-allegro form (also known as *sonata form*): Most important musical structure of the Classical era. It is based on the concept of dramatic interaction between two contrasting themes and structured in four parts, sometimes with an introduction to the exposition or first part. The exposition introduces the main themes that will be developed in the development section. The themes return in the recapitulation section, and the movement is closed with a coda.

stringendo (It.): Compressing time; getting faster.

string quartet: (1) Ensemble of four stringed instruments: two violins, viola, and cello. (2) Composition for such an ensemble.

Sturm und Drang (Ger.): "Storm and stress"; late 18th-century literary movement.

symphony: Large-scale instrumental composition for orchestra, containing several movements. The Viennese Classical symphony usually had four movements.

symphonic poem: One-movement orchestral composition depicting a story and usually based on literature.

syncopation: Displacement of the expected accent from a strong beat to a weak beat and vice versa.

theme and variations: Musical form in which a theme is introduced, then treated to a series of variations on some aspect of that theme.

tone poem: See **symphonic poem**.

tonic: First note of the scale; main key of a composition or musical section.

transition (or **bridge**): Musical passage linking two sections.

triad: Chord consisting of three notes: the root, the third, and the fifth, e.g., C-E-G, the triad of C major.

trio: (1) Ensemble of three instruments. (2) Composition for three instruments. (3) Type of minuet, frequently rustic in nature and paired with another minuet to form a movement in a Classical-era symphony.

triplet: Three notes occurring in the space of one beat.

tritone: Interval of six semi-tones that produces an extreme dissonance and begs for immediate resolution.

tutti (It.): The whole orchestra plays together.

Viennese Classical style: Style that dominated European music in the late 18th century. It is characterized by clarity of melodies, harmonies, and rhythms and balanced, proportional musical structures.

voice: A pitch or register, commonly used to refer to the four melodic pitches: soprano, alto, tenor, and bass.

List of Symphonists

Pre-Classical:

Giovanni Battista Pergolesi (1710–1736)

Giovanni Battista Sammartini (c.1700–1775)

Franz Xaver Richter (1709–1789)

Ignaz Holzbauer (1711–1783)

Carl Philipp Emanuel Bach (1714–1788)

Georg Christoph Wagenseil (1715–1777)

Jan Vaclav Stamitz (1717–1757)

Classical:

Christian Cannabich (1731–1798)

Joseph Haydn (1732–1809)

François Gossec (1734–1829)

Johann Christian Bach (1735–1782)

Michael Haydn (1737–1806)

Carl Ditters von Dittersdorf (1739–1799)

Jan Ignatius Vanhal (1739–1813)

Luigi Boccherini (1743–1805)

Wolfgang Mozart (1756–1791)

Franz Schubert (1797–1828)

His Own Category:

Ludwig van Beethoven (1770–1827)

Romantic:

Hector Berlioz (1803–1869)

Felix Mendelssohn (1809–1847)

Robert Schumann (1810–1856)

César Franck (1822–1890)

Anton Bruckner (1824–1896)

Alexander Borodin (1833–1887)

Johannes Brahms (1833–1897)

Camille Saint-Saens (1835–1921)

Mily Balakirev (1837–1910)

John Knowles Paine (1839–1906)

Peter Tchaikovsky (1840–1893)

Antonin Dvorak (1841–1904)

Nicolai Rimsky Korsakov (1844–1908)

Edward Elgar (1857–1934)

Gustav Mahler (1860–1911)

20th Century:

Carl Nielsen (1865–1931)

Alexander Glazunov (1865–1936)

Jean Sibelius (1865–1957)

Ralph Vaughn Williams (1872–1958)

Charles Ives (1874–1954)

Sergei Prokofiev (1891–1953)

Roy Harris (1898–1979)

Aaron Copland (1900–1990)

Dmitri Shostakovich (1906–1975)

Olivier Messiaen (1908–1992)

Samuel Barber (1910–1981)

William Schuman (1910–1992)

Annotated Bibliography

Brown, A. Peter. *The Symphonic Repertoire, Volume II*. Bloomington: University of Indiana Press, 2002. This book offers a comprehensive and highly technical exploration of the symphonies of Haydn, Mozart, Beethoven, and Schubert. As such, it is not for the casual reader, but it is an essential source for anyone who is looking for a detailed and scholarly examination of the key symphonic composers of the Classical era.

Downes, Edward. *Guide to Symphonic Music*. New York: Walker and Company, 1981. A huge collection of essays on orchestral works from the 17th century through the mid-20th century, arranged alphabetically by composer. Most of the essays first appeared as program notes for the New York Philharmonic Orchestra, and as such, they are written for the non-specialist. Along with the Steinberg book (see below), this is the indispensable source for general information about the orchestral repertoire.

Holomon, D. Kern, ed. *The Nineteenth Century Symphony*. New York: Schirmer Books, 1997. An excellent collection of essays by leading musicologists spanning the symphonies of Schubert to Sibelius. Though prepared as a textbook, the essays are extremely readable and often quite entertaining.

Layton, Robert, ed. *A Guide to the Symphony*. Oxford and New York: Oxford University Press, 1995. Another excellent collection of essays, this one by mostly English musicologists. It starts with the origin of the symphony in the 17th century and ends with American and English symphonies in the 20th century. The appendices include an excellent list of "Recommended Further Reading," as well as a "CD Checklist."

Schonberg, Harold. *The Lives of the Great Composers*. New York: W.W. Norton, 1970. A genuinely entertaining series of sketches of the "great" composers, from the 18th century to the 20th. Schonberg was the chief music critic for the *New York Times* for many years, and he writes with the concision and irreverence of the born journalist. A must-have book for any music fan.

Steinberg, Michael. *The Symphony: A Listener's Guide*. Oxford and New York: Oxford University Press, 1995. This book is a collection of program notes written over the years by Michael Steinberg, music critic for the *Boston Globe* and artistic advisor and program note writer for the Boston Symphony, the San Francisco Symphony, and the New York Philharmonic.

They are everything program notes should be: packed with information, witty, erudite but never stuffy. Along with the Downes book (above), this is the indispensable source for the symphonic repertoire.

Bibliography

Badley, Allan. *Carl Philipp Emanuel Bach: Hamburg Sinfonia Nos. 1–6*, program note. Naxos CD 8.553285, 1996.

———. *Johann Stamitz: Symphonies Volume 1*, program note. Naxos CD 8.553194, 1994.

Berlioz, Hector. *Memoirs of Hector Berlioz, 1803 to 1865*. New York: Tudor Publishing, 1935.

Brown, A. Peter. *The Symphonic Repertoire*, Vol. II. Bloomington, IN: University of Indiana Press, 2002.

Cairns, David. *Responses*. New York: Knopf, 1973.

Cardus, Neville. *Gustav Mahler: His Mind and His Music*. London: Gollancz Ltd., 1965.

Chase, Gilbert. *America's Music from the Pilgrims to the Present*, 3rd ed. Urbana and Chicago, IL: University of Illinois Press, 1987.

Chesky, Annette, and Jeffrey Chesky. *Franck: Symphonic Music of Cesar Franck*, program note. Chesky CD CD87, 1993.

Chusid, Martin. *Schubert: Symphony in B Minor*, Norton Critical Score. New York: W.W. Norton, 1961.

Cone, Edward. *Berlioz: Fantastic Symphony*, Norton Critical Score. New York: W.W. Norton, 1971.

Copland, Aaron. *Copland on Music*. New York: W.W. Norton, 1960.

———. Symphony No. 2 program note. Columbia LP MS7223.

Copland, Aaron, and Vivian Perlis. *Copland: 1900 through 1942*. New York: St. Martin's Press, 1984.

Cowell, Henry, and Sidney Cowell. *Charles Ives and His Music*. Oxford and New York: Oxford University Press, 1969.

Daverio, John. *Robert Schumann: Herald of a "New Poetic Age."* New York and Oxford: Oxford University Press, 1997.

Debussy, Claude. *Monsieur Croche: The Dilettante Hater*. New York: Lear Publishers, 1948.

Di Ascoli, Arturo. *Quartetto Milanese ottocentesco: lettere di G. Verdi, G. Strepponi, C. Maffei, C. Tenca e di altri personaggi del mondo politico e artistico dell'epoce*. Rome: Archivi Edizioni, 1974.

Downes, Olin. *Symphonic Masterpieces*. New York: Tudor Publishing, 1939.

Echols, Paul. *Ives Symphony No. 4*, program note. Sony CD SK 44939, 1991.

Fanning, David. *The Breath of the Symphonist: Shostakovich's Tenth*. London: Royal Musical Association, 1988.

Fleming, Michael. *Roy Harris: Symphony No. 3*, program note. Chandos CD 9474, 1996.

Garden, Edward. *Balakirev: Symphony No. 1 in C Major*, program note. Hyperion CDD22030, 1998.

Goodwin, Noel. *Sergei Prokofiev: Symphony No. 1 in D Major, Op. 25*, program note. Chandos CD 8400, 1985.

Goss, Madeline. *Modern Music-Makers: Contemporary American Composers*. New York: E.P. Dutton & Co., 1952.

Grout, Donald, and Claude Palisca. *A History of Western Music*, 4th ed. New York: W.W. Norton, 1988.

Grout, Donald. *A Short History of Opera*, 2nd ed. New York: Columbia University Press, 1965.

Grove, George. *Beethoven and His Nine Symphonies*. New York: Dover, 1962.

Hildesheimer, Wolfgang. *Mozart*. New York: Vintage, 1983.

Hitchcock, H. Wiley. *Music in the United States: A Historical Introduction*. Englewood Cliffs, NJ: Prentice-Hall, 1969.

Ho, Allan Benedict, and Dmitry Feofanov. *Shostakovich Reconsidered*. London: Toccata Press, 1998.

Hogwood, Christopher. *Haydn: Symphonies Nos. 100 and 104*, program note. L'Oiseau-Lyre CD 411 833-2, 1984.

Holden, Anthony. *Tchaikovsky: A Biography*. New York: Random House, 1995.

Holomon, D. Kern, ed. *The Nineteenth Century Symphony*. New York: Schirmer Books, 1997.

Hopkins, Antony. *The Nine Symphonies of Beethoven*. Seattle: University of Washington Press, 1981.

Horne, Alistair. *Seven Ages of Paris*. New York: Knopf, 2003.

Ives, Charles. *Essays before a Sonata*. New York: W.W. Norton, 1962.

————. Symphony No. 2 program note. Columbia CD MK 42407.

Johnson, David. *The Late Symphonies of Mozart*, program note. Columbia LP.

Johnson, Robert Sherlaw. *Messiaen*. London: J.M. Dent & Sons, 1989.

Kennedy, Michael. *Ralph Vaughn Williams: Symphony No. 6 in E Minor*, program note. EMI CDC 7 472152, 1986.

Kerman, Joseph. *The Beethoven Quartets*. New York: Knopf, 1971.

Kupferberg, Herbert. *Felix Mendelssohn: His Life, His Family, His Music*. London: Encore, 1972.

Landon, H. C. Robbins. *Mozart: The Golden Years*. New York: Schirmer Books, 1989.

Lang, Paul Henry. *Music in Western Civilization*. New York: W.W. Norton, 1969.

LaRue, Jan. *A Catalog of 18th-Century Symphonies*, Vol. 1. Bloomington, IN: University of Indiana Press, 1988.

Layton, Robert, ed. *A Guide to the Symphony*. Oxford and New York: Oxford University Press, 1995.

————. *Sibelius*. New York: Schirmer Books, 1992.

Levitin, Yuri. *The Year 1948*. Shostakovichiana.com.

Litzmann, Berthold. *Clara Schumann: An Artist's Life*, 3 vols. Leipzig: Breitkopf and Hartel, 1925.

Mitchell, Donald. *Gustav Mahler: The Wunderhorn Years*. Boulder, CO: Westview Press, 1976.

Nabokov, Nicholas. *Old Friends and New Music*. London: Little, Brown, 1951.

Neef, Sigrid. *Nicolai Rimsky-Korsakov: Symphony No. 3*, program note. Melodiya CD 74321-40065 2, 1984.

Newbould, Brian. *Schubert: The Man and the Music*. Berkeley and Los Angeles: University of California Press, 1997.

Orga, Ates. *Francois-Joseph Gossec: Four Symphonies*, program note. ASV CD DCA 1123, 2001.

Osborne, Charles. *Schubert and His Vienna*. New York: Knopf, 1985.

Peyser, Joan, ed. *The Orchestra: Origins and Transformation*. New York: Billboard Books, 2000.

Pollack, Howard. *Aaron Copland: The Life and Work of an Uncommon Man.* New York: Henry Holt, 1999.

Randel, Don Michael, ed. *The New Harvard Dictionary of Music.* Cambridge, MA: Harvard University Press, 1986.

Raynor, Henry. *Mahler.* London: Macmillan, 1975.

Remnick, David. *Lenin's Tomb.* New York: Random House, 1993.

Richards, Denby. *Dittersdorf: Six Symphonies after Ovid's Metamorphoses,* program note. Chandos CD CHAN 8564/5, 1987.

Rollum-Larsen, Claus. *Carl Nielsen: Symphony No. 4,* program note. Dacapo CD 8.224156, 2000.

Rossiter, Frank R. *Charles Ives and His America.* New York: Liverlight, 1975.

Sadie, Stanley, ed. *New Grove Dictionary of Music and Musicians.* New York: Macmillan, 1980.

Saint-Foix, Georges Poullain. *The Symphonies of Mozart,* translated by Leslie Orrey. London: Dobson, 1947.

Schonberg, Harold. *The Lives of the Great Composers.* New York: W.W. Norton, 1970.

Schruff, Christian. *Ignaz Holzbauer: Five Symphonies,* program note. CPO CD 999 585-2, 1999.

Schweizer, Klaus. *Messiaen: Turangalila Symphony,* program note. Teldec 8573-82043-2, 2000.

Shostakovich, Dmitri, and Solomon Volkov. *Testimony: The Memoirs of Dmitri Shostakovich.* New York: Harper and Row, 1979.

Simpson, Robert. *Carl Nielson, Symphonist.* New York: Taplinger, 1979.

———, ed. *The Symphony.* Vol. 1: *Haydn to Dvorak.* Baltimore, MD: Penguin Books, 1966.

———, ed. *The Symphony.* Vol. 2: *Elgar to Present Day.* Baltimore, MD: Penguin Books, 1967.

Slonimsky, Nicolas. *Lexicon of Musical Invective.* Seattle: University of Washington Press, 1975.

Solomon, Maynard. *Mozart: A Life.* New York: Harper Collins, 1995.

Stedman, Preston. *The Symphony,* 2nd ed. Upper Saddle River, NJ: Prentice Hall, 1992.

Steinberg, Michael. *The Symphony: A Listener's Guide*. Oxford and New York: Oxford University Press, 1995.

Stravinsky, Igor, and Robert Craft. *Memories and Commentaries*. Berkeley and Los Angeles: University of California Press, 1959/1981.

Swafford, Jan. *Charles Ives: A Life with Music*. New York: W.W. Norton, 1996.

Tchaikovsky, Modest. *The Life and Letters of Peter Ilyich Tchaikovsky*; abridged and translated by Rosa Newmarch (1905). New York: M.S.G. Haskell House, 1970.

Tovey, Donald Francis. *Essays in Musical Analysis*, Vol. II. London: Oxford University Press, 1936.

Vaughn Williams, Ralph. *National Music and Other Essays* (1934). 2nd ed. New York: Oxford University Press, 1996.

Vignal, Marc. *Ives: Symphony No. 4*, program note. Columbia/Sony CD MPK 46726, 1991.

Walker, Alan, ed. *Robert Schumann: The Man and His Music*. London: Faber & Faber, 1976.

Weiss, Piero, and Richard Taruskin. *Music in the Western World: A History in Documents*. New York: Schirmer Books, 1984.

Werner, Eric. *Mendelssohn*. London: Collier-Macmillan, 1963.

Wilson, Elizabeth. *Shostakovich: A Life Remembered*. Princeton: Princeton University Press, 1994.

Web sites
http://www.andante.com
http://www.classical.com
http://classicalmusic.about.com
http://www.classical.net

Notes

Notes

Notes

Notes

Notes

Notes

Notes